A GUIDE TO CRITICAL REVIEWS

Part I: *American Drama, 1909-1982.*
                 3d ed. 1984.

Part II: *The Musical, 1909-1974.*
                 2d ed. 1976.

Part III: *Foreign Drama, 1909-1977.*
                 2d ed. 1979.

Part IV: *The Screenplay from*
                 "The Jazz Singer" to
                 "Dr. Strangelove."
                 2 vols. 1971.

Part IV: *The Screenplay, Supplement*
                 One: 1963-1980. 1982.

A Guide to Critical Reviews:

Part I:
American Drama, 1909-1982

Third Edition

by
JAMES M. SALEM

The Scarecrow Press, Inc.
Metuchen, N.J., & London
1984

Ref.
Z
5781
.S16
1984
pt.1.
C.2

Library of Congress Cataloging in Publication Data

Salem, James M.
    A guide to critical reviews.

    Includes indexes.
    Contents: pt. 1. American drama, 1909-1982.
    1. Theater--New York (N.Y.)--Reviews--Indexes.
2. Moving-pictures--United States--Reviews--Indexes.
I. Title.
Z5781.S16 1984   [PN2266]   016.8092   84-1370
ISBN 0-8108-1690-3 (v. 1)

To Dr. James Nardin

FOREWORD

The purpose of Part I of A Guide to Critical Reviews (third edition) is to provide a bibliography of critical reviews of American plays from the 1909-1910 season to the season of 1981-1982. I have included almost 2, 500 plays by some 350 dramatists. Broadway, Off-Broadway, and Off-Off-Broadway productions are represented.

Playwrights included in this bibliography are presented alphabetically, with plays listed alphabetically under each dramatist. Opening dates and performance totals are provided for most productions; however, in the case of plays premiering in university or regional theaters, indicated by an asterisk (*), I have listed reviews only. My key source of production information is The Best Plays of the Year series (New York: Dodd, Mead), begun by Burns Mantle and currently directed by Otis L. Guernsey, Jr.

The reviews cited in this volume are those which appeared in American or Canadian periodicals and in the New York Times. With the exception of some now defunct dramatic periodicals like the Dramatic Mirror and the New York Clipper, most of the reviews should be available in college and public libraries. Reviews in other New York newspapers have not been indexed, but New York Theatre Critics' Reviews--which has reprinted reviews from the New York Journal-American, Daily News, Post, Mirror, World Telegram and Sun, Herald Tribune, and Times since 1940--has been cited for plays produced after that date.

Indexes at the end of this volume can assist in finding the author of an American non-musical play, the first year of production, adapters or original authors, long-running plays, award-winning plays, or birthdates and places of birth of American dramatists.

James M. Salem

University, Alabama
September 1983

CONTENTS

vii

x

ABBOTT, GEORGE

Broadway (see entry under Dunning, Philip)

Coquette (with Ann Preston Bridgers)
    Productions:
    Opened November 8, 1927 for 366 performances.
    Reviews:
    American Mercury 13:120-21, Jan 1928
    Dial 84:80, Jan 1928
    Drama 18:241-2, May 1928
    Dramatist 19:1360-61, Jan 1927
    Independent 119:606, Dec 17, 1927
    Life (NY) 90:21, Dec 8, 1927
    New York Times IX, p. 2, Oct 16, 1927
                    p.23, Nov 9, 1927
                    IX, p. 1, Nov 13, 1927
                    p. 27, Apr 25, 1928
                    p. 26, Apr 26, 1928
    Outlook 147:369, Nov 23, 1927
    Theatre Arts 12:17-18, Jan 1928
    Theatre Magazine 47:24-6+, Feb 1928
    Vogue 71:64-5+, Jan 1, 1928

The Fall Guy (see entry under Gleason, James)

Four Walls (with Dana Burnet)
    Productions:
    Opened September 19, 1927 for 144 performances.
    Reviews:
    Dramatist 18:354-5, Oct 1927
    Nation 125:343-4, Oct 5, 1927
    New York Times p. 33, Sep 20, 1927
                    VIII, p. 1, Oct 2, 1927
                    VIII, p. 2, Oct 2, 1927
    Vogue 70:166, Nov 15, 1927

Heat Lightning (with Leon Abrams)
    Productions:
    Opened September 15, 1933 for 44 performances.
    Reviews:
    Catholic World 138:219, Nov 1933
    Literary Digest 116:18, Oct 14, 1933

1

Nation 137:390-1, Oct 4, 1933
New York Times p. 9, Sep 16, 1933

A Holy Terror (see entry under Smith, Winchell)

Ladies' Money (Based on a play by Lawrence Hazard and Richard Flour-
noy)
Productions:
Opened November 1, 1934 for 36 performances.
Reviews:
Catholic World 140:343, Dec 1934
New York Times p. 26, Nov 2, 1934
Newsweek 4:27, Nov 10, 1934
Theatre Arts 18:904, Dec 1934

Lilly Turner (see entry under Dunning, Philip)

Love 'Em and Leave 'Em (with John V.A. Weaver)
Productions:
Opened February 3, 1926 for 152 performances.
Reviews:
Bookman 63:217, Apr 1926
Life (NY) 87:21, Mar 4, 1926
New York Times p. 20, Feb 4, 1926
              VIII, p. 1, Feb 14, 1926
              VIII, p. 1, Mar 28, 1926
Theatre Magazine 43:26-8+, May 1926
                 44:22+, Nov 1926
Vogue 67:94-5, Apr 1, 1926

Ringside (with Edward E. Paramore and Hyatt Daab)
Productions:
Opened August 29, 1928 for 37 performances.
Reviews:
Life (NY) 92:11, Sep 21, 1928
New York Times p. 13, Aug 30, 1928
              IX, p. 1, Sep 9, 1928
Theatre Magazine 48:30+, Oct 1928
                 48:47-8, Nov 1928
Vogue 72:110, Oct 27, 1928

Sweet River (Adapted from Harriet Beecher Stowe's Uncle Tom's Cabin)
Productions:
Opened October 28, 1936 for 5 performances.
Reviews:
New Republic 89:78, Nov 18, 1936
New York Times X, p. 2, Oct 18, 1936
              p. 30, Oct 29, 1936
Theatre Arts 20:935, Dec 1936

Those We Love (with S.K. Lauren)

Productions:
Opened February 19, 1930 for 77 performances.
Reviews:
New York Times p. 22, Feb 20, 1930
Outlook 154:390, Mar 5, 1930
Theatre Magazine 51:47-8, Apr 1930

Three Men on a Horse (with John Cecil Holm)
Productions:
Opened January 30, 1935 for 835 performances.
Opened October 9, 1942 for 28 performances.
Opened October 16, 1969 for 100 performances.
(Off Off Broadway) April 20, 1979 (IRT).
Reviews:
America 121:545, Nov 29, 1969
Catholic World 140:723-4, Mar 1935
Commonweal 21:458, Feb 15, 1935
Literary Digest 119:20, Feb 9, 1935
New York Theatre Critics' Reviews 1942:209
    1969:226
New York Times p. 22, Jan 22, 1935
    p. 22, Jan 31, 1935
    p. 16, Feb 19, 1936
    p. 22, Mar 11, 1936
    X, p. 2, Mar 15, 1936
    p. 26, Mar 24, 1936
    IX, p. 1, Jun 2, 1936
    p. 10, Oct 10, 1942
    p. 35, Oct 17, 1969
    II, p. 1, Oct 26, 1969
    II, p. 3, Jan 11, 1970
New Yorker 45:138-9, Oct 25, 1969
Vanity Fair 44:41, Apr 1935

ADE, GEORGE

The County Chairman
Productions:
Opened May 25, 1936 for 8 performances.
Reviews:
Commonweal 24:190, Jun 12, 1936
Literary Digest 121:20, Jan 6, 1936
New York Times IX, p. 2, May 24, 1936
    p. 26, May 26, 1936
    X, p. 1, May 31, 1936

Mrs. Peckham's Carouse
Productions:
Opened April 21, 1913 for 24 performances.
Reviews:
Dramatic Mirror 69:6, Apr 23, 1913

Nettie
Productions:
Opened October 17, 1914 in repertory (The Princess Players).
Reviews:
Bookman 40:550, Jan 1915
Dramatic Mirror 72:8, Dec 2, 1914
Green Book 13:383-4, Feb 1915
New York Times p. 11, Mar 25, 1919

AKINS, ZOË

The Crown Prince (Adapted from the Hungarian of Ernest Vajda)
Productions:
Opened March 23, 1927 for 45 performances.
Reviews:
Bookman 65:448, Jun 1927
Life (NY) 89:18, Apr 14, 1927
New York Times VII, p. 4, Feb 27, 1927
                    p. 23, Mar 24, 1927

Daddy's Gone A-Hunting
Productions:
Opened August 31, 1921 for 129 performances.
Reviews:
Bookman 54:230, Nov 1921
Dial 76:94, Jan 1924
Dramatic Mirror 84:376, Sep 10, 1921
Everybody's 45:93-100, Dec 1921
Life (NY) 78:18, Sep 22, 1921
Nation 113:324-5, Sep 21, 1921
New York Clipper 69:20, Sep 7, 1921
New York Times p. 18, Sep 1, 1921
                    VI, p. 1, Sep 4, 1921
                    VI, p. 1, Sep 25, 1921
                    VII, p. 1, Oct 2, 1921
Theatre Magazine 34:315, Nov 1921
Weekly Review 5:234, Sep 10, 1921

Déclassée
Productions:
Opened October 6, 1919 for 257 performances.
(Off Off Broadway) February 25, 1981 for 24 performances
    (Lion Theater Co.).
Reviews:
Current Opinion 68:187-93, Feb 1920
Dial 76:94, Jan 1924
Dramatic Mirror 80:1612, Oct 16, 1919
Dramatist 11:999-1000, Apr 1920
Hearst 37:46-7+, Jan 1920
Nation 109:548, Oct 25, 1919

New Republic 22:95, Mar 17, 1920
New York Times p. 22, Oct 7, 1919
             p. 20, Aug 6, 1935
Theatre Magazine 30:440, Dec 1919

*Did It Really Happen?
Reviews:
New York Times p. 9, Nov 27, 1916

First Love (Adapted from Louis Verneuil's Pile ou Face)
Productions:
Opened November 8, 1926 for 50 performances.
Reviews:
Life (NY) 88:23, Nov 25, 1926
New York Times p. 31, Nov 9, 1926
Theatre Magazine 45:16+, Feb 1927

Footloose (Adapted from For-get-me-not by Herman Merivale and F.C.
    Grove)
Productions:
Opened May 10, 1920 for 32 performances.
Reviews:
Dramatic Mirror 82:994, May 15, 1920
Dramatist 17:1294, Jan 1926
Forum 64:98, Jul 1920
Life (NY) 75:992, May 27, 1920
New York Clipper 68:16, May 19, 1920
New York Times p. 12, May 11, 1920
             VI, p. 1, May 16, 1920
Theatre Magazine 31:526, Jan 1920

The Furies
Productions:
Opened March 7, 1928 for 45 performances.
Reviews:
Dial 84:438-9, May 1928
Nation 126:356, Mar 28, 1928
New Republic 54:155-6, Mar 21, 1928
New York Times p. 23, Mar 8, 1928
Outlook 148:545, Apr 4, 1928
Theatre Arts 12:317+, May 1928
Vogue 71:136+, May 1, 1928

The Greeks Had a Word for It
Productions:
Opened September 25, 1930 for 253 performances.
Reviews:
Bookman 73:70, Mar 1931
Life (NY) 96:18, Oct 17, 1930
National Magazine 59:138, Dec 1930
New York Times p. 16, Sep 26, 1930

p. 22, Nov 23, 1934
Vanity Fair 35:92, Dec 1930
Vogue 76:126+, Nov 24, 1930

The Happy Days (Adapted from Claude-André Puget's Les Jours
    Heureux)
    Productions:
    Opened May 13, 1941 for 23 performances.
    Reviews:
        Commonweal 34:135, May 30, 1941
        Nation 152:648, May 31, 1941
        New York Theatre Critics' Reviews 1941:324
        New York Times p. 24, May 14, 1941
        Time 37:44, May 26, 1941

*I Am Different
    Reviews:
        New York Times IX, p. 2, Aug 28, 1938

The Love Duel (Adapted from the play by Lili Hatvany)
    Productions:
    Opened April 15, 1929 for 88 performances.
    Reviews:
        Catholic World 129:332-3, Jun 1929
        Life (NY) 93:24, May 10, 1929
        New York Times p. 32, Apr 16, 1929
        Outlook 152:72, May 8, 1929
        Theatre Magazine 49:44, Jun 1929

The Magical City (with Pierre Patelin)
    Productions:
    Season of 1915-16 in repertory (Washington Square Players).
    Reviews:
        Current Opinion 60:331, May 1916
        Dramatic Mirror 75:8, Apr 1, 1916
        Forum 55:507-50, May 1916
        New York Times p. 9, Mar 21, 1916
                      II, p. 8, Mar 26, 1916
                      p. 9, Sep 19, 1916

Mrs. January and Mr. Ex
    Productions:
    Opened March 31, 1944 for 43 performances.
    Reviews:
        Catholic World 159:170, May 1944
        Commonweal 40:14-5, Apr 21, 1944
        Nation 158:456, Apr 15, 1944
        New Republic 110:532, Apr 15, 1944
        New York Theatre Critics' Reviews 1944:235
        New York Times p. 10, Apr 1, 1944
        New Yorker 20:44, Apr 8, 1944

Newsweek 23:92, Apr 10, 1944
Theatre Arts 28:328+, Jun 1944
Time 43:44, Apr 10, 1944

The Moon-Flower (Adapted from the Hungarian of Lajos Biro)
Productions:
Opened February 25, 1924 for 48 performances.
Reviews:
American Mercury 1:497-8, Apr 1924
Independent 112:231-2, Apr 26, 1924
Life (NY) 83:20, Mar 13, 1924
New York Times VII, p. 2, Jan 27, 1924
p. 15, Feb 26, 1924
VIII, p. 1, Mar 2, 1924
Theatre Magazine 39:19, May 1924

O Evening Star
Productions:
Opened January 8, 1936 for 5 performances.
Reviews:
Commonweal 23:356, Jan 24, 1936
Literary Digest 121:19, Jan 18, 1936
New York Times p. 20, Dec 26, 1935
p. 24, Jan 9, 1936
IX, p. 1, Jan 19, 1936
Pictorial Review 37:50, Apr 1936

The Old Maid (Based on a novel by Edith Wharton)
Productions:
Opened January 7, 1935 for 305 performances.
(Off Off Broadway) March 18, 1978 (Encompass Theater).
Reviews:
Catholic World 140:602, Feb 1935
Commonweal 21:375, Jan 25, 1935
New Republic 82:162, Mar 20, 1935
New York Times p. 26, Jan 8, 1935
IX, p. 1, Jan 13, 1935
p. 21, May 7, 1935
p. 17, May 8, 1935
p. 21, May 8, 1935
XI, p. 1, May 26, 1935
p. 19, Feb 24, 1937
p. 20, Jan 27, 1949
Newsweek 5:25, May 18, 1935
Player's Magazine 11:11, Mar-Apr 1935
Theatre Arts 19:168+, Mar 1935
Time 25:25, Jan 21, 1935

Papa
Productions:
Opened April 10, 1919 for 12 performances.

Reviews:
New York Times p. 9, Apr 11, 1919
               IV, p. 2, Apr 20, 1919
Theatre Magazine 29:344, Jun 1919

Plans for Tomorrow (see Mrs. January and Mr. Ex)

A Royal Fandango
Productions:
Opened November 12, 1923 for 24 performances.
Reviews:
American Mercury 1:118-19, Jan 1924
Independent 111:257, Nov 24, 1923
Nation 117:615, Nov 28, 1923
New York Times VIII, p. 2, Nov 11, 1923
                  p. 25, Nov 13, 1923
                VIII, p. 1, Nov 18, 1923

The Texas Nightingale
Productions:
Opened November 20, 1922 for 32 performances.
Reviews:
Bookman 56:746-7, Feb 1923
New York Clipper 70:20, Nov 29, 1922
New York Times p. 15, Nov 21, 1922
               VIII, p. 1, Dec 3, 1922
Theatre Magazine 37:19, Jan 1923

*Thou Desperate Pilot
Reviews:
Life (NY) 89:21, Mar 24, 1927
New York Times p. 23, Mar 8, 1927

*Two Mothers
Reviews:
New York Times p. 19, Feb 24, 1937

The Varying Shore
Productions:
Opened December 5, 1921 for 66 performances.
Reviews:
Dramatic Mirror 84:845, Dec 10, 1921
Nation 113:763, Dec 28, 1921
New York Clipper 69:20, Dec 14, 1921
New York Times p. 24, Dec 6, 1921
             VI, p. 1, Dec 11, 1921
Theatre Magazine 35:75+, Feb 1922

ALBEE, EDWARD

Albee Directs Albee (Consists of Zoo Story, American Dream, Sand-

box, Fam & Yam, Box and Quotations from Chairman Mao-Tse-Tung, Counting the Ways, and Listening)
Productions:
(Off Off Broadway) February 1979 (Columbia University).
No Reviews.

All Over
Productions:
Opened March 28, 1971 for 42 performances.
Reviews:
America 124:593-5, Jun 5, 1971
Commonweal 94:166-7, Apr 23, 1971
Nation 212:476-7, Apr 12, 1971
  212:571-2, May 3, 1971
National Review 23:602-4, Jun 1, 1971
New Republic 164:24+, Apr 17, 1971
New York Theatre Critics' Reviews 1971:320
New York Times p. 41, Mar 29, 1971
  II, p. 1, Apr 4, 1971
  p. 49, Apr 20, 1971
New Yorker 47:95, Apr 3, 1971
Newsweek 77:52, Apr 5, 1971
Saturday Review 54:54, Apr 17, 1971
Time 97:69, Apr 5, 1971

The American Dream
Productions:
(Off Broadway) January 24, 1961 for 370 performances.
(Off Broadway) February 11, 1962 for 55 performances.
(Off Broadway) September 4, 1962 for 30 performances.
(Off Broadway) May 28, 1963 for 143 performances.
(Off Broadway) April 21, 1964 for 48 performances.
Opened October 2, 1968 in repertory for 12 performances.
See also Albee Directs Albee.
Reviews:
America 108:891-2, Jun 22, 1963
Catholic World 193:335-6, Aug 1961
Christian Century 78:275, Mar 1, 1961
Horizon 3:117, Jul 1961
Nation 192:125-6, Feb 11, 1961
New Republic 144:30, Mar 27, 1961
New York Times p. 28, Jan 25, 1961
  p. 33, Oct 25, 1961
  p. 27, Feb 12, 1962
  VI, p. 30, Feb 25, 1962
  p. 39, May 29, 1963
  p. 72, Oct 20, 1963
  p. 10, Feb 13, 1965
  p. 55, Oct 3, 1968
New Yorker 36:62+, Feb 4, 1961
Saturday Review 44:54, Feb 11, 1961
Theatre Arts 45:68, Mar 1961

Time 77:53+, Feb 3, 1961

The Ballad of the Sad Cafe (Adapted from the story by Carson Mc-
　　Cullers)
　　Productions:
　　　　Opened October 30, 1963 for 123 performances.
　　　　(Off Off Broadway) October 13, 1977 for 16 performances (WPA
　　　　　　Theater).
　　Reviews:
　　　　America 110:26, Jan 4, 1964
　　　　Catholic World 198:264, Jan 1964
　　　　Commonweal 79:256, Nov 22, 1963
　　　　Nation 197:353-4, Nov 23, 1963
　　　　National Review 16:34-5, Jan 14, 1964
　　　　New Republic 149:28-9, Nov 16, 1963
　　　　New York Theatre Critics' Reviews 1963:212
　　　　New York Times II, p. 1, Oct 27, 1963
　　　　　　　　　　　　p. 27, Oct 31, 1963
　　　　　　　　　　　　II, p. 1, Nov 10, 1963
　　　　　　　　　　　　III, p. 20, Nov 3, 1977
　　　　New Yorker 39:95, Nov 9, 1963
　　　　Newsweek 62:76, Nov 11, 1963
　　　　Saturday Review 46:54, Nov 16, 1963
　　　　Time 82:67, Nov 8, 1963
　　　　Vogue 143:20, Jan 1, 1964

Box
　　Productions:
　　　　Opened September 30, 1968 in repertory for 12 performances.
　　　　See also Albee Directs Albee.
　　Reviews:
　　　　Commonweal 89:120+, Oct 25, 1968
　　　　Nation 206:420, Mar 25, 1968
　　　　New York Theatre Critics' Reviews 1968:213
　　　　　　　　　　　　　　　　　　　　1968:228
　　　　New York Times p. 48, Mar 8, 1968
　　　　　　　　　　　　II, p. 1, Mar 17, 1968
　　　　　　　　　　　　p. 39, Oct 1, 1968
　　　　　　　　　　　　II, p. 5, Oct 13, 1968
　　　　New Yorker 44:103-4+, Oct 12, 1968
　　　　Newsweek 71:109, Mar 18, 1968
　　　　Saturday Review 51:34, Mar 23, 1968
　　　　Time 92:73, Oct 11, 1968
　　　　Vogue 152:92, Nov 15, 1968

Box-Mao-Box (see entries under Box and Quotations from Chairman
　　Mao-Tse-Tung.)

*Counting the Ways
　　Productions:
　　　　See Albee Directs Albee.

Reviews:
New York Times III, p. 3, Feb 4, 1977
XXIII, p. 17, Feb 27, 1977
Newsweek 89:69, Feb 14, 1977
Saturday Review 4:36, Apr 2, 1977

The Death of Bessie Smith
Productions:
(Off Broadway) March 1, 1961 for 328 performances.
Opened October 2, 1968 in repertory for 12 performances.
Reviews:
Catholic World 193:335, Aug 1961
Horizon 3:116, Jul 1961
Nation 192:242, Mar 18, 1961
New Republic 144:29-30, Mar 27, 1961
New York Times p. 33, Oct 25, 1961
p. 19, Mar 2, 1961
p. 29, Jun 11, 1963
p. 55, Oct 3, 1968
New Yorker 37:114, Mar 11, 1961
Theatre Arts 45:56, May 1961

A Delicate Balance
Productions:
Opened September 22, 1966 for 132 performances.
Reviews:
America 115:432-3, Oct 8, 1966
Christian Century 83:55-6, Oct 14, 1966
Life 61:119, Oct 28, 1966
Nation 203:361-3, Oct 10, 1966
National Review 19:99, Jan 24, 1967
New Republic 155:35-6, Oct 8, 1966
New York Theatre Critics' Reviews 1966:294
New York Times p. 35, Aug 16, 1966
p. 44, Sep 23, 1966
II, p. 1, Oct 2, 1966
p. 35, Oct 28, 1967
New Yorker 42:121, Oct 1, 1966
Newsweek 68:98, Oct 3, 1966
Reporter 35:52-3, Oct 20, 1966
Saturday Review 49:90, Oct 8, 1966
Time 88:88, Sep 20, 1966
Vogue 148:150, Nov 1, 1966

Everything in the Garden (Based on the play by Giles Cooper)
Productions:
Opened November 29, 1967 for 84 performances.
(Off Off Broadway) Season of 1973-74 (Theater Arts Repertory Co.).
(Off Off Broadway) January 3, 1980 (Actors Studio).
Reviews:
America 118:19, Jan 6, 1968

Commonweal 87:444+, Jan 12, 1968
Life 64:16, Feb 2, 1968
Nation 205:669, Dec 18, 1967
New Republic 157:25-7, Dec 16, 1967
New York Theatre Critics' Reviews 1967:204
                                   1967:211
New York Times p. 50, Oct 24, 1967
              II, p. 1, Nov 26, 1967
              p. 60, Nov 30, 1967
              II, p. 5, Dec 10, 1967
Newsweek 70:96, Dec 11, 1967
Reporter 37:38-9, Dec 28, 1967
Saturday Review 50:24, Dec 16, 1967
Time 90:96, Dec 8, 1967
Vogue 151:28, Jan 15, 1968

Fam and Yam
Productions:
(Off Broadway) Season of 1960-1961.
See also Albee Directs Albee.
Reviews:
New York Times p. 44, Oct 26, 1960

The Lady from Dubuque
Productions:
Opened January 31, 1980 for 12 performances.
Reviews:
Nation 230:221, Feb 23, 1980
New Republic 182:26-7, Mar 8, 1980
New York Magazine 13:74-5, Feb 11, 1980
New York Theatre Critics' Reviews 1980:384
New York Times III, p. 5, Feb 1, 1980
              XXIII, p. 16, Jun 15, 1980
              XXI, p. 15, Sep 26, 1982
New Yorker 55:63-4, Feb 11, 1980
Newsweek 95:102-3, Feb 11, 1980
Saturday Review 7:34-5, Mar 15, 1980
Time 115:69, Feb 11, 1980

*Listening
Productions:
See Albee Directs Albee.
Reviews:
New York Times III, p. 3, Feb 4, 1977
              XXIII, p. 17, Feb 27, 1977
Newsweek 89:69, Feb 14, 1977
Saturday Review 4:36, Apr 2, 1977

Lolita (Adapted from the novel by Vladimir Nabokov)
Productions:
Opened March 19, 1981 for 12 performances.

Reviews:
Maclean's 94:62, Apr 6, 1981
Nation 232:474-6, Apr 18, 1981
New Republic 184:27-8, Apr 11, 1981
New York Magazine 14:35-9, Mar 16, 1981
               14:34, Mar 30, 1981
New York Theatre Critics' Reviews 1981:312
New York Times III, p. 2, Jan 2, 1981
           II, p. 1, Mar 1, 1981
          III, p. 3, Mar 20, 1981
           II, p. 3, Mar 29, 1981
          III, p. 17, Apr 16, 1981
New Yorker 57:62, Mar 30, 1981
Newsweek 97:85, Mar 30, 1981
People 15:44-6, Apr 6, 1981
Saturday Review 8:78-9, May 1981
Time 117:65, Mar 30, 1981

Malcolm (Based on James Purdy's novel)
Productions:
Opened January 11, 1966 for 7 performances.
Reviews:
Commonweal 83:584-5, Feb 18, 1966
New Republic 154:34+, Jan 29, 1966
New York Theatre Critics' Reviews 1966:392
New York Times II, p. 1, Jan 7, 1966
            p. 29, Jan 12, 1966
New Yorker 41:74, Jan 22, 1966
Newsweek 67:82, Jan 24, 1966
Time 87:50, Jan 21, 1966
Vogue 147:56, Feb 15, 1966

Quotations from Chairman Mao-Tse-Tung
Productions:
Opened September 30, 1968 in repertory for 12 performances.
See also Albee Directs Albee.
Reviews:
Commonweal 89:120+, Oct 25, 1968
Nation 206:420, Mar 25, 1968
New York Theatre Critics' Reviews 1968:213
                             1968:228
New York Times p. 48, Mar 8, 1968
         II, p. 1, Mar 17, 1968
         p. 39, Oct 1, 1968
         II, p. 5, Oct 13, 1968
New Yorker 44:103-4+, Oct 12, 1968
Newsweek 71:109, Mar 18, 1968
Saturday Review 51:34, Mar 23, 1968
Time 92:73, Oct 11, 1968
Vogue 152:92, Nov 15, 1968

The Sandbox
Productions:
  (Off Broadway) Season of 1959-1960.
  (Off Broadway) February 11, 1968 for 55 performances.
  See also Albee Directs Albee.
Reviews:
  New York Times p. 42, May 17, 1960
              p. 27, Feb 12, 1962
              VI, p. 30, Feb 25, 1962

Seascape
Productions:
  Opened January 26, 1975 for 65 performances.
Reviews:
  America 132:136-7, Feb 22, 1975
  Nation 220:314, Mar 15, 1975
  New Republic 172:22, Feb 22, 1975
  New York Magazine 8:55, Feb 10, 1075
  New York Theatre Critics' Reviews 1975:368
  New York Times p. 20, Jan 27, 1975
              II, p. 5, Feb 2, 1975
  Newsweek 85:75, Feb 10, 1975
  Playboy 22:42, May 1975
  Saturday Review 2:40, Mar 8, 1975
  Time 105:57, Feb 10, 1975

Tiny Alice
Productions:
  Opened December 29, 1964 for 167 performances.
  Opened September 29, 1969 for 10 performances.
Reviews:
  America 112:336-7, Mar 6, 1965
          121:342, Oct 18, 1969
  Catholic World 200:384, Mar 1965
  Commonweal 81:543, Jan 22, 1965
            84:583-5, Sep 16, 1966
  Esquire 63:58+, Apr 1965
  Life 58:14, Jan 29, 1965
  Nation 200:65, Jan 18, 1965
        209:451, Oct 27, 1969
  National Review 21:1334, Dec 30, 1969
  New Republic 152:33-4+, Jan 23, 1965
            161:22+, Nov 1, 1969
  New York Theatre Critics' Reviews 1964:95
                                1969:251, 254
  New York Times p. 38, Dec 18, 1964
              II, p. 1, Dec 27, 1964
              p. 14, Dec 30, 1964
              p. 14, Dec 31, 1964
              II, p. 1, Jan 10, 1965
              p. 22, Jan 21, 1965

                    p. 33, Mar 23, 1965
                    II, p. 1, Apr 11, 1965
                    p. 42, Sep 30, 1969
                    II, p. 9, Oct 12, 1969
                    p. 24, Jan 17, 1970
                    p. 46, Apr 17, 1972
New Yorker 40:84, Jan 9, 1965
           45:85-6, Oct 11, 1969
Newsweek 65:75, Jan 11, 1965
         74:125, Oct 13, 1969
Reporter 32:53-4, Jan 28, 1965
Saturday Review 48:40, Jan 16, 1965
                48:38-9+, Jan 30, 1965
                48:21, Feb 20, 1965
                52:20, Oct 18, 1969
Texas Monthly 5:138+, Mar 1977
Time 85:32, Jan 8, 1965
     85:68+, Jan 15, 1965
     94:72, Oct 17, 1969
Vogue 145:50, Feb 15, 1965

Tse-Tung (see Box and Quotations from Chairman Mao-Tse-Tung)

Who's Afraid of Virginia Woolf?
    Productions:
        Opened October 13, 1962 for 664 performances.
        Opened April 1, 1976 for 141 performances.
    Reviews:
        America 107:1105-6, Nov 17, 1962
                134:362-3, Apr 24, 1976
        Atlantic 213:122+, Apr 1964
        Catholic World 196:263-4, Jan 1963
        Commentary 35:296-301, Apr 1963
                   36:272+, Oct 1963
        Commonweal 77:175-6, Nov 9, 1962
        Esquire 60:69+, Dec 1963
        Life 53:107-8, Dec 14, 1962
        Nation 195:273-4, Oct 27, 1962
               222:507-8, Apr 24, 1976
        National Review 14:35-6, Jan 15, 1963
        New Republic 147:29-30, Nov 3, 1962
        New York Magazine 9:93, Apr 19, 1976
        New York Theatre Critics' Reviews 1962:251
                                          1976:310
        New York Times II, p. 1, Oct 7, 1962
                       p. 33, Oct 15, 1962
                       p. 79, Oct 16, 1962
                       II, p. 1, Oct 28, 1962
                       p. 15, Aug 16, 1963
                       p. 68, Oct 6, 1963
                       p. 15, Nov 9, 1963

p. 15, Feb 8, 1964
p. 52, Nov 26, 1964
p. 71, Oct 15, 1972
p. 20, Apr 2, 1976
II, p. 1, Apr 11, 1976
XI, p. 9, May 13, 1979
II, p. 1, May 4, 1980
XXI, p. 4, May 18, 1980
New Yorker 38:85, Oct 20, 1962
52:101, Apr 12, 1976
Newsweek 60:52, Oct 29, 1962
87:109+, Apr 12, 1976
Psychology Today 10:26, Oct 1976
Reporter 28:48, Apr 25, 1963
Saturday Review 45:29, Oct 27, 1962
51:34, Jul 20, 1968
Theatre Arts 46:10, Nov 1962
Time 80:84+, Oct 26, 1962
107:82-3, Apr 12, 1976

The Zoo Story
Productions:
(Off Broadway) January 14, 1960 for 582 performances.
(Off Broadway) September 12, 1961 for 32 performances.
(Off Broadway) February 11, 1962 for 55 performances.
(Off Broadway) September 4, 1962 for 30 performances.
(Off Broadway) May 28, 1963 for 143 performances.
(Off Broadway) June 8, 1965 for 168 performances.
Opened October 9, 1968 in repertory for 5 performances.
(Off Off Broadway) Season of 1971-72 (New Old Reliable Theater).
See also Albee Directs Albee.
Reviews:
America 108:891-2, Jun 22, 1963
Commonweal 82:501-2, Jul 9, 1965
Esquire 55:48-50, Apr 1961
Nation 190:153, Feb 13, 1960
New Republic 142:21, Feb 22, 1960
New York Times p. 45, Sep 29, 1959
p. 37, Jan 15, 1960
II, p. 1, Jan 31, 1960
p. 23, Feb 15, 1960
p. 13, Aug 26, 1960
p. 39, May 29, 1963
p. 29, Jun 11, 1963
p. 10, Feb 13, 1965
p. 42, Jun 9, 1965
p. 41, Oct 11, 1968
New Yorker 35:75-6, Jan 23, 1960
Saturday Review 43:32, Feb 6, 1960

ALFRED, WILLIAM

*Agamemnon
  Reviews:
    New York Times p. 29, Jan 12, 1966
                  II, p. 8, Nov 19, 1972

The Curse of an Aching Heart (music by Claibe Richardson)
  Productions:
    Opened January 25, 1982 for 32 performances.
  Reviews:
    New Republic 186:24, Feb 24, 1982
    New York Magazine 15:44-5, Feb 8, 1982
    New York Theatre Critics' Reviews 1982:388
    New York Times II, p. 1, Jan 24, 1982
                  III, p. 7, Jan 26, 1982
                  II, p. 3, Feb 7, 1982
    New Yorker 57:115, Feb 1, 1982
    Newsweek 99:76, Feb 8, 1982
    Saturday Review 9:46-7, Mar 1982
    Time 119:81, Feb 8, 1982

Hogan's Goat
  Productions:
    (Off Broadway) November 11, 1965 for 607 performances.
  Reviews:
    Catholic World 202:318-20, Feb 1966
    Commonweal 83:441, Jan 14, 1966
                109:146-7, Mar 12, 1982
    Life 60:17, Feb 4, 1966
    Nation 201:427-8, Nov 29, 1965
    New Republic 153:46, Nov 27, 1965
    New York Times p. 56, Nov 12, 1965
                  p. 14, Nov 13, 1965
                  II, p. 1, Nov 21, 1965
                  II, p. 5, Nov. 21, 1965
    New Yorker 41:150-2, Nov 20, 1965
    Newsweek 66:92, Dec 6, 1965
    Reporter 34:47-8, Feb 24, 1966
    Time 87:65, Feb 18, 1966

ALLEN, JAY

Forty Carats (Adapted from a play by Pierre Barillet and Jean-
    Pierre Gredy)
  Productions:
    Opened December 26, 1968 for 780 performances.
  Reviews:
    America 120:148, Feb 1, 1969
    Life 66:10, Feb 14, 1969

Nation 208:125, Jan 27, 1969
New York Theatre Critics' Reviews 1968:119
New York Times p. 45, Dec 27, 1968
   II, p. 1, Jan 5, 1969
   II, p. 5, Feb 9, 1969
   p. 48, Jan 6, 1970
New Yorker 44:59, Jan 4, 1969
Newsweek 73:57, Jan 6, 1969
Time 93:64+, Jan 3, 1969
Vogue 153:54, Feb 15, 1969

The Prime of Miss Jean Brodie
 Productions:
  Opened January 16, 1968 for 378 performances.
  (Off Off Broadway) October 1974 (Manhattan Theater Club).
 Reviews:
  America 118:330, Mar 9, 1968
  Christian Century 86:92-3, Jan 15, 1969
  Commonweal 87:592-3, Feb 16, 1968
  Life 64:14, Apr 5, 1968
  Nation 206:186, Feb 5, 1968
  New York Theatre Critics' Reviews 1968:376
              1968:381
  New York Times p. 39, Jan 17, 1968
       II, p. 1, Jan 28, 1968
  New Yorker 42:85, Jul 9, 1966
      43:84, Jan 27, 1968
  Newsweek 71:76, Jan 29, 1968
  Reporter 38:43-4, Mar 7, 1968
  Saturday Review 51:45, Feb 3, 1968
  Time 91:45, Jan 26, 1968
  Vogue 151:104, Mar 1, 1968

ALLEN, WOODY

Don't Drink the Water
 Productions:
  Opened November 17, 1966 for 598 performances.
 Reviews:
  America 116:26, Jan 7, 1967
  Commonweal 85:348, Dec 23, 1966
  Nation 203:652, Dec 12, 1966
  New York Theatre Critics' Reviews 1966:246
  New York Times p. 37, Nov 18, 1966
      II, p. 1, Dec 25, 1966
      XXIII, p. 6, Nov 20, 1977
  New Yorker 42:155, Dec 3, 1966
  Saturday Review 49:69, Dec 3, 1966
  Time 88:8, Nov 25, 1966

*An Evening by Woody Allen (Consists of God, Without Feathers, and
Getting Even)
Reviews:
Los Angeles 22:235, Oct 1977
Los Angeles Times IV, p. 13, Aug 4, 1977

The Floating Light Bulb
Productions:
Opened April 27, 1981 for 65 performances.
Reviews:
America 144:487, Jun 13, 1981
Commonweal 108:500-1, Sep 11, 1981
New Leader 64:20, Jun 1, 1981
New Republic 184:26+, May 23, 1981
New York Magazine 14:58+, May 11, 1981
New York Theatre Critics' Reviews 1981:255
New York Times III, p. 17, Mar 19, 1981
III, p. 7, Apr 28, 1981
II, p. 3, May 10, 1981
XXI, p. 15, Aug 29, 1982
New Yorker 57:101-2, May 4, 1981
Newsweek 97:93, May 11, 1981
Time 117:83, May 11, 1981

Getting Even (see An Evening by Woody Allen)

God (see An Evening by Woody Allen)

Play It Again, Sam
Productions:
Opened February 12, 1969 for 453 performances.
Reviews:
America 120:434, Apr 5, 1969
Commonweal 90:438, Jul 11, 1969
Nation 208:282-3, Mar 3, 1969
New York Theatre Critics' Reviews 1969:360
New York Times II, p. 1, Feb 9, 1969
p. 52, Feb 13, 1969
p. 26, Feb 14, 1969
II, p. 1, Feb 23, 1969
p. 25, Feb 7, 1970
New Yorker 45:89, Feb 22, 1969
Saturday Review 52:45, Mar 1, 1969
Time 93:42, Feb 21, 1969
Vogue 153:150, Apr 1, 1969

Without Feathers (see An Evening by Woody Allen)

ANDERSON, MAXWELL

Anne of the Thousand Days

Productions:
Opened December 8, 1948 for 286 performances.
Reviews:
Catholic World 168:321-2, Jan 1949
Commonweal 49:281, Dec 24, 1948
Forum 111:92-3, Feb 1949
Life 26:74-6, Jan 17, 1949
Nation 168:24-5, Jan 1, 1949
New Republic 119:29, Dec 27, 1948
New York Theatre Critics' Reviews 1948:128
New York Times p. 49, Dec 9, 1948
             II, p. 3, Dec 19, 1948
             II, p. 1, Sep 18, 1949
New York Times Magazine, pp. 40-1, Nov 28, 1948
New Yorker 24:48+, Dec 18, 1948
Newsweek 32:72, Dec 20, 1948
Saturday Review 31:24-26, Dec 25, 1948
Theatre Arts 32:11-12, Oct 1948
             33:52+, Mar 1949
Time 52:60, Dec 20, 1948
Vogue 113:113, Jan 1949

Bad Seed (Adapted from William March's novel)
Productions:
Opened December 8, 1954 for 332 performances.
Reviews:
America 92:346, Dec 25, 1954
Catholic World 180:387-8, Feb 1955
Commonweal 61:358-9, Dec 31, 1954
Life 38:53-4+, Jan 10, 1955
Nation 179:556-7, Dec 25, 1954
New Republic 131:21, Dec 27, 1954
New York Theatre Critics' Reviews 1954:223
New York Times p. 41, Dec 9, 1954
             II, p. 3, Dec 19, 1954
             VI, p. 22, Jan 16, 1955
             II, p. 3, May 1, 1955
New Yorker 30:61, Dec 18, 1954
Newsweek 44:57 Dec 20, 1954
Saturday Review 37:22, Dec 25, 1954
             38:26, Apr 30, 1955
Theatre Arts 39:18-20, Feb 1955
             39:26, Apr 1955
             39:33-4, Dec 1955
Time 64:59, Dec 20, 1954

Barefoot in Athens
Productions:
Opened October 31, 1951 for 30 performances.
Reviews:
Catholic World 174:226-7, Dec 1951

Commonweal 55:142-3, Nov 16, 1951
Nation 173:430-1, Nov 17, 1951
New York Theatre Critics' Reviews 1951:183
New York Times II, p. 1, Oct 28, 1951
           p. 35, Nov 1, 1951
           II, p. 1, Nov 11, 1951
New Yorker 27:66+, Nov 10, 1951
Newsweek 38:92, Nov 12, 1951
Saturday Review 34:26-8, Nov 24, 1951
           35:28, Feb 23, 1952
Theatre Arts 35:3, Dec 1951
           36:81, Jan 1952
Time 58:60+, Nov 12, 1951

Both Your Houses
Productions:
   Opened March 6, 1933 for 120 performances.
Reviews:
   Catholic World 173:80-1, Apr 1933
   Commonweal 17:582, Mar 22, 1933
   Literary Digest 115:15, Mar 25, 1933
   Nation 136:355, Mar 29, 1933
   New Outlook 161:46, Apr 1933
   New Republic 74:188, Mar 29, 1933
   New York Times p. 20, Mar 7, 1933
              IX, p. 1, Mar 12, 1933
              p. 22, May 23, 1933
   Newsweek 1:29, Mar 18, 1933
   Stage 10:6+, Apr 1933
   Theatre Arts 17:338-40, May 1933
   Time 21:40, Mar 13, 1933
   Vanity Fair 40:31-2+, May 1933
   Vogue 81:84, May 1, 1933

The Buccaneer (with Laurence Stallings)
Productions:
   Opened October 2, 1925 for 20 performances.
Reviews:
   Nation 121:469, Oct 21, 1925
   New York Times p. 10, Oct 3, 1925
   Theatre Magazine 42:16, Dec 1925

Candle in the Wind
Productions:
   Opened October 22, 1941 for 95 performances.
Reviews:
   Catholic World 154:334-5, Dec 1941
   Commonweal 35:71, Nov 7, 1941
   Current History ns 1:379-80, Dec 1941
   Nation 153:462, Nov 8, 1941
   New Republic 105:621 Nov 10, 1941

New York Theatre Critics' Reviews 1941:258
New York Times p. 19, Sep 16, 1941
           p. 26, Oct 23, 1941
           IX, p. 1, Nov 2, 1941
New Yorker 17:40+, Nov 1, 1941
Newsweek 18:58, Nov 3, 1941
Player's Magazine 18:11, Jan 1942
Theatre Arts 25:861-2+, Dec 1941
           26:80, Feb 1942

City Forgotten   (see Night over Taos)

The Day the Money Stopped (with Brendan Gill. Based on Brendan
     Gill's novel)
Productions:
Opened February 20, 1958 for 4 performances.
Reviews:
New York Theatre Critics' Reviews 1958:349
New York Times p. 19, Feb 21, 1958
New Yorker 34:56+, Mar 1, 1958
Time 71:74, Mar 3, 1958

Elizabeth and Essex   (see Elizabeth the Queen)

Elizabeth the Queen
Productions:
Opened November 3, 1930 for 147 performances.
(Off Broadway) November 9, 1962 for 9 performances (Equity
     Library Theatre).
Opened November 3, 1966 for 14 performances (City Center
     Drama Company).
Reviews:
Bookman 72:628, Feb 1931
Catholic World 132:335, Dec 1930
Collier's 87:10, Feb 7, 1931
Commonweal 13:76, Nov 19, 1930
Drama Magazine 21:11-12, Dec 1930
Life (NY) 96:14, Nov 21, 1930
Literary Digest 107:17-18, Nov 22, 1930
Nation 131:562, Nov 1930
National Review 19:99, Jan 24, 1967
New Republic 65:17-19, Nov 19, 1930
New York Times IX, p. 4, Oct 5, 1930
               p. 37, Nov 4, 1930
               IX, p. 1, Nov 9, 1930
               p. 18, Nov 9, 1935
               p. 23, Jul 28, 1936
               p. 25, Oct 30, 1936
               p. 24, Aug 25, 1937
               p. 30, Nov 4, 1966
Outlook 156:472, Nov 19, 1930

Theatre Arts 15:10-12, Jan 1931
Theatre Magazine 53:66, Jan 1931
Vanity Fair 35:30, Jan 1931
Woman's Journal ns 15:15, Dec 1930

The Eve of St. Mark
Productions:
  Opened October 7, 1942 for 307 performances.
Reviews:
  Catholic World 156:214-15, Nov 1942
  Commonweal 37:15, Oct 23, 1942
  Current History ns 3:264-5, Nov 1942
  Independent Woman 21:368, Dec 1942
  Life 13:51-2+, Oct 19, 1942
  Nation 155:425, Oct 24, 1942
  New Republic 107:546, Oct 26, 1942
  New York Theatre Critics' Reviews 1942:211
  New York Times VIII, p. 1, Oct 4, 1942
                  p. 30, Oct 8, 1942
                  VIII, p. 1, Oct 18, 1942
                  p. 8, Jan 25, 1943
  New Yorker 18:36, Oct 17, 1942
  Newsweek 20:76-8, Oct 19, 1942
  Player's Magazine 19:12, Dec 1942
  Scholastic 41:20, Nov 9, 1942
  Theatre Arts 26:735-7+, Dec 1942
                33:54, May 1949
  Time 40:60+, Oct 19, 1942

First Flight (with Laurence Stallings)
Productions:
  Opened September 17, 1925 for 12 performances.
Reviews:
  American Mercury 6:376-7, Nov 1925
  Nation 121:390-1, Oct 7, 1925
  New York Times p. 26, Sep 18, 1925
                 VII, p. 1, Sep 27, 1925

Gods of the Lightning (with Harold Hickerson)
Productions:
  Opened October 24, 1928 for 29 performances.
  (Off Broadway) November 4, 1961 for 10 performances (Equity
    Library Theatre).
Reviews:
  Catholic World 128:338-9, Dec 1928
  Dial 86:80-2, Jan 1929
  Life (NY) 92:14, Nov 9, 1928
  Nation 127:528, Nov 14, 1928
         127:593, Dec 5, 1928
  New Republic 56:326-7, Nov 7, 1928
  New York Times p. 27, Oct 25, 1928

                    p. 17, Nov 27, 1935
        Theatre Arts 13:11-13, Jan 1929
        Theatre Magazine 49:47, Jan 1929
        Vogue 72:99, Dec 8, 1928

The Golden Six
    Productions:
        (Off Broadway) Season of 1958-59.
    Reviews:
        Commonweal 69:175-6, Nov 14, 1958
        New York Times p. 31, May 2, 1958
                       p. 31, Oct 27, 1958
        New Yorker 34:91-3, Nov 8, 1958
        Theatre Arts 43:66, Jan 1959
        Time 72:50, Nov 3, 1958

Gypsy
    Productions:
        Opened January 14, 1929 for 64 performances.
    Reviews:
        Catholic World 128:724-5, Mar 1929
        Commonweal 9:406, Feb 6, 1929
        Life (NY) 93:23, Feb 1, 1929
        Nation 128:168, Feb 6, 1929
        New York Times p. 22, Jan 15, 1929
                       IX, p. 1, Jan 27, 1929
                       IX, p. 2, Oct 13, 1929
        Outlook 151:171, Jan 30, 1929

High Tor
    Productions:
        Opened Jan 9, 1937 for 171 performances.
    Reviews:
        Catholic World 144:728-9, Mar 1937
        Commonweal 25:388 Jan 29, 1937
                   26:132, May 28, 1937
        Forum 97:353, Jun 1937
        Literary Digest 123:21, Jan 23, 1937
        Nation 144:136, Jan 30, 1937
        New Republic 89:411-12, Feb 3, 1937
                     90:295, Apr 14, 1937
        New York Times X, p. 3, Dec 27, 1936
                       p. 20, Dec 31, 1936
                       p. 15, Jan 11, 1937
                       X, p. 1, Jan 17, 1937
                       X, p. 2, Feb 14, 1937
                       X, p. 1, Feb 21, 1937
                       X, p. 1, Apr 4, 1937
        Newsweek 9:32, Jan 16, 1937
        Scribner's Magazine 101:65-6, Jun 1937
        Stage 14:40-42, Jan 1937

14:73-6, Feb 1937
14:41-4, Mar 1937
Theatre Arts 21:175-9, Mar 1937
Time 29:47, Jan 18, 1937

Joan of Lorraine
  Productions:
    Opened November 18, 1946 for 199 performances.
    (Off Off Broadway) March 1974 (Alan Arkin).
  Reviews:
    Catholic World 164:357-8, Jan 1947
    Commonweal 45:200, Dec 6, 1946
    Life 21:51-2+, Dec 2, 1946
    Nation 163:671 Dec 7, 1946
    New Republic 115:726, Dec 2, 1946
    New York Theatre Critics' Reviews 1946:255
    New York Times p. 29, Oct 30, 1946
                 VI, p. 22, Nov 10, 1946
                    p. 40, Nov 19, 1946
                 II, p. 1, Nov 24, 1946
                 II, p. 3, Dec 1, 1946
                    p. 29, Nov 14, 1947
                    p. 12, Mar 26, 1955
                    p. 28, Mar 19, 1974
                    p. 24, Mar 12, 1976
    New York Times Magazine p. 22-3, Nov 30, 1946
    New Yorker 22:58, Nov 30, 1946
    Newsweek 28:94+, Dec 2, 1946
             29:84, Jan 27, 1947
    Saturday Review 29:24-5, Dec 21, 1946
    Theatre Arts 31:12-13+, Jan 1947
    Time 48:54, Dec 2, 1946

Journey to Jerusalem
  Productions:
    Opened October 5, 1940 for 17 performances.
  Reviews:
    American Mercury 51:481-3, Dec 1940
    Arts and Decoration 52:40, Nov 1940
    Catholic World 152:216-17, Nov 1940
    Commonweal 32:530, Oct 18, 1940
    Nation 151:373, Oct 19, 1940
    New Republic 103:557, Oct 21, 1940
    New York Theatre Critics' Reviews 1940:262
    New York Times IX, p. 1, Sep 29, 1940
                      p. 21, Oct 7, 1940
    New Yorker 16:46, Oct 12, 1940
    Newsweek 16:74, Oct 14, 1940
    Theatre Arts 24:850+, Dec 1940
    Time 36:62, Oct 14, 1940

Key Largo
    Productions:
        Opened November 27, 1939 for 105 performances.
        (Off Off Broadway) September 25, 1975 (Soho Repertory).
    Reviews:
        Catholic World 150:467-8, Jan 1940
        Commonweal 31:163, Dec 8, 1939
        Forum 103:32, Jan 1940
        Nation 149:656+, Dec 9, 1939
        New Republic 101:230, Dec 13, 1939
        New York Theatre Critics' Reviews 1940:451
        New York Times p. 26, Oct 31, 1939
                      X, p. 3, Nov 19, 1939
                      p. 30, Nov 28, 1939
                      IX, p. 5, Dec 3, 1939
                      X, p. 3, Dec 10, 1939
                      VIII, p. 1, Jun 21, 1942
        Newsweek 14:34, Dec 11, 1939
        One Act Play Magazine 3:179-80, Feb 1940
        Theatre Arts 24:81-3+, Feb 1940
        Time 34:49, Dec 11, 1939

Mary of Scotland
    Productions:
        Opened November 27, 1933 for 248 performances.
    Reviews:
        Canadian Forum 15:275, Apr 1935
        Catholic World 138:473-5, Jan 1934
        Commonweal 19:189-90, Dec 15, 1933
        Nation 137:688+, Dec 13, 1933
        New Outlook 163:42, Jan 1934
        New Republic 77:130-1, Dec 13, 1933
        New York Times p. 28, Nov 28, 1933
                      IX, p. 5, Dec 3, 1933
                      IX, p. 2, Apr 14, 1935
        Newsweek 2:32, Dec 9, 1933
        Player's Magazine 10:32, May-Jun 1934
        Review of Reviews 89:39, Feb 1934
        Saturday Review 10:496, Feb 17, 1934
        Stage 11:10-11, Dec 1933
              11:8+, Jan 1934
        Theatre Arts 18:14-18, Jan 1934
        Time 22:48-9, Dec 4, 1983
        Vanity Fair 41:41, Feb 1934

The Masque of Kings
    Productions:
        Opened February 8, 1937 for 89 performances.
    Reviews:
        Catholic World 144:731-2, Mar 1937
        Commonweal 25:502, Feb 26, 1937

26:216, Jun 18, 1937
Literary Digest 123:24, Feb 20, 1937
Nation 144:221-2, Feb 20, 1937
New Republic 90:111-12, Mar 3, 1937
New York Times p. 28, Jan 19, 1937
    XI, p. 2, Jan 31, 1937
    X, p. 2, Feb 7, 1937
    p. 19, Feb 9, 1937
    X, p. 1, Feb 21, 1937
    X, p. 1, May 8, 1938
Newsweek 9:24, Feb 20, 1937
Saturday Review 15:23, Mar 13, 1937
Theatre Arts 21:260-1, Apr 1937
Time 29:39, Feb 15, 1937

Night over Taos
 Productions:
  Opened March 9, 1932 for 13 performances.
 Reviews:
  Arts and Decoration 37:56, May 1932
  Catholic World 135:76, Apr 1932
  Nation 134:378, Mar 30, 1932
  New Republic 70:181-2, Mar 30, 1932
  New York Times p. 24, Feb 24, 1932
       p. 25, Mar 10, 1932
  Stage 9:32-5, May 1932
  Theatre Arts 16:60-2, May 1932
  Theatre Guild Magazine 9:3, Apr 1932
  Vogue 79:100+, May 15, 1932

Outside Looking In
 Productions:
  Opened September 7, 1925 for 113 performances.
 Reviews:
  Independent 115:393, Oct 3, 1925
  Life (NY) 86:20, Sep 24, 1925
  Nation 121:338, Sep 23, 1925
  New Republic 44:123-4, Sep 23, 1925
  New York Times p. 28, Sep 8, 1925
       VIII, p. 1, Sep 13, 1925
       IX, p. 2, Oct 4, 1925
       VIII, p. 2, Oct 11, 1925
       VIII, p. 2, Oct 25, 1925
       VIII, p. 2, Nov 15, 1935
       VIII, p. 2, Jun 23, 1929
  Survey 55:46-7, Oct 1, 1925
  Theatre Arts 9:710-11, Nov 1925
  Theatre Magazine 42:16, Nov 1925

Saturday's Children
 Productions:

Opened January 26, 1927 for 310 performances.
Opened April 9, 1928 for 16 performances.
Reviews:
American Mercury 10:503-4, Apr 1927
Bookman 65:207, Apr 1927
Life (NY) 89:19, Feb 17, 1927
Nation 124:194, Feb 16, 1927
New Republic 49:357, Jan 27, 1927
New York Times p. 13, Jan 27, 1927
                VII, p. 1, Feb 6, 1927
                p. 32, Apr 10, 1928
                p. 17, Jul 30, 1935
                p. 22, Jul 7, 1936
                IX, p. 3, May 12, 1940
Theatre Magazine 45:22, May 1927
                46:24-5+, Jul 1927
Vogue 69:132, Apr 1, 1927

The Star Wagon
Productions:
Opened September 29, 1937 for 223 performances.
Reviews:
Catholic World 146:215-16, Nov 1937
Commonweal 26:580, Oct 15, 1937
Independent Woman 16:351+, Nov 1937
Nation 145:411, Oct 16, 1937
New Republic 92:302, Oct 20, 1937
New York Times p. 28, Sep 17, 1937
                p. 18, Sep 30, 1937
                XI, p. 1, Oct 10, 1937
Newsweek 10:27, Oct 11, 1937
One Act Play Magazine 1:857, Jan 1938
Scribner's Magazine 102:53-4, Dec 1937
Stage 15:69, Nov 1937
Theatre Arts 21:838+, Nov 1937
Time 30:52-3, Oct 11, 1937
Vogue 90:90, Nov 1, 1937

Storm Operation
Productions:
Opened January 11, 1944 for 23 performances.
Reviews:
Catholic World 158:489-90, Feb 1944
Commonweal 39:398-9, Feb 4, 1944
Nation 158:105-7, Jan 22, 1944
New Republic 110-148, Jan 31, 1944
New York Theatre Critics' Reviews 1944:289
New York Times II, p. 1, Sep 19, 1943
                p. 28, Jan 12, 1944
New York Times Magazine pp. 10-11, Dec 26, 1943
New Yorker 19:34, Jan 22, 1944

Theatre Arts 28:133-6, Mar 1944
Time 43:40, Jan 24, 1944

Truckline Cafe
    Productions:
        Opened February 27, 1946 for 13 performances.
    Reviews:
        Commonweal 43:533-4, Mar 15, 1946
        Forum 105:753-5, Apr 1946
        Nation 162:324, Mar 16, 1946
        New Republic 114:349, Mar 11, 1946
        New York Theatre Critics' Reviews 1946:441
        New York Times II, p. 1, Feb 24, 1946
                        p. 19, Feb 28, 1946
        New Yorker 22:43-4, Mar 9, 1946
        Newsweek 27:82, Mar 11, 1946
        Theatre Arts 30:260+, May 1946
        Time 47:86, Mar 11, 1946

Valley Forge
    Productions:
        Opened December 10, 1934 for 58 performances.
    Reviews:
        Catholic World 140:596-7, Feb 1935
        Commonweal 21:264, Dec 28, 1934
        Literary Digest 118:22, Dec 22, 1934
        Nation 139:750, Dec 26, 1934
        New Republic 81:196, Dec 26, 1934
        New York Times p. 26, Nov 27, 1934
                       p. 28, Dec 11, 1934
                       IX, p. 1, Dec 23, 1934
        Newsweek 4:24, Dec 22, 1934
        Stage 12:24-7, Jan 1935
        Theatre Arts 19:94-6, Feb 1935
        Time 24:46-8, Dec 10, 1934
        Vanity Fair 43:37-8, Feb 1935

What Price Glory? (with Laurence Stallings)
    Productions:
        Opened September 3, 1924 for 299 performances.
    Reviews:
        American Mercury 3:372-3, Nov 1924
        Bookman 60:328, Nov 1924
        Canadian Magazine 64:74, Apr 1925
        Classic 20:46, Dec 1924
        Current Opinion 77:612+, Nov 1924
        Dial 77:440, Nov 1924
        Drama Magazine 15:4, Oct 1924
        Independent 113:403, Nov 15, 1924
        Life (NY) 84:18, Sep 24, 1924
        Literary Digest 83:30-1, Oct 4, 1924

                    84:30-1, Jan 10, 1925
                    92:24-5, Mar 5, 1927
                    117:21, Jun 30, 1934
        Living Age 324:68, Jan 3, 1925
        Nation 119:316-7, Sep 24, 1924
        New Republic 40:98, Sep 24, 1924
                    40:160-61, Oct 15, 1924
        New York Times p. 14, Sep 6, 1924
                    VIII, p. 1, Sep 14, 1924
                    VII, p. 1, Sep 21, 1924
                    p. 14, Sep 27, 1924
                    VII, p. 1, Sep 27, 1924
                    p. 14, Sep 29, 1924
                    p. 22, Oct 2, 1924
                    IV, p. 7, Oct 12, 1924
                    VIII, p. 1, Jun 28, 1925
                    IX, p. 2, Apr 28, 1929
                    p. 25, Oct 30, 1936
                    IX, p. 1, Sep 24, 1939
                    p. 33, Mar 3, 1949
        Outlook 138:439-41, Nov 19, 1924
        Saturday Review 28:18, Dec 8, 1945
        Theatre Arts 11:659, Sep 1927
                    25:578, Aug 1941
        Theatre Magazine 39:14-15, Nov 1924
                    40:15, Nov 1924
                    40:28, Dec 1924
                    41:19, Jan 1925
                    44:7, Jul 1926
        Vogue 101:80, Feb 1, 1943
        Woman Citizen 9:11, Oct 18, 1924

White Desert
    Productions:
        Opened October 18, 1923 for 12 performances.
    Reviews:
        New York Times p. 17, Oct 19, 1923

The Wingless Victory
    Productions:
        Opened December 23, 1936 for 110 performances.
    Reviews:
        Catholic World 144:598-9, Feb 1937
        Commonweal 25:304, Jan 8, 1937
        Forum 97:354, Jun 1937
        Nation 144:53-4, Jan 9, 1937
        New Republic 89:411, Feb 3, 1937
        New York Times p. 17, Nov 25, 1936
                    p. 20, Dec 24, 1936
                    X, p. 1, Jan 3, 1937
                    X, p. 1, Feb 21, 1937

Newsweek 9:22, Jan 2, 1937
Scholastic 30:19, Feb 13, 1937
Scribner's Magazine 101:69-70, Mar 1937
Stage 14:38-9+, Jan 1937
Theatre Arts 21:89-95, Feb 1937
          29:309, May 1945
Time 29:29, Jan 4, 1937
Vogue 89:64, Feb 1, 1937

Winterset
  Productions:
    Opened September 25, 1935 for 195 performances.
    (Off Broadway) February 9, 1966 for 30 performances.
    (Off Off Broadway) May 12, 1976 (Jean Cocteau).
  Reviews:
    Catholic World 142:211-12, Nov 1935
    Commonweal 22:585, Oct 11, 1935
              24:218, Jun 19, 1936
    Forum 95:345-6, Jun 1936
    Literary Digest 120:20, Oct 5, 1935
    Nation 141:420, Oct 9, 1935
          141:638, Dec 4, 1935
          142:484-5, Apr 15, 1936
    New Republic 84:274, Oct 16, 1935
              84:365, Nov 6, 1935
              85:257, Jan 8, 1936
    New York Times p. 19, Sep 26, 1935
              XI, p. 1, Oct 6, 1935
              IX, p. 1, Feb 16, 1936
              p. 35, Jun 2, 1936
              p. 32, Feb 10, 1966
              p. 28, Jul 23, 1968
    Newsweek 6:32-3, Oct 5, 1935
           7:32, Apr 4, 1936
           8:20, Dec 5, 1936
    Player's Magazine 12:2+, Jan-Feb, 1936
    Saturday Review 12:16, Oct 12, 1935
    Stage 13:56-8, Nov 1935
    Theatre Arts 19:815-20, Nov 1935
           20:465, Jun 1936
           31:30, Nov 1947
    Time 26:38+, Oct 7, 1935
    Vanity Fair 45:39, Dec 1935

ANDERSON, ROBERT

All Summer Long (Adapted from Donald Wetzel's novel)
  Productions:
    Opened September 23, 1954 for 60 performances.

Reviews:
America 92:110, Oct 23, 1954
Catholic World 180:144-5, Nov 1954
Commonweal 61:60, Oct 22, 1954
Nation 179:314, Oct 9, 1954
New Republic 131:22, Oct 4, 1954
New York Theatre Critics' Reviews 1954:304
New York Times p. 23, Jan 29, 1953
          II, p. 3, Sep 19, 1954
          p. 26, Sep 24, 1954
          II, p. 1, Oct 3, 1954
New Yorker 30:63, Oct 2, 1954
Newsweek 44:83, Oct 4, 1954
Saturday Review 37:26, Oct 9, 1954
Theatre Arts 38:20, 90, Dec 1954
Time 64:56, Oct 4, 1954

Come Marching Home
Productions:
Opened May 18, 1946 for 19 performances.
Reviews:
Commonweal 44:166, May 31, 1946
New York Times p. 18, May 20, 1946

The Days Between
Productions:
(Off Broadway) June 6, 1979 for 23 performances.
(Off Off Broadway) November 29, 1979 (Park Royal Theater).
Reviews:
Life 59:20, Nov 19, 1965
New York Times p. 28, Feb 19, 1965
          p. 39, Jun 4, 1965
          II, p. 1, Jun 27, 1965
          III, p. 5, Jun 8, 1979

Double Solitaire (see Solitaire/Double Solitaire)

The Footsteps of Doves (see You Know I Can't Hear You When the Water's Running)

I Never Sang for My Father
Productions:
Opened January 25, 1968 for 124 performances.
(Off Off Broadway) Season of 1975-76 (Elysian Playhouse).
Reviews:
America 118:356, Mar 16, 1968
Christian Century 85:405-6, Mar 27, 1968
Life 64:10, Mar 1, 1968
Nation 206:221, Feb 12, 1968
New York Theatre Critics' Reviews 1968:367
                           1968:373

New York Times p. 30, Jan 26, 1968
II, p. 1, Feb 4, 1968
New Yorker 43:77, Feb 3, 1968
Newsweek 71:81, Feb 5, 1968
Saturday Review 51:39, Feb 10, 1968
Time 91:47, Feb 2, 1968
Vogue 151:44, Mar 15, 1968

I'll Be Home for Christmas   (see You Know I Can't Hear You When
the Water's Running)

I'm Herbert   (see You Know I Can't Hear You When the Water's Running)

The Shock of Recognition   (see You Know I Can't Hear You When the
Water's Running)

Silent Night, Lonely Night
Productions:
Opened December 3, 1959 for 124 performances.
(Off Broadway) Season of 1967-68.
Reviews:
America 102:428, Jan 9, 1960
Christian Century 77:16, Jan 6, 1960
Commonweal 71:395, Jan 1, 1960
Nation 189:476, Dec 19, 1959
New York Theatre Critics' Reviews 1959:204
New York Times p. 12, Nov 14, 1959
p. 36, Dec 4, 1959
II, p. 3, Dec 13, 1959
New Yorker 35:102-3, Dec 12, 1959
Saturday Review 42:24, Dec 19, 1959
Time 74:77, Dec 14, 1959

Solitaire/Double Solitaire
Productions:
Opened September 30, 1971 for 36 performances.
Reviews:
America 125:322, Oct 23, 1971
Nation 213:380, Oct 18, 1971
New York Theatre Critics' Reviews 1971:248
New York Times p. 29, Mar 2, 1971
p. 33, Oct 1, 1971
II, p. 1, Oct 10, 1971
New Yorker 47:95-6, Oct 9, 1971
Saturday Review 54:35, Oct 16, 1971
Time 98:74, Oct 11, 1971

Tea and Sympathy
Productions:
Opened September 30, 1953 for 712 performances.

Reviews:
America 90:107+, Oct 24, 1953
Catholic World 178:148-9, Nov 1953
Commonweal 59:90, Oct 30, 1953
Life 35:121-3, Oct 19, 1953
Nation 177:317-18, Oct 17, 1953
New Republic 129:20-1, Oct 19, 1953
New York Theatre Critics' Reviews 1953:266
New York Times II, p. 3, Sep 27, 1953
            p. 35, Oct 1, 1953
            II, p. 1, Oct 11, 1953
            VI, p. 14, Oct 11, 1953
            II, p. 3, Nov 8, 1953
            II, p. 1, Aug 15, 1954
            p. 50, Dec 4, 1956
            p. 22, Apr 26, 1957
New Yorker 29:71, Oct 10, 1953
Newsweek 42:84, Oct 12, 1953
            42:60, Dec 21, 1953
Saturday Review 36:35, Oct 17, 1953
            36:45, Dec 12, 1953
Theatre Arts 37:62-7, Nov 1953
            37:18-19, Dec 1953
Time 62:49, Oct 12, 1953

You Know I Can't Hear You When the Water's Running ("The Shock of Recognition," "The Footsteps of Doves," "I'll be Home for Christmas," "I'm Herbert")
Productions:
Opened March 13, 1967 for 755 performances.
Reviews:
America 116:793, May 27, 1967
Christian Century 84:1048-9, Aug 16, 1967
Commonweal 86:175-6, Apr 28, 1967
Life 62:23, Apr 28, 1967
Nation 204:444, Apr 3, 1967
New York Theatre Critics' Reviews 1967:343
New York Times p. 54, Mar 14, 1967
            p. 54, Mar 15, 1967
            II, p. 1, Mar 26, 1967
            p. 33, Mar 29, 1968
New Yorker 43:119, Mar 25, 1967
Newsweek 69:110, Mar 27, 1967
Reporter 36:43-4, Apr 20, 1967
Saturday Review 50:42, Apr 1, 1967
Time 89:69, Mar 24, 1967

ANSPACHER, LOUIS K.

Dagmar (Adapted from a play by Ferencz Herczeg)

Productions:
  Opened January 22, 1923 for 56 performances.
Reviews:
    Life (NY) 81:18, Feb 8, 1923
    New York Clipper 70:14, Jan 31, 1923
    New York Times p. 18, Jan 23, 1923

Our Children
  Productions:
  Opened September 10, 1915 for 18 performances.
Reviews:
    Dramatic Mirror 74:8, Sep 15, 1915
    Life (NY) 66:566, Sep 23, 1915
    Nation 101:364-5, Sep 16, 1915
    New York Drama News 61:19, Sep 18, 1915
    Theatre Magazine 22:167-8, Oct 1915

The Rhapsody
  Productions:
  Opened September 15, 1930 for 16 performances.
Reviews:
    Commonweal 12:555, Oct 1, 1930
    Nation 131:355, Oct 1, 1930
    New York Times p. 30, Sep 16, 1930

That Day
  Productions:
  Opened October 3, 1922 for 15 performances.
Reviews:
    Dramatic Mirror 77:34, Aug 11, 1917
    Dramatist 13:1131-2, Oct 1922
    New York Times p. 11, Jul 4, 1922
                    p. 27, Oct 4, 1922

The Unchastened Woman
  Productions:
  Opened October 9, 1915 for 193 performances.
  Opened February 15, 1926 for 31 performances.
Reviews:
    Book News 34:181-2, Dec 1915
    Bookman 42:380+, Dec 1915
    Current Opinion 59:400-4, Dec 1915
    Drama 22:285-93, May 1916
    Dramatic Mirror 74:9, Oct 16, 1915
    Dramatist 7:638-9, Jan 1916
    Green Book 15:18-19, Jan 1916
    Hearst 29:106-8+, Feb 1916
    Nation 101:476-7, Oct 14, 1915
    New York Drama News 61:17, Oct 16, 1915
    New York Times p. 12, Feb 17, 1926
                    VII, p. 1, Feb 21, 1926

Smart Set 47:147, Dec 1915

A Woman of Impulse
Productions:
Opened March 1, 1909 for 16 performances.
Reviews:
Forum 41:337-9, Apr 1909
Theatre Magazine 9:105+, Apr 1909

ARCHIBALD, WILLIAM

The Cantilevered Terrace
Productions:
(Off Broadway) January 17, 1962 for 39 performances.
Reviews:
America 106:632, Feb 10, 1962
New York Times p. 24, Jan 18, 1962
II, p. 1, Jan 28, 1962
New Yorker 37:73-4+, Jan 27, 1962
Saturday Review 45:38, Feb 17, 1962
Time 79:56, Jan 26, 1962

The Innocents (Based on Henry James's The Turn of the Screw)
Productions:
Opened February 1, 1950 for 141 performances.
(Off Broadway) Season of 1958-1959.
Opened October 21, 1976 for 12 performances.
Reviews:
Catholic World 170:469, Mar 1950
189:321, Jul 1959
Commonweal 51:509, Feb 17, 1950
Life 28:91-2+, Apr 3, 1950
Nation 170:141, Feb 11, 1950
New Republic 122:20, Feb 27, 1950
New York Magazine 9:74, Nov 8, 1976
New York Theatre Critics' Reviews 1950:359
1976:142
New York Times p. 30, Feb 2, 1950
II, p. 1, Feb 12, 1950
II, p. 3, Mar 26, 1950
II, p. 2, Apr 23, 1950
p. 9, Jul 4, 1952
p. 41, Apr 21, 1959
III, p. 3, Oct 22, 1976
New Yorker 25:44, Feb 11, 1950
35:97-9, May 2, 1959
52:99-100, Nov 1, 1976
Newsweek 35:80, Feb 13, 1950
Saturday Review 33:32+, Feb 25, 1950
School and Society 71:214-15, Apr 8, 1950

Theatre Arts 34:16, Apr 1950
                34:22-3+, Jun 1950
Time 55:52-3, Feb 13, 1950

Portrait of a Lady (Based on Henry James's novel)
  Productions:
    Opened December 21, 1954 for 7 performances.
  Reviews:
    America 92:407, Jan 15, 1955
    Commonweal 61:429, Jan 21, 1955
    Nation 180:36, Jan 8, 1955
    New York Theatre Critics' Reviews 1954:211
    New York Times II, p. 3, Dec 19, 1954
                     p. 30, Dec 21, 1954
                     p. 27, Dec 22, 1954
    New Yorker 30:42+, Jan 1, 1955
    Newsweek 45:43, Jan 3, 1955
    Saturday Review 38:25, Jan 8, 1955
    Time 65:35, Jan 3, 1955

ARDREY, ROBERT

Casey Jones
  Productions:
    Opened February 19, 1938 for 25 performances.
  Reviews:
    Commonweal 27:554, Mar 11, 1938
    Nation 146:281, Mar 5, 1938
    New York Times p. 14, Feb 21, 1938
    One Act Play Magazine 1:1021-2, Mar 1938
    Theatre Arts 22:248-50, Apr 1938

How to Get Tough About It
  Productions:
    Opened February 8, 1938 for 23 performances.
  Reviews:
    Catholic World 146:730, Mar 1938
    Commonweal 27:496, Feb 25, 1938
    New York Times p. 16, Feb 9, 1938
    One Act Play Magazine 1:943-4, Feb 1938
    Theatre Arts 22:250-1, Apr 1938
    Time 31:42, Feb 21, 1938

Jeb
  Productions:
    Opened February 21, 1946 for 9 performances.
  Reviews:
    Forum 105:753, Apr 1946
    New Republic 114:349, Mar 11, 1946
    New York Theatre Critics' Reviews 1946:446

New York Times II, p. 1, Feb 17, 1946
p. 20, Feb 22, 1946
II, p. 1, Mar 3, 1946
New Yorker 22:41-3, Mar 2, 1946
Newsweek 27:79, Mar 4, 1946
Theatre Arts 30:203-5, Apr 1946

Shadow of Heroes (Stone and Star)
Productions:
(Off Broadway) December 5, 1961 for 20 performances.
Reviews:
Commonweal 75:389, Jan 5, 1962
New York Times p. 59, Dec 6, 1961
New Yorker 37:98+, Dec 16, 1961
Reporter 26:38, Jan 4, 1962
Saturday Review 45:25, Jan 6, 1962
Theatre Arts 46:74-5, Feb 1962

Sing Me No Lullaby
Productions:
Opened October 14, 1954 for 30 performances.
Reviews:
America 92:221, Nov 20, 1954
Commentary 18:522-5, Dec 1954
Commonweal 61:189, Nov 19, 1954
Nation 179:390, Oct 30, 1954
New Republic 131:23, Nov 1, 1954
New York Theatre Critics' Reviews 1954:279
New York Times p. 17, Oct 15, 1954
II, p. 1, Oct 24, 1954
New Yorker 30:79, Oct 23, 1954
Newsweek 44:93, Oct 25, 1954
Saturday Review 37:27, Oct 30, 1954
Theatre Arts 38:81, 92, Dec 1954
Time 64:42, Oct 25, 1954

Star Spangled
Productions:
Opened March 10, 1936 for 23 performances.
Reviews:
Catholic World 143:89, Apr 1936
Literary Digest 121:19, Mar 21, 1936
New York Times p. 25, Mar 6, 1936
p. 23, Mar 11, 1936

Stone and Star   (see Shadow of Heroes)

Thunder Rock
Productions:
Opened November 14, 1939 for 23 performances.
(Off Off Broadway) February 8, 1973 (Equity Library Theater).

(Off Off Broadway) October 23, 1975 (Joseph Jefferson).
Reviews:
    Commonweal 31:137, Dec 1, 1939
    Nation 149:586, Nov 25, 1939
    New York Times p. 18, Nov 15, 1939
                X, p. 3, Nov 19, 1939
                p. 10, Jul 29, 1940
                IV, p. 2, Aug 4, 1940
                IX, p. 2, Aug 11, 1940
                p. 18, Feb 27, 1956
                p. 27, Feb 13, 1973
                p. 47, Oct 29, 1975
    Newsweek 14:23, Nov 27, 1939
    Theatre Arts 24:16-17+, Jan 1940
    Time 36:52, Aug 12, 1940

ATLAS, LEOPOLD

But for the Grace of God
Productions:
    Opened January 12, 1937 for 42 performances.
Reviews:
    Commonweal 25:418, Feb 5, 1937
    Nation 144:108, Jan 23, 1937
    New York Times X, p. 3, Jan 10, 1937
                p. 21, Jan 13, 1937
    Theatre Arts 21:182-3, Mar 1937

Wednesday's Child
Productions:
    Opened January 16, 1934 for 56 performances.
Reviews:
    Catholic World 138:732, Mar 1934
    Literary Digest 117:23, Feb 24, 1934
    New Outlook 163:33, Mar 1934
    New York Times p. 23, Jan 17, 1934
                X, p. 2, Jan 21, 1934
                IX, p. 1, Jan 28, 1934
    Newsweek 3:33, Jan 27, 1934
    Review of Reviews 89:47, Mar 1934
    Stage 11:10-11, Mar 1934
    Theatre Arts 18:170-1, Mar 1934
    Time 23:34, Jan 29, 1934

AURTHUR, ROBERT ALAN

Carry Me Back to Morningside Heights
Productions:
    Opened February 27, 1968 for 7 performances.

Reviews:
New York Theatre Critics' Reviews 1968:343
New York Times p. 41, Feb 28, 1968

A Very Special Baby
Productions:
Opened November 14, 1956 for 5 performances.
Reviews:
Nation 183:485, Dec 1, 1956
New York Theatre Critics' Reviews 1956:206
New York Times p. 43, Nov 15, 1956
New Yorker 32:123, Nov 24, 1956
Saturday Review 39:50, Dec 1, 1956
Theatre Arts 41:27, Jan 1957
Time 68:58, Nov 26, 1956

AXELROD, GEORGE

Goodbye, Charlie
Productions:
Opened December 16, 1959 for 109 performances.
Reviews:
Commonweal 71:630-1, Mar 4, 1960
New York Theatre Critics' Reviews 1959:186
New York Times p. 50, Dec 17, 1959
New Yorker 35:48+, Dec 26, 1959
Newsweek 54:43, Dec 28, 1959
Saturday Review 43:30, Jan 2, 1960

The Seven Year Itch
Productions:
Opened November 20, 1952 for 1,141 performances.
Reviews:
Catholic World 176:307, Jan 1953
Commonweal 57:259, Dec 12, 1952
Life 33:145-8, Dec 1952
Nation 175:563, Dec 13, 1952
New York Theatre Critics' Reviews 1952:186
New York Times p. 21, Nov 21, 1952
                    II, p. 1, Nov 30, 1952
                    II, p. 3, Mar 1, 1953
                    p. 26, May 18, 1953
New Yorker 28:67, Dec 6, 1952
Newsweek 40:79, Dec 1, 1952
Saturday Review 35:25, Dec 13, 1952
Theatre Arts 37:27-8, Feb 1953
Time 60:78+, Dec 1, 1952

*Souvenir (with Peter Viertel)
Reviews:
Los Angeles 20:136+, Dec 1975

Will Success Spoil Rock Hunter?
Productions:
    Opened October 13, 1955 for 444 performances.
    (Off Off Broadway) July 17, 1980 (Manhattan Punch Line).
Reviews:
    America 94:138, Oct 29, 1955
    Catholic World 182:226, Dec 1955
    Commonweal 63:141, Nov 11, 1955
    Nation 181:405, Nov 5, 1955
    New Republic 134:20, Jan 2, 1956
    New York Theatre Critics' Reviews 1955:246
    New York Times p. 22, Oct 14, 1955
    New Yorker 31:88, Oct 22, 1955
    Newsweek 46:54, Oct 24, 1955
    Saturday Review 38:20, Oct 29, 1955
    Theatre Arts 39:26, Dec 1955
    Time 66:86, Oct 24, 1955

BABE, THOMAS

Billy Irish
Productions:
    (Off Off Broadway) January 27, 1977 (Manhattan Theatre Club).
No Reviews.

Cathleen
Productions:
    (Off Off Broadway) May 26, 1980 (Actors Studio).
No Reviews.

Fathers and Sons
Productions:
    (Off Off Broadway) November 11, 1978 for 24 performances (New
        York Shakespeare Festival Public Theater).
Reviews:
    Los Angeles 25:274+, May 1980
    New York Magazine 11:146, Dec 4, 1978
    New York Times II, p. 3, Nov 26, 1978

Kid Champion
Productions:
    (Off Broadway) January 28, 1975 for 48 performances.
Reviews:
    New York Magazine 8:78, Mar 10, 1975
    New York Times p. 38, Feb 20, 1975
                    II, p. 5, Mar 2, 1975
    New Yorker 51:71-2, Mar 3, 1975

A Prayer for My Daughter
Productions:

(Off Off Broadway) September 30, 1977 for 18 performances (New York Shakespeare Festival Public Theater).
(Off Broadway) December 27, 1977 for 127 performances.
Reviews:
America 138:124, Feb 18, 1978
Harper's 256:84-5, May 1978
Nation 226:154, Feb 11, 1978
New Leader 61:25-6, Feb 13, 1978
New York Magazine 11:60, Jan 30, 1978
New York Theatre Critics' Reviews 1978:353
New York Times III, p. 16, Jan 18, 1978
          II, p. 3, Jan 22, 1978
New Yorker 53:45-6, Jan 13, 1978
Time 111:70, Jan 30, 1978

Rebel Women
Productions:
(Off Broadway) May 6, 1976 for 40 performances.
Reviews:
New York Magazine 9:64+, Jun 21, 1976
New York Times III, p. 6, Jun 4, 1976
          II, p. 5, Jun 13, 1976
New Yorker 52:78-9, Jun 14, 1976

Salt Lake City Skyline
Productions:
(Off Broadway) January 23, 1980 for 31 performances.
Reviews:
New York Magazine 13:57-8, Feb 4, 1980
New York Theatre Critics' Reviews 1980:339
New York Times III, p. 15, Jan 24, 1980
New Yorker 55:96+, Feb 4, 1980
Newsweek 95:84, Feb 4, 1980

Taken in Marriage
Productions:
(Off Broadway) February 2, 1979 for 46 performances.
(Off Broadway) November 1, 1981 for 25 performances.
Reviews:
Nation 228:285, Mar 17, 1979
New Republic 180:25, Apr 21, 1979
New York Magazine 12:95, Mar 26, 1979
New York Theatre Critics' Reviews 1979:318
New York Times III, p. 3, Feb 16, 1979
          III, p. 7, Feb 27, 1979
          II, p. 3, Mar 18, 1979
New Yorker 55:108, Mar 12, 1979
Newsweek 93:103, Mar 12, 1979
Time 113:90, Mar 19, 1979

BALDERSTON, JOHN

Berkeley Square (Suggested by Henry James's "A Sense of the
    Past")
    Productions:
    Opened November 4, 1929 for 229 performances.
    Reviews:
    American Mercury 19:116-17, Jan 1930
    Catholic World 130:464-6, Jan 1930
    Commonweal 11:85, Nov 20, 1929
    Life (NY) 94:24, Nov 22, 1929
                95:18, Jun 6, 1930
    Literary Digest 103:19, Nov 30, 1929
    Nation 129:604-5, Nov 20, 1929
    New Republic 60:374-5, Nov 20, 1929
    New York Times p. 19, Oct 7, 1926
                    VIII, p. 2, Oct 24, 1926
                    p. 32, Nov 5, 1929
                    X, p. 1, Nov 9, 1929
                    X, p. 1, Dec 1, 1929
                    p. 25, Aug 20, 1935
    Outlook 153:470, Nov 20, 1929
    Sketch Book 7:29, Jan 1930
    Theatre Arts 14:11-12, Jan 1930
    Theatre Magazine 50:76, Dec 1929
                    51:32-5+, Jan 1930

Dracula (with Hamilton Deane. Based on Bram Stoker's novel)
    Productions:
    Opened October 5, 1927 for 261 performances.
    Opened April 13, 1931 for 8 performances.
    Opened October 20, 1977 for 925 performances.
    Reviews:
    America 137:334, Nov 12, 1977
    Crawdaddy pp. 26-33, Jun 1978
    Los Angeles 23:322+, Nov 1978
    New West 3:122+, Nov 6, 1978
    New York Magazine 10:75, Nov 7, 1977
    New York Theatre Critics' Reviews 1977:166
    New York Times p. 29, Oct 6, 1927
                    VIII, p. 3, Dec 25, 1927
                    p. 33, Apr 14, 1931
                    III, p. 3, Oct 21, 1977
                    II, p. 5, Oct 31, 1977
                    III, p. 17, Dec 19, 1979
    New York Times Magazine pp. 40-2+, Oct 16, 1977
    New Yorker 53:115, Oct 31, 1977
    Newsweek 82:80, Jul 16, 1973
                90:74-5+, Oct 31, 1977
    Theatre Magazine 46:84, Dec 1927

Time 110:93, Oct 31, 1977
Vogue 70:172, Dec 1, 1927

Red Planet (with J. E. Hoare)
Productions:
Opened December 17, 1932 for 7 performances.
Reviews:
Commonweal 17:271, Jan 4, 1933
Nation 136:27-8, Jan 4, 1933
New York Times p. 19, Dec 19, 1932
Stage 10:8-9, Feb 1933
Theatre Arts 17:105-6, Feb 1933

BALDWIN, JAMES

The Amen Corner
Productions:
Opened April 15, 1965 for 84 performances.
(Off Off Broadway) Season of 1977-78 (Afro American Total
Theater).
Reviews:
America 112:690, May 8, 1965
Catholic World 201:215-6, Jun 1965
Commonweal 82:221-2, May 7, 1965
Life 58:16, May 14, 1965
Nation 200:514-5, May 10, 1965
New York Theatre Critics' Reviews 1965:349
New York Times p. 37, Mar 5, 1965
II, p. 1, Apr 11, 1965
p. 35, Apr 16, 1965
II, p. 1, Apr 25, 1965
p. 82, Jun 13, 1965
p. 19, Aug 9, 1965
p. 54, Apr 23, 1978
XI, p. 26, Dec 20, 1981
New Yorker 41:85, Apr 25, 1965
Newsweek 65:90, Apr 26, 1965
Saturday Review 48:49, May 1, 1965
Time 85:59, Apr 23, 1965
Vogue 145:68, Jun 1965

Blues for Mr. Charlie
Productions:
Opened April 23, 1964 for 148 performances.
(Off Off Broadway) August 1974 (Manhattan Theater Club).
Reviews:
America 110:776-7, May 30, 1964
Catholic World 199:263-4, Jul 1964
Commonweal 80:299-300, May 29, 1964
Ebony 19:188, Jun 1964

Nation 198:495-6, May 11, 1964
National Review 16:780-1, Sep 8, 1964
New Republic 150:35-7, May 16, 1964
New York Theatre Critics' Reviews 1964:276
New York Times II, p. 1, Apr 19, 1964
         p. 24, Apr 24, 1964
         II, p. 1, May 3, 1964
         p. 18, Jun 29, 1964
         p. 52, May 5, 1965
New Yorker 40:143, May 9, 1964
Newsweek 63:46, May 4, 1964
Saturday Review 47:27-8, May 2, 1964
         47:36, May 9, 1964
Time 83:50, May 1, 1964
     83:96, Jun 5, 1964
Vogue 144:32, Jul 1964

A Deed from the King of Spain
    Productions:
        (Off Off Broadway) January 24, 1974 (ACSTA).
    Reviews:
        New York Times p. 29, Feb 26, 1974

BARAKA, IMAMU AMIRI

Amiri Baraka: Poetry of the 50's, 60's and 70's
    Productions:
        (Off Off Broadway) November 1, 1980 for 5 performances (New
          Federal Theater).
    No Reviews.

The Baptism
    Productions:
        (Off Broadway) May 1, 1964 for 3 performances.
        (Off Off Broadway) October 7, 1972 (Players' Workshop).
    No Reviews.

A Black Mass
    Productions:
        (Off Off Broadway) Season of 1972-73 (Afro American Studio).
    Reviews:
        New York Times p. 18, Sep 30, 1972

A Black Quartet (Consists of Great Goodness of Life and Ed Bullins'
    The Gentleman Caller)
    Productions:
        (Off Broadway) July 30, 1969 for 111 performances.
    Reviews:
        New York Times p. 92, Apr 27, 1969
               II, p. 1, May 4, 1969

p. 28, Jul 31, 1969
II, p. 1, Aug 3, 1969
p. 36, Sep 22, 1969

Boy and Tarzan Appear in a Clearing
    Productions:
        (Off Off Broadway) October 9, 1981 for 12 performances (New
        Federal Theater).
    Reviews:
        New York Times III, p. 18, Oct 15, 1981

Dante
    Productions:
        (Off Broadway) October 29, 1961 for 16 performances.
    No Reviews.

Dutchman
    Productions:
        (Off Broadway) January 12, 1964 for 2 performances (Theater
        1964 Playwrights' Unit).
        (Off Broadway) March 23, 1964 for 80 performances.
        (Off Off Broadway) Season of 1975-76.
        (Off Off Broadway) February 10, 1977 (Perry Street Theater).
    Reviews:
        American Imago 29:215-32, Fall 1972
        New York Times p. 46, Mar 25, 1964
                       p. 34, Jun 28, 1965
                       p. 53, Nov 17, 1965
        New Yorker 40:78-9, Apr 4, 1964
        Newsweek 63:60, Apr 13, 1964
        Vogue 144:32, Jul 1964

Experimental Death Unit No. 1 (Presented in repertory with Junkies
        Are Full of Shhh and Great Goodness of Life)
    Productions:
        (Off Off Broadway) October 1, 1972 (Afro American Studio)
    Reviews:
        New York Times p. 41, Sep 20, 1972

Great Goodness of Life
    Productions:
        (Off Broadway) July 30, 1969 for 111 performances, (as part of
        a bill called A Black Quartet).
        (Off Off Broadway) October 1, 1972 in repertory (see Experi-
        mental Death Unit No. 1).
    Reviews:
        New York Times p. 92, Apr 27, 1969
                       II, p. 1, May 4, 1969
                       p. 28, Jul 31, 1969
                       II, p. 1, Aug 3, 1969
                       p. 36, Sep 22, 1969
                       p. 41, Sep 20, 1972

Junkies Are Full of Shhh
Productions:
(Off Off Broadway) October 1, 1972 in repertory (see Experimental Death Unit No. 1).
Reviews:
New York Times p. 41, Sep 20, 1972

Mad Heart
Productions:
(Off Off Broadway) Season of 1972-73 (Afro American Studio).
Reviews:
New York Times p. 18, Sep 30, 1972

The Motion of History
Productions:
(Off Off Broadway) May 27, 1977 (New York Theater Ensemble).
No Reviews.

A Recent Killing
Productions:
(Off Off Broadway) Season of 1972-73 (New Federal Theater).
Reviews:
Nation 216:218-19, Feb 12, 1973
New York Times p. 25, Jan 30, 1973
              II, p. 3, Feb 4, 1973
New Yorker 48:75, Feb 10, 1973
Newsweek 81:75, Feb 19, 1973

S-1
Productions:
(Off Off Broadway) July 1976 (Washington Square Methodist Church).
Reviews:
New York Times p. 18, July 29, 1976

Sidnee, Poet Heroical
Productions:
(Off Off Broadway) May 15, 1975 (New Federal Theater)
Reviews:
New York Times p. 54, May 21, 1975
Saturday Review 2:52, Jul 12, 1975

The Slave
Productions:
(Off Broadway) December 16, 1964 for 151 performances.
(Off Off Broadway) Season of 1971-72 (ACSTA).
(Off Off Broadway) Season of 1972-73 (ACSTA).
(Off Off Broadway) February 7, 1974 (ACSTA).
(Off Off Broadway) February 27, 1976 (ACSTA).
Reviews:
Nation 200:16-17, Jan 4, 1965

National Review 17:249, Mar 23, 1965
New Republic 152:32-3, Jan 23, 1965
New York Times p. 51, Dec 17, 1964
            p. 53, Nov 17, 1965
            p. 29, Feb 26, 1974
New Yorker 40:50+, Dec 26, 1964
Newsweek 64:56, Dec 28, 1964
Saturday Review 48:46, Jan 9, 1965
Time 84:62-3, Dec 25, 1964
Vogue 145:98, Feb 1, 1965

Slave Ship
　　Productions:
　　　　(Off Off Broadway) Season of 1969-70 (Chelsea Theater Center).
　　　　(Off Broadway) January 13, 1970 for 4 performances.
　　Reviews:
　　　　Nation 210:125, Feb 2, 1970
　　　　New York Times p. 46, Nov 22, 1969
　　　　　　　　II, p. 3, Nov 23, 1969
　　　　New Yorker 45:168, Dec 6, 1969
　　　　Newsweek 74:86, Dec 1, 1969

The Toilet
　　Productions:
　　　　(Off Broadway) December 16, 1964 for 151 performances.
　　Reviews:
　　　　Nation 200:16, Jan 4, 1965
　　　　National Review 17:249, Mar 23, 1965
　　　　New Republican 152:32-3, Jan 23, 1965
　　　　New York Times p. 51, Dec 17, 1964
　　　　New Yorker 40:50+, Dec 26, 1964
　　　　Newsweek 64:56, Dec 28, 1964
　　　　Saturday Review 48:46, Jan 9, 1965
　　　　Time 84:62, Dec 25, 1964
　　　　Vogue 145:98, Feb 1, 1965

BARKER, JAMES NELSON

No productions.

BARRY, PHILIP

The Animal Kingdom
　　Productions:
　　　　Opened January 12, 1932 for 183 performances.
　　Reviews:
　　　　Arts and Decoration 36:63-4, Mar 1932
　　　　Bookman 74:562-3, Jan 1932

Catholic World 134:714-15, Mar 1932
Commonweal 15:441-2, Feb 17, 1932
Nation 134:141, Feb 3, 1932
New Republic 69:293-4, Jan 27, 1932
New York Times p. 26, Jan 13, 1932
      VIII, p. 1, Jan 24, 1932
      p. 14, Jul 27, 1938
      p. 16, Jul 4, 1974
      III, p. 5, Jul 23, 1982
North American Review 234:173, Aug 1932
Outlook 160:118, Jan 27, 1932
Theatre Arts 16:187-8, Mar 1932
Theatre Guild Magazine 9:15-17, Mar 1932
Vogue 79:100, Mar 1, 1932

Bright Star
 Productions:
  Opened October 15, 1935 for 7 performances.
 Reviews:
  Commonweal 23:19, Nov 1, 1935
  Nation 141:520, Oct 30, 1935
  New York Times IX, p. 1, Oct 13, 1935
       p. 26, Oct 16, 1935
  Theatre Arts 19:899-900, Dec 1935
  Time 26:39, Oct 28, 1935

Cock Robin (with Elmer Rice)
 Productions:
  Opened January 12, 1928 for 100 performances.
 Reviews:
  American Mercury 13:376-7, Mar 1928
  Life (NY) 91:21, Feb 2, 1928
  Nation 126:130, Feb 1, 1928
  New York Times p. 26, Jan 13, 1928
       VIII, p. 2, Jan 15, 1928
  Outlook 148:423, Mar 14, 1928
  Theatre Arts 12:172, Mar 1928
  Theatre Magazine 47:40, Mar 1928
  Vogue 71:83+, Mar 1, 1928

Foolish Notion
 Productions:
  Opened March 13, 1945 for 104 performances.
 Reviews:
  Catholic World 161:70, Apr 1945
  Commonweal 41:589, Mar 30, 1945
  Nation 160:340-1, Mar 24, 1945
  New Republic 112:421, Mar 26, 1945
  New York Theatre Critics' Reviews 1945:254
  New York Times VI, p. 24, Feb 25, 1945
       p. 23, Mar 14, 1945

II, p. 1, Mar 18, 1945
New York Times Magazine p. 24-5, Feb 25, 1945
New Yorker 21:48, Mar 24, 1945
Newsweek 25:88, Mar 26, 1945
Saturday Review 28:18-19, Mar 24, 1945
Theatre Arts 29:199, Apr 1945
29:269-70, May 1945
Time 45:70+, Mar 26, 1945

Here Come the Clowns

Productions:
Opened December 7, 1938 for 88 performances.
(Off Broadway) Season of 1960-61.
(Off Broadway) May 13, 1966 for 9 performances (Equity Theatre).

Reviews:
America 104:100, Oct 15, 1960
Catholic World 148:473-4, Jan 1939
179:308, Jul 1954
Commonweal 29:244, Dec 23, 1938
29:552, Mar 10, 1939
Forum 101:72, Feb 1939
Nation 147:700, Dec 24, 1938
New Republic 97:230, Dec 28, 1938
New York Times p. 36, Dec 8, 1938
p. 30, Dec 20, 1938
IX, p. 3, Jan 8, 1939
p. 36, May 5, 1954
p. 48, Sep 20, 1960
New Yorker 36:131-2, Oct 1, 1960
Newsweek 12:25, Dec 19, 1938
North American Review 247, no. 1:156-7, Mar 1939
One Act Play Magazine 2:671-3, Jan 1939
Theatre Arts 23:89-91+, Feb 1939
Time 32:43-4, Dec 19, 1938

Holiday

Productions:
Opened November 26, 1928 for 229 performances.
Opened December 26, 1973 for 28 performances.

Reviews:
American Mercury 16:245, Feb 1929
Bookman 68:684-5, Feb 1929
Commonweal 9:405, Feb 6, 1929
Drama 19:103, 128, Jan 1929
Los Angeles 25:294+, Nov 1980
Nation 218:61-2, Jan 12, 1974
New Republic 57:96-7, Dec 12, 1928
New York Magazine 7:66+, Jan 14, 1974
New York Theatre Critics' Reviews 1973:128
New York Times p. 36, Nov 27, 1928

p. 26, Nov 28, 1928
X, p. 1, Dec 9, 1928
p. 21, Feb 6, 1930
p. 15, Jul 23, 1941
p. 45, Dec 27, 1973
II, p. 1, Jan 6, 1974
XXIII, p. 13, Aug 15, 1982
New Yorker 49:44+, Jan 7, 1974
Newsweek 83:62, Jan 7, 1974
Outlook 151:11, Jan 2, 1929
Review of Reviews 79:160, Feb 1929
Theatre Magazine 49:78, Feb 1929
49:18, Apr 1929
50:15, Jul 1929
52:47, Aug 1930
Time 103:71, Jan 7, 1974

Hotel Universe
Productions:
Opened April 14, 1930 for 81 performances.
(Off Off Broadway) Season of 1971-72 (American Theater Co.).
Reviews:
Catholic World 131:327-8, Jun 1930
Commonweal 11:741, Apr 30, 1930
Life (NY) 95:18, May 2, 1930
Nation 130:525-6, Apr 30, 1930
New Republic 62:326-8, May 7, 1930
New York Times p. 29, Apr 15, 1930
VIII, p. 1, Apr 20, 1930
Outlook 154:711, Apr 30, 1930
Review of Reviews 81:130, Jun 1930
Sketch Book 7:29, Jul 1930
Theatre Arts 14:462-3, Jun 1930
Theatre Magazine 51:43-4+, Jun 1930
Vogue 75:122, Jun 7, 1930

In a Garden
Productions:
Opened November 16, 1925 for 73 performances.
Reviews:
Bookman 62:705, Feb 1926
Dial 80:73, Jan 1926
Independent 116:48, Jan 9, 1926
Life (NY) 86:18, Dec 10, 1925
New York Times p. 29, Nov 17, 1925
VIII, p. 1, Nov 22, 1925
Theatre Magazine 43:15, Jan 1926
Vogue 67:87, Jan 15, 1926

John
Productions:

Opened November 2, 1927 for 11 performances.
(Off Off Broadway) May 5, 1976 (Joseph Jefferson).
Reviews:
Dial 84:81, Jan 1928
Life (NY) 90:23, Nov 24, 1927
Nation 125:582-3, Nov 23, 1927
New York Times p. 16, Nov 5, 1927
p. 22, May 22, 1976
Theatre Arts 12:4, Jan 1928
12:19, Jan 1928

The Joyous Season
Productions:
Opened January 29, 1934 for 16 performances.
Reviews:
Catholic World 138:729-30, Mar 1934
Commonweal 19:413, Feb 9, 1934
19:469, Feb 23, 1934
Literary Digest 117:23, Feb 24, 1934
Nation 138:200-2, Feb 14, 1934
New Republic 78:21, Feb 14, 1934
New York Times p. 16, Jan 30, 1934
II, p. 9, Nov 24, 1935
Newsweek 3:39, Feb 10, 1934
Review of Reviews 89:47, Mar 1934
Stage 11:17, Mar 1934
Theatre Arts 18:244, Apr 1934
Time 23:34, Feb 5, 1934
Vanity Fair 42:45-6, Apr 1934

Liberty Jones
Productions:
Opened February 5, 1941 for 22 performances.
Reviews:
Catholic World 152:725-6, Mar 1941
Commonweal 33:447, Feb 21, 1941
Nation 152:192, Feb 15, 1941
New Republic 104:276, Feb 24, 1941
New York Theatre Critics' Reviews 1941:391
New York Times p. 24, Feb 6, 1941
New Yorker 17:30, Feb 15, 1941
Newsweek 17:67, Feb 17, 1941
Theatre Arts 25:261, Apr 1941
Time 37:85, Feb 17, 1941

My Name Is Aquilon (Adapted from the play by Jean Pierre Aumont)
Productions:
Opened February 9, 1949 for 31 performances.
Reviews:
Nation 168:256, Feb 26, 1949
New York Theatre Critics' Reviews 1949:362

New York Times p. 38, Feb 10, 1949
New Yorker 24:60, Feb 19, 1949
Newsweek 33:79, Feb 21, 1949
Theatre Arts 33:24-5, May 1949
Time 53:76, Feb 21, 1949

Paris Bound

Productions:
Opened December 27, 1927 for 234 performances.
Reviews:
American Mercury 13:376-7, Mar 1928
Bookman 67:288-90, May 1928
Drama Magazine 18:139, Feb 1928
Life (NY) 91:21, Jan 19, 1928
Nation 126:75-6, Jan 18, 1928
New Republic 53:273, Jan 25, 1928
New York Times p. 26, Dec 28, 1927
VIII, p. 1, Jan 1, 1928
VIII, p. 1, Jan 15, 1928
X, p. 1, Dec 2, 1928
p. 28, May 1, 1929
IX, p. 1, May 19, 1929
Outlook 148:147, Jan 25, 1928
Saturday Review 4:515-6, Jan 14, 1928
Theatre Arts 12:166, 169, Mar 1928
Theatre Magazine 47:40, Mar 1928
Vogue 71:86-7, Feb 15, 1928

The Philadelphia Story

Productions:
Opened March 28, 1939 for 417 performances.
(Off Off Broadway) November 1974 (Manhattan Theater Club).
Opened November 14, 1980 for 60 performances.
Reviews:
America 143:391, Dec 13, 1980
Catholic World 149:216-17, May 1939
Commonweal 29:692, Apr 14, 1939
Life 6:39-40+, Apr 24, 1939
Nation 148:410-11, Apr 8, 1939
231:620, Dec 6, 1980
New Leader 63:22-3, Dec 1, 1980
New Republic 183:25-6, Dec 27, 1980
New West 5:SC-25, Jun 2, 1980
New York Magazine 13:68, Dec 1, 1980
New York Theatre Critics' Reviews 1950:487
1980:89
New York Times p. 14, Feb 17, 1939
XI, p. 2, Mar 19, 1929
p. 21, Mar 29, 1939
X, p. 1, Apr 2, 1939
p. 8, Jun 4, 1949

p. 32, Jun 28, 1949
p. 3, Sep 27, 1949
p. 46, Jun 22, 1967
p. 11, Apr 22, 1978
II, p. 1, Nov 9, 1980
III, p. 15, Nov 17, 1980
II, p. 3, Nov 23, 1980
New Yorker 56:134-5, Nov 24, 1980
Newsweek 13:28-9, Apr 10, 1939
96:83, Dec 1, 1980
North American Review 247:366, Summer 1939
Stage 16:16-18, Apr 1, 1939
Theatre Arts 23:324-25, May 1939
Time 33:56, Apr 10, 1939
116:98, Dec 1, 1980
Vogue 93:90, May 1, 1939

Second Threshold (with revisions by Robert E. Sherwood)
Productions:
Opened January 2, 1951 for 126 performances.
Reviews:
Catholic World 172:385, Feb 1951
Christian Science Monitor Magazine p. 6, Jan 6, 1951
Commonweal 53:398, Jan 26, 1951
Life 30:53-4, Jan 29, 1951
Nation 172:44, Jan 13, 1951
New Republic 124:22, Feb 5, 1951
New York Theatre Critics' Reviews 1951:398
New York Times II, p. 1, Dec 31, 1950
p. 23, Jan 3, 1951
II, p. 1, Jan 14, 1951
VI, p. 32, Jan 14, 1951
p. 38, Sep 25, 1952
II, p. 3, Oct 12, 1952
New Yorker 26:42+, Jan 13, 1951
Newsweek 37:78, Jan 15, 1951
Saturday Review 34:25-7, Jan 27, 1951
School and Society 73:183, Mar 24, 1951
Theatre Arts 35:16, Mar 1951
35:17, Sep 1951
Time 57:39, Jan 15, 1951

Spring Dance
Productions:
Opened August 25, 1936 for 24 performances.
Reviews:
Commonweal 24:487, Sep 18, 1936
Literary Digest 122:19, Jul 25, 1936
122:24, Sep 5, 1936
Nation 143:284, Sep 5, 1936
New Republic 88:160, Sep 16, 1936

New York Times p. 22, Jul 7, 1936
          p. 17, Aug 26, 1936
Newsweek 8:27, Sep 5, 1936
Time 28:53, Sep 7, 1936

Tomorrow and Tomorrow

Productions:
   Opened January 13, 1931 for 206 performances.
Reviews:
   Arts and Decoration 34:84, Mar 1931
   Bookman 73:72-3, Mar 1931
   Catholic World 132:717-18, Mar 1931
   Commonweal 13:357-8, Jan 28, 1931
   Drama Magazine 21:10-11, Mar 1931
   Dramatist 22:1431, Jan 1931
   Life (NY) 97:18, Jan 30, 1931
   Nation 132:108, Jan 28, 1931
   New Republic 65:322-3, Feb 4, 1931
   New York Times p. 26, Jan 14, 1931
             VIII, p. 2, Feb 1, 1931
             p. 17, Jun 24, 1941
   Outlook 157:152, Jan 28, 1931
   Theatre Arts 15:185-6, Mar 1931
   Theatre Magazine 53:24, Mar 1931
             53:33-5+, May 1931
   Vogue 77:59, Mar 1, 1931

White Wings

Productions:
   Opened October 15, 1926 for 27 performances.
Reviews:
   Dial 82:77, Jan 1927
   Life (NY) 88:23, Nov 11, 1926
   New York Times p. 15, Oct 16, 1926
             VIII, p. 1, Oct 24, 1926
   Theatre Magazine 44:72, Dec 1926
   Vogue 68:77+, Dec 15, 1926

Without Love

Productions:
   Opened November 10, 1942 for 113 performances.
Reviews:
   Catholic World 156:336-7, Dec 1942
   Commonweal 37:144, Nov 27, 1942
   Current History ns 3:456, Jan 1943
   Life 12:78+, May 11, 1942
   Nation 155:553-4, Nov 21, 1942
   New Republic 107:679-80, Nov 23, 1942
   New York Theatre Critics' Reviews 1942:182
   New York Times p. 20, Mar 5, 1942
             p. 17, Apr 28, 1942

IV, p. 2, May 3, 1942
VII, p. 12, Nov 8, 1942
p. 28, Nov 11, 1942
VIII, p. 1, Nov 29, 1942
New Yorker 18:36+, Nov 21, 1942
Newsweek 20:73, Nov 23, 1942
Theatre Arts 27:15, Jan 1943
Time 39:61, Apr 27, 1942
40:53, Nov 23, 1942

You and I
Productions:
Opened February 19, 1923 for 136+ performances.
Reviews:
Bookman 57:318-9, May 1923
58:58-9, Sep 1923
Current Opinion 74:702-7, Jun 1923
Dial 75:100-101, Jun 1923
Dramatist 14:1153-4, Apr 1923
Hearst 44:85-7+, Oct 1923
Independent 110:207, Mar 17, 1923
Life (NY) 81:18, Mar 15, 1923
Nation 116:346, Mar 21, 1923
New York Clipper 71:14, Feb 28, 1923
New York Times p. 12, Feb 20, 1923
VII, p. 1, Feb 25, 1923
p. 29, Oct 20, 1925
Scribner's Magazine 74:69, Jul 1923
Theatre Magazine 37:16, Apr 1923
38:28+, Jul 1923

The Youngest
Productions:
Opened December 22, 1924 for 104 performances.
Reviews:
American Mercury 4:247-8, Feb 1925
Current Opinion 78:436-44, Apr 1925
Life (NY) 85:18, Jan 8, 1925
New York Times p. 17, Dec 23, 1924
Theatre Arts 9:151, Mar 1925
Theatre Magazine 41:19, Mar 1925

BEACH, LEWIS

*Ann Vroome
Reviews:
New York Times VIII, p. 2, Jul 27, 1930

Brothers
Productions:

(Off Broadway) Season of 1919-20.
Reviews:
New York Times p. 14, Dec 6, 1919

The Clod
Productions:
Season of 1915-16 in repertory (Washington Square Players).
Reviews:
Bookman 43:23, Mar 1916
Dramatic Mirror 75:8, Jan 22, 1916
New York Times p. 11, Jan 11, 1916
p. 11, Jun 6, 1916

The Goose Hangs High
Productions:
Opened January 29, 1924 for 159+ performances.
Reviews:
Bookman 59:203, Apr 1924
Drama 16:66, Nov 1925
Dramatist 15:1210-11, Apr 1924
Life (NY) 83:18, Feb 14, 1924
New York Times p. 16, Jan 30, 1924
VII, p. 1, Feb 3, 1924
Theatre Magazine 39:15-16, Apr 1924

Merry Andrew
Productions:
Opened January 21, 1929 for 24 performances.
Reviews:
Commonweal 4:431, Feb 13, 1929
Life (NY) 93:25, Feb 15, 1929
Nation 128:168, Feb 6, 1929
New York Times VIII, p. 2, Jan 13, 1929
p. 22, Jan 22, 1929
Vogue 73:150, Mar 16, 1929

A Square Peg
Productions:
Opened January 27, 1923 for 41 performances.
Reviews:
Bookman 57:194-5, Apr 1923
Life (NY) 81:18, Feb 15, 1923
Nation 116:224, Feb 21, 1923
New York Clipper 71:14, Feb 7, 1923
New York Times p. 10, Jan 29, 1923
VII, p. 1, Feb 11, 1923

BEHRMAN, S. N.

Amphitryon 38 (Adapted from the original by Jean Giraudoux)
Productions:

Opened November 1, 1937 for 153 performances.
(Off Off Broadway) November 5, 1978 (Soho Repertory).
Reviews:
Catholic World 146:338-9, Dec 1937
Commonweal 27:78, Nov 12, 1937
Life 3:70, Jul 1937
Literary Digest 1:35, Nov 20, 1935
Nation 145:539, Nov 13, 1937
New Republic 93:44, Nov 17, 1937
        94:132, Mar 9, 1938
New York Times p. 30, Jun 24, 1937
        p. 32, Nov 2, 1937
        XI, p. 1, Nov 7, 1937
Newsweek 10:20-1, Jul 3, 1937
        10:22, Nov 8, 1937
Scribner's Magazine 102:66+, Dec 1937
Stage 15:46-9, Oct 1937
     15:94, Nov 1937
     15:44-5, Jan 1938
Theatre Arts 21:924, Dec 1937
Time 30:25, Nov 8, 1937

Biography
Productions:
Opened December 12, 1932 for 267 performances.
Opened February, 1934 for 283 performances.
(Off Broadway) February 26, 1980 for 48 performances.
Reviews:
Arts and Decoration 38:56, Feb 1933
Catholic World 136:590, Feb 1933
Commonweal 17:245, Dec 28, 1932
Nation 135:654, Dec 28, 1932
     136:327-8, Mar 22, 1933
New Outlook 161:46, Jan 1933
New Republic 73:188-9, Dec 28, 1932
New York Magazine 13:88-9, Mar 31, 1980
New York Times p. 25, Dec 13, 1932
        IX, p. 1, Jan 22, 1933
        p. 24, Feb 6, 1934
        IX, p. 2, May 20, 1934
        II, p. 12, Apr 11, 1937
        p. 14, Aug 3, 1938
        III, p. 5, Feb 23, 1979
        III, p. 13, Mar 17, 1980
        XXI, p. 15, May 4, 1980
Player's Magazine 9:11, Mar-Apr 1933
Saturday Review 9:438, Feb 18, 1933
Stage 10:1+, Feb 1933
Theatre Arts 17:103-5, Feb 1933
     18:495-6, Jul 1934

Vanity Fair 39:60, Feb 1933
Vogue 81:56+, Feb 1, 1933

Brief Moment
    Productions:
        Opened November 9, 1931 for 129 performances.
    Reviews:
        Arts and Decoration 36:78, Jan 1932
        Catholic World 134:469-70, Jan 1932
        Commonweal 15:134, Dec 2, 1931
        Nation 133:621-2, Dec 2, 1931
        New Republic 69:70, Dec 2, 1931
                69:136, Dec 16, 1931
        New York Times p. 16, Feb 25, 1932
                VIII, p. 1, Feb 28, 1932
                VIII, p. 2, Oct 25, 1931
                p. 28, Nov 10, 1931
        Outlook 159:407, Nov 25, 1931
        Theatre Arts 16:20, Jan 1932
        Theatre Guild Magazine 9:4-6, Dec 1931

But for Whom Charlie
    Productions:
        Opened March 12, 1964 for 34 performances (Repertory Theatre
           of Lincoln Center).
    Reviews:
        America 110:657, May 9, 1964
        Commonweal 80:90, Apr 10, 1964
        Nation 198:335-6, Mar 30, 1964
        New York Theatre Critics' Reviews 1964:322
        New York Times II, p. 5, Mar 8, 1964
                p. 42, Mar 13, 1964
        New Yorker 40:64, Mar 21, 1964
        Newsweek 63:70, Mar 23, 1964
        Saturday Review 47:21, Mar 28, 1964
        Time 83:55, Mar 20, 1964
        Vogue 143:62, May 1964

The Cold Wind and the Warm
    Productions:
        Opened December 8, 1958 for 120 performances.
        (Off Off Broadway) October 27, 1977 (Jewish Repertory The-
           ater).
    Reviews:
        America 100:438, Jan 10, 1959
        Catholic World 188:421, Feb 1959
        Commentary 27:256-60, Mar 1959
        Commonweal 69:496-7, Feb 6, 1959
        New York Theatre Critics' Reviews 1958:175
        New York Times II, p. 8, Dec 7, 1958

p. 55, Dec 9, 1958
II, p. 1, Jan 18, 1959
New Yorker 34:69, Dec 20, 1958
Newsweek 52:46, Dec 22, 1958
Theatre Arts 43:201, Feb 1959
Time 72:54, Dec 22, 1958

Dunnigan's Daughter

Productions:
Opened December 26, 1945 for 38 performances.
Reviews:
Catholic World 162:456, Feb 1946
Nation 162:81, Jan 19, 1946
New York Theatre Critics' Reviews 1945:54
New York Times p. 16, Dec 27, 1945
II, p. 1, Jan 6, 1946
New Yorker 21:43-4, Jan 5, 1946
Theatre Arts 30:138, Mar 1946
Time 47:86+, Jan 7, 1946

End of Summer

Productions:
Opened February 17, 1936 for 153 performances.
(Off Off Broadway) November 24, 1974 (Manhattan Theater
Club).
Reviews:
Catholic World 143:86-7, Apr 1936
Commonweal 23:497, Feb 28, 1936
Literary Digest 121:19, Feb 29, 1936
Los Angeles 22:187, Mar 1977
Nation 142:291-2, Mar 4, 1936
New Republic 86:113, Mar 4, 1936
86:141, Mar 11, 1936
New York Times p. 17, Jan 31, 1936
X, p. 2, Feb 9, 1936
p. 26, Feb 18, 1936
IX, p. 1, Mar 1, 1936
p. 30, Nov 26, 1974
Newsweek 7:31-2, Feb 29, 1936
Stage 13:28-9, Mar 1936
Theatre Arts 20:258-60, Apr 1936
Time 27:59, Mar 2, 1936

I Know My Love (Adapted from Marcel Achard's Auprès de Ma Blonde)

Productions:
Opened November 2, 1949 for 246 performances.
Reviews:
Catholic World 170:229, Dec 1949
Forum 112:337-8, Dec 1949
Nation 169:498, Nov 19, 1949
New Republic 121:19, Nov 21, 1949

New York Theatre Critics' Reviews 1949:233
New York Times p. 29, Feb 24, 1949
          p. 36, Nov 3, 1949
          VI, p. 24, Nov 13, 1949
          II, p. 1, Nov 20, 1949
New Yorker 25:54+, Nov 12, 1949
Newsweek 34:84, Nov 14, 1949
Saturday Review 32:54-5, Dec 3, 1949
Theatre Arts 34:13, Jan 1950
Time 53:58, Mar 7, 1949
     54:49, Nov 14, 1949

Jacobowsky and the Colonel (Based on the play by Franz Werfel)
  Productions:
    Opened March 14, 1944 for 417 performances.
  Reviews:
    Catholic World 159:169-70, May 1944
                   159:457-8, Aug 1944
    Commonweal 39:589-90, Mar 31, 1944
    Life 16:49-50+, Apr 10, 1944
    Nation 158:373, Mar 25, 1944
           158:429-30, Apr 8, 1944
    New Republic 110:407, Mar 27, 1944
    New York Theatre Critics' Reviews 1944:243
    New York Times II, p. 3, Jan 9, 1944
                   VI, p. 24, Mar 5, 1944
                   II, p. 1, Mar 12, 1944
                   p. 17, Mar 15, 1944
                   II, p. 1, Mar 19, 1944
                   VI, p. 16, Apr 9, 1944
                   II, p. 1, May 21, 1944
                   II, p. 1, Jun 24, 1945
    New Yorker 20:52, Mar 25, 1944
    Newsweek 23:105-6, Mar 27, 1944
    Theatre Arts 28:143-50, Mar 1944
                 28:204, Apr 1944
                 28:261-2+, May 1944
    Time 43:60+, Mar 27, 1944

Jane (Suggested by a story of W. Somerset Maugham's)
  Productions:
    Opened February 1, 1952 for 100 performances.
  Reviews:
    Catholic World 174:465, Mar 1952
    Commonweal 55:496, Feb 22, 1952
    Nation 174:162, Feb 16, 1952
    New Republic 126:23, Feb 18, 1952
    New York Theatre Critics' Reviews 1952:376
    New York Times p. 10, Feb 2, 1952
                   II, p. 1, Feb 10, 1952
    New Yorker 27:56-7, Feb 9, 1952

Newsweek 39:82, Feb 11, 1952
Saturday Review 35:34, Feb 16, 1952
School and Society 75:325, May 24, 1952
Theatre Arts 31:59, Apr 1947
           36:71, Apr 1952
Time 59:79, Feb 11, 1952

Lord Pengo (Based on Behrman's The Days of Duveen)
   Productions:
     Opened November 19, 1962 for 175 performances.
   Reviews:
     America 108:52, Jan 12, 1963
     Life 54:51-2, Feb 22, 1963
     Nation 196:214, Mar 9, 1963
     New York Theatre Critics' Reviews 1962:192
     New York Times II, p. 1, Nov 18, 1962
                     p. 41, Nov 20, 1962
     New Yorker 38:118, Dec 1, 1962
     Newsweek 60:63, Dec 3, 1962
     Theatre Arts 47:11, Jan 1963
     Time 80:53, Nov 30, 1962

Love Is Like That (with Kenyon Nicholson)
   Productions:
     Opened April 18, 1927 for 24 performances.
   Reviews:
     Life (NY) 89:25, May 5, 1927
     New York Times p. 24, Apr 19, 1927
     Theatre Magazine 45:25, Jun 1927

The Mechanical Heart (see The Talley Method)

Meteor
   Productions:
     Opened December 23, 1929 for 92 performances.
   Reviews:
     Catholic World 130:724-5, Mar 1930
     Commonweal 11:310, Jan 15, 1930
     Life (NY) 95:20, Jan 10, 1930
     Nation 130:78-9, Jan 15, 1930
     New Republic 61:250, Jan 22, 1930
     New York Times X, p. 2, Dec 8, 1929
                   p. 15, Dec 24, 1929
                   p. 24, Jan 20, 1930
     Outlook 154:73, Jan 8, 1930
     Sketch Book 7:21, Mar 1930
     Theatre Magazine 51:45-6, Mar 1930
                     51:8, Apr 1930
     Vogue 75:118, Feb 15, 1930

No Time for Comedy
   Productions:

Opened April 17, 1939 for 185 performances.
Reviews:
Catholic World 149:344-5, Jun 1939
Commonweal 30:48, May 5, 1939
Nation 148:509-10, Apr 29, 1939
New Republic 98:378, May 3, 1939
New York Times p. 18, Mar 31, 1939
                p. 26, Apr 18, 1939
                XI, p. 1, Apr 30, 1939
                X, p. 2, May 7, 1939
                p. 47, Mar 31, 1940
                III, p. 17, Dec 7, 1978
Newsweek 13:45, May 1, 1939
North American Review 247 no 2:367-8, Jun 1939
Stage 16:22, Apr 1, 1939
      16:18-21, Apr 15, 1939
Theatre Arts 23:395-6, Jun 1939
Time 33:61, May 1, 1939

The Pirate (Suggested by a play by Ludwig Fulda)
Productions:
Opened November 25, 1942 for 177 performances.
Reviews:
Catholic World 156:475-6, Jan 1943
Commonweal 37:206, Dec 11, 1942
Current History ns 3:455, Jan 1943
Independent Woman 21:367, Dec 1942
Life 13:89-92, Oct 5, 1942
Nation 155:659, Dec 12, 1942
New Republic 107:792-3, Dec 14, 1942
New York Theatre Critics' Reviews 1942:162
New York Times p. 18, Sep 15, 1942
                p. 39, Nov 26, 1942
                VIII, p. 1, Dec 6, 1942
                p. 18, May 26, 1943
New York Times Magazine pp. 16-17, Oct 4, 1942
Newsweek 20:74, Dec 7, 1942
Poet Lore 49:286, Autumn 1943
Theatre Arts 26:605, Oct 1942
             27:12+, Jan 1943
Time 40:54-5, Dec 7, 1942

Rain from Heaven
Productions:
Opened December 24, 1934 for 99 performances.
Reviews:
Canadian Forum 15:194-5, Feb 1935
Catholic World 140:599, Feb 1935
Commonweal 21:318, Jan 11, 1935
Nation 140:55-6, Jan 9, 1935
New Republic 81:308, Jan 23, 1935

New York Times p. 26, Dec 11, 1934
XI, p. 2, Dec 16, 1934
p. 28, Dec 25, 1934
IX, p. 3, Dec 30, 1934
IX, p. 1, Jan 6, 1935
Stage 12:2-3, Feb 1935
Theatre Arts 19:96, Feb 1935
Time 25:40, Jan 7, 1935
Vanity Fair 44:47, Mar 1935

The Second Man

Productions:
Opened April 11, 1927 for 178 performances.
(Off Off Broadway) June 1, 1977 (Joseph Jefferson).
(Off Off Broadway) January 4, 1980 (Soho Repertory).
Reviews:
American Mercury 11:249-50, Jun 1927
Dial 82:535-6, Jun 1927
Dramatist 18:1343, Jun 1927
Life (NY) 89:19, Apr 28, 1927
Nation 124:484, Apr 27, 1927
New Republic 50:274, Apr 27, 1927
New York Times p. 24, Apr 12, 1927
VII, p. 1, Apr 24, 1927
VIII, p. 2, Feb 12, 1928
IX, p. 2, May 25, 1930
Theatre Magazine 46:18, Jul 1927
Vogue 69:75+, Jun 1, 1927
70:118, Oct 1, 1927

Serena Blandish

Productions:
Opened January 23, 1929 for 93 performances.
Reviews:
Catholic World 128:722-3, Mar 1929
Commonweal 9:430-1, Feb 13, 1929
Life (NY) 93:25, Feb 15, 1929
Nation 128:212-14, Feb 13, 1929
New Republic 57:346-7, Feb 13, 1929
New York Times VIII, p. 2, Jan 13, 1929
p. 30, Jan 24, 1929
IX, p. 2, Jan 27, 1929
VIII, p. 1, Feb 3, 1929
Outlook 151:262, Feb 13, 1929
Theatre Magazine 49:45, Apr 1929
50:14, Jul 1929
Vogue 73:104, Mar 16, 1929

The Talley Method

Productions:
Opened February 24, 1941 for 56 performances.

Reviews:
American Mercury 52:355-6, Mar 1941
Catholic World 153:85-6, Apr 1941
Commonweal 33:519, Mar 14, 1941
Nation 152:277, Mar 8, 1941
New Republic 104:340, Mar 10, 1941
New York Theatre Critics' Reviews 1941:373
New York Times p. 26, Feb 23, 1941
p. 26, Feb 25, 1941
IX, p. 1, Mar 2, 1941
IX, p. 4, Mar 23, 1941
IX, p. 3, Mar 30, 1941
New Yorker 17:34+, Mar 8, 1941
Newsweek 17:66, Mar 10, 1941
Theatre Arts 25:256+, Apr 1941
Time 37:44, Mar 10, 1941

Wine of Choice
Productions:
Opened February 21, 1938 for 43 performances.
Reviews:
Catholic World 147:85, Apr 1938
Commonweal 27:554, Mar 11, 1938
Nation 146:280-1, Mar 5, 1938
New Republic 94:132, Mar 9, 1938
New York Times p. 32, Dec 14, 1937
p. 18, Feb 22, 1938
X, p. 1, Feb 27, 1938
One Act Play Magazine 1:953-4, Feb 1938
1:1023-4, Mar 1938
Theatre Arts 22:253-4, Apr 1938
Time 31:52, Mar 7, 1938

BELASCO, DAVID

The Comedian (Adapted from a play by Sacha Guitry)
Productions:
Opened March 13, 1923 for 87 performances
Reviews:
Dial 74:635-6, Jun 1923
Hearst 44:85-7+, Jul 1923
Life (NY) 81:20, Apr 5, 1923
New York Clipper 71:14, Mar 21, 1923
New York Times p. 14, Mar 14, 1923
VIII, p. 1, Mar 25, 1923
Theatre Magazine 37:14+, May 1923

Fanny (with Willard Mack)
Productions:
Opened September 21, 1926 for 63 performances.

Reviews:
    Bookman 64:481, Dec 1926
    New York Times p. 30, Sep 22, 1926
    Theatre Magazine 44:15, Nov 1926
    Vogue 68:106, Nov 15, 1926

Girl of the Golden West
  Productions:
    (Off Broadway) Season of 1957-68.
  Reviews:
    New York Times p. 44, Nov 6, 1957
    Theatre Arts 42:25, Jan 1958

Kiki (Adapted from the French of André Picard.)
  Productions:
    Opened November 29, 1921 for 600 performances.
  Reviews:
    Bookman 54:573, Feb 1922
    Current Opinion 72:342-51, Mar 1922
    Dramatic Mirror 84:809, Dec 3, 1921
    Dramatist 13:1102-3, Apr 1922
    Hearst 42:85-7+, Jul 1922
    Life (NY) 78:18, Dec 15, 1921
    Nation 113:736, Dec 21, 1921
    New York Clipper 69:20, Dec 7, 1921
    New York Times p. 13, Nov 30, 1921
            VII, p. 1, Dec 4, 1921
    Theatre Magazine 35:97-8+, Feb 1922

Laugh, Clown, Laugh! (with Tom Cushing. Adapted from Faurto
    Martini's Ridi Pagliaccio.)
  Productions:
    Opened November 28, 1923 for 133 performances.
  Reviews:
    Life (NY) 82:18, Dec 20, 1923
    New Republic 37:94-5, Dec 19, 1923
    New York Times VIII, p. 2, Oct 28, 1923
              p. 30, Nov 29, 1923
              IX, p. 1, Dec 9, 1923
    Theatre Magazine 39:15-16, Feb 1924

The Lily (Adapted from the French of Pierre Wolff and Gaston
    Leroux)
  Productions:
    Opened December 23, 1909 for 164 performances.
  Reviews:
    Burr McIntosh Monthly 22:222-3, Mar 1910
    Current Literature 48:204, Feb 1910
    Dramatic Mirror 63:5, Jan 1, 1910
    Dramatist 1:45-8, Apr 1913
    Forum 43:190, Feb 1910

Green Book 3:516-19, Mar 1910
Hampton 24:407-8, Mar 1910
Life (NY) 55:37, Jan 6, 1910
Metropolitan Magazine 31:818-9, Mar 1910
Nation 89:659, Dec 30, 1909
Pearson 23:368-72, Mar 1910
Theatre Magazine 11:42-4, Feb 1910
Twentieth Century Magazine 2:507-10, Sep 1910

Mima (Adapted from Ferenc Molnar's The Red Mill)
Productions:
    Opened December 12, 1928 for 180 performances.
Reviews:
    American Mercury 16:249, Feb 1929
    Bookman 68:686, Feb 1929
    Catholic World 128:593-4, Feb 1929
    Life (NY) 93:23, Jan 18, 1929
    New York Times p. 24, Dec 13, 1928
                  VIII, p. 1, Dec 23, 1928
    Scientific American 140:244-5, Mar 1929
    Theatre Magazine 49:49, Feb 1929
    Vogue 73:118, Feb 2, 1929

The Return of Peter Grimm
Productions:
    Opened October 17, 1911 for 231 performances.
    Opened September 21, 1921 for 78 performances.
Reviews:
    American Magazine 73:490, Feb 1912
    American Playwright 1:26-7, Jan 1912
                       1:89-96, Mar 1912
    Blue Book 13:9-11, May 1911
    Book News 31:194, Nov 1912
    Bookman 35:362-7, Dec 1911
    Current Literature 52:447-54, Apr 1912
    Dramatic Mirror 66:7, Oct 25, 1911
                    84:484, Oct 1, 1921
    Dramatist 3:210-12, Jan 1912
    Everybody's 26:91-5, Jan 1912
    Independent 72:503, Mar 7, 1912
    Life (NY) 58:762, Nov 2, 1911
    Munsey 46:427-8, Dec 1911
    New York Clipper 69:17, Sep 28, 1921
    New York Times p. 12, Sep 22, 1921
                   VI, p. 1, Sep 25, 1921
    Pearson 26:764-9, Dec 1911
    Red Book 18:561+, Jan 1912
    Theatre Magazine 14:xi-xii, Nov 1911
                     34:388+, Dec 1921
    World Today 21:1501-16, Dec 1911

The Son-Daughter (with George Scarborough)
    Productions:
        Opened November 19, 1919 for 223 performances.
    Reviews:
        Dramatic Mirror 80:1861, Dec 4, 1919
        Dramatist 11:991-2, Apr 1920
        Life (NY) 74:898, Nov 27, 1919
        New York Times p. 11, Nov 20, 1919
        Theatre Magazine 31:17, Jan 1920

*Van der Decker
    Reviews:
        New York Times p. 8, Dec 8, 1915

BELLOW, SAUL

The Last Analysis
    Productions:
        Opened October 1, 1964 for 28 performances.
        (Off Broadway) June 23, 1971 for 46 performances.
    Reviews:
        Life 57:17, Oct 30, 1964
        Nation 199:256-7, Oct 19, 1964
        New Republic 151:25-6, Oct 24, 1964
        New York Theatre Critics' Reviews 1964:206
        New York Times II, p. 1, Sep 27, 1964
                        p. 30, Oct 2, 1964
                        II, p. 1, Oct 11, 1964
                        p. 34, Jun 24, 1971
                        II, p. 3, Jul 4, 1971
                        p. 18, Jul 26, 1977
        Newsweek 64:105, Oct 12, 1964
        Saturday Review 47:29, Oct 27, 1964
        Time 84:92, Oct 9, 1964
        Vogue 144:64, Nov 15, 1964

Orange Souffle (see Under the Weather)

Out from Under (see Under the Weather)

Under the Weather (Out from Under, Orange Souffle, and The Wen)
    Productions:
        Opened October 27, 1966 for 12 performances.
    Reviews:
        Commonweal 85:199-201, Nov 18, 1966
        Nation 203:5234, Nov 14, 1966
        New York Theatre Critics' Reviews 1966:254
        New York Times p. 42, Jun 8, 1966
                        p. 14, Jul 16, 1966

p. 35, Oct 28, 1966
II, p. 1, Dec 25, 1966
New Yorker 42:127, Nov 5, 1966
Newsweek 68:96, Nov 7, 1966
Saturday Review 49:34, Nov 12, 1966
Time 88:85, Nov 4, 1966

The Wen (see Under the Weather)

BENET, STEVEN VINCENT

Devil and Daniel Webster (see Archibald MacLeish's Scratch)

John Brown's Body (Adapted by Charles Laughton)
    Productions:
        Opened February 14, 1953 for 65 performances.
        (Off Broadway) Season of 1960-61.
        (Off Broadway) March 3, 1969 for 3 performances.
        (Off Off Broadway) Season of 1971-72 (Manhattan Theater Club).
        (Off Off Broadway) October 14, 1977 (WPA Theater).
    Reviews:
        Colliers 130:24-7, Dec 6, 1952
        New York Theatre Critics' Reviews 1953:358
        New York Times p. 25, Nov 3, 1952
                       p. 43, Dec 16, 1952
                       p. 17, Feb 16, 1953
                       II, p. 1, Feb 22, 1953
                       II, p. 3, Mar 8, 1953
                       p. 31, Jun 22, 1960
                       II, p. 1, Aug 21, 1960
                       p. 33, Jun 29, 1964
                       p. 49, Feb 13, 1968
        Newsweek 40:88, Nov 24, 1952

Nerves (with John Farrar)
    Productions:
        Opened September 1, 1924 for 16 performances.
    Reviews:
        New York Times p. 22, Sep 2, 1924
                       VI, p. 1, Sep 7, 1924
                       VII, p. 2, Sep 7, 1924

That Awful Mrs. Eaton (with John Farrar)
    Productions:
        Opened September 29, 1924 for 16 performances.
    Reviews:
        New York Times VII, p. 1, Jul 20, 1924
                       p. 27, Sep 30, 1924
        Theatre Magazine 39:19, Dec 1924

BENTHAM, JOSEPHINE

Janie (with Herschel Williams)
    Productions:
        Opened September 10, 1942 for 642 performances
    Reviews:
        Catholic World 156:90-1, Oct 1942
        Commonweal 36:543, Sep 25, 1942
        Independent Woman 21:378, Dec 1942
        Life 13:119-22+, Sep 28, 1942
        Nation 155:278, Sep 26, 1942
        New York Theatre Critics' Reviews 1942:244
        New York Times p. 24, Sep 11, 1942
                      II, p. 2, Dec 17, 1944
        New Yorker 18:34, Sep 19, 1942
        Newsweek 20:78, Sep 21, 1942
        Theatre Arts 26:674+, Nov 1942
        Time 40:42, Sep 21, 1942

BERG, GERTRUDE

Dear Me, the Sky Is Falling (see entry under Spigelgass, Leonard)

Me and Molly
    Productions:
        Opened February 26, 1948 for 156 performances.
        (Off Off Broadway) October 15, 1980 (Jewish Repertory The-
            ater).
    Reviews:
        Catholic World 167:71, Apr 1948
        Commonweal 47:546, Mar 12, 1948
        New York Theatre Critics' Reviews 1948:322
        New York Times p. 27, Feb 27, 1948
                      II, p. 1, Mar 7, 1948
                     III, p. 3, Oct 31, 1980
        New Yorker 24:52, Mar 6, 1948
        Newsweek 31:75, Mar 8, 1948
        Theatre Arts 32:31, Apr 1948
        Time 51:50, Mar 8, 1948
        Vogue 111:151, Apr 1, 1948

BERRIGAN, DANIEL

The Trial of the Catonsville Nine (Text prepared by Saul Levitt)
    Productions:
        (Off Broadway) February 7, 1971 for 130 performances and trans-
            ferred to Broadway.
        Opened on Broadway June 2, 1971 for 29 performances (159 in
            all).

Reviews:
America 124:208-9, Feb 27, 1971
Christian Century 88:412-13, Mar 31, 1971
Commonweal 93:525, Feb 26, 1971
Life 70:16-17, Apr 16, 1971
Nation 212:254, Feb 22, 1971
National Review 22:1173, Nov 3, 1970
23:490-1, May 4, 1971
New Republic 164:28-30, Mar 6, 1971
New York Theatre Critics' Reviews 1971:357
New York Times p. 34, Aug 10, 1970
II, p. 1, Aug 16, 1970
p. 40, Feb 8, 1971
II, p. 3, Feb 14, 1971
p. 38, Jun 16, 1971
New Yorker 47:90, Feb 20, 1971
Newsweek 77:67, Feb 22, 1971
77:14-15, Mar 1, 1971
Saturday Review 54:21, Mar 6, 1971
Time 97:52, Feb 22, 1971
Vogue 157:126, Apr 15, 1971

BIRD, ROBERT MONTGOMERY

The Gladiator
    Productions:
        (Off Off Broadway) Season of 1970-71 (American Theater Club).
    No Reviews.

BOKER, GEORGE HENRY
    No productions.

BOLTON, GUY

Adam and Eva (with George Middleton)
    Productions:
        Opened September 13, 1919 for 312 performances.
    Reviews:
        Current Opinion 68:782-8, Jun 1920
        Dramatic Mirror 80:1503, Sep 25, 1919
        Dramatist 10:969-70, Oct 1919
        Hearst 38:41-3+, Jul 1920
        Life (NY) 74:548-9, Sep 25, 1919
        New York Times p. 15, Sep 16, 1919
                    IV, p. 2, Sep 21, 1919

Anastasia (Adapted from a play by Marcelle Maurette)
    Productions:

Opened December 29, 1954 for 272 performances.
Reviews:
America 92:461, Jan 29, 1955
Catholic World 180:386, Feb 1955
Commonweal 61:582-3, Mar 4, 1955
Life 38:32-3, Feb 14, 1955
Nation 180:24, Jan 22, 1955
New Republic 132:22, Feb 7, 1955
New York Theatre Critics' Reviews 1954:192
New York Times II, p. 3, Dec 26, 1954
              p. 13, Dec 30, 1954
             II, p. 1, Jan 16, 1955
New Yorker 30:66, Jan 8, 1955
Newsweek 45:62, Jan 10, 1955
Saturday Review 38:31, Jan 15, 1955
Theatre Arts 39:19+, Mar 1955
             39:28+, Jun 1955
             40:34-61, May 1956
Time 65:35, Jan 10, 1955

The Cave Girl (with George Middleton)
Productions:
Opened August 18, 1920 for 37 performances.
Reviews:
Dramatic Mirror p. 9, Jul 3, 1920
                p. 371, Aug 28, 1920
Independent 103:261, Sep 4, 1920
New York Clipper 68:19, Aug 25, 1920
New York Times p. 12, Aug 19, 1920
Theatre Magazine 32:242, Oct 1920

Chicken Feed (Wages for Wives)
Productions:
Opened September 24, 1923 for 144 performances.
Reviews:
Nation 117:412, Oct 10, 1923
New York Times p. 10, Sep 25, 1923
Theatre Magazine 38:56+, Nov 1923

Child of Fortune (Adapted from Wings of the Dove by Henry James)
Productions:
Opened November 13, 1956 for 23 performances.
Reviews:
Commonweal 65:383, Jan 11, 1957
New York Theatre Critics' Reviews 1956:209
New York Times p. 41, Nov 14, 1956
New Yorker 32:124, Nov 24, 1956
Saturday Review 39:50, Dec 1, 1956
Theatre Arts 41:27, Jan 1957
Time 68:58, Nov 26, 1956

Children (with Tom Carlton)
    Productions:
        Opened October 4, 1915 in repertory (Washington Square Play-
           ers).
    Reviews:
        Dramatic Mirror 75:8, Apr 1, 1916
        New York Times p. 9, Mar 21, 1916

The Fallen Idol
    Productions:
        Opened January 23, 1915 for nine performances.
    Reviews:
        Current Opinion 58:177-8, Mar 1915
        Dramatic Mirror 73:24, Jan 27, 1915
        Green Book 13:765-6, Apr 1915
        Life (NY) 65:196, Feb 4, 1915
        New York Dramatic News 60:17, Jan 30, 1915
        New York Times p. 9, Jan 25, 1915
        Theatre Magazine 21:149, Mar 1915

The Five Million (with Frank Mandel)
    Productions:
        Opened July 8, 1919 for 91 performances.
    Reviews:
        Current Opinion 67:160-4, Sep 1919
        Forum 62:243-4, Aug 1919
        Hearst 36:42-3+, Oct 1919
        New York Times p. 14, Jul 9, 1919
        Theatre Magazine 30:149, Sep 1919

Golden Wings (R.A.F.) (with William Jay)
    Productions:
        Opened December 8, 1941 for six performances.
    Reviews:
        New York Theatre Critics' Reviews 1941:178
        New York Times p. 33, Nov 25, 1941
                   p. 46, Dec 9, 1941
        Newsweek 18:61, Dec 22, 1941
        Theatre Arts 26:79, Feb 1942

Grounds for Divorce (Adapted from the Hungarian of Ernest Vajda)
    Productions:
        Opened September 23, 1924 for 127 performances.
    Reviews:
        Nation 119:394-5, Oct 8, 1924
        New York Times VIII, p. 2, Mar 2, 1924
                   p. 20, Sep 24, 1924

Hit-the-Trail-Holiday (see entry under Cohan, George M.)

*Larger Than Life
    Reviews:

New York Times p. 33, Feb 8, 1950
II, p. 3, Mar 12, 1950

The Light of the World (with George Middleton)
Productions:
Opened January 6, 1920 for 31 performances.
Reviews:
Dramatic Mirror 82:51, Jan 15, 1920
Life (NY) 75:148, Jan 22, 1920
New York Clipper 67:25, Jan 14, 1920
New York Times p. 17, Jan 7, 1920
Theatre Magazine 31:142, Feb 1920

The Nightcap (with Max Marcin)
Productions:
Opened August 15, 1921 for 96 performances.
Reviews:
Dramatic Mirror 84:285, Aug 20, 1921
New York Clipper 69:24, Aug 14, 1921
New York Times p. 18, Aug 16, 1921
Theatre Magazine 34:236, Oct 1921
Weekly Review 5:215, Sep 3, 1921

Nobody Home (with Paul Rubens)
Productions:
Opened April 20, 1915 for 135 performances.
Reviews:
Dramatic Mirror 73:8, Apr 28, 1915
Green Book 14:59-60, Jul 1915
14:191-2, Jul 1915
Life (NY) 65:808, May 16, 1915
Theatre Magazine 21:280+, Jun 1915

Nobody's Business (with Frank Mandel)
Productions:
Opened October 22, 1923 for 40 performances.
Reviews:
New York Times p. 17, Oct 23, 1923
VIII, p. 1, Oct 28, 1923

Polly Preferred
Productions:
Opened January 11, 1923 for 184 performances.
Reviews:
New York Clipper 70:14, Jan 17, 1923
New York Times p. 13, Jan 12, 1923

Polly with a Past (with George Middleton)
Productions:
Opened September 8, 1917 for 315 performances.

Reviews:
Bookman 46:284-5, Nov 1917
Dramatic Mirror 77:5+, Sep 15, 1917
Green Book 18:774-8, Nov 1917
Life (NY) 70:466, Sep 20, 1917
New York Dramatic News 64:6, Sep 15, 1917
New York Times p. 7, Sep 7, 1917
    II, p. 5, Sep 16, 1917
    p. 13, Mar 3, 1921
Theatre Magazine 26:197+, Oct 1917

R.A.F. (see Golden Wings)

The Rule of Three
    Productions:
    Opened February 16, 1914 for 80 performances.
    Reviews:
    Bookman 39:145, Apr 1914
    Dramatic Mirror 71:6, Feb 18, 1914
    Green Book 11:776, May 1914
           11:972-4, Jun 1914
           11:1058-68, Jun 1914
    Hearst 25:685-700, May 1914
    Life (NY) 63:409, Mar 5, 1914
    Munsey 51:585, Apr 1914
    New York Dramatic News 59:20, Feb 21, 1914
    New York Times p. 11, Feb 17, 1914
    Theatre Magazine 19:170+, Apr 1914

Theatre (with W. Somerset Maugham)
    Productions:
    Opened November 12, 1914 for 69 performances.
    Reviews:
    Catholic World 154:473, Jan 1942
    Commonweal 35:144, Nov 28, 1941
    New Republic 105:762, Dec 8, 1941
    New York Theatre Critics' Reviews 1941:226
    New York Times IX, p. 2, Oct 26, 1941
           p. 34, Nov 13, 1941
    Theatre Arts 26:15, Jan 1942

Wages for Wives (see Chicken Feed)

BOOTHE, CLARE

Abide with Me
    Productions:
    Opened November 21, 1935 for 36 performances.
    Reviews:
    Commonweal 23:162, Dec 6, 1935

New York Times p. 19, Nov 22, 1935
Theatre Arts 20:20, Jan 1936
Time 26:68, Dec 2, 1935

Child of the Morning
Productions:
(Off Broadway) Season of 1957-58.
Reviews:
America 99:151, Apr 26, 1958
Catholic World 187:311, Jul 1958
Commonweal 68:153-4, May 9, 1958
New York Times p. 40, Apr 22, 1958
      p. 37, Feb 18, 1959

Kiss the Boys Good-bye
Productions:
Opened September 28, 1938 for 286 performances.
Reviews:
Catholic World 148:212-13, Nov 1938
Commonweal 28:644, Oct 14, 1938
Independent Woman 17:348+, Nov 1938
Life 5:66-9, Oct 17, 1938
Nation 147:362, Oct 8, 1938
New Republic 96:331, Oct 26, 1938
New York Times p. 30, Sep 29, 1938
Theatre Arts 22:778+, Nov 1938
Time 32:48, Oct 10, 1938
Vogue 92:75, Nov 1, 1935

Margin for Error
Productions:
Opened November 3, 1939 for 264 performances.
Reviews:
Catholic World 150:339, Dec 1939
Commonweal 31:118, Nov 24, 1939
Forum 103:33, Jan 1940
Life 7:60-61, Nov 20, 1939
New York Theatre Critics' Reviews 1940:460
New York Times p. 48, Oct 15, 1939
      p. 11, Nov 4, 1939
      IX, p. 1, Nov 12, 1939
      IX, p. 2, Aug 11, 1940
Newsweek 14:36, Nov 20, 1939
Spectator 156:146, Aug 9, 1940
Theatre Arts 24:18-19, Jan 1940
Time 34:58, Nov 13, 1939

*Slam the Door Softly
Reviews:
New York Times p. 26, Jun 28, 1971

The Women
  Productions:
    Opened December 26, 1936 for 657 performances.
    Opened April 25, 1973 for 63 performances.
  Reviews:
    America 128:495, May 26, 1973
    Catholic World 144:599-600, Feb 1937
    Commonweal 25:332, Jan 15, 1937
    Life 2:38+, Jan 25, 1937
      13:4-6, Dec 21, 1942
    Literary Digest 123:24-5, Jan 9, 1937
    Ms. 2:42+, Aug 1973
    Nation 216:636, May 14, 1973
    New Republic 90:263, Apr 7, 1937
    New York Magazine 6:97, May 14, 1973
    New York Theatre Critics' Reviews 1973:286
    New York Times p. 30, Dec 8, 1936
                   p. 13, Dec 28, 1936
                   X, p. 3, Oct 31, 1937
                   II, p. 2, May 22, 1938
                   p. 14, Nov 5, 1938
                   X, p. 3, Mar 5, 1939
                   p. 21, Apr 21, 1939
                   X, p. 2, May 7, 1939
                   p. 14, Jun 10, 1939
                   p. 53, Apr 26, 1973
                   II, p. 1, May 6, 1973
                   p. 56, Jun 13, 1973
    Newsweek 9:22, Jan 2, 1937
             81:109, May 7, 1973
    Playboy 20:39, Aug 1973
    Stage 14:50, Jan 1937
          14:48-9, Feb 1937
          14:41-4, Mar 1937
    Theatre Arts 21:101-2, Feb 1937
    Time 29:30, Jan 4, 1937
         101:88, May 7, 1973
    Vogue 89:78-9, Jan 15, 1937
          101:44-5, Jan 1, 1943

BOUCICAULT, DION

*After Dark
  Reviews:
    Life (NY) 93:21, Feb 22, 1929
    Literary Digest 101:24-6, Apr 6, 1929
    Nation 128:54, Jan 9, 1929
    New York Times p. 35, Dec 11, 1928
    Theatre Magazine 49:51+, Feb 1929

Forbidden Fruit
    Productions:
        (Off Off Broadway) Dec 7, 1976 (adaptation by George Wolf
            Reily, No Smoking Playhouse).
    Reviews:
        New York Times III, p. 5, Jan 7, 1977

Life in Louisiana (see The Octoroon)

London Assurance
    Productions:
        Opened February 18, 1937 for 5 performances.
        Adapted by Ronald Eyre. Opened December 5, 1976 for 46
            performances.
    Reviews:
        New York Magazine 7:62+, Dec 23, 1974
        New York Theatre Critics' Reviews 1974:159
        New York Times p. 14, Feb 19, 1937
                       p. 55, Jun 25, 1970
                       p. 26, Aug 7, 1970
                       p. 30, Dec 6, 1974
                       II, p. 5, Dec 15, 1974

The Octoroon (or Life in Louisiana)
    Productions:
        Opened March 12, 1929.
        Opened January 27, 1961 for 45 performances.
    Reviews:
        America 104:714, Feb 25, 1961
        Commonweal 73:636, Mar 17, 1961
        Life 50:39-40+, Feb 24, 1961
        Nation 128:380, Mar 27, 1929
               192:126, Feb 11, 1961
        New York Theatre Critics' Reviews 1961:382
        New York Times p. 28, Mar 13, 1929
                       p. 24, Sep 1, 1936
                       II, p. 3, Jan 22, 1961
                       p. 13, Jan 28, 1961
        New Yorker 36:75-6+, Feb 11, 1961
        Saturday Review 44:41, Feb 25, 1961

Rip Van Winkle (Based on the story by Washington Irving)
    Productions:
        (Off Off Broadway) July 1974 (Joseph Jefferson).
        (Off Off Broadway) July 14, 1975 (Joseph Jefferson).
        (Off Off Broadway) July 21, 1976 (Joseph Jefferson).
    Reviews:
        New York Times II, p. 3, Aug 11, 1974
                       p. 24, Jul 22, 1975
                       p. 14, Dec 23, 1975

*The Shaughraun
    Reviews:
        New York Times p. 54, May 22, 1968

The Streets of New York, or Poverty Is No Crime
    Productions:
        Opened October 6, 1931 for 87 performances.
        (Off Off Broadway) October 30, 1980 (Soho Repertory).
    Reviews:
        Bookman 74:564, Jan-Feb 1932
        Catholic World 134:210, Nov 1931
        Commonweal 19:608, Oct 21, 1931
        Literary Digest 111:19, Nov 14, 1931
        Nation 133:467-8, Oct 28, 1931
        New Republic 68:301, Oct 28, 1931
        New York Times p. 29, Apr 26, 1929
                     VIII, p. 4, Oct 4, 1931
                     p. 29, Oct 7, 1931
                     p. 14, Jul 21, 1934
                     p. 67, Nov 16, 1980
        Outlook 159:248, Oct 21, 1931
        Stage 9:10, Jul 1932
        Theatre Arts 15:984, Dec 1931
        Vogue 78:60-61, Dec 1, 1931

BOWLES, JANE

In the Summer House
    Productions:
        Opened December 29, 1953 for 55 performances.
        (Off Broadway) March 25, 1964 for 15 performances.
        (Off Off Broadway) May 4, 1977 (Manhattan Theater Club).
        (Off Off Broadway) May 28, 1980 (Interart Theater and La Mama
            ETC).
    Reviews:
        America 90:406, Jan 16, 1954
        Catholic World 178:386, Feb 1954
        Commonweal 59:449-50, Feb 5, 1954
        Nation 178:58, Jan 16, 1954
               224:668-9, May 28, 1977
        New Republic 130:20-1, Jan 11, 1954
        New York Magazine 10:86, May 23, 1977
        New York Theatre Critics' Reviews 1953:168
        New York Times II, p. 5, Dec 27, 1953
                 p. 17, Dec 30, 1953
                 II, p. 1, Jan 10, 1954
                 p. 43, Mar 26, 1964
        New Yorker 29:61-2, Jan 9, 1954
               53:83-4, May 23, 1977

Saturday Review 37:31, Jan 16, 1954
         37:61-2, Jan 23, 1954
Theatre Arts 38:19, Mar 1954
Time 63:67, Jan 11, 1954

BREIT, HARVEY

The Disenchanted   (see entry under Schulberg, Budd)

The Guide (with Patricia Rinehart. Based on the novel by R. K.
    Naryan)
    Productions:
        Opened March 6, 1968 for 5 performances.
    Reviews:
        New York Theatre Critics' Reviews 1968:329
        New York Times p. 50, Mar 7, 1968
        New Yorker 44:130, Mar 16, 1968

BRIDGERS, ANN

Coquette   (see entry under Abbott, George)

BROKAW, CLARE   (see Boothe, Clare)

BROWNE, PORTER EMERSON

The Bad Man
    Productions:
        Opened August 30, 1920 for 342 performances.
    Reviews:
        Bookman 53:407+, Jul 1921
        Current Opinion 69:812-22, Dec 1920
        Dramatic Mirror p. 415, Sep 4, 1920
        Dramatist 12:1054, Apr 1921
        Hearst 39:41-3+, Jan 1921
        Life (NY) 76:500, Sep 16, 1920
        New York Clipper 68:29, Sep 8, 1920
        New York Times p. 7, Aug 31, 1920
        Outlook 126:183, Sep 29, 1920
        Theatre Magazine 32:278-9, Nov 1920

Chains (Adapted from the play by Elizabeth Baker)
    Productions:
        Opened December 16, 1912 for one matinee.
    Reviews:
        American Playwright 2:7-9, Jan 1913
        Bookman 36:640-1, Feb 1913

Dramatic Mirror 68:6, Dec 18, 1912
Munsey 48:845, Feb 1913
New York Drama News 57:26, Dec 21, 1912
Theatre Magazine 17:xv+, Feb 1913

A Fool There Was
Productions:
Opened March 24, 1909 for 93 performances.
Reviews:
Collier's 43:20, May 22, 1909
Dramatist 7:621-2, Oct 1915
Forum 41:449-50, May 1909
Green Book 2:257-83, Aug 1909
Hampton 23:109-111, Jul 1909
Theatre Magazine 9:135-6+, May 1909

The Spendthrift
Productions:
Opened April 11, 1910 for 88 performances.
Reviews:
Collier's 45:34, May 7, 1910
Dramatic Mirror 63:7-8, Apr 23, 1910
Dramatist 2:105-6, Oct 1910
Green Book 4:98-9, Jul 1910
         4:929-50, Nov 1910
Hampton 24:824-5, Jun 1910
Leslies' Weekly 110:437, May 5, 1910
Metropolitan Magazine 32:538-9, Jul 1910
World Today 19:1099-105, Oct 1910

BUCK, PEARL S.

A Desert Incident
Productions:
Opened March 24, 1959 for 7 performances.
Reviews:
New York Theatre Critics' Reviews 1959:332
New York Times p. 40, Mar 25, 1959
New Yorker 35:112+, Apr 4, 1959
Saturday Review 42:35, Apr 11, 1959
Theatre Arts 43:11, Jun 1959

The First Wife
Productions:
(Off Broadway) December 1945 (Chinese Theatre).
No Reviews.

*Flight into China
Reviews:
New York Times p. 28, Sep 12, 1939

The Good Earth (see entry under Davis, Owen)

BULLINS, ED

A Black Quartet (Consists of The Gentleman Caller and Amiri Ba-
    raka's Great Goodness of Life)
    Productions:
        (Off Broadway) July 30, 1969 for 111 performances.
    Reviews:
        New York Times p. 92, Apr 27, 1969
                    II, p. 1, May 4, 1969
                        p. 28, Jul 31, 1969
                    II, p. 1, Aug 3, 1969
                        p. 36, Sep 22, 1969

Clara's Ole Man
    Productions:
        (Off Broadway) March 6, 1968 for 90 performances, as part of
            a bill called The Electronic Nigger and Others (American
            Place Theater).
        (Off Off Broadway) Season of 1969-70 (Afro American Studio).
        (Off Off Broadway) January 22, 1977 (Theater for the New City).
        (Off Off Broadway) February 1977 (The Family).
        (Off Off Broadway) April 2, 1977 (Afro American Theater).
        (Off Off Broadway) Season of 1981-82 (La Mama ETC).
    Reviews:
        New York Times p. 16, Oct 31, 1981
        New Yorker 57:154-5, Nov 9, 1981
        See also The Electronic Nigger and Others

The Corner
    Productions:
        (Off Broadway) January 28-29, 1971 (Negro Ensemble Co.).
        (Off Broadway) May 16, 1972, as part of a bill called Four
            for One (Joseph Papp's Theater at the Outer Stage).
        (Off Broadway) June 22, 1972 for 46 performances (New York
            Shakespeare Festival).
    Reviews:
        New York Times p. 21, Jun 23, 1972
                        p. 15, Jul 21, 1972
        New Yorker 48:53, Jul 1, 1972

Daddy
    Productions:
        (Off Off Broadway) June 9, 1977 for 18 performances (New
            Federal Theater).
    Reviews:
        New York Times III, p. 12, Jun 17, 1977
        New Yorker 53:89, Jun 20, 1977

The Devil Catcher
Productions:
(Off Off Broadway) October 17, 1976 (Cathedral of St. John the
Divine).
No Reviews.

Dialect Determinism   (see Short Bullins)

The Duplex
Productions:
(Off Broadway) March 9, 1972 for 28 performances (Repertory
Theater of Lincoln Center).
Reviews:
Nation 214:412, Mar 27, 1972
New York Theatre Critics' Reviews 1972:330
New York Times p. 46, Mar 10, 1972
II, p. 1, Mar 19, 1972
New Yorker 48:85, Mar 18, 1972
Newsweek 79:98-9, Mar 20, 1972
Time 99:81, Mar 27, 1972

The Electronic Nigger and Others (with A Son, Come Home and
Clara's Ole Man)
Productions:
(Off Broadway) March 6, 1968 for 90 performances (American
Place Theater).
Reviews:
Ebony 23:97-8+, Sep 1968
Nation 206:420-1, Mar 25, 1968
New York Times p. 33, Mar 9, 1968
p. 50, Apr 11, 1968
New Yorker 44:133-4, Mar 9, 1968
Newsweek 71:110, Mar 18, 1968

The Fabulous Miss Marie
Productions:
(Off Off Broadway) Season of 1970-71 (New Lafayette Thea-
ter).
Reviews:
New York Times p. 28, Mar 12, 1971
New Yorker 47:94-5, Mar 20, 1971

Four for One   (see The Corner and You Gonna Let Me Take You Out
Tonight, Baby?)

The Gentleman Caller
Productions:
(Off Broadway) July 30, 1969 for 111 performances, as part
of a bill called A Black Quartet.
Reviews:
New York Times II, p. 3, Apr 13, 1969

p. 92, Apr 27, 1969
II, p. 1, May 4, 1969
p. 28, Jul 31, 1969
II, p. 1, Aug 3, 1969
p. 36, Sep 22, 1969

Goin' A Buffalo
Productions:
> (Off Off Broadway) Season of 1971-72 (Workshop of the Players Art).

Reviews:
> New York Times p. 28, Feb 16, 1972
> Newsweek 48:83, Mar 4, 1972

Home Boy
Productions:
> (Off Off Broadway) September 23, 1976 (Perry Street Theater).

Reviews:
> New York Times p. 42, Sep 27, 1976
> New Yorker 52:81, Oct 11, 1976

House Party
Productions:
> (Off Broadway) October 16, 1973 for 42 performances (American Place Theater).

Reviews:
> New York Magazine 6:75, Nov 12, 1973
> New York Theatre Critics' Reviews 1973:173
> New York Times p. 35, Oct 30, 1973
> II, p. 7, Nov 4, 1973
> New Yorker 49:89-91, Nov 5, 1973

How Do You Do
Productions:
> (Off Off Broadway) December 27, 1980 (Solid Productions).
> See also Short Bullins.

Reviews:
> New York Times III, p. 3, Apr 13, 1969
> III, p. 9, Dec 31, 1980
> See also Short Bullins

I Am Lucy Terry: An Historical Fantasy for Young Americans
Productions:
> (Off Broadway) February 11, 1976 for 12 performances.

Reviews:
> New York Times p. 42, Feb 12, 1976
> New Yorker 52:82+, Feb 23, 1976

In New England Winter
Productions:
> (Off Off Broadway) Season of 1970-71 (New Federal Theater).

(Off Broadway) January 26, 1971 for 8 performances.
Reviews:
New York Times p. 28, Jan 27, 1971
            II, p. 3, Feb 7, 1971
New Yorker 46:72, Feb 6, 1971

In the Wine Time
    Productions:
        (Off Off Broadway) April 21, 1976 (Manhattan Theater Club).
    Reviews:
        Negro History Bulletin 32:18-19, Apr 1969
        New York Times II, p. 7, Dec 22, 1968
                    III, p. 4, Apr 30, 1976
        New Yorker 52:104-5, May 10, 1976

It Has No Choice   (see Short Bullins)

Jo Anne!
    Productions:
        (Off Off Broadway) October 7, 1977 (Theater of the Riverside
            Church).
    Reviews:
        New York Times p. 53, Oct 19, 1976
        New Yorker 52:62+, Oct 25, 1976

Michael (music by Gregory Saint Strickland)
    Productions:
        (Off Off Broadway) May 1978 (New Heritage Repertory Thea-
            ter).
        (Off Off Broadway) June 20, 1978 for 72 performances, as
            part of a bill called Man-Wo-Man (New York Shakespeare
            Festival Public Theater).
    Reviews:
        New Yorker 54:91-2, May 22, 1978

Man-Wo-Man   (see Michael)

A Minor Scene   (see Short Bullins)

The Mystery of Phyllis Wheatley
    Productions:
        (Off Off Broadway) February 1976 (New Federal Theater).
    Reviews:
        New York Times p. 42, Feb 4, 1976

The Pig Pen
    Productions:
        (Off Broadway) April 29, 1970 for 46 performances (American
            Place Theater).
    Reviews:
        Nation 210:668, Jun 1, 1970

New York Times p. 47, May 21, 1970
                  II, p. 3, May 31, 1970
New Yorker 46:72-3, May 30, 1970

Short Bullins (Consists of How Do You Do, A Minor Scene, Dialect
    Determinism, and It Has No Choice)
Productions:
    (Off Broadway) Season of 1971-72 (La Mama ETC).
Reviews:
    New York Times p. 59, Mar 5, 1972

A Son Come Home
Productions:
    (Off Off Broadway) April 2, 1977 (Afro American Theater).
    (Off Off Broadway) July 1977 (Stage 73).
    (Off Off Broadway) December 27, 1980 (Solid Productions).
    See also The Electronic Nigger and Others.
Reviews:
    New York Times III, p. 9, Dec 31, 1980
    See also The Electronic Nigger and Others

Street Sounds
Productions:
    (Off Off Broadway) Season of 1970-71 (La Mama).
    (Off Off Broadway) October 7, 1972 (Player's Workshop).
Reviews:
    New York Times p. 32, Oct 23, 1970

The Taking of Miss Janie
Productions:
    (Off Off Broadway) March 13, 1975 (New Federal Theater).
    (Off Broadway) May 4, 1975 for 42 performances.
Reviews:
    America 132:427, May 31, 1975
    Essence 6:16, Jul 1975
    Nation 220:414, Apr 5, 1975
    New Republic 172:20, Jun 7, 1975
    New York Magazine 8:93, May 19, 1975
    New York Theatre Critics' Reviews 1975:243
    New York Times p. 29, Mar 18, 1975
                  p. 40, May 5, 1975
                  II, p. 5, May 11, 1975
    New Yorker 51:61-3, Mar 24, 1975
    Saturday Review 2:52, Jul 12, 1975
    Time 105:80, May 19, 1975

Three Plays by Ed Bullins   (see The Electronic Nigger and Others)

A Trio of Vignettes
Productions:
    (Off Off Broadway) February 1976 (New Genesis).
No Reviews.

You Gonna Let Me Take You Out Tonight, Baby?
Productions:
(Off Broadway) May 16, 1972, as part of a bill called Four for
One.
(Off Off Broadway) December 27, 1980 (Solid Productions).
Reviews:
New York Times III, p. 9, Dec 31, 1980

BURROWS, ABE

Betty (see Four on a Garden)

Cactus Flower (Based on a play by Pierre Barillet and Jean Pierre
Gredy)
Productions:
Opened December 8, 1965 for 1,234 performances.
Reviews:
America 114:54, Jan 8, 1966
Commonweal 83:410, Jan 7, 1966
Life 60:35-6, Feb 11, 1966
National Review 18:739-40, Jul 26, 1966
New York Theatre Critics' Reviews 1965:229
New York Times p. 60, Dec 9, 1965
p. 58, Dec 10, 1965
II, p. 2, Jul 31, 1966
p. 48, Dec 16, 1967
New Yorker 41:152, Dec 18, 1965
Newsweek 66:72, Dec 20, 1965
Saturday Review 48:41, Dec 25, 1965
Time 86:40, Dec 17, 1965
Vogue 147:99, Feb 1, 1966

Four on a Garden (Consists of House of Dunkelmayer, Betty, Tore-
ador, and The Swingers. Based on the plays of Pierre Barillet
and Jean Pierre Gredy)
Productions:
Opened January 30, 1971 for 57 performances.
Reviews:
New York Theatre Critics' Reviews 1971:372
New York Times p. 25, Feb 1, 1971
II, p. 1, Feb 7, 1971
New Yorker 46:72, Feb 6, 1971
Time 97:60, Feb 15, 1971

House of Dunkelmayer (see Four on a Garden)

The Swingers (see Four on a Garden)

Toreador (see Four on a Garden)

BUTLER, RACHEL BARTON

Mama's Affair
  Productions:
    Opened January 19, 1920 for 98 performances.
  Reviews:
    Dramatic Mirror 82:132, Jan 29, 1920
    Life (NY) 75:184, Jan 29, 1920
    Nation 110:211, Feb 14, 1920
    New York Clipper 67:25, Jan 28, 1920
    New York Times p. 10, Jan 20, 1920
                   VIII, p. 2, Jan 25, 1920
    Theatre Magazine 31:181+, Mar 1920

CALDWELL, ERSKINE

Journeyman (see entry under Hayes, Alfred)

Tobacco Road (see entry under Kirkland, Jack)

*Trouble in July
  Reviews:
    New York Times p. 36, Dec 2, 1949

CAPOTE, TRUMAN

The Grass Harp (Based on his novel)
  Productions:
    Opened March 27, 1952 for 36 performances.
  Reviews:
    Catholic World 175:147-8, May 1952
                   177:228, Jun 1953
    Commonweal 56:68-9, Apr 25, 1952
               58:179, May 22, 1953
    Life 32:142+, Apr 14, 1952
    Nation 174:353, Apr 12, 1952
           176:421, May 16, 1953
    New Republic 126:22-3, Apr 14, 1952
    New York Theatre Critics' Reviews 1952:328
    New York Times II, p. 1, Mar 23, 1952
                   p. 26, Mar 28, 1952
                   II, p. 1, Apr 6, 1952
                   p. 32, Apr 28, 1953
                   II, p. 1, May 24, 1953
    New Yorker 28:70, Apr 5, 1952
    Newsweek 39:94, Apr 7, 1952
    Saturday Review 35:43-4, Apr 19, 1952
                    36:30, May 16, 1953
    School and Society 75:323-4, May 24, 1952

Theatre Arts 36:17-18, Jun 1952
37:16, Jul 1953
Time 59:77, Apr 7, 1952

CAROLE, JOSEPH

Separate Rooms (with Alan Dinehart)
  Productions:
    Opened March 23, 1940 for 613 performances.
  Reviews:
    New York Theatre Critics' Reviews 1940:359
                                      1941:487
    New York Times p. 10, Mar 25, 1940
                   IX, p. 2, Aug 18, 1940
    Stage 1:17, Nov 1940
          1:18, Dec 1940

Thanks for My Wife (see Separate Rooms)

CARTER, STEVE

*Dame Lorraine
  Reviews:
    Chicago 30:70+, May 1981
    Chicago Tribune II, p. 11, Apr 2, 1981

Eden
  Productions:
    (Off Broadway) March 3, 1976 for 181 performances.
  Reviews:
    Nation 222:381, Mar 27, 1976
    New York Magazine 9:60, Aug 2, 1976
    New York Theatre Critics' Reviews 1976:278
    New York Times p. 25, Mar 4, 1976
                   II, p. 5, Mar 14, 1976
                   p. 42, May 17, 1976
    New Yorker 52:51-2, Mar 15, 1976

Nevis Mountain Dew
  Productions:
    (Off Broadway) December 7, 1978 for 14 performances.
    (Off Broadway) Reopened February 22, 1978 for 61 perform-
      ances.
  Reviews:
    New Republic 180:25, Apr 21, 1979
    New York Magazine 12:88-9, Dec 25, 1978
    New York Times III, p. 3, Dec 8, 1978
                    II, p. 1, Apr 15, 1979
    New Yorker 54:51, Dec 18, 1978

Terraces
    Productions:
        (Off Broadway) April 2, 1974 for 8 performances (Negro Ensemble Co.).
    Reviews:
        New York Times p. 39, Apr 3, 1974
        New Yorker 50:103-4, Apr 22, 1974

CHAPMAN, ROBERT

Billy Budd (see entry under Coxe, Louis O.)

Uniform of Flesh (see entry under Coxe, Louis O.)

CHASE, MARY COYLE

Bernadine
    Productions:
        Opened October 16, 1952 for 157 performances.
    Reviews:
        Catholic World 176:227-8, Dec 1952
        Commonweal 57:119, Nov 7, 1952
        Life 33:83-4+, Nov 24, 1952
        Nation 175:414, Nov 1, 1952
        New York Theatre Critics' Reviews 1952:231
        New York Times p. 33, Oct 17, 1952
                 II, p. 1, Nov 9, 1952
                 II, p. 1, Nov 23, 1952
        New Yorker 28:74, Oct 25, 1952
        Newsweek 40:78, Oct 27, 1952
        Saturday Review 35:26, Nov 1, 1952
        School and Society 76:403, Dec 20, 1952
        Theatre Arts 36:26-8, Dec 1952
        Time 60:75, Oct 27, 1952

Harvey
    Productions:
        Opened November 1, 1944 for 1,775 performances.
        Opened February 24, 1970 for 79 performances.
    Reviews:
        America 122:313, Mar 21, 1970
        Catholic World 160:260, Dec 1944
        Commonweal 41:124, Nov 17, 1944
        Cosmopolitan 119:34-5+, Jul 1945
        Life 17:96-8+, Nov 27, 1944
           18:55-8+, Jan 8, 1945
        Nation 59:624, Nov 18, 1944
           210:349, Mar 23, 1970
        New Republic 111:661, Nov 20, 1944

New York Theatre Critics' Reviews 1944:95
                                   1970:357
New York Times p. 23, Nov 2, 1944
        II, p. 1, Nov 12, 1944
        VI, p. 28, Jan 7, 1945
        p. 16, May 8, 1945
        II, p. 1, May 13, 1945
        p. 36, Mar 11, 1947
        II, p. 3, Mar 16, 1947
        p. 27, Jul 15, 1947
        II, p. 1, Sep 7, 1947
        II, p. 1, Oct 26, 1947
        p. 31, Nov 24, 1947
        p. 30, Apr 7, 1948
        p. 29, Oct 19, 1948
        p. 29, Jan 6, 1949
        II, p. 1, Jan 16, 1949
        II, p. 3, Feb 13, 1949
        p. 34, Mar 24, 1949
        p. 14, Feb 13, 1950
        p. 10, Oct 21, 1950
        II, p. 5, Nov 26, 1950
        II, p. 3, Dec 31, 1950
        II, p. 2, Jun 3, 1951
        p. 41, Feb 25, 1970
        II, p. 1, Mar 8, 1970
New Yorker 20:44, Nov 11, 1944
        23:40+, Jul 26, 1947
        46:83, Mar 7, 1970
Newsweek 24:82-3, Nov 13, 1944
        30:78-9, Jul 28, 1947
        75:97, Mar 9, 1970
Player's Magazine 22:5, Sep-Oct 1945
Saturday Review 27:10-11, Dec 30, 1944
        53:26, Mar 14, 1970
Theatre Arts 29:2, 5-6+, Jan 1945
        29:85, Feb 1945
        32:20, Fall 1948
Time 44:60, Nov 13, 1944
        49:74, Jun 16, 1947
        53:31, Apr 25, 1949
        95:54, Mar 9, 1970

Midgie Purvis
    Productions:
    Opened February 1, 1961 for 21 performances.
    Reviews:
    Nation 192:155-6, Feb 18, 1961
    New York Theatre Critics' Reviews 1961:375
    New York Times p. 25, Feb 2, 1961
            II, p. 1, Feb 12, 1961

New Yorker 36:75, Feb 11, 1961
Saturday Review 44:41, Feb 25, 1961
Time 77:68, Feb 10, 1961

Mrs. McThing
Productions:
Opened February 20, 1952 for 350 performances.
Reviews:
Catholic World 175:68, Apr 1952
Commonweal 55:567, Mar 14, 1952
Life 32:149-50+, Mar 10, 1952
Nation 174:258, Mar 15, 1952
New Republic 126:22, Mar 17, 1952
New York Theatre Critics' Reviews 1952:359
New York Times II, p. 1, Feb 17, 1952
            p. 22, Feb 21, 1952
          II, p. 1, Mar 2, 1952
          II, p. 3, Mar 30, 1952
New Yorker 28:58, Mar 1, 1952
Newsweek 39:61, Mar 3, 1952
Saturday Review 35:28, Mar 15, 1952
School and Society 75:182-3, Mar 22, 1952
Theatre Arts 36:28-9, 38-41, May 1952
Time 59:63, Mar 3, 1952

The Next Half Hour
Productions:
Opened October 29, 1945 for 8 performances.
Reviews:
New Republic 113:639, Nov 12, 1945
New York Theatre Critics' Reviews 1945:130
New York Times II, p. 1, Nov 4, 1945
New Yorker 21:44+, Nov 10, 1945
Theatre Arts 30:12, Jan 1946

Now You've Done It
Productions:
Opened March 5, 1937 for 43 performances.
Reviews:
New York Times p. 10, Mar 6, 1937

CHAYEFSKY, PADDY

Gideon
Productions:
Opened November 9, 1961 for 236 performances.
(Off Off Broadway) November 1974 (York Players).
Reviews:
America 106:453-4, Jan 6, 1962
Catholic World 194:216-21, Jan 1962

Christian Century 78:1500-1, Dec 13, 1961
Commonweal 75:257-9, Dec 1, 1961
Life 51:118-19, Dec 15, 1961
Nation 193:437-8, Nov 25, 1961
New Republic 145:21-3, Nov 27, 1961
New York Theatre Critics' Reviews 1961:174
New York Times II, p. 1, Nov 5, 1961
       p. 38, Nov 10, 1961
       II, p. 1, Nov 19, 1961
New Yorker 37:96, Nov 18, 1961
Newsweek 58:69, Nov 20, 1961
Reporter 25:62, Dec 7, 1961
Saturday Review 44:27, Dec 9, 1961
       45:30, May 19, 1962
Theatre Arts 46:10-11, Jan 1962
Time 78:71, Nov 17, 1961

*The Latent Heterosexual
  Reviews:
    Life 64:16, Apr 20, 1968
    New York Times p. 52, Mar 22, 1968
            II, p. 3, Mar 31, 1968
    Newsweek 71:87, Apr 1, 1968
    Saturday Review 51:20, Apr 6, 1968
    Time 91:91, Mar 29, 1968

Middle of the Night
  Productions:
    Opened February 8, 1956 for 477 performances.
    (Off Off Broadway) December 9, 1971 (Equity Library Thea-
    ter).
  Reviews:
    America 94:619, Mar 3, 1956
    Catholic World 183:66, Apr 1956
    Commonweal 63:663, Mar 30, 1956
    Life 40:99-100+, Feb 27, 1956
    Nation 182:166, Feb 25, 1956
    New Republic 134:21, Feb 27, 1956
    New York Theatre Critics' Reviews 1956:370
    New York Times p. 39, Feb 9, 1956
            II, p. 1, Feb 19, 1956
            II, p. 1, Jul 15, 1956
            p. 22, Dec 11, 1971
            p. 36, Dec 27, 1971
    New York Times Magazine p. 78, Jan 29, 1956
    New Yorker 31:60+, Feb 18, 1956
    Newsweek 47:93, Feb 20, 1956
    Saturday Review 39:26, Feb 25, 1956
    Theatre Arts 40:20, Apr 1956
    Time 67:90, Feb 20, 1956

The Passion of Josef D.
Productions:
Opened February 11, 1964 for 15 performances.
Reviews:
Commonweal 79:693, Mar 6, 1964
New York Theatre Critics' Reviews 1964:354
New York Times II, p. 1, Feb 9, 1964
                 p. 29, Feb 12, 1964
                 p. 25, Feb 17, 1964
                 II, p. 1, Feb 23, 1964
New Yorker 40:92, Feb 22, 1964
Newsweek 63:61, Feb 24, 1964
Saturday Review 47:26, Feb 29, 1964
Time 83:62, Feb 21, 1964

The Tenth Man
Productions:
Opened November 5, 1959 for 623 performances.
Opened November 8, 1967 for 23 performances.
(Off Off Broadway) April 1980 (American Jewish Theater).
Reviews:
America 102:362, Dec 12, 1959
Christian Century 76:1528-9, Dec 30, 1959
Commentary 28:523-7, Dec 1959
Life 47:127-8+, Dec 7, 1959
Los Angeles 22:190+, Apr 1977
Nation 189:388, Nov 21, 1959
New Republic 141:21-2, Nov 23, 1959
New West 2:SC-33, Apr 11, 1977
New York Theatre Critics' Reviews 1959:232
New York Times p. 24, Nov 6, 1959
               II, p. 1, Nov 15, 1959
               VI, p. 106, Nov 15, 1959
               p. 68, Feb 7, 1960
               p. 23, Apr 14, 1961
               p. 46, Oct 3, 1962
               p. 54, Nov 9, 1967
               XXI, p. 6, Feb 3, 1980
               III, p. 15, Apr 21, 1980
New Yorker 35:118+, Nov 14, 1959
Newsweek 54:109, Nov 16, 1959
Reporter 21:39, Dec 10, 1959
Saturday Review 42:31+, Nov 21, 1959
                50:70, Nov 25, 1967
Time 74:57, Nov 16, 1959

CHODOROV, EDWARD

Common Ground
Productions:
Opened April 25, 1945 for 69 performances.

Reviews:
  Catholic World 161:261, Jun 1945
  Commonweal 42:93, May 11, 1945
  New York Theatre Critics' Reviews 1945:221
  New York Times p. 19, Apr 12, 1945
               p. 27, Apr 26, 1945
               p. 16, May 1, 1945
               II, p. 1, May 6, 1945
  New Yorker 21:42, May 5, 1945
  Newsweek 25:81, May 7, 1945
  Theatre Arts 29:389, Jul 1945
  Time 45:74, May 7, 1945

Cue for Passion (with H. S. Kraft)
  Productions:
  Opened December 19, 1940 for 12 performances.
  Reviews:
  New York Theatre Critics' Reviews 1940:185
  New York Times p. 33, Dec 20, 1940
  New Yorker 16:29, Dec 28, 1940
  Theatre Arts 25:98, Feb 1941

Decision
  Productions:
  Opened February 2, 1944 for 160 performances.
  Reviews:
  Catholic World 158:585-6, Mar 1944
  Commonweal 39:447, Feb 18, 1944
  Life 16:47-8+, May 27, 1944
  Nation 158:235, Feb 19, 1944
  New Republic 110:242, Feb 21, 1944
  New York Theatre Critics' Reviews 1944:265
  New York Times p. 23, Feb 3, 1944
               II, p. 1, Feb 13, 1944
               II, p. 1, May 21, 1944
  Newsweek 23:72, Feb 14, 1944
  Theatre Arts 28:197-99+, Apr 1944
  Time 43:62, Feb 14, 1944

Kind Lady (Adapted from a story by Hugh Walpole)
  Productions:
  Opened April 23, 1935 for 102 performances.
  Opened September 9, 1935 for 20 performances.
  Opened September 3, 1940 for 107 performances.
  (Off Off Broadway) December 4, 1980 (Equity Library Theater).
  Reviews:
  Catholic World 141:340-1, Jun 1935
               152:88, Oct 1940
  Commonweal 22:47, May 10, 1935
             32:449, Sep 20, 1940
  Literary Digest 119:16, May 4, 1935

Nation 140:554, May 8, 1935
New Republic 82:370, May 8, 1935
New York Theatre Critics' Reviews 1940:286
New York Times p. 24, Apr 24, 1935
　　　　　　　　X, p. 1, Apr 28, 1935
　　　　　　　　p. 24, Jul 23, 1935
　　　　　　　　p. 27, Nov 19, 1935
　　　　　　　　p. 19, Jun 12, 1936
　　　　　　　　p. 22, Jul 14, 1936
　　　　　　　　p. 23, Jul 6, 1937
　　　　　　　　p. 19, Jul 21, 1937
　　　　　　　　p. 14, Jul 11, 1938
　　　　　　　　p. 28, Sep 4, 1940
Newsweek 5:24, May 4, 1935
Stage 1:14, Nov 1940
Theatre Arts 24:775+, Nov 1940
　　　　　　 24:779, Nov 1940
Time 25:40, May 6, 1935

Last Judgment (see Cue for Passion)

Oh, Men! Oh Women!
　　Productions:
　　　　Opened December 17, 1953 for 382 performances.
　　Reviews:
　　　　America 90:386, Jan 9, 1954
　　　　Catholic World 178:389, Feb 1954
　　　　Commonweal 59:403, Jan 22, 1954
　　　　Life 36:49-50+, Jan 11, 1954
　　　　Nation 178:57, Jan 16, 1954
　　　　New Republic 130:21, Jan 4, 1954
　　　　　　　　　　 130:21, May 31, 1954
　　　　New York Theatre Critics' Reviews 1953:184
　　　　New York Times p. 37, Dec 18, 1953
　　　　New Yorker 29:38-9, Jan 2, 1954
　　　　Newsweek 42:47, Dec 28, 1953
　　　　Saturday Review 37:30, Jan 9, 1954
　　　　Theatre Arts 38:17, Mar 1954
　　　　Time 62:34, Dec 28, 1953

Those Endearing Young Charms
　　Productions:
　　　　Opened June 16, 1943 for 61 performances.
　　Reviews:
　　　　Catholic World 157:523, Aug 1943
　　　　Commonweal 38:234-5, Jul 2, 1943
　　　　New York Theatre Critics' Reviews 1943:318
　　　　New York Times p. 16, Jun 17, 1943
　　　　New Yorker 19:33, Jun 26, 1943

Wonder Boy (with Arthur Barton)
　　Productions:

Opened October 22, 1931 for 44 performances.
Reviews:
Commonweal 15:102, Nov 25, 1931
Nation 133:525-6, Nov 11, 1931
New York Times p. 20, Oct 24, 1931
Vogue 78:57, Dec 15, 1931

CHODOROV, JEROME

Anniversary Waltz (with Joseph A. Fields)
Productions:
Opened April 7, 1954 for 615 performances.
Reviews:
America 91:116, Apr 24, 1954
Catholic World 179:226, Jun 1954
Commonweal 60:143, May 14, 1954
Nation 178:370, Apr 24, 1954
New York Theatre Critics' Reviews 1954:339
New York Times p. 34, Apr 8, 1954
II, p. 1, Apr 25, 1954
p. 18, Apr 8, 1955
p. 31, Dec 2, 1955
II, p. 7, Dec 11, 1955
New Yorker 30:66-8, Apr 17, 1954
Newsweek 43:66, Apr 19, 1954
Saturday Review 37:24, Apr 24, 1954
Theatre Arts 38:20, Jun 1954
Time 63:88, Apr 19, 1954

The French Touch (see entry under Fields, Joseph A.)

Junior Miss (with Joseph A. Fields)
Productions:
Opened November 18, 1941 for 710 performances.
Reviews:
Catholic World 154:471-2, Jan 1942
Commonweal 35:178, Dec 5, 1941
Life 11:103, Dec 15, 1941
15:82, Aug 2, 1943
Nation 153:548, Nov 29, 1941
New Republic 113:161, Aug 1, 1945
New York Theatre Critics' Reviews 1941:211
New York Times p. 28, Nov 19, 1941
IV, p. 2, Nov 23, 1941
IX, p. 1, Nov 30, 1941
p. 23, Jan 7, 1942
II, p. 1, Apr 18, 1943
New Yorker 17:39, Nov 29, 1941
Newsweek 18:71, Dec 1, 1941
Theatre Arts 26:9+, Jan 1942
Time 38:67, Dec 1, 1941

My Sister Eileen (see entry under Fields, Joseph A.)

The Ponder Heart (see entry under Fields, Joseph A.)

Schoolhouse on the Lot (see entry under Fields, Joseph A.)

A Talent for Murder (with Norman Panama)
    Productions:
        Opened October 1, 1981 for 77 performances.
    Reviews:
        New Leader 64:20, Nov 2, 1981
        New York Magazine 14:86, Oct 12, 1981
        New York Theatre Critics' Reviews 1981:165
        New York Times III, p. 3, Oct 2, 1981
                      III, p. 2, Nov 20, 1981
        New Yorker 57:148, Oct 12, 1981
        Time 118:96, Oct 12, 1981

3 Bags Full (Based on a play by Claude Magnier)
    Productions:
        Opened March 6, 1966 for 33 performances.
    Reviews:
        America 114:453, Apr 2, 1966
        New York Theatre Critics' Reviews 1966:339
        New York Times p. 22, Mar 7, 1966
        New Yorker 42:160, May 19, 1966
        Newsweek 67:97, Mar 21, 1966
        Time 87:80, Mar 18, 1966
        Vogue 147:145, May 1966

CLEMENTS, COLIN

Glamour Preferred (see entry under Ryerson, Florence)

Harriet (see entry under Ryerson, Florence)

Morality Clause (see Glamour Preferred)

Strange Bedfellows (see entry under Ryerson, Florence)

COBURN, D. L.

*Bluewater Cottage
    Reviews:
        Los Angeles Times V, p. 1, Sep 18, 1979
        New West 4:SC-38, Oct 22, 1979

The Gin Game
    Productions:
        Opened October 6, 1977 for 517 performances.

Reviews:
America 137:334, Nov 12, 1977
Los Angeles 24:236+, Feb 1979
Nation 225:445, Oct 29, 1977
New Republic 177:24, Nov 12, 1977
New West 4:80+, Jan 29, 1979
New York Magazine 10:85, Oct 24, 1977
New York Theatre Critics' Reviews 1977:178
New York Times III, p. 3, Oct 7, 1977
                II, p. 5, Oct 16, 1977
                III, p. 9, Nov 22, 1978
                III, p. 20, Dec 6, 1978
                XI, p. 30, Oct 18, 1981
                XXI, p. 6, Jun 13, 1982
New Yorker 53:93, Oct 17, 1977
           53:36-7, Oct 24, 1977
Newsweek 90:117, Oct 17, 1977
Texas Monthly 6:134, Jun 1978
              10:150, Jul 1982
Time 110:94, Oct 17, 1977

COFFEE, LEONORE (MRS. W. J. COWEN)

Family Portrait (with William Joyce Cowen)
  Productions:
    Opened March 8, 1939 for 111 performances.
    (Off Broadway) Season of 1958-59.
  Reviews:
    Catholic World 149:89-90, Apr 1939
    Commonweal 29:609, Mar 24, 1939
    New York Times p. 18, Mar 9, 1939
                   XI, p. 1, Mar 19, 1939
                   IX, p. 2, Jun 30, 1940
                   p. 48, May 6, 1959
    New Yorker 35:87-8, May 16, 1959
    Newsweek 13:33, Mar 20, 1939
    North American Review 247:No 2:370-1, Jun 1939
    Player's Magazine 17:11-12, Jan 1941
    Stage 16:24-5, Mar 15, 1939
    Theatre Arts 23:318-19+, May 1939
    Time 33:60-61, Mar 20, 1939

COHAN, GEORGE M.

American Born
  Productions:
    Opened October 5, 1925 for 88 performances.
  Reviews:
    Life (NY) 86:18, Oct 29, 1925
    New York Times p. 31, Oct 6, 1925

Baby Cyclone
  Productions:
    Opened September 12, 1927 for 184 performances.
  Reviews:
    Life (NY) 90:21, Oct 6, 1927
    New York Times VII, p. 2, Aug 14, 1927
                   p. 37, Sep 13, 1927
    Theatre Magazine 46:23, Nov 1927

Broadway Jones
  Productions:
    Opened September 23, 1912 for 176 performances.
  Reviews:
    Blue Book 16:229-34, Dec 1912
    Bookman 36:281, Nov 1912
    Dramatic Mirror 68:6-7, Sep 25, 1912
    Dramatist 4:377-9, Jul 1913
    Everybody's 27:817-18, Dec 1912
    Green Book 8:924-6+, Dec 1912
                9:534-52, Mar 1913
    Hearst 23:315-26, Feb 1913
    Leslies' Weekly 115:490, Nov 14, 1912
    Life (NY) 60:1912, Oct 3, 1912
    Munsey 48:354, Nov 1912
    New York Times p. 3, Feb 4, 1914
    Red Book 20:374-7+, Dec 1912
    Theatre Magazine 16:134, Nov 1912

*Confidential Service
  Reviews:
    New York Times VIII, p. 2, Apr 3, 1932

Dear Old Darling
  Productions:
    Opened March 2, 1936 for 16 performances.
  Reviews:
    Commonweal 23:580, Mar 20, 1936
    Literary Digest 121:19, Mar 14, 1936
    Nation 142:359-60, Mar 18, 1936
    New Republic 86:169, Mar 18, 1936
    New York Times p. 10, Dec 31, 1935
                   IX, p. 1, Feb 2, 1936
                   p. 25, Mar 3, 1936
    Newsweek 7:39-40, Mar 14, 1936
    Stage 13:29-30, Jan 1936
    Theatre Arts 20:260-1, Apr 1936
    Time 27:42, Mar 9, 1936

Friendship
  Productions:
    Opened August 31, 1931 for 24 performances.

Reviews:
Arts and Decoration 36:73, Nov 1931
Commonweal 14:470, Sep 16, 1931
Life (NY) 98:18, Sep 18, 1931
New York Times VIII, p. 2, May 10, 1931
     p. 30, Sep 1, 1931
     IX, p. 1, Sep 13, 1931
Outlook 159:86, Sep 16, 1931
Theatre Arts 15:887-8, Nov 1931
Vogue 78:106, Nov 1, 1931

Fulton of Oak Falls (Based on a story by Parker Fennelly)
Productions:
Opened February 10, 1937 for 37 performances.
Reviews:
New York Times p. 15, Jan 2, 1937
     p. 18, Feb 11, 1937
Newsweek 9:21-4, Feb 20, 1937
Stage 14:65, Feb 1937
Time 29:46, Feb 22, 1937

Gambling
Productions:
Opened August 26, 1929 for 152 performances.
Reviews:
Catholic World 130:209-10, Nov 1929
Commonweal 10:645, Oct 23, 1929
Life (NY) 94:20, Sep 20, 1929
New York Times IX, p. 2, May 19, 1929
     p. 31, Aug 27, 1929
Outlook 153:72, Sep 11, 1929
Theatre Magazine 50:42, Oct 1929

Get-Rich-Quick Wallingford (Adapted from the novel by George Randolph Chester)
Productions:
Opened September 19, 1910 for 424 performances.
Opened May 7, 1917 for 16 performances.
Reviews:
Blue Book 12:638-9, Jan 1911
Collier's 46:17, Dec 24, 1910
Current Literature 51:185-91, Aug 1911
Dramatist 2:118-19, Jan 1911
Green Book 4:1222-23, Dec 1910
     5:239+, Feb 1911
Hampton 25:828-9, Dec 1910
Literary Digest 44:1356, Jun 29, 1912
Metropolitan Magazine 33:404-5, Dec 1910
Munsey 44:410, Dec 1910
New York Times p. 9, May 9, 1917
     VIII, p. 7, May 13, 1917

Pearson 24:806-7, Dec 1910
Red Book 16:566-71, Jan 1911
Theatre Magazine 12:141+, Nov 1910
Worlds' Work 21:14112-21, Mar 1911
　　　　　　22:14322-8, May 1911
　　　　　　22:14274-9, Jun 1911

Hit-the-Trail-Holiday (Suggested by George Middleton and Guy Bolton)
Productions:
Opened September 13, 1915 for 336 performances.
Reviews:
Bookman 42:267-8, Nov 1915
Dramatic Mirror 74:8, Sep 15, 1915
　　　　　　　　75:2+, Jan 8, 1916
Everybody's 34:502, Apr 1916
Green Book 14:973-5, Dec 1915
　　　　　　14:981-2, Dec 1915
Life (NY) 66:566, Sep 23, 1915
National Magazine 43:379-80, Nov 1915
New Republic 4:211, Sep 25, 1915
New York Drama News 61:19, Sep 18, 1915
New York Times p. 11, Sep 14, 1915

The Home Towners
Productions:
Opened August 23, 1926 for 64 performances.
Reviews:
Bookman 64:341-2, Nov 1926
Dial 81:520, Dec 1926
Independent 117:421, Oct 9, 1926
Life (NY) 88:20, Sep 16, 1926
New York Times VIII, p. 2, May 16, 1926
　　　　　　　　p. 19, Aug 24, 1926
　　　　　　　VII, p. 1, Aug 29, 1926
　　　　　　　VII, p. 1, Sep 5, 1926
Theatre Magazine 44:66+, Oct 1926
Vogue 68:80+, Oct 15, 1926

The Little Millionaire
Productions:
Opened September 25, 1911 for 192 performances.
Reviews:
Blue Book 14:463-5, Jan 1912
Dramatic Mirror 66:11, Sep 27, 1911
Green Book 6:1195-6, Dec 1911
Leslies' Weekly 113:409, Oct 12, 1911
Life (NY) 58:618, Oct 12, 1911
Munsey 46:426, Dec 1911

Madeleine and the Movies
Productions:
Opened March 6, 1922 for 80 performances.

Reviews:
Bookman 55:283, May 1922
Life (NY) 79:18, Mar 23, 1922
New York Clipper 70:22, Mar 15, 1922
New York Times p. 11, Mar 7, 1922
                p. 17, Mar 9, 1922
Theatre Magazine 35:336, May 1922

The Miracle Man (Based on Frank L. Packard's story)
  Productions:
    Opened September 21, 1914 for 97 performances.
  Reviews:
    American Magazine 79:87-8, Feb 1915
    Book News 33:230-1, Jan 1915
    Bookman 40:256-8, Nov 1914
    Dramatic Mirror 72:8, Sep 30, 1914
    Dramatist 6:530-1, Jan 1915
    Everybody's 31:702, Nov 1914
    Green Book 12:1140, Dec 1914
    Life (NY) 64:584, Oct 1, 1914
    Munsey 53:360, Nov 1914
    Nation 99:415, Oct 1, 1914
    New Republic 1:23, Nov 14, 1914
    New York Drama News 59:18, Sep 26, 1914
    New York Times VIII, p. 6, Jul 19, 1914
                        p. 11, Sep 22, 1914
                   VII, p. 8, Nov 15, 1914
    Theatre Magazine 20:205+, Nov 1914

Pigeons and People
  Productions:
    Opened January 16, 1933 for 70 performances.
  Reviews:
    Arts and Decoration 38:42, Mar 1933
    Catholic World 136:716-17, Mar 1933
    Commonweal 17:385, Feb 1, 1933
    Nation 136:160, Feb 8, 1933
    New Outlook 161:49, Mar 1933
    New York Times IX, p. 2, Jan 1, 1933
                       p. 22, Jan 17, 1933
    Stage 10:11, Feb 1933
    Theatre Arts 17:180+, Mar 1933
                 19:325, May 1935
    Time 21:22, Jan 30, 1933
    Vogue 81:51+, Mar 15, 1933

A Prince There Was (Based on a story by Dorrough Aldrich)
  Productions:
    Opened December 24, 1918 for 159 performances.
  Reviews:
    Dramatic Mirror 80:47-8, Jan 11, 1919

Nation 108:104, Jan 18, 1919
New Republic 18:279, Mar 29, 1919
New York Times p. 13, Dec 25, 1918

The Return of the Vagabond
Productions:
Opened May 17, 1940 for 7 performances.
Reviews:
Commonweal 32:129, May 31, 1940
Life 8:72-4, May 27, 1940
New York Theatre Critics' Reviews 1940:307
New York Times p. 19, Apr 12, 1940
                p. 20, Apr 13, 1940
                IX, p. 1, Apr 21, 1940
                p. 27, May 14, 1940
Newsweek 15:48, May 27, 1940

Seven Keys to Baldpate (Based on the novel by Earl Derr Biggers)
Productions:
Opened September 22, 1913 for 320 performances.
Opened May 27, 1935 for 8 performances.
Reviews:
American Magazine 2:303-5, Oct 1913
                  5:447-9, Apr 1914
Blue Book 18:836-7, Mar 1914
Bookman 38:262-3, Nov 1913
Commonweal 22:190, Jun 14, 1935
Current Opinion 55:408-12, Dec 1913
Dramatic Mirror 70:10, Sep 24, 1913
Green Book 10:960-3, Dec 1913
           10:1058-60, Dec 1913
Life (NY) 62:567, Oct 2, 1913
Literary Digest 119:23, Jun 1, 1935
Munsey 50:299, Nov 1913
New York Drama News 58:19-20, Sep 27, 1913
New York Times p. 11, Sep 23, 1913
                p. 11, Jun 2, 1914
                p. 3, Apr 2, 1919
                p. 25, Jan 8, 1930
                IX, p. 1, May 19, 1935
                p. 30, May 28, 1935
Newsweek 5:22-3, Jun 8, 1935
Stage 12:6-9, May 1935
      12:32-5, Jul 1935
Theatre Magazine 18:161+, Nov 1913

The Song and Dance Man
Productions:
Opened December 31, 1923 for 96 performances.
Opened June 16, 1930 for 16 performances.

Reviews:
Metropolitan Magazine 59:38+, Apr 1924
New York Times p. 21, Jan 1, 1924
                 VIII, p. 1, Jun 15, 1930
                 p. 25, Jun 17, 1930
Theatre Magazine 39:16, Mar 1924

The Tavern
 Productions:
  Opened May 23, 1921 for 27 performances.
  Opened May 19, 1930 for 32 performances.
  (Off Broadway) April 3, 1962 for 11 performances (APA Rep-
    ertory).
  (Off Broadway) March 5, 1964 for 12 performances (Association
    of Producing Artists).
  (Off Off Broadway) December 1975 (Bert Wheeler Theater).
  (Off Broadway) June 24, 1976 for 18 performances.
  (Off Off Broadway) June 24, 1976 (Playwrights Horizons).
 Reviews:
  Commonweal 12:134-5, Jun 4, 1930
  Dramatic Mirror p. 591, Oct 2, 1920
                  83:929, May 28, 1921
  Life (NY) 76:680, Oct 14, 1920
            77:840, Jun 9, 1921
            95:18, Jun 6, 1930
  New Republic 146:38, May 14, 1962
  New York Clipper 68:29, Oct 6, 1920
                   69:23, Jun 1, 1921
  New York Times VI, p. 1, Oct 10, 1920
                 p. 20, May 18, 1921
                 p. 20, May 24, 1921
                 VIII, p. 1, May 18, 1930
                 p. 32, May 20, 1930
                 VIII, p. 4, Nov 16, 1930
                 p. 29, Apr 5, 1962
                 p. 39, Mar 6, 1964
                 p. 21, Jun 28, 1976
  New Yorker 38:108, Apr 14, 1962
  Outlook 155:193, Jun 4, 1930
  Saturday Review 45:38, Apr 28, 1962
  Theatre Magazine 32:370+, Dec 1930
                   52:40-41, Jul 1930

The Voice of McConnell
 Productions:
  Opened December 25, 1918 for 30 performances.
 Reviews:
  Dramatic Mirror 80:48, Jan 11, 1919
  Forum 61:246, Feb 1919
  Life (NY) 73:56, Jan 9, 1919
  New York Times p. 9, Dec 26, 1918

Theatre Magazine 29:79+, Feb 1919

Whispering Friends
Productions:
Opened February 20, 1928 for 112 performances.
Reviews:
Life (NY) 91:19, Mar 22, 1928
New York Times p. 18, Feb 21, 1928

CONKLE, E. P.

Afternoon Storm
Productions:
Opened April 11, 1948 for 8 performances.
Reviews:
New York Times p. 24, Apr 12, 1948

Minnie Field
Productions:
(Off Broadway) Season of 1940-41.
No Reviews

Prologue to Glory
Productions:
Opened March 17, 1938 for 70 performances.
Reopened September 19, 1938 for 99 performances.
Reviews:
Catholic World 147:213-14, May 1938
Commonweal 27:636, Apr 1, 1938
Life 4:41-2+, Apr 11, 1938
Nation 146:395, Apr 2, 1938
New York Times p. 22, Mar 18, 1938
                X, p. 1, Mar 27, 1938
One Act Play Magazine 1:1122-3, Apr 1938
Theatre Arts 22:329-30, May 1938
Time 31:24, Mar 28, 1938

200 Were Chosen
Productions:
Opened November 20, 1936 for 35 performances.
Reviews:
Catholic World 144:472, Jan 1937
Commonweal 25:162, Dec 4, 1936
Literary Digest 122:19-20, Dec 5, 1936
Nation 143:677, Dec 5, 1936
New York Times XI, p. 3, Nov 15, 1936
                p. 21, Nov 21, 1936
                XII, p. 1, Nov 29, 1936
Newsweek 8:20, Nov 28, 1936
Survey 26:41, Jan 1937

Theatre Arts 21:17-18, Jan 1937
Time 28:54, Nov 30, 1936

What D'You Call It
    Productions:
        Opened March 19, 1940 for 38 performances.
    Reviews:
        New York Times p. 36, Mar 20, 1940

CONNELLY, MARC

Beggar on Horseback (see entry under Kaufman, George S.)

The Deep Tangled Wildwood (see entry under Kaufman, George S.)

Dulcy (see entry under Kaufman, George S.)

Everywhere I Roam (with Arnold Sundguard)
    Productions:
        Opened December 29, 1918 for 13 performances.
    Reviews:
        Catholic World 148:597, Feb 1939
        Commonweal 29:330, Jan 13, 1939
        Nation 148:73-4, Jan 14, 1939
        New York Times p. 15, Apr 22, 1938
                       p. 10, Dec 30, 1938
                       IX, p. 1, Jan 8, 1939
                       IX, p. 2, Jan 15, 1939
                       IX, p. 8, Jan 22, 1939
        Stage 16:39, Jan 1939
        Theatre Arts 23:164, Mar 1939
        Time 33:25, Jan 9, 1939

The Farmer Takes a Wife (with Frank B. Elser. Based on Walter
        D. Edmonds' Rome Haul)
    Productions:
        Opened October 30, 1934 for 104 performances.
    Reviews:
        Catholic World 140:340, Dec 1934
        Commonweal 21:122, Nov 23, 1934
        Literary Digest 118:20, Nov 17, 1934
        Nation 139:573, Nov 14, 1934
        New Republic 81:21, Nov 14, 1934
        New York Times p. 17, Oct 9, 1934
                       IX, p. 3, Oct 28, 1934
                       p. 17, Oct 31, 1934
                       IX, p. 1, Nov 11, 1934
                       IX, p. 1, Jan 6, 1935
        Newsweek 4:27, Nov 10, 1934

Stage 12:12, Nov 1934
  12:28-9, Dec 1934
Theatre Arts 18:902-3, Dec 1934
Time 24:36+, Nov 12, 1934

The Flowers of Virtue
  Productions:
    Opened February 5, 1942 for 4 performances.
  Reviews:
    Catholic World 154:732, Mar 1942
    Commonweal 35:437, Feb 20, 1942
    New York Theatre Critics' Reviews 1942:354
    New York Times p. 22, Feb 6, 1942
    New Yorker 17:28, Feb 14, 1942
    Theatre Arts 26:225, Apr 1942

Green Pastures (Based on Roark Bradford's Ol' Man Adam an' His
    Chillun')
  Productions:
    Opened February 26, 1930 for 640 performances.
    Opened February 26, 1935 for 73 performances.
    Opened March 15, 1951 for 44 performances.
  Reviews:
    Arts and Decoration 33:105, May 1930
    Bookman 71:340, Jun 1930
      73:294-5, May 1931
    Catholic World 131:210-11, May 1930
      133:596-8, Aug 1931
      173:145, May 1951
    Christian Century 47:1278-81, Oct 22, 1930
      49:1316, Oct 26, 1932
      52:399-401, Mar 27, 1935
    Collier's 85:23+, May 10, 1930
    Commonweal 11:561, Mar 19, 1930
      17:481, Mar 1, 1933
      53:646, Apr 6, 1951
    Dramatist 22:1435-6, Jan 1931
    Ladies Home Journal 52:8-9+, Sep 1935
    Life (NY) 95:18+, Mar 21, 1930
      95:16, May 23, 1930
    Life 30:67-9, Apr 16, 1951
    Literary Digest 104:20-1, Mar 22, 1930
      105:22-3, Jun 21, 1930
      105:18, Jun 28, 1930
      107:19-20, Dec 20, 1930
      119:25, Mar 9, 1935
    Living Age 338:501, Jun 15, 1930
    Nation 130:376, Mar 26, 1930
      130:415, Apr 9, 1930
      130:600, May 21, 1930

172:305, Mar 31, 1951
National Magazine 59:172, Jan 1931
Negro History Bulletin 42:42-3, Apr 1979
New Republic 62:128-9, Mar 18, 1930
    63:128, Jun 18, 1930
    63:150-1, Jun 25, 1930
    124:30, Apr 16, 1951
New York Theatre Critics' Reviews 1951:312
New York Times p. 26, Feb 27, 1930
    IX, p. 1, Mar 9, 1930
    p. 26, Mar 19, 1930
    VIII, p. 1, May 18, 1930
    IX, p. 1, Jun 8, 1930
    VIII, p. 5, Jun 29, 1930
    VIII, p. 1, Mar 1, 1931
    p. 14, Aug 31, 1931
    p. 17, Aug 3, 1932
    p. 24, Sep 1, 1932
    p. 26, Oct 11, 1932
    p. 17, Oct 17, 1932
    X, p. 2, Sep 10, 1933
    p. 24, Oct 5, 1933
    IX, p. 1, Oct 22, 1933
    X, p. 3, Jan 7, 1934
    IX, p. 3, Feb 25, 1934
    p. 26, Mar 22, 1934
    X, p. 3, Sep 23, 1934
    p. 19, Oct 4, 1934
    VIII, p. 2, Feb 3, 1935
    p. 16, Feb 27, 1935
    VIII, p. 2, Mar 3, 1935
    p. 35, Mar 16, 1951
    II, p. 1, Apr 1, 1951
New Yorker 27:56+, Mar 24, 1951
Newsweek 5:28-9, Mar 9, 1935
    37:90, Mar 26, 1951
Outlook 154:429, Mar 12, 1930
Review of Reviews 81:145, Apr 1930
Saturday Review 34:28-30, Apr 7, 1951
School and Society 73:246-7, Apr 21, 1951
Sketch Book 7:37, May 1930
Survey 64:156, May 1, 1930
Theatre Arts 14:369-70, May 1930
    35:22, May 1951
    42:64-6+, Nov 1958
Theatre Magazine 51:46, Mar 1930
    51:15-16, Apr 1930
    51:46, Mar 1930
    51:23+, Jun 1930
    53:14, Mar 1931
Time 25:35-7, Mar 4, 1935

             35:68, Jan 29, 1940
             57:67, Mar 26, 1951
        Vogue 75:82-3+, May 10, 1930
             110:181, Sep 1, 1947

*Hunger's Moon
    Reviews:
    New York Times II, p. 3, Mar 16, 1958

Merton of the Movies   (see entry under Kaufman, George S.)

*The Stitch in Time
    Reviews:
    New York Times III, p. 17, Jan 8, 1981

A Story for Strangers
    Productions:
    Opened September 21, 1948 for 15 performances.
    Reviews:
    Commonweal 48:618, Oct 8, 1948
    Nation 167:381, Oct 2, 1948
    New York Theatre Critics' Reviews 1948:231
    New York Times p. 39, Sep 22, 1948
    New Yorker 24:51, Oct 2, 1948
    Time 52:59, Oct 4, 1948

To the Ladies   (see entry under Kaufman, George S.)

The Wild Man of Borneo (with Herman J. Mankiewicz)
    Productions:
    Opened September 13, 1927 for 15 performances.
    Reviews:
    New Republic 52:148-9, Sep 28, 1927
    New York Times p. 29, Sep 14, 1927
                VIII, p. 1, Sep 25, 1927

The Wisdom Tooth
    Productions:
    Opened February 15, 1926 for 160 performances.
    Reviews:
    Bookman 63:341, May 1926
    Dramatist 17:1300-1, Apr 1926
    Independent 116:332, Mar 20, 1926
    Life (NY) 87:22, Mar 18, 1926
    Nation 122:238, Mar 3, 1926
    New Republic 46:45, Mar 3, 1926
    New York Times p. 22, Feb 16, 1926
                VIII, p. 1, Feb 28, 1926
                VIII, p. 1, Mar 14, 1926
    Theatre Magazine 43:16, May 1926
                43:30, May 1926
                43:26+, Jun 1926

Vogue 67:117+, Apr 15, 1926

CORMACK, BARTLETT

*Hey Diddle Diddle
Reviews:
New York Times p. 24, Jan 22, 1937

The Racket
Productions:
Opened November 22, 1927 for 119 performances.
Reviews:
Life (NY) 90:21, Dec 8, 1927
New York Times p. 28, Nov 23, 1927
IX, p. 1, Dec 18, 1927

COWEN, WILLIAM JOYCE

Family Portrait (see Coffee, Leonore)

COXE, LOUIS O.

Billy Budd (with Robert Chapman. Based on the novel by Herman
Melville)
Productions:
Opened February 10, 1951 for 105 performances.
(Off Broadway) Season of 1954-55.
(Off Broadway) Season of 1958-59 (Equity Library Theatre).
Reviews:
Commonweal 53:518, Mar 2, 1951
Nation 172:189, Feb 24, 1951
New York Theatre Critics' Reviews 1951:353
New York Times p. 18, Feb 12, 1951
II, p. 1, Feb 18, 1951
II, p. 1, Apr 15, 1951
II, p. 1, May 6, 1951
II, p. 3, Oct 21, 1951
p. 35, May 4, 1955
p. 13, Feb 28, 1959
New Yorker 27:70, Feb 17, 1951
Newsweek 37:82-3, Feb 19, 1951
Time 57:68+, Feb 19, 1951

Uniform of Flesh (with R. H. Chapman. Based on Herman Melville's
Billy Budd)
Productions:
(Off Broadway) Season of 1948-49 (Experimental Theatre).
Reviews:
New York Times p. 15, Jan 31, 1949

The Witchfinders
    Productions:
        (Off Broadway) Season of 1955-56.
    Reviews:
        New York Times p. 22, May 11, 1956

CRAVEN, FRANK

The First Year
    Productions:
        Opened October 20, 1920 for 760 performances.
    Reviews:
        Bookman 53:408-10, Jul 1921
        Current Opinion 70:343-51, Mar 1921
        Dramatic Mirror p. 795, Oct 30, 1920
        Dramatist 12:1055-6, Apr 1921
        Everybody's 44:54-5, Feb 1921
        Hearst 39:21-3+, Mar 1921
        Independent 104:177, Nov 6, 1920
        Life (NY) 76:872, Nov 11, 1920
        New York Clipper 68:28, Oct 27, 1920
        New York Times p. 11, Oct 21, 1920
                        VI, p. 1, Oct 31, 1920
                        VII, p. 6, Dec 19, 1926
        Theatre Magazine 33:27+, Jan 1921
                        33:402+, Jun 1921

Money from Home
    Productions:
        Opened February 28, 1927 for 32 performances.
    Reviews:
        Life (NY) 89:21, Mar 24, 1927
        New York Times p. 30, Mar 1, 1927
        Vogue 69:138, May 1, 1927

New Brooms
    Productions:
        Opened November 17, 1924 for 88 performances.
    Reviews:
        American Mercury 4:120, Jan 1925
        Current Opinion 78:60-65, Jan 1925
        New York Times p. 23, Nov 18, 1924
        Overland 86:51, Feb 1928
        Theatre Magazine 40:16, Feb 1925

The 19th Hole
    Productions:
        Opened October 11, 1927 for 119 performances.
    Reviews:
        Life (NY) 90:23, Nov 10, 1927

New York Times VIII, p. 4, Oct 2, 1927
                 p. 30, Oct 12, 1927
Outlook 148:23, Jan 4, 1928
Theatre Magazine 46:42-3, Dec 1927
Vogue 70:172, Dec 1, 1927

Spite Corner
  Productions:
    Opened September 25, 1922 for 121 performances.
  Reviews:
    Dramatic Mirror 84:85, Jul 16, 1921
    Hearst 43:93-5+, Jan 1923
    New York Clipper 70:21, Oct 4, 1922
    New York Times p. 18, Sep 26, 1922

That's Gratitude
  Productions:
    Opened September 11, 1930 for 197 performances.
    Opened June 16, 1932 for 8 performances.
  Reviews:
    Arts and Decoration 34:67, Nov 1930
    Catholic World 135:595-6, Aug 1932
    Drama 21:15-16, Nov 1930
    Life (NY) 96:18, Oct 3, 1930
    Nation 131:355, Oct 1, 1930
    National Magazine 59:138, Dec 1930
    New York Times p. 28, Sep 12, 1930
                   IX, p. 1, Sep 21, 1930
                   p. 23, Feb 2, 1931
                   p. 24, Jun 17, 1932
    Sketch Book 8:29, Nov 1930
    Theatre Magazine 52:24-5, Nov 1930
    Vogue 76:116, Nov 10, 1930

This Way Out
  Productions:
    Opened August 30, 1917 for 28 performances.
  Reviews:
    Dramatic Mirror 77:8, Sep 8, 1917
    New York Times p. 8, Aug 31, 1917
    Theatre Magazine 26:206, Oct 1917

Too Many Cooks
  Productions:
    Opened February 24, 1914 for 223 performances.
  Reviews:
    American Magazine 77:105-6, Jun 1914
    American Playwright 3:129-30, Apr 1914
    Book News 32:404, Apr 1914
    Bookman 39:143-5, Apr 1914
    Dramatic Mirror 71:6, Mar 4, 1914

Dramatist 5:478-9, Jul 1914
Green Book 11:712-13, May 1914
    11:773-5, May 1914
Munsey 51:588, Apr 1914
New York Drama News 59:19, Mar 7, 1914
New York Times p. 9, Jan 27, 1914
      p. 9, Feb 26, 1914
Theatre Magazine 19:170-1+, Apr 1914

CRISTOFER, MICHAEL

*Black Angel
 Reviews:
  New West 3:SC-21, Jun 19, 1978

*Lady and the Clarinet
 Reviews:
  Los Angeles 25:260, Oct 1980
  New West 5:89, Sep 22, 1980

The Shadow Box
 Productions:
  Opened March 31, 1977 for 315 performances.
 Reviews:
  America 136:397, Apr 30, 1977
  Los Angeles 20:138+, Dec 1975
  Nation 224:507, Apr 23, 1977
  New York Magazine 10:82, Apr 18, 1977
  New York Theatre Critics' Reviews 1977:288
  New York Times p. 28, Jan 25, 1977
      II, p. 3, Feb 6, 1977
      III, p. 3, Apr 1, 1977
      II, p. 5, Apr 10, 1977
      III, p. 17, Dec 22, 1977
  New Yorker 53:85, Apr 11, 1977
  Newsweek 89:89-90, Apr 25, 1977
  Saturday Review 4:42-3, May 14, 1977
  Texas Monthly 6:142+, May 1978
  Time 109:60, Feb 7, 1977

CROTHERS, RACHEL

As Husbands Go
 Productions:
  Opened March 5, 1931 for 148 performances.
  Opened January 19, 1933 for 148 performances.
 Reviews:
  Arts and Decoration 35:88, May 1931
  Bookman 73:296, May 1931

Catholic World 133:205, May 1931
Commonweal 13:552-3, Mar 18, 1931
Drama 21:11, Apr 1931
Life (NY) 97:25, Mar 27, 1931
Nation 132:338, Mar 25, 1931
New York Times p. 26, Mar 6, 1931
　　　　　IX, p. 1, Mar 15, 1931
　　　　　p. 20, Jan 20, 1933
　　　　　p. 24, Jul 2, 1935
Theatre Arts 15:370-1, May 1931
Vogue 77:59+, May 1, 1931

*Bon Voyage
　Reviews:
　　New York Times VIII, p. 4, Dec 29, 1929

Caught Wet
　Productions:
　　Opened November 4, 1931 for 13 performances.
　Reviews:
　　Catholic World 134:334, Dec 1931
　　New York Times p. 29, Nov 5, 1931

Everyday
　Productions:
　　Opened November 16, 1921 for 30 performances.
　Reviews:
　　Dramatic Mirror 84:773, Nov 26, 1921
　　New York Clipper 69:20, Nov 23, 1921
　　New York Times p. 15, Nov 17, 1921

Expressing Willie
　Productions:
　　Opened April 16, 1924 for 69+ performances.
　　(Off Off Broadway) March 16, 1978 (Encompass Theater).
　Reviews:
　　American Mercury 2:246, Jun 1924
　　Arts and Decoration 21:38, Jul 1924
　　Bookman 59:452, Jun 1924
　　Classic 19:46+, Aug 1924
　　Current Opinion 76:799-807, Jun 1924
　　Dramatist 15:1239, Oct 1924
　　New York Times p. 22, Apr 17, 1924
　　　　　　　VIII, p. 1, Apr 27, 1924
　　　　　　　VIII, p. 1, May 4, 1924
　　Theatre Magazine 39:15-16, Jun 1924
　　　　　　　39:14, Jul 1924
　　　　　　　39:26+, Aug 1924
　　Woman Citizen ns 8:13, May 17, 1924

He and She
　Productions:

Opened February 12, 1920 for 28 performances.
(Off Off Broadway) Season of 1970-71 (American Theater Club).
(Off Broadway) May 22, 1980 for 27 performances.
Reviews:
Dramatic Mirror 82:310, Feb 21, 1920
Dramatist 11:994-5, Apr 1920
New York Clipper 68:21, Feb 18, 1920
New York Magazine 13:88, Jun 16, 1980
New York Times p. 16, Feb 13, 1920
III, p. 5, Feb 22, 1920
III, p. 6, Feb 22, 1920
II, p. 3, May 25, 1980
III, p. 5, May 30, 1980
New Yorker 56:112+, Jun 9, 1980
Review 2:262+, Mar 13, 1920
Theatre Magazine 31:269-70, Apr 1920

*The Heart of Paddy Whack
Reviews:
New York Times p. 13, Nov 24, 1914

A Lady's Virtue
Productions:
Opened November 23, 1925 for 136 performances.
Reviews:
New York Times p. 28, Nov 24, 1925
VIII, p. 5, Dec 6, 1925
VII, p. 2, Feb 21, 1926

Let Us Be Gay
Productions:
Opened February 19, 1929 for 132 performances.
Reviews:
American Mercury 17:118-9, May 1929
Arts and Decoration 31:64, May 1929
Catholic World 129:82-3, Apr 1929
Commonweal 9:750, May 1, 1929
Life (NY) 93:20, Mar 22, 1929
New York Times p. 19, Feb 22, 1929
X, p. 4, Mar 10, 1929
p. 18, Jun 29, 1937
Outlook 151:423, Mar 13, 1929
Theatre Arts 13:330-3, May 1929
Theatre Magazine 49:28-9+, Jun 1929

A Little Journey
Productions:
Opened December 26, 1918 for 252 performances.
Reviews:
Dramatic Mirror 80:47, Jan 11, 1919
Dramatist 11:1001-2, Apr 1920

Hearst 36:42-3+, Aug 1919
Life (NY) 73:57, Jan 9, 1919
    73:615, Apr 10, 1919
New York Times p. 9, Dec 27, 1918
Theatre Magazine 29:77+, Feb 1919

A Man's World
    Productions:
        Opened February 8, 1910 for 71 performances.
    Reviews:
        Bookman 31:139-42, Apr 1910
        Burr McIntosh Monthly 22:394-5, May 1910
        Dial 59:326, Oct 14, 1915
        Dramatic Mirror 63:6, Feb 19, 1910
        Everybody's 22:703+, May 1910
        Green Book 3:697, Apr 1910
            3:1006-8, May 1910
        Hampton 24:579, Apr 1910
        Harper's Weekly 54:24, Mar 26, 1910
        Life (NY) 55:324, Feb 24, 1910
        Metropolitan Magazine 32:266-7, May 1910
        Nation 90:146, Feb 10, 1910
        Pearson 23:552, Apr 1910
        Theatre Magazine 11:68-9, Mar 1910

Mary the Third
    Productions:
        Opened February 5, 1923 for 152+ performances.
    Reviews:
        Nation 116:278, Mar 7, 1923
        New York Clipper 71:14, Feb 14, 1923
        New York Times p. 14, Feb 6, 1923
        Scribner's Magazine 74:269, Jul 1923
        Theatre Magazine 37:20, Apr 1923

Mother Carey's Chickens (with Kate Douglas Wiggin. Based on Miss
        Wiggin's novel)
    Productions:
        Opened September 25, 1917 for 39 performances.
    Reviews:
        Dramatic Mirror 77:7, Oct 16, 1917
        Dramatist 9:873-4, Jan 1918
        New York Drama News 64:10, Sep 29, 1917
        New York Times p. 11, Sep 26, 1917
            III, p. 8, Sep 30, 1917
        Theatre Magazine 26:279+, Nov 1917

Nice People
    Productions:
        Opened March 2, 1921 for 120+ performances.
    Reviews:
        Bookman 53:275, May 1921

Dramatist 15:1201-2, Jan 1924
Everybody's 45:87-94, Nov 1921
Hearst 40:25-7+, Jul 1921
Independent 105:281, Mar 19, 1921
Life (NY) 77:428, Mar 24, 1921
New York Clipper 69:23, Mar 9, 1921
New York Times p. 11, Mar 3, 1921
Scribner's Magazine 72:105, Jul 1922
Theatre Magazine 33:339, May 1921
            34:16+, Jul 1921
Weekly Review 4:345-6, Apr 13, 1921

Old Lady 31 (Suggested by Louise Forsslund's novel)
   Productions:
      Opened October 30, 1916 for 160 performances.
   Reviews:
      Book News 36:304-5, Apr 1918
      Bookman 44:396-8, Dec 1916
      Collier's 58:8+, Jan 27, 1917
      Current Opinion 61:389-92, Dec 1916
      Dramatic Mirror 76:10, Sep 16, 1916
                     76:7, Nov 11, 1916
      Everybody's 36:65-6, Jan 1917
      Green Book 17:4-5+, Jan 1917
      Life (NY) 68:858-9, Nov 16, 1916
      Nation 103:470, Nov 16, 1916
      New Republic 9:217-18, Dec 23, 1916
      New York Drama News 63:14, Nov 4, 1916
      New York Times p. 11, Oct 31, 1916
                     II, p. 6, Nov 5, 1916
      Theatre Magazine 24:357, Dec 1916
      Woman's Home Companion 44:45, Apr 1917

Once upon a Time
   Productions:
      Opened April 15, 1918 for 24 performances.
   Reviews:
      Dramatic Mirror 78:584-5, Apr 27, 1918
      Green Book 20:14-17, Jul 1918
      New York Times p. 11, Apr 16, 1918

Ourselves
   Productions:
      Opened November 12, 1913 for 29 performances.
   Reviews:
      Bookman 38:496-9, Jan 1914
      Dramatic Mirror 70:6-7, Nov 19, 1913
      Dramatist 5:421-2, Jan 1914
      Everybody's 30:264, Feb 1914
      Green Book 11:346-7, Feb 1914
      Harper's Weekly 58:12-17, Dec 6, 1913
                     58:26, Jan 10, 1914

Life (NY) 62:922-3, Nov 27, 1913
Munsey 51:124, Feb 1914
New York Drama News 58:20, Nov 22, 1913
New York Times p. 13, Nov 11, 1913
                p. 11, Nov 14, 1913
Theatre Magazine 18:xviii+, Dec 1913

*Rector
    Reviews:
    New York Times p. 7, Apr 26, 1926

Revenge, or the Pride of Lilian LeMar
    Productions:
    Opened February 25, 1913 for one matinee.
    No reviews.

Susan and God
    Productions:
    Opened October 7, 1937 for 288 performances.
    Opened December 13, 1944 for 8 performances.
    Reviews:
    Catholic World 146:219-20, Nov 1937
    Commonweal 26:606, Oct 22, 1937
    Independent Woman 16:351, Nov 1937
    Life 4:31, Feb 21, 1938
    Literary Digest 123:20+, May 15, 1937
                    125:21, Jan 8, 1939
    Nation 145:455-6, Oct 23, 1937
    New Republic 92:342, Oct 27, 1937
    New York Times II, p. 12, Apr 11, 1937
                    X, p. 2, Apr 25, 1937
                    p. 26, Oct 8, 1937
                    XI, p. 1, Oct 17, 1937
                    XI, p. 3, Nov 7, 1937
                    p. 29, Jun 8, 1938
                    X, p. 10, Jun 12, 1938
                    p. 17, Nov 24, 1943
                    II, p. 3, Dec 12, 1943
                    p. 30, Dec 14, 1943
    Newsweek 10:25, Oct 25, 1937
    Stage 15:7-8, Mar 1938
    Theatre Arts 21:918-19, Dec 1937
    Time 30:36, Oct 18, 1937

*Talent
    Reviews:
    New York Times p. 18, Aug 4, 1933
                   IX, p. 3, Dec 31, 1933

39 East
    Productions:
    Opened March 31, 1919 for 160 performances.

Reviews:
Dramatist 11:987, Jan 1920
Forum 61:629, May 1919
Independent 102:309, Jun 5, 1920
New York Times p. 9, Apr 1, 1919
Review 1:131-2, Jun 21, 1919
Theatre Magazine 29:275+, May 1919

Venus
Productions:
Opened December 26, 1927 for 8 performances.
Reviews:
New York Times p. 26, Dec 26, 1927

When It Strikes Home   (see Ourselves)

When Ladies Meet
Productions:
Opened October 6, 1932 for 173 performances.
Opened Spring, 1933 for 18 performances.
Reviews:
Catholic World 136:208-9, Nov 1932
Commonweal 16:621, Oct 26, 1932
Nation 135:408, Oct 26, 1932
New Outlook 161:46, Nov 1932
New York Times IX, p. 1, Aug 14, 1932
p. 19, Oct 7, 1932
IX, p. 1, Oct 16, 1932
p. 15, Apr 27, 1933
Player's Magazine 9:20, Nov-Dec, 1932
Stage 10:11, Nov 1932
10:8-9, Dec 1932
Theatre Arts 16:958, Dec 1932
Town and Country 87:22-3, Nov 1, 1932
Vogue 80:61, Dec 1, 1932

Young Wisdom
Productions:
Opened January 5, 1914 for 56 performances.
Reviews:
American Playwright 3:6-7, Jan 1914
Book News 32:403-4, Apr 1914
Bookman 39:66, Mar 1914
Collier's 52:24, Feb 21, 1914
Dramatic Mirror 71:10, Jan 7, 1914
Green Book 11:408-10, Mar 1914
11:525-6, Mar 1914
Harper's Weekly 58:5, Jan 31, 1914
Life (NY) 63:150-1, Jan 22, 1914
Munsey 51:341, Mar 1914
New York Drama News 58:13, Jan 10, 1914

New York Times p. 6, Jan 6, 1914
Theatre Magazine 19:60-1+, Feb 1914

CROUSE, RUSSEL

The Great Sebastians (see entry under Lindsay, Howard)

I'd Rather Be Right (see State of the Union)

Life with Father (see entry under Lindsay, Howard)

Life with Mother (see entry under Lindsay, Howard)

The Prescott Proposals (see entry under Lindsay, Howard)

Remains to Be Seen (see entry under Lindsay, Howard)

State of the Union (see entry under Lindsay, Howard)

Strip for Action (see entry under Lindsay, Howard)

Tall Story (see entry under Lindsay, Howard)

CROWLEY, MART

The Boys in the Band
    Productions:
        (Off Broadway) April 15, 1968 for 1,000 performances.
    Reviews:
        America 118:652, May 11, 1968
        Commonweal 88:335, May 31, 1968
        Life 64:18, May 24, 1968
        Nation 206:580, Apr 29, 1968
        New York Theatre Critics' Reviews 1968:260
        New York Times p. 48, Apr 15, 1968
                      II, p. 1, Apr 28, 1968
                      II, p. 3, Sep 29, 1968
                      p. 52, Feb 13, 1969
                      p. 36, Feb 18, 1969
                      II, p. 23, Jun 1, 1969
                      p. 21, Sep 20, 1969
                      p. 34, Apr 18, 1970
                      p. 17, Aug 14, 1970
        New Yorker 44:84+, Apr 27, 1968
        Newsweek 71:93-4, Apr 29, 1968
        Saturday Review 51:26, May 11, 1968
        Time 91:97, Apr 26, 1968
        Vogue 152:64, Aug 1, 1968

A Breeze from the Gulf
    Productions:
        (Off Broadway) October 15, 1973 for 48 performances.
    Reviews:
        Nation 217:477-8, Nov 5, 1973
        New York Magazine 6:79, Oct 29, 1973
        New York Theatre Critics' Reviews 1973:179
        New York Times p. 53, Oct 16, 1973
                II, p. 1, Oct 21, 1973

*Remote Asylum
    Reviews:
        New York Times II, p. 3, Dec 13, 1970

CUMMINGS, E. E.

Him
    Productions:
        Opened April 18, 1928 for 27 performances.
        (Off Off Broadway) April 14, 1974 (Circle Repertory Theater
          Co.).
    Reviews:
        Dial 85:77-81, Jul 1928
        Nation 218:605-5, May 11, 1974
        New Republic 54:325-6, May 2, 1928
                54:383, May 16, 1928
                119:26, Aug 9, 1948
        New York Times IX, p. 4, Apr 15, 1928
                p. 23, Apr 19, 1928
                IX, p. 1, Apr 22, 1928
                IX, p. 2, Apr 27, 1928
                p. 16, Apr 20, 1974
        Newsweek 83:108, Apr 29, 1974
        Theatre Arts 12:392-3, Jun 1928
        Vogue 71:98, Jun 15, 1928

Santa Claus
    Productions:
        (Off Broadway) Season of 1956-57 (ANTA).
        (Off Broadway) Season of 1960-61.
    Reviews:
        New York Times p. 42, Dec 18, 1957
                p. 13, Jul 22, 1960

DALY, AUGUSTIN

Under the Gaslight
    Productions:
        Opened April 2, 1929 for 23 performances.

(Off Broadway) December 8, 1967 for 9 performances (Equity
    Theatre).
(Off Off Broadway) June 28, 1977 (Stage 73).
Reviews:
    Life (NY) 93:20, Apr 26, 1929
    New York Times p. 27, Apr 3, 1929

DAVIS, BILL C.

Mass Appeal
Productions:
    (Off Off Broadway) October 21, 1979.
    (Off Broadway) April 22, 1980 for 46 performances (Manhattan
        Theater Club) and transferred to Broadway.
    Opened on Broadway November 12, 1981 for 214 performances.
Reviews:
    America 145:417-18, Dec 26, 1981
        146:35, Jan 16, 1982
    Commonweal 109:50-1, Jan 29, 1982
    Nation 230:731, Jun 14, 1980
        234:155-6, Feb 6, 1982
    New Leader 65:20, Nov 30, 1981
    New York Magazine 13:49-50, Jun 2, 1980
        14:85-6, Nov 23, 1981
    New York Theatre Critics' Reviews 1981:118
    New York Times III, p. 13, May 12, 1980
        II, p. 1, Jun 22, 1980
        III, p. 5, Nov 13, 1980
    New Yorker 57:69, Nov 23, 1981
    Newsweek 95:106, Jun 9, 1980
        98:123, Nov 23, 1981
    Saturday 9:55, Jan 1982
    Time 115:84, May 26, 1980
    U.S. Catholic 47:41, Jan 1982

DAVIS, J. FRANK

The Ladder
Productions:
    Opened October 22, 1926 for 789 performances.
Reviews:
    Collier's 81:17+, Feb 18, 1928
    New York Times p. 15, Oct 23, 1926
        p. 28, Dec 20, 1926
        p. 30, Dec 26, 1926
        p. 30, Jan 9, 1927
        p. 30, Apr 5, 1927
        VII, p. 2, Aug 28, 1927
        p. 24, Oct 7, 1927

> p. 28, Nov 23, 1927
> p. 22, Nov 24, 1927
> p. 24, Nov 25, 1927
> p. 29, Dec 9, 1927
> p. 19, Feb 22, 1928
> p. 8, Feb 26, 1928
> p. 25, Jul 12, 1928
> VIII, p. 1, Jul 15, 1928
> p. 24, Aug 22, 1928
> p. 20, Aug 23, 1928
> p. 21, Nov 10, 1928
> p. 30, Nov 11, 1928
> p. 26, Nov 14, 1928

Outlook 149:63, May 9, 1928
Theatre Arts 48:15-16+, Nov 1928

DAVIS, OSSIE

Purlie Victorious
　　Productions:
　　　　Opened September 28, 1961 for 261 performances.
　　　　(Off Broadway) March 7, 1969 for 9 performances (Equity Library Theater).
　　Reviews:
　　　　America 106:376, Dec 9, 1961
　　　　Ebony 17:55-6+, Mar 1962
　　　　Nation 193:254-5, Oct 14, 1961
　　　　New Republic 145:22, Nov 6, 1961
　　　　New York Theatre Critics' Reviews 1961:256
　　　　New York Times II, p. 1　Sep 24, 1961
　　　　　　　　　　　　p. 29, Sep 29, 1961
　　　　　　　　　　　　II, p. 1, Oct 8, 1961
　　　　New Yorker 37:130, Oct 7, 1961
　　　　Reporter 25:52, Oct 26, 1961
　　　　Saturday Review 44:78, Oct 14, 1961
　　　　Theatre Arts 45:12, Dec 1961
　　　　Time 78:88, Oct 6, 1961

DAVIS, OWEN

Any House
　　Productions:
　　　　Opened February 14, 1916 for 16 performances.
　　Reviews:
　　　　Dramatic Mirror 75:8, Feb 19, 1916
　　　　　　　　　　　75:4, Feb 26, 1916
　　　　　　　　　　　75:2, Mar 4, 1916
　　　　New York Dramatic News 62:17-18, Feb 9, 1916
　　　　New York Times p. 9, Feb 15, 1916
　　　　　　　　　　　II, p. 7, Feb 20, 1916

At 9:45
  Productions:
    Opened June 28, 1919 for 139 performances.
  Reviews:
    Dramatist 10:967-8, Oct 1919
    Forum 62:243, Aug 1919
    Independent 99:169, Aug 9, 1919
    New York Times p. 16, Jun 30, 1919
    Theatre Magazine 30:81+, Aug 1919

Beware of Widows
  Productions:
    Opened December 1, 1925 for 55 performances.
  Reviews:
    Life (NY) 86:18, Dec 24, 1925
    New York Times p. 22, Dec 2, 1925
    Vogue 67:108+, Feb 1, 1926

*The Big Deal
  Reviews:
    New York Times p. 13, Mar 7, 1953

Big Jim Garrity
  Productions:
    Opened October 16, 1914 for 27 performances.
  Reviews:
    American Playwright 3:371-3, Nov 1914
    Dramatic Mirror 72:8, Oct 28, 1914
    Green Book 12:1095-1107, Dec 1914
    Munsey 53:557, Dec 1914
    New York Dramatic News 60:16-17, Oct 24, 1914
    New York Times p. 11, Oct 17, 1914

The Bronx Express (Adapted from the Russian of Ossip Dymow)
  Productions:
    Opened April 26, 1922 for 58+ performances.
  Reviews:
    Life (NY) 79:18, May 18, 1922
    New York Clipper 70:20, May 3, 1922
    New York Times p. 12, Apr 27, 1922
    Theatre Magazine 36:7+, Jul 1922

Carry On
  Productions:
    Opened January 23, 1928 for 8 performances.
  Reviews:
    New York Times p. 26, Jan 24, 1928
    Vogue 71:158, Mar 15, 1928

*Coming Spring
  Reviews:
    New York Times X, p. 2, Sep 23, 1934

The Detour
    Productions:
        Opened August 23, 1921 for 48 performances.
    Reviews:
        Bookman 54:147-8, Oct 1921
        Current Opinion 71:603-12, Nov 1921
        Dramatic Mirror 84:85, Jul 16, 1921
                        84:305, Aug 21, 1921
        Dramatist 13:1119, Jul 1922
        Independent 106:113, Sep 17, 1921
        Life (NY) 78:18, Sep 15, 1921
        Nation 113:299, Sep 14, 1921
        New York Clipper 69:17, Aug 31, 1921
        New York Times p. 12, Aug 24, 1921
                        VI, p. 1, Sep 24, 1921
        Theatre Magazine 34:313, Nov 1921

The Donovan Affair
    Productions:
        Opened August 30, 1926 for 128 performances.
    Reviews:
        Independent 117:421, Oct 9, 1926
        Life 88:21, Sep 23, 1926
        New York Times p. 15, Aug 31, 1926
        Theatre Magazine 44:16+, Nov 1926
        Vogue 68:90-91, Nov 1, 1926

*Dread
    Reviews:
        New York Times IX, p. 2, Oct 27, 1929

Dreams for Sale
    Productions:
        Opened September 13, 1922 for 13 performances.
    Reviews:
        New York Clipper 70:22, Sep 20, 1922
        New York Times p. 24, Sep 14, 1922

Easy Come, Easy Go
    Productions:
        Opened October 26, 1925 for 180 performances.
    Reviews:
        Life (NY) 68:20, Nov 19, 1925
        New York Times p. 20, Oct 27, 1925

Ethan Frome (with Donald Davis. Based on Edith Wharton's novel)
    Productions:
        Opened January 21, 1936 for 120 performances.
        (Off Broadway) July 7, 1947 (On Stage).
        (Off Off Broadway) January 18, 1979 for 12 performances (WPA
            Theater).

Reviews:
  Catholic World 142:723-4, Mar 1936
  Commonweal 23:414, Feb 7, 1936
  Literary Digest 121:19, Feb 1, 1936
  Nation 142:167-8, Feb 5, 1936
  New Republic 86:78, Feb 26, 1936
  New York Times p. 24, Jan 7, 1936
            p. 15, Jan 22, 1936
            IX, p. 1, Feb 2, 1936
            X, p. 3, Feb 9, 1936
            p. 68, Apr 25, 1982
  Newsweek 7:33, Feb 1, 1936
  Player's Magazine 14:28, Dec 1937
  Stage 13:20-25, Feb 1936
        13:37, Mar 1936
  Theatre Arts 20:181-2, Mar 1936
  Time 27:25, Feb 3, 1936
  Vogue 37:50, Feb 15, 1936

The Family Cupboard
  Productions:
  Opened August 21, 1913 for 140 performances.
  Reviews:
  American Playwright 2:281-3, Sep 1913
  Blue Book 18:10-12+, Nov 1913
  Bookman 38:134, Oct 1913
  Current Opinion 55:325-8, Nov 1913
  Dramatic Mirror 70:6, Aug 27, 1913
                 70:5, Nov 12, 1913
  Dramatist 5:415, Oct 1913
  Everybody's 29:684, Nov 1913
  Green Book 10:722-3, Nov 1913
            10:866-7, Nov 1913
            10:1043-57, Dec 1913
  Munsey 50:297, Nov 1913
  New York Times p. 9, Aug 22, 1913
  Theatre Magazine 18:x-xi, Oct 1913

Forever After
  Productions:
  Opened September 9, 1918 for 312 performances.
  Reviews:
  Dramatic Mirror 79:301, Aug 31, 1918
                 79:434-5, Sep 21, 1918
  Life (NY) 72:417, Sep 19, 1918
  New York Times p. 11, Sep 10, 1918
                IV, p. 2, Sep 22, 1918

Gentle Grafters
  Productions:
  Opened October 27, 1926 for 13 performances.

Reviews:
New York Times p. 23, Oct 28, 1926

The Good Earth (with Donald Davis and Pearl Buck)
Productions:
Opened October 17, 1932 for 56 performances.
Reviews:
Arts and Decoration 38:57, Dec 1932
Catholic World 136:338-9, Dec 1932
Commonweal 17:23-4, Nov 2, 1932
Literary Digest 114:17, Nov 5, 1932
Nation 135:438, Nov 2, 1932
New Outlook 161:47, Dec 1932
New Republic 72:330-1, Nov 2, 1932
73:19-20, Nov 16, 1932
New York Times IX, p. 1, Sep 25, 1932
p. 23, Oct 18, 1932
IX, p. 1, Oct 23, 1932
Stage 10:13-16, Nov 1932
Theatre Arts 17:16-17, Jan 1933
Town and Country 87:22, Nov 15, 1932
Vogue 80:61+, Dec 1, 1932

The Great Gatsby (Adapted from the novel by F. Scott Fitzgerald)
Productions:
Opened February 2, 1926 for 112 performances.
Reviews:
Bookman 63:216, Apr 1926
Life (NY) 87:21, Mar 4, 1926
88:24, Dec 16, 1926
Nation 122:211-12, Feb 24, 1926
New Republic 46:145, Mar 24, 1926
New York Times p. 22, Feb 3, 1926
VII, p. 1, Feb 7, 1926
Theatre Magazine 43:19+, Apr 1926
Vogue 67:126, Apr 1, 1926

*Harbor Light
Reviews:
New York Times IX, p. 2, Aug 7, 1932

The Haunted House
Productions:
Opened September 2, 1924 for 103 performances.
Reviews:
New York Times p. 12, Sep 3, 1924
Theatre Magazine 39:19+, Nov 1924

Home Fires
Productions:
Opened August 20, 1923 for 48 performances.

Reviews:
    Bookman 58:181-2, Oct 1923
    Life (NY) 82:20, Sep 6, 1923
    New York Times VI, p. 1, Sep 2, 1923
    Theatre Magazine 38:16+, Oct 1923

Icebound
    Productions:
        Opened February 10, 1923 for 145+ performances.
    Reviews:
        Bookman 57:317-18, May 1923
              58:59:60, Sep 1923
        Current Opinion 74:574-9, May 1923
        Hearst 44:85-7+, Sep 1923
        Life (NY) 81:18, Mar 1, 1923
        New York Clipper 71:14, Feb 21, 1923
        New York Times p. 16, Feb 12, 1923
        Theatre Magazine 37:20, Apr 1923
              37:28+, May 1923

The Insect Comedy   (see The World We Live In)

Jezebel
    Productions:
        Opened December 19, 1933 for 32 performances.
    Reviews:
        Catholic World 138:604-5, Feb 1934
        Commonweal 19:273, Jan 5, 1934
        Nation 138:28, Jan 3, 1934
        New Republic 77:226, Jan 3, 1934
        New York Times p. 26, Dec 20, 1933
        Newsweek 2:30, Dec 30, 1933
        Stage 11:19-21, Feb 1934
        Theatre Arts 18:95-7, Feb 1934
        Time 23:23, Jan 1, 1934

Just to Remind You
    Productions:
        Opened September 7, 1931 for 16 performances.
    Reviews:
        Arts and Decoration 36:73, Nov 1931
        Literary Digest 110:15, Sep 26, 1931
        Nation 133:316, Sep 23, 1931
        New York Times p. 39, Sep 8, 1931
        Outlook 159:119, Sep 23, 1931
        Theatre Arts 15:891-2, Nov 1931
        Vogue 78:68+, Nov 1, 1931

Lazybones
    Productions:
        Opened September 22, 1924 for 79 performances.

Reviews:
New York Times p. 23, Sep 23, 1924

Making Good
    Productions:
        Opened February 5, 1912 for 8 performances.
    Reviews:
        American Playwright 1:71-5, Mar 1912
        Dramatic Mirror 67:7, Feb 7, 1912
        Theatre Magazine 15:xiv-xv, Mar 1912

Marry the Poor Girl
    Productions:
        Opened September 25, 1920 for 18 performances.
    Reviews:
        Dramatic Mirror p. 591, Oct 2, 1920
        New York Clipper 68:19, Sep 29, 1920
        New York Times p. 18, Sep 27, 1920

Mile-a-Minute Kendall
    Productions:
        Opened November 28, 1916 for 47 performances.
    Reviews:
        Dramatic Mirror 76:7+, Dec 9, 1916
        Dramatist 8:763-4, Jan 1917
        Green Book 17:204-7, Feb 1917
        New York Times p. 9, Nov 29, 1916
        Theatre Magazine 25:23, Jan 1917

Mr. and Mrs. North (Based on the stories by Frances and Richard
    Lockridge)
    Productions:
        Opened January 12, 1941 for 163 performances.
    Reviews:
        Catholic World 152:727-8, Mar 1941
        Commonweal 33:375, Jan 31, 1941
        Nation 152:109, Jan 25, 1941
        New Republic 104:116, Jan 27, 1941
        New York Theatre Critics' Reviews 1941:413
        New York Times p. 11, Jan 13, 1941
                      IX, p. 1, Feb 23, 1941
        Stage 1:25, Feb 1941
        Theatre Arts 25:189, Mar 1941

The Nervous Wreck (Based on a story by E. J. Rath)
    Productions:
        Opened October 9, 1923 for 279 performances.
    Reviews:
        Bookman 58:439-40, Dec 1923
        Classic 19:46, Mar 1924
        Dramatist 15:1206-7, Apr 1924

Life (NY) 82:20, Nov 1, 1923
New York Times p. 16, Oct 10, 1923
      VIII, p. 1, Oct 21, 1923
      VIII, p. 2, Oct 19, 1924
      p. 28, Dec 16, 1924
      X, p. 4, Dec 9, 1928
Theatre Magazine 38:68+, Dec 1923

The 9th Guest
    Productions:
    Opened August 25, 1930 for 72 performances.
    Reviews:
    Life (NY) 96:16, Sep 12, 1930
    National Magazine 59:137, Dec 1930
    New York Times p. 24, Aug 26, 1930
    Outlook 156:71, Sep 10, 1930
    Vogue 76:116, Oct 13, 1930

No Way Out
    Productions:
    Opened October 30, 1944 for 8 performances.
    Reviews:
    New York Theatre Critics' Reviews 1944:100
    New York Times p. 23, Oct 31, 1944

Opportunity
    Productions:
    Opened July 30, 1920 for 138 performances.
    Reviews:
    Dramatic Mirror p. 229, Aug 7, 1920
    New York Clipper 68:23, Aug 4, 1920
    New York Times p. 5, Jul 31, 1920
    Theatre Magazine 32:188, Oct 1920

*Peacocks
    Reviews:
    New York Times VIII, p. 2, Mar 2, 1924

*Robin Hood and His Merry Men
    Reviews:
    New York Times IV, p. 7, Apr 26, 1914

Sandalwood (with Fulton Oursler)
    Productions:
    Opened September 22, 1926 for 39 performances.
    Reviews:
    Bookman 64:480-1, Dec 1926
    Life (NY) 88:23, Oct 14, 1926
    Nation 123:384-5, Oct 13, 1926
    New York Times p. 23, Sep 23, 1926
          VIII, p. 1, Oct 3, 1926

Theatre Magazine 44:15, Nov 1926
Vogue 68:79+, Nov 15, 1926

A Saturday Night
    Productions:
        Opened February 28, 1933 for 40 performances.
    Reviews:
        Arts and Decoration 38:49+, Apr 1933
        Catholic World 137:78-9, Apr 1933
        Commonweal 17:553, Mar 15, 1933
        Nation 136:300, Mar 15, 1933
        New Outlook 161:47, Apr 1933
        New York Times p. 13, Mar 1, 1933
                        IX, p. 1, Mar 19, 1933
        Theatre Arts 17:343, May 1933
        Vanity Fair 40:32+, May 1933
        Vogue 81:84, May 1, 1933

The Scrap of Paper (with Arthur Somers Roche)
    Productions:
        Opened September 17, 1917 for 40 performances.
    Reviews:
        Dramatic Mirror 77:4+, Sep 29, 1917
        Life (NY) 70:549, Oct 4, 1917
        New York Times p. 7, Sep 18, 1917
        Theatre Magazine 26:278, Nov 1917

Sinners
    Productions:
        Opened January 7, 1915 for 220 performances.
    Reviews:
        American Playwright 4:41-4, Feb 1915
        Bookman 40:641-2, Feb 1915
        Current Opinion 58:177, Mar 1915
        Dramatic Mirror 73:8, Jan 13, 1915
        Dramatist 7:648-9, Jan 1916
        Green Book 13:477-8, Mar 1915
                   13:619-33, Apr 1915
        Hearst 27:440-3, May 1915
        Life (NY) 65:112-13, Jan 21, 1915
        Munsey 54:338-9, Mar 1915
        Nation 100:61, Jan 14, 1915
        New York Drama News 60:14-15, Jan 16, 1915
        New York Times p. 11, Jan 8, 1915
        Smart Set 45:285-6, Mar 1915
        Theatre Magazine 21:101, Feb 1915

The Snark Was a Boojum (Based on Richard Shattuck's novel)
    Productions:
        Opened September 1, 1943 for 5 performances.
    Reviews:
        New York Theatre Critics' Reviews 1943:288

New York Times p. 14, Sep 2, 1943
New Yorker 19:44, Sep 11, 1943

Spring Freshet
    Productions:
        Opened October 4, 1934 for 12 performances.
    Reviews:
        New York Times p. 19, Oct 2, 1934
                       p. 28, Oct 5, 1934
        Vanity Fair 43:46, Dec 1934

*Ten Minute Alibi
    Reviews:
        New York Times p. 24, Jun 11, 1935
                       p. 19, Jul 20, 1937

Those Who Walk in Darkness
    Productions:
        Opened August 14, 1919 for 28 performances.
    Reviews:
        New York Times p. 12, Aug 15, 1919
                       VI, p. 2, Aug 24, 1919
        Theatre Magazine 30:224-5, Oct 1919

Tonight at 12
    Productions:
        Opened November 13, 1928 for 60 performances.
    Reviews:
        New York Times p. 28, Nov 16, 1928
        Theatre Magazine 49:45, Jan 1929
        Vogue 73:67+, Jan 5, 1929

Too Many Boats (Based on a novel by Charles L. Clifford)
    Productions:
        Opened September 11, 1934 for 7 performances.
    Reviews:
        New York Times p. 26, Sep 12, 1934
        Vogue 84:74, Oct 15, 1934

The Triumphant Bachelor
    Productions:
        Opened September 15, 1927 for 12 performances.
    Reviews:
        New York Times p. 21, Sep 16, 1927

*Two Time Mary
    Reviews:
        New York Times p. 20, Aug 3, 1937

Up the Ladder
    Productions:
        Opened March 6, 1922 for 117+ performances.

Reviews:
    Dramatist 13:1106-7, Apr 1922
    New York Clipper 70:20, Mar 29, 1922
    New York Times p. 11, Mar 7, 1922

What Happened to Mary
    Productions:
        Opened March 24, 1913 for 56 performances.
    Reviews:
        American Playwright 2:115-16, Apr 1913
        Blue Book 17:448-50, Jul 1913
        Dramatic Mirror 69:6, Mar 26, 1913
        Dramatist 4:343, Apr 1913
        Green Book 9:932-4+, Jun 1913
                  9:1079-80, Jun 1913
        Life (NY) 61:734, Apr 10, 1913
        New York Drama News 57:20-21, Mar 29, 1913
        New York Times p. 8, Mar 25, 1913
        Red Book 21:315-17, Jun 1913
        Theatre Magazine 17:130, May 1913

*Wife's Away
    Reviews:
        New York Times IX, p. 3, Nov 23, 1930

The World We Live In (The Insect Comedy) (Adapted from the play
        by Josef and Karel Capek)
    Productions:
        Opened October 31, 1922 for 111 performances.
        Opened June 3, 1948 for 14 performances.
    Reviews:
        Bookman 56:610-11, Jan 1923
        Catholic World 116:501-3, Jan 1923
        Commonweal 43:235, Jun 18, 1948
        Drama 13:130-1, Jun 1923
        Forum 110:20-2, Jul 1948
        Independent 109:320-1, Nov 25, 1922
        Living Age 313:617-20, Jun 3, 1922
        Nation 115:556, Nov 22, 1922
        New Republic 118:28-9, Jun 21, 1948
        New York Clipper 70:20, Nov 8, 1922
        New York Times p. 16, Nov 1, 1922
                       p. 26, Jun 4, 1948
        School and Society 67:478, Jun 26, 1948

DAYTON, KATHERINE

First Lady (with George S. Kaufman)
    Productions:
        Opened November 26, 1935 for 246 performances.
        Opened May 28, 1952 for 16 performances.

Reviews:
Catholic World 142:468-9, Jan 1936
                175:309, Jul 1952
Commonweal 23:188, Dec 13, 1935
            56:269, Jun 20, 1952
Literary Digest 120:20, Dec 7, 1935
Nation 141:694+, Dec 11, 1935
New Republic 85:175, Dec 18, 1935
New York Theatre Critics' Reviews 1952:273
New York Times p. 21, Nov 11, 1935
               p. 17, Nov 17, 1935
               X, p. 3, Dec 8, 1935
               p. 17, Oct 9, 1937
               p. 16, May 23, 1952
               II, p. 3, May 25, 1952
               p. 18, May 29, 1952
Newsweek 6:41, Dec 7, 1935
Stage 13:22+, Jan 1936
Theatre Arts 20:16+, Jan 1936
             20:379-83, May 1936
             36:72, Aug 1952
Time 26:52, Dec 9, 1935

Save Me the Waltz
    Productions:
        Opened February 28, 1938 for 8 performances.
    Reviews:
        Commonweal 27:608, Mar 25, 1938
        Nation 146:310, Mar 12, 1938
        New York Times p. 19, Mar 1, 1938
        Newsweek 11:22, Mar 14, 1938
        Stage 15:26, Mar 1938

DELL, FLOYD

Cloudy with Showers (with Thomas Mitchell)
    Productions:
        Opened September 1, 1931 for 71 performances.
    Reviews:
        Arts & Decoration 36:51, Nov 1931
        Life (NY) 98:18, Sep 18, 1931
        New York Times VIII, p. 2, Aug 23, 1931
                       p. 17, Sep 2, 1931
                       VIII, p. 3, Oct 4, 1931
        Outlook 159:86, Sep 16, 1931
        Sketch Book 8:21, Oct 1931

Little Accident (with Thomas Mitchell)
    Productions:
        Opened October 9, 1928 for 303 performances.

Reviews:
  Commonweal 9:431, Feb 13, 1929
  Life (NY) 92:21, Nov 2, 1928
  New York Times p. 32, Oct 10, 1928
  Outlook 150:1031, Oct 24, 1928
  Theatre Magazine 48:46-7, Dec 1928
  Vogue 72:76-7, Nov 24, 1928

*Sweet and Twenty
  Reviews:
  New York Times p. 28, Nov 8, 1921

DENKER, HENRY

A Case of Libel (Based on Louis Nizer's My Life in Court)
  Productions:
  Opened October 10, 1963 for 242 performances.
  Reviews:
  America 109:751, Dec 7, 1963
  Commonweal 79:194, Nov 8, 1963
  Nation 197:306+, Nov 9, 1963
  New York Theatre Critics' Reviews 1963:244
  New York Times p. 43, Oct 11, 1963
                 II, p. 1, Oct 27, 1963
                 p. 79, Feb 12, 1968
  New Yorker 39:99, Oct 19, 1963
  Newsweek 62:104, Oct 21, 1963
  Saturday Review 46:18, Nov 2, 1963
  Theatre Arts 48:66, Jan 1964
  Time 82:78, Oct 18, 1963

A Far Country
  Productions:
  Opened April 4, 1961 for 271 performances.
  Reviews:
  America 105-408+, Jun 3, 1961
  Nation 192:359, Apr 22, 1961
  New Republic 144:20-2, Apr 17, 1961
  New York Theatre Critics' Reviews 1961:310
  New York Times II, p. 3, Mar 26, 1961
                 p. 32, Apr 5, 1961
                 II, p. 1, Apr 16, 1961
  New Yorker 37:76, Apr 15, 1961
  Newsweek 57:69, Apr 17, 1961
  Saturday Review 44:31, Apr 22, 1961
  Theatre Arts 45:28-9, Jun 1961
  Time 77:106, Apr 14, 1961
  Vogue 138:22, Sep 1, 1961

Horowitz and Mrs. Washington
  Productions:

Opened April 2, 1980 for 6 performances.
Reviews:
New York Theatre Critics' Reviews 1980:298
New York Times III, p. 11, Apr 3, 1980
Time 115:112, Apr 14, 1980

Something Old, Something New
Productions:
Opened January 1, 1977 for one performance.
Reviews:
New York Magazine 10:50, Jan 17, 1977
New York Theatre Critics' Reviews 1977:398
New York Times p. 27, Jan 3, 1977

Time Limit! (with Ralph Berkey)
Productions:
Opened January 24, 1956 for 127 performances.
Reviews:
America 94:599, Feb 25, 1956
Commonweal 63:542-3, Feb 24, 1956
Life 40:65-6+, Feb 6, 1956
Nation 182:125-6, Feb 11, 1956
New York Theatre Critics' Reviews 1956:381
New York Times II, p. 1, Jan 22, 1956
              p. 27, Jan 25, 1956
              II, p. 1, Feb 5, 1956
New Yorker 31:60, Feb 4, 1956
Newsweek 47:42, Feb 6, 1956
Saturday Review 39:22, Feb 11, 1956
Theatre Arts 40:17, Apr 1956
Time 67:67, Feb 6, 1956

Venus at Large
Productions:
Opened April 12, 1962 for 4 performances.
Reviews:
New York Theatre Critics' Reviews 1962:296
New York Times p. 30, Apr 13, 1962
New Yorker 38:85, Apr 21, 1962
Saturday Review 45:38, Apr 28, 1962

What Did We Do Wrong?
Productions:
Opened October 22, 1967 for 48 performances.
Reviews:
America 117:623, Nov 18, 1967
New York Theatre Critics' Reviews 1967:231
                                  1967:247
New York Times p. 56, Oct 23, 1967
              II, p. 5, Nov 12, 1967
New Yorker 43:162, Nov 4, 1967

DODD, LEE WILSON

The Changelings
Productions:
    Opened September 17, 1923 for 128 performances.
Reviews:
    Bookman 58:307-8, Nov 1923
    Life (NY) 82:22, Oct 4, 1923
    Nation 117:359-60, Oct 3, 1923
    New York Times p. 16, Sep 18, 1923
              II, p. 1, Sep 30, 1923
    Theatre Magazine 38:16, Nov 1923
              38:26+, Dec 1923

His Majesty Bunker Bean (Adapted from Harry Leon Wilson's novel)
Productions:
    Opened October 2, 1916 for 72 performances.
Reviews:
    Dramatic Mirror 76:7, Oct 7, 1916
    Green Book 16:970-2, Dec 1916
    Nation 103:358, Oct 12, 1916
    New York Drama News 63:10-11, Oct 7, 1916
    New York Times p. 9, Oct 3, 1916
    Theatre Magazine 23:152, Mar 1916
              24:284, Nov 1916

Pals First (Based on Francis Perry Elliott's novel)
Productions:
    Opened February 26, 1917 for 152 performances.
Reviews:
    Dramatic Mirror 77:7+, Mar 3, 1917
    Green Book 17:779+, May 1917
    Life (NY) 69:444, Mar 15, 1917
    New York Drama News 64:2, Mar 3, 1917
    New York Times p. 9, Feb 27, 1917
    Theatre Magazine 25:215+, Apr 1917

The Return of Eve
Productions:
    Opened March 17, 1909 for 29 performances.
Reviews:
    Collier's 43:20, May 22, 1909
    Dramatist 1:27-9, Jan 1910
    Forum 41:341-2, Apr 1909
    Theatre Magazine 9:134-5, May 1909

Speed
Productions:
    Opened September 9, 1911 for 33 performances.
Reviews:
    American Playwright 1:26, Jan 1912

Blue Book 14:475-7, Jan 1912
Collier's 48:17, Sep 30, 1911
Dramatic Mirror 66:9, Sep 13, 1911
Dramatist 3:191-2, Oct 1911
Green Book 6:996, Nov 1911
      6:1199-1200, Dec 1911
Life (NY) 58:478, Sep 21, 1911
Munsey 46:279, Nov 1911
Red Book 14:186-9, Nov 1911
Theatre Magazine 14:114+, Oct 1911

A Strong Man's House
  Productions:
    Opened September 16, 1929 for 24 performances.
  Reviews:
    Commonweal 10:592, Oct 9, 1929
    Life (NY) 94:24, Oct 11, 1929
    New York Times VIII, p. 1, Jun 30, 1929
              p. 34, Sep 17, 1929
    Theatre Magazine 50:47, Nov 1929

DOS PASSOS, JOHN

*Airways, Inc.
  Reviews:
    Dial 86:442, May 1929
    New York Times p. 30, Feb 21, 1929

The Garbage Man (see The Moon Is a Gong)

The Moon Is a Gong
  Productions:
    Opened March 12, 1926 for 18 performances.
  Reviews:
    New Republic 46:174, Mar 31, 1926
    New York Times p. 21, Mar 13, 1926
            VIII, p. 2, Mar 21, 1926
    Theatre Magazine 43:16+, Jun 1926

U.S.A. (with Paul Shyre. Based on Dos Passos' novel)
  Productions:
    (Off Broadway) October 28, 1959 for 256 performances.
    (Off Broadway) October 1, 1972 for 3 performances (City Cen-
      ter Acting Co.).
    (Off Off Broadway) May 6, 1974 (Theater at St. Clements).
    (Off Off Broadway) October 27, 1976 (Joseph Jefferson).
  Reviews:
    Nation 189:367, Nov 14, 1959
    New York Times II, p. 5, Oct 25, 1959
            p. 38, Oct 29, 1959

II, p. 1, Nov 8, 1959
p. 43, Oct 2, 1972
New Yorker 35:88, Nov 7, 1959
Theatre Arts 44:24-50, Jun 1960

DREISER, THEODORE

The Girl in the Coffin
Productions:
Opened October 31, 1917 in repertory (Washington Square
Players).
Reviews:
New York Times p. 11, Dec 4, 1917
Theatre Magazine 27:15+, Jan 1918

The Hand of the Potter
Productions:
Opened December 5, 1921 for 21 performances.
Reviews:
Nation 109:340, Sep 6, 1919
113:762-3, Dec 28, 1921

DUBERMAN, MARTIN

Electric Map, a Melodrama   (see Memory Bank)

In White America
Productions:
(Off Broadway) October 31, 1963 for 493 performances.
(Off Broadway) May 18, 1965 for 32 performances.
(Off Off Broadway) Dec 7, 1972 (Equity Library Theater).
Reviews:
America 109:754, Dec 7, 1963
Commonweal 79:693, Mar 6, 1964
Nation 199:254-6, Oct 19, 1964
New Republic 149:28-9, Nov 16, 1963
New York Times p. 26, Nov 1, 1963
p. 55, Aug 2, 1964
p. 42, Feb 9, 1965
p. 63, Dec 14, 1972
New Yorker 39:98-9, Nov 9, 1963

Memory Bank (Consists of The Recorder, a History and Electric
Map, a Melodrama)
Productions:
(Off Broadway) January 11, 1970 for 25 performances.
Reviews:
Nation 210:124, Feb 2, 1970
New York Theatre Critics' Reviews 1970:300

New York Times p. 24, Jan 12, 1970
II, p. 1, Jan 25, 1970
New Yorker 45:58, Jan 24, 1970

Metaphors
   Productions:
   (Off Broadway) May 8, 1968 for 80 performances.
   Reviews:
   Harper's Bazaar 237:113-15, Oct 1968
   Nation 206:772+, Jun 10, 1968
   New York Times p. 55, May 9, 1968
              II, p. 1, May 19, 1968
   New Yorker 44:74, May 18, 1968

The Recorder, a History (see Memory Bank)

Visions of Kerouac
   Productions:
   (Off Off Broadway) November 26, 1976 (Lion Theater Co.).
   Reviews:
   Los Angeles 22:255, Nov 1977
   New York Magazine 9:85, Dec 20, 1976
   New York Times III, p. 4, Dec 3, 1976
              p. 56, Dec 7, 1976

DUNLAP, WILLIAM

A Spy for the British
   Productions:
   (Off Off Broadway) June 23, 1976 (West Park Theater).
   No Reviews.

DUNNING, PHILIP

Broadway (with George Abbott)
   Productions:
   Opened September 16, 1926 for 603 performances.
   (Off Off Broadway) October 18, 1973 (Equity Library Theater).
   Reviews:
   American Mercury 9:504, Dec 1926
   Dial 82:77, Jan 1927
   Dramatist 17:1317-18, Oct 1926
   Independent 118:21, Jan 1, 1927
   Life (NY) 88:23, Oct 14, 1926
   Nation 123:330, Oct 6, 1926
   New Republic 50:45, Mar 2, 1927
   New York Times p. 19, Sep 17, 1926
              VIII, p. 1, Sep 26, 1926
              p. 23, Dec 23, 1926

VII, p. 2, Jan 9, 1927
VIII, p. 2, Oct 23, 1927
VIII, p. 2, Feb 12, 1928
p. 5, Mar 11, 1928
IX, p. 4, Apr 15, 1928
p. 34, Oct 12, 1928
p. 34, Dec 6, 1928
p. 47, Oct 22, 1973
Texas Monthly 8:160+, Mar 1980
Theatre Magazine 44:66, Nov 1926
45:26+, Jan 1927
Vogue 68:78-9, Nov 15, 1926

Dawn Glory (see Night Hostess)

East of Broadway (see Night Hostess)

Get Me in the Movies (with Charlton Andrews)
Productions:
Opened May 21, 1928 for 32 performances.
Reviews:
Life (NY) 91:26, Jun 7, 1928
New York Times p. 18, May 22, 1928
VIII, p. 1, May 27, 1928
Vogue 17:98, Jul 15, 1928

Kill That Story (with Harry Madden)
Productions:
Opened August 29, 1934 for 117 performances.
Reviews:
New York Times p. 22, Aug 30, 1934

Lilly Turner (with George Abbott)
Productions:
Opened September 19, 1932 for 24 performances.
Reviews:
New York Times p. 26, Sep 20, 1932
Theatre Arts 16:868+, Nov 1932
Vogue 80:89, Nov 1, 1932

Night Hostess
Productions:
Opened September 12, 1928 for 117 performances.
Reviews:
Drama 19:44, Nov 1928
Life (NY) 92:15, Oct 5, 1928
Nation 127:327-8, Oct 3, 1928
New York Times VII, p. 2, Jul 29, 1928
p. 31, Sep 13, 1928
Vogue 72:150, Nov 10, 1928

Page Miss Glory (with Joseph Schrank)
    Productions:
        Opened November 27, 1934 for 63 performances.
    Reviews:
        Catholic World 140:469, Jan 1935
        Golden Book 21:28a+, Feb 1935
        New York Times p. 24, Nov 28, 1934
                     X, p. 2, Dec 9, 1934
        Newsweek 4:26, Dec 8, 1934
        Time 24:51, Dec 10, 1934

Remember the Day (with Philo Higley)
    Productions:
        Opened September 25, 1935 for 122 performances.
    Reviews:
        Catholic World 142:213-14, Nov 1935
        Commonweal 22:585, Oct 11, 1935
        New York Times p. 24, Jul 9, 1935
                       p. 19, Sep 26, 1935
                      XI, p. 2, Oct 6, 1935
                      IX, p. 1, Oct 13, 1935
                       X, p. 2, Nov 3, 1935
        Stage 13:72, Dec 1935
        Theatre Arts 19:825, Nov 1935
        Time 26:38, Oct 7, 1935

Sweet Land of Liberty
    Productions:
        Opened September 23, 1929 for 8 performances.
    Reviews:
        New York Times p. 29, Sep 24, 1929
        Theatre Magazine 50:72, Nov 1929

DURANG, CHRISTOPHER

The Actor's Nightmare
    Productions:
        (Off Broadway) October 21, 1981 for 247 performances (Play-
            wrights Horizons).
    Reviews:
        New York Times III, p. 21, Oct 22, 1981
                        II, p. 3, Nov 8, 1981
        New Yorker 57:66, Nov 2, 1981
        Time 118:119, Nov 9, 1981

Beyond Therapy
    Productions:
        (Off Broadway) January 1, 1981 for 30 performances.
        Revised version opened on Broadway May 26, 1982 for 6+ per-
            formances (still running on Jun 1, 1982).

Reviews:
    New York Magazine 14:40, Jan 19, 1981
                      15:62, Jun 7, 1982
    New York Theatre Critics' Reviews 1981:363
                                      1982:260
    New York Times III, p. 11, Jan 6, 1981
                     III, p. 19, May 27, 1982
                      II, p. 3, Jun 26, 1982
    New Yorker 56:91, Jan 19, 1981
               58:112, Jun 7, 1982
    Newsweek 99:63, Jun 7, 1982
    Time 119:70, Jun 7, 1982

*A History of the American Film
    Reviews:
        Horizon 21:25-31, Mar 1978
        Los Angeles 22:181+, Jun 1977
        Nation 226:443, Apr 15, 1978
        New Republic 178:25, Apr 22, 1978
        New West 2:SC-23, May 9, 1977
        New York Magazine 10:66, Jun 6, 1977
                          11:100, Apr 17, 1978
        New York Theatre Critics' Reviews 1978:310
        New York Times p. 41, Mar 21, 1977
                       II, p. 4, May 27, 1977
                       XXII, p. 20, Apr 3, 1977
                       p. 22, May 23, 1977
                       II, p. 3, Jun 5, 1977
        New Yorker 54:91-2, Apr 10, 1978
        Newsweek 91:63, Apr 10, 1978
        Saturday Review 5:42, May 27, 1978
        Time 109:108, May 23, 1977

I Don't Generally Like Poetry but Have You Read Trees? (see entry
    under Innaurato, Albert)

Invitational (see Sister Mary Ignatius Explains It All for You)

The Nature and Purpose of the Universe
    Productions:
        (Off Off Broadway) September 3, 1975 (Direct Theater).
        (Off Off Broadway) February 21, 1979 for 26 performances
            (Direct Theater).
    Reviews:
        New York Times p. 15, Feb 24, 1979

Sister Mary Ignatius Explains It All for You
    Productions:
        (Off Off Broadway) November/December 1979 as part of a bill
            called Invitational (Playwrights Horizons).
        (Off Broadway) October 21, 1981 for 247 performances (with
            The Actor's Nightmare, Playwrights Horizons).

Reviews:
America 145:417-18, Dec 26, 1981
Commonweal 109:50-1, Jan 29, 1982
Los Angeles 27:340+, Nov 1982
Nation 233:649-50, Dec 12, 1981
New Republic 185:24-5, Dec 9, 1981
New York Magazine 15:40-3, Mar 15, 1982
New York Theatre Critics' Reviews 1981:90
New York Times III, p. 5, Dec 21, 1979
            III, p. 21, Oct 22, 1981
            II, p. 3, Nov 8, 1981
            II, p. 1, Jan 3, 1982
New Yorker 57:66, Nov 2, 1981
Newsweek 98:101, Nov 9, 1981
Time 118:119, Nov 9, 1981
U.S. Catholic 47:40, Jan 1982

Titanic
Productions:
(Off Broadway) May 10, 1976 for 8 performances.
Reviews:
New York Times p. 34, Mar 17, 1976
                p. 26, May 11, 1976

D'USSEAU, ARNAUD

Deep Are the Roots (with James Gow)
Productions:
Opened September 26, 1945 for 477 performances.
(Off Broadway) Season of 1959-60.
Reviews:
Catholic World 162:164, Nov 1945
Commonweal 42:624, Oct 12, 1945
Life 19:51-2+, Oct 15, 1945
Nation 161:384, Oct 13, 1945
New Republic 113:499, Oct 15, 1945
              114:446, Apr 1, 1946
New York Theatre Critics' Reviews 1945:160
New York Times p. 24, Sep 27, 1945
                II, p. 1, Oct 7, 1945
                II, p. 1, Oct 14, 1945
                p. 26, Apr 28, 1947
                p. 17, Jul 10, 1947
                II, p. 2, Aug 24, 1947
                p. 47, Oct 4, 1960
New Yorker 21:46+, Oct 6, 1945
Newsweek 26:94-5, Oct 8, 1945
Saturday Review 28:38+, Oct 13, 1945
Theatre Arts 29:622-4, Nov 1945
              29:678, Dec 1945
              31:37, Oct 1947

Time 46:77, Oct 8, 1945

The Ladies of the Corridor (see entry under Parker, Dorothy)

Legend of Sarah (see entry under Gow, James)

Tomorrow the World (see entry under Gow, James)

ELIOT, T. S.

The Cocktail Party
    Productions:
        Opened January 21, 1950 for 409 performances.
        Opened October 7, 1968 for 44 performances (A.P.A. Phoenix).
        (Off Off Broadway) October 1974.
        (Off Off Broadway) November 21, 1975.
        (Off Off Broadway) November 4, 1977.
        (Off Broadway) June 10, 1980 for 8 performances.
    Reviews:
        America 119:445-7, Nov 9, 1968
        American Mercury 70:557-8, May 1950
        Catholic World 170:466, Mar 1950
                      171:469-70, Sep 1950
        Christian Science Monitor Magazine, p. 6, May 27, 1950
        Commonweal 51:463, Feb 3, 1950
                   51:507-8, Feb 17, 1950
        Fortnightly 174 (ns 168):391-8, Dec 1950
        Life 27:16+, Sep 26, 1949
        Nation 170:94-5, Jan 28, 1950
        New Republic 122:30, Feb 13, 1950
        New York Theatre Critics' Reviews 1950:376
                                          1968:219
        New York Times p. 28, Aug 23, 1949
                       II, p. 2, Sep 11, 1949
                       p. 17, Jan 23, 1950
                       II, p. 1, Jan 29, 1950
                       VI, p. 14, Jan 29, 1950
                       II, p. 1, Apr 16, 1950
                       p. 33, May 4, 1950
                       II, p. 2, May 7, 1950
                       II, p. 3, May 21, 1950
                       II, p. 3, Dec 17, 1950
                       p. 42, Oct 8, 1968
                       II, p. 1, Oct 20, 1968
                       III, p. 3, Jan 11, 1980
                       III, p. 5, Jun 13, 1980
        New Yorker 25:47, Jan 28, 1950
                   26:26-9, Apr 1, 1950
                   44:159, Oct 19, 1968
        Newsweek 35:66, Jan 30, 1950

Saturday Review 33:28-30, Feb 4, 1950
                33:48, Feb 11, 1950
School and Society 72:180-2, Sep 16, 1950
Theatre Arts 34:8, May 1950
              34:10, Apr 1950
Time 54:58, Sep 5, 1949
     55:37, Jan 30, 1950
     92:72+, Oct 18, 1968

The Confidential Clerk
Productions:
Opened February 11, 1954 to 117 performances.
Reviews:
America 90:608+, Mar 6, 1954
Catholic World 179:68-9, Apr 1954
Commentary 17:367-72, Apr 1954
Commonweal 59:475-6, Feb 12, 1954
            59:599, Mar 19, 1954
Life 36:56-8+, Feb 1, 1954
Nation 178:184+, Feb 27, 1954
New Republic 129:17-18, Sep 21, 1953
             130:22, Feb 22, 1954
             131:124-5, Nov 22, 1954
New York Theatre Critics' Reviews 1954:370
New York Times p. 20, Dec 22, 1952
               p. 22, Aug 26, 1953
               p. 21, Aug 27, 1953
               II, p. 2, Aug 30, 1953
               II, p. 3, Oct 11, 1953
               II, p. 1, Feb 7, 1954
               p. 22, Feb 12, 1954
               II, p. 1, Feb 21, 1954
New York Times Magazine pp. 36-7, Sep 6, 1953
                        p. 16, Feb 21, 1954
New Yorker 29:110-11, Oct 10, 1953
           30:62+, Feb 20, 1954
Newsweek 43:94, Feb 22, 1954
Saturday Review 36:26-8, Aug 29, 1953
                36:44-6, Sep 12, 1953
                37:26-8, Feb 27, 1954
Theatre Arts 37:81-2, Nov 1953
             38:22-3, Apr 1954
             38:22-5, May 1954
Time 63:80+, Feb 22, 1954
Vogue 123:130-1, Mar 1, 1954

*The Elder Statesman
Reviews:
Life 45:108, Nov 24, 1958
New York Times p. 21, Aug 20, 1958
               p. 35, Aug 26, 1958
               II, p. 3, Aug 31, 1958

New Yorker 34:168, Nov 1, 1958
Saturday Review 41:30-1, Sep 13, 1958
Texas Monthly 7:118+, Jan 1979
Time 72:43+, Sep 8, 1958

The Family Reunion
  Productions:
    (Off Broadway) December, 1947 (On Stage).
    Opened October 20, 1958 for 20 performances.
    (Off Broadway) November 20, 1967 for 3 performances (Equity
      Theatre).
  Reviews:
    America 100:174, Nov 8, 1958
    Catholic World 188:331, Jan 1959
    Christian Century 75:1380-2, Nov 26, 1958
    Commonweal 69:232-4, Nov 28, 1958
    Nation 148:676, Jun 10, 1939
           187:347, Nov 8, 1958
    New Republic 98:384-5, May 3, 1939
    New York Theatre Critics' Reviews 1958:255
    New York Times X, p. 1, Apr 9, 1939
                    p. 9, Nov 29, 1947
                    p. 13, Jun 9, 1956
                    p. 39, Oct 21, 1958
                   II, p. 1, Oct 26, 1958
                    p. 26, Dec 10, 1960
    New Yorker 34:99-101, Nov 1, 1958
    One Act Play Magazine 3:82, Jan 1940
    Reporter 19:35, Nov 27, 1958
    Saturday Review 19:12, Apr 1, 1939
                    41:25, Nov 8, 1958
    Theatre Arts 41:23-4, May 1957
                 42:64, Dec 1958
    Time 72:48, Nov 3, 1958
    Yale Review 28:836-8, Summer, 1939

Murder in the Cathedral
  Productions:
    Opened March 20, 1936 for 38 performances.
    Opened February 16, 1938 for 21 performances.
    (Off Off Broadway) January 14, 1977 (York Players).
  Reviews:
    Catholic World 143:209-11, May 1936
    Christian Century 52:1636, Dec 18, 1935
    Commonweal 23:636, Apr 3, 1936
               27:524, Mar 4, 1938
    Forum 95:346-7, Jun 1936
    Life 19:123-7, Oct 1, 1945
    Nation 141:417, Oct 9, 1935
           142:459-60, Apr 8, 1936
    New Republic 85:290, Jan 15, 1936

86:253, Apr 8, 1936
94:101, Mar 2, 1938
New York Times p. 12, Nov 2, 1935
                IX, p. 1, Feb 16, 1936
                p. 13, Mar 21, 1936
                IX, p. 1, Mar 29, 1936
                p. 16, Feb 17, 1938
                XI, p. 1, Feb 20, 1938
                II, p. 1, Apr 26, 1953
                p. 12, Mar 22, 1958
                p. 38, Jun 21, 1966
New Yorker 29:87, May 2, 1953
Newsweek 7:26, Mar 28, 1936
Saturday Review 12:10-11, Oct 12, 1935
                49:41, Jul 9, 1966
Stage 13:97, Nov 1935
Theatre Arts 20:25-6, Jan 1936
                20:341-3, May 1936
                22:254-5, Apr 1938
Time 31:34, Feb 28, 1938
Yale Review 25:427-9, Winter 1936

Old Possum's Book of Practical Cats (Adapted by Jonathan Foster)
    Productions:
        (Off Off Broadway) Season of 1979-1980 (Soho Rep).
    No Reviews.

EMERY, GILBERT

Episode
    Productions:
        Opened February 4, 1925 for 21 performances.
    Reviews:
        American Mercury 4:502-3, Apr 1925
        Nation 120:221-2, Feb 25, 1925
        New York Times p. 23, Feb 5, 1925
                        VII, p. 1, Feb 8, 1925
                        VII, p. 1, Feb 15, 1925
        Theatre Magazine 41:18, Apr 1925

Far-Away Horses (with Michael Birmingham)
    Productions:
        Opened March 21, 1933 for 4 performances.
    Reviews:
        Nation 136:382, Apr 5, 1933
        New York Times p. 21, Mar 22, 1933

The Hero
    Productions:
        Opened March 14, 1921 for 5 matinees.

Opened September 5, 1921 for 80 performances.
Reviews:
    Bookman 53:276, May 1921
            54:229-30, Nov 1921
    Current Opinion 71:751-60, Dec 1921
    Dramatist 83:488, Mar 19, 1921
            84:376, Sep 10, 1921
    Everybody's 46:123-30, Mar 1922
    Life (NY) 77:464-5, Mar 31, 1921
    Nation 113:381, Oct 5, 1921
    New York Drama News 69:19, Mar 16, 1921
            69:23, Sep 14, 1921
    New York Times p. 14, Mar 15, 1921
            VI, p. 1, Mar 20, 1921
            p. 13, Sep 6, 1921
            VI, p. 1, Sep 11, 1921
    Review 4:301-3, Mar 30, 1921
    Theatre Magazine 35:16+, Jan 1922
    Weekly Review 4:302-3, Mar 30, 1921
            5:255-6, Sep 17, 1921

Housewarming
    Productions:
        Opened April 7, 1932 for 4 performances.
    Reviews:
        New York Times p. 25, Apr 8, 1932

Love in a Mist (with Amelie Rives)
    Productions:
        Opened April 12, 1926 for 118 performances.
    Reviews:
        Life (NY) 87:21, Apr 29, 1926
        Nation 122:484, Apr 28, 1926
        New York Times p. 28, Apr 13, 1926

Tarnish
    Productions:
        Opened October 1, 1923 for 248 performances.
    Reviews:
        Bookman 58:440, Dec 1923
        Current Opinion 76:186-94, Feb 1924
        Dramatist 15:1190-91, Jan 1924
        Life (NY) 82:18, Oct 25, 1923
        Nation 117:444, Oct 17, 1923
        New York Times p. 10, Oct 2, 1923
        Theatre Magazine 38:18+, Dec 1923
                39:26+, Feb 1924

FAULKNER, WILLIAM

Requiem for a Nun (with Ruth Ford. Adapted from Faulkner's novel)

Productions:
Opened January 30, 1959 for 43 performances.
Reviews:
America 100:614, Feb 21, 1959
Catholic World 189:61, Apr 1959
Nation 188:193-4, Feb 28, 1959
New Republic 140:22, Mar 9, 1959
New York Theatre Critics' Reviews 1959:390
New York Times II, p. 1, Jan 25, 1959
      p. 32, Jan 30, 1959
      p. 13, Jan 31, 1959
      II, p. 1, Feb 8, 1959
New Yorker 34:82+, Feb 7, 1959
Newsweek 53:56+, Feb 9, 1959
Saturday Review 42:32, Feb 14, 1959
Theatre Arts 43:23+, Apr 1959
Time 73:70, Feb 9, 1959

FEIFFER, JULES

Collision Course (see The Unexpurgated Memoirs of Bernard Mergendeiler)

Feiffer's People
Productions:
(Off Off Broadway) August 2, 1973 (Lolly's Theater Club).
No Reviews.

Grown Ups
Productions:
Opened December 10, 1981 for 83 performances.
Reviews:
Nation 234:123-4, Jan 30, 1982
New Leader 65:21-2, Feb 8, 1982
New York Magazine 14:46-7, Jul 20, 1981
                14:81, Dec 21, 1981
New York Theatre Critics' Reviews 1981:72
New York Times III, p. 18, Jun 18, 1981
        III, p. 3, Dec 11, 1981
        III, p. 9, Dec 15, 1981
        II, p. 3, Dec 20, 1981
        II, p. 1, Jan 3, 1982
        III, p. 3, Jan 15, 1982
New Yorker 57:98, Dec 21, 1981
Newsweek 97:83, Jun 29, 1981
        98:77, Dec 21, 1981
Saturday Review 9:50-1, Feb 1982
Time 118:80, Dec 21, 1980

Hold Me! (see Jules Feiffer's Hold Me!)

Jules Feiffer's Hold Me!
Productions:
(Off Broadway) February 14, 1977 for 100 performances.
Reviews:
Los Angeles 22:198+, Jul 1977
Nation 224:189, Feb 12, 1977
New York Magazine 10:87, Mar 21, 1977
New York Theatre Critics' Reviews 1977:318
New York Times p. 19, Jan 24, 1977
II, p. 3, Mar 13, 1977
III, p. 25, May 5, 1977
New Yorker 53:65, Mar 14, 1977
Newsweek 89:93, Mar 7, 1977

Knock Knock
Productions:
(Off Broadway) January 18, 1976 for 41 performances.
Opened February 24, 1976 for 192 performances.
Reviews:
Nation 222:188, Feb 14, 1976
New Republic 174:18-19, May 20, 1976
175:20, Jul 3, 1976
New York Magazine 9:64, Feb 2, 1976
9:64+, Jun 21, 1976
New York Theatre Critics' Reviews 1976:229
1976:357
New York Times p. 21, Jan 19, 1976
II, p. 1, Feb 1, 1976
p. 48, Jun 3, 1976
II, p. 5, Jun 13, 1976
p. 20, Jul 1, 1976
III, p. 21, Feb 16, 1977
New Yorker 51:67, Feb 2, 1976
52:51, Mar 15, 1976
Newsweek 87:68, Feb 2, 1976
Time 107:55, Feb 2, 1976

Little Murders
Productions:
Opened April 25, 1967 for 7 performances.
(Off Broadway) January 5, 1969 for 400 performances.
(Off Off Broadway) November 18, 1977 (TRG Repertory Co.).
Reviews:
Nation 208:94, Jan 20, 1969
New York Theatre Critics' Reviews 1967:315
New York Times p. 38, Apr 26, 1967
p. 23, Apr 29, 1967
II, p. 1, Jun 4, 1967
p. 38, Jan 6, 1969
II, p. 3, Jan 26, 1969
p. 54, Oct 2, 1969

XXI, p. 11, Dec 23, 1979
XXI, p. 15, Nov 15, 1981
New Yorker 44:100, Feb 8, 1969
Newsweek 69:116, May 8, 1967
Saturday Review 50:66, May 13, 1967
52:22, Feb 1, 1969
Time 93:69, Jan 17, 1969

*Think Piece
Reviews:
New York Times III, p. 7, Jun 29, 1982
II, p. 3, Jul 4, 1982

The Unexpurgated Memoirs of Bernard Mergendeiler
Productions:
(Off Broadway) May 8, 1968 for 80 performances (bill called
Collision Course).
Reviews:
Harper's Bazaar 237:113-15, Oct 1968
Nation 206:772+, Jun 10, 1968
New York Times p. 55, May 9, 1968
II, p. 1, May 19, 1968
New Yorker 44:74, May 18, 1968

The White House Murder Case
Productions:
(Off Broadway) February 18, 1970 for 119 performances.
Reviews:
Commonweal 92:143-5, Apr 24, 1970
Nation 210:285, Mar 9, 1970
New York Theatre Critics' Reviews 1970:287
New York Times p. 59, Feb 19, 1970
II, p. 3, Mar 1, 1970
II, p. 3, Mar 15, 1970
New Yorker 46:78-9, Feb 28, 1970
Newsweek 75:78, Mar 2, 1970
Saturday Review 53:12, Mar 7, 1970
Time 95:69, Mar 2, 1970

FERBER, EDNA

Bravo! (with George S. Kaufman)
Productions:
Opened November 11, 1948 for 44 performances.
Reviews:
Commonweal 49:195, Dec 3, 1948
New Republic 119:28-9, Nov 29, 1948
New York Theatre Critics' Reviews 1948:165
New York Times p. 31, Nov 12, 1948
New Yorker 24:58+, Nov 20, 1948

Newsweek 32:80, Nov 22, 1948
School and Society 68:454-5, Dec 25, 1948
Time 52:85, Nov 22, 1948

Dinner at Eight (see entry under Kaufman, George S.)

The Land Is Bright (see entry under Kaufman, George S.)

Minick (see entry under Kaufman, George S.)

Old Man Minick (see Minick)

Our Mrs. McChesney (with George V. Hobert. Adapted from the
    Ferber stories)
  Productions:
    Opened October 19, 1915 for 151 performances.
  Reviews:
    American Magazine 80:40-42+, Nov 1915
    Book News 34:179-80, Dec 1915
    Bookman 42:384+, Dec 1915
    Dramatic Mirror 74:8, Oct 30, 1915
    Dramatist 7:635-6, Jan 1916
    Harper's Weekly 61:440, Nov 6, 1915
    Nation 101:527-8, Oct 28, 1915
    National Magazine 43:244-7, Nov 1915
    New York Drama News 61:18, Oct 23, 1915
    New York Times p. 11, Oct 20, 1915
                   VI, p. 6, Oct 24, 1915

The Royal Family (see entry under Kaufman, George S.)

Stage Door (see entry under Kaufman, George S.)

Theatre Royal (see The Royal Family)

FERRIS, WALTER

Death Takes a Holiday (Adapted from the Italian of Alberto Casella)
  Productions:
    Opened December 26, 1929 for 180 performances.
    Opened February 16, 1931 for 32 performances.
    (Off Off Broadway) February 12, 1981 (Equity Library The-
      atre).
  Reviews:
    Catholic World 130:725-6, Mar 1930
    Commonweal 11:369, Jan 29, 1930
    Life (NY) 95:20, Jan 17, 1930
    Literary Digest 104:18, Jan 18, 1930
    Nation 138:342, Mar 21, 1934

New Republic 61:675-6, Jan 29, 1930
New York Times X, p. 4, Nov 24, 1929
    p. 26, Dec 27, 1929
    VIII, p. 2, Jan 5, 1930
    p. 22, Jan 29, 1930
    p. 29, Feb 17, 1931
Theatre Arts 14:191-2, Mar 1930
Vogue 75:122, Feb 15, 1930

The First Stone (Based on a story by Mary Heaton Vorse)
Productions:
Opened January 16, 1928 for 3 performances.
Reviews:
Drama 18:201, Apr 1928
New York Times p. 12, Jan 14, 1928

Judas (with Basil Rathbone)
Productions:
Opened January 24, 1929 for 12 performances.
Reviews:
Life (NY) 93:25, Feb 15, 1929
New York Times p. 20, Jan 25, 1929

FIELD, SALISBURY

The Rented Earl
Productions:
Opened February 8, 1915 for 16 performances.
Reviews:
Current Opinion 58:249-50, Apr 1915
Dramatic Mirror 72:7, Sep 16, 1914
    73:8, Feb 17, 1915
Green Book 13:958, May 1915
New York Times p. 9, Feb 9, 1915

Twin Beds (with Margaret Mayo)
Productions:
Opened August 14, 1914 for 411 performances.
Reviews:
Bookman 40:186, Oct 1914
Dramatic Mirror 72:8, Aug 19, 1914
Dramatist 6:533-4, Jan 1915
Green Book 12:90+, Jul 1914
    12:697-9, Oct 1914
    12:940-7, Nov 1914
Munsey 53:358-9, Nov 1914
New York Drama News 59:11, Aug 22, 1914
New York Times p. 9, Aug 15, 1914
Theatre Magazine 20:154+, Oct 1914

Wedding Bells
    Productions:
        Opened November 10, 1919 for 168 performances.
    Reviews:
        Dramatic Mirror 80:1825, Nov 27, 1919
        Dramatist 11:998-9, Apr 1920
        New York Times p. 11, Nov 13, 1919
                    IX, p. 2, Dec 7, 1919
        Theatre Magazine 30:367, Dec 1919

Zander the Great
    Productions:
        Opened April 9, 1923 for 80+ performances.
    Reviews:
        Bookman 57:438-9, Jun 1923
        Current Opinion 75:189-94+, Aug 1923
        Hearst 44:85-7+, Aug 1923
        Independent 110:302, Apr 28, 1923
        Life (NY) 81:18, Apr 26, 1923
        New York Clipper 71:14, Apr 18, 1923
        New York Times p. 24, Apr 10, 1923
                    VII, p. 1, Apr 15, 1923
        Theatre Magazine 37:14+, Jun 1923

FIELDS, JOSEPH

Anniversary Waltz   (see entry under Chodorov, Jerome)

The Doughgirls
    Productions:
        Opened December 30, 1942 for 671 performances.
    Reviews:
        Catholic World 156:599-600, Feb 1943
        Commonweal 37:350, Jan 22, 1943
        Independent Woman 22:144, May 1943
        Life 14:68-9, Feb 1, 1943
        Nation 156:103, Jan 16, 1943
        New York Theatre Critics' Reviews 1942:124
        New York Times p. 19, Dec 31, 1942
                    VIII, p. 1, Jan 10, 1943
                    II, p. 2, Jan 9, 1944
        Theatre Arts 27:139-40, Mar 1943
        Time 41:64, Jan 11, 1943

The French Touch (with Jerome Chodorov)
    Productions:
        Opened December 8, 1945 for 33 performances.
    Reviews:
        Commonweal 43:287, Dec 28, 1945
        Harper's Bazaar 79:128, Dec 1945

New York Theatre Critics' Reviews 1945:77
New York Times p. 18, Dec 10, 1945
New Yorker 21:60, Dec 15, 1945
Theatre Arts 30:79, Feb 1946
-Time 46:72, Dec 17, 1945

I Gotta Get Out (with Ben Sher)
Productions:
Opened September 25, 1947 for 4 performances.
Reviews:
New York Theatre Critics' Reviews 1947:343
New York Times II, p. 1, Sep 21, 1947
p. 27, Sep 26, 1947
New Yorker 23:50, Oct 4, 1947

Junior Miss (see entry under Chodorov, Jerome)

My Sister Eileen (with Jerome Chodorov. Based on the stories of
Ruth McKenney)
Productions:
Opened December 26, 1940 for 865 performances.
(Off Broadway) April 26, 1948.
Reviews:
Life 10:49, Feb 17, 1941
Nation 152:53, Jan 11, 1941
New Republic 104:84, Jan 20, 1941
New York Theatre Critics' Reviews 1940:175
1941:445
New York Times p. 23, Dec 27, 1940
IX, p. 1, Jan 5, 1941
IX, p. 2, May 18, 1941
Newsweek 17:52, Jan 6, 1941
Stage 1:20-21, Feb 1941
Theatre Arts 25:94, Feb 1941
Time 37:41, Jan 6, 1941

The Ponder Heart (with Jerome Chodorov)
Productions:
Opened February 16, 1956 for 149 performances.
Reviews:
America 94:703, Mar 24, 1956
Catholic World 183:64-5, Apr 1956
Commonweal 64:22, Apr 6, 1956
Life 40:111-12+, Mar 5, 1956
Nation 182:204, Mar 10, 1956
New Republic 134:29, Mar 12, 1956
New York Theatre Critics' Reviews 1956:358
New York Times VI, p. 44, Jan 22, 1956
p. 26, Feb 1, 1956
p. 14, Feb 17, 1956
II, p. 1, Feb 26, 1956

New Yorker 32:90, Feb 25, 1956
Newsweek 47:61, Mar 5, 1956
Saturday Review 39:22, Mar 3, 1956
Theatre Arts 40:22-3, Apr 1956
Time 67:61, Feb 27, 1956

Schoolhouse on the Lot (with Jerome Chodorov)
  Productions:
    Opened March 22, 1938 for 55 performances.
  Reviews:
    Catholic World 147:217, May 1938
    New York Times p. 18, Mar 23, 1938
    Newsweek 11:22, Mar 14, 1938
             11:25, Apr 4, 1938
    One Act Play Magazine 2:69-70, May 1938
    Time 31:22, Apr 4, 1938

The Tunnel of Love (with Peter DeVries. Based on DeVries' novel)
  Productions:
    Opened February 13, 1957 for 417 performances.
  Reviews:
    America 96:629, Mar 2, 1957
    Catholic World 185:69, Apr 1957
    Commonweal 65:662, Mar 29, 1957
    New York Theatre Critics' Reviews 1957:347
    New York Times VI, p. 62, Feb 3, 1957
                   p. 31, Feb 14, 1957
                   p. 47, Dec 5, 1957
    New York Times Magazine p. 62, Feb 3, 1957
    New Yorker 33:69, Feb 23, 1957
    Newsweek 49:75, Feb 25, 1957
    Saturday Review 40:26, Mar 2, 1957
    Theatre Arts 41:18, Apr 1957
    Time 69:52, Feb 25, 1957

FIERSTEIN, HARVEY

Flatbush Tosca
  Productions:
    (Off Off Broadway) May 22, 1975 (New York Theater Ensem-
    ble).
  No Reviews.

Freaky Pussy
  Productions:
    (Off Broadway) February 15, 1974 (New York Theater Ensem-
    ble).
  No Reviews.

Fugue in a Nursery (part of Torch Song Trilogy)
  Productions:

(Off Off Broadway) February 1, 1979 (La Mama ETC).
(Off Broadway) December 12, 1979 for 53 performances.
See also Torch Song Trilogy.
Reviews:
New York Times p. 24, Dec 15, 1979
(See also Torch Song Trilogy)

The International Stud (part of Torch Song Trilogy)
Productions:
(Off Off Broadway) Fall 1976 (Theater for the New City).
(Off Off Broadway) February 2, 1978 (La Mama ETC).
(Off Broadway) May 22, 1978 for 72 performances.
See also productions of Torch Song Trilogy.
Reviews:
New York Times III, p. 6, May 23, 1978
(See also Torch Song Trilogy)

Search of the Cobra Jewels
Productions:
(Off Broadway) October 4, 1972 (Playwrights' Workshop Club at
Bastiano's).
No Reviews.

Spookhouse
Productions:
(Off Off Broadway) March 15, 1982 (Circle Repertory Projects).
No Reviews.

Torch Song Trilogy (Consists of The International Stud, Fugue in a
Nursery, and Widows and Children First!)
Productions:
(Off Off Broadway) October 16, 1981 (Richard Allen Center).
(Off Broadway) January 15, 1982 for 117 performances.
See also individual entries.
Reviews:
America 146:320, Apr 24, 1982
New York Magazine 14:110-11, Dec 14, 1981
New York Times p. 81, Nov 1, 1981
II, p. 3, Jun 27, 1982
New Yorker 57:116, Feb 1, 1982
Newsweek 99:63, Mar 15, 1982
Saturday Review 9:46-7, Mar 1982
Time 119:70, Feb 22, 1982
(See also individual entries)

Widows and Children First! (part of Torch Song Trilogy)
Productions:
(Off Off Broadway) October 24, 1979 (La Mama ETC).
See also Torch Song Trilogy.
Reviews:
See Torch Song Trilogy

FISHER, ROBERT (BOB)

Happiness Is Just a Little Thing Called a Rolls Royce (with Arthur
Alsberg)
Productions:
Opened May 11, 1968 for 1 performance.
Reviews:
New York Theatre Critics' Reviews 1968:277
New York Times p. 54, May 13, 1968
p. 39, May 14, 1968
New Yorker 44:73, May 18, 1968

The Impossible Years (with Arthur Marx)
Productions:
Opened October 13, 1965 for 670 performances.
Reviews:
Commonweal 83:243, Nov 26, 1965
Life 59:72B, Nov 5, 1965
New York Theatre Critics' Reviews 1965:311
New York Times II, p. 10, Apr 22, 1965
p. 55, Oct 14, 1965
Newsweek 66:102, Oct 25, 1965
Time 86:103A, Oct 22, 1965

FITCH, CLYDE

The Bachelor
Productions:
Opened March 15, 1909 for 56 performances.
Reviews:
Forum 41:340-1, Apr 1909

Beau Brummell
Productions:
Opened April 24, 1916 for 24 performances.
Reviews:
Dramatic Mirror 75:8, Apr 29, 1916
Green Book 16:79+, Jul 1916
Munsey 58:521, Aug 1916
Nation 102:483, May 4, 1916
New York Times p. 11, Apr 26, 1916
VII, p. 7, Apr 30, 1916
Stage 14:93, Aug 1937
Theatre Magazine 23:334-5, Jun 1916

Captain Jinks of the Horse Marines
Productions:
Opened January 25, 1938 for 2 performances (WPA Federal
Theatre Project).
Reviews:
New York Times p. 16, Jan 28, 1938

The City
   Productions:
      Opened December 21, 1909 for 190 performances.
   Reviews:
      Bookman 31:63-6, Mar 1910
      Burr McIntosh Monthly 22:226, Mar 1910
      Colliers 44:7, Jan 15, 1910
      Current Literature 48:201-2, Feb 1910
      Dramatic Mirror 63:5-6, Jan 1, 1910
      Dramatist 1:39-41, Apr 1910
      Forum 43:190-1, Feb 1910
      Green Book 3:513-16, Mar 1910
      Hampton 24:401-4, Mar 1910
      Harper's Weekly 54:24, Jan 15, 1910
                      54:24, Apr 16, 1910
      Life (NY) 55:36, Jan 6, 1910
      Metropolitan Magazine 32:114-15, Apr 1910
      Pearson 23:373-6, Mar 1910
      Theatre Magazine 11:34+, Feb 1910

Girls
   Productions:
      Opened March 23, 1908 for 64 performances.
      Opened February 8, 1909 for one week.
   Reviews:
      New York Times p. 3, Sep 11, 1913
      Theatre Magazine 8:vii+, May 1908

The Happy Marriage
   Productions:
      Opened April 12, 1909 for 24 performances.
   Reviews:
      Dramatic Mirror 61:3, Apr 24, 1909
      Forum 41:455-7, May 1909
      Independent 66:90, Apr 29, 1909
      Nation 88:392, Apr 15, 1909

*House of Mirth (from Edith Wharton's novel. New adaptation by
   John Tillinger)
   Reviews:
      New York Times p. 8, Apr 17, 1976
      Newsweek 87:105, Apr 26, 1976

*Nathan Hale
   Reviews:
      New York Times p. 11, May 1, 1926

The Truth
   Productions:
      Opened April 14, 1914 for 55 performances.
      (Off Off Broadway) Season of 1969-70 (American Theater Club).

Reviews:
    Book News 32:456-7, May 1914
    Current Opinion 57:24-7, Jul 1914
    Dramatic Mirror 71:12, Apr 15, 1914
    Green Book 11:1015-17, Jun 1914
                12:462-71, Sep 1914
    Harper's Weekly 58:21, May 2, 1914
    Life (NY) 63:740-1, Apr 23, 1914
    Nation 98:418+, Apr 16, 1914
    New York Times VIII, p. 6, Apr 12, 1914
                    p. 11, Apr 13, 1914
    Theatre Magazine 7:301+, Feb 1907
                19:265, May 1914

FITZGERALD, F. SCOTT

The Great Gatsby (see entry under Davis, Owen)

The Vegetable
    Productions:
        Opened April 10, 1929 for 13 performances.
        (Off Broadway) October 26, 1963 for 8 performances (Equity
            Library Theater).
    Reviews:
        Bookman 56:57-8, Sep 1923
        Dramatist 14:1183-4, Oct 1923
        Life (NY) 93:24, May 3, 1929
        New York Times p. 32, Apr 11, 1929

FLAVIN, MARTIN

Achilles Had a Heel
    Productions:
        Opened October 13, 1935 for 8 performances.
    Reviews:
        Commonweal 23:19, Nov 1, 1935
        New York Times X, p. 1, Apr 28, 1935
                        p. 20, Oct 14, 1935
        Time 26:51, Oct 21, 1935

Around the Corner
    Productions:
        Opened December 28, 1936 for 16 performances.
    Reviews:
        New York Times p. 17, Dec 29, 1936
        Theatre Arts 21:102, Feb 1937

Broken Dishes
    Productions:

Opened November 5, 1929 for 178 performances.
Reviews:
Catholic World 130:466-7, Jan 1930
Commonweal 11:115-16, Nov 27, 1929
Life (NY) 94:48, Dec 6, 1929
New York Times p. 28, Nov 6, 1929
Theatre Magazine 51:45-6+, Jan 1930
Vogue 75:118, Feb 15, 1930

Children of the Moon
Productions:
Opened August 17, 1923 for 117 performances.
Reviews:
Bookman 58:180-1, Oct 1923
Dramatist 14:1184-5, Oct 1923
Life (NY) 82:18, Sep 13, 1923
Metropolitan Magazine 58:38+, Jan 1924
Nation 117:273, Sep 12, 1923
New York Times p. 10, Aug 18, 1923
                VI, p. 2, Sep 2, 1923
                VIII, p. 1, Nov 7, 1926
                XI, p. 3, May 4, 1930
Theatre Magazine 38:14-15, Oct 1923
                38:26+, Nov 1923

The Criminal Code
Productions:
Opened October 2, 1929 for 173 performances.
Reviews:
Catholic World 180:331-2, Dec 1929
Commonweal 11:115, Nov 27, 1929
Drama 21:26-7, Mar 1931
Life (NY) 94:22, Oct 25, 1929
Literary Digest 103:19-20, Nov 2, 1929
New York Times p. 28, Oct 2, 1929
                IX, p. 1, Oct 13, 1929
                IX, p. 4, Oct 20, 1929
                p. 30, Dec 19, 1929
Outlook 153:314, Oct 23, 1929
Review of Reviews 80:156, Dec 1929
Theatre Arts 13:875-6, Dec 1929
Theatre Magazine 50:41-2+, Dec 1929
Vogue 74:116, Nov 23, 1929

Cross Roads
Productions:
Opened November 11, 1929 for 28 performances.
Reviews:
Commonweal 11:116, Nov 27, 1929
Life (NY) 94:48, Dec 26, 1929
Nation 129:640-2, Nov 27, 1929

New York Times p. 34, Nov 12, 1929
Theatre Magazine 51:46, Jan 1930

Grist of the Mill (see Cross Roads)

Lady of the Rose
    Productions:
        Opened May 19, 1925 for 8 performances.
    Reviews:
        New York Times p. 26, May 20, 1925

Service for Two
    Productions:
        Opened August 30, 1926 for 24 performances.
    Reviews:
        New York Times p. 15, Aug 31, 1926
                    VII, p. 1, Sep 5, 1926
        Theatre Magazine 44:18, Nov 1926

Tapestry in Gray
    Productions:
        Opened December 27, 1935 for 24 performances.
    Reviews:
        Catholic World 142:602, Feb 1936
        Commonweal 23:330, Jan 17, 1936
        Literary Digest 121:20, Jan 11, 1936
        New York Times p. 10, Dec 28, 1935

FORBES, JAMES

The Commuters
    Productions:
        Opened August 15, 1910 for 160 performances.
    Reviews:
        Blue Book 12:661-3, Feb 1911
        Bookman 32:349-, Dec 1910
        Dramatic Mirror 64:7-8, Aug 27, 1910
        Dramatist 2:102-5, Oct 1910
        Green Book 5:307-8, Feb 1911
        Hampton 25:524, Oct 1910
        Life (NY) 56:434, Sep 15, 1910
        Metropolitan Magazine 33:122-3, Oct 1910
        Munsey 44:125, Oct 1910
        Theatre Magazine 12:xv, Sep 1910

The Endless Chain
    Productions:
        Opened September 4, 1922 for 40 performances.
    Reviews:
        Life (NY) 80:18, Sep 21, 1922

New York Clipper 70:20, Sep 13, 1922
New York Times p. 21, Sep 5, 1922

The Famous Mrs. Fair
    Productions:
    Opened December 22, 1919 for 183 performances.
    Reviews:
    Current Opinion 69:192-9, Aug 1920
    Dramatic Mirror 81:2023, Jan 1, 1920
    Dramatist 12:1039-40, Jan 1921
    Forum 63:246, Feb 1920
    Life (NY) 75:72, Jan 8, 1920
    Nation 110:210-11, Feb 14, 1920
    New York Times p. 12, Dec 23, 1919
                 p. 20, Apr 24, 1920
    Theatre Magazine 21:83+, Feb 1920

*Final Fling
    Reviews:
    New York Times IX, p. 2, Oct 7, 1928

Matrimony PFD (with Grace George. Adapted from the play by Louis
    Verneuil)
    Productions:
    Opened November 12, 1936 for 61 performances.
    Reviews:
    Catholic World 144:473, Jan 1937
    Nation 143:642, Nov 28, 1936
    New York Times p. 28, Nov 6, 1936
                 p. 26, Nov 13, 1936
    Theatre Arts 21:22, Jan 1937
    Time 28:36, Nov 23, 1936

Precious
    Productions:
    Opened January 14, 1929 for 24 performances.
    Reviews:
    New York Times p. 22, Jan 15, 1929

A Rich Man's Son
    Productions:
    Opened November 4, 1912 for 32 performances.
    Reviews:
    Blue Book 16:692-5, Feb 1913
    Bookman 36:377, Dec 1912
    Dramatic Mirror 68:5, Nov 13, 1912
    Everybody's 28:257-8, Feb 1913
    New York Drama News 56:19-20, Nov 16, 1912

The Show Shop
    Productions:
    Opened December 31, 1914 for 156 performances.

Reviews:
    American Magazine 79:85-6, May 1915
    Bookman 40:641, Feb 1915
    Current Opinion 58:328-31, May 1915
    Dramatic Mirror 73:8-9, Jan 6, 1915
    Dramatist 6:558-60, Apr 1915
    Green Book 13:474-6, Mar 1915
                13:763-4, Apr 1915
    Life (NY) 65:68, Jan 14, 1915
    Nation 100:31, Jan 7, 1915
    New Republic 2:131, Mar 6, 1915
    New York Drama News 60:18, Jan 9, 1915
    New York Times p. 17, Jan 1, 1915
                VII, p. 6, Jan 24, 1915
    Smart Set 45:285, Mar 1915
    Theatre Magazine 21:57-8, Feb 1915

Young Blood
    Productions:
    Opened November 24, 1925 for 73 performances.
    Reviews:
    New York Times p. 15, Nov 25, 1925
                VIII, p. 1, Nov 29, 1925
    Theatre Magazine 43:18, Feb 1926

FORD, RUTH

Requiem for a Nun (see entry under Faulkner, William)

FOSTER, PAUL

Balls
    Productions:
    (Off Broadway) February 10, 1965 for 23 performances (The-
        atre 1965 New Playwrights Series).
    Reviews:
    New York Times II, p. 1, Feb 7, 1965
                p. 45, Feb 11, 1965
    Newsweek 65:93, Feb 22, 1965

Elizabeth I (music by David Sheridan Spangler)
    Productions:
    Opened April 5, 1972 for 5 performances.
    (Off Off Broadway) June 7, 1979 (La Mama ETC).
    (Off Broadway) April 29, 1980 for 7 performances.
    Reviews:
    New York Theatre Critics' Reviews 1972:324
    New York Times p. 52, Apr 6, 1972
                p. 14, May 3, 1980
    Texas Monthly 8:160+, Mar 1980

Hurrah for the Bridge
    Productions:
        (Off Off Broadway) Season of 1981-82 (La Mama ETC).
    No Reviews.

*Marcus Brutus
    Reviews:
        New York Times p. 46, Jan 19, 1975
        Time 105:57, Feb 10, 1975

Rags to Riches to Rags
    Productions:
        (Off Off Broadway) December 1974 (La Mama ETC).
    No Reviews.

The Recluse
    Productions:
        (Off Broadway) April 12, 1966 for 16 performances.
    Reviews:
        Nation 202:405-6, Apr 4, 1966
        New York Times II, p. 15, Apr 10, 1966
                         p. 36, Apr 13, 1966

Silver Queen (music by John Braden)
    Productions:
        (Off Off Broadway) April 11, 1973 (La Mama ETC).
    No Reviews.

Tom Paine
    Productions:
        (Off Broadway) March 25, 1968 for 295 performances.
    Reviews:
        America 118:652, May 11, 1968
        Nation 206:516, Apr 15, 1968
        New York Times p. 38, Mar 26, 1968
                      II, p. 1, May 12, 1968
                       p. 71, Mar 30, 1969
        New Yorker 44:110-11, Apr 6, 1968
        Newsweek 71:131, Apr 8, 1968
        Saturday Review 51:40, May 4, 1968

FRANKEN, ROSE

Another Language
    Productions:
        Opened April 25, 1932 for 344 performances.
        Opened May 8, 1933 for 89 performances.
        (Off Off Broadway) December 4, 1975 (Equity Library Thea-
            ter).
    Reviews:
        Arts and Decoration 37:58, Sep 1932

Bookman 75:176-7, May 1932
Catholic World 135:338, Jun 1932
Commonweal 16:76-7, May 18, 1932
Literary Digest 113:17, May 28, 1932
Nation 134:580, May 18, 1932
New Republic 70:351-2, May 11, 1932
New York Times p. 25, Apr 26, 1932
                VIII, p. 1, May 15, 1932
                IX, p. 1, Dec 25, 1932
                IX, p. 1, Jan 8, 1933
                p. 20, May 9, 1933
                p. 42, Dec 8, 1975
North American Review 234:172-3, Aug 1932
Player's Magazine 9:13, Sep-Oct, 1932
Stage 9:14-17, Jun 1932
Town and Country 87:24, Jun 1, 1932
Vogue 79:41+, Jun 15, 1932

Claudia

Productions:
    Opened February 12, 1941 for 722 performances.
    Reopened May 24, 1942 for 24 performances.
Reviews:
    Commonweal 33:475, Feb 28, 1941
    Life 10:120-23, Mar 31, 1941
         11:118-22+, Nov 17, 1941
    Nation 152:221, Feb 22, 1941
    New York Theatre Critics' Reviews 1941:378
    New York Times p. 24, Feb 13, 1941
                   IX, p. 1, Mar 9, 1941
                   IX, p. 3, Apr 20, 1941
                   IX, p. 1, Jul 27, 1941
                   IX, p. 1, Aug 10, 1941
                   p. 28, Jul 28, 1942
                   VIII, p. 2, Sep 27, 1942
                   VIII, p. 2, Oct 4, 1942
    Newsweek 17:60, Feb 24, 1941
    Player's Magazine 17:11, May 1941
    Theatre Arts 25:258+, Apr 1941
                 25:262, Apr 1941
    Time 37:58, Feb 24, 1941

Doctors Disagree

Productions:
    Opened December 28, 1943 for 23 performances.
Reviews:
    Commonweal 39:328, Jan 14, 1944
    New York Theatre Critics' Reviews 1943:186
    New York Times p. 15, Dec 29, 1943
    New Yorker 19:38, Jan 8, 1944
    Newsweek 23:89, Jan 10, 1944

Theatre Arts 28:141, Mar 1944
Time 43:72, Jan 10, 1944

The Hallams
Productions:
Opened March 4, 1948 for 12 performances.
Reviews:
Commonweal 47:566, Mar 19, 1948
New Republic 118:34, Mar 22, 1948
New York Theatre Critics' Reviews 1948:313
New York Times p. 18, Mar 5, 1948
New Yorker 24:48, Mar 13, 1948
Newsweek 31:79, Mar 15, 1948
Time 51:65, Mar 15, 1948
Vogue 111:151, Apr 1, 1948

Outrageous Fortune
Productions:
Opened November 3, 1943 for 77 performances.
Reviews:
Catholic World 159:298, Dec 1943
Commonweal 39:116, Nov 19, 1943
New Republic 109:686, Nov 15, 1943
New York Theatre Critics' Reviews 1943:237
New York Times p. 28, Nov 4, 1943
            II, p. 1, Nov 21, 1943
Newsweek 22:96, Nov 15, 1943
Player's Magazine 20:13, Jan 1944
Theatre Arts 28:8-11, Jan 1944

Soldier's Wife
Productions:
Opened October 4, 1944 for 253 performances.
Reviews:
Catholic World 160:169-70, Nov 1944
Nation 159:482-3, Oct 21, 1944
New Republic 111:521, Oct 23, 1944
New York Theatre Critics' Reviews 1944:121
New York Times p. 18, Oct 5, 1944
            II, p. 1, Oct 15, 1944
            p. 13, Sep 2, 1946
New Yorker 20:42, Oct 14, 1944
Newsweek 24:85, Oct 16, 1944
Theatre Arts 28:696+, Dec 1944
Time 44:52, Oct 16, 1944

FREEMAN, DAVID

Battering Ram
Productions:

(Off Off Broadway) April 24, 1975 (Manhattan Theater Club).
No Reviews.

Creeps
   Productions:
      (Off Broadway) December 4, 1973 for 15 performances.
   Reviews:
      New York Magazine 6:72, Dec 24, 1973
      New York Theatre Critics' Reviews 1973:144
      New York Times p. 52, Dec 5, 1973
                     II, p. 5, Dec 16, 1973

Jesse and the Bandit Queen
   Productions:
      (Off Off Broadway) October 3, 1975 (New York Shakespeare
         Festival Public Theater).
      (Off Broadway) October 17, 1975 for 155 performances.
      (Off Off Broadway) February 8, 1980 (IRT).
   Reviews:
      Los Angeles 22:255, Nov 1977
      New York Magazine 8:91+, Nov 24, 1975
      New York Theatre Critics' Reviews 1975:103
      New York Times p. 48, Nov 3, 1975
                     II, p. 28, Nov 16, 1975
                     p. 22, Feb 26, 1976
      New Yorker 51:124-5, Nov 17, 1975

You're Gonna Be Alright, Jamie Boy
   Productions:
      (Off Off Broadway) May 1977 (Performing Garage).
   No Reviews.

FRIEDMAN, BRUCE JAY

A Foot in the Door
   Productions:
      (Off Off Broadway) February 23, 1979 for 12 performances
         (American Place Theater).
   Reviews:
      New York Times III, p. 17, Mar 8, 1979

Scuba Duba
   Productions:
      (Off Broadway) October 10, 1967 for 692 performances.
   Reviews:
      America 117:486-7, Oct 28, 1967
      Commentary 44:84, Dec 1967
      Commonweal 87:624, Feb 23, 1968
      Life 63:119-20+, Nov 17, 1967
      Nation 205:438-9+, Oct 30, 1967

New Republic 157:31-3, Oct 28, 1967
New York Times p. 36, Oct 11, 1967
        II, p. 3, Oct 22, 1967
        VI, p. 13, Jan 14, 1968
        p. 51, Apr 7, 1969
New York Times Magazine p. 30-2+, Jan 14, 1968
New Yorker 43:82+, Oct 21, 1967
Newsweek 70:113+, Oct 23, 1967
Reporter 38:43, Jan 25, 1968
Time 90:82+, Oct 20, 1967

Steambath
  Productions:
    (Off Broadway) June 30, 1970 for 128 performances.
  Reviews:
    Commonweal 93:95, Oct 23, 1970
    New York Theatre Critics' Reviews 1970:198
    New York Times p. 49, Jul 1, 1970
               p. 30, Jul 2, 1970
               II, p. 1, Jul 12, 1970
               II, p. 28, Oct 11, 1970
    New Yorker 46:48, Jul 11, 1970
    Newsweek 76:101, Jul 13, 1970
    Saturday Review 53:28, Aug 8, 1970

FRINGS, KETTI

Look Homeward, Angel (Based on Thomas Wolfe's novel)
  Productions:
    Opened November 28, 1957 for 564 performances.
    (Off Off Broadway) January 1975 (Manhattan Theater Club).
  Reviews:
    America 98:551, Feb 8, 1957
    Catholic World 186:385-6, Feb 1958
    Christian Century 75:469, Apr 16, 1958
    Commonweal 68:16-18, Apr 4, 1958
    Life 43:79-82, Dec 16, 1957
    Los Angeles 20:105, Oct 1975
    Nation 185:463-4, Dec 14, 1957
    New York Theatre Critics' Reviews 1957:166
    New York Times II, p. 1, Nov 24, 1957
               p. 33, Nov 29, 1957
               II, p. 5, Dec 8, 1957
               VI, p. 18, Dec 15, 1957
               II, p. 1, Aug 31, 1958
    New York Times Magazine p. 18+, Dec 15, 1957
    New Yorker 33:95-6, Dec 7, 1957
    Newsweek 50:70-1, Dec 9, 1957
    Reporter 17:33, Dec 26, 1957

Saturday Review 40:27-8, Nov 23, 1957
40:22, Dec 14, 1957
Theatre Arts 42:18-19, Feb 1958
Time 70:72, Dec 9, 1957

The Long Dream (Based on Richard Wright's novel)
Productions:
Opened February 17, 1960 for 5 performances.
Reviews:
New York Theatre Critics' Reviews 1960:362
New York Times p. 36, Feb 18, 1960
New Yorker 36:120, Mar 5, 1960
Reporter 22:38-9, Mar 17, 1960

Mr. Sycamore (Based on a story by Robert Ayre)
Productions:
Opened November 13, 1942 for 19 performances.
Reviews:
Commonweal 37:144, Nov 27, 1942
Current History 3:456, Jan 1943
Independent Woman 21:378, Dec 1942
Nation 155:598, Nov 28, 1942
New Republic 107:714, Nov 30, 1942
New York Theatre Critics' Reviews 1942:179
New York Times p. 13, Nov 14, 1942
VIII, p. 1, Nov 29, 1942
Newsweek 20:73, Nov 23, 1942
Theatre Arts 27:20, Jan 1943
Time 40:53, Nov 23, 1942

FROST, ROBERT

Fire and Ice
Productions:
(Off Off Broadway) May 13, 1975 (Theater at St. Clements).
No Reviews.

Masque of Reason
Productions:
(Off Broadway) Season of 1959-60 (ANTA).
(Off Off Broadway) Season of 1972-73 (American Theater Co.).
Reviews:
New York Times p. 19, Nov 25, 1959

FULLER, CHARLES

The Brownsville Raid
Productions:
(Off Broadway) December 5, 1976 for 112 performances.

Reviews:
Essence 7:8, Mar 1977
Nation 223:701-2, Dec 25, 1976
New York Theatre Critics' Reviews 1976:76
New York Times p. 46, Dec 6, 1976
II, p. 5, Dec 12, 1976
New Yorker 52:84, Dec 20, 1976
Time 108:58, Dec 20, 1976

Candidate
Productions:
(Off Off Broadway) March 14, 1974 (New Federal Theater).
No Reviews.

In the Deepest Part of Sleep
Productions:
(Off Broadway) Jun 4, 1974 for 32 performances (Negro En-
semble Co.).
Reviews:
New York Magazine 7:76, Jun 17, 1974
New York Times p. 54, Jun 5, 1974
New Yorker 50:84, Jun 17, 1974

The Perfect Party (revised version of The Village: A Party)
Productions:
(Off Broadway) March 20, 1969 for 21 performances.
Reviews:
New York Times p. 42, Mar 21, 1969
(See also The Village: A Party)

A Soldier's Play
Productions:
(Off Broadway) November 20, 1981 for 221+ performances (still
running on June 1, 1982).
Reviews:
America 146:343, May 1, 1982
Los Angeles 27:254+, Oct 1982
Nation 234:90, Jan 23, 1982
New Leader 65:21-2, Jul 12-26, 1982
New York Magazine 14:159, Dec 7, 1981
New York Theatre Critics' Reviews 1982:363
New York Times III, p. 3, Nov 27, 1981
II, p. 3, Dec 6, 1981
II, p. 1, Jan 3, 1982
III, p. 13, Jan 11, 1982
II, p. 4, Apr 13, 1982
New Yorker 57:110+, Dec 7, 1981
Newsweek 98:77, Dec 21, 1981
People 17:85-6, Jun 20, 1982
Time 119:87, Jan 18, 1982

*The Village: A Party (original version of The Perfect Party)
Reviews:
    New York Times p. 39, Nov 13, 1968
    (See also The Perfect Party)

Zooman and the Sign
    Productions:
        (Off Broadway) December 7, 1980 for 33 performances.
        (Off Broadway) June 20, 1981 for 44 performances.
    Reviews:
        Commonweal 108:178-9, Mar 27, 1981
        New York Times III, p. 13, Dec 8, 1970
                       III, p. 3, Dec 21, 1980
                       II, p. 9, Jun 7, 1981
        New Yorker 56:55-6, Dec 22, 1980

FUNT, JULIAN

The Dancer (with Milton Lewis)
    Productions:
        Opened June 5, 1946 for 5 performances.
    Reviews:
        New York Theatre Critics' Reviews 1946:368
        New York Times p. 16, Jun 6, 1946
        New Yorker 22:40, Jun 15, 1946

The Magic and the Loss
    Productions:
        Opened April 9, 1954 for 27 performances.
    Reviews:
        America 91:145, May 1, 1954
        Commonweal 60:175, May 21, 1954
        Nation 178:390, May 1, 1954
        New Republic 130:21, May 3, 1954
        New York Theatre Critics' Reviews 1954:332
        New York Times p. 10, Apr 10, 1954
        New Yorker 30:63, Apr 17, 1954
        Newsweek 43:66, Apr 19, 1954
        Saturday Review 37:24, Apr 24, 1954
        Theatre Arts 38:21, Jun 1954
        Time 63:86+, Apr 19, 1954

GALE, ZONA

Miss Lulu Bett
    Productions:
        Opened December 27, 1920 for 198+ performances.
        (Off Off Broadway) March 9, 1978 (Encompass Theater).
    Reviews:
        Bookman 52:567-8, Feb 1921

Colliers 67:13, Jan 29, 1921
Current Opinion 70:487-95, Apr 1921
Dramatic Mirror 83:40, Jan 1, 1921
Hearst 40:25-7+, Sep 1921
Independent 105:57, Jan 15, 1921
Life (NY) 77:64-5, Jan 13, 1921
      80:18, Jul 13, 1922
Literary Digest 68:26-7, Feb 12, 1921
Nation 112:189, Feb 2, 1921
New Republic 25:204-5, Jan 19, 1921
New York Clipper 68:19, Jan 5, 1921
New York Times p. 11, Dec 27, 1920
      p. 9, Dec 28, 1920
      VI, p. 1, Jan 9, 1921
      VI, p. 1, Jan 23, 1921
      VI, p. 1, Feb 6, 1921
Outlook 127:579-80, Apr 13, 1921
Theatre Magazine 33:180-81+, Mar 1921
Weekly Review 4:90, Jan 26, 1921

Mr. Pitt
  Productions:
    Opened January 22, 1924 for 87 performances.
  Reviews:
    American Mercury 1:374-5, Mar 1924
    Freeman 8:520-1, Feb 6, 1924
    Life (NY) 83:20, Feb 7, 1924
    New York Times VII, p. 1, Jan 6, 1924
              p. 15, Jan 23, 1924
    Theatre Magazine 39:17, Apr 1924

Neighbors
  Productions:
    Opened October 31, 1917 in repertory (Washington Square
      Players).
  Reviews:
    Dial 50:112-13, Aug 15, 1915
    Dramatic Mirror 75:8, Apr 1, 1916
    New York Times p. 13, Oct 22, 1917
              p. 11, Dec 4, 1917

GARDNER, DOROTHY

Eastward in Eden
  Productions:
    Opened November 18, 1947 for 15 performances.
    (Off Broadway) Season of 1955-56.
  Reviews:
    Commonweal 47:196, Dec 5, 1947
    Nation 165:628-9, Dec 6, 1947
    New Republic 117:31, Dec 1, 1947

New York Theatre Critics' Reviews 1947:261
New York Times p. 33, Nov 19, 1947
                 p. 25, Apr 18, 1956
New Yorker 23:58+, Nov 29, 1947
Newsweek 30:80, Dec 1, 1947
Theatre Arts 32:12, 14, Jan 1948
Time 50:66, Dec 1, 1947

GARDNER, HERB

The Goodbye People
    Productions:
        Opened December 3, 1968 for 7 performances.
        Opened April 30, 1979 for one performance.
    Reviews:
        Los Angeles 24:234+, Feb 1979
        New West 4:81, Jan 29, 1979
        New York Theatre Critics' Reviews 1968:157
                                          1979:267
        New York Times p. 52, Dec 4, 1968
                       p. 59, Dec 9, 1968
                       II, p. 5, Dec 15, 1968
                       III, p. 7, May 1, 1979
                       III, p. 23, May 2, 1979
        New Yorker 44:180, Dec 14, 1968
        Newsweek 72:114, Dec 16, 1968

Thieves
    Productions:
        Opened April 7, 1974 for 312 performances.
    Reviews:
        New York Magazine 7:81, Apr 29, 1974
        New York Theatre Critics' Reviews 1974:317
        New York Times p. 44, Apr 8, 1974
                       II, p. 3, May 5, 1974
                       p. 22, Dec 7, 1974
        New Yorker 50:104+, Apr 15, 1974

A Thousand Clowns
    Productions:
        Opened April 5, 1962 for 428 performances.
        (Off Off Broadway) October 1, 1975 (Elysian Playhouse).
    Reviews:
        Commonweal 76:116-17, Apr 27, 1962
        Life 52:57-8, Jun 15, 1962
        Nation 194:408, May 5, 1962
        New York Theatre Critics' Reviews 1962:302
        New York Times p. 31, Apr 6, 1962
                       II, p. 1, Apr 13, 1962
        New Yorker 38:106+, Apr 14, 1962

Newsweek 59:100, Apr 16, 1962
Saturday Review 45:46, Apr 21, 1962
Theatre Arts 46:57-8, Jun 1962
Time 79:82, Apr 13, 1962

GAZZO, MICHAEL V.

A Hatful of Rain
    Productions:
    Opened November 9, 1955 for 398 performances.
    (Off Off Broadway) April 9, 1970 for 12 performances (Equity
        Library Theater).
    (Off Off Broadway) February 12, 1976 (18th St. Players).
    Reviews:
    America 94:286, Dec 3, 1955
    Catholic World 182:309-10, Jan 1956
    Commonweal 63:331, Dec 30, 1955
    Life 39:85-6+, Dec 19, 1955
    Nation 181:465, Nov 26, 1955
    New Republic 134:20, Jan 2, 1956
    New York Theatre Critics' Reviews 1955:213
    New York Times VI, p. 76, Oct 30, 1955
                    p. 44, Nov 10, 1955
                    II, p. 1, Dec 4, 1955
                    XXI, p. 13, Oct 18, 1979
    New Yorker 31:121-3, Nov 19, 1955
    Newsweek 46:66+, Nov 21, 1955
    Saturday Review 38:26, Nov 26, 1955
    Theatre Arts 40:22, Jan 1956
    Time 66:110, Nov 21, 1955

The Night Circus
    Productions:
    Opened December 2, 1958 for 7 performances.
    Reviews:
    New York Theatre Critics' Reviews 1958:183
    New York Times II, p. 3, Sep 14, 1958
                    p. 44, Dec 3, 1958
    New Yorker 34:106-7, Dec 13, 1958
    Saturday Review 41:32, Dec 20, 1958
    Time 72:44, Dec 15, 1958

GELBART, LARRY

Sly Fox (Based on Ben Jonson's Volpone)
    Productions:
    Opened December 14, 1976 for 495 performances.
    Reviews:
    America 136:60, Jan 22, 1977

Los Angeles 23:214+, Aug 1978
New Republic 176:24, Jan 15, 1977
New West 3:87, Aug 14, 1978
New York Magazine 10:95, Dec 27, 1976/Jan 3, 1977
New York Theatre Critics' Reviews 1976:66
New York Times III, p. 19, Dec 15, 1976
            II, p. 3, Jan 2, 1977
               p. 28, May 24, 1977
            II, p. 3, Jul 31, 1977
New Yorker 52:42, Dec 27, 1976
Newsweek 88:39, Dec 27, 1976
Time 108:39, Dec 27, 1976

GELBER, JACK

The Apple
Productions:
    (Off Broadway) December 7, 1961 for 64 performances.
Reviews:
    Christian Century 79:233-4, Feb 21, 1962
    Commentary 33:331-4, Apr 1962
    Commonweal 75:364-5, Dec 29, 1961
    National Review 12:68, Jan 30, 1962
    New Republic 145:20+, Dec 25, 1961
    New York Times II, p. 3, Nov 26, 1961
                     p. 44, Dec 8, 1961
                      p. 22, Apr 20, 1962
                      p. 33, Apr 23, 1962
    New Yorker 37:97-8, Dec 16, 1961
    Newsweek 58:72, Dec 18, 1961
    Theatre Arts 46:13-14, Feb 1962

Barbary Shore (Adapted from the novel by Norman Mailer)
Productions:
    (Off Broadway) December 18, 1973 for 48 performances.
Reviews:
    New York Magazine 7:64, Feb 4, 1974
    New York Times p. 16, Jan 11, 1974
                 II, p. 4, Jan 20, 1974
    New Yorker 49:61-2, Jan 21, 1974

The Connection
Productions:
    (Off Broadway) July 15, 1959 for 722 performances.
    (Off Broadway) September 12, 1961 for 120 performances.
    (Off Off Broadway) October 23, 1980 (New Federal Theater).
Reviews:
    Esquire 55:45-7, Apr 1961
    Harper's Bazaar 220:26-8, Apr 1960
    Nation 189:80, Aug 15, 1959

New Republic 141:29-30, Sep 28, 1959
New York Times p. 30, Jul 16, 1959
        II, p. 1, Feb 7, 1960
        p. 23, Feb 15, 1960
        p. 30, Feb 23, 1961
        p. 17, Mar 4, 1961
        p. 29, Jun 16, 1961
        III, p. 16, Oct 27, 1980
New Yorker 35:126-9, Oct 10, 1959
        56:174-5, Nov 10, 1980
Saturday Review 42:27, Sep 26, 1959
Time 75:61, Jan 25, 1960

The Cuban Thing
    Productions:
        Opened September 24, 1968 for one performance.
    Reviews:
        New Republic 159:36, Oct 19, 1968
        New York Theatre Critics' Reviews 1968:245
        New York Times p. 39, Sep 13, 1968
                II, p. 1, Sep 15, 1968
                p. 36, Sep 25, 1968
        New Yorker 44:95-6, Oct 5, 1968

Jack Gelber's New Play: Rehearsal
    Productions:
        (Off Broadway) September 28, 1976 for 32 performances.
    Reviews:
        New York Magazine 9:77, Oct 25, 1976
        New York Theatre Critics' Reviews 1976:130
        New York Times III, p. 4, Oct 8, 1976
                II, p. 3, Oct 17, 1976

Rehearsal   (see Jack Gelber's New Play: Rehearsal)

Sleep
    Productions:
        (Off Broadway) February 10, 1972 for 32 performances (American Place Theater).
    Reviews:
        New York Times p. 30, Feb 23, 1972
                II, p. 3, Feb 27, 1972

Square in the Eye
    Productions:
        (Off Broadway) May 19, 1965 for 31 performances.
    Reviews:
        Commonweal 82:474, Jul 2, 1965
        New Republic 152:30, Jun 26, 1965
        New York Times p. 54, May 20, 1965
                p. 18, May 22, 1965

II, p. 1, Jun 6, 1965
p. 44, Jun 15, 1965
New Yorker 41:56+, May 29, 1965
Newsweek 65:76, May 31, 1965
Reporter 33:42, Jul 1, 1965
Time 85:83, May 28, 1965
Vogue 146:38, Jul 1965

GERSHE, LEONARD

Butterflies Are Free
  Productions:
    Opened October 21, 1969 for 1,128 performances.
  Reviews:
    America 121:545, Nov 29, 1969
    Commonweal 92:15-16, Mar 13, 1970
    Life 68:57-8, Feb 6, 1970
    Nation 209:518, Nov 10, 1969
    New York Theatre Critics' Reviews 1969:221
    New York Times p. 30, Oct 22, 1969
                II, p. 1, Nov 2, 1969
                p. 60, Dec 3, 1970
                p. 52, Sep 16, 1971
                II, p. 1, Sep 19, 1971
                XI, p. 4, Sep 7, 1980
    New Yorker 45:127, Nov 1, 1969
    Newsweek 74:93-4, Nov 3, 1969
    Saturday Review 52:28, Nov 8, 1969
    Time 94:55, Oct 31, 1969

GIBBS, WOLCOTT

Season in the Sun
  Productions:
    Opened September 28, 1950 for 367 performances.
  Reviews:
    Catholic World 172:149-50, Nov 1950
    Christian Science Monitor Magazine p. 11, Oct 7, 1950
    Commonweal 53:42, Oct 20, 1950
    Life 29:111-14, Oct 9, 1950
    Nation 171:320-1, Oct 7, 1950
    New Republic 123:22, Oct 16, 1950
    New York Theatre Critics' Reviews 1950:258
    New York Times p. 31, Sep 29, 1950
                II, p. 1, Oct 8, 1950
                II, p. 3, Oct 13, 1950
                II, p. 3, Nov 26, 1950
    New Yorker 26:54+, Oct 7, 1950
    Newsweek 36:84, Oct 9, 1950

Saturday Review 33:26-7+, Oct 21, 1950
School and Society 73:184, Mar 24, 1951
Theatre Arts 34:15, Nov 1950
     35:82, Sep 1951
Time 56:85, Oct 9, 1950

GIBSON, WILLIAM

The Butterfingers Angel, Mary and Joseph, Herod the Nut, and
    The Slaughter of 12 Hit Carols in a Pear Tree
Productions:
    (Off Off Broadway) November 27, 1980 for 20 performances
      (Quaigh Theater).
Reviews:
    New York Times III, p. 12, Dec 9, 1980

A Cry of Players
Productions:
    Opened November 14, 1968 for 72 performances.
Reviews:
    America 119:634, Dec 14, 1968
    Nation 207:604-5, Dec 2, 1968
    New York Theatre Critics' Reviews 1968:179
    New York Times p. 40, Nov 15, 1968
        II, p. 9, Nov 24, 1968
        II, p. 1, Dec 1, 1968
    New Yorker 44:122+, Nov 23, 1968
    Newsweek 72:126, Nov 25, 1968
    Saturday Review 51:60, Nov 30, 1968
    Vogue 152:170, Dec 1968

Dinny and the Witches
Productions:
    (Off Broadway) December 9, 1959 for 29 performances.
Reviews:
    America 102:482, Jan 16, 1960
    New York Times p. 53, Dec 10, 1959
    New Yorker 35:82+, Dec 19, 1959
    Saturday Review 42:24-5, Dec 26, 1959

Golda
Productions:
    Opened November 14, 1977 for 108 performances.
Reviews:
    America 137:423, Dec 10, 1977
    Nation 225:605, Dec 3, 1977
    New Republic 177:18-19, Dec 3, 1977
    New York Magazine 10:138, Dec 5, 1977
    New York Theatre Critics' Reviews 1977:142
    New York Times p. 53, Nov 15, 1977

II, p. 3, Nov 27, 1977
II, p. 3, Feb 19, 1978

New Yorker 53:81, Nov 28, 1977
Newsweek 90:80, Nov 28, 1977
Time 110:103, Nov 28, 1977

Herod the Nut (see The Butterfingers Angel ...)

*John and Abigail
   Reviews:
     New York Times p. 42, Jan 14, 1971
                II, p. 16, Jan 31, 1971

Mary and Joseph (see The Butterfingers Angel ...)

The Miracle Worker (Based on the life of Helen Keller)
   Productions:
     Opened October 19, 1959 for 700 performances.
     (Off Off Broadway) January 4, 1979 (Equity Library Theater).
   Reviews:
     America 102:217, Nov 14, 1959
     Christian Century 76:1470, Dec 16, 1959
     Commonweal 71:289, Dec 4, 1959
     Life 47:127-8, Sep 28, 1959
     Nation 189:366, Nov 14, 1959
     New Republic 141:28-9, Nov 9, 1959
     New York Theatre Critics' Reviews 1959:254
     New York Times VI, p. 67, Sep 27, 1959
                II, p. 1, Oct 18, 1959
                p. 44, Oct 20, 1959
                II, p. 1, Nov 1, 1959
                II, p. 5, Dec 20, 1959
                II, p. 1, Mar 5, 1961
                p. 19, Mar 10, 1961
                p. 22, Mar 20, 1961
                p. 40, Mar 28, 1961
                p. 11, Apr 1, 1961
                p. 31, Apr 5, 1961
                p. 43, Apr 11, 1961
                p. 29, Apr 21, 1961
                p. 35, May 1, 1961
                p. 22, May 19, 1961
                p. 28, May 31, 1961
                p. 20, Aug 21, 1961
                p. 43, Jan 7, 1979
     New Yorker 35:132-4, Oct 31, 1959
     Newsweek 54:97, Nov 2, 1959
     Saturday Review 42:28, Nov 7, 1959
     Theatre Arts 43:14, Dec 1959
                44:26-9+, Jan 1960
     Time 74:51, Oct 5, 1959

74:30, Nov 2, 1959
74:46-8+, Dec 21, 1959
Vogue 135:112-13+, Jan 1, 1959

The Slaughter of 12 Hit Carols in a Pear Tree   (see The Butterfingers
   Angel ...)

Two for the Seesaw
   Productions:
      Opened January 16, 1958 for 750 performances.
      (Off Off Broadway) April 1976 (Playwrights Horizons).
   Reviews:
      America 98:552, Feb 8, 1959
      Catholic World 187:67-8, Apr 1958
      Commonweal 67:540-1, Feb 21, 1958
      Life 44:95-6, Feb 17, 1958
      Nation 186:107, Feb 1, 1958
      New York Theatre Critics' Reviews 1958:394
      New York Times II, p. 1, Jan 12, 1958
                       p. 15, Jan 17, 1958
                       II, p. 1, Jan 26, 1958
                       VII, p. 5, Mar 15, 1959
                       II, p. 1, Apr 12, 1959
                       p. 34, Sep 4, 1963
                       XI, p. 29, Nov 4, 1979
      New Yorker 33:56+, Jan 25, 1958
      Newsweek 51:63, Jan 27, 1958
      Reporter 18:36, Mar 6, 1958
      Saturday Review 41:25, Feb 1, 1958
      Theatre Arts 42:9, Mar 1958
      Time 71:86+, Jan 27, 1958

GILLETTE, WILLIAM

All The Comforts of Home (Adapted from a play by Carl Laufs)
   Productions:
      Opened May 25, 1942 for 8 performances.
   Reviews:
      New York Theatre Critics' Reviews 1942:280
      New York Times p. 24, May 26, 1942

The Dream Maker
   Productions:
      Opened November 21, 1921 for 82 performances.
   Reviews:
      Bookman 54:573-4, Feb 1922
      Dramatic Mirror 84:773, Nov 26, 1921
      New York Clipper 69:20, Nov 30, 1921
      New York Times p. 17, Nov 22, 1921

Electricity
  Productions:
    Opened October 31, 1910 for 16 performances.
  Reviews:
    Blue Book 12:863, Feb 1911
    Bookman 32:352, Dec 1910
    Dramatic Mirror 64:7, Nov 2, 1910
    Dramatist 2:118-20, Jan 1911
    Leslies' Weekly 111:515, Nov 17, 1910
    Life (NY) 56:864, Nov 17, 1910
    Metropolitan Magazine 33:666-7, Feb 1911
    Munsey 44:561, Jan 1911
    Theatre Magazine 12:165+, Dec 1910

Held by the Enemy
  Productions:
    Opened December 5, 1910 in repertory.
  Reviews:
    Dramatic Mirror 65:7, Mar 29, 1911
    Leslies' Weekly 112:617, Jan 1, 1911

The Private Secretary
  Productions:
    Opened December 5, 1910 in repertory.
    (Off Off Broadway) April 17, 1975 (American Theater Co.).
  Reviews:
    Dramatic Mirror 64:8, Dec 14, 1910

Secret Service
  Productions:
    Opened December 5, 1910 in repertory.
    Opened November 8, 1915 for two weeks.
    Opened April 12, 1976 for 13 performances.
  Reviews:
    Dramatic Mirror 74:8, Nov 13, 1915
    Dramatist 7:649-50, Jan 1916
    Munsey 45:286, May 1911
    Nation 222:541-2, May 1, 1976
    New Republic 174:18-19, May 8, 1976
    New York Magazine 9:88, Apr 26, 1976
    New York Theatre Critics' Reviews 1976:305
    New York Times p. 9, Nov 9, 1915
                   VI, p. 8, Nov 14, 1915
                   p. 28, Apr 13, 1976
                   II, p. 5, Apr 25, 1976
    New Yorker 52:111, Apr 26, 1976
    Theatre Arts 27:471, Aug 1943

Sherlock Holmes (Based on the novels of Arthur Conan Doyle)
  Productions:
    Opened December 5, 1910 in repertory.

Opened October 11, 1915 for four weeks.
Opened February 20, 1928 for 16 performances.
Opened November 25, 1929 for 45 performances.
Opened November 12, 1974 for 471 performances.
Reviews:
America 131:349, Nov 30, 1974
Commentary 59:75-7, Apr 1975
Commonweal 11:198, Dec 18, 1929
Current Literature 50:73-81, Jan 1911
Dramatic Mirror 74:9, Oct 16, 1915
Los Angeles 21:162+, May 1976
Nation 219:573, Nov 30, 1974
New Republic 172:22, Jan 4, 1975
New York Magazine 7:67, Aug 26, 1974
                  7:88, Dec 2, 1974
New York Theatre Critics' Reviews 1974:186
New York Times p. 11, Oct 12, 1915
            VI, p. 8, Oct 17, 1915
            p. 18, Feb 21, 1928
            V, p. 14, Nov 10, 1929
            p. 28, Nov 26, 1929
            p. 24, Aug 9, 1974
            p. 36, Nov 13, 1974
            II, p. 7, Nov 24, 1974
            p. 27, May 29, 1975
            II, p. 1, Oct 5, 1975
            p. 16, Dec 31, 1975
New Yorker 50:131, Nov 25, 1974
Playboy 22:41, Mar 1975
Saturday Review 13:18, Jan 4, 1936
Stage 13:76, Oct 1935
      14:90-91, Aug 1937
Theatre Arts 14:105+, Feb 1930
Theatre Magazine 51:68, Feb 1930
Time 104:108, Nov 25, 1974
Vogue 165:234-5+, Feb 1975

Too Much Johnson
    Productions:
        Opened December 5, 1910 in repertory.
        (Off Broadway) January 15, 1964 for 23 performances.
        (Off Off Broadway) November 29, 1978 (Joseph Jefferson).
    Reviews:
        Los Angeles 20:132+, Nov 1975
        New York Times p. 29, Jan 26, 1964
                III, p. 9, Dec 5, 1978
        New Yorker 39:74+, Jan 25, 1964

GILROY, FRANK D.

Come Next Tuesday (see Present Tense)

Dreams of Glory
    Productions:
        (Off Off Broadway) June 1979 as part of a bill called Marathon
            (Ensemble Studio Theater).
    No Reviews.

Last Licks
    Productions:
        Opened November 20, 1979 for 15 performances.
    Reviews:
        New York Theatre Critics' Reviews 1979:91
        New York Times II, p. 6, Nov 18, 1979
                        III, p. 11, Nov 21, 1979
                        III, p. 22, Nov 28, 1979
        New Yorker 55:108, Dec 3, 1979

The Next Contestant
    Productions:
        (Off Off Broadway) April 1978 as part of a bill called Mara-
            thon '78 (Ensemble Studio Theater).
    No Reviews.

The Only Game in Town
    Productions:
        Opened May 20, 1968 for 16 performances.
        (Off Off Broadway) February 17, 1978 (Ensemble Studio The-
            ater).
    Reviews:
        Commonweal 88:382+, Jun 14, 1968
        New York Theatre Critics' Reviews 1968:274
        New York Times p. 42, May 21, 1968
        New Yorker 44:102, Jun 1, 1968
        Newsweek 71:102, Jun 3, 1968

Present Tense (consists of Come Next Tuesday, Twas Brillig, So
        Please Be Kind, and Present Tense)
    Productions:
        (Off Broadway) July 18, 1972 for 8 performances.
    Reviews:
        New York Times p. 23, Jul 19, 1972

So Please Be Kind (see Present Tense)

The Subject Was Roses
    Productions:
        Opened May 25, 1964 for 832 performances.
        (Off Off Broadway) September 1974 (Manhattan Theater Club).
        (Off Off Broadway) January 11, 1980 (York Players).
    Reviews:
        America 110:853, Jun 20, 1964
        Life 56:17, Jun 19, 1964
              57:71-3, Sep 4, 1964

Nation 198:611, Jun 15, 1964
New York Theatre Critics' Reviews 1964:252
New York Times p. 45, May 26, 1964
    II, p. 1, Jun 7, 1964
    p. 25, Jul 2, 1964
    III, p. 20, Jan 16, 1980
    XXII, p. 17, Mar 16, 1980
New Yorker 40:86, Jun 6, 1964
Newsweek 63:69, Jun 8, 1964
Saturday Review 47:44, Jun 13, 1964
Time 83:75, Jun 5, 1964
Vogue 144:30, Aug 1, 1964

That Summer--That Fall
Productions:
Opened March 16, 1967 for 12 performances.
Reviews:
Commonweal 86:153-4, Apr 21, 1967
New York Theatre Critics' Reviews 1967:340
New York Times p. 33, Mar 17, 1967
    II, p. 3, Apr 2, 1967
Newsweek 69:110, Mar 27, 1967
Saturday Review 50:42, Apr 1, 1967
Time 89:69, Mar 24, 1967

Twas Brillig (see Present Tense)

Who'll Save the Plowboy?
Productions:
(Off Broadway) January 9, 1962 for 56 performances.
Reviews:
America 106:605, Feb 3, 1962
Nation 194:127, Feb 10, 1962
New Republic 146:29-30, Feb 5, 1962
New York Times p. 24, Jan 10, 1962
    II, p. 1, Jan 28, 1962
New Yorker 37:69, Jan 20, 1962
Reporter 26:48, Mar 1, 1962
Theatre Arts 46:61-2, Mar 1962
Time 79:56, Jan 26, 1962

GLASPELL, SUSAN

Alison's House
Productions:
Opened December 1, 1930 for 41 performances
(Off Off Broadway) March 23, 1978 (Encompass Theater).
Reviews:
Bookman 72:514, Jan 1931
Catholic World 132:591-2, Feb 1931

Commonweal 13:127, Dec 13, 1930
Drama Magazine 21:13, Jan 1931
Life (NY) 97:18, Jan 2, 1931
Nation 132:590-1, May 27, 1931
New York Times p. 31, Dec 2, 1930
              VIII, p. 1, May 10, 1931
              IX, p. 3, Nov 13, 1932
Outlook 156:711, Dec 31, 1930
Sketch Book 8:23, Feb 1931
Theatre Arts 15:99+, Feb 1931
Theatre Magazine 53:25, Feb 1931
Vogue 77:84, Feb 1, 1931

*Bernice
  Reviews:
    New York Times IV, p. 2, Mar 30, 1919

Chains of Dew
  Productions:
    Opened April 27, 1922 for 16 performances.
  Reviews:
    Nation 114:627, May 24, 1922
    New York Times p. 20, Apr 28, 1922

*Close the Book
  Reviews:
    New York Times p. 11, May 14, 1918

The Comic Artist (with Norman Matson)
  Productions:
    Opened April 19, 1933 for 21 performances.
  Reviews:
    Commonweal 18:49-50, May 12, 1933
    Nation 136:539-40, May 10, 1933
    New Republic 74:365-6, May 10, 1933
    New York Times VIII, p. 1, Jul 22, 1928
                p. 20, Apr 20, 1933
    Newsweek 1:26, Apr 29, 1933
    Player's Magazine 9:15, May-Jun 1933
    Stage 10:11, Jun 1933
    Theatre Arts 17:418, Jun 1933
    Time 21:43, May 1, 1933

Inheritors
  Productions:
    Season of 1920-21.
    Opened March 15, 1927 for 17 performances.
  Reviews:
    Bookman 53:526-8, Aug 1921
    Independent 105:329, Apr 2, 1921
    Nation 112:515, Apr 6, 1921
           116:393, Apr 4, 1923

New York Times VII, p. 1, Mar 27, 1921
              p. 24, Sep 28, 1925
              p. 23, Mar 8, 1927
            VIII, p. 1, Mar 20, 1927
Review 4:344-6, Apr 13, 1921
Vogue 69:138, May 1, 1927

Suppressed Desires (with George Cram Cook)
  Productions:
    Opened October 31, 1917 in repertory (Washington Square Players).
  Reviews:
    New York Times p. 7, Jan 24, 1918

*Tickless Time (with George Cram Cook)
  Reviews:
    New York Times p. 13, Dec 21, 1918

Trifles
  Productions:
    Opened August 30, 1916 in repertory. (Washington Square Players).
    (Off Off Broadway) June 1, 1979 for 12 performances, as part of a bill called Wed-Lock (IRT).
  Reviews:
    Dramatic Mirror 76:7, Nov 25, 1916
    New York Times p. 8, Nov 14, 1916
    Theatre Magazine 25:21+, Jan 1917

The Verge
  Productions:
    Opened November 14, 1921 for 38 performances.
  Reviews:
    Nation 113:708-9, Dec 14, 1921
    New Republic 29:47, Dec 7, 1921
    New York Clipper 69:20, Nov 23, 1921
    New York Times p. 23, Nov 15, 1921
                 VI, p. 1, Nov 20, 1921

A Woman's Honor
  Productions:
    Opened April 18, 1918 in repertory. (Greenwich Village Players).
  Reviews:
    Dramatic Mirror 78:766, Jun 1, 1918
    New York Times p. 13, May 21, 1918

GLEASON, JAMES

The Fall Guy (with George Abbott)
  Productions:

Opened March 10, 1925 for 95 performances.
Reviews:
American Mercury 5:119, May 1925
Nation 120:362-3, Apr 1, 1925
New York Times VII, p. 1, Jul 20, 1924
    p. 19, Mar 11, 1925
Theatre Magazine 42:26+, Sep 1925

Is Zat So? (with Richard Taber)
Productions:
Opened January 5, 1925 for 618 performances.
Reviews:
American Mercury 5:119, May 1925
Bookman 61:338, May 1925
Life (NY) 85:18, Jan 29, 1925
Literary Digest 85:26-7, May 16, 1925
New Republic 42:160+, Apr 1, 1925
New York Times p. 23, Jan 6, 1925
    VII, p. 1, Feb 1, 1925
    p. 12, Feb 17, 1926
    p. 25, Jun 25, 1926
Theatre Magazine 41:17-18, Apr 1925

*Puffy
Reviews:
New York Times VII, p. 2, Jul 29, 1928

Shannons of Broadway
Productions:
Opened Septebmer 26, 1927 for 288 performances.
Reviews:
Life (NY) 90:25, Oct 20, 1927
New York Times p. 30, Sep 27, 1927
    VIII, p. 1, Oct 9, 1927
Outlook 147:213-14, Oct 19, 1927
Theatre Magazine 46:74, Nov 1927

GODFREY, THOMAS
No productions.

GOETZ, RUTH and AUGUSTUS

The Heiress (Suggested by Henry James's Washington Square)
Productions:
Opened September 29, 1947 for 410 performances.
Opened February 8, 1950 for 16 performances.
Opened April 20, 1976 for 23 performances.
Reviews:
Catholic World 166:168, Nov 1947

Commonweal 47:16, Oct 17, 1947
Forum 108:370-1, Dec 1947
Life 23:149-50+, Nov 3, 1947
Nation 165:425-6, Oct 18, 1947
    222:574, May 8, 1976
New Republic 117:36, Oct 13, 1947
New York Magazine 9:79, May 3, 1976
New York Theatre Critics' Reviews 1947:335
    1976:290
New York Times p. 22, Sep 30, 1947
    II, p. 1, Oct 5, 1947
    II, p. 3, Nov 16, 1947
    p. 34, Feb 9, 1950
    p. 65, Feb 15, 1976
    p. 22, Apr 21, 1976
    p. 15, May 8, 1976
New Yorker 23:50, Oct 11, 1947
    52:75, May 3, 1976
Newsweek 30:80, Oct 13, 1947
Publisher's Weekly 153:1130, Feb 28, 1948
School and Society 67:167, Feb 28, 1948
Theatre Arts 31:12-13, Dec 1947
    32:32, Apr 1948
    32:21, Oct 1948
    34:18, Apr 1950
Time 50:70+, Oct 13, 1947
    107:75-6, May 3, 1976
Vogue 110:190, Nov 15, 1947

The Hidden River (Based on Storm Jameson's novel)
  Productions:
    Opened January 23, 1957 for 61 performances.
  Reviews:
    Catholic World 185:69, Apr 1957
    Commonweal 65:569, Mar 1, 1957
    Nation 184:146, Feb 16, 1957
    New York Theatre Critics' Reviews 1957:378
    New York Times II, p. 1, Jan 20, 1957
        p. 32, Jan 24, 1957
        p. 41, Apr 14, 1959
    New Yorker 32:70+, Feb 2, 1957
    Newsweek 49:78, Feb 4, 1957
    Reporter 16:40, Mar 7, 1957
    Saturday Review 40:25, Feb 9, 1957
    Theatre Arts 41:14, Apr 1957
    Time 69:56, Feb 4, 1957

The Immoralist (Based on André Gide's novel)
  Productions:
    Opened February 8, 1954 for 96 performances.
    (Off Broadway) November 7, 1963 for 210 performances.

Reviews:
America 90:581, Feb 27, 1954
Catholic World 179:70, Apr 1954
Commonweal 79:283-4, Nov 29, 1963
Nation 178:156, Feb 20, 1954
New Republic 130:21, Mar 22, 1954
New York Theatre Critics' Reviews 1954:373
New York Times II, p. 1, Jan 31, 1954
p. 22, Feb 9, 1954
II, p. 1, Feb 14, 1954
p. 36, Nov 8, 1963
New Yorker 29:61, Feb 13, 1954
Newsweek 43:94, Feb 22, 1954
Saturday Review 37:28, Feb 27, 1954
Theatre Arts 38:17, Apr 1954
Time 63:80, Feb 22, 1954

One-Man Show
Productions:
Opened February 8, 1945 for 36 performances.
Reviews:
Catholic World 160:551, Mar 1945
Commonweal 41:475, Feb 23, 1945
Nation 160:229, Feb 24, 1945
New Republic 112:295, Feb 26, 1945
New York Theatre Critics' Reviews 1945:269
New York Times p. 21, Feb 9, 1945
II, p. 1, Feb 18, 1945
Newsweek 25:84, Feb 19, 1945
Theatre Arts 29:204, Apr 1945
Time 45:69, Feb 19, 1945

GOLDBERG, DICK

Family Business
Productions:
(Off Broadway) April 12, 1978 for 438 performances (Honey
Waldman).
(Off Broadway) May 29, 1979 for 32 performances (Roundabout
Theater Co.).
Reviews:
New York Times III, p. 17, Apr 13, 1978
II, p. 5, Apr 30, 1978

GOLDMAN, JAMES

Blood, Sweat, and Stanley Poole (with William Goldman)
Productions:
Opened October 5, 1961 for 84 performances.

Reviews:
America 106:134, Oct 28, 1961
New York Theatre Critics' Reviews 1961:244
New York Times p. 31, Oct 6, 1961
New Yorker 37:165, Oct 14, 1961
Newsweek 58:102, Oct 16, 1961
Theatre Arts 45:13+, Dec 1961
Time 78:58, Oct 13, 1961

The Lion in Winter
Productions:
Opened March 3, 1966 for 92 performances.
(Off Off Broadway) November 11, 1977 (Nat Horne Theater).
Reviews:
America 114:452, Apr 2, 1966
Commonweal 84:114, Apr 15, 1966
Nation 202:374, Mar 28, 1966
New Republic 154:37, Aug 26, 1966
New York Theatre Critics' Reviews 1966:344
New York Times p. 23, Mar 4, 1966
II, p. 1, Mar 13, 1966
XXII, p. 16, Oct 30, 1977
New Yorker 42:110, May 12, 1966
Newsweek 62:94, Mar 14, 1966
Saturday Review 49:55, Mar 19, 1966
Time 87:52, Mar 11, 1966
Vogue 147:145, May 1966

GOLDSMITH, CLIFFORD

What a Life
Productions:
Opened April 13, 1938 for 538 performances.
(Off Off Broadway) May 21, 1982 (Manhattan Punch Line).
Reviews:
Catholic World 147:347, Jun 1938
Commonweal 28:21, Apr 29, 1938
Life 4:48-51, Jun 6, 1938
New York Times p. 26, Apr 14, 1938
IX, p. 3, Feb 26, 1939
p. 17, Aug 2, 1939
p. 59, Jun 6, 1982
One Act Play Magazine 2:77-8, May 1938
Stage 15:28, May 1938
Theatre Arts 22:396+, Jun 1938
Time 31:39-40, Apr 25, 1938

GOODHART, WILLIAM

Generation

Productions:
  Opened October 6, 1965 for 299 performances.
Reviews:
  Commonweal 83:125-6, Oct 28, 1965
  Life 59:72A-72B, Nov 5, 1965
  New York Theatre Critics' Reviews 1965:262
  New York Times p. 5, Oct 8, 1965
  New Yorker 41:195-6, Oct 16, 1965
  Newsweek 66:114, Oct 18, 1965
  Saturday Review 48:74, Oct 23, 1965
  Time 86:75, Oct 15, 1965
  Vogue 146:68, Nov 15, 1965

GOODMAN, RUTH (see Goetz, Ruth)

GOODRICH, FRANCES

Bridal Wise (see entry under Hackett, Albert)

The Diary of Anne Frank (with Albert Hackett. Based on Anne
        Frank: The Diary of a Young Girl)
Productions:
  Opened October 5, 1955 for 717 performances.
  (Off Off Broadway) Season of 1971-72 (Manhattan Theater
    Club).
  (Off Off Broadway) October 13, 1976 (Hudson Guild Theater).
  (Off Broadway) December 28, 1978 for 78 performances.
Reviews:
  America 94:110+, Oct 22, 1955
          140:36, Jan 20, 1979
  Catholic World 182:223, Dec 1955
  Commentary 20:464-7, Nov 1955
  Commonweal 63:91-2, Oct 28, 1955
          65:87, Oct 26, 1956
  Life 39:162-3, Oct 17, 1955
  Nation 181:370, Oct 29, 1955
  New Republic 134:20, Jan 2, 1956
  New York Theatre Critics' Reviews 1955:257
                                    1978:132
  New York Times VI, p. 47, Sep 25, 1955
                 II, p. 1, Oct 2, 1955
                 p. 24, Oct 6, 1955
                 II, p. 1, Oct 16, 1955
                 II, p. 3, Oct 23, 1955
                 II, p. 1, Sep 30, 1956
                 p. 39, Oct 2, 1956
                 p. 30, Oct 3, 1956
                 p. 18, Oct 6, 1956
                 VI, p. 2, Oct 7, 1956
                 II, p. 1, Oct 14, 1956

p. 43, Nov 29, 1956
II, p. 7, Dec 9, 1956
III, p. 3, Mar 10, 1978
XXIII, p. 24, Dec 10, 1978
III, p. 4, Dec 29, 1978
II, p. 3, Jan 7, 1979
II, p. 1, Dec 2, 1979
New Yorker 31:75-6, Oct 15, 1955
54:88-9, Jan 15, 1979
Newsweek 46:103, Oct 17, 1955
48:112, Oct 15, 1956
Reporter 13:31, Dec 29, 1955
Saturday Review 38:27, Oct 22, 1955
6:48, Mar 3, 1979
Theatre Arts 39:24, Dec 1955
41:29-30, May 1957
Time 66:51, Oct 17, 1955
68:50+, Oct 15, 1956
113:70, Jan 8, 1979

The Great Big Doorstep (with Albert Hackett. Based on E. P.
O'Donell's novel)
Productions:
Opened November 26, 1942 for 28 performances.
Reviews:
Catholic World 156:474, Jan 1943
Commonweal 37:206, Dec 11, 1942
Current History 3:457, Jan 1943
New York Theatre Critics' Reviews 1942:160
New York Times p. 26, Nov 27, 1942
p. 8, Mar 18, 1950
Newsweek 20:76, Dec 7, 1942
Theatre Arts 27:17, Jan 1943
Time 40:54, Dec 7, 1942

Up Pops the Devil (see entry under Hackett, Albert)

*Western Union (with Albert Hackett)
Reviews:
New York Times p. 22, Jul 13, 1937

GORDON, RUTH

The Leading Lady
Productions:
Opened October 18, 1948 for 8 performances.
Reviews:
Commonweal 49:94, Nov 5, 1948
New Republic 119:25-6, Nov 8, 1948
New York Theatre Critics' Reviews 1948:190

New York Times p. 38, Sep 25, 1948
                p. 30, Oct 18, 1948
                p. 33, Oct 19, 1948
New Yorker 24:42+, Oct 30, 1948
Newsweek 32:74, Nov 1, 1948
Time 52:52, Nov 1, 1948

Miss Jones (see Years Ago)

Over 21
  Productions:
    Opened January 3, 1944 for 221 performances.
  Reviews:
    Catholic World 158:488, Feb 1944
    Commonweal 359:351-2, Jan 21, 1944
    Life 16:107-8+, Feb 14, 1944
    Nation 158:107, Jan 22, 1944
    New York Theatre Critics' Reviews 1944:297
    New York Times p. 20, Jan 4, 1944
                  II, p. 1, Jan 9, 1944
    New Yorker 19:36, Jan 15, 1944
    Newsweek 23:70, Jan 17, 1944
    Theatre Arts 28:137-8, Mar 1944
    Time 43:90, Jan 17, 1944

A Very Rich Woman (Based on a play by Phillippe Heriat)
  Productions:
    Opened September 30, 1965 for 28 performances.
  Reviews:
    Commonweal 83:98, Oct 22, 1965
    New York Theatre Critics' Reviews 1965:268
    New York Times p. 5, Oct 5, 1965
    New Yorker 41:184, Oct 9, 1965
    Newsweek 66:93, Oct 11, 1965
    Saturday Review 48:75, Oct 16, 1965
    Time 86:68, Oct 8, 1965
    Vogue 146:71, Nov 15, 1965

Years Ago
  Productions:
    Opened December 3, 1946 for 206 performances.
  Reviews:
    Catholic World 164:359, Jan 1947
    Commonweal 45:254, Dec 20, 1946
    Life 22:58-60, Jan 6, 1947
    Nation 163:738, Dec 21, 1946
    New Republic 115:878, Dec 23, 1946
    New York Theatre Critics' Reviews 1946:229
    New York Times VI, p. 38, Dec 1, 1946
                      p. 44, Dec 4, 1946
                   II, p. 3, Dec 15, 1946

II, p. 1, Jan 12, 1947
II, p. 3, May 11, 1947
New Yorker 22:60+, Dec 14, 1946
Newsweek 28:94, Dec 16, 1946
Saturday Review 30:30-2, Mar 22, 1947
Scholastic 50:20, Feb 3, 1947
Theatre Arts 31:16+, Feb 1947
Time 48:70, Dec 16, 1946

GORDONE, CHARLES

*Gordone Is a Muthah
 Reviews:
 New York Times p. 72, May 10, 1970

The Last Chord
 Productions:
 (Off Off Broadway) August 1976 (Billie Holiday Theater).
 Reviews:
 New York Times p. 39, May 18, 1976

No Place to Be Somebody
 Productions:
 (Off Broadway) Season of 1968-69 (The Other Stage).
 (Off Broadway) May 4, 1969 for 250 performances.
 Opened December 30, 1969 for 16 performances.
 (Off Broadway) January 20, 1970 for 312 performances.
 Opened September 9, 1971 for 39 performances.
 Reviews:
 America 121:145, Sep 6, 1969
 Nation 208:644, May 19, 1969
 New York Theatre Critics' Reviews 1969:265
                                    1971:253
 New York Times p. 53, May 5, 1969
                II, p. 1, May 18, 1969
                II, p. 22, May 18, 1969
                II, p. 1, Jun 8, 1969
                p. 17, Dec 31, 1969
                II, p. 1, Jan 25, 1970
                II, p. 1, May 17, 1970
                p. 43, Sep 10, 1971
                II, p. 1, Sep 19, 1971
                XXII, p. 20, May 31, 1981
 New Yorker 45:112+, May 17, 1969
            45:64, Jan 10, 1970
 Newsweek 73:101, Jun 2, 1969
 Saturday Review 52:18, May 31, 1969
 Time 93:85-6, May 16, 1969

A Qualification for Anabiosis
 Productions:

(Off Off Broadway) April 1978 as part of a bill called Marathon
'78 (Ensemble Studio Theater).
No Reviews.

GOW, JAMES

Deep are the Roots (see entry under d'Usseau, Arnaud)

Legend of Sarah (with Arnaud d'Usseau)
    Productions:
        Opened October 11, 1950 for 29 performances.
    Reviews:
        Christian Science Monitor Magazine p. 6, Oct 21, 1950
        Commonweal 53:95, Nov 3, 1950
        Nation 171:370, Oct 21, 1950
        New York Theatre Critics' Reviews 1950:247
        New York Times p. 42, Oct 12, 1950
        New Yorker 26:55-7, Oct 21, 1950
        Newsweek 36:85, Oct 23, 1950
        Theatre Arts 34:14, Dec 1950
        Time 56:58, Oct 23, 1950

Tomorrow the World (with Arnaud d'Usseau)
    Productions:
        Opened April 14, 1943 for 500 performances.
    Reviews:
        Catholic World 157:298-9, Jun 1943
        Commonweal 38:40, Apr 30, 1943
        Life 14:63-4+, May 31, 1943
        Nation 156:642, May 1, 1943
        New Republic 108:637, May 10, 1943
        New York Theatre Critics' Reviews 1943:334
        New York Times p. 22, Apr 15, 1943
                      II, p. 1, Apr 25, 1943
                      II, p. 1, May 2, 1943
                      p. 24, Apr 26, 1944
        New Yorker 19:28, Apr 24, 1943
        Newsweek 21:86, Apr 26, 1943
        Theatre Arts 27:331-2+, Jun 1943
        Time 41:66, Apr 26, 1943

GREEN, PAUL

*Common Glory
    Reviews:
        New York Times p. 11, Jul 19, 1947
                      II, p. 1, Jul 27, 1947
                      II, p. 13, Jun 26, 1949

*The Confederacy
Reviews:
New York Times p. 20, Jul 3, 1958
II, p. 1, Jul 13, 1958
IV, p. 8, Jul 20, 1958

*The Cross and the Sword
Reviews:
New York Times p. 32, Jun 28, 1965

*Enchanted Maze
Reviews:
New York Times p. 10, Dec 14, 1935
XI, p. 5, Dec 15, 1935

*Faith of Our Fathers
Reviews:
New York Times II, p. 1, Jul 1, 1950
p. 72, Aug 6, 1950
II, p. 1, Aug 13, 1950
p. 5, May 26, 1951

The Field God
Productions:
Opened April 21, 1927 for 45 performances.
Reviews:
Life (NY) 89:24, Jun 2, 1927
Nation 125:510-11, May 4, 1927
New York Times p. 18, Apr 22, 1927
VIII, p. 1, May 1, 1927
Theatre Magazine 46:19, Jul 1927

*The Founders
Reviews:
New York Times p. 14, Aug 24, 1956
II, p. 3, May 12, 1957
p. 39, May 14, 1957

*Highland Call
Reviews:
New York Times p. 19, Nov 21, 1939
North Carolina Historical Review 19:305-7, Jul 1942

The House of Connelly
Productions:
Opened September 28, 1931 for 91 performances.
Reviews:
Arts and Decoration 36:68, Dec 1931
Bookman 74:298-9, Nov 1931
75:290, Jun-Jul, 1932
Catholic World 134:207-8, Nov 1931

Commonweal 14:583-4, Oct 14, 1931
Literary Digest 111:17, Oct 24, 1931
Nation 133:408, Oct 14, 1931
New Republic 68:234-6, Oct 14, 1931
New York Times p. 22, Sep 29, 1931
        VIII, p. 1, Oct 4, 1931
Outlook 159:215, Oct 14, 1931
Saturday Review 8:199+, Oct 17, 1931
Theatre Arts 15:75-7, Dec 1931
        16:92+, Feb 1932
Vogue 78:100, Dec 1, 1931

Hymn to the Rising Sun

Productions:
  Opened May 6, 1937 for 10 performances (Federal Theatre
    Project).
  Season of 1937-38 in repertory for 22 performances (Federal
    Theatre Project).

Reviews:
  New York Times p. 14, Jul 13, 1936
             p. 28, May 7, 1937
  Newsweek 9:29, May 22, 1937

In Abraham's Bosom

Productions:
  Opened December 30, 1926 for 200 performances.
  Opened September 6, 1927 for 88 performances.

Reviews:
  Bookman 65:706-7, Aug 1927
  Drama 17:136, Feb 1927
  Dramatist 18:1347, Jul 1927
  Life (NY) 89:24, Jun 2, 1927
  Literary Digest 93:27-8, May 28, 1927
  Nation 124:73, Jan 19, 1927
       124:510-11, May 4, 1927
  New Republic 50:46-7, Mar 2, 1927
  New York Times p. 10, Dec 31, 1926
          VII, p. 1, Feb 20, 1927
          VII, p. 1, May 8, 1927
          p. 26, May 9, 1927
          p. 35, Sep 7, 1927
          X, p. 1, Dec 2, 1928
  Survey 57:591, Feb 1, 1927
  Theatre Magazine 46:18, Jul 1927
              46:24-6+, Aug 1927

Johnny Johnson (with Kurt Weill)

Productions:
  Opened November 19, 1936 for 68 performances.
  (Off Broadway) May 2, 1941 (Theatre Associates).
  (Off Broadway) Season of 1956-57.

Reviews:
 Catholic World 144:468-9, Jan 1937
 Commonweal 25:162, Dec 4, 1936
 Forum 97:354, Jun 1937
 Literary Digest 123:23, Jan 2, 1937
 Nation 143:674+, Dec 5, 1936
  183:439, Nov 17, 1956
 New Republic 89:179, Dec 9, 1936
 New York Times p. 26, Nov 20, 1936
  XI, p. 2, Nov 22, 1936
  XII, p. 1, Nov 29, 1936
  p. 20, May 3, 1941
  p. 24, Oct 22, 1956
 Newsweek 8:19, Nov 28, 1936
 Scribner's Magazine 101:66-7, Jun 1937
 Theatre Arts 21:15-17, Jan 1937
  21:426-7, Jun 1937
 Time 28:54, Nov 30, 1936

*Last of the Lowries
 Reviews:
 New York Times p. 15, May 7, 1927

*The Lone Star
 Reviews:
 Texas Monthly 7:124+, Aug 1979

*Lost Colony
 Reviews:
 Holiday 1:74-6, Jun 1946
 Life 7:58-9, Jul 31, 1939
 Magazine of Art 31:690-3+, Dec 1938
 New York Times X, p. 2, Jul 11, 1937
  X, p. 1, Aug 15, 1937
  p. 14, Jun 30, 1952
 Player's Magazine 16:10+, Apr 1940
 Reader's Digest 37:30, Jul 1940
 Saturday Review 39:31, Aug 4, 1956
 Theatre Arts 23:518-22, Jul 1939
  36:72-3, Jul 1952
  40:69-70+, Jul 1956
 Time 34:48, Jul 10, 1939

Native Son (with Richard Wright. Based on Richard Wright's novel)
 Productions:
 Opened March 24, 1941 for 114 performances.
 Opened October 23, 1942 for 84 performances.
 (Off Off Broadway) October 19, 1973 (Players' Workshop).
 (Off Off Broadway) March 7, 1978 for 16 performances (Perry
  St. Theater).
 Reviews:
 Catholic World 153:217, May 1941

Commonweal 33:622, Apr 11, 1941
Independent Woman 21:378, Dec 1942
Life 10:94-6, Apr 7, 1941
Nation 152:417, Apr 5, 1941
New Republic 104:468-9, Apr 7, 1941
New York Theatre Critics' Reviews 1941:349
New York Times p. 26, Mar 25, 1941
      IX, p. 1, Mar 30, 1941
      IX, p. 1, Apr 6, 1941
      p. 10, Oct 24, 1942
      VIII, p. 1, Nov 1, 1942
      p. 50, Mar 28, 1978
Theatre Arts 25:329-32, May 1941
      25:467-70, Jun 1941
      26:744, Dec 1942
Time 37:76, Apr 7, 1941

Peer Gynt (Adapted from Henrik Ibsen's play)
Productions:
  Opened January 28, 1951 for 32 performances.
Reviews:
  Catholic World 172:464, Mar 1951
  Commonweal 53:468-9, Feb 16, 1951
  Nation 172:139-40, Feb 10, 1951
  New Republic 124:22-3, Mar 5, 1951
  New York Theatre Critics' Reviews 1951:373
  New York Times II, p. 3, Jan 21, 1951
      p. 15, Jan 29, 1951
      II, p. 1, Feb 4, 1951
  New Yorker 26:61, Feb 10, 1951
  School and Society 73:184, Mar 24, 1951
  Theatre Arts 35:14, Apr 1951

The Potter's Field (see Roll, Sweet Chariot)

Roll, Sweet Chariot
Productions:
  Opened October 2, 1934 for 7 performances.
Reviews:
  New York Times IX, p. 1, Sep 30, 1934
      p. 24, Oct 3, 1934
      X, p. 1, Oct 14, 1934
  Stage 12:5, Nov 1934
  Theatre Arts 18:813-14, Nov 1934
  Vanity Fair 43:46, Dec 1934

*Salvation on a String
Reviews:
  America 91:425, Jul 24, 1954
  New York Times p. 23, Jul 7, 1954

Saturday Night
    Productions:
        (Off Broadway) Season of 1940-41.
    No Reviews.

*Shroud My Body Down
    Reviews:
        New York Times II, p. 1, Dec 9, 1934
        Theatre Arts 19:311, Apr 1935
                    19:961-2, Dec 1935

*Texas
    Reviews:
        Texas Monthly 7:124+, Aug 1979

*Tread the Green Grass
    Reviews:
        New York Times IX, p. 1, Jul 24, 1932
                        p. 19, Apr 21, 1950
        Player's Magazine 9:10, Sep-Oct 1932
        Theatre Arts 16:1003, Dec 1932

Unto Such Glory
    Productions:
        Opened May 6, 1937 for 10 performances (Federal Theatre
            Project).
        Season of 1937-38 in repertory for 22 performances (Federal
            Theatre Project).
    Reviews:
        New York Times p. 14, Jan 13, 1936
                        p. 28, May 7, 1937
        Newsweek 9:29, May 22, 1937

*Wilderness Road
    Reviews:
        New York Times p. 43, Jun 19, 1955
                        p. 17, Jun 30, 1955
                        p. 20, Jun 30, 1955
        Saturday Review 39:30, Aug 4, 1956

GUARE, JOHN

Bosoms and Neglect
    Productions:
        Opened May 3, 1979 for 4 performances.
    Reviews:
        Maclean's 93:46, Aug 4, 1980
        New York Magazine 12:77, May 21, 1979
        New York Theatre Critics' Reviews 1979:263
        New York Times III, p. 3, May 4, 1979

II, p. 5, May 13, 1979
p. 63, Oct 14, 1979
New Yorker 55:83, May 14, 1979
Newsweek 93:85-6, May 14, 1979
Saturday Review 6:40, Jul 7, 1979

Cop-Out (consists of Home Fires and Cop Out)
Productions:
Opened April 7, 1969 for 8 performances.
Reviews:
New York Theatre Critics' Reviews 1969:310
New York Times p. 42, Apr 8, 1969
II, p. 1, Apr 20, 1969
New Yorker 45:98, Apr 19, 1969

A Day for Surprises
Productions:
(Off Off Broadway) June 13, 1975 (Greenwich Mews Theater).
(Off Off Broadway) September 15, 1978 (Gene Frankel).
No Reviews.

Gardenia
Productions:
(Off Broadway) April 13, 1982 for 48 performances (Manhattan Theater Club).
Reviews:
New Republic 186:24-5, May 19, 1982
New York Magazine 15:75-6, May 10, 1982
New York Theatre Critics' Reviews 1982:270
New York Times III, p. 20, Apr 29, 1982
II, p. 5, May 2, 1982
New Yorker 58:148, May 10, 1982
Newsweek 99:89, May 10, 1982

Home Fires
Productions:
(Off Off Broadway) Season of 1979-80 (Soho Repertory).
See also Cop-Out.
Reviews:
New York Times p. 42, Apr 8, 1969
See also Cop-Out.

House of Blue Leaves
Productions:
(Off Broadway) February 10, 1971 for 337 performances.
Reviews:
Nation 212:285-6, Mar 1, 1971
New York Theatre Critics' Reviews 1971:354
New York Times p. 54, Feb 11, 1971
II, p. 9, Feb 21, 1971
II, p. 3, Apr 4, 1971

New Yorker 47:90, Feb 20, 1971
Saturday Review 54:10, Mar 20, 1971

In Fireworks Lie Secret Codes
    Productions:
        (Off Off Broadway) May 26, 1980 (Actors Studio).
        (Off Broadway) March 5, 1981 for 37 performances, as part
        of a bill called One Act Play Festival.
    Reviews:
        New York Times III, p. 5, Mar 6, 1981
        New Yorker 57:66, Mar 16, 1981

Landscape of the Body
    Productions:
        (Off Broadway) September 27, 1977 for 64 performances.
    Reviews:
        Nation 225:505, Nov 12, 1977
        New York Magazine 10:94+, Oct 31, 1977
        New York Theatre Critics' Reviews 1977:128
        New York Times III, p. 17, Oct 13, 1977
                        II, p. 5, Oct 23, 1977
        New Yorker 53:144, Oct 24, 1977
        Newsweek 90:86, Oct 24, 1977

The Loveliest Afternoon of the Year
    Productions:
        (Off Off Broadway) August 1977 (Academy Arts Theater Co.).
        (Off Off Broadway) Season of 1978-79 (Lion Theater Co.).
        (Off Off Broadway) May 18, 1978 (Theater of the Riverside
        Church).
        (Off Off Broadway) July-August 1980 as part of a bill called
        A Company in Progress (Shelter West).
    No Reviews.

Lydie Breeze
    Productions:
        (Off Broadway) February 25, 1982 for 29 performances.
    Reviews:
        Nation 234:409-10, Apr 3, 1982
        New Republic 18:26-7, Mar 24, 1982
        New York Magazine 15:81, Mar 8, 1982
        New York Theatre Critics' Reviews 1982:344
        New York Times III, p. 3, Feb 26, 1982
                        II, p. 5, May 2, 1982
        New Yorker 58:96+, Mar 8, 1982
                   58:33-5, Mar 15, 1982
        Newsweek 99:94, Mar 8, 1982
        Time 119:86, Mar 8, 1982

Marco Polo Sings a Solo
    Productions:
        (Off Broadway) January 12, 1977 for 64 performances.

Reviews:
New York Magazine 10:62, Feb 21, 1977
New York Theatre Critics' Reviews 1977:344
New York Times p. 30, Feb 7, 1977
    II, p. 3, Feb 20, 1977
    II, p. 3, Mar 6, 1977
New Yorker 52:53-4, Feb 14, 1977
Newsweek 89:66+, Feb 14, 1977
Time 109:57, Feb 21, 1977

Muzeeka
Productions:
(Off Broadway) April 28, 1968 for 65 performances.
Reviews:
Commonweal 88:384, Jun 14, 1968
New York Times p. 47, Apr 29, 1968
    p. 55, Jun 3, 1968
New Yorker 44:91-2, May 11, 1968

Rich & Famous
Productions:
(Off Broadway) January 13, 1976 for 78 performances.
Reviews:
America 134:208, Mar 13, 1976
Los Angeles 27:380+, Aug 1982
Nation 222:318, Mar 13, 1976
New Republic 174:28-9, Mar 13, 1976
New York Magazine 9:77, Mar 8, 1976
New York Theatre Critics' Reviews 1976:332
New York Times p. 15, Feb 20, 1976
    II, p. 5, Feb 29, 1976
New Yorker 52:76-7, Mar 1, 1976
Newsweek 87:57, Mar 1, 1976
Time 107:51, Mar 1, 1976

Something I'll Tell You Tuesday
Productions:
(Off Off Broadway) October 13, 1977 (Academy Arts Theater
Co.).
(Off Off Broadway) Season of 1978-79 (Lion Theater Co.).
No Reviews.

GURNEY, A. R., JR.

Children (Based on John Cheever's "Goodbye, My Brother")
Productions:
(Off Off Broadway) October 20, 1976 (Manhattan Theater Club).
Reviews:
Nation 223:509-10, Nov 13, 1976
New York Theatre Critics' Reviews 1976:94

New York Times p. 47, Oct 26, 1976
III, p. 3, Nov 12, 1976
New Yorker 52:167, Nov 8, 1976
Newsweek 88:109, Nov 8, 1976

The David Show
Productions:
(Off Broadway) October 31, 1968 for one performance.
(Off Broadway) June 10, 1969 for 24 performances as part of
a bill called Tonight in Living Color.
Reviews:
New York Times p. 34, Nov 1, 1968
p. 27, Nov 2, 1968
p. 43, Jun 11, 1969
New Yorker 44:115-16, Nov 9, 1968

The Dining Room
Productions:
(Off Broadway) February 24, 1982 for 131+ performances (Play-
wrights Horizons, still running June 1, 1982).
Reviews:
Commonweal 109:243-4, Apr 23, 1982
New Republic 186:25-8, May 12, 1982
New York Magazine 15:81-2, Mar 8, 1982
New York Theatre Critics' Reviews 1982:352
New York Times III, p. 15, Feb 15, 1982
III, p. 15, Feb 25, 1982
III, p. 17, Apr 29, 1982
New Yorker 58:94+, Mar 1, 1982
Newsweek 99:64, Mar 15, 1982
Time 119:79, Mar 22, 1982

The Golden Fleece
Productions:
(Off Broadway) June 10, 1969 for 24 performances as part of
a bill called Tonight in Living Color.
(Off Off Broadway) January 9, 1976 (Hartley House).
(Off Off Broadway) February 9, 1981 (Quaigh Theater).
Reviews:
New York Times p. 43, Jun 11, 1969

The Love Course
Productions:
(Off Off Broadway) June 18, 1976 (York Players).
No Reviews.

The Middle Ages
Productions:
(Off Off Broadway) March 1982 (Ark Theater Co.).
Reviews:
New York Times p. 64, Mar 14, 1982
New Yorker 58:165, Apr 5, 1982

The Problem
    Productions:
        (Off Off Broadway) January 19, 1978 for 12 performances
           (IRT).
    No Reviews.

The Rape of Bunny Stunte
    Productions:
        (Off Off Broadway) December 1975 (TOSOS).
    No Reviews.

Scenes from American Life
    Productions:
        (Off Broadway) March 25, 1971 for 30 performances.
        (Off Off Broadway) November 4, 1979 (Urban Arts Corps.).
    Reviews:
        New York Theatre Critics' Reviews 1971:271
        New York Times p. 33, Mar 26, 1971
        New Yorker 47:95-7, Apr 3, 1971

Tonight in Living Color   (see The Golden Fleece and The David
    Show)

The Wayside Motor Inn
    Productions:
        (Off Off Broadway) November 2, 1977 for 20 performances
           (Manhattan Theater Club).
    Reviews:
        Nation 225:604-5, Dec 3, 1977
        New York Times p. 13, Nov 12, 1977
        New Yorker 53:143-4, Nov 21, 1977

What I Did Last Summer
    Productions:
        (Off Off Broadway) December 7, 1981 (Circle Repertory Proj-
           ects).
    No Reviews.

Who Killed Richard Cory?
    Productions:
        (Off Broadway) March 10, 1976 for 31 performances.
    Reviews:
        Los Angeles 24:316, Nov 1979
        New York Times p. 25, Mar 12, 1976

HACKETT, ALBERT

Bridal Wise (with Frances Goodrich)
    Productions:
        Opened May 30, 1932 for 128 performances.

Reviews:
Catholic World 135:464-5, Jul 1932
Commonweal 16:188, Jun 15, 1932
New York Times p. 15, May 31, 1932
Stage 9:2-3, Jul 1932

The Diary of Anne Frank   (see entry under Goodrich, Frances)

The Great Big Doorstep   (see entry under Goodrich, Frances)

Up Pops the Devil (with Frances Goodrich)
    Productions:
        Opened September 1, 1930 for 148 performances.
    Reviews:
        Arts and Decoration 34:96, Nov 1930
        Catholic World 132:205, Nov 1930
        Drama 21:15, Nov 1930
        Life (NY) 96:16, Sep 19, 1930
        National Magazine 59:107, Nov 1930
        New York Times p. 19, Sep 2, 1930
                      VIII, p. 1, Sep 14, 1930
        Outlook 156:113, Sep 17, 1930
        Theatre Magazine 52:25-6, Nov 1930
        Vogue 76:100, Oct 27, 1930

Western Union   (see entry under Goodrich, Frances)

HAGAN, JAMES

Guns
    Productions:
        Opened August 6, 1928 for 48 performances.
    Reviews:
        New York Times p. 25, Aug 7, 1928

Mid-West
    Productions:
        Opened January 7, 1936 for 22 performances.
    Reviews:
        Commonweal 23:356, Jan 24, 1936
        Literary Digest 121:19, Jan 18, 1936
        Nation 142:112, Jan 22, 1936
        New York Times p. 21, Jan 2, 1936
                      IX, p. 3, Jan 5, 1936
                      p. 22, Jan 8, 1936
        Theatre Arts 20:175-6, Mar 1936

One Sunday Afternoon
    Productions:
        Opened February 15, 1933 for 322 performances.

(Off Off Broadway) August 1974 (Manhattan Theater Club).
Reviews:
    Arts and Decoration 38:58, Apr 1933
    Catholic World 137-38, Apr 1933
    Commonweal 17:610, Mar 29, 1933
    Nation 136:272, Mar 8, 1933
    New Outlook 161:47, Apr 1933
    New York Times p. 23, Feb 16, 1933
                IX, p. 2, Mar 26, 1933
                 X, p. 2, Sep 17, 1933
                    p. 25, Aug 13, 1974
    Player's Magazine 9:25, May-Jun 1933
    Stage 10:28-9, Apr 1933
    Theatre Arts 17:262-4, Apr 1933
    Vanity Fair 40:60, May 1933
    Vogue 81:86, Apr 15, 1933

HAINES, WILLIAM WISTER

Command Decision
Productions:
    Opened October 1, 1947 for 408 performances.
Reviews:
    Catholic World 166:170, Nov 1947
    Commonweal 47:16, Oct 17, 1947
    Forum 108:368-70, Dec 1947
    Life 23:107-8+, Oct 20, 1947
    Nation 165:480-1, Nov 1, 1947
    New Republic 117:36, Oct 13, 1947
    New York Theatre Critics' Reviews 1947:328
    New York Times p. 59, Sep 21, 1947
                VI, p. 30, Sep 28, 1947
                   p. 30, Oct 2, 1947
                II, p. 1, Oct 12, 1947
                II, p. 3, Nov 23, 1947
    New Yorker 23:50+, Oct 11, 1947
    Newsweek 30:80, Oct 13, 1947
    Saturday Review 30:30-3, Oct 25, 1947
    School and Society 66:326-7, Oct 25, 1947
    Theatre Arts 31:13-14, 60, Dec 1947
                32:30, Apr 1948
    Time 50:70, Oct 13, 1947
    Vogue 110:112, Nov 15, 1947

HANLEY, WILLIAM

Mrs. Dally
Productions:
    Opened September 22, 1965 for 53 performances.

Reviews:
America 113:508, Oct 30, 1965
Commonweal 83:61-2, Oct 15, 1965
New York Theatre Critics' Reviews 1965:270
New York Times p. 5, Sep 25, 1965
New Yorker 41:176, Oct 2, 1965
Newsweek 66:94, Oct 4, 1965
Saturday Review 48:34, Oct 9, 1965
Time 86:67, Oct 1, 1965
See also Mrs. Dally Has a Lover

Mrs. Dally Has a Lover
Productions:
(Off Broadway) October 1, 1962 for 48 performances.
(Off Off Broadway) Season of 1970-71 (Cubiculo).
(Off Off Broadway) Season of 1974-75 (Corner Loft Theater).
Reviews:
Commonweal 77:123, October 26, 1962
New York Times p. 47, Oct 2, 1962
New Yorker 38:183, Oct 13, 1962
See also Mrs. Dally

Slow Dance on the Killing Ground
Productions:
Opened November 30, 1964 for 88 performances.
(Off Broadway) May 13, 1970 for 36 performances.
Reviews:
America 113:508, Oct 30, 1965
Commonweal 81:485-6, Jan 8, 1965
        83:61-2, Oct 15, 1965
Life (NY) 58:10, Jan 15, 1965
Nation 199:523-4, Dec 28, 1964
New Republic 152:32, Jan 23, 1965
New York Theatre Critics' Reviews 1964:127
New York Times p. 50, Dec 1, 1964
        p. 56, Dec 2, 1964
        II, p. 5, Dec 13, 1964
        p. 43, May 14, 1970
        p. 55, Jun 16, 1970
New Yorker 41:176, Oct 2, 1965
Newsweek 64:84+, Dec 14, 1964
        66:94, Oct 4, 1965
Saturday Review 47:24-5, Dec 19, 1964
        48:34, Oct 9, 1965
Time 84:73, Dec 11, 1964
        86:67, Oct 1, 1965
Vogue 145:27, Jan 15, 1965

Whisper into My Good Ear
Productions:
(Off Broadway) October 1, 1962 for 48 performances.

Reviews:
Commonweal 77:123, Oct 26, 1962
New York Times p. 47, Oct 2, 1962
New Yorker 38:182, Oct 13, 1962

HANSBERRY, LORRAINE

Les Blancs (Final text adapted by Robert Nemiroff)
Productions:
Opened November 15, 1970 for 40 performances.
Reviews:
Commonweal 93:397, Jan 22, 1971
Nation 211:573, Nov 30, 1970
211:606, Dec 7, 1970
New York Theatre Critics' Reviews 1970:152, 154
New York Times p. 48, Nov 16, 1970
II, p. 3, Nov 29, 1970
New Yorker 46:104, Nov 21, 1970
Newsweek 76:98, Nov 30, 1970

A Raisin in the Sun
Productions:
Opened March 11, 1959 for 530 performances.
(Off Off Broadway) January 19, 1979 (New Federal Theater).
Reviews:
America 101:286-7, May 2, 1959
Catholic World 189:159, May 1959
190:31-5, Oct 1959
Commentary 27:527-30, Jun 1959
Commonweal 70:81, Apr 17, 1959
Life 46:137-8, Apr 27, 1959
Nation 188:301-2, Apr 4, 1959
New Republic 140:21, Apr 13, 1959
New York Theatre Critics' Reviews 1959:344
New York Times II, p. 3, Mar 8, 1959
p. 27, Mar 12, 1959
p. 25, Mar 13, 1959
II, p. 1, Mar 29, 1959
p. 32, Aug 5, 1959
p. 19, Jul 27, 1965
III, p. 17, Jan 24, 1979
New Yorker 35:100-2, Mar 21, 1959
Newsweek 53:76, Mar 23, 1959
Reporter 20:34-5, Apr 16, 1959
Saturday Review 42:28, Apr 4, 1959
Theatre Arts 43:22-3, May 1959
43:58-61, Jul 1959
Time 73:58+, Mar 23, 1959

The Sign in Sidney Brustein's Window
Productions:

Opened October 15, 1964 for 101 performances.
Opened January 26, 1972 for 5 performances.
(Off Off Broadway) August 27, 1980 (Shelter West).
Reviews:
America 111:758, Dec 5, 1964
Commonweal 81:197, Nov 6, 1964
Nation 199:340, Nov 9, 1964
National Review 17:250, Mar 23, 1965
New York Theatre Critics' Reviews 1964:190
                                   1972:382
New York Times II, p. 1, Oct 11, 1964
              p. 32, Oct 16, 1964
              II, p. 1, Nov 1, 1964
              II, p. 7, Jun 27, 1971
              p. 44, Jan 27, 1972
New Yorker 40:93, Oct 24, 1964
Newsweek 64:101, Oct 26, 1964
Saturday Review 47:31-, Oct 31, 1964
Time 84:67, Oct 23, 1964

To Be Young, Gifted and Black (Adapted by Robert Nemiroff)
    Productions:
    (Off Broadway) January 2, 1969 for 380 performances.
    (Off Off Broadway) Season of 1973-74 (Lincoln Center Per-
        forming Arts).
    (Off Off Broadway) November 27, 1975 (Afro American Studio).
    (Off Off Broadway) May 21, 1976 (Afro American Studio).
    Reviews:
    Commonweal 90:542-3, Sep 5, 1969
    Nation 208:548, Apr 28, 1969
    New York Times p. 15, Jan 3, 1969
                  II, p. 1, May 25, 1969
                  p. 36, Sep 22, 1969

The World of Lorraine Hansberry (see To Be Young, Gifted and
    Black)

HARRIGAN, EDWARD

Mulligan Guard Ball
    Productions:
    (Off Off Broadway) January 20, 1977 (American Theater Co.).
    No Reviews.

HART, MOSS

The American Way (see entry under Kaufman, George S.)

Christopher Blake
    Productions:

Opened November 30, 1946 for 114 performances.
Reviews:
Catholic World 164:357-8, Jan 1947
Commonweal 45:255, Dec 20, 1946
Life (NY) 22:95-6+, Jan 13, 1947
Nation 163:738, Dec 21, 1946
New Republic 115:824, Dec 16, 1946
New York Theatre Critics' Reviews 1946:233
New York Times p. 33, Dec 2, 1946
          II, p. 5, Dec 8, 1946
New Yorker 22:67-9, Dec 7, 1946
Newsweek 28:92, Dec 9, 1946
Theatre Arts 31:12-13+, Feb 1947
Time 48:83, Dec 9, 1946

The Climate of Eden (Based on Edgar Mittelholzer's novel Shadows
    Move Among Them)
Productions:
Opened November 14, 1952 for 20 performances.
(Off Off Broadway) February 18, 1976 (Quaigh Theater).
Reviews:
Commonweal 57:223, Dec 5, 1952
Nation 175:473, Nov 22, 1952
New York Theatre Critics' Reviews 1952:204
New York Times II, p. 1, Nov 2, 1952
          p. 20, Nov 7, 1952
          II, p. 1, Nov 16, 1952
          p. 11, Nov 21, 1953
New Yorker 28:69, Nov 15, 1952
Newsweek 40:74, Nov 17, 1952
Saturday Review 35:37-8, Nov 22, 1952
Theatre Arts 37:23-4, Jan 1953
Time 60:102+, Nov 17, 1952

The Fabulous Invalid (with George S. Kaufman)
Productions:
Opened October 8, 1938 for 65 performances.
Reviews:
Catholic World 148:210-11, Nov 1938
Commonweal 28:677, Oct 21, 1938
Independent Woman 17:347, Nov 1938
Nation 147:432, Oct 22, 1938
New Republic 96:334, Oct 26, 1938
New York Times p. 15, Oct 10, 1938
          IX, p. 1, Oct 16, 1938
          IX, p. 3, Oct 1930
          p. 23, Jan 26, 1950
Newsweek 12:34, Oct 24, 1938
Publishers' Weekly 134:1581, Oct 29, 1938
Stage 16:7+, Nov 1938
      16:34, Nov 1938

Theatre Arts 22:862-4, Dec 1938
Time 32:50, Oct 17, 1938

George Washington Slept Here (see entry under Kaufman, George
    S.)

Light Up the Sky
  Productions:
    Opened November 18, 1948 for 216 performances.
  Reviews:
    Catholic World 168:324, Jan 1949
    Commonweal 49:196, Dec 3, 1948
    Forum 111:92, Feb 1949
    Life 25:115-16+, Dec 6, 1948
    Nation 167:674, Dec 11, 1948
    New Republic 119:37-8, Dec 6, 1948
    New York Theatre Critics' Reviews 1948:148
    New York Times p. 34, Nov 19, 1948
         II, p. 5, Dec 5, 1948
         II, p. 1, Jan 2, 1949
    New Yorker 24:55, Nov 27, 1948
    Newsweek 32:82, Nov 29, 1948
    Saturday Review 31:24-5, Dec 11, 1948
    School and Society 69:154, Feb 26, 1949
    Time 52:78, Nov 29, 1948
         54:59, Aug 8, 1949
    Vogue 113:116, Jan 1949

The Man Who Came to Dinner (with George S. Kaufman)
  Productions:
    Opened October 16, 1939 for 739 performances.
    (Off Off Broadway) October 1975 (Drama Comm. Repertory
        Theater).
    Opened June 26, 1980 for 85 performances.
  Reviews:
    Catholic World 150:339-40, Dec 1939
    Commonweal 31:47, Nov 3, 1939
    Life 7:88-9, Oct 30, 1939
    Los Angeles 24:202+, Jan 1979
    Nation 149:474-5, Oct 28, 1939
    New Republic 100:368, Nov 1, 1939
    New West 4:75+, Jan 1, 1979
    New York Magazine 13:51, Jul 21, 1980
    New York Theatre Critics' Reviews 1940:472
                                      1941:492
                                      1980:207
    New York Times p. 21, Sep 26, 1939
         IX, p. 2, Oct 1, 1939
         p. 31, Oct 17, 1939
         IX, p. 1, Oct 22, 1939
         IX, p. 1, Oct 29, 1939
         p. 19, Feb 10, 1940

IX, p. 3, Feb 18, 1940
p. 17, Feb 26, 1941
IV, p. 2, Mar 2, 1941
IX, p. 1, Mar 23, 1941
p. 13, Jul 29, 1941
IX, p. 4, Dec 14, 1941
XXIII, p. 6, Dec 25, 1977
III, p. 3, Jun 27, 1980
II, p. 1, Jul 6, 1980
III, p. 5, Sep 12, 1980
New Yorker 56:58, Jul 7, 1980
Newsweek 14:38, Oct 30, 1939
Stage 1:18, Nov 1940
1:19, Dec 1940
1:13, Jan 1941
Theatre Arts 23:770, 788-98, Nov 1939
23:851-2+, Dec 1939
24:407, Jun 1940
Time 34:42, Oct 30, 1939
35:50, Jan 22, 1940
38:31, Aug 11, 1941
116:64, Jul 28, 1980
Vogue 94:63-4, Nov 15, 1939

Merrily We Roll Along   (see entry under Kaufman, George S.)

Once in a Lifetime   (see entry under Kaufman, George S.)

Winged Victory
    Productions:
        Opened November 20, 1943 for 212 performances.
    Reviews:
        American Magazine 137:28-9, Jun 1944
        Catholic World 158:392, Jan 1944
        Commonweal 39:204-5, Dec 10, 1943
        Life 15:58-64, Nov 29, 1943
        Nation 157:675, Dec 4, 1943
        New Republic 109:808, Dec 4, 1943
        New York Theatre Critics' Reviews 1943:216
        New York Times p. 22, Nov 3, 1943
                    VI, p. 8, Nov 7, 1943
                    p. 56, Nov 21, 1943
                    p. 24, Nov 22, 1943
                    II, p. 1, Nov 28, 1943
        New Yorker 19:51-2, Dec 4, 1943
        Newsweek 22:86, Nov 29, 1943
        Theatre Arts 27:723, Dec 1943
                    28:6-8, Jan 1944
                    28:88+, Feb 1944
        Time 42:43-4, Nov 29, 1943
                45:84, Apr 16, 1945

You Can't Take It with You (with George S. Kaufman)
    Productions:
        Opened December 14, 1936 for 837 performances.
        Opened March 26, 1945 for 17 performances.
        Opened November 23, 1965 for 255 performances.
        Opened February 10, 1967 for 16 performances (APA Repertory
        Co.).
    Reviews:
        America 113:762-3, Dec 11, 1965
        Catholic World 144:597-8, Feb 1937
        Commonweal 25:249, Dec 25, 1936
        Life 2:54-5, Jun 28, 1937
            56:16, Dec 17, 1965
        Literary Digest 122:22, Dec 26, 1936
        Nation 143:770, Dec 26, 1936
            201:484, Dec 13, 1965
        New Republic 89:273, Dec 30, 1936
            153:28, Dec 8, 1965
        New York Theatre Critics' Reviews 1965:248
        New York Times p. 30, Dec 1, 1936
                    XII, p. 6, Dec 6, 1936
                    p. 31, Dec 15, 1936
                    XI, p. 3, Dec 20, 1936
                    X, p. 1, Aug 29, 1937
                    X, p. 3, Oct 31, 1937
                    X, p. 1, Jan 9, 1938
                    X, p. 1, Jan 16, 1938
                    p. 23, Mar 27, 1945
                    p. 8, Apr 7, 1951
                    II, p. 1, Nov 21, 1965
                    p. 32, Nov 24, 1965
                    p. 66, Nov 25, 1965
                    II, p. 5, Dec 5, 1965
        Newsweek 8:38, Dec 26, 1936
            25:87, Apr 9, 1945
        Saturday Review 15:3-4, May 8, 1937
        Stage 14:52-3, Jan 1937
            14:41-4, May 1937
        Theatre Arts 21:96-7, Feb 1937
        Time 28:33, Dec 28, 1936
        Vogue 89:69, Jan 15, 1937

HAWTHORNE, RUTH

Mrs. Partridge Presents (see entry under Kennedy, Mary)

Queen Bee (with Louise Fox Connell)
    Productions:
        Opened November 12, 1929 for 21 performances.
    Reviews:
        New York Times p. 25, Nov 13, 1929

HAYDEN, JOHN

Lost Horizons (Based on a play by Harry Segall)
  Productions:
    Opened October 15, 1934 for 56 performances.
  Reviews:
    Catholic World 140:338, Dec 1934
    Commonweal 20:618, Oct 26, 1934
    Literary Digest 118:24, Oct 27, 1934
    Nation 139:517, Oct 31, 1934
    New Republic 80:341, Oct 31, 1934
    New York Times p. 31, Oct 16, 1934
                  IX, p. 1, Oct 21, 1934
    Theatre Arts 18:903-4, Dec 1934
    Time 24:44, Oct 29, 1934

HAYES, ALFRED

The Girl on the Via Flaminia
  Productions:
    Opened February 9, 1954 for 111 performances.
  Reviews:
    America 90:581, Feb 27, 1954
    Catholic World 179:69, Apr 1954
    Life 36:57-8+, Mar 15, 1954
    Nation 178:184+, Feb 27, 1954
    New Republic 130:21, May 3, 1954
    New York Theatre Critics' Reviews 1954:349
    New York Times p. 37, Feb 10, 1954
                  II, p. 3, May 16, 1954
                  p. 26, Oct 13, 1954
    New Yorker 30:65, Feb 20, 1954
    Saturday Review 37:25, Mar 6, 1954
    Theatre Arts 38:22, Jun 1954
    Time 63:74, Apr 12, 1954

Journeyman (with Leon Alexander. Based on Erskine Caldwell's
    novel)
  Productions:
    Opened January 29, 1938 for 41 performances.
  Reviews:
    Nation 146:190, Feb 12, 1938
    New York Times p. 14, Jan 31, 1938
    One Act Play Magazine 1:945, Feb 1938

HAYES, JOSEPH

Calculated Risk (Based on a play by George Ross and Campbell
    Singer)
  Productions:

Opened October 31, 1962 for 221 performances.
Reviews:
Commonweal 77:280, Dec 7, 1962
New York Theatre Critics' Reviews 1962:214
New York Times p. 33, Oct 17, 1962
         p. 35, Nov 1, 1962
New Yorker 38:146, Nov 10, 1962
Newsweek 60:62, Nov 12, 1962
Theatre Arts 46:12-3, Dec 1962
Time 80:64, Nov 9, 1962

The Desperate Hours (Based on his novel)
Productions:
Opened February 10, 1955 for 212 performances.
(Off Off Broadway) December 5, 1974 (Equity Library Theater).
Reviews:
America 92:685-6, Mar 26, 1955
Catholic World 181:65-6, Apr 1955
Life 38:75-6+, Feb 28, 1955
Nation 180:186, Feb 26, 1955
New Republic 132:19-20, Mar 7, 1955
New York Theatre Critics' Reviews 1955:370
New York Times II, p. 1, Jan 30, 1955
         p. 20, Feb 11, 1955
         II, p. 1, Feb 20, 1955
         II, p. 3, May 1, 1955
         II, p. 3, Jun 2, 1955
         p. 22, Dec 7, 1974
New Yorker 31:76-7, Feb 19, 1955
Newsweek 45:90, Feb 21, 1955
Saturday Review 38:22, Feb 26, 1955
Theatre Arts 39:20-1, 24-5, Apr 1955
Time 65:54, Feb 21, 1955

*Is Anyone Listening?
Reviews:
Saturday Review 54:16, 38, Feb 20, 1971

Leaf and Bough
Productions:
Opened January 21, 1949 for 3 performances.
Reviews:
New York Theatre Critics' Reviews 1949:381
New York Times p. 10, Jan 22, 1949
New Yorker 24:42+, Jan 29, 1949
Newsweek 33:71, Jan 31, 1949
Saturday Review 31:24, Apr 3, 1948
Time 53:44, Jan 31, 1949

*Midnight Sun
Reviews:
New York Times p. 26, Nov 6, 1959

HECHT, BEN

The Egotist
Productions:
Opened December 25, 1922 for 48 performances.
Reviews:
New York Clipper 70:20, Jan 10, 1923
New York Times p. 12, Dec 27, 1922
Theatre Magazine 37:19, Mar 1923

A Flag Is Born
Productions:
Opened September 5, 1946 for 120 performances.
Reviews:
Catholic World 164:71, Oct 1946
Life 21:87-8, Sep 30, 1946
New Republic 115:351, Sep 23, 1946
New York Theatre Critics' Reviews 1946:348
New York Times p. 10, Sep 7, 1946
II, p. 21, Sep 15, 1946
p. 19, Oct 16, 1946
New Yorker 22:48+, Sep 14, 1946
Newsweek 28:92, Sep 16, 1946
30:74, Nov 10, 1947
Time 48:85, Sep 16, 1946

The Front Page (with Charles MacArthur)
Productions:
Opened August 14, 1928 for 276 performances.
Opened September 4, 1946 for 79 performances.
Opened May 10, 1969 for 64 performances.
Opened May 10, 1969 for 64 performances, closed June 5,
1969, and reopened.
Opened October 18, 1969 for 158 performances.
(Off Off Broadway) December 11, 1980 (Manhattan Punch Line).
Reviews:
America 120:673-4, Jun 7, 1969
121:434, Nov 8, 1969
127:470-1, Dec 2, 1972
American Mercury 15:251, Oct 1928
Catholic World 128:211-12, Nov 1928
164:72, Oct 1946
Commonweal 90:437-8, Jul 11, 1969
Dial 86:82-3, Jan 1929
Life (NY) 92:12, Aug 30, 1928
Life 21:78-80, Sep 23, 1946
Literary Digest 98:29, Sep 29, 1928
Nation 127:207, Aug 29, 1928
208:676, May 26, 1969
New Republic 56:73-4, Sep 5, 1928
115:351, Sep 23, 1946

New York Theatre Critics' Reviews 1946:355
                                             1969:287
New York Times p. 19, Aug 15, 1928
                VII, p. 1, Aug 26, 1928
                VIII, p. 4, Jan 6, 1929
                p. 27, Nov 12, 1937
                p. 22, Sep 5, 1946
                II, p. 21, Sep 15, 1946
                p. 85, Oct 20, 1968
                p. 52, May 12, 1969
                p. 54, May 12, 1969
                II, p. 1, May 25, 1969
                p. 86, Nov 2, 1969
                p. 67, Feb 2, 1970
                II, p. 10, Jul 30, 1972
                p. 24, Aug 9, 1972
                II, p. 3, Dec 10, 1972
                III, p. 15, Dec 23, 1980
                III, p. 31, Jun 10, 1982
New Yorker 22:46, Sep 14, 1946
           45:112, May 17, 1969
           44:160, Oct 19, 1968
Newsweek 28:92, Sep 16, 1946
         73:133, May 26, 1969
Outlook 149:705, Aug 29, 1928
Saturday Review 5:706, Feb 23, 1929
                29:24-6, Oct 26, 1946
Theatre Arts 12:701-6, Oct 1928
Theatre Magazine 48:24-6+, Aug 1928
                  48:40, Oct 1928
Time 48:85, Sep 16, 1946
     93:75, May 23, 1969
Vogue 72:94-5+, Oct 13, 1928

The Great Magoo (with Gene Fowler)
    Productions:
        Opened December 2, 1932 for 11 performances.
    Reviews:
        Nation 135:625-6, Dec 21, 1932
        New York Times IX, p. 2, Nov 27, 1932
                    p. 20, Dec 3, 1932
        Theatre Arts 17:112, Feb 1933
        Vanity Fair 39:41, Feb 1933

The Hero of Santa Maria (with Kenneth Goodman)
    Productions:
        Opened August 30, 1916 in repertory (Washington Square
           Players).
    Reviews:
        Dramatic Mirror 77:7, Feb 24, 1917
        New York Times p. 7, Feb 14, 1917
        Theatre Magazine 25:213+, Apr 1917

Ladies and Gentlemen   (see entry under MacArthur, Charles)

Lily of the Valley
    Productions:
        Opened January 26, 1942 for 8 performances.
    Reviews:
        Catholic World 154:732, Mar 1942
        Commonweal 35:418, Feb 13, 1942
        New Republic 106:204, Feb 9, 1942
        New York Theatre Critics' Reviews 1942:365
        New York Times p. 25, Jan 27, 1942
                        IX, p. 1, Feb 1, 1942
        Theatre Arts 26:225, Apr 1942

*Man Eating Tiger
    Reviews:
        New York Times VIII, p. 4, Sep 25, 1927

The Stork (Adapted from the play by Laszlo Fodor)
    Productions:
        Opened January 26, 1925 for 8 performances.
    Reviews:
        New York Times p. 14, Jan 27, 1925

Swan Song (with Charles MacArthur. Based on a story by Ramon
        Romero and Harriet Hinsdale)
    Productions:
        Opened May 15, 1946 for 158 performances.
    Reviews:
        Catholic World 163:360, Jul 1946
        New York Theatre Critics' Reviews 1946:386
        New York Times p. 29, May 16, 1946
        New Yorker 22:46-7, May 25, 1946
        Time 47:66, May 27, 1946

To Quito and Back
    Productions:
        Opened October 6, 1937 for 46 performances.
    Reviews:
        Catholic World 146:218-19, Nov 1937
        Commonweal 26:606, Oct 22, 1937
        Independent Woman 16:368, Nov 1937
        Life 3:120-22+, Oct 11, 1937
        Nation 145:412, Oct 16, 1937
        New Republic 92:342, Oct 27, 1937
        New York Times XI, p. 2, Sep 19, 1937
                        p. 29, Sep 21, 1937
                        XI, p. 3, Sep 26, 1937
                        p. 30, Oct 7, 1937
        Newsweek 10:25, Oct 18, 1937
        Theatre Arts 21:919, 20, Dec 1937
        Time 30:32+, Oct 18, 1937

20th Century (with Charles MacArthur)
  Productions:
    Opened December 29, 1932 for 152 performances.
  Reviews:
    Arts and Decoration 38:63, Mar 1933
    Catholic World 136:589, Feb 1933
                172:387-8, Feb 1951
    Commonweal 17:329, Jan 18, 1933
                53:349, Jan 12, 1951
    Christian Science Monitor Magazine p. 9, Dec 30, 1950
    Life 30:117-18+, Feb 19, 1951
    Nation 136:75, Jan 18, 1933
                172:18, Jan 6, 1951
    New Outlook 161:48, Feb 1933
    New Republic 124:22, Jan 8, 1951
    New York Theatre Critics' Reviews 1950:163
    New York Times p. 15, Dec 30, 1932
                IX, p. 3, Jan 1, 1933
                IX, p. 3, Jan 29, 1933
                IX, p. 1, Feb 12, 1933
                II, p. 4, Dec 24, 1950
                    p. 23, Dec 25, 1950
    New Yorker 26:54+, Jan 6, 1951
    Newsweek 37:80, Jan 22, 1951
    Saturday Review 34:25-7, Mar 24, 1951
    Stage 10:32-3, Feb 1933
    Theatre Arts 17:178, Mar 1933
                35:12, 22-3, Mar 1951
    Time 21:40, Jan 9, 1933
                57:30, Jan 8, 1951

Winkelberg
  Productions:
    (Off Broadway) Season of 1957-58.
  Reviews:
    New Republic 138:21, Feb 3, 1958
    New York Times II, p. 3, Jan 12, 1958
                p. 26, Jan 15, 1958
    Saturday Review 41:25, Feb 1, 1958

HEGGEN, THOMAS

Mister Roberts (see entry under Logan, Joshua)

HELLER, JOSEPH

*Catch-22
  Reviews:
    Intellectual Digest 4:55+, Oct 1973

New York Times p. 14, Jul 23, 1971
p. 55, Apr 29, 1976

We Bombed in New Haven

Productions:
Opened October 16, 1968 for 85 performances.
(Off Broadway) September 24, 1972 for one performance.
Reviews:
America 119:447, Nov 9, 1968
Life 64:14, Jan 12, 1968
Nation 206:26-7, Jan 1, 1968
207:477-8, Nov 4, 1968
New York Theatre Critics' Reviews 1968:206
New York Times II, p. 1, Dec 3, 1967
p. 58, Dec 7, 1967
II, p. 3, Dec 17, 1967
p. 49, Sep 10, 1968
p. 51, Oct 17, 1968
II, p. 1, Oct 27, 1968
p. 49, Sep 25, 1972
New Yorker 44:139, Oct 26, 1968
Newsweek 70:96, Dec 18, 1967
72:135, Oct 28, 1968
Reporter 38:44, Jan 25, 1968
Saturday Review 51:53, Nov 2, 1968
Time 90:87, Dec 15, 1967
92:69, Oct 25, 1968

HELLMAN, LILLIAN

Another Part of the Forest

Productions:
Opened November 20, 1946 for 182 performances.
Reviews:
Catholic World 164:360, Jan 1947
Commonweal 45:201, Dec 6, 1946
Life 21:71-2+, Dec 9, 1946
Nation 163:671, Dec 7, 1946
New Republic 115:822, Dec 16, 1946
New York Theatre Critics' Reviews 1946:247
New York Times II, p. 1, Nov 17, 1946
VI, p. 68, Nov 17, 1946
p. 42, Nov 21, 1946
II, p. 1, Dec 1, 1946
II, p. 3, Feb 16, 1947
p. 19, Oct 17, 1949
p. 34, Oct 18, 1949
p. 83, Nov 13, 1949
New Yorker 22:58+, Nov 30, 1946
Newsweek 28:94, Dec 14, 1946

Saturday Review 29:20-3, Dec 14, 1946
School and Society 65:251, Apr 5, 1947
Theatre Arts 31:14, 17, Jan 1947
Time 48:56, Dec 2, 1946

The Autumn Garden

Productions:
Opened March 7, 1951 for 101 performances.
(Off Off Broadway) April 17, 1975.

Reviews:
Catholic World 173:67, Apr 1951
Commonweal 53:645, Apr 6, 1951
Nation 172:257, Mar 17, 1951
New Republic 124:21-2, Mar 26, 1951
New York Theatre Critics' Reviews 1951:325
New York Times II, p. 1, Feb 25, 1951
                 p. 36, Mar 8, 1951
                 II, p. 1, Mar 18, 1951
                 p. 30, Apr 23, 1975
                 p. 52, Nov 16, 1976
                 II, p. 3, Nov 28, 1976
New Yorker 27:52+, Mar 17, 1951
Newsweek 37:84, Mar 19, 1951
Theatre Arts 35:18, May 1951
             35:17+, Sep 1951
Time 57:51, Mar 19, 1951

The Children's Hour

Productions:
Opened November 20, 1934 for 691 performances.
Opened December 18, 1952 for 189 performances.
(Off Off Broadway) March 28, 1976 (Drama Comm. Repertory
    Theater).

Reviews:
Catholic World 140:466-7, Jan 1935
               176:388, Feb 1953
Commonweal 57:377, Jan 16, 1953
Golden Book 21:28A, Feb 1935
Life 34:51+, Jan 19, 1953
Literary Digest 118:20, Dec 1, 1934
                120:20, Dec 28, 1935
Nation 139:656-7, Dec 5, 1934
       140:610, May 22, 1935
       176:18, Jan 3, 1953
New Republic 81:169, Dec 19, 1934
             128:30-1, Jan 5, 1953
New York Theatre Critics' Reviews 1952:151
New York Times p. 23, Nov 21, 1934
               X, p. 1, Dec 2, 1934
               IX, p. 3, Nov 17, 1935
               VI, p. 11, Dec 22, 1935

IX, p. 1, Jun 7, 1936
p. 27, Nov 13, 1936
XII, p. 2, Nov 29, 1936
II, p. 3, Dec 14, 1952
p. 35, Dec 19, 1952
II, p. 1, Dec 28, 1952
p. 39, Nov 10, 1953
p. 12, Jul 29, 1978
New Yorker 28:30, Jan 3, 1953
Newsweek 40:40, Dec 29, 1952
Saturday Review 11:523, Mar 2, 1935
11:528, Mar 16, 1935
36:30, Jan 10, 1953
School and Society 77:117-18, Feb 21, 1953
Stage 12:28-9, Jan 1935
Theatre Arts 19:13-15, Jan 1935
Time 24:24, Dec 3, 1934
60:55, Dec 29, 1952
Vanity Fair 43:37, Feb 1935

Days to Come
Productions:
Opened December 15, 1936 for 7 performances.
(Off Off Broadway) October 19, 1978 for 12 performances (WPA Theater).
Reviews:
Commonweal 25:276, Jan 1, 1937
Literary Digest 122:22, Dec 26, 1936
Nation 143:769-70, Dec 26, 1936
227:588, Nov 25, 1978
New Republic 89:274, Dec 30, 1936
New York Times XI, p. 4, Dec 13, 1936
p. 35, Dec 16, 1936

Ladies and Gentlemen (see Another Part of the Forest)

The Lark (Adapted from the play by Jean Anouilh)
Productions:
Opened November 17, 1955 for 229 performances.
(Off Off Broadway) November 10, 1975 (Theater Off Park).
Reviews:
America 90:420-1, Jan 23, 1954
94:363, Dec 24, 1955
95:109-10, Apr 28, 1956
Catholic World 182:308-9, Jan 1952
Commonweal 63:304, Dec 23, 1955
Holiday 19:77+, Mar 1956
Life 39:113-114+, Dec 12, 1955
Nation 181:485-6, Dec 3, 1955
New Republic 133:21, Dec 5, 1955
New York Theatre Critics' Reviews 1955:206

New York Times II, p. 1, Nov 13, 1955
                II, p. 1, Nov 27, 1955
New Yorker 31:112+, Dec 3, 1955
Newsweek 46:110, Nov 28, 1955
Reporter 13:31, Dec 29, 1955
Saturday Review 38:24, Feb 19, 1955
Theatre Arts 39:23, Apr 1955
            40:63-4+, Mar 1956
            40:8-10, May 1956
Time 66:76+, Nov 28, 1955

The Little Foxes
    Productions:
        Opened February 15, 1939 for 410 performances.
        Opened October 26, 1967 for 100 performances (Repertory Theatre of Lincoln Center).
        Opened May 7, 1981 for 126 performances.
    Reviews:
        America 117:723, Dec 9, 1967
                145:35, Jul 18-25, 1981
        Catholic World 149:87-8, Apr 1939
        Christian Century 85:332, Mar 13, 1968
        Commonweal 29:525, Mar 3, 1939
                    87:304-5, Dec 1, 1967
        Harper's Bazaar 80:220, Dec 1946
        Life 6:70-73, Mar 6, 1939
        Los Angeles 20:111, Jul 1975
                    26:338+, Nov 1981
        Nation 148:244, Feb 25, 1939
                232:770+, Jun 20, 1981
        New Leader 64:19-20, Jun 1, 1981
        New Republic 98:279, Apr 12, 1939
        New York Magazine 14:50, May 18, 1981
        New York Review of Books 20:33+, Sep 20, 1973
        New York Theatre Critics' Reviews 1940:490
                                          1967:237
                                          1981:228
        New York Times p. 16, Feb 16, 1939
                       IX, p. 1, Feb 26, 1939
                       VIII, p. 2, Nov 1, 1942
                       II, p. 1, Oct 22, 1967
                       p. 53, Oct 27, 1967
                       II, p. 1, Nov 5, 1967
                       p. 24, Jan 6, 1968
                       XXIII, p. 14, Mar 4, 1979
                       III, p. 3, May 8, 1981
                       II, p. 7, May 17, 1981
        New Yorker 43:162, Nov 4, 1967
                   57:142, May 18, 1981
        Newsweek 13:26, Feb 27, 1939
                 70:86, Nov 6, 1967
                 97:129, May 18, 1981

One Act Play Magazine 2:748-9, Feb 1939
People 15:149-51, Apr 6, 1981
      15:32-3, May 25, 1981
Reporter 38:36, Jan 11, 1968
Saturday Review 50:26, Nov 11, 1967
      8:86-7, Jul 1981
Stage 16:36-7+, Apr 1, 1939
Theatre Arts 23:244+, Apr 1939
Time 33:38+, Feb 27, 1939
      90:64+, Nov 3, 1967
      117:76-7, Mar 30, 1981
      117:81, May 18, 1981

Montserrat (Adapted from the French of Emmanuel Robles)
   Productions:
      Opened October 29, 1949 for 65 performances.
      (Off Broadway) Season of 1960-61.
   Reviews:
      America 104:577, Jan 28, 1961
      Catholic World 170:227-8, Dec 1949
      Commonweal 51:179-80, Nov 1949
      Forum 112:338-9, Dec 1949
      Nation 169:478, Nov 12, 1949
      New Republic 121:21-2, Dec 5, 1949
      New York Theatre Critics' Reviews 1949:244
      New York Times p. 21, Oct 31, 1949
                II, p. 3, May 11, 1952
                p. 34, May 26, 1954
                p. 30, Jan 9, 1961
      New Yorker 36:68-70, Jan 21, 1961
            25:62+, Nov 5, 1949
      Newsweek 34:80-1, Nov 7, 1949
      Saturday Review 32:53-4, Nov 19, 1949
      School and Society 71:25-6, Jan 14, 1950
      Theatre Arts 34:10, Jan 1950
      Time 54:79, Nov 7, 1949

My Mother, My Father and Me (Based on Burt Blechman's How
     Much?)
   Productions:
      Opened March 23, 1963 for 17 performances.
      (Off Off Broadway) January 3, 1980 for 16 performances (WPA
        Theater).
   Reviews:
      Nation 196:334, Apr 20, 1963
      New York Theatre Critics' Reviews 1963:302
      New York Times p. 5, Mar 25, 1963
                III, p. 17, Jan 10, 1980
      New Yorker 39:108, Mar 30, 1963
      Newsweek 61:85, Apr 8, 1963
      Reporter 28:48, Apr 25, 1963

Saturday Review 46:27, Apr 27, 1963
Theatre Arts 47:69-70, May 1963
Time 81:56, Apr 5, 1963

The Searching Wind
Productions:
Opened April 12, 1944 for 318 performances.
Reviews:
Catholic World 159:170-1, May 1944
Commonweal 40:40, Apr 28, 1944
Life 16:43-4+, May 1, 1944
Nation 158:494, Apr 22, 1944
New Republic 110:604, May 1, 1944
New York Theatre Critics' Reviews 1944:217
New York Times II, p. 1, Apr 9, 1944
             p. 25, Apr 13, 1944
             II, p. 1, Apr 23, 1944
New York Times Magazine p. 19, Apr 23, 1944
New Yorker 20:42+, Apr 22, 1944
Newsweek 23:86+, Apr 24, 1944
Quarterly Journal of Speech 31:22-8, Feb 1945
Theatre Arts 28:331-3, Jun 1944
Time 43:72, Apr 24, 1944

Toys in the Attic
Productions:
Opened February 25, 1960 for 556 performances.
(Off Off Broadway) May 1978 (Theater Three).
Reviews:
America 103:323, May 28, 1960
Christian Century 77:511, Apr 27, 1960
Life 48:53-4+, Apr 4, 1960
Nation 190:261, Mar 19, 1960
New Republic 142:22, Mar 14, 1960
New York Theatre Critics' Reviews 1960:345
New York Times II, p. 3, Feb 21, 1960
             p. 23, Feb 26, 1960
             II, p. 1, Mar 6, 1960
             p. 12, Mar 4, 1978
New Yorker 36:124-5, Mar 5, 1960
Newsweek 55:89, Mar 7, 1960
Reporter 22:43, Mar 31, 1960
Saturday Review 43:71-2, Mar 12, 1960
Time 75:50, Mar 7, 1960

Watch on the Rhine
Productions:
Opened April 1, 1941 for 378 performances.
Opened January 3, 1980 for 36 performances.
Reviews:
America 142:104, Feb 9, 1980

Catholic World 153:215-16, May 1941
Commonweal 34:15-16, Apr 25, 1941
Life 10:81-2+, Apr 14, 1941
Nation 152:453, Apr 12, 1941
  230:93, Jan 26, 1980
New Republic 104:498-9, Apr 14, 1941
New York Magazine 13:71-2, Jan 14, 1980
New York Theatre Critics' Reviews 1941:341
         1980:396
New York Times p. 26, Mar 25, 1941
      p. 26, Apr 2, 1941
      IV, p. 8, Apr 6, 1941
      IX, p. 1, Apr 13, 1941
      IX, p. 1, Apr 20, 1941
      p. 20, Apr 24, 1941
      VI, p. 2, Apr 27, 1941
      IX, p. 1, Aug 24, 1941
      VIII, p. 1, May 3, 1942
      p. 10, Feb 26, 1945
      III, p. 20, Oct 16, 1979
      III, p. 3, Jan 4, 1980
      II, p. 2, Jan 21, 1980
New Yorker 17:32, Apr 12, 1941
    55:55, Jan 14, 1980
Newsweek 17:70, Apr 14, 1941
Theatre Arts 25:409-11, Jun 1941
    25:791, Nov 1941
Time 37:64, Apr 14, 1941
  38:56, Nov 3, 1941
  115:76, Feb 4, 1980

HEMINGWAY, ERNEST

A Farewell to Arms (see entry under Stallings, Laurence)

The Fifth Column (Adapted by Benjamin Glazer from Hemingway's
  published play)
 Productions:
  Opened March 6, 1940 for 87 performances.
 Reviews:
  Catholic World 151:97-8, Apr 1940
  Commonweal 31:475, Mar 22, 1940
  Forum 103:272, May 1940
  Life 8:100-1, Mar 25, 1940
  Nation 150:371-2, Mar 16, 1940
  New Republic 102:408, Mar 25, 1940
  New York Theatre Critics' Reviews 1940:370
  New York Times p. 9, Jan 27, 1940
        IX, p. 1, Feb 4, 1940
        p. 18, Mar 7, 1940
        X, p. 1, Mar 17, 1940

New Yorker 16:44, Mar 16, 1940
Newsweek 15:52, Mar 18, 1940
Theatre Arts 24:310-11+, May 1940
Time 35:65-7, Mar 18, 1940

HENLEY, BETH

Am I Blue
    Productions:
        (Off Off Broadway) May 1980 (Circle Repertory).
        (Off Broadway) January 10, 1982 for 36 performances, as
            part of a bill called Confluence (Circle Repertory Co.).
    Reviews:
        New York Magazine 15:56, Jan 25, 1982
        New York Theatre Critics' Reviews 1982:360
        New York Times III, p. 14, Jan 11, 1982
                        II, p. 3, Jan 24, 1982

Confluence   (see Am I Blue)

Crimes of the Heart
    Productions:
        (Off Off Broadway) December 9, 1980 for 35 performances
            (Manhattan Theater Club) and transferred to Broadway.
        Opened on Broadway November 4, 1981 for 239+ performances
            (still running on June 1, 1982).
    Reviews:
        New Leader 64:19, Nov 30, 1981
        New Republic 185:25-7, Dec 23, 1981
        New York Magazine 14:42+, Jan 12, 1981
                        14:125-6, Nov 16, 1981
        New York Theatre Critics' Reviews 1981:136
        New York Times III, p. 16, Dec 22, 1980
                        III, p. 21, Nov 5, 1981
                        II, p. 3, Nov 15, 1981
        New Yorker 56:81, Jan 12, 1981
                    57:182-3, Nov 16, 1981
        Newsweek 98:123, Nov 16, 1981
        People 16:124-5, Dec 21, 1981
        Saturday Review 8:40+, Nov 1981
                        9:54, Jan 1982
        Time 118:122, Nov 16, 1981

HERBERT, F. HUGH

The Best House in Naples (Adapted from the play by Eduardo de
        Felippo)
    Productions:
        Opened October 26, 1956 for 3 performances.

Reviews:
New York Theatre Critics' Reviews 1956:243
New York Times p. 16, Oct 27, 1956
New Yorker 32:73, Nov 3, 1956
Theatre Arts 41:20, Jan 1957

For Keeps
Productions:
Opened June 14, 1944 for 29 performances.
Reviews:
Catholic World 159:459, Aug 1944
Commonweal 40:255, Jun 30, 1944
New York Theatre Critics' Reviews 1944:169
New York Times p. 17, Jun 15, 1944
New Yorker 20:47, Jun 1944

For Love or Money
Productions:
Opened November 4, 1947 for 265 performances.
Reviews:
Catholic World 166:267, Dec 1947
New Republic 117:32, Nov 17, 1947
New York Theatre Critics' Reviews 1947:271
New York Times II, p. 1, Nov 2, 1947
                p. 36, Nov 5, 1947
New Yorker 23:54+, Nov 15, 1947
Newsweek 30:84, Nov 17, 1947
School and Society 66:421-2, Nov 29, 1947
Time 50:87, Nov 17, 1947

A Girl Can Tell
Productions:
Opened October 29, 1953 for 60 performances.
Reviews:
America 90:215, Nov 21, 1953
Catholic World 178:231, Dec 1953
Commonweal 59:164, Nov 20, 1953
Nation 177:434, Nov 21, 1953
New York Theatre Critics' Reviews 1953:237
New York Times II, p. 3, Oct 25, 1953
                p. 28, Oct 30, 1953
New Yorker 29:76+, Nov 7, 1953
Newsweek 42:60, Nov 9, 1953
Saturday Review 36:38, Nov 14, 1953
Theatre Arts 38:17, Jan 1954
Time 62:72, Nov 9, 1953

Kiss and Tell
Productions:
Opened March 17, 1943 for 956 performances.

Reviews:
Catholic World 157:18, May 6, 1943
Commonweal 37:590, Apr 2, 1943
Independent Woman 22:155, May 1943
Life 14:41-2, Apr 12, 1943
Nation 156:534, Apr 10, 1943
New York Theatre Critics' Reviews 1943:356
New York Times p. 22, Mar 8, 1943
          II, p. 1, Mar 28, 1943
          II, p. 1, Apr 4, 1943
Newsweek 21:58, May 29, 1943
Theatre Arts 27:276, May 1943
Time 41:55, Mar 29, 1943

The Moon Is Blue
Productions:
Opened March 8, 1951 for 924 performances.
(Off Broadway) Opened June 7, 1961 in repertory.
Reviews:
Catholic World 173:147, May 1951
Commonweal 53:618, Mar 30, 1951
Life 30:87-8, Apr 2, 1951
New Republic 124:21, Apr 9, 1951
New York Theatre Critics' Reviews 1951:322
New York Times p. 29, Mar 9, 1951
          II, p. 3, Mar 25, 1951
          p. 24, Jul 8, 1953
          II, p. 1, Aug 9, 1953
          p. 29, Aug 9, 1961
New Yorker 27:56, Mar 17, 1951
Newsweek 37:84, Mar 19, 1951
Theatre Arts 35:19, May 1951
Time 57:52, May 19, 1951

Quiet Please (with Hanz Kraly. Based on a story by Ferdinand
Reyher)
Productions:
Opened November 8, 1940 for 16 performances.
Reviews:
Commonweal 33:127, Nov 22, 1940
New York Theatre Critics' Reviews 1940:224
New York Times IX, p. 2, Oct 20, 1940
          p. 20, Nov 9, 1940
Newsweek 16:60, Nov 18, 1940

HERNE, JAMES A.

*Drifting Apart, or the Fisherman's Child
Reviews:
New York Times p. 16, Aug 20, 1941

HEYWARD, DOROTHY AND DUBOSE

Brass Ankle (Dubose Heyward)
Productions:
Opened April 23, 1931 for 44 performances.
Reviews:
Arts and Decoration 35:82, Jul 1931
Catholic World 133:335-7, Jun 1931
Commonweal 14:16, May 6, 1931
Drama Magazine 21:10-11, May 1931
Life (NY) Vol. 97, May 8, 1931
Nation 132:538-9, May 13, 1931
New Republic 66:357, May 13, 1931
New York Times p. 26, Apr 24, 1931
Outlook 158:26, May 6, 1931
Vogue 77:100, Jun 15, 1931

Cinderelative (Dorothy Heyward with Dorothy De Jagers)
Productions:
Opened September 18, 1930 for 4 performances.
Reviews:
New York Times p. 18, Sep 19, 1930

The Dud (see Nancy Ann)

Mamba's Daughters (from Dubose Heyward's novel)
Productions:
Opened January 3, 1939 for 162 performances.
Opened March 23, 1940 for 17 performances.
Reviews:
Catholic World 148:597-8, Feb 1939
Commonweal 29:358, Jan 20, 1939
Life 6:49-51, Jan 23, 1939
Nation 148:74, Jan 14, 1939
New Republic 97:315, Jan 18, 1939
New York Times IX, p. 3, Jan 1, 1939
p. 24, Jan 4, 1939
IX, p. 1, Jan 15, 1939
p. 10, Mar 25, 1940
p. 12, Mar 21, 1953
North American Review 247 no. 2:366-7, Jun 1939
Newsweek 13:26, Jan 16, 1939
Theatre Arts 23:169, Mar 1939
Time 33:41, Jan 16, 1939

Nancy Ann (Dorothy Heyward)
Productions:
Opened March 31, 1924 for 40 performances.
Reviews:
Dramatist 15:1205-6, Apr 1924
Life (NY) 83:20, Apr 17, 1924

New York Times VIII, p. 2, Mar 9, 1924
             p. 18, Apr 1, 1924
             VIII, p. 1, Apr 6, 1924
Theatre Magazine 39:19, Jun 1924

Porgy
Productions:
    Opened October 10, 1927 for 367 performances.
    Opened September 13, 1929 for 34 performances.
Reviews:
    Dial 83:529-30, Dec 1927
    Independent 119:606, Dec 17, 1927
    Literary Digest 95:27-8, Nov 5, 1927
    Nation 125:457-8, Oct 26, 1927
    New Republic 52:261-2, Oct 26, 1927
    New York Times p. 26, Oct 11, 1927
              IX, p. 1, Oct 16, 1927
              IX, p. 2, Apr 29, 1928
              p. 17, May 29, 1928
              VIII, p. 1, Jul 1, 1928
              X, p. 1, Dec 2, 1928
              p. 32, Apr 11, 1929
              IX, p. 1, Apr 28, 1929
              p. 28, May 9, 1929
              p. 17, Sep 14, 1929
    Outlook 147:402-3, Nov 30, 1927
    Saturday Review 4:251, Oct 29, 1927
    Survey 57:465-6, Jan 1, 1928
    Theatre Arts 11:901-4, Dec 1927
    Theatre Magazine 46:82, Dec 1927
    Vogue 70:87, Dec 1, 1927

Set My People Free (Dorothy Heyward)
Productions:
    Opened November 3, 1948 for 36 performances.
    (Off Broadway) Season of 1948-49 (Neighborhood Playhouse).
Reviews:
    Catholic World 168:241-2, Dec 1948
    Commonweal 49:142, Nov 19, 1948
    Forum 110:353-4, Dec 1948
    Nation 167:586, Nov 20, 1948
    New Republic 119:28-9, Nov 22, 1948
    New York Theatre Critics' Reviews 1948:171
    New York Times p. 38, Nov 4, 1948
              II, p. 1, Nov 14, 1948
    New Yorker 24:60+, Nov 13, 1948
    Newsweek 32:82, Nov 15, 1948
    School and Society 68:389, Dec 4, 1948
    Time 52:84, Nov 15, 1948
    Vogue 112:183, Dec 1948

South Pacific (Dorothy Heyward with Howard Rigsby)
    Productions:
        Opened December 29, 1943 for 5 performances.
    Reviews:
        Commonweal 29:328-9, Jan 14, 1944
        New York Theatre Critics' Reviews 1943:184
        New York Times p. 11, Dec 30, 1943
        New Yorker 19:38, Jan 8, 1944
        Newsweek 23:89, Jan 10, 1944
        Theatre Arts 28:136-7, Mar 1944
        Time 43:72, Jan 10, 1944

HOPKINS, ARTHUR

Burlesque (see entry under Watters, George Manker)

Conquest
    Productions:
        Opened February 18, 1933 for 10 performances.
    Reviews:
        Commonweal 17:526, Mar 8, 1933
        Nation 136:270, Mar 8, 1933
        New Republic 74:159, Mar 22, 1933
        New York Times p. 11, Feb 20, 1933
        Theatre Arts 17:343-4, May 1933
        Vogue 81:86, Apr 15, 1933

The Fatted Calf
    Productions:
        Opened February 19, 1912 for 8 performances.
    Reviews:
        Dramatic Mirror 67:6, Feb 28, 1912
        Dramatist 3:247, Apr 1912
        Green Book 7:1068-9, May 1912

*Moonshine
    Reviews:
        Dramatic Mirror 68:7, Sep 25, 1912
        New York Times III, p. 7, Jun 23, 1918
                       p. 11, Sep 17, 1918

HOROVITZ, ISRAEL

Acrobats
    Productions:
        (Off Broadway) February 15, 1971 for 32 performances.
    Reviews:
        Nation 212:314, Mar 8, 1971
        New York Theatre Critics' Reviews 1971:349

New York Times p. 26, Feb 16, 1971
II, p. 3, Mar 7, 1971
New Yorker 47:82-4, Feb 27, 1971

Alfred Dies
    Productions:
    (Off Off Broadway) January 14, 1977 (Actors Studio).
    No Reviews.

Alfred the Great
    Productions:
    (Off Off Broadway) February 1, 1978 (Actors Studio).
    Reviews:
    New York Times p. 28, Aug 14, 1974

Cappella (with David Boorstin. Adapted from Israel Horovitz's
    novel)
    Productions:
    (Off Off Broadway) January 6, 1978 for 18 performances (Off
    Center Theater).
    Reviews:
    New York Times p. 13, Feb 4, 1978

Dr. Hero
    Productions:
    (Off Off Broadway) March 19, 1973 (Shade Co.).
    (Off Off Broadway) April 5, 1976 (Cubiculo).
    Reviews:
    New York Times p. 55, Mar 22, 1973
                    II, p. 11, Apr 22, 1973
    Time 101:71, Apr 2, 1973

The First, the Middle, and the Last
    Productions:
    (Off Off Broadway) December 1974 (Cubiculo).
    No Reviews.

The Good Parts
    Productions:
    (Off Off Broadway) May 1979 (Actors Studio).
    (Off Broadway) January 7, 1982 for 22 performances.
    Reviews:
    America 146:135, Feb 20, 1982
    New York Magazine 15:70, Jan 18, 1982
    New York Times III, p. 3, Jan 8, 1982

Hero
    Productions:
    (Off Off Broadway) Season of 1970-71 (The Other Stage).
    No Reviews.

The Honest-to-God Schnozzola
    Productions:
        (Off Broadway) April 21, 1969 for 8 performances.
    Reviews:
        New York Times p. 40, Apr 22, 1969
        New Yorker 45:108-9, May 3, 1969
        Newsweek 73:118, May 5, 1969

Hopscotch
    Productions:
        (Off Off Broadway) Season of 1973-74 (Manhattan Theater
            Club).
        See also The Quannapowitt Quartet Part One: Hopscotch.
    No Reviews.

The Indian Wants the Bronx
    Productions:
        (Off Broadway) January 17, 1968 for 204 performances.
        (Off Off Broadway) February 27, 1976 (ACSTA).
    Reviews:
        Nation 206:221, Feb 12, 1968
        New York Theatre Critics' Reviews 1968:268
        New York Times p. 47, Jan 18, 1968
                       p. 72, Dec 16, 1971
        New Yorker 43:86-7, Jan 27, 1968
        Reporter 38:35, May 2, 1968
        Vogue 151:166, May 1968

It's Called the Sugar Plum
    Productions:
        (Off Broadway) January 17, 1968 for 204 performances.
        (Off Off Broadway) January 1974 (Courtyard Players).
    Reviews:
        New York Times p. 47, Jan 18, 1968
        New Yorker 43:87, Jan 27, 1968

Leader
    Productions:
        (Off Broadway) Opened April 21, 1969 for 8 performances.
    Reviews:
        New York Times p. 40, Apr 22, 1969
        New Yorker 45:108-9, May 3, 1969
        Newsweek 73:118, May 5, 1969

Line
    Productions:
        (Off Broadway) Season of 1967-1968 (La Mama Experimental
            Theatre Club).
        (Off Off Broadway) February 1976 (13th St. Repertory Co.).
    Reviews:
        Nation 212:314, Mar 8, 1971

New York Times p. 26, Feb 16, 1971
        II, p. 3, Mar 7, 1971
        p. 20, Mar 22, 1976
New Yorker 47:82-4, Feb 27, 1971
Time 97:67, Mar 1, 1971

The Lounge Player
    Productions:
        (Off Off Broadway) May 1978 (Actors Studio).
    No Reviews.

Morning
    Productions:
        Opened November 28, 1968 for 52 performances.
    Reviews:
        Commonweal 89:471-2, Jan 10, 1969
        Nation 207:665-6, Dec 16, 1968
        New York Theatre Critics' Reviews 1968:168
        New York Times p. 52, Nov 29, 1968
                II, p. 7, Dec 8, 1968
                p. 54, Dec 10, 1968
        New Yorker 44:139-40, Dec 7, 1968
        Time 92:71-2, Dec 6, 1968

Our Father's Failing
    Productions:
        (Off Off Broadway) Season of 1973-74 (Manhattan Theater Club).
    No Reviews.

Park Your Car in the Harvard Yard
    Productions:
        (Off Off Broadway) May 1980 (Actors Studio).
    No Reviews.

The Primary English Class
    Productions:
        (Off Off Broadway) June 4, 1975 (Cubiculo).
        (Off Broadway) February 16, 1976 for 120 performances.
    Reviews:
        Nation 222:283-4, Mar 6, 1976
        New York Magazine 9:60, Mar 1, 1976
        New York Theatre Critics' Reviews 1976:335
        New York Times p. 38, Feb 17, 1976
                II, p. 5, Feb 29, 1976
        New Yorker 52:79, Mar 1, 1976
        Time 107:51, Mar 1, 1976

The Quannapowitt Quartet Part One: Hopscotch
    Productions:
        (Off Off Broadway) March 3, 1978 for 4 performances (New
        York Shakespeare Festival Public Theater).

See also Hopscotch.
No Reviews.

The Quannapowitt Quartet Part Two: The 75th
    Productions:
        (Off Off Broadway) April 22, 1978 for 8 performances (New
            York Shakespeare Festival Public Theater).
        See also The 75th.
    No Reviews.

The Quannapowitt Quartet Part Three: Stage Directions
    Productions:
        (Off Off Broadway) December 22, 1978 for 12 performances
            (New York Shakespeare Festival Public Theater).
    Reviews:
        New York Times III, p. 21, Mar 7, 1979

Rats
    Productions:
        (Off Broadway) May 8, 1968 for 80 performances.
        (Off Off Broadway) Season of 1975-76 (13th St. Repertory
            Co.).
        (Off Off Broadway) June 1976 (13th St. Repertory Co.).
        (Off Off Broadway) February 1977 (Direct Theater).
    Reviews:
        Harper's Bazaar 237:113-15, Oct 1968
        Nation 206:772+, Jun 10, 1968
        New York Times p. 55, May 9, 1968
                        II, p. 1, May 19, 1968
        New Yorker 44:74, May 18, 1968

The Reason We Eat
    Productions:
        (Off Off Broadway) June 1976 (Cubiculo).
        (Off Off Broadway) June 1977 (Cubiculo).
    No Reviews.

The 75th
    Productions:
        (Off Off Broadway) June 1977 (Cubiculo).
        See also The Quannapowitt Quartet Part Two: The 75th.
    No Reviews.

Shooting Gallery
    Productions:
        (Off Off Broadway) February 1976 (13th St. Repertory Co.).
    Reviews:
        New York Times p. 20, Mar 22, 1976

Spared
    Productions:

(Off Off Broadway) Season of 1973-74 (Manhattan Theater Club).
No Reviews.

Stage Directions (see The Quannapowitt Quartet Part 3: Stage Directions)

Sunday Runners in the Rain
Productions:
(Off Off Broadway) April 18, 1980 for 21 performances (New York Shakespeare Festival Public Theater).
Reviews:
New York Times III, p. 17, May 5, 1980

The Wakefield Plays
Productions:
(Off Off Broadway) December 2, 1976 (New Dramatists).
No Reviews.

The Widow's Blind Date
Productions:
(Off Off Broadway) May 2, 1979 (Actors Studio/New York Playwright's Lab).
Reviews:
Los Angeles 25:297, Nov 1980

HOWARD, GEORGE BRONSON

The Henrietta (see The New Henrietta under Smith, Winchell)

The Only Law (with Wilson Mizner)
Productions:
Opened August 2, 1909 for 48 performances.
Reviews:
Dramatic Mirror 62:5, Aug 14, 1909
Forum 42:360-1, Oct 1909
Green Book 2:777-9, Oct 1909
Hampton 23:542, Oct 1909
Metropolitan Magazine 31:126-7, Oct 1909
Munsey 42:248-53, Nov 1909
Pearson 22:506, Oct 1909
Theatre Magazine 10:73-4, Sep 1909
World To-Day 17:912, Sep 1909

HOWARD, SIDNEY

Alien Corn
Productions:
Opened February 20, 1933 for 98 performances.
Reviews:
Arts and Decoration 38:48-9, Apr 1933

Catholic World 137:77, Apr 1933
Commonweal 17:553, Mar 15, 1933
Literary Digest 115:20, Mar 11, 1933
Nation 136:299-300, Mar 15, 1933
New Outlook 161:46, Apr 1933
New Republic 74:101-2, Mar 8, 1933
New York Times p. 19, Feb 14, 1933
            p. 17, Feb 21, 1933
            IX, p. 1, Feb 26, 1933
            X, p. 3, Jan 20, 1935
            p. 26, Jul 6, 1939
            IX, p. 2, Jul 23, 1939
Newsweek 1:26, Feb 25, 1933
Stage 10:7-9, Mar 1933
      10:12-13, Mar 1933
Theatre Arts 17:342, May 1933
Time 21:18, Feb 27, 1933
Vanity Fair 40:31-2, May 1933
Vogue 81:61+, Apr 15, 1933

Bewitched (see entry under Sheldon, Edward)

Casanova (Adapted from the play by Lorenzo de Azertis)
    Productions:
        Opened September 26, 1923 for 77 performances.
    Reviews:
        Nation 117:412, Oct 10, 1923
        New Republic 36:180-1, Oct 10, 1923
        New York Times p. 10, Sep 27, 1923
        Theatre Magazine 38:13+, Nov 1923

Dodsworth (Based on the novel by Sinclair Lewis)
    Productions:
        Opened February 24, 1934 for 147 performances.
        Opened August 20, 1934 for 168 performances.
    Reviews:
        Catholic World 139:86-7, Apr 1934
        Collier's 95:16+, Jan 12, 1935
        Commonweal 19:554, Mar 16, 1934
        Golden Book Magazine 20:376, Oct 1934
        Literary Digest 117:22, Mar 17, 1934
        Nation 138:311-12+, Mar 14, 1934
        New Outlook 163:44, Apr 1934
        New Republic 78:134, Mar 14, 1934
        New York Times p. 20, Feb 26, 1934
                    p. 12, Aug 21, 1934
                    IX, p. 2, Apr 5, 1936
                    p. 26, Feb 23, 1938
                    XI, p. 3, Mar 13, 1938
        Newsweek 3:34, Mar 3, 1934
        Review of Reviews 89:48, Apr 1934

Saturday Review 10:569-70, Mar 24, 1934
Stage 11:6+, Mar 1934
        12:9-10, Oct 1934
Theatre Arts 18:325-6, May 1934
Time 23:40, Mar 5, 1934

*Gather Ye Rosebuds (with R. Littell)
    Reviews:
    New York Times p. 33, Nov 29, 1934
                   X, p. 1, Dec 2, 1934

The Ghost of Yankee Doodle
    Productions:
    Opened November 22, 1937 for 48 performances.
    Reviews:
    Catholic World 146:467, Jan 1938
    Commonweal 27:191, Dec 10, 1937
    Nation 145:664, Dec 11, 1937
    New York Times p. 28, Oct 28, 1937
                   XI, p. 2, Nov 7, 1937
                   XI, p. 2, Nov 21, 1937
                   p. 26, Nov 23, 1937
    Newsweek 10:32, Dec 6, 1937
    Theatre Arts 22:20-1, Jan 1938
    Time 30:41, Dec 6, 1937

Half Gods
    Productions:
    Opened December 21, 1929 for 17 performances.
    Reviews:
    Drama Magazine 20:138, Feb 1930
    Life (NY) 95:20, Jan 10, 1930
    Nation 130:52, Jan 8, 1930
    New York Times p. 18, Dec 23, 1929
    Theatre Arts 14:109, Feb 1930
    Theatre Magazine 51:66, Feb 1930
    Vogue 75:118, Feb 15, 1930

The Late Christopher Bean (Adapted from the French of Rene
    Fauchois)
    Productions:
    Opened October 31, 1932 for 224 performances.
    Reviews:
    Arts and Decoration 38:50, Jan 1933
    Catholic World 136:335-6, Dec 1932
    Commonweal 17:75, Nov 16, 1932
    Los Angeles 24:391, Dec 1979
    Nation 135:484-5, Nov 16, 1932
    New Outlook 161:46, Dec 1932
    New York Times p. 24, Nov 1, 1932
                   p. 15, May 17, 1933
                   p. 13, Aug 28, 1935

Player's Magazine 9:13, Nov-Dec 1932
Stage 10:35, Dec 1932
Theatre Arts 17:18+, Jan 1933
Town and Country 87:26+, Dec 1, 1932
Vogue 80:48, Dec 15, 1932

Lucky Sam McCarver
   Productions:
      Opened October 21, 1925 for 29 performances.
   Reviews:
      Life (NY) 86:20, Nov 12, 1925
      New York Times p. 22, Oct 22, 1925
               VIII, p. 1, Nov 1, 1925
               VII, p. 1, Feb 21, 1926
               p. 10, Apr 15, 1950
      Theatre Arts 10:15-16, Jan 1926

Madam Will You Walk
   Productions:
      Opened December 1, 1953 for 42 performances.
   Reviews:
      America 90:346, Dec 26, 1953
      Catholic World 178:307, Jan 1954
      Commonweal 59:330, Jan 1, 1954
      Nation 177:554, Dec 19, 1953
      New York Theatre Critics' Reviews 1953:201
      New York Times p. 20, Nov 14, 1939
               p. 2, Dec 2, 1953
      New Yorker 29:87-8, Dec 12, 1953
      Newsweek 42:61, Dec 14, 1953
      Saturday Review 36:28, Dec 19, 1953
      Time 62:94, Dec 14, 1953

Marseilles (Adapted from the French of Marcel Pagnol)
   Productions:
      Opened November 17, 1930 for 16 performances.
   Reviews:
      Commonweal 13:160, Dec 10, 1930
      New York Times IX, p. 3, Nov 9, 1930
               p. 28, Nov 18, 1930
      Theatre Arts 15:18-19, Jan 1931

Muse of All Work (see The Late Christopher Bean)

Ned McCobb's Daughter
   Productions:
      Opened November 29, 1926 for 156 performances.
   Reviews:
      Bookman 64:731, Feb 1927
      Dramatist 18:1331-2, Jan 1927
      Independent 118:270, Mar 5, 1927

Life (NY) 88:19, Dec 23, 1926
Nation 123:697, Dec 29, 1926
New Republic 49:108-9, Dec 15, 1926
New York Times p. 26, Nov 30, 1926
        VIII, p. 2, Dec 5, 1926
        VII, p. 2, Feb 6, 1927
        VIII, p. 2, Mar 20, 1927
        p. 29, Jan 7, 1948
Theatre Magazine 45:15, Feb 1927
Vogue 16:120, Feb 1, 1927
Yale Review 17:175, Oct 1927

Ode to Liberty (Adapted from the French of Michel Duran)
   Productions:
      Opened December 21, 1934 for 67 performances.
   Reviews:
      Catholic World 140:598-9, Feb 1935
      New York Times p. 28, Dec 11, 1934
                 p. 20, Dec 22, 1934
                 p. 24, Jul 9, 1935
                 p. 20, Aug 6, 1935
      Time 24:24, Dec 31, 1934

Paths of Glory (Adapted from Humphrey Cobb's novel)
   Productions:
      Opened September 26, 1935 for 23 performances.
   Reviews:
      Catholic World 142:212-13, Nov 1935
      Commonweal 22:585, Oct 11, 1935
      Literary Digest 121:19, Jan 4, 1936
      New Republic 84:302, Oct 23, 1935
      New York Times p. 29, Sep 19, 1935
                 p. 24, Sep 27, 1935
                 IX, p. 1, Oct 13, 1935
                 p. 16, Oct 14, 1935
                 p. 23, Mar 19, 1936
      Newsweek 6:33, Oct 5, 1935
      Theatre Arts 19:813-15, Nov 1935
                20:74-6, Jan 1936
      Time 26:38, Oct 7, 1935

Salvation (with Charles MacArthur)
   Productions:
      Opened January 31, 1928 for 31 performances.
   Reviews:
      Dial 84:351-2, Apr 1928
      Life (NY) 91:19, Feb 23, 1928
      Nation 126:220, Feb 22, 1928
      New Republic 54:18-19, Feb 22, 1928
      New York Times p. 31, Feb 1, 1928
                 VIII, p. 1, Feb 12, 1928
      Vogue 71:142, Apr 1, 1928

The Silver Cord
    Productions:
        Opened December 20, 1926 for 112 performances.
    Reviews:
        Bookman 65:70-71, Mar 1927
        Dial 82:259-60, Mar 1927
        Drama Magazine 17:171, Mar 1927
        Dramatist 18:1337-8, Apr 1927
        Independent 118:270, Mar 5, 1927
        Life (NY) 89:21, Jan 6, 1927
        Nation 124:20-1, Jan 5, 1927
        New Republic 49:328, Feb 9, 1927
        New York Times p. 21, Dec 21, 1926
                     p. 29, Sep 14, 1927
                     VIII, p. 1, Oct 2, 1927
                     IX, p. 2, Oct 16, 1927
                     IX, p. 2, Apr 29, 1928
        Theatre Magazine 45:58, Feb 1927
                      45:19, Mar 1927
                      45:50, Mar 1927
        Vogue 69:80-81+, Feb 15, 1927

Swords
    Productions:
        Opened September 1, 1921 for 36 performances.
    Reviews:
        Bookman 54:228-9, Nov 1921
        Dramatic Mirror 84:376, Sep 10, 1921
        Independent 106:137, Sep 24, 1921
        Life (NY) 78:18, Sep 22, 1921
        Nation 113:325, Sep 21, 1921
        New Republic 28:77, Sep 14, 1921
        New York Clipper 69:22, Sep 7, 1921
        New York Times p. 9, Sep 2, 1921
                     VI, p. 1, Nov 20, 1921
        Theatre Magazine 34:16, Nov 1921
        Weekly Review 5:255, Sep 17, 1921

They Knew What They Wanted
    Productions:
        Opened November 24, 1924 for 192 performances.
        Opened October 2, 1939 for 24 performances.
        Opened February 16, 1949 for 61 performances.
        Opened January 27, 1976 for 30 performances.
    Reviews:
        Bookman 60:741, Feb 1925
        Catholic World 150:217, Nov 1939
                      169:64, Apr 1949
        Commonweal 30:587, Oct 20, 1939
                    49:591, Mar 25, 1949

Current Opinion 78:188-95, Feb 1925
Dial 78:82, Jan 1925
Forum 111:287-8, May 1949
Independent 114:51, Jan 10, 1925
Motion Picture Classic 21:46+, Mar 1925
Nation 119:662-3, Dec 10, 1924
      168:312, Mar 12, 1949
      222:252-3, Feb 28, 1976
New York Magazine 9:71, Feb 9, 1976
New York Theatre Critics' Reviews 1949:354
                                         1976:379
New York Times VIII, p. 1, Nov 20, 1924
                 p. 27, Nov 25, 1924
                 p. 19, Apr 27, 1925
                 p. 14, Jun 4, 1925
                 p. 17, Jul 7, 1936
                 p. 14, Jul 8, 1936
                 p. 10, Jul 30, 1938
                 p. 19, Oct 3, 1939
                 II, p. 1, Feb 13, 1949
                 p. 28, Feb 17, 1949
                 p. 26, Jan 28, 1976
                 II, p. 5, Feb 8, 1976
New Yorker 25:50-1, Feb 26, 1949
        51:78, Feb 9, 1976
Newsweek 14:44, Oct 16, 1939
        33:73, Feb 28, 1949
School and Society 69:233, Mar 26, 1949
Theatre Arts 9:77, Feb 1925
           23:862, Dec 1939
           33:24, 26, May 1949
Theatre Magazine 41:19, Feb 1925
                  41:19, Mar 1925
                  42:7, Jul 1925
                  42:26+, Aug 1925
Time 34:56, Oct 16, 1939
    53:57, Feb 28, 1949

Yellow Jack (with Paul de Kruif)
    Productions:
        Opened March 6, 1934 for 79 performances.
        Opened February 27, 1947 for 21 performances.
        (Off Broadway) December 11, 1964 for 9 performances (Equity
           Library Theater).
    Reviews:
        Catholic World 139:89-90, Apr 1934
                   165:71, Apr 1947
        Commonweal 19:580, Mar 23, 1934
              45:566, Mar 21, 1947
        Literary Digest 117:32, Mar 31, 1934
        Nation 138:340-1, Mar 21, 1934
          164:312-3, Mar 15, 1947

New Outlook 163:44, Apr 1934
New Republic 116:41, Mar 17, 1947
New York Theatre Critics' Reviews 1947:443
New York Times p. 22, Mar 7, 1934
     X, p. 1, Mar 11, 1934
     IX, p. 1, Mar 18, 1934
     p. 26, Feb 28, 1947
New Yorker 23:56, Mar 8, 1947
Newsweek 3:38, Mar 17, 1934
    29:82, Mar 10, 1947
Review of Reviews 89:49, May 1934
Saturday Review 10:569-70, Mar 24, 1934
School and Society 65:252, Apr 5, 1947
Stage 11:8-10, Apr 1934
Survey Graphic 23:241, May 1934
Theatre Arts 18:326-8, May 1934
Time 23:35-6, Mar 19, 1934
   49:46, Mar 10, 1947

HOWELLS, WILLIAM DEAN
No productions.

HOYT, CHARLES HALE

*Temperance Town
Reviews:
New York Times VIII, p. 2, Aug 11, 1929

Texas Steer
Productions:
(Off Broadway) Season of 1968-69 (American Theatre Club).
Reviews:
New York Times p. 39, Nov 13, 1968

HUGHES, HATCHER

Hell-Bent fer Heaven
Productions:
Opened January 4, 1924 for 122 performances.
Reviews:
Arts and Decoration 20:24, Apr 1924
Life (NY) 83:20, Feb 7, 1924
Nation 118:68-9, Jan 16, 1924
New York Times p. 9, Dec 31, 1923
     p. 10, Jan 5, 1924
     p. 21, Feb 5, 1924
     VII, p. 1, Feb 10, 1924
Theatre Magazine 39:19, Apr 1924
     39:26+, Jul 1924

*Honeymooning on High
    Reviews:
        New York Times VII, p. 4, Feb 27, 1927

It's a Grand Life (with Alan Williams)
    Productions:
        Opened February 10, 1930 for 25 performances.
    Reviews:
        Commonweal 11:480, Feb 26, 1930
        Nation 130:254, Feb 26, 1930
        New Republic 62:47, Feb 26, 1930
        New York Times VIII, p. 2, Feb 2, 1930
                        p. 30, Feb 11, 1930

The Lord Blesses the Bishop
    Productions:
        Opened November 27, 1934 for 7 performances.
    Reviews:
        New York Times p. 24, Nov 28, 1934

"Ruint"
    Productions:
        Opened April 7, 1925 for 30 performances.
    Reviews:
        American Mercury 5:247, Jun 1925
        Nation 120:473-4, Apr 22, 1925
        New York Times p. 24, Apr 8, 1925

Wake Up, Jonathan! (with Elmer Rice)
    Productions:
        Opened January 17, 1921 for 105 performances.
    Reviews:
        Dramatic Mirror 83:163, Jan 22, 1921
        Life (NY) 77:172, Feb 3, 1921
        Nation 112:189, Feb 2, 1921
        New York Clipper 68:19, Jan 26, 1921
        New York Times p. 14, Jan 18, 1921
                        VI, p. 1, Jan 23, 1921
        Review 4:112-14, Feb 2, 1921
        Theatre Magazine 33:261, Apr 1921
        Weekly Review 4:112-14, Feb 2, 1921

HUGHES, LANGSTON

Black Nativity
    Productions:
        (Off Broadway) December 11, 1961 for 57 performances.
        (Off Broadway) Season of 1968-69 in repertory (Afro-American
            Studio).
        (Off Off Broadway) December 30, 1980 (Richard Allen Center).

Reviews:
New York Times p. 54, Dec 12, 1961
p. 37, Aug 15, 1962
III, p. 5, Dec 30, 1980

Don't You Want to Be Free?
Productions:
(Off Broadway) June 10, 1938 in repertory (New Theatre League).
No Reviews.

Jerico-Jim Crow
Productions:
(Off Broadway) January 12, 1964 for 31 performances.
(Off Broadway) Season of 1967-68.
Reviews:
New York Times p. 25, Jan 13, 1964
p. 22, Mar 23, 1968

Mulatto
Productions:
Opened October 24, 1935 for 373 performances.
(Off Broadway) Season of 1967-68.
Reviews:
New York Times p. 13, Aug 8, 1935
p. 25, Oct 25, 1935
p. 61, Nov 16, 1967
Theatre Arts 19:902, Dec 1935
Time 26:58+, Nov 4, 1935

The Prodigal Son
Productions:
(Off Broadway) May 20, 1965 for 141 performances.
Reviews:
America 113:62, Jul 10, 1965
New York Times p. 19, May 21, 1965

Shakespeare in Harlem
Productions:
(Off Broadway) Season of 1959-60.
Reviews:
America 102:747, Mar 19, 1960
New York Times p. 43, Feb 10, 1960
II, p. 1, Feb 21, 1960

HURLBUT, WILLIAM J.

Are You a Crook? (with Frances Whitehouse)
Productions:
Opened May 1, 1913 for 12 performances.

Reviews:
  Blue Book 17:652-5, Aug 1913
  Dramatic Mirror 69:6, May 7, 1913
  Dramatist 4:376-7, Jul 1913
  Green Book 10:10-12+, Jul 1913
  Life (NY) 61:980-1, May 15, 1913
  New York Drama News 57:18, May 10, 1913
  New York Times p. 11, May 2, 1913
  Red Book 21:507-11, Jul 1913
  Theatre Magazine 17:181, Jun 1913

The Bride
  Productions:
  Opened September 27, 1913 in repertory (The Princess Play-
    ers).
  No Reviews.

Bride of the Lamb
  Productions:
  Opened March 30, 1926 for 109 performances.
  Reviews:
  Dramatic Mirror 70:6, Oct 15, 1913
  Dramatist 17:1306-7, Jul 1926
  Green Book 10:1064, Dec 1913
  Life (NY) 87:21, Apr 22, 1926
  Nation 121:426-7, Apr 14, 1926
  New Republic 46:301-2, Apr 28, 1926
  New York Times p. 20, Mar 31, 1926
            p. 26, Mar 29, 1934
  Theatre Magazine 18:143, Nov 1913
            43:5+, Jun 1926
            44:26-8+, Aug 1926
  Vogue 67:80+, Jun 1, 1926

Chivalry
  Productions:
  Opened December 15, 1925 for 23 performances.
  Reviews:
  New York Times p. 22, Dec 16, 1925
  Theatre Magazine 43:16, Mar 1926

The Cup
  Productions:
  Opened November 12, 1923 for 16 performances.
  Reviews:
  New York Times p. 25, Nov 13, 1923

Hail and Farewell
  Productions:
  Opened February 19, 1923 for 40 performances.
  Reviews:

New York Clipper 71:14, Feb 28, 1923
New York Times p. 12, Feb 20, 1923

Hidden
Productions:
Opened October 4, 1927 for 79 performances.
Reviews:
Dramatist 18:1353-4, Oct 1927
Life (NY) 90:25, Oct 20, 1927
New York Times VIII, p. 4, Sep 25, 1927
p. 30, Oct 5, 1927
Theatre Magazine 46:43-4, Dec 1927

Lilies of the Field
Productions:
Opened October 4, 1921 for 169 performances.
Reviews:
Dramatic Mirror 84:520, Oct 8, 1921
New York Clipper 69:20, Oct 12, 1921
New York Times p. 20, Oct 5, 1921
Theatre Magazine 34:363+, Dec 1921

New York
Productions:
Opened October 17, 1910 for 16 performances.
Reviews:
Blue Book 12:431-3, Jan 1911
Dramatic Mirror 64:7, Oct 19, 1910
Life (NY) 56:704, Oct 27, 1910

On the Stairs
Productions:
Opened September 25, 1922 for 80 performances.
Reviews:
New York Clipper 70:21, Oct 4, 1922
New York Times p. 18, Sep 26, 1922

Paradise
Productions:
Opened December 26, 1927 for 8 performances.
Reviews:
New York Times p. 26, Dec 26, 1927

A Primer for Lovers
Productions:
Opened November 18, 1929 for 24 performances.
Reviews:
Nation 129:669, Dec 4, 1929
New York Times p. 26, Nov 19, 1929

Romance and Arabella
Productions:

Opened October 17, 1917 for 29 performances.
Reviews:
Dramatic Mirror 77:7, Oct 27, 1917
Life (NY) 70:714-15, Nov 1, 1917
New York Drama News 64:6, Oct 27, 1917
New York Times p. 13, Oct 18, 1917

Saturday to Monday
Productions:
Opened October 1, 1917 for 16 performances.
Reviews:
Dramatic Mirror 77:15, Jun 2, 1917
77:8, Oct 13, 1917
Life (NY) 70:591, Oct 11, 1917
New York Times p. 11, Oct 2, 1917
Theatre Magazine 26:265+, Nov 1917

*Story to Be Whispered
Reviews:
New York Times p. 21, Aug 20, 1937

The Strange Woman
Productions:
Opened November 17, 1913 for 88 performances.
Reviews:
Blue Book 18:631-3, Feb 1914
Book News 32:257-8, Jan 1913
Bookman 38:495, Jan 1914
Collier's 52:30, Jan 10, 1914
Dramatic Mirror 70:10, Nov 16, 1913
Green Book 11:238-9, Feb 1914
11:350-1, Feb 1914
Hearst 25:275-86, Feb 1914
Munsey 50:728, Jan 1914
New York Times p. 11, Nov 18, 1913
Theatre Magazine 19:6-8, Jan 1914

Trimmed in Scarlet
Productions:
Opened February 2, 1920 for 14 performances.
Reviews:
Dramatic Mirror 82:206, Feb 7, 1920
Life (NY) pp. 322-3, Feb 19, 1920
New York Times p. 18, Feb 3, 1920
Theatre Magazine 31:185+, Mar 1920

The Writing on the Wall
Productions:
Opened April 26, 1909 for 32 performances.
Reviews:
Forum 41:548-9, Jun 1909

Hampton 23:111, Jul 1909
Nation 88:447, Apr 29, 1909
New York Times p. 25, Jul 3, 1923
Theatre Magazine 9:169-70+, Jun 1909

HUSTON, JOHN

In Time to Come   (see entry under Koch, Howard)

HWANG, DAVID

The Dance and the Railroad
  Productions:
    (Off Off Broadway) March 21, 1981 (New Federal Theater).
    (Off Broadway) July 16, 1981 for 181 performances.
  Reviews:
    Commonweal 108:688+, Dec 4, 1981
    Nation 233:554-5, Nov 21, 1981
    New Republic 185:28-9, Oct 14, 1981
    New York Magazine 14:68-70, Aug 24, 1981
    New York Times III, p. 5, Mar 31, 1981
    New Yorker 57:52, Jul 27, 1981

Family Devotions
  Productions:
    (Off Broadway) October 18, 1981 for 76 performances.
  Reviews:
    Commonweal 108:688+, Dec 4, 1981
    Nation 233:554-5, Nov 21, 1981
    New York Magazine 14:71, Nov 2, 1981
    New York Theatre Critics' Reviews 1981:93
    New York Times III, p. 17, Oct 19, 1981

FOB
  Productions:
    (Off Off Broadway) May 27, 1980.
    (Off Broadway) June 8, 1980 for 42 performances.
  Reviews:
    New York Times III, p. 6, Jun 10, 1980
    New Yorker 56:96-7, Jun 16, 1980

INGE, WILLIAM

Bus Stop
  Productions:
    Opened March 2, 1955 for 478 performances.
    (Off Off Broadway) January 23, 1975 (Manhattan Theater
      Club).

(Off Off Broadway) February 6, 1975 (Equity Library Theater).
Reviews:
America 93:54, Apr 9, 1955
Catholic World 181:147, May 1955
Commonweal 62:14, Apr 8, 1955
Life 38:77-80, Mar 28, 1955
Nation 180:245, Mar 19, 1955
New Republic 132:22, May 2, 1955
New York Theatre Critics' Reviews 1955:346
New York Times II, p. 3, Feb 27, 1955
                     p. 23, Mar 3, 1955
                     II, p. 1, Mar 13, 1955
                     II, p. 1, Apr 3, 1955
New York Times Magazine p. 59, Mar 20, 1955
New Yorker 31:62+, Mar 12, 1955
Newsweek 45:99, Mar 14, 1955
Saturday Review 38:24, Mar 19, 1955
Theatre Arts 39:16, 22, May 1955
Time 65:58, Mar 14, 1955

Come Back Little Sheba
  Productions:
    Opened February 15, 1950 for 123 performances.
    (Off Off Broadway) August 22, 1974 (Queen's Playhouse).
    (Off Off Broadway) February 10, 1977 (Equity Library Theater).
  Reviews:
    Catholic World 171:67, Apr 1950
    Christian Science Monitor Magazine p. 4, Feb 25, 1950
    Commonweal 51:558, Mar 3, 1950
    Life 28:93+, Apr 17, 1950
    New Republic 122:22-3, Mar 13, 1950
    New York Magazine 7:67, Sep 9, 1974
    New York Theatre Critics' Reviews 1950:348
    New York Times p. 28, Feb 16, 1950
                  II, p. 1, Feb 26, 1950
                  II, p. 3, Apr 2, 1950
                  II, p. 1, Jul 23, 1950
                  p. 17, Aug 23, 1974
                  p. 20, Feb 15, 1977
    New Yorker 26:68+, Feb 25, 1950
    Newsweek 35:74, Feb 27, 1950
    School and Society 71:345, Jan 3, 1950
    Theatre Arts 34:20, Apr 1950
                34:22-3, May 1950
    Time 55:81, Feb 27, 1950

The Dark at the Top of the Stairs
  Productions:
    Opened December 5, 1957 for 468 performances.
    (Off Off Broadway) October 25, 1976 (IRT).
    (Off Broadway) November 29, 1979 for 62 performances.

Reviews:
    America 98:436, Jan 11, 1958
    Catholic World 186:385, Feb 1958
    Christian Century 75:17-18, Jan 1, 1958
    Commonweal 67:615-16, Mar 14, 1958
    Life 44:74-7, Jan 6, 1958
    Los Angeles 26:276+, Sep 1981
    Nation 185:483, Dec 21, 1957
    New Republic 137:21, Dec 30, 1957
    New York Theatre Critics' Reviews 1957:158
    New York Times II, p. 1, Dec 1, 1957
                   p. 38, Dec 6, 1957
                   II, p. 3, Dec 15, 1957
                   II, p. 1, Mar 16, 1958
                   p. 30, Apr 11, 1974
                   III, p. 3, Nov 30, 1979
    New York Times Magazine pp. 80-1, Nov 24, 1957
    New Yorker 33:83, Dec 14, 1957
    Newsweek 50:81, Dec 16, 1957
    Reporter 17:34, Dec 26, 1957
    Saturday Review 40:27, Dec 21, 1957
    Theatre Arts 42:20-21, Feb 1958
                 42:62-4, Jul 1958
    Time 70:42+, Dec 16, 1957

*Farther Off from Heaven
    Reviews:
    New York Times p. 33, Jun 4, 1947

Glory in the Flower
    Productions:
    (Off Broadway) Season of 1958-1959 (ANTA).
    Reviews:
    New York Times p. 57, Dec 9, 1959

The Last Pad
    Productions:
    (Off Off Broadway) December 1970 (4 A Productions).
    Reviews:
    New York Times p. 61, Dec 8, 1970

A Loss of Roses
    Productions:
    Opened November 28, 1959 for 25 performances.
    Reviews:
    America 102:402+, Jan 2, 1960
    Christian Century 77:15, Jan 6, 1960
    Commonweal 71:395, Jan 1, 1960
    Nation 189:475, Dec 19, 1959
    New Republic 141:23-4, Dec 21, 1959
    New York Theatre Critics' Reviews 1959:211

New York Times II, p. 3, Nov 22, 1959
　　　　　　　 p. 27, Nov 30, 1959
　　　　　　　 II, p. 5, Dec 6, 1959
New Yorker 35:99-100, Dec 12, 1959
Newsweek 54:96, Dec 7, 1959
Saturday Review 42:24, Dec 19, 1959
Theatre Arts 44:10-13, Feb 1960
Time 74:56, Dec 7, 1959

The Love Death Plays of William Inge (Part I)
　Productions:
　　(Off Off Broadway) July 10, 1975 (Billy Munk Theater).
　Reviews:
　　Nation 221:157-8, Aug 30, 1975
　　New York Times p. 19, Jul 10, 1975

The Love Death Plays of William Inge (Part II)
　Productions:
　　(Off Off Broadway) July 17, 1975 (Billy Munk Theater).
　Reviews:
　　New York Times p. 14, Jul 19, 1975

Natural Affection
　Productions:
　　Opened January 31, 1963 for 36 performances.
　Reviews:
　　Commonweal 77:598, Mar 1, 1963
　　Nation 196:148, Feb 16, 1963
　　New Republic 148:29, Feb 23, 1963
　　New York Theatre Critics' Reviews 1963:383
　　New York Times p. 5, Feb 2, 1963
　　　　　　　　 p. 59, Jun 14, 1973
　　New Yorker 38:66+, Feb 9, 1963
　　Newsweek 61:84, Feb 11, 1963
　　Reporter 28:48-9, Apr 25, 1963
　　Saturday Review 46:25, Feb 16, 1963
　　Theatre Arts 47:58-9, Mar 1963
　　Time 81:56, Feb 8, 1963

Overnight
　Productions:
　　(Off Off Broadway) July 11, 1974 (URGENT).
　Reviews:
　　New York Times p. 24, Jul 17, 1974

Picnic
　Productions:
　　Opened February 19, 1953 for 477 performances.
　　(Off Off Broadway) April 4, 1975 (WPA Theater).
　　See also productions of Summer Brave.

Reviews:
    America 88:632, Mar 7, 1953
           89:147, May 2, 1953
    Catholic World 177:69, Apr 1953
    Commonweal 57:603, Mar 20, 1953
    Life 34:136-7, Mar 16, 1953
    Nation 176:213, Mar 7, 1953
    New Republic 128:22-3, Mar 16, 1953
    New York Theatre Critics' Reviews 1953:348
    New York Times II, p. 3, Feb 15, 1953
                    p. 14, Feb 20, 1953
                    II, p. 1, Mar 1, 1953
                    II, p. 1, Aug 30, 1953
                    p. 32, Feb 21, 1957
                    p. 43, Apr 22, 1975
    New Yorker 29:65, Feb 28, 1953
    Newsweek 41:84, Mar 2, 1953
    Saturday Review 36:33, Mar 7, 1953
    Theatre Arts 37:14-15, May 1953
                 37:28-9, Oct 1953
                 37:66-7, Jul 1953
                 38:32-3, Apr 1954
    Time 61:72+, Mar 2, 1953

Summer Brave ("Final, revised version" of Picnic)
    Productions:
    (Off Off Broadway) April 5, 1973 (Equity Library Theater).
    Opened October 26, 1975 for 16 performances.
    Reviews:
    New York Magazine 8:84+, Nov 10, 1975
    New York Theatre Critics' Reviews 1975:174
    New York Times p. 49, Apr 9, 1973
                   p. 46, Sep 9, 1975
                   p. 47, Sep 10, 1975
                   p. 24, Oct 27, 1975
    New Yorker 51:122, Nov 3, 1975

Where's Daddy?
    Productions:
    Opened March 2, 1966 for 22 performances.
    Reviews:
    Commonweal 84:83, Apr 8, 1966
    New Republic 154:36, Mar 26, 1966
    New York Theatre Critics' Reviews 1966:347
    New York Times p. 27, Mar 3, 1966
    New Yorker 42:110, Mar 12, 1966
    Newsweek 67:94, Mar 14, 1966
    Saturday Review 49:55, Mar 19, 1966
    Time 87:52, Mar 11, 1966
    Vogue 147:64, Apr 5, 1966

INNAURATO, ALBERT

Earthworms
Productions:
(Off Off Broadway) May 17, 1977 (Playwrights Horizons).
Reviews:
New York Magazine 10:67, Jun 6, 1977
New York Times III, p. 3, May 27, 1977

Gemini
Productions:
(Off Broadway) March 13, 1977 for 63 performances and transferred to Broadway.
Opened on Broadway May 21, 1977 for 1,788 performances.
Reviews:
America 136:363, Apr 16, 1977
Harper's 256:85-6, May 1978
Nation 224:410-11, Apr 2, 1977
New York Magazine 10:86, May 23, 1977
New York Theatre Critics' Reviews 1977:305
New York Times p. 36, Mar 14, 1977
III, p. 17, Apr 6, 1977
p. 31, May 24, 1977
p. 12, Sep 5, 1981
New Yorker 53:84, Mar 28, 1977
Time 109:95, Mar 28, 1977

I Don't Generally Like Poetry But Have You Read Trees? (with Chris Durang)
Productions:
(Off Broadway) December 14, 1972 (Manhattan Theater Club).
No Reviews.

Monsters (see The Transfiguration of Benno Blimpie)

Passione
Productions:
(Off Off Broadway) May 17, 1980 for 28 performances (Playwrights Horizons).
Opened September 23, 1980 for 16 performances.
Reviews:
Nation 231:387, Oct 18, 1980
New York Magazine 13:58, Jun 9, 1980
13:75-6, Oct 6, 1980
New York Theatre Critics' Reviews 1980:162
New York Times III, p. 5, May 23, 1980
III, p. 23, Sep 24, 1980
II, p. 5, Sep 28, 1980
New Yorker 56:147, Oct 6, 1980
Newsweek 96:108, Oct 6, 1980
Time 115:68, Jun 2, 1980

The Transfiguration of Benno Blimpie
    Productions:
        (Off Off Broadway) April 3, 1975 (Ensemble Studio Theater).
        (Off Off Broadway) April 22, 1976 (Direct Theater).
        (Off Broadway) March 10, 1977 for 61 performances as part of a
            bill called Monsters.
    Reviews:
        America 136:363-4, Apr 16, 1977
        Los Angeles 23:219+, Mar 1978
        Nation 224:410-11, Apr 2, 1977
        New York Magazine 10:70, Mar 28, 1977
        New York Theatre Critics' Reviews 1977:308
        New York Times p. 15, May 8, 1976
        New Yorker 53:77, Mar 21, 1977
        Saturday Review 4:42-3, May 14, 1977
        Time 109:95, Mar 28, 1977

Ulysses in Traction
    Productions:
        (Off Broadway) December 8, 1977 for 47 performances (Circle
            Repertory Co.).
    Reviews:
        Horizon 21:62, Jan 1978
        New Leader 61:28-9, Jan 2, 1978
        New York Magazine 11:87+, Dec 26, 1977/Jan 2, 1978
        New York Times III, p. 3, Dec 9, 1977
                        p. 37, Jan 3, 1978
        New Yorker 53:112, Dec 19, 1977

Urlicht
    Productions:
        (Off Broadway) March 26, 1974 (Playwrights Horizons).
    No Reviews.

IRVING, WASHINGTON

Charles the Second or, The Merry Monarch (see entry under Payne,
    John Howard)

Rip Van Winkle (see entry under Boucicault, Dion)

IRWIN, JAMES (see Moore, Edward J.)

JAMES, DANIEL L.

Winter Soldiers
    Productions:
        Opened November 29, 1942 for 25 performances.

Reviews:
American Mercury 56:237-8, Feb 1943
Current History 3:459, Jan 1943
New York Times p. 19, Nov 30, 1942
Theatre Arts 27:79+, Feb 1943

JAMES, HENRY

Disengaged
Productions:
Opened March 11, 1909 for 1 performance.
Reviews:
Forum 41:342-3, Apr 1909
Theatre Magazine 9:xii-xiii, Apr 1909

Innocents (see entry under Archibald, William)

Portrait of a Lady (see entry under Archibald, William)

Pyramus and Thisbe
Productions:
(Off Broadway) Season of 1968-69 (American Theatre Club).
No Reviews

The Salon
Productions:
(Off Broadway) Season of 1968-69 in repertory (American Theatre Club).
No Reviews

"A Sense of the Past" (see Berkeley Square under Balderston, John)

The Turn of the Screw (see The Innocents under Archibald, William)

Washington Square (see The Heiress under Goetz, Ruth)

Wings of the Dove (see Child of Fortune under Bolton, Guy)

JEFFERS, ROBINSON

Cretan Woman
Productions:
(Off Broadway) Season of 1954-1955.
Reviews:
Catholic World 179:469-71, Sep 1954
Commonweal 60:558, Sep 10, 1954
Life 37:142+, Sep 13, 1954

New York Times p. 17, May 21, 1954
p. 18, Jul 8, 1954
II, p. 1, Sep 5, 1954
Saturday Review 37:25, Jun 5, 1954

Dear Judas (Adapted by Michael Myerberg)
Productions:
Opened October 5, 1947 for 17 performances.
Reviews:
Commonweal 47:71, Oct 31, 1947
Forum 108:371, Dec 1947
New York Theatre Critics' Reviews 1947:315
New York Times II, p. 1, Aug 3, 1947
p. 26, Aug 5, 1947
II, p. 1, Oct 5, 1947
II, p. 3, Oct 5, 1947
p. 26, Oct 6, 1947
II, p. 6, Oct 19, 1947
New Yorker 23:59-61, Oct 18, 1947
Newsweek 30:91, Oct 20, 1947
Time 50:59, Aug 25, 1947
50:73, Oct 20, 1947

The Double Axe
Productions:
(Off Broadway) Season of 1968-69 (American Theatre Club).
No Reviews.

Medea (Adapted from the tragedy by Euripides)
Productions:
Opened October 20, 1947 for 214 performances.
Opened May 2, 1949 for 16 performances.
(Off Broadway) Season of 1960-61.
(Off Broadway) Opened November 28, 1965 for 77 performances.
Opened May 2, 1982 for 33+ performances (still running on
June 1, 1982).
Reviews:
America 147:13, June 26/July 3, 1982
Catholic World 166:263-4, Dec 1947
169:228-9, Jun 1949
Commonweal 47:94, Nov 7, 1947
Life 23:112-14, Nov 17, 1947
Nation 165:509-10, Nov 8, 1947
New Leader 65:19-20, May 31, 1982
New Republic 117:36, Nov 3, 1947
New York Magazine 15:76+, May 17, 1982
New York Theatre Critics' Reviews 1947:295
1982:311
New York Times VI, p. 56, Oct 12, 1947
II, p. 1, Oct 19, 1947
p. 27, Oct 21, 1947

II, p. 1, Oct 26, 1947
II, p. 1, Nov 9, 1947
II, p. 4, Dec 14, 1947
p. 9, Sep 4, 1948
p. 32, Sep 30, 1948
p. 31, May 3, 1949
p. 22, Sep 14, 1951
II, p. 9, Sep 16, 1951
p. 24, Oct 6, 1955
p. 25, Jul 26, 1960
p. 46, Nov 29, 1965
III, p. 10, May 3, 1982
II, p. 8, May 16, 1982
New Yorker 23:44, Nov 1, 1947
58:110+, May 17, 1982
Newsweek 30:76, Nov 3, 1947
99:90, May 17, 1982
Saturday Review 30:24-7, Nov 22, 1947
School and Society 67:163-4, Feb 28, 1948
Survey 31:31-4, Nov 1937
Theatre Arts 31:10-12, 36, Dec 1947
Time 50:68, Nov 3, 1947
119:74, May 31, 1982
Vogue 110:168-9, Dec 1947

Medea and Jason (Adapted by Eugenie Leontovich from Jeffers' version
of Euripides' Medea)
Productions:
Opened October 2, 1974 for one performance.
Reviews:
New York Theatre Critics' Reviews 1974:239
New York Times p. 51, Oct 3, 1974

The Tower Beyond Tragedy (Based on the works of Aeschylus)
Productions:
Opened November 26, 1950 for 32 performances.
Reviews:
Catholic World 172:308, Jan 1951
Christian Science Monitor Magazine p. 5, Dec 9, 1950
Commonweal 53:279, Dec 22, 1950
New Republic 124:22, Jan 8, 1951
New York Theatre Critics' Reviews 1950:180
New York Times II, p. 1, Nov 26, 1950
p. 29, Nov 27, 1950
II, p. 5, Dec 10, 1950
New Yorker 26:62+, Dec 9, 1950
School and Society 72:416-19, Dec 23, 1950
Theatre Arts 35:15, Feb 1951
Time 56:65, Dec 4, 1950

JONES, LE ROI   (see Baraka, Imamu Amiri)

JONES, PRESTON

The Last Meeting of the Knights of the White Magnolia (part of A
      Texas Trilogy)
   Productions:
      Opened September 22, 1976 for 22 performances as part of A
         Texas Trilogy.
   Reviews:
      Los Angeles 21:196+, Aug 1976
      New York Theatre Critics' Reviews 1976:178
      See also reviews of A Texas Trilogy

Lu Ann Hampton Laverty Oberlander (part of A Texas Trilogy)
   Productions:
      Opened September 21, 1976 for 21 performances as part of A
         Texas Trilogy.
   Reviews:
      New York Theatre Critics' Reviews 1976:181
      See also reviews of A Texas Trilogy

The Oldest Living Graduate (part of A Texas Trilogy)
   Productions:
      Opened September 23, 1976 for 20 performances as part of A
         Texas Trilogy.
   Reviews:
      Los Angeles 25:229, Jun 1980
      New West 2:SC-39, Dec 5, 1977
              5:103, Jun 16, 1980
      New York Theatre Critics' Reviews 1976:175
      Texas Monthly 8:175+, Jun 1980
      See also reviews of A Texas Trilogy

*A Place on the Magdalena Flats
   Reviews:
      Texas Monthly 4:84, Aug 1976

*Santa Fe Sunshine
   Reviews:
      Texas Monthly 5:104+, Jul 1977

A Texas Trilogy (consists of Lu Ann Hampton Laverty Oberlander,
      The Last Meeting of the Knights of the White Magnolia, and
      The Oldest Living Graduate)
   Productions:
      See individual entries for exact openings.
   Reviews:
      America 135:260-1, Oct 23, 1976
      Mademoiselle 82:178, Nov 1976

Nation 223:348-50, Oct 9, 1976
New Republic 175:20-1, Oct 23, 1976
New York Magazine 9:88+, Oct 11, 1976
New York Theatre Critics' Reviews 1976:175, 178, 181
New York Times II, p. 1, May 30, 1976
  p. 30, Sep 22, 1976
  p. 51, Sep 23, 1976
  III, p. 3, Sep 24, 1976
  II, p. 3, Oct 3, 1976
  p. 37, Oct 23, 1976
New Yorker 52:75-6, Oct 4, 1976
Newsweek 87:95-6, May 17, 1976
  88:97, Oct 4, 1976
Smithsonian 7:48-55, Oct 1976
Time 108:67-8, Sep 27, 1976
See also reviews of individual entries

KANIN, FAY

Goodbye, My Fancy
    Productions:
    Opened November 17, 1948 for 446 performances.
    Reviews:
    Catholic World 168:323, Jan 1949
    Commonweal 49:196, Dec 3, 1948
    Independent Woman 28:38-40, Feb 1949
    Life 25:69-72, Dec 13, 1948
    Nation 167:646-7, Dec 4, 1948
    New Republic 119:30, Dec 13, 1948
    New York Theatre Critics' Reviews 1948:152
    New York Times p. 35, Nov 18, 1948
                  II, p. 1, Nov 28, 1948
                  II, p. 4, Dec 19, 1948
                  p. 19, Jul 1, 1952
    New Yorker 24:56+, Nov 27, 1948
    Newsweek 32:81, Nov 29, 1948
    Saturday Review 32:30-2, Jan 8, 1949
    Theatre Arts 33:13, Jan 1949
    Time 52:76, Nov 29, 1948
    Vogue 113:117, Jan 1949

His and Hers (with Michael Kanin)
    Productions:
    Opened January 7, 1954 for 76 performances.
    Reviews:
    America 90:463, Jan 30, 1954
    Catholic World 178:467, Mar 1954
    New York Theatre Critics' Reviews 1954:393
    New York Times p. 18, Jan 8, 1954
    New Yorker 29:54-6, Jan 16, 1954
    Newsweek 43:59, Jan 18, 1954

Saturday Review 37:27, Jan 30, 1954
Theatre Arts 38:15, Mar 1954
Time 63:54, Jan 18, 1954

Rashomon (with Michael Kanin. Based on the stories of Ryunosuke
    Akutagawa)
  Productions:
    Opened January 27, 1959 for 159 performances.
    (Off Off Broadway) December 6, 1973 (Equity Library Theater).
    (Off Off Broadway) September 30, 1981 (Shelter West).
  Reviews:
    America 100:670-1, Mar 7, 1959
    Catholic World 189:59, Apr 1959
    Commonweal 69:650, Mar 20, 1959
    Nation 188:146, Feb 14, 1959
    Coronet 46:12, May 1959
    New York Theatre Critics' Reviews 1959:397
    New York Times II, p. 1, Jan 18, 1959
                    p. 36, Jan 28, 1959
                    II, p. 1, Feb 8, 1959
                    p. 56, May 10, 1973
                    p. 58, Dec 10, 1973
                    p. 16, Sep 14, 1974
    New Yorker 34:81-2, Feb 7, 1959
    Newsweek 53:56, Feb 9, 1959
    Reporter 20:39, Mar 19, 1959
    Saturday Review 42:32, Feb 14, 1959
    Theatre Arts 43:12-13+, Feb 1959
                 43:9, Apr 1959
    Time 73:70+, Feb 9, 1959
    Vogue 133:112-13, Mar 1, 1959

KANIN, GARSON

Born Yesterday
  Productions:
    Opened February 4, 1946 for 1,642 performances.
    (Off Broadway) Season of 1957-58 (Equity Library Theater).
    (Off Off Broadway) Season of 1973-1974 (Manhattan Theater
        Club).
    (Off Off Broadway) July 15, 1976 (Playwrights Horizons).
  Reviews:
    Catholic World 162:552, Mar 1946
    Commonweal 43:479, Feb 22, 1946
    Life 20:81-2+, Feb 25, 1946
    Nation 162:205, Feb 16, 1946
    New Republic 114:254, Feb 18, 1946
                 114:280-2, Feb 25, 1946
    New York Theatre Critics' Reviews 1946:466
    New York Times p. 18, Feb 5, 1946

II, p. 1, Feb 10, 1946
II, p. 1, Apr 7, 1946
II, p. 1, May 5, 1946
II, p. 1, Jul 21, 1946
p. 32, Nov 5, 1946
II, p. 3, Feb 2, 1947
II, p. 3, Feb 9, 1947
II, p. 1, May 18, 1947
II, p. 1, Jul 27, 1947
II, p. 1, Oct 12, 1947
II, p. 3, Dec 28, 1947
VI, p. 16, Mar 4, 1951
p. 16, Jan 1, 1954
p. 12, Mar 22, 1958
p. 17, Feb 23, 1974
New Yorker 22:46+, Feb 16, 1946
Newsweek 27:92, Feb 18, 1946
Theatre Arts 30:200-1+, Apr 1946
31:58, Apr 1947
Time 47:49, Feb 18, 1946

Come On Strong
Productions:
Opened October 4, 1962 for 36 performances.
(Off Off Broadway) November 1977 (Greenwich Mews).
Reviews:
New York Theatre Critics' Reviews 1962:256
New York Times p. 29, Oct 5, 1962
p. 12, Oct 6, 1962
p. 19, Oct 8, 1962
New Yorker 38:180+, Oct 13, 1962
Newsweek 60:68, Oct 15, 1962
Theatre Arts 46:12-13, Nov 1962

Dreyfus in Rehearsal (Adapted from the original of Jean-Claude Grumberg)
Productions:
Opened October 17, 1974 for 12 performances.
Reviews:
Nation 210:476, Nov 9, 1974
New York Magazine 7:88, Nov 4, 1974
New York Theatre Critics' Reviews 1974:210
New York Times p. 26, Oct 18, 1974
p. 28, Oct 25, 1974
II, p. 5, Oct 27, 1974
New Yorker 50:65-6, Oct 28, 1974

A Gift of Time (Based on Lael Tucker Wertenbaker's Death of a Man)
Productions:
Opened February 22, 1962 for 92 performances.
Reviews:
Catholic World 195:127-8, May 1962

Commonweal 76:16, Mar 30, 1962
Nation 194:221-2, Mar 10, 1962
New York Theatre Critics' Reviews 1962:340
New York Times p. 34, Feb 23, 1962
                II, p. 1, Mar 4, 1962
New Yorker 38:93, Mar 3, 1962
Newsweek 59:73, Mar 5, 1962
Saturday Review 45:32, Mar 10, 1962
Theatre Arts 46:61, Apr 1962
Time 79:42, Mar 2, 1962

The Good Soup (Adapted from the play by Felicien Marceau)
    Productions:
        Opened March 2, 1960 for 21 performances.
    Reviews:
        America 103:27, Apr 2, 1960
        Nation 190:263, Mar 19, 1960
        New York Theatre Critics' Reviews 1960:330
        New York Times VI, p. 79, Feb 21, 1960
                II, p. 1, Feb 28, 1960
                p. 26, Mar 3, 1960
        New Yorker 36:113-14, Mar 12, 1960
        Saturday Review 43:26-7, Mar 19, 1960
        Theatre Arts 43:14, Jul 1959
        Time 75:73, Mar 14, 1960

The Live Wire
    Productions:
        Opened August 17, 1950 for 28 performances.
    Reviews:
        Christian Science Monitor Magazine p. 8, Aug 26, 1950
        Commonweal 52:510, Sep 1, 1950
        New Republic 123:23, Sep 4, 1950
        New York Theatre Critics' Reviews 1950:277
        New York Times p. 26, Jul 19, 1950
                p. 16, Aug 18, 1950
                II, p. 1, Aug 27, 1950
        New Yorker 26:50, Aug 26, 1950
        Newsweek 36:75, Aug 28, 1950
        Theatre Arts 34:11, Oct 1950
        Time 56:70, Aug 28, 1950

The Rat Race
    Productions:
        Opened December 22, 1949 for 84 performances.
    Reviews:
        Catholic World 170:386, Feb 1950
        Commonweal 51:390, Jan 13, 1950
        New Republic 122:31, Jan 16, 1950
        New York Theatre Critics' Reviews 1949:190
        New York Times p. 16, Dec 23, 1949

New Yorker 25:40-1, Dec 31, 1949
Newsweek 35:48, Jan 2, 1950
Theatre Arts 34:9, Mar 1950
Time 55:52, Jan 2, 1950

The Smile of the World
    Productions:
        Opened January 12, 1949 for 5 performances.
    Reviews:
        Forum 111:161, Mar 1949
        New Republic 120:30, Jan 31, 1949
        New York Theatre Critics' Reviews 1949:396
        New York Times p. 26, Jan 13, 1949
        New Yorker 24:44-6, Jan 22, 1949
        Newsweek 33:70, Jan 24, 1949
        Theatre Arts 33:17, Apr 1949
        Time 53:52, Jan 24, 1949

KAUFMAN, GEORGE S.

The American Way (with Moss Hart)
    Productions:
        Opened January 21, 1939 for 164 performances.
        Opened July 17, 1939 for 80 performances.
    Reviews:
        Catholic World 148:728-9, Mar 1939
        Commonweal 29:441, Feb 10, 1939
        Life 6:32, Feb 6, 1939
        Nation 148:157-8, Feb 4, 1939
        New Republic 98:14, Feb 8, 1939
        New York Times p. 9, Jan 23, 1939
                      IX, p. 1, Jan 29, 1939
        Newsweek 13:24, Feb 6, 1939
        North American Review 247, no. 1:153-5, Mar 1939
        One Act Play Magazine 2:746-7, Feb 1939
        Theatre Arts 23:162-4, Mar 1939
        Time 33:28, Jan 30, 1939

Beggar on Horseback (with Marc Connelly)
    Productions:
        Opened February 12, 1924 for 144+ performances.
        Opened March 23, 1925 for 16 performances.
        Opened May 14, 1970 for 52 performances.
    Reviews:
        American Mercury 1:499-500, Apr 1924
        Bookman 59:201, Apr 1924
        Classic 19:46+, Jul 1924
        Dial 76:384, Apr 1924
        Freeman 8:617-18, Mar 5, 1924
        Life (NY) 83:20, Mar 6, 1924

Metropolitan Magazine 59:48, Jul 1924
Nation 118:238-9, Feb 27, 1924
    210:668, Jun 1, 1970
New Republic 38:45-6, Mar 5, 1924
New York Theatre Critics' Reviews 1970:253
New York Times p. 17, Feb 13, 1924
        VII, p. 1, Feb 17, 1924
        p. 22, May 8, 1925
        p. 24, Nov 12, 1925
        p. 18, Nov 12, 1925
        p. 47, May 15, 1970
        II, p. 1, May 24, 1970
New Yorker 46:73-4, May 23, 1970
Newsweek 75:95, May 25, 1970
Theatre Magazine 39:19, 62, Apr 1924
    53:49, Feb 1931

Bravo! (see entry under Ferber, Edna)

The Butter and Egg Man
  Productions:
    Opened September 23, 1925 for 243 performances.
    (Off Broadway) October 17, 1966 for 32 performances.
  Reviews:
    America 115:524, Oct 29, 1966
    Bookman 62:480, Dec 1925
    Independent 116:20, Jan 2, 1926
    Nation 203:493, Nov 7, 1966
    New Republic 44:202, Oct 14, 1925
    New York Times p. 28, Sep 24, 1925
               p. 28, Aug 23, 1927
               p. 19, Aug 31, 1927
               p. 15, Sep 17, 1927
               p. 49, Oct 18, 1966
               p. 34, Nov 4, 1966
               II, p. 3, Jul 29, 1979
    New Yorker 42:98-9, Oct 29, 1966

The Channel Road (with Alexander Woollcott)
  Productions:
    Opened October 17, 1929 for 60 performances.
  Reviews:
    Catholic World 130:333-4, Dec 1929
    Life (NY) 94:28, Nov 8, 1929
    Nation 129:530, Nov 6, 1929
    New York Times p. 24, Oct 18, 1929
               IX, p. 1, Oct 27, 1929
    Outlook 153:389, Nov 6, 1929
    Theatre Arts 13:881-2, Dec 1929
    Theatre Magazine 50:24, Dec 1929

The Dark Tower (with Alexander Woollcott)
    Productions:
        Opened November 25, 1933 for 57 performances.
    Reviews:
        Catholic World 138:475-6, Jan 1934
        Commonweal 19:160, Dec 8, 1933
        Nation 137:690, Dec 13, 1933
        New Outlook 163:42, Jan 1934
        New Republic 81:78, Nov 28, 1934
        New York Times p. 20, Nov 27, 1933
                    IX, p. 5, Dec 3, 1933
        Stage 11:18-19, Jan 1934
        Time 22:48, Dec 4, 1933
        Vanity Fair 41:42, Feb 1934

The Deep Tangled Wildwood (with Marc Connelly)
    Productions:
        Opened November 5, 1923 for 16 performances.
    Reviews:
        Life (NY) 82:18, Nov 22, 1923
        New York Times p. 22, Nov 6, 1923

Dinner at Eight (with Edna Ferber)
    Productions:
        Opened October 22, 1932 for 232 performances.
        Opened September 27, 1966 for 127 performances.
    Reviews:
        America 115:524, Oct 29, 1966
        Arts and Decoration 38:51, Dec 1932
        Christian Century 84:144, Feb 1, 1967
        Commonweal 17:49, Nov 9, 1932
                    85:78, Oct 21, 1966
        Life 61:127-30, Nov 25, 1966
        Nation 135:464-5, Nov 9, 1932
                203:397-8, Oct 17, 1966
        National Review 19:99, Jan 24, 1967
        New Outlook 161:46, Dec 1932
        New Republic 72:355-7, Nov 9, 1932
        New York Theatre Critics' Reviews 1966:289
        New York Times p. 18, Oct 24, 1932
                    IX, p. 3, Oct 30, 1932
                    IX, p. 1, Nov 6, 1932
                    p. 11, Jan 7, 1933
                    IX, p. 1, Jan 29, 1933
                    IX, p. 1, Apr 9, 1933
                    p. 21, Oct 6, 1933
                    p. 26, Oct 17, 1933
                    II, p. 1, Sep 25, 1966
                    p. 38, Sep 28, 1966
                    II, p. 1, Oct 9, 1966
        Newsweek 68:104, Oct 10, 1966

Saturday Review 49:63, Oct 15, 1966
Stage 10:13-16, Dec 1932
Theatre Arts 17:22, Jan 1933
Time 88:92, Oct 9, 1966
Town and Country 87:26, Dec 1, 1932
Vanity Fair 39:25, Nov 1932
Vogue 80:92, Dec 1, 1932

Dulcy (with Marc Connelly)
   Productions:
      Opened August 13, 1921 for 246 performances.
      (Off Off Broadway) October 27, 1980 for 19 performances
         (Quaigh).
   Reviews:
      Bookman 54:144-6, Oct 1921
      Dramatic Mirror 83:408, Mar 5, 1921
                       84:265, Aug 20, 1921
      Hearst 40:21-3+, Oct 1921
      Life (NY) 78:18, Sep 1, 1921
      Nation 113:299, Sep 14, 1921
      New Republic 28:33, Aug 31, 1921
      New York Clipper 69:24, Aug 17, 1921
      New York Times p. 14, Aug 15, 1921
                     VI, p. 1, Aug 21, 1921
                     VI, p. 1, Nov 6, 1921
                     II, p. 1, Jun 22, 1947
                     III, p. 5, Oct 28, 1980
      Theatre Magazine 34:234, Oct 1921
                       34:237, Oct 1921
                       34:372+, Dec 1921
      Weekly Review 5:216, Sep 3, 1921

Eldorado   (see entry under Stallings, Laurence)

The Fabulous Invalid   (see entry under Hart, Moss)

Fancy Meeting You Again (with Leueen MacGrath)
   Productions:
      Opened January 14, 1952 for 8 performances.
   Reviews:
      Commonweal 55:423, Feb 1, 1952
      New York Theatre Critics' Reviews 1952:392
      New York Times p. 23, Jan 15, 1952
      New Yorker 27:54, Jan 26, 1952
      Saturday Review 35:30, Feb 2, 1952
      Theatre Arts 36:71, Mar 1952

First Lady   (see entry under Dayton, Katherine)

George Washington Slept Here (with Moss Hart)
   Productions:
      Opened October 18, 1940 for 173 performances.

(Off Off Broadway) April 29, 1976 (Playwrights Horizons).
Reviews:
  American Mercury 51:483-5, Dec 1940
  Catholic World 152:335, Dec 1940
  Commonweal 33:80, Nov 8, 1940
  Nation 151:430, Nov 2, 1940
  New Republic 103:629, Nov 4, 1940
  New York Theatre Critics' Reviews 1940:246
                           1941:466
  New York Times p. 27, Sep 24, 1940
             p. 20, Oct 19, 1940
             IX, p. 1, Oct 27, 1940
             X, p. 5, Dec 15, 1940
             p. 27, Jul 1, 1941
  New Yorker 16:36, Oct 26, 1940
  Newsweek 16:62, Nov 4, 1940
  Stage 1:10, Nov 1940
      1:10, Dec 1940
      1:39, Feb 1941
  Theatre Arts 24:849, Dec 1940
  Time 36:67, Oct 28, 1940

The Good Fellow (with Herman J. Mankiewicz)
  Productions:
    Opened October 5, 1926 for 7 performances.
  Reviews:
    New York Times p. 22, Oct 6, 1926
    Theatre Magazine 44:18, Dec 1926

June Moon (see entry under Lardner, Ring)

The Land Is Bright (with Edna Ferber)
  Productions:
    Opened October 28, 1941 for 79 performances.
  Reviews:
    Catholic World 154:337-8, Dec 1941
    Commonweal 35:93, Nov 14, 1941
    Current History 1:379-80, Dec 1941
    Life 11:53-6, Dec 1, 1941
    Nation 153:491, Nov 15, 1941
    New York Theatre Critics' Reviews 1941:253
    New York Times p. 28, Oct 21, 1941
               p. 26, Oct 29, 1941
               p. 22, Oct 30, 1941
               IV, p. 2, Nov 2, 1941
               IX, p. 1, Nov 2, 1941
               IX, p. 1, Nov 9, 1941
    New Yorker 17:36+, Nov 8, 1941
    Newsweek 18:70, Nov 10, 1941
    Theatre Arts 26:10, Jan 1942
    Time 38:55, Nov 10, 1941

The Late George Apley (see entry under Marquand, John P.)

The Man Who Came To Dinner (see entry under Hart, Moss)

Merrily We Roll Along (with Moss Hart)
    Productions:
        Opened September 29, 1934 for 155 performances.
    Reviews:
        Catholic World 140:209, Nov 1934
        Commonweal 20:589, Oct 19, 1934
        Golden Book 20:636+, Dec 1934
        Literary Digest 118:18, Oct 13, 1934
        Nation 139:460, Oct 17, 1934
        New York Times p. 14, Oct 1, 1934
                    IX, p. 1, Oct 7, 1934
                    X, p. 3, Oct 14, 1934
                    II, p. 2, Jan 13, 1935
                    p. 15, Jun 30, 1936
        Scholastic 25:3, Oct 20, 1934
        Stage 12:2, 6, Nov 1934
              12:13-14, Dec 1934
              12:26, May 1935
        Theatre Arts 18:815-16, Nov 1934
        Time 24:46, Oct 8, 1934
        Vanity Fair 43:45, Dec 1934
        Vogue 84:51, Oct 15, 1934

Merton of the Movies (with Marc Connelly. Adapted from Harry
    Leon Wilson's story)
    Productions:
        Opened November 13, 1922 for 248+ performances.
    Reviews:
        Life (NY) 80:18, Nov 30, 1922
        Los Angeles 22:183, Jun 1977
        New West 2:SC-48, May 23, 1977
        New York Clipper 70:20, Nov 22, 1922
        New York Times p. 16, Nov 14, 1922
                    VII, p. 1, Nov 19, 1922
                    p. 20, Apr 13, 1923
                    p. 20, Apr 27, 1923
                    p. 62, Sep 26, 1968
                    p. 46, Apr 13, 1980
                    III, p. 18, Apr 23, 1981
        Theatre Magazine 37:25, Jan 1923

Minick (with Edna Ferber)
    Productions:
        Opened September 24, 1924 for 141 performances.
    Reviews:
        American Mercury 3:376-7, Nov 1924
        Current Opinion 77:732-9, Dec 1924
        Independent 113:551, Dec 20, 1924
        Life (NY) 84:18, Oct 16, 1924

Motion Picture Classic 28:48+, Jan 1925
Nation 119:423-4, Oct 15, 1924
New York Times VII, p. 1, Aug 24, 1924
              p. 20, Sep 25, 1924
Overland 86:19, Jan 1928
Survey 53:162-4, Nov 1, 1924
Theatre Arts 8:804+, Dec 1924
Theatre Magazine 40:16, Dec 1924
              40:18, Dec 1924

Old Man Minick (see Minick)

Once in a Lifetime (with Moss Hart)
    Productions:
        Opened September 24, 1930 for 406 performances.
        (Off Broadway) January 28, 1964 for one performance.
        (Off Off Broadway) Season of 1974-75 (ETC).
        Opened June 15, 1978 for 85 performances.
    Reviews:
        Bookman 74:72, Sep 1931
        Catholic World 132:204-5, Nov 1930
        Commonweal 12:584, Oct 8, 1930
        Drama 21:15-16, Nov 1930
        Life (NY) 96:18, Oct 17, 1930
        Nation 131:386, Oct 8, 1930
              132:392, Apr 8, 1931
        New York Magazine 11:74, Jul 3, 1978
        New York Theatre Critics' Reviews 1978:236
        New York Times IX, p. 2, Sep 7, 1930
                       p. 22, Sep 25, 1930
                       IX, p. 1, Dec 7, 1930
                       VIII, p. 1, Feb 1, 1931
                       p. 13, Feb 24, 1933
                       p. 30, Oct 30, 1962
                       p. 20, Jan 29, 1964
                       p. 22, Apr 4, 1975
                       III, p. 3, Jun 16, 1978
                       II, p. 5, Jun 25, 1978
        New Yorker 54:51, Jun 26, 1978
        Outlook 156:233, Oct 8, 1930
        Sketch Book 8:31, Dec 1930
        Theatre Magazine 52:26, Dec 1930
                       52:35-7+, Dec 1930
        Time 112:83, Jul 17, 1978
        Vanity Fair 35:46+, Dec 1930
        Vogue 76:69+, Nov 24, 1930

The Royal Family (with Edna Ferber)
    Productions:
        Opened December 28, 1927 for 345 performances.
        Opened January 10, 1951 for 15 performances.

(Off Broadway) December 17, 1975 for 15 performances.
Opened December 30, 1975 for 232 performances.
Reviews:
America 134:74-5, Jan 31, 1976
American Mercury 13:378, Mar 1928
Commonweal 32:390, Aug 30, 1940
Dramatist 19:1366-7, Apr 1928
Life (NY) 91:21, Jan 19, 1928
Life 9:46-8, Sep 23, 1940
Literary Digest 96:26-7, Jan 21, 1928
Nation 222:28, Jan 3, 1976
National Review 28:686, Jun 25, 1976
New York Magazine 9:70, Jan 12, 1976
New York Theatre Critics' Reviews 1951:392
1975:87
New York Times p. 26, Dec 29, 1927
VIII, p. 1, Jan 8, 1928
IX, p. 1, Apr 12, 1931
p. 24, Oct 24, 1934
IX, p. 1, Nov 11, 1934
p. 15, Jul 16, 1936
p. 15, Aug 12, 1936
p. 15, Aug 13, 1940
IV, p. 2, Aug 18, 1940
p. 28, Jan 11, 1951
p. 64, Dec 18, 1975
II, p. 7, Jan 11, 1976
p. 60, Apr 4, 1976
New Yorker 51:43, Dec 29, 1975
Newsweek 87:81, Jan 19, 1976
Outlook 148:67, Jan 11, 1928
Saturday Review 4:531-2, Jan 21, 1928
School and Society 73:102-103, Feb 17, 1951
Texas Monthly 6:174, Sep 1978
Theatre Arts 12:171-2, Mar 1928
35:18, Mar 1951
Theatre Magazine 47:28-30+, Mar 1928
Time 107:61, Jan 12, 1976
Vogue 71:124, Feb 15, 1928

The Small Hours (with Leueen MacGrath)
Productions:
Opened February 15, 1951 for 20 performances.
Reviews:
Commonweal 53:542, Mar 9, 1951
New York Theatre Critics' Reviews 1951:344
New York Times II, p. 1, Feb 11, 1951
p. 22, Feb 16, 1951
New Yorker 27:66+, Feb 24, 1951
Newsweek 37:49, Feb 26, 1951
Theatre Arts 35:20, Apr 1951
Time 57:50, Feb 26, 1951

The Solid Gold Cadillac (with Howard Teichmann)
Productions:
    Opened November 5, 1953 for 526 performances.
Reviews:
    American 90:278, Dec 5, 1953
    Business Week pp. 128+, Nov 14, 1953
    Catholic World 178:306-7, Jan 1954
    Commonweal 59:306, Dec 25, 1953
    Fortune 48:100, Dec 1953
    Harpers 208:93-4, Jan 1954
    Life 35:65-6+, Nov 23, 1953
    Nation 177:433, Nov 21, 1953
    New York Theatre Critics' Reviews 1953:222
    New York Times II, p. 3, Nov 1, 1953
                    p. 24, Nov 6, 1953
                    II, p. 1, Nov 15, 1953
    New Yorker 29:70+, Nov 14, 1953
    Newsweek 42:60, Nov 16, 1953
             42:60, Dec 21, 1953
    Saturday Review 36:50, Nov 21, 1953
                    35:46, Dec 12, 1953
    Theatre Arts 38:19, Jan 1954
    Time 62:90, Nov 16, 1953

Some One in the House (with Larry Evans and Walter Percival)
Productions:
    Opened September 9, 1918 for 32 performances.
Reviews:
    Dramatic Mirror 79:435, Sep 21, 1918
    Independent 95:370, Sep 21, 1918
    New York Times p. 11, Sep 10, 1918
                   VIII, p. 1, Sep 15, 1918
    Theatre Magazine 28:274+, Nov 1918

Stage Door (with Edna Ferber)
Productions:
    Opened October 22, 1936 for 169 performances.
    (Off Off Broadway) April 29, 1977 (IRT).
    (Off Off Broadway) May 7, 1977 (Playwrights Horizons).
Reviews:
    Catholic World 144:471, Jan 1937
    Commonweal 25:51, Nov 6, 1936
    Nation 143:557, Nov 7, 1936
    New Republic 89:50, Nov 11, 1936
    New York Times p. 35, Sep 29, 1936
                   IX, p. 2, Oct 4, 1936
                   p. 26, Oct 23, 1936
                   X, p. 3, Oct 25, 1936
                   X, p. 1, Nov 1, 1936
                   p. 19, Mar 15, 1939
    Newsweek 8:24, Oct 31, 1936

Stage 14:48-9, Nov 1936
Theatre Arts 20:923-4, Dec 1936
Time 28:46, Nov 2, 1936

Theatre Royal (see The Royal Family)

To the Ladies (with Marc Connelly)
Productions:
Opened February 20, 1922 for 128 performances.
Reviews:
Life (NY) 79:18, Mar 9, 1922
Nation 114:294, Mar 8, 1922
New York Clipper 70:22, Mar 8, 1922
New York Times p. 20, Feb 21, 1922
VI, p. 1, Mar 5, 1922
VI, p. 1, Mar 12, 1922
Theatre Magazine 35:307-8, May 1922

You Can't Take It with You (see entry under Hart, Moss)

KELLY, GEORGE

Behold the Bridegroom
Productions:
Opened December 26, 1927 for 88 performances.
Reviews:
American Mercury 13:375-6, Mar 1928
Dramatist 19:1359-60, Jan 1928
Life (NY) 91:21, Jan 12, 1928
Nation 126:51, Jan 11, 1928
New Republic 53:246-7, Jan 18, 1928
New York Times p. 24, Dec 27, 1927
VIII, p. 1, Jan 1, 1928
IX, p. 4, Apr 1, 1928
Outlook 148:105, Jan 18, 1928
Saturday Review 4:547-8, Jan 28, 1928
Theatre Arts 12:169-71, Mar 1928
Theatre Magazine 47:38, Mar 1928
47:28-30+, Apr 1928
Vogue 71:87, Feb 15, 1928

Craig's Wife
Productions:
Opened October 12, 1925 for 360 performances.
(Off Broadway) February 1946 (Playhouse des Artistes).
Opened February 12, 1947 for 69 performances.
(Off Off Broadway) October 1974 (WPA Theater).
Reviews:
American Mercury 6:504-5, Dec 1925
Bookman 62:596, Jan 1926

Catholic World 165:72, Apr 1947
Commonweal 45:492, Feb 28, 1947
Dramatist 17:1305-6, Jul 1926
Independent 115:586, Nov 21, 1925
Mentor 14:36-7, Jun 1926
Nation 121:521-2, Nov 4, 1925
      164:256, Mar 1, 1947
New Republic 44:281-2, Nov 4, 1925
      116:40, Feb 24, 1947
New York Theatre Critics' Reviews 1947:457
New York Times p. 21, Oct 13, 1925
      IX, p. 1, Oct 18, 1925
      II, p. 1, Feb 9, 1947
      p. 35, Feb 13, 1947
      II, p. 1, Mar 30, 1947
New Yorker 23:53, Feb 22, 1947
Newsweek 29:92, Feb 24, 1947
Outlook 142:49-50, Jan 13, 1926
Saturday Review 30:32-4, Mar 8, 1947
Theatre Arts 31:19, Apr 1947
Theatre Magazine 42:15, Dec 1925
      43:29, Jan 1926
      43:26+, Apr 1926
      44:9+, Oct 1926
Time 49:58, Feb 24, 1947

Daisy Mayme
  Productions:
    Opened October 25, 1926 for 112 performances.
  Reviews:
    Bookman 64:618-20, Jan 1927
    Independent 118:21, Jan 1, 1927
    Life (NY) 88:23, Nov 11, 1926
    Nation 123:488, Nov 10, 1926
    New Republic 48:375-6, Nov 17, 1926
    New York Times p. 24, Oct 26, 1926
          VIII, p. 1, Oct 31, 1926
    Theatre Arts 11:11-12, Jan 1927
    Theatre Magazine 45:16, Jan 1927
    Vogue 68:76-7, Dec 15, 1926

The Deep Mrs. Sykes
  Productions:
    Opened March 19, 1945 for 72 performances.
  Reviews:
    Commonweal 41:625, Apr 6, 1945
    Nation 160:395, Apr 7, 1945
    New Republic 112:447, Apr 2, 1945
    New York Theatre Critics' Reviews 1945:246
    New York Times p. 22, Mar 20, 1945
          II, p. 1, Mar 25, 1945

New Yorker 21:40+, Mar 31, 1945
Newsweek 25:84, Apr 2, 1945
Theatre Arts 29:271, May 1945
Time 45:58+, Apr 2, 1945

Fatal Weakness

Productions:
Opened November 19, 1946 for 119 performances.
Reviews:
Catholic World 164:359, Jan 1947
Commonweal 45:201, Dec 6, 1946
Nation 164:81, Jan 18, 1947
New Republic 115:764, Dec 9, 1946
New York Theatre Critics' Reviews 1946:251
New York Times p. 43, Nov 20, 1946
II, p. 3, Feb 9, 1947
New Yorker 22:60, Nov 30, 1946
Newsweek 28:94, Dec 2, 1946
Saturday Review 29:23, Dec 21, 1946
Theatre Arts 31:21, 30, Jan 1947
Time 48:54, Dec 2, 1946

Maggie the Magnificent

Productions:
Opened October 21, 1929 for 32 performances.
Reviews:
Commonweal 11:21, Nov 6, 1929
Life (NY) 94:28, Nov 8, 1929
New Republic 60:323-5, Nov 6, 1929
New York Times p. 26, Oct 22, 1929
IX, p. 1, Nov 3, 1929
Review of Reviews 80:158-9, Dec 1929
Theatre Arts 14:17-18, Jan 1930
Theatre Magazine 50:68, Dec 1929

Philip Goes Forth

Productions:
Opened January 12, 1931 for 97 performances.
Reviews:
Bookman 73:70-1, Mar 1931
Catholic World 132:722, Mar 1931
Commonweal 13:241, Dec 31, 1930
Drama 21:13, Feb 1931
Nation 132:107, Jan 28, 1931
New Republic 65:301-2, Jan 28, 1931
New York Times VIII, p. 2, Jan 4, 1931
p. 35, Jan 13, 1931
VIII, p. 1, Jan 18, 1931
VIII, p. 3, Feb 8, 1931
Outlook 157:152, Jan 28, 1931
Sketch Book 8:25, Mar 1931

Theatre Arts 15:183-5, Mar 1931
Theatre Magazine 53:24-5, Mar 1931
Vogue 77:59, Mar 1, 1931

Reflected Glory
Productions:
Opened September 21, 1936 for 127 performances.
(Off Off Broadway) November 29, 1979 (No Smoking Playhouse).
Reviews:
Catholic World 144:217-18, Nov 1936
Commonweal 24:560, Oct 9, 1936
Literary Digest 122:18-19, Aug 8, 1936
122:19, Oct 3, 1936
Nation 143:401-2, Oct 3, 1936
New Republic 88:257, Oct 7, 1936
New York Times p. 23, Jul 22, 1936
p. 19, Sep 18, 1936
p. 30, Sep 22, 1936
X, p. 1, Sep 27, 1936
p. 14, Apr 17, 1937
II, p. 10, May 2, 1937
Newsweek 8:22, Aug 1, 1936
Player's Magazine 13:8, Nov-Dec, 1936
Theatre Arts 20:849-50, Nov 1936
Time 28:42, Oct 5, 1936

The Show-Off
Productions:
Opened February 5, 1924 for 571 performances.
Opened December 12, 1932 for 119 performances.
Opened May 31, 1950 for 6 performances.
Opened December 5, 1967 for 81 performances.
Opened September 13, 1968 for 19 performances.
(Off Broadway) Opened April 25, 1978 for 89 performances.
(Off Off Broadway) June 9, 1979 (Playwrights Horizons).
Reviews:
America 118:131, Jan 27, 1968
American Mercury 1:500-501, Apr 1924
Bookman 59:204-5, Apr 1924
Canadian Forum 10:347, Jun 1930
Canadian Magazine 64:104-5+, May 1925
Catholic World 171:309, July 1950
Christian Science Monitor Magazine p. 9, Jun 17, 1950
Classic 19:46+, Jun 1924
Commonweal 17:187, Dec 14, 1932
17:245, Dec 28, 1932
87:471, Jan 19, 1968
Current Opinion 76:673-6+, May 1924
Freeman 8:592-3, Feb 27, 1924
Life (NY) 83:18, Feb 21, 1924
Metropolitan Magazine 59:46, Aug 1924

Nation 118:351-2, Mar 26, 1924
 135:654, Dec 28, 1932
 170:603, Jun 17, 1950
 206:27, Jan 1, 1968
New Republic 122:21, Jun 19, 1950
 158:41-2, Jan 6, 1968
New York Theatre Critics' Reviews 1950:292
 1967:201
New York Times VII, p. 2, Jan 20, 1924
 p. 16, Feb 6, 1924
 VII, p. 1, Feb 17, 1924
 VII, p. 1, Feb 15, 1925
 p. 25, Dec 13, 1932
 p. 24, Jun 1, 1950
 II, p. 1, Jun 11, 1950
 p. 40, Dec 6, 1967
 p. 61, Dec 7, 1967
 II, p. 3, Dec 17, 1967
 p. 43, Nov 25, 1975
 III, p. 3, May 19, 1978
Newsweek 35:83, Jun 12, 1950
 70:94, Dec 18, 1967
Reporter 38:37, Jan 11, 1968
Saturday Review 51:26, Jan 6, 1968
Theatre Magazine 39:16, 19, Apr 1924
 39:26+, Sep 1924
Time 55:57, Jun 12, 1950
 90:87, Dec 15, 1967

The Torch Bearers
 Productions:
 Opened August 29, 1922 for 135 performances.
 Reviews:
 Bookman 57:324-5, Nov 1922
 58:56-7, Sep 1923
 Dramatist 14:1175, Jul 1923
 Independent 109:397-8, Dec 23, 1922
 Life (NY) 80:18, Sep 21, 1922
 Nation 115:286, Sep 20, 1922
 New Republic 32:100-101, Sep 20, 1922
 New York Clipper 70:20, Sep 27, 1922
 New York Times p. 10, Aug 30, 1922
 VI, p. 1, Sep 3, 1922
 p. 30, Mar 22, 1929
 Playground 16:357-60, Nov 1922
 Theatre Magazine 36:298, Nov 1922
 38:42, Jul 1923

KENNEDY, ADRIANNE

A Beast's Story (see Cities in Bezique)

Cities in Bezique (The Owl Answers and A Beast's Story)
Productions:
    (Off Broadway) January 4, 1969 for 67 performances (New York
    Shakespeare Festival Public Theatre).
Reviews:
    New York Times p. 26, Jan 13, 1969
                   II, p. 3, Jan 19, 1969
    New Yorker 44:77, Jan 25, 1969

Funnyhouse of a Negro
Productions:
    (Off Broadway) January 14, 1964 for 46 performances.
Reviews:
    New York Times p. 25, Jan 15, 1964
    New Yorker 39:76+, Jan 25, 1964

*In His Own Write (with John Lennon and Victor Spinetti)
Reviews:
    New York Times p. 50, Jun 20, 1968
                p. 30, Jul 9, 1968
              II, p. 4, Jul 14, 1968

Lesson in a Dead Language
Productions:
    (Off Off Broadway) Season of 1970-71 (Theater Genesis).
No Reviews.

A Movie Star Has to Star in Black and White
Productions:
    (Off Off Broadway) November 1976 (NY Sh Fest Pub Th).
No Reviews.

The Owl Answers (see Cities in Bezique)

A Rat's Mass
Productions:
    (Off Off Broadway) Season of 1969-70 (La Mama).
    (Off Off Broadway) March 1976 (La Mama).
Reviews:
    New York Times p. 39, Nov 1, 1969
                p. 42, Mar 11, 1976

KENNEDY, CHARLES RANN

The Admiral
Productions:
    Opened April 17, 1924 for 4 performances.
Reviews:
    Living Age 322:664, Sep 27, 1924
    New York Times p. 20, Apr 25, 1924
                 VIII, p. 1, May 4, 1924

The Army with Banners
    Productions:
        Opened April 9, 1918 for 17 performances.
    Reviews:
        Dramatic Mirror 78:584+, Apr 27, 1918
        New Republic 14:360, Apr 20, 1928
        New York Times IV, p. 6, Apr 14, 1918
        Theatre Magazine 27:285-6, May 1918

The Chastening
    Productions:
        Opened March 12, 1923 for 18 performances.
    Reviews:
        Literary Digest 77:36-7, Apr 7, 1923
        New York Clipper 71:14, Feb 21, 1923
        New York Times p. 9, Feb 17, 1923

The Flower of the Palace of Han (with Louis Laloy. Adapted from
    the Chinese)
    Productions:
        Opened March 19, 1912 for 39 performances.
    Reviews:
        Blue Book 15:252-4, Jun 1912
        Bookman 35:246, May 1912
        Dramatic Mirror 67:6, Mar 27, 1912
        Green Book 7:1094-5+, Jun 1912
                8:352-68, Aug 1912
        Life (NY) 59:700, Apr 4, 1912
        New York Drama News 55:26, Mar 30, 1912
        Red Book 19:568-70, Jul 1912
        Theatre Magazine 15:139-40+, May 1912

The Servant in the House
    Productions:
        Opened April 24, 1918 for 21 performances.
        Opened May 2, 1921 for 3 performances.
        Opened April 7, 1925 for 8 performances.
        Opened May 3, 1926 for 12 performances.
    Reviews:
        Arena 41:57-73, Jan 1909
        Book News 27:611-2, Apr 1909
        Bookman 63:590, Jul 1926
        Dramatic Mirror 78:656, May 11, 1918
        Dramatist 3:234-5, Apr 1912
        Everybody's 22:122-7, Jan 1910
        New York Clipper 69:19, May 11, 1921
        New York Times p. 10, Apr 25, 1918
                IV, p. 9, Apr 28, 1918
                p. 20, May 3, 1921
                p. 24, Apr 8, 1925
                p. 30, May 4, 1926

Poet Lore 20:438-43, Nov-Dec 1909
Theatre Magazine 8:90, Apr 1908
8:116-7+, May 1908
14:24-6, Jul 1911
27:349, Jun 1918
Weekly Review 4:496, May 21, 1921

The Seventh Trumpet
Productions:
Opened November 21, 1941 for 11 performances.
Reviews:
Commonweal 35:178, Dec 5, 1941
New York Theatre Critics' Reviews 1941:204
New York Times p. 10, Nov 22, 1941

The Terrible Meek
Productions:
Opened March 19, 1912 for 39 performances.
Reviews:
Blue Book 15:680-1, Aug 1912
Book News 31:60-1, Sep 1912
Bookman 35:246-7, May 1912
Collier's 49:21, Apr 6, 1912
Dramatic Mirror 67:6, Mar 27, 1912
Dramatist 3:235-6, Apr 1912
Green Book 7:1185-7, Jun 1912
7:1204, Jun 1912
Life (NY) 59:700, Apr 4, 1912
Literary Digest 44:644-5, Mar 30, 1912
44:758, Apr 13, 1912
Nation 94:294-5, Mar 21, 1912
New York Drama News 55:26, Mar 30, 1912
New York Times XI, p. 3, May 4, 1930
Red Book 19:566+, Jul 1912
Theatre Magazine 15:139-40, May 1912

KENNEDY, MARY

Mrs. Partridge Presents (with Ruth Hawthorne)
Productions:
Opened January 5, 1925 for 144 performances.
Reviews:
Life (NY) 85:18, Jan 29, 1925
New York Times p. 23, Jan 6, 1925
VII, p. 1, Jan 11, 1925
p. 10, Feb 29, 1936
Theatre Magazine 40:16+, Mar 1925
Woman Citizen 9:9, Feb 7, 1925

KERR, JEAN

Finishing Touches
Productions:
   Opened February 8, 1973 for 164 performances.
Reviews:
   America 128:190, Mar 3, 1973
   Commonweal 98:215, May 4, 1973
   Nation 216:284, Feb 26, 1973
   National Review 25:316-17, Mar 16, 1973
   New York Magazine 6:66, Feb 26, 1973
   New York Theatre Critics' Reviews 1973:364
   New York Times p. 30, Feb 9, 1973
                 II, p. 1, Feb 18, 1973
                    p. 54, Jun 21, 1973
                    XI, p. 12, Jul 29, 1979
   New Yorker 48:79, Feb 17, 1973
   Newsweek 81:75, Feb 19, 1973
   Playboy 20:52, May 1973
   Saturday Review (Arts) 1:55, Mar 1973
   Time 101:58, Feb 19, 1973

Jenny Kissed Me
Productions:
   Opened December 23, 1948 for 20 performances.
Reviews:
   Catholic World 168:403, Feb 1949
   New York Theatre Critics' Reviews 1948:112
   New York Times p. 12, Dec 24, 1948
   New Yorker 24:36, Jan 1, 1949
   Newsweek 33:54, Jan 3, 1949
   Time 53:49, Jan 3, 1949

King of Hearts (with Eleanor Brooke)
Productions:
   Opened April 1, 1954 for 279 performances.
   (Off Off Broadway) September 24, 1981 (Equity Library The-
      atre).
Reviews:
   America 91:114+, Apr 24, 1954
   Catholic World 179:149, May 1954
   Commonweal 60:143, May 14, 1954
   Life 36:97-8+, Apr 26, 1954
   Nation 178:342, Apr 17, 1954
   New Republic 130:21, May 31, 1954
   New York Theatre Critics' Reviews 1954:342
   New York Times II, p. 1, Mar 28, 1954
                    p. 23, Apr 2, 1954
                 II, p. 1, Apr 11, 1954
                    p. 16, Aug 4, 1955
   New Yorker 30:60+, Apr 10, 1954

Newsweek 43:92, Apr 12, 1954
Saturday Review 37:22, Apr 17, 1954
Theatre Arts 38:17, Jun 1954
            38:17, Jul 1954
Time 63:74, Apr 12, 1954

Lunch Hour
    Productions:
    Opened November 12, 1980 for 262 performances.
    Reviews:
    New York Magazine 13:67, Dec 1, 1980
    New York Theatre Critics' Reviews 1980:95
    New York Times II, p. 1, Nov 9, 1980
                III, p. 19, Nov 13, 1980
                    p. 21, Jun 13, 1981
    New York Times Magazine pp. 42-3+, Nov 9, 1980
    New Yorker 56:134, Nov 24, 1980
    Newsweek 96:129+, Nov 24, 1980
    Time 116:64, Nov 24, 1980

Mary, Mary
    Productions:
    Opened March 8, 1961 for 1,572 performances.
    Reviews:
    America 105:27, Apr 1, 1961
    Commonweal 74:79-80, Apr 14, 1961
    Coronet 50:16, Jun 1961
    Nation 192:311, Apr 8, 1961
    New York Theatre Critics' Reviews 1961:335
    New York Times p. 24, Mar 9, 1961
                p. 16, Jul 29, 1963
                p. 14, Mar 7, 1964
                p. 55, Dec 8, 1964
    New Yorker 37:124, Mar 18, 1961
    Newsweek 57:88, Mar 20, 1961
    Reporter 24:46, Apr 13, 1961
    Saturday Review 44:27, Mar 18, 1961
                44:35, Mar 25, 1961
    Theatre Arts 45:58, May 1961
    Time 77:42, Mar 17, 1961

Poor Richard
    Productions:
    Opened December 2, 1964 for 118 performances.
    Reviews:
    Look 29:67-70, Mar 9, 1965
    New York Theatre Critics' Reviews 1964:120
    New York Times p. 59, Dec 3, 1964
                p. 37, Mar 5, 1965
    New Yorker 40:152+, Dec 12, 1964
    Newsweek 64:84, Dec 14, 1964

Saturday Review 47:25, Dec 19, 1964
Time 84:73, Dec 11, 1964
Vogue 145:27, Jan 15, 1965

The Song of Bernadette (with Walter Kerr. Adapted from Franz Wer-
    fel's novel)
Productions:
    Opened March 26, 1946 for 3 performances.
Reviews:
    America 99:179, May 3, 1958
    New York Theatre Critics' Reviews 1946:418
    New York Times p. 22, Mar 27, 1946

KESSELRING, JOSEPH O.

Arsenic and Old Lace
    Productions:
    Opened January 10, 1941 for 1,444 performances.
    (Off Off Broadway) April 14, 1977 (Equity Library Theater).
Reviews:
    Catholic World 152:599, Feb 1941
    Commonweal 33:351, Jan 24, 1941
    Life 16:57-8+, Apr 3, 1944
    Nation 152:108-9, Jan 25, 1941
    New Republic 104:116, Jan 27, 1941
    New York Theatre Critics' Reviews 1941:417
    New York Times p. 13, Jan 11, 1941
                    IX, p. 1, Jan 12, 1941
                    IX, p. 3, Jan 19, 1941
                    IX, p. 3, Feb 9, 1941
                    IX, p. 1, Feb 23, 1941
                    IX, p. 1, Jun 22, 1941
                    IX, p. 2, Sep 7, 1941
                    IX, p. 3, Feb 1, 1942
                    p. 25, Mar 24, 1942
                    p. 26, Jan 1, 1943
                    VIII, p. 1, Jan 10, 1943
                    p. 16, Feb 26, 1943
                    II, p. 1, May 30, 1943
                    p. 7, Jul 3, 1944
                    p. 59, Nov 5, 1970
                    p. 16, Apr 16, 1977
    New Yorker 16:34, Jan 18, 1941
    Newsweek 17:63, Jan 20, 1941
             19:56, May 18, 1942
    Stage 1:24-5, Feb 1941
    Theatre Arts 25:185-6+, Mar 1941
    Time 37:40, Jan 20, 1941
         46:64, Jul 9, 1945
    Vogue 97:77, Mar 1, 1941

Cross-Town
    Productions:
        Opened March 17, 1937 for 5 performances.
    Reviews:
        New York Times p. 21, Mar 18, 1937

Four Twelves Are 48
    Productions:
        Opened January 17, 1951 for 2 performances.
    Reviews:
        Commonweal 53:447, Feb 9, 1951
        New York Theatre Critics' Reviews 1951:384
        New York Times p. 30, Jan 18, 1951
        New Yorker 26:54, Jan 27, 1951
        Newsweek 37:83, Jan 29, 1951
        Theatre Arts 35:20, Mar 1951
        Time 57:49, Jan 29, 1951

There's Wisdom in Women
    Productions:
        Opened October 30, 1935 for 46 performances.
    Reviews:
        Catholic World 142:343, Dec 1935
        Commonweal 23:76, Nov 15, 1935
        New York Times p. 24, Jul 16, 1935
                       p. 17, Oct 31, 1935
        Vanity Fair 45:46, Jan 1936

KINGSLEY, SIDNEY

Darkness at Noon (Based on the novel by Arthur Koestler)
    Productions:
        Opened January 13, 1951 for 186 performances.
        (Off Broadway) March 29, 1963 for 9 performances (Equity Library Theatre).
        (Off Off Broadway) Opened March 10, 1981 for 12 performances (Quaigh Theater).
    Reviews:
        Catholic World 172:465, Mar 1951
        Commonweal 53:425, Feb 2, 1951
        Life 30:77-8+, Feb 5, 1951
        Nation 172:92-3, Jan 27, 1951
        New Republic 124:22-3, Feb 5, 1951
        New York Theatre Critics' Reviews 1951:388
        New York Times II, p. 1, Jan 7, 1951
                       p. 13, Jan 15, 1951
                       II, p. 1, Jan 21, 1951
                       II, p. 3, Feb 4, 1951
                       II, p. 1, Mar 18, 1951
                       p. 34, Apr 4, 1951
                       II, p. 2, Mar 28, 1981

New Yorker 26:54, Jan 20, 1951
Newsweek 37:80, Jan 22, 1951
Saturday Review 34:22-4, Feb 3, 1951
School and Society 73:105-6, Feb 17, 1951
Theatre Arts 35:19, 42, Mar 1951
    35:41+, 373, Sep 1951
Time 57:38, Jan 22, 1951

Dead End
Productions:
Opened October 28, 1935 for 687 performances.
(Off Off Broadway) April 25, 1978 (Quaigh Theater).
Reviews:
Catholic World 142:339-40, Dec 1935
Commonweal 23:48, Nov 8, 1935
    23:76, Nov 15, 1935
Literary Digest 120:17, Nov 9, 1935
Nation 141:575-6, Nov 13, 1935
New Republic 85:21, Nov 13, 1935
    85:49, Nov 20, 1935
New York Times p. 17, Oct 29, 1935
    X, p. 1, Nov 3, 1935
    IX, p. 1, Nov 10, 1935
    XI, p. 5, Dec 15, 1935
    X, p. 3, Nov 1, 1936
    p. 17, Jan 15, 1937
    p. 18, Jun 29, 1937
    p. 23, Aug 17, 1937
    III, p. 3, May 5, 1978
Newsweek 6:26, Nov 9, 1935
Player's Magazine 12:13+, Jan-Feb, 1936
Stage 13:26-8, Dec 1935
    13:66, Jan 1936
Survey Graphic 25:52, Jan 1936
Theatre Arts 19:888-93, Dec 1935
    20:462-3, Jun 1936
Time 26:40, Nov 11, 1935
Vanity Fair 45:45+, Jan 1936

Detective Story
Productions:
Opened March 23, 1949 for 581 performances.
(Off Broadway) Season of 1953-54 (Equity Library Theater).
(Off Off Broadway) March 26, 1976 (Courtyard Playhouse).
Reviews:
Catholic World 169:144, May 1949
Christian Science Monitor Magazine p. 7, Apr 15, 1950
Commonweal 49:638, Apr 8, 1949
Life 28:131-2+, May 2, 1949
Nation 168:424-5, Apr 9, 1949
New Republic 120:25, Apr 11, 1949

New York Theatre Critics' Reviews 1949:330
New York Times II, p. 1, Mar 20, 1949
        p. 34, Mar 24, 1949
        II, p. 1, Apr 3, 1949
        p. 18, Mar 27, 1950
        II, p. 2, Jun 3, 1951
        p. 11, Feb 13, 1954
        p. 37, May 11, 1968
New Yorker 25:50, Apr 2, 1949
Newsweek 33:78, Apr 4, 1949
Saturday Review 32:50-2, Apr 16, 1949
School and Society 70:362-3, Dec 3, 1949
Theatre Arts 33:11, Jan 1949
Time 53:75-6, Apr 4, 1949
Vogue 113:116-17, May 1, 1949

Lunatics and Lovers
    Productions:
        Opened December 13, 1954 for 336 performances.
    Reviews:
        America 92:366, Jan 1, 1955
        Catholic World 180:388, Feb 1955
        Commonweal 61:406, Jan 14, 1955
        Life 38:57-8+, Jan 17, 1955
        Nation 180:18, Jan 1, 1955
        New Republic 132:20, Mar 7, 1955
        New York Theatre Critics' Reviews 1954:219
        New York Times II, p. 3, Dec 12, 1954
                p. 44, Dec 14, 1954
                p. 31, Dec 21, 1954
        New Yorker 30:44-6, Dec 25, 1954
        Newsweek 45:43, Jan 3, 1955
        Saturday Review 38:62, Jan 1, 1955
        Theatre Arts 39:17, 90, Feb 1955
        Time 64:32, Dec 27, 1954

Men in White
    Productions:
        Opened September 26, 1933 for 351 performances.
        (Off Off Broadway) Opened July 10, 1979 for 18 performances
            (Quaigh Theater).
    Reviews:
        Catholic World 138:215-17, Nov 1933
        Commonweal 18:563-4, Oct 13, 1933
        Hygeia 12:358-60, Apr 1934
        Literary Digest 116:19, Nov 4, 1933
        Nation 137:419-20, Oct 11, 1933
        New Outlook 162:43, Nov 1933
        New Republic 76:241-2, Oct 11, 1933
        New York Times p. 24, Sep 27, 1933
                IX, p. 1, Oct 1, 1933

IX, p. 2, Oct 15, 1933
p. 16, Jun 29, 1934
p. 13, Feb 26, 1955
III, p. 14, Jul 12, 1979
Newsweek 2:29, Oct 7, 1933
Review of Reviews 89:39, Feb 1934
Stage 11:27-9, Nov 1933
Theatre Arts 17:915-16, Dec 1933

Night Life
Productions:
Opened December 15, 1962 for 63 performances.
Reviews:
Catholic World 196:199, Dec 1962
Commonweal 77:232, Nov 23, 1962
New York Theatre Critics' Reviews 1962:234
New York Times p. 27, May 26, 1962
p. 45, Oct 2, 1962
II, p. 3, Oct 21, 1962
p. 44, Oct 24, 1962
New Yorker 38:111, Nov 3, 1962
Newsweek 60:75, Nov 5, 1962
Saturday Review 45:28, Nov 10, 1962
Theatre Arts 46:12-13, Dec 1962
Time 80:82, Nov 2, 1962

The Patriots
Productions:
Opened January 29, 1943 for 173 performances.
Opened December 20, 1943 for 8 performances.
Reviews:
American Mercury 56:486-7, Apr 1943
Catholic World 156:726-7, Mar 1943
Commonweal 37:422, Feb 12, 1943
Current History ns 4:88-91, Mar 1943
Independent Woman 22:143, May 1943
Life 14:57-8+, Mar 8, 1943
Nation 156:248, Feb 13, 1943
New Republic 108:211, Feb 15, 1943
New York Theatre Critics' Reviews 1943:385
New York Times p. 11, Jan 30, 1943
V, p. 16, Jan 31, 1943
II, p. 1, Feb 7, 1943
p. 22, Dec 21, 1943
New York Times Magazine pp. 16-17, Jan 31, 1943
New Yorker 18:31, Feb 6, 1943
Newsweek 21:82+, Feb 8, 1943
Saturday Review 26:26+, Apr 17, 1943
Scholastic 42:20, Mar 15, 1943
Theatre Arts 27:201-4, Apr 1943
Time 41:36, Feb 8, 1943

Ten Million Ghosts
  Productions:
    Opened October 23, 1936 for 11 performances.
  Reviews:
    Nation 143:558, Nov 7, 1936
    New York Times p. 23, Oct 24, 1936
    Stage 14:50, Nov 1936
    Theatre Arts 20:932, Dec 1936
    Time 28:49, Nov 2, 1936

The World We Make (Based on Millen Brand's The Outward Room)
  Productions:
    Opened Nov. 20, 1939 for 80 performances.
  Reviews:
    Catholic World 150:470, Jan 1940
    Forum 103:32-3, Jan 1940
    Life 8:27-9, Jan 1, 1940
    Nation 149:627-9, Dec 2, 1939
    New York Theatre Critics' Reviews 1940:454
    New York Times p. 19, Nov 21, 1939
              IX, p. 1, Nov 26, 1939
              IX, p. 5, Dec 3, 1939
              IX, p. 3, Dec 17, 1939
    Newsweek 14:39, Dec 4, 1939
    North American Review 248 No. 2:402-3 (Dec) 1939
    Theatre Arts 24:15, Jan 1940
    Time 34:38+, Dec 4, 1939

KIRKLAND, JACK

Frankie and Johnnie
  Productions:
    Opened September 25, 1930 for 61 performances
  Reviews:
    Life (NY) 90:19, Oct 17, 1930
    National Magazine 59:136, Dec 1920
    New York Times p. 16, Sep 26, 1930
    Theatre Arts 16:456-8, Jun 1932

I Must Love Someone (with Leyla Georgie)
  Productions:
    Opened February 7, 1939 for 191 performances.
  Reviews:
    New York Times p. 18, Feb 8, 1939
    Time 33:55, Feb 20, 1939

The Man with the Golden Arm
  Productions:
    (Off Broadway) Season of 1955-56.

Reviews:
New York Times p. 28, May 22, 1956
Saturday Review 39:32, Jun 16, 1956

Mandingo (Based on Kyle Onstott's novel)
Productions:
Opened May 22, 1961 for 8 performances.
Reviews:
New York Times p. 43, May 23, 1961
New Yorker 37:90, Jun 3, 1961
Theatre Arts 45:10, Jul 1961
Time 77:85-6, Jun 2, 1961

Mr. Adam (Based on Pat Frank's novel)
Productions:
Opened May 25, 1949 for 5 performances.
Reviews:
New York Theatre Critics' Reviews 1949:292
New York Times p. 34, May 26, 1949
New Yorker 25:46+, Jun 4, 1949
Theatre Arts 33:5, Aug 1949
Time 53:70, Jun 6, 1949

Suds in Your Eye (Based on a novel by Mary Lasswell)
Productions:
Opened January 12, 1944 for 37 performances.
Reviews:
Catholic World 150:490, Feb 1944
New York Theatre Critics' Reviews 1944:287
New York Times p. 15, Jan 13, 1944
Theatre Arts 28:141, Mar 1944
Time 43:40, Jan 24, 1944

Tobacco Road (Based on Erskine Caldwell's novel)
Productions:
Opened December 4, 1933 for 3,182 performances.
Opened September 5, 1942 for 34 performances.
Opened September 4, 1943 for 66 performances.
Opened March 6, 1950 for 7 performances.
(Off Broadway) Season of 1959-60.
Reviews:
Catholic World 138:603-4, Feb 1934
Commonweal 34:185, Jun 13, 1941
39:140-1, Nov 26, 1943
Golden Book Magazine 20:246+, Sep 1934
Life 2:36-7, Jan 11, 1937
9:30, Dec 16, 1940
Literary Digest 118:18+, Dec 15, 1934
Nation 137:718, Dec 20, 1933
New Outlook 163:43, Jan 1934
New Republic 77:168-9, Dec 20, 1933

New York Theatre Critics' Reviews 1940:498
                          1941:498
                          1950:333
New York Times p. 31, Dec 5, 1933
        IX, p. 3, Jan 28, 1934
        p. 24, Jun 20, 1934
        X, p. 1, Jul 1, 1934
        X, p. 2, Dec 2, 1934
        p. 17, Oct 30, 1935
        p. 17, Nov 27, 1935
        XI, p. 7, Dec 1, 1935
        II, p. 1, Jan 19, 1936
        p. 25, Jan 23, 1936
        XI, p. 1, Mar 22, 1936
        p. 31, Apr 7, 1936
        XII, p. 1, Nov 29, 1936
        XI, p. 2, Mar 21, 1937
        p. 16, May 20, 1937
        p. 27, Nov 23, 1937
        XI, p. 2, Nov 21, 1937
        IX, p. 3, Nov 27, 1937
        IX, p. 3, Nov 27, 1938
        p. 17, Nov 4, 1939
        VII, p. 6, Nov 12, 1939
        IX, p. 3, Nov 12, 1939
        VII, p. 12, Dec 24, 1939
        XI, p. 1, Mar 10, 1940
        X, p. 3, Dec 1, 1940
        p. 32, Dec 5, 1940
        p. 18, May 24, 1941
        p. 20, Jun 3, 1941
        IX, p. 3, Nov 30, 1941
        p. 34, Sep 7, 1942
        p. 21, Sep 6, 1943
        p. 26, Aug 26, 1947
        p. 27, Aug 11, 1949
        p. 23, Mar 7, 1950
        p. 44, May 11, 1960
        XI, p. 16, Oct 14, 1979
Newsweek 7:32, Apr 4, 1936
      8:22, Dec 5, 1936
      14:32-3, Nov 27, 1939
      17:58, Jun 9, 1941
Photoplay 18:50-51, Apr 1941
Review of Reviews 89:47, Mar 1934
Stage 11:29, Jan 1934
    1:20, Nov 1940
    1:19, Dec 1940
Theatre Arts 18:93-5, Feb 1934
           31:67-9, Apr 1947
           34:16, May 1950

Time 22:31, Dec 18, 1933
24:32, Jul 2, 1934
24:50-51, Dec 17, 1934
30:57, Dec 13, 1937
37:53, Jun 9, 1941
55:61, Mar 20, 1950

Tortilla Flat (Based on John Steinbeck's novel)
    Productions:
        Opened January 12, 1938 for 5 performances.
    Reviews:
        New York Times p. 16, Jan 13, 1938
        Time 31:47, Jan 24, 1938

KOBER, ARTHUR

Having Wonderful Time
    Productions:
        Opened February 20, 1937 for 372 performances.
    Reviews:
        Catholic World 145:85, Apr 1937
        Commonweal 25:528, Mar 5, 1937
        Literary Digest 123:25, Mar 6, 1937
        Nation 144:276-7, Mar 6, 1937
        New York Times X, p. 1, Feb 14, 1937
                        p. 12, Feb 22, 1937
                        XI, p. 1, Feb 28, 1937
                        XI, p. 1, Mar 21, 1937
        Newsweek 9:22-4, Feb 27, 1937
        Stage 14:50-53, Mar 1937
              14:78, Apr 1937
        Theatre Arts 21:262, Apr 1937
        Time 29:47-8, Mar 1, 1937

A Mighty Man Is He (with George Oppenheimer)
    Productions:
        Opened January 6, 1960 for 5 performances.
    Reviews:
        New York Theatre Critics' Reviews 1960:397
        New York Times p. 25, Jan 7, 1960
        New Yorker 35:86+, Jan 16, 1960

KOCH, HOWARD

Give Us This Day
    Productions:
        Opened October 27, 1933 for 3 performances.
    Reviews:
        New York Times p. 20, Oct 28, 1933

In Time to Come (with John Huston)
    Productions:
        Opened December 28, 1941 for 40 performances.
    Reviews:
        Catholic World 154:599-600, Feb 1942
        Commonweal 35:344-5, Jan 23, 1942
        Current History 1:568, Feb 1942
        Life 12:33-4+, Feb 2, 1942
        Nation 154:74, Jan 17, 1942
        New Republic 106:147, Feb 2, 1942
        New York Theatre Critics' Reviews 1941:158
        New York Times p. 20, Dec 29, 1941
                IX, p. 1, Jan 4, 1942
        Scholastic 39:24, Jan 19, 1942
        Theatre Arts 26:149-50, Mar 1942
                28:606, Oct 1944
        Time 39:42, Jan 12, 1942
        Vogue 99:61, Feb 15, 1942

KOPIT, ARTHUR

An Arthur Kopit Festival (Part One)
    Productions:
        (Off Off Broadway) Season of 1976-77 (IRT). Plays presented
           included:
           Chamber Music
           The Conquest of Everest
           The Day the Whores Came Out to Play Tennis
           The Hero
           The Questioning of Nick
           Sing to Me Through Open Windows
    No Reviews.

Chamber Music (see An Arthur Kopit Festival)

Conquest of Everest
    Productions:
        (Off Off Broadway) May 18, 1973 (Playwrights Cooperative).
        See also An Arthur Kopit Festival.
    No Reviews.

The Day the Whores Came Out to Play Tennis
    Productions:
        (Off Broadway) March 15, 1965 for 24 performances.
        See also An Arthur Kopit Festival.
    Reviews:
        Nation 200:374, Apr 5, 1965
        New Republic 152:24, Apr 10, 1965
        New York Times p. 45, Mar 16, 1965
        New Yorker 41:146-7, May 27, 1965

Newsweek 65:82, Mar 29, 1965
Time 85:58, Mar 26, 1965
Vogue 145:142, May 1965

Good Help Is Hard to Find
    Productions:
        (Off Off Broadway) May-June, 1981 (Ensemble Studio Theater).
    Reviews:
        New York Times p. 66, Jun 14, 1981

Hero
    Productions:
        (Off Off Broadway) May 18, 1973 (Playwrights Cooperative).
        See also An Arthur Kopit Festival.
    No Reviews.

Indians
    Productions:
        Opened October 13, 1969 for 96 performances.
        (Off Off Broadway) December 7, 1972 (The Cubiculo).
    Reviews:
        America 121:432+, Nov 8, 1969
        Commonweal 91:185-6, Nov 7, 1969
        Dance Magazine 43:30-1, Dec 1969
        Nation 209:485-6, Nov 3, 1969
        New Republic 161:24+, Nov 8, 1969
        New York Theatre Critics' Reviews 1969:233
        New York Times p. 30, Jul 9, 1968
                      II, p. 12, Jul 21, 1968
                      II, p. 3, May 18, 1969
                      p. 43, May 27, 1969
                      p. 51, Oct 14, 1969
                      p. 37, Oct 15, 1969
                      II, p. 1, Oct 19, 1969
        New Yorker 45:149-50, Oct 18, 1969
        Newsweek 72:97, Jul 29, 1968
                 74:137-8, Oct 27, 1969
        Saturday Review 52:24, Jun 7, 1969
                        52:55-6+, Oct 25, 1969
        Time 93:96, Jun 6, 1969
             94:68, Oct 24, 1969
        Vogue 154:58, Nov 15, 1969

Oh Dad, Poor Dad, Mamma's Hung You in the Closet and I'm Feelin'
    So Sad
    Productions:
        (Off Broadway) February 26, 1962 for 454 performances.
        Opened August 27, 1963 for 47 performances.
    Reviews:
        Commonweal 76:41, Apr 6, 1962
        National Review 12:416-17, Jun 5, 1962

New Republic 146:31, Mar 19, 1962
New York Theatre Critics' Reviews 1963:294
New York Times p. 19, Jul 6, 1961
           p. 28, Feb 27, 1962
           II, p. 1, Mar 11, 1962
           p. 28, Aug 28, 1963
New Yorker 38:84-5, Mar 10, 1962
Saturday Review 45:35, Mar 17, 1962
Theatre Arts 46:60-1, May 1962

The Questioning of Nick
    Productions:
        (Off Off Broadway) Season of 1973-74 (Manhattan Theater Club).
        See also An Arthur Kopit Festival.
    No Reviews.

Sing to Me Through Open Windows
    Productions:
        (Off Broadway) March 15, 1965 for 24 performances.
        See also An Arthur Kopit Festival.
    Reviews:
        Nation 200:373-4, Apr 5, 1965
        New Republic 152:24, Apr 10, 1965
        New York Times p. 45, Mar 16, 1965
        Newsweek 65:82, Mar 29, 1965

Wings
    Productions:
        (Off Broadway) June 21, 1978 for 15 performances.
        Transferred to Broadway, January 28, 1979 for 113 perform-
           ances.
    Reviews:
        Commonweal 105:594, Sep 15, 1978
        New York Magazine 11:66-7, Jul 10, 1978
        New York Theatre Critics' Reviews 1978:178
                            1979:385
        New York Times III, p. 16, Mar 8, 1978
                II, p. 1, Jun 4, 1978
                III, p. 20, Jun 22, 1978
                II, p. 1, Jul 2, 1978
                II, p. 3, Jan 28, 1979
                III, p. 13, Jan 29, 1979
                II, p. 3, Mar 25, 1979
                II, p. 1, Apr 15, 1979
                III, p. 10, May 1, 1979
        Newsweek 54:70, Jul 3, 1978
        Time 112:86, Jul 3, 1978

KRAMM, JOSEPH

*Build with One Hand

Reviews:
New York Times p. 42, Nov 29, 1956

Giants, Sons of Giants
Productions:
Opened January 6, 1962 for 9 performances.
Reviews:
New York Theatre Critics' Reviews 1962:388
New York Times p. 26, Jan 8, 1962

The Shrike
Productions:
Opened January 15, 1952 for 161 performances.
Opened November 25, 1953 for 15 performances.
(Off Broadway) February 1, 1964 for 8 performances (Equity
    Library Theater).
Reviews:
America 90:306, Dec 12, 1953
Catholic World 174:465, Mar 1952
            178:309, Jan 1954
Commonweal 55:422, Feb 1, 1952
New Republic 126:23, Feb 4, 1952
New York Theatre Critics' Reviews 1952:389
New York Times p. 20, Jan 16, 1952
            II, p. 1, Jan 27, 1952
            II, p. 1, Feb 24, 1952
            p. 51, Nov 26, 1953
New Yorker 27:53, Jan 26, 1952
Newsweek 39:83, Jan 28, 1952
Saturday Review 35:22-3, Feb 9, 1952
            35:28, May 17, 1952
School and Society 75:181-2, Mar 22, 1952
Theatre Arts 36:71, Mar 1952
            36:4, Jul 1952
            38:20, Feb 1954
Time 59:43, Jan 28, 1952

KRASNA, NORMAN

Bunny
Productions:
(Off Off Broadway) August 6, 1979 (Actors Studio).
Reviews:
New York Times III, p. 13, Aug 2, 1979

Dear Ruth
Productions:
Opened December 13, 1944 for 683 performances.
(Off Off Broadway) June 2, 1976 (Playwrights Horizons).
Reviews:
Catholic World 160:454, Feb 1945

Commonweal 41:275, Dec 29, 1944
Life 18:57-8+, Jan 22, 1944
Nation 159:810, Dec 30, 1944
New York Theatre Critics' Reviews 1944:56
New York Times p. 29, Dec 14, 1944
        II, p. 1, Dec 31, 1944
        II, p. 1, Jan 7, 1945
        p. 14, Jan 27, 1945
        p. 26, Oct 24, 1945
        p. 17, Mar 1, 1946
New Yorker 20:38, Dec 23, 1944
Newsweek 24:69, Dec 25, 1944
Saturday Review 28:24, Mar 17, 1945
Theatre Arts 29:74-5, Feb 1945
        29:334, Jun 1945
Time 44:56, Dec 25, 1944

John Loves Mary

Productions:
    Opened February 4, 1947 for 423 performances.
Reviews:
    Catholic World 164:552, Mar 1947
    Commonweal 45:469, Feb 21, 1947
    Life 22:125-6+, Apr 14, 1947
    New Republic 116:40, Feb 17, 1947
    New York Theatre Critics' Reviews 1947:465
    New York Times II, p. 1, Feb 2, 1947
            p. 29, Feb 5, 1947
            II, p. 1, Apr 13, 1947
            II, p. 1, Jul 13, 1947
    New Yorker 22:48+, Feb 15, 1947
    Newsweek 29:88, Feb 17, 1947
    School and Society 66:327-8, Oct 25, 1947
    Theatre Arts 31:18, Apr 1947
    Time 49:53, Feb 17, 1947

Kind Sir

Productions:
    Opened November 4, 1953 for 166 performances.
Reviews:
    America 90:249+, Nov 28, 1953
    Catholic World 178:310, Jan 1954
    Commonweal 59:224-5, Dec 4, 1953
    Life 35:160-4, Oct 12, 1953
    Nation 177:434, Nov 21, 1953
    New York Theatre Critics' Reviews 1953:225
    New York Times VI, p. 19, Sep 20, 1953
            p. 21, Sep 28, 1953
            II, p. 3, Oct 18, 1953
            p. 41, Nov 5, 1953
    New Yorker 29:69-70, Nov 14, 1953

Newsweek 42:60, Dec 21, 1953
42:56+, Nov 9, 1953
Saturday Review 36:47, Nov 21, 1953
Theatre Arts 37:11, Aug 1953
38:18, Jan 1954
Time 62:90, Nov 16, 1953

Louder, Please
Productions:
Opened November 12, 1931 for 68 performances.
Reviews:
New York Times p. 26, Nov 13, 1931
Theatre Guild Magazine 9:34-5, Jan 1932

Love in E-Flat
Productions:
Opened February 13, 1967 for 24 performances.
Reviews:
New York Theatre Critics' Reviews 1967:367
New York Times p. 38, Feb 14, 1967

The Man with Blond Hair
Productions:
Opened November 4, 1941 for 7 performances.
Reviews:
New York Theatre Critics' Reviews 1941:241
New York Times p. 30, Nov 5, 1941

Small Miracle
Productions:
Opened September 26, 1934 for 117 performances.
Reviews:
Catholic World 140:213-14, Nov 1934
Golden Book 20:510, Nov 1934
New York Times p. 24, Sep 27, 1934
Stage 12:2+, Nov 1934
Time 24:46, Oct 8, 1934

Sunday in New York
Productions:
Opened November 29, 1961 for 188 performances.
Reviews:
America 106:453, Jan 6, 1962
New York Theatre Critics' Reviews 1961:158
New York Times p. 40, Nov 30, 1961
New Yorker 37:160, Dec 9, 1961
Newsweek 58:65, Dec 11, 1961
Reporter 26:38, Jan 4, 1962
Theatre Arts 46:12-13, Feb 1962
Time 78:75, Dec 8, 1961

Time for Elizabeth (with Groucho Marx)
Productions:
  Opened September 27, 1948 for 8 performances.
Reviews:
  Nation 167:410, Oct 9, 1948
  New Republic 119:27, Oct 18, 1948
  New York Theatre Critics' Reviews 1948:218
  New York Times p. 32, Sep 28, 1948
  New Yorker 24:62, Oct 9, 1948
  Time 52:78+, Oct 11, 1948

We Interrupt This Program ...
Productions:
  Opened April 1, 1975 for 7 performances.
Reviews:
  New York Theatre Critics' Reviews 1975:281
  New York Times p. 24, Apr 2, 1975

Who Was That Lady I Saw You With?
Productions:
  Opened March 3, 1958 for 208 performances.
Reviews:
  America 99:93+, Apr 12, 1958
  Catholic World 187:145-6, May 1958
  Commonweal 68:128, May 2, 1958
  Nation 186:261, Mar 22, 1958
  New York Theatre Critics' Reviews 1958:337
  New York Times p. 33, Mar 4, 1958
  New Yorker 34:89-90, Mar 15, 1958
  Newsweek 51:91, Mar 17, 1958
  Saturday Review 41:56, Mar 15, 1958
  Time 71:86, Mar 17, 1958

KUMMER, CLARE

Amourette
Productions:
  Opened September 27, 1933 for 22 performances.
Reviews:
  Catholic World 138:217, Nov 1933
  Commonweal 18:544, Oct 13, 1933
  Stage 11:5-6, Oct 1933

Banco (Adapted from the French of Alfred Savoir)
Productions:
  Opened September 20, 1922 for 69 performances.
Reviews:
  Life (NY) 80:10, Oct 12, 1922
  New York Clipper 70:39, Oct 4, 1922

New York Times p. 18, Sep 21, 1922
Theatre Magazine 36:297, Nov 1922

Be Calm, Camilla
    Productions:
        Opened October 31, 1918 for 84 performances.
    Reviews:
        Dramatic Mirror 79:723, Nov 16, 1918
        Independent 96:193, Nov 16, 1918
        Life (NY) 72:712, Nov 14, 1918
        New York Drama News 65:11, Nov 9, 1918
        New York Times p. 13, Nov 1, 1918
                        IV, p. 2, Nov 10, 1918
        Theatre Magazine 28:380, Dec 1918

Bridges
    Productions:
        Opened February 28, 1921 for 5 Matinees.
    Reviews:
        Dramatic Mirror 83:408+, Mar 5, 1921

Good Gracious Annabelle
    Productions:
        Opened October 31, 1916 for 111 performances.
    Reviews:
        Dramatic Mirror 76:7, Nov 11, 1916
        Green Book 17:10+, Jan 1917
        International 11:29, Jan 1917
        Nation 103:470, Nov 16, 1916
        National Magazine 45:576-7, Jan 1917
        New Republic 9:331, Jan 20, 1917
        New York Times p. 9, Nov 1, 1916
                        II, p. 6, Nov 5, 1916
                        II, p. 7, Nov 12, 1916
        Theatre Magazine 24:358, Dec 1916

Her Master's Voice
    Productions:
        Opened October 23, 1933 for 224 performances.
        (Off Broadway) December 26, 1964 for 18 performances.
    Reviews:
        Catholic World 138:341, Dec 1933
        Commonweal 19:104, Nov 24, 1933
        Nation 137:550, Nov 8, 1933
        New Outlook 162:46, Dec 1933
        New York Times p. 24, Oct 24, 1933
                        IX, p. 7, Dec 3, 1933
                        X, p. 1, Dec 10, 1933
                        p. 33, Dec 28, 1964
        New Yorker 40:84+, Jan 9, 1965
        Newsweek 2:28, Nov 4, 1933

Stage 11:7, Dec 1933
Theatre Arts 17:920, Dec 1933
Vanity Fair 41:42, Jan 1934

Many Happy Returns
Productions:
Opened January 5, 1945 for 3 performances.
Reviews:
New York Theatre Critics' Reviews 1945:296
New York Times p. 15, Jan 6, 1945
New Yorker 20:40, Jan 13, 1945

The Mountain Man
Productions:
Opened December 12, 1921 for 163 performances.
Reviews:
Dramatic Mirror 84:881, Dec 17, 1921
Life (NY) 79:18, Jan 5, 1922
New Republic 29:309-10, Feb 8, 1922
New York Clipper 69:12, Dec 21, 1921
New York Times p. 24, Dec 13, 1921
Theatre Magazine 35:128, Feb 1922

Pomeroy's Past
Productions:
Opened April 19, 1926 for 94 performances.
Reviews:
Life (NY) 87:23, May 13, 1926
Nation 122:510, May 5, 1926
New York Times p. 24, Apr 20, 1926
VIII, p. 1, May 2, 1926
Theatre Magazine 44:16, Jul 1926
44:26, Oct 1926
Vogue 67:79+, Jun 15, 1926

The Rescuing Angel
Productions:
Opened October 8, 1917 for 32 performances.
Reviews:
Dramatic Mirror 77:7, Oct 20, 1917
Life (NY) 70:672, Oct 25, 1917
New York Drama News 64:7, Oct 13, 1917
New York Times p. 9, Oct 9, 1917
III, p. 6, Oct 14, 1917
Theatre Magazine 27:349+, Dec 1917

The Robbery
Productions:
Opened February 28, 1921 for 5 matinees.
Reviews:
Dramatic Mirror 83:408+, Mar 5, 1921

New York Times p. 18, Mar 1, 1921
VIII, p. 1, Mar 13, 1921

Rollo's Wild Oat
Productions:
Opened November 23, 1920 for 228 performances.
Reviews:
Collier's 66:11, Dec 25, 1920
Dramatic Mirror p. 1051, Dec 4, 1920
Hearst 39:21-3+, May 1921
Independent 104:385, Dec 18, 1920
New York Clipper 67:25, Feb 4, 1920
68:23, Dec 1, 1920
New York Times p. 14, Nov 24, 1920
VI, p. 1, Jan 23, 1921
Theatre Magazine 33:83+, Feb 1921

Spring Thaw
Productions:
Opened March 21, 1938 for 8 performances.
Reviews:
New York Times p. 18, Mar 22, 1938
Newsweek 11:25, Apr 4, 1938
One Act Play Magazine 2:69, May 1938
Stage 15:31, Apr 1938

A Successful Calamity
Productions:
Opened February 5, 1917 for 144 performances.
Opened February 12, 1934 in repertory.
Reviews:
American Magazine 85:30, Feb 1918
Book News 35:283, Mar 1917
Current Opinion 62:249-52, Apr 1917
Dramatic Mirror 77:7, Feb 10, 1917
Green Book 17:581+, Apr 1917
International 11:95, Mar 1917
Nation 104:198, Feb 15, 1917
New York Drama News 63:6, Feb 10, 1917
New York Times p. 10, Feb 6, 1917
II, p. 2, Feb 11, 1917
p. 11, Mar 19, 1921
Theatre Magazine 25:145+, Mar 1917

LAPINE, JAMES

Table Settings
Productions:
(Off Off Broadway) March 21, 1979 (Playwrights Horizons).
(Off Broadway) January 14, 1980 for 264 performances.

Reviews:
America 142:192, Mar 8, 1980
Los Angeles 26:316+, May 1981
New York Theatre Critics' Reviews 1980:342
New York Times p. 10, Mar 24, 1979
                III, p. 7, Jan 15, 1980
                III, p. 13, Aug 22, 1980
New Yorker 55:96, Jan 21, 1980
Newsweek 95:58, Jan 28, 1980
Time 115:89, Jan 28, 1980

Twelve Dreams
Productions:
(Off Off Broadway) March 8, 1978 (Lenox Arts Center).
(Off Broadway) December 22, 1981 (New York Shakespeare Festival Public Theater).
Reviews:
New Republic 186:26, Feb 10, 1982
New York Magazine 15:53, Jan 11, 1982
New York Times III, p. 9, Dec 23, 1981
New Yorker 57:53+, Jan 4, 1982

LARDNER, RING

Elmer the Great
Productions:
Opened September 24, 1928 for 40 performances.
Reviews:
Drama 19:43-4, Nov 1928
Life (NY) 92:17, Oct 12, 1928
New York Times p. 29, Sep 25, 1928
                IX, p. 1, Sep 30, 1928
                p. 32, Nov 1, 1940
Theatre Arts 12:775+, Nov 1928
Time 36:44, Aug 5, 1940

June Moon (with George S. Kaufman)
Productions:
Opened October 9, 1929 for 273 performances.
Opened May 15, 1933 for 49 performances.
(Off Off Broadway) October 21, 1971 (Equity Library Theater).
Reviews:
American Mercury 18:502-3, Dec 1929
Life (NY) 94:22, Nov 1, 1929
New York Times VIII, p. 1, Aug 4, 1929
                IX, p. 4, Oct 6, 1929
                p. 34, Oct 10, 1929
                p. 50, Oct 26, 1971
Outlook 153:431, Nov 13, 1929
Theatre Arts 13:880-1, Dec 1929

Theatre Magazine 50:47-8, Dec 1929
                 51:32-5+, Feb 1930
Vogue 74:164, Dec 7, 1929

The Love Nest (see entry under Sherwood, Robert E.)

A Round with Ring (Based on the works of Ring Lardner, adapted
    by Nathan R. Teitel and Haila Stoddard)
  Productions:
    (Off Off Broadway) October 27, 1969 for 2 performances (ANTA
        Matinee Theater Series).
  Reviews:
    New York Times p. 56, Oct 30, 1969

LAURENTS, ARTHUR

The Bird Cage
  Productions:
    Opened February 22, 1950 for 21 performances.
  Reviews:
    Commonweal 51:607, Mar 17, 1950
    Nation 170:236, Mar 11, 1950
    New Republic 122:23, Mar 13, 1950
    New York Theatre Critics' Reviews 1950:341
    New York Times p. 32, Feb 23, 1950
    New Yorker 26:58, Mar 4, 1950
    Newsweek 35:82, Mar 6, 1950
    Theatre Arts 34:14, May 1950
    Time 55:71, Mar 6, 1950

A Clearing in the Woods
  Productions:
    Opened January 10, 1957 for 36 performances.
    (Off Broadway) Season of 1958-59.
  Reviews:
    America 96:510, Feb 2, 1957
    Catholic World 184:470, Mar 1957
    Christian Century 74:235, Feb 20, 1957
    Commonweal 65:489, Feb 8, 1957
    New York Theatre Critics' Reviews 1957:393
    New York Times p. 20, Jan 11, 1957
                 II, p. 1, Jan 20, 1957
                    p. 32, Feb 13, 1959
    New Yorker 32:57, Jan 19, 1957
    Saturday Review 40:23, Jan 26, 1957
                    42:25, Feb 28, 1959
    Theatre Arts 41:20, Mar 1957
    Time 69:72, Jan 21, 1957

The Enclave
  Productions:

(Off Broadway) November 15, 1973 for 22 performances.
Reviews:
Nation 217:638, Dec 10, 1973
New York Magazine 6:105, Dec 3, 1973
New York Times p. 31, Nov 16, 1973
New Yorker 49:147, Dec 3, 1973

Home of the Brave
Productions:
Opened December 27, 1945 for 69 performances.
(Off Broadway) Season of 1946-47 (Associated Playwright, Inc.).
(Off Off Broadway) March 3, 1977 (New York Theater Ensemble).
Reviews:
Catholic World 162:457, Feb 1946
Forum 105:657-9, Mar 1946
New York Theatre Critics' Reviews 1945:51
New York Times p. 13, Dec 28, 1945
        II, p. 1, Jan 6, 1946
        II, p. 1, Jan 13, 1946
        p. 12, Nov 15, 1980
New Yorker 21:42-4, Jan 12, 1946
Newsweek 27:82, Jan 7, 1946
Theatre Arts 30:141, 145-6, Mar 1946
Time 47:88, Jan 7, 1946

Invitation to a March
Productions:
Opened October 29, 1960 for 113 performances.
(Off Broadway) Season of 1966-67 for 10 performances (Equity Theatre).
Reviews:
America 104:352, Dec 3, 1960
Christian Century 77:1382, Nov 23, 1960
Nation 191:420-1, Nov 26, 1960
New Republic 143:20-1, Nov 14, 1960
New York Theatre Critics' Reviews 1960:191
New York Times II, p. 1, Oct 23, 1960
            p. 27, Oct 31, 1960
New Yorker 36:116, Nov 5, 1960
Newsweek 56:61, Nov 14, 1960
Saturday Review 43:73, Nov 12, 1960
Theatre Arts 45:73, Jan 1961
Time 76:84, Nov 14, 1960

My Mother Was a Fortune Teller
Productions:
(Off Off Broadway) May 5, 1978 for 24 performances (Hudson Guild Theater).
Reviews:
New York Times III, p. 13, May 8, 1978

*Scream
    Reviews:
        Texas Monthly 6:204+, Dec 1978

The Time of the Cuckoo
    Productions:
        Opened October 15, 1952 for 263 performances.
        (Off Broadway) Season of 1958-59.
        (Off Off Broadway) February 7, 1980 (Equity Library Theater).
    Reviews:
        Catholic World, 176:229-30, Dec 1952
        Commonweal 57:118, Nov 7, 1952
        Nation 175:413, Nov 1, 1952
        New York Theatre Critics' Reviews 1952:235
        New York Times II, p. 3, Oct 12, 1952
                          p. 37, Oct 16, 1952
                          II, p. 1, Nov 2, 1952
                          II, p. 1, Jan 4, 1953
                          p. 40, Oct 28, 1958
                          p. 55, Feb 10, 1980
        New Yorker 28:77-8, Oct 25, 1952
        Newsweek 40:77, Oct 27, 1952
        Saturday Review 35:28, Oct 18, 1952
                        35:26, Nov 1, 1952
        School and Society 77:117, Feb 21, 1953
        Theatre Arts 36:26-7, Dec 1952
        Time 60:75, Oct 27, 1952

*The Way Back
    Reviews:
        New York Times p. 9, Jan 29, 1949

LAVERY, EMMET

*Dawn's Early Light
    Reviews:
        New York Times p. 76, Aug 9, 1959

The First Legion
    Productions:
        Opened October 1, 1934 for 112 performances.
    Reviews:
        Catholic World 140:210, Nov 1934
        Commonweal 20:563, Oct 12, 1934
                   21:654, Apr 3, 1935
                   23:104, Nov 22, 1935
        New York Times p. 18, Oct 2, 1934
                       VIII, p. 2, Mar 10, 1935
                       p. 19, Mar 12, 1936
                       p. 30, Jun 8, 1937
                       X, p. 2, Aug 15, 1937

Stage 12:13, Nov 1934
12:63-4, Dec 1934
Theatre Arts 20:89, Feb 1936

The Gentleman from Athens
Productions:
Opened December 9, 1947 for 7 performances.
Reviews:
New York Theatre Critics' Reviews 1947:241
New York Times p. 78, Nov 30, 1947
II, p. 5, Dec 7, 1947
p. 42, Dec 10, 1947
New Yorker 23:48+, Dec 20, 1947
Newsweek 30:76, Dec 22, 1947
Time 50:74, Dec 22, 1947

The Magnificent Yankee
Productions:
Opened January 22, 1946 for 160 performances.
Reviews:
Catholic World 162:550-1, Mar 1946
Commonweal 43:429, Feb 8, 1946
43:456, Feb 15, 1946
Forum 105:659, Mar 1946
Life 20:56-8, Feb 11, 1946
New Republic 114:189, Feb 11, 1946
New York Theatre Critics' Reviews 1946:477
New York Times p. 23, Jan 2, 1946
VI, p. 28, Jan 13, 1946
p. 21, Jan 23, 1946
II, p. 1, Feb 3, 1946
II, p. 1, Mar 31, 1946
New Yorker 21:36-8, Feb 2, 1946
Newsweek 27:80, Feb 4, 1946
Saturday Review 29:28-30, Feb 23, 1946
Theatre Arts 30:140, Mar 1946
Time 47:62, Feb 4, 1946

LAWRENCE, JEROME

Auntie Mame (with Robert E. Lee. Based on Patrick Dennis' novel)
Productions:
Opened October 31, 1956 for 639 performances.
Opened August 11, 1958 for 24 performances.
Reviews:
America 96:310, Dec 8, 1956
Catholic World 184:305-6, Jan 1957
Commonweal 65:382, Jan 11, 1957
Life 41:129-30+, Nov 12, 1956
Nation 183:485, Dec 1, 1956

New York Theatre Critics' Reviews 1956:229
New York Times VI, p. 17, Oct 28, 1956
     p. 47, Nov 1, 1956
     II, p. 1, Nov 11, 1956
     II, p. 3, Nov 18, 1956
     II, p. 1, Jun 8, 1958
     p. 3, Aug 12, 1958
New Yorker 32:110+, Nov 10, 1956
Newsweek 48:54, Nov 12, 1956
Saturday Review 39:28, Nov 17, 1956
Theatre Arts 41:22-3, Jan 1957
    41:33+, Aug 1957
    42:25-6+, Nov 1958
Time 68:71, Nov 12, 1956

A Call on Kuprin (with Robert E. Lee)
 Productions:
  Opened May 25, 1961 for 12 performances.
 Reviews:
  Nation 192:504+, Jun 10, 1961
  New York Theatre Critics' Reviews 1961:282
  New York Times II, p. 1, May 21, 1961
       p. 29, May 26, 1961
       II, p. 1, Jun 4, 1961
  New Yorker 37:94, Jun 10, 1961
  Newsweek 57:85, Jun 5, 1961
  Theatre Arts 45:9-11, Jul 1961
  Time 77:85, Jun 2, 1961

Diamond Orchid (with Robert E. Lee)
 Productions:
  Opened February 10, 1965 for 5 performances.
 Reviews:
  New York Theatre Critics' Reviews 1965:378
  New York Times p. 44, Feb 11, 1965

First Monday in October (with Robert E. Lee)
 Productions:
  Opened October 3, 1978 for 79 performances.
 Reviews:
  America 139:314, Nov 4, 1978
  Encore 7:36, Nov 6, 1978
  Nation 227:452, Oct 28, 1978
  New Leader 61:21-2, Oct 23, 1978
  New Republic 179:26, Oct 28, 1978
  New York Magazine 11:131+, Oct 16, 1978
  New York Theatre Critics' Reviews 1978:206
  New York Times p. 18, Nov 7, 1975
       p. 46, Oct 5, 1978
       p. 54, Nov 6, 1978
  New Yorker 54:86, Oct 16, 1978

Newsweek 92:94, Oct 16, 1978
Saturday Review 5:45, Oct 1978
Time 106:86+, Nov 3, 1975
   112:130, Oct 16, 1978

The Gang's All Here (with Robert E. Lee)
   Productions:
      Opened October 1, 1959 for 132 performances.
   Reviews:
      America 102:213-14, Nov 14, 1959
      Commonweal 71:186, Nov 6, 1959
      Nation 189:239, Oct 17, 1959
      New York Theatre Critics' Reviews 1959:289
      New York Times p. 23, Oct 2, 1959
                  II, p. 1, Oct 11, 1959
      New Yorker 35:125-6, Oct 10, 1959
      Newsweek 54:70, Oct 12, 1959
      Reporter 21:37, Nov 12, 1959
      Saturday Review 42:65, Oct 17, 1959
      Theatre Arts 43:15, Dec 1959
      Time 74:70, Oct 12, 1959

The Incomparable Max (with Robert E. Lee. Based on stories by
      Max Beerbohm)
   Productions:
      Opened October 19, 1971 for 23 performances.
      (Off Off Broadway) June 1980 for 16 performances (Manhattan
         Punch Line).
   Reviews:
      America 125:427, Nov 20, 1971
      New York Theatre Critics' Reviews 1971:236
      New York Times p. 52, Oct 20, 1971
                  II, p. 1, Oct 31, 1971
                  II, p. 17, Oct 31, 1971
                  III, p. 14, Jun 16, 1980
      New Yorker 47:101, Oct 30, 1971
      Time 98:95, Nov 1, 1971

Inherit the Wind (with Robert E. Lee)
   Productions:
      Opened April 21, 1955 for 806 performances.
      (Off Off Broadway) October 26, 1977 (Joseph Jefferson).
   Reviews:
      America 93:250, May 28, 1955
      Catholic World 181:225-6, Jun 1955
      Commonweal 62:278, Jun 17, 1955
      Life 38:119-20+, May 9, 1955
      Nation 180:410, May 7, 1955
      New York Theatre Critics' Reviews 1955:322
      New York Times p. 24, Jan 12, 1955
                  p. 28, Apr 5, 1955

II, p. 1, Apr 17, 1955
p. 20, Apr 22, 1955
VI, p. 17, May 22, 1955
II, p. 1, Sep 25, 1955
p. 31, Jun 3, 1957
p. 36, Feb 18, 1960
p. 50, Jun 23, 1967
p. 41, Oct 8, 1973
II, p. 1, Nov 18, 1973
III, p. 3, Nov 11, 1977
New Yorker 31:67, Apr 30, 1955
Newsweek 45:82, May 2, 1955
Saturday Review 38:25, May 14, 1955
Theatre Arts 39:18-19, 23, Jul 1955
41:34-62, Aug 1957
Time 65:78, May 2, 1955

The Night Thoreau Spent in Jail (with Robert E. Lee)
Productions:
(Off Off Broadway) October 1974 (The Nighthouse).
(Off Off Broadway) November 6, 1975 (Walden Theater).
Reviews:
Nation 70:17, Apr 16, 1971
National Review 23:45-6, Jan 12, 1971
New York Times II, p. 1, Oct 18, 1970
p. 66, Nov 2, 1970
p. 16, Dec 23, 1970

Only in America (with Robert E. Lee. Based on Harry Golden's book)
Productions:
Opened November 19, 1959 for 28 performances.
Reviews:
Commonweal 71:321, Dec 11, 1959
Nation 189:427, Dec 5, 1959
New York Theatre Critics' Reviews 1959:224
New York Times p. 46, Nov 18, 1959
p. 35, Nov 20, 1959
New Yorker 35:97, Dec 5, 1959
Newsweek 54:100, Nov 30, 1959
Saturday Review 42:29, Dec 5, 1959
Time 74:64, Nov 30, 1959

LAWSON, JOHN HOWARD

Gentlewoman
Productions:
Opened March 22, 1934 for 12 performances.
Reviews:
Nation 138:424, Apr 11, 1934
New York Times p. 28, Mar 23, 1934

Stage 11:10, Apr 1934
Time 23:26, Apr 2, 1934

The International
Productions:
Opened January 12, 1928 for 27 performances.
Reviews:
Life (NY) 92:21, Feb 2, 1928
Nation 126:130, Feb 1, 1928
New York Times p. 24, Jan 16, 1928

Loud Speaker
Productions:
Opened March 7, 1927 for 42 performances.
(Off Off Broadway) April 17, 1979 (Shelter West).
Reviews:
Bookman 65:332, May 1927
Independent 118:445, Apr 23, 1927
Life (NY) 89:21, Mar 24, 1927
Nation 124:324, Mar 23, 1927
New York Times p. 27, Mar 3, 1927
VII, p. 1, Mar 20, 1927
III, p. 8, May 1, 1979
Vogue 69:82-3, May 1, 1927

Marching Song
Productions:
Opened February 17, 1937 for 61 performances.
Reviews:
Catholic World 145:85-6, Apr 1937
Commonweal 25:258, Mar 5, 1937
Nation 144:248-9, Feb 27, 1937
New Republic 90:166-7, Mar 17, 1937
New York Times p. 18, Feb 18, 1937
XI, p. 2, Feb 28, 1937
Theatre Arts 21:265, Apr 1937
Time 29:47, Mar 1937

Nirvana
Productions:
Opened March 3, 1926 for 6 performances.
Reviews:
Nation 122:295, Mar 17, 1926
New Republic 46:173, Mar 31, 1926
New York Times p. 19, Mar 4, 1926
Theatre Magazine 43:16, May 1926

Processional
Productions:
Opened January 12, 1925 for 96 performances.
Opened October 13, 1937 for 81 performances (WPA Federal
Theatre Project).

Reviews:
    American Mercury 4:372-3, Mar 1925
    Bookman 61:74-5, Mar 1925
    Catholic World 146:341-2, Dec 1937
    Dial 78:341-4, Apr 1925
    Drama 15:129-30, Mar 7, 1925
    Independent 114:275, Mar 7, 1925
    Independent Woman 16:368, Nov 1937
    Life (NY) 85:18, Feb 5, 1925
    Nation 120:99-100, Jan 28, 1925
          145:456, Oct 23, 1937
    New Republic 41:261, Jan 28, 1925
    New York Times p. 17, Jan 13, 1925
                 VII, p. 1, Jan 18, 1925
                 VII, p. 1, Jan 25, 1925
                 IV, p. 18, Feb 1, 1925
                 VII, p. 2, Feb 1, 1925
                 VII, p. 2, Feb 8, 1925
                 XI, p. 2, Oct 10, 1937
                 p. 23, Oct 14, 1937
                 XI, p. 1, Oct 24, 1937
    Theatre Magazine 40:19, Mar 1925

The Pure in Heart
    Productions:
    Opened March 20, 1934 for 7 performances.
    Reviews:
    New York Times p. 9, May 21, 1932
                 IX, p. 3, Oct 9, 1932
                 p. 24, Mar 21, 1934
    Stage 11:10, Apr 1934

Roger Bloomer
    Productions:
    Opened March 1, 1923 for 50 performances.
    Reviews:
    Bookman 57:319, May 1923
    Freeman 7:111-12, Apr 11, 1923
    Independent 110:206, Mar 17, 1923
    Nation 116:346, Mar 21, 1923
    New Republic 34:100-1, Mar 21, 1923
    New York Clipper 71:14, Mar 7, 1923
    New York Times p. 18, Mar 2, 1923
                 VIII, p. 1, Mar 11, 1923
    Theatre Magazine 37:15, Apr 1923

Success Story
    Productions:
    Opened September 26, 1932 for 121 performances.
    (Off Off Broadway) December 3, 1980 (Jewish Repertory Theater).

Reviews:
  Catholic World 136:207-8, Nov 1932
  Commonweal 16:566, Oct 12, 1932
  Nation 135:336-7, Oct 12, 1932
  New Outlook 161:46, Jan 1933
  New Republic 72:233-5, Oct 12, 1932
  New York Times p. 24, Sep 27, 1932
            IX, p. 1, Oct 2, 1932
            p. 17, Jan 2, 1934
            III, p. 9, Dec 23, 1980
  Theatre Arts 16:955-6, Dec 1932
  Vogue 80:59+, Nov 15, 1932

LEE, ROBERT E.

Auntie Mame (see entry under Lawrence, Jerome)

A Call on Kuprin (see entry under Lawrence, Jerome)

Diamond Orchid (see entry under Lawrence, Jerome)

First Monday in October (see entry under Lawrence, Jerome)

The Gang's All Here (see entry under Lawrence, Jerome)

The Incomparable Max (see entry under Lawrence, Jerome)

Inherit the Wind (see entry under Lawrence, Jerome)

The Night Thoreau Spent in Jail (see entry under Lawrence, Jerome)

Only in America (see entry under Lawrence, Jerome)

LEVIN, IRA M.

Break a Leg
  Productions:
    (Off Off Broadway) Season of 1974-75 (ETC).
    (Off Off Broadway) May 13, 1974 (URGENT).
    Opened April 29, 1979 for one performance.
  Reviews:
    New York Theatre Critics' Reviews 1979:270
    New York Times III, p. 13, Apr 30, 1979
            III, p. 10, May 1, 1979
            II, p. 5, May 20, 1979
    New Yorker 55:130, May 7, 1979

Critic's Choice
  Productions:
    Opened December 14, 1960 for 189 performances.

Reviews:
    America 104:548, Jan 21, 1961
    Nation 191:531, Dec 31, 1960
    New York Theatre Critics' Reviews 1960:138
    New York Times p. 61, Dec 15, 1960
                p. 53, Dec 7, 1961
    New Yorker 36:38+, Dec 24, 1960
    Newsweek 56:53, Dec 26, 1960
    Saturday Review 43:28, Dec 31, 1960
    Theatre Arts 45:11, Feb 1961

Deathtrap
Productions:
    Opened February 26, 1978 for 1,809+ performances (still running on June 1, 1982).
Reviews:
    Los Angeles 24:251, Jun 1979
    New West 4:SC-45, May 7, 1979
    New York Magazine 11:72, Mar 13, 1978
    New York Theatre Critics' Reviews 1978:372
    New York Times III, p. 15, Feb 27, 1978
                II, p. 1, Mar 5, 1978
                 XXI, p. 4, Jul 22, 1979
                 II, p. 3, Feb 21, 1982
                 III, p. 15, Jun 8, 1982
    New Yorker 54:56, Mar 13, 1978
    Newsweek 91:93+, Mar 13, 1978
    Saturday Review 5:26, Apr 29, 1978
    Time 111:75, Mar 13, 1978

Dr. Cook's Garden
Productions:
    Opened September 25, 1967 for 8 performances.
Reviews:
    New York Theatre Critics' Reviews 1967:290
    New York Times p. 52, Sep 26, 1967
    New Yorker 43:131, Oct 7, 1967

General Seeger
Productions:
    Opened February 28, 1962 for 2 performances.
Reviews:
    New York Theatre Critics' Reviews 1962:334
    New York Times p. 26, Mar 1, 1962
    New Yorker 38:83, Mar 10, 1962

Interlock
Productions:
    Opened February 6, 1958 for 4 performances.
Reviews:
    New Republic 138:22, Mar 3, 1958

New York Theatre Critics' Reviews 1958:363
New York Times p. 18, Feb 7, 1958
New Yorker 33:58+, Feb 15, 1958
Theatre Arts 42:25, Apr 1958

No Time for Sergeants (Adapted from Mac Hyman's novel)
    Productions:
        Opened October 20, 1955 for 796 performances.
    Reviews:
        America 94:167, Nov 5, 1955
        Catholic World 182:226, Dec 1955
        Colliers 137:6, Mar 2, 1956
        Commonweal 63:141-2, Nov 11, 1955
        Life 39:113+, Nov 7, 1955
        Nation 181:406, Nov 5, 1955
        New York Theatre Critics' Reviews 1955:238
        New York Times VI, p. 38, Oct 9, 1955
                       p. 32, Oct 21, 1955
                       II, p. 1, Nov 6, 1955
                       p. 15, Aug 24, 1956
        New Yorker 31:88+, Oct 29, 1955
        Newsweek 46:55, Oct 31, 1955
        Saturday Review 38:26, Nov 5, 1955
        Theatre Arts 39:28-9, Dec 1955
        Time 66:73+, Oct 31, 1955

Veronica's Room
    Productions:
        Opened October 25, 1973 for 75 performances.
        (Off Broadway) March 8, 1981 for 97 performances.
    Reviews:
        New York Magazine 6:75, Nov 12, 1973
        New York Theatre Critics' Reviews 1973:210
        New York Times p. 50, Oct 26, 1973
                       II, p. 1, Nov 4, 1973
                       p. 15, Dec 29, 1973
                       p. 53, Mar 15, 1981
        New Yorker 49:89, Nov 5, 1973
        Newsweek 82:75, Nov 5, 1973
        Time 102:135, Nov 12, 1973

LEVITT, SAUL

The Andersonville Trial
    Productions:
        Opened December 29, 1959 for 179 performances.
    Reviews:
        America 102:482-3, Jan 16, 1960
        Christian Century 77:136-7, Feb 3, 1960
        Commonweal 71:469, Jan 22, 1960

Life 48:125-6, Feb 8, 1960
Nation 190:87-8, Jan 23, 1960
New Republic 142:21-2, Jan 18, 1960
New York Theatre Critics' Reviews 1959:181
New York Times p. 15, Oct 31, 1959
                p. 15, Dec 30, 1959
               II, p. 1, Jan 10, 1960
                p. 33, Nov 25, 1960
New Yorker 35:69-70+, Jan 9, 1960
Newsweek 55:60, Jan 11, 1960
Saturday Review 43:54, Jan 16, 1960
Theatre Arts 44:12, Mar 1960
Time 75:46, Jan 11, 1960

Lincoln
    Productions:
        (Off Broadway) November 30, 1976 for 32 performances.
    Reviews:
        New York Times III, p. 20, Dec 20, 1976

The Trial of the Catonsville Nine   (see entry under Berrigan, Daniel)

LEWIS, SINCLAIR

*Angela Is Twenty-Two
    Reviews:
        New York Times p. 6, Dec 31, 1938

Dodsworth   (see entry under Howard, Sidney)

Hobohemia
    Productions:
        Opened Feburary 8, 1919 for 89 performances.
    Reviews:
        Dramatic Mirror 80:267, Feb 22, 1919
        Life (NY) 73:293, Feb 20, 1919
        New York Times p. 20, Feb 9, 1919
        Theatre Magazine 29:205-6+, Apr 1919

It Can't Happen Here (with John C. Moffitt. Based on the novel by
        Sinclair Lewis)
    Productions:
        Opened October 26, 1936 for 95 performances.
    Reviews:
        Catholic World 144:338, Dec 1936
        Commonweal 25:76, Nov 13, 1936
        Nation 143:558, Nov 7, 1936
        New Republic 89:50, Nov 11, 1936
        New York Times p. 30, Oct 28, 1936
                      X, p. 1, Nov 8, 1936
                       p. 22, Jul 26, 1938

Newsweek 8:40, Nov 7, 1936
Stage 14:78, Dec 1936
Theatre Arts 20:930-1, Dec 1936
Time 28:21, Nov 9, 1936

Jayhawker (with Lloyd Lewis)
    Productions:
        Opened November 5, 1934 for 24 performances.
    Reviews:
        Catholic World 140:342, Dec 1934
        Nation 139:600-1, Nov 21, 1934
        New York Times IX, p. 3, Nov 4, 1934
                         p. 34, Nov 6, 1934
                       VIII, p. 3, Feb 17, 1935
        Stage 12:26-7, Dec 1934
        Theatre Arts 19:9-10, Jan 1935
        Time 24:36, Nov 12, 1934

LINDSAY, HOWARD

The Great Sebastians (with Russel Crouse)
    Productions:
        Opened January 4, 1956 for 174 performances.
    Reviews:
        America 94:515, Feb 4, 1956
        Commonweal 63:428, Jan 27, 1956
        Life 40:107-8+, Jan 30, 1956
        Nation 182:58, Jan 21, 1956
        New York Theatre Critics' Reviews 1956:397
        New York Times p. 27, Jan 5, 1956
                       II, p. 1, Jan 11, 1956
                       II, p. 1, Jan 15, 1956
        New Yorker 31:60+, Jan 14, 1956
        Newsweek 47:50, Jan 16, 1956
        Saturday Review 39:40, Jan 21, 1956
        Theatre Arts 40:18, Feb 1956
                     40:16, Mar 1956
        Time 67:79, Jan 16, 1956

I'd Rather Be Left (see State of the Union)

Life with Father (with Russel Crouse. Based on the book by Clarence Day).
    Productions:
        Opened November 8, 1939 for 3,224 performances.
        Opened October 19, 1967 for 22 performances (City Center Drama Co.).
    Reviews:
        Catholic World 150:336, Dec 1939
                       156:90, Oct 1942

161:508-9, Sep 1945
163:554, Sep 1946
Collier's 115:18+, Apr 21, 1945
Commonweal 31:118, Nov 24, 1939
40:399-400, Aug 11, 1944
Cosmopolitan 123:8, Sep 1947
Forum 103:33, Jan 1940
Ladies Home Journal 58:20-21+, May 1941
Life 7:39-40+, Nov 27, 1939
9:110+, Dec 2, 1940
Nation 149:560, Nov 18, 1939
New Republic 101:169, Nov 29, 1939
New York Theatre Critics' Reviews 1940:457
1941:489
New York Times p. 14, Aug 15, 1939
IX, p. 1, Nov 5, 1939
p. 26, Nov 9, 1939
X, p. 1, Nov 19, 1939
X, p. 5, Dec 10, 1939
X, p. 2, Mar 3, 1940
p. 29, Jul 28, 1940
IX, p. 1, Aug 18, 1940
IX, p. 2, Jun 1, 1941
p. 20, Sep 30, 1941
IX, p. 3, Nov 16, 1941
p. 26, Mar 25, 1942
VIII, p. 1, Nov 1, 1942
p. 8, Jun 19, 1943
p. 34, Dec 16, 1943
II, p. 1, Nov 5, 1944
p. 15, Aug 1, 1945
VI, p. 34, Nov 3, 1946
II, p. 3, Nov 24, 1946
II, p. 3, Apr 20, 1947
p. 34, Apr 30, 1947
p. 27, Jun 6, 1947
II, p. 1, Jun 8, 1947
p. 26, Jun 10, 1947
p. 52, Jun 14, 1947
p. 58, Oct 16, 1967
p. 53, Oct 20, 1967
p. 32, Jan 19, 1968
XXIII, p. 16, Jun 29, 1980
New York Times Magazine pp. 34-5, Nov 3, 1946
New Yorker 21:16-17, Jun 16, 1945
Newsweek 14:36, Nov 20, 1939
29:86, Jun 16, 1947
30:77, Aug 18, 1947
North American Review 248:no.2:401, Dec 1939
Saturday Review 21:8-9, Nov 18, 1939
Stage 1:14, Nov 1940
1:14, Dec 1940

Theatre Arts 24:13-15, Jan 1940
24:397+, Jun 1940
26:26-30, Jan 1942
30:672, Nov 1946
31:69, Apr 1947
31:58+, Jul 1947
Time 34:69, Nov 20, 1939
40:40, Sep 14, 1942
49:27+, Mar 24, 1947
49:74, Jun 16, 1947
50:43, Jul 21, 1947
Vogue 95:38-9, Jan 1, 1940
Yale Review 30:421, Winter 1941

Life with Mother (with Russel Crouse. Based on the book by Clarence Day)
Productions:
Opened October 20, 1948 for 265 performances.
Reviews:
Catholic World 168:241, Dec 1948
Commonweal 49:118, Nov 12, 1948
Life 25:53-4, Jul 5, 1948
25:149-50, Nov 15, 1948
26:41, Feb 7, 1949
Nation 167:528, Nov 6, 1948
New Republic 119:26, Nov 8, 1948
New York Theatre Critics' Reviews 1948:182
New York Times p. 36, Jun 9, 1948
VI, p. 16, Jun 27, 1948
II, p. 3, Oct 17, 1948
p. 32, Oct 21, 1948
II, p. 1, Oct 31, 1948
II, p. 1, Mar 27, 1949
New York Times Magazine pp. 16-17, Jun 27, 1948
New Yorker 24:40+, Oct 30, 1948
Newsweek 32:74, Nov 1, 1948
Saturday Review 31:25-8, Nov 20, 1948
32:30, Dec 31, 1949
School and Society 68:455-6, Dec 25, 1948
Theatre Arts 32:10-14, Aug 1948
32:28-9, Oct 1948
Time 52:51, Nov 1, 1948
Vogue 112:183, Dec 1948

Oh, Promise Me (with Bertrand Robinson)
Productions:
Opened November 24, 1930 for 145 performances.
Reviews:
Commonweal 13:218, Dec 24, 1930
Drama 21:12-13, Jan 1931
Life (NY) 96:18, Dec 26, 1930

New York Times p. 31, Nov 25, 1930
Vogue 77:98, Jan 15, 1931

The Prescott Proposals (with Russel Crouse)
    Productions:
        Opened December 16, 1953 for 125 performances.
    Reviews:
        America 90:385, Jan 9, 1954
        Catholic World 178:386-7, Feb 1954
        Commonweal 59:404, Jan 22, 1954
        Life 36:75-7, Jan 18, 1954
        Nation 178:57, Jan 16, 1954
        New Republic 130:21, Jan 4, 1954
        New York Theatre Critics' Reviews 1953:187
        New York Times II, p. 7, Dec 13, 1953
                      p. 53, Dec 17, 1953
                   II, p. 3, Dec 27, 1953
        New Yorker 42:47, Dec 28, 1953
        Saturday Review 37:55-6, Jan 2, 1954
        Theatre Arts 38:21, Mar 1954
        Time 62:34, Dec 28, 1953

Remains to Be Seen (with Russel Crouse)
    Productions:
        Opened October 3, 1951 for 199 performances.
    Reviews:
        Catholic World 174:148, Nov 1951
        Commonweal 55:37-8, Oct 19, 1951
        Life 31:169-70+, Oct 15, 1951
        Nation 173:334, Oct 20, 1951
        New York Theatre Critics' Reviews 1951:223
        New York Times II, p. 3, Sep 30, 1951
                      p. 37, Oct 4, 1951
                   II, p. 3, Jan 25, 1953
        New Yorker 27:84, Oct 13, 1951
        Newsweek 38:85, Oct 15, 1951
        Saturday Review 34:25-6, Oct 20, 1951
        School and Society 75:185, Mar 22, 1952
        Theatre Arts 35:3, 78, Dec 1951
        Time 58:74, Oct 15, 1951

She Loves Me Not (Adapted from Edward Hope's novel)
    Productions:
        Opened November 20, 1933 for 360 performances.
    Reviews:
        Catholic World 138:477, Jan 1934
        Literary Digest 118:23, Jul 14, 1934
        Nation 137:662, Dec 6, 1933
        New Outlook 163:42, Jan 1934
        New York Times IX, p. 3, Nov 19, 1933
                      p. 22, Nov 21, 1933

IX, p. 5, Dec 17, 1933
IX, p. 3, Feb 18, 1934
p. 18, Mar 26, 1934
p. 25, May 2, 1934
X, p. 2, May 27, 1934
Newsweek 2:32, Nov 25, 1933
Review of Reviews 81:49, Jun 1934
Stage 11:20-22, Jan 1934
Theatre Arts 18:9-11+, Jan 1934
Time 22:49, Dec 4, 1933

A Slight Case of Murder (with Damon Runyon)
    Productions:
    Opened September 11, 1935 for 69 performances.
    Reviews:
    Commonweal 22:528, Sep 27, 1935
    Literary Digest 120:22, Sep 28, 1935
    Nation 141:364, Sep 25, 1935
        122:24, Sep 5, 1936
    New York Times p. 28, Sep 12, 1935
        X, p. 1, Sep 22, 1935
    Newsweek 8:27, Sep 5, 1936
    Theatre Arts 19:822, Nov 1935
    Time 26:54-5, Sep 23, 1935
    Vanity Fair 45:41, Nov 1935

State of the Union (with Russel Crouse)
    Productions:
    Opened November 14, 1945 for 765 performances.
    Reviews:
    Catholic World 162:357, Jan 1946
    Commonweal 43:169, Nov 30, 1945
    Forum 105:466-8, Jan 1946
    Harper's Bazaar 79:128, Dec 1945
    Life 19:84-5+, Dec 10, 1945
    Nation 161:604, Dec 1, 1945
    New Republic 113:711, Nov 26, 1945
    New York Theatre Critics' Reviews 1945:102
    New York Times VI, p. 24, Nov 4, 1945
        p. 21, Nov 7, 1945
        p. 25, Nov 15, 1945
        II, p. 1, Nov 25, 1945
        II, p. 1, Apr 7, 1946
        II, p. 1, Aug 4, 1946
        II, p. 1, Sep 8, 1946
        II, p. 1, Nov 10, 1946
        II, p. 1, Jan 26, 1947
        II, p. 3, May 18, 1947
        p. 26, Jul 15, 1947
        II, p. 1, Jul 20, 1947
    New York Times Magazine pp. 24-5, Nov 4, 1945

New Yorker 21:48+, Nov 24, 1945
Newsweek 26:96, Nov 26, 1945
Player's Magazine 25:21, Oct 1948
Saturday Review 28:18-20, Nov 24, 1945
Theatre Arts 29:677, Dec 1945
           30:5-6, Jan 1946
Time 46:48, Nov 26, 1945
Vogue 106:61, Dec 15, 1945

Strip for Action (with Russel Crouse)
   Productions:
      Opened September 30, 1942 for 110 performances.
   Reviews:
      New Republic 107:545, Oct 26, 1942
      New York Theatre Critics' Reviews 1942:220
      New York Times p. 26, Oct 1, 1942
                  VIII, p. 1, Oct 11, 1942
                  p. 18, Dec 14, 1942
      Newsweek 20:82+, Oct 12, 1942
      Theatre Arts 26:741, Dec 1942

Tall Story (with Russel Crouse. Suggested by Howard Nemerov's
      The Homecoming Game)
   Productions:
      Opened January 29, 1959 for 108 performances.
   Reviews:
      America 100:614, Feb 21, 1959
      Catholic World 189:60-1, Apr 1959
      Commonweal 69:600, Mar 6, 1959
      New York Theatre Critics' Reviews 1959:393
      New York Times p. 33, Jan 30, 1959
      New Yorker 34:87-8, Feb 7, 1959
      Newsweek 53:56, Feb 9, 1959
      Saturday Review 42:34, Feb 21, 1959
      Theatre Arts 43:21-2, Apr 1959
      Time 73:73, Feb 9, 1959

Tommy (with Bertrand Robinson)
   Productions:
      Opened January 10, 1927 for 232 performances.
      Opened August 7, 1933 for 24 performances.
   Reviews:
      Life (NY) 89:19, Feb 17, 1927
      New York Times p. 36, Jan 11, 1927
                  VII, p. 1, Mar 27, 1927
                  p. 22, Aug 8, 1933
      Theatre Magazine 45:24+, May 1927
      Vogue 69:110+, Mar 1, 1927

Your Uncle Dudley (with Bertrand Robinson)
   Productions:

Opened November 18, 1929 for 96 performances.
Reviews:
Commonweal 11:145, Dec 4, 1929
New York Times p. 26, Nov 19, 1929
Theatre Magazine 51:46-7, Jan 1930
Vogue 75:106, Jan 18, 1930

LOGAN, JOSHUA

Mister Roberts (with Thomas Heggen. Based on Thomas Heggen's
novel)
Productions:
Opened February 18, 1948 for 1,157 performances.
Opened December 5, 1956 for 15 performances.
(Off Broadway) September 28, 1962 for 9 performances (Equity
Library Theater).
Reviews:
Catholic World 167:70, Apr 1948
Christian Science Monitor Magazine p. 7, Aug 5, 1950
Commonweal 47:521, Mar 5, 1948
Life 24:93-6+, Mar 1, 1948
Nation 166:402-3, Apr 10, 1948
New Republic 118:29, Mar 8, 1948
New York Theatre Critics' Reviews 1948:388
                                   1956:169
New York Times p. 27, Feb 19, 1948
              II, p. 1, Feb 29, 1948
              p. 8, Feb 18, 1950
              II, p. 1, May 21, 1950
              p. 22, Jul 20, 1950
              II, p. 1, Jul 23, 1950
              p. 20, Feb 9, 1951
              p. 29, Apr 2, 1951
              II, p. 3, Feb 10, 1952
              p. 46, Dec 6, 1956
New York Times Magazine p. 12-13, Feb 8, 1948
New Yorker 24:46+, Feb 28, 1948
Newsweek 31:65-6, Mar 1, 1948
         31:56, Apr 19, 1948
Saturday Review 31:24-6, Mar 6, 1948
Theatre Arts 32:28-9, Apr 1948
Theatre Guild Magazine 32:32, Summer 1948
                       32:23, Fall 1948
                       33:12+, Nov 1949
Time 51:63, Mar 1, 1948
     51:52, Apr 19, 1948
Vogue 111:150, Apr 1, 1948
      112:144-5+, Aug 15, 1948

The Wisteria Trees (Based on Anton Chekhov's The Cherry Orchard)
Productions:

Opened March 29, 1950 for 165 performances.
Opened February 2, 1955 for 15 performances.
Reviews:
Catholic World 171:147, May 1950
      180:468, Mar 1955
Christian Science Monitor Magazine p. 4, Apr 1, 1950
Commonweal 52:69-70, Apr 28, 1950
Life 28:68-70, Apr 24, 1950
Nation 170:354-5, Apr 15, 1950
New Republic 122:22, Apr 10, 1958
New York Theatre Critics' Reviews 1950:320
      1955:377
New York Times p. 22, Feb 7, 1950
     II, p. 1, Mar 26, 1950
     p. 39, Mar 30, 1950
     II, p. 1, Apr 9, 1950
     p. 20, Feb 3, 1955
New York Times Magazine pp. 32-3, Mar 5, 1950
New Yorker 26:63+, Apr 8, 1950
     30:60, Feb 12, 1955
Newsweek 35:77, Apr 10, 1950
Saturday Review 38:24, Feb 19, 1955
Theatre Arts 34:15, Jun 1950
     39:22+, Apr 1955
Time 55:68, Apr 10, 1950

LONG, JOHN LUTHER

Kassa
Productions:
Opened January 23, 1909 for 65 performances.
Reviews:
Hampton 22:543+, Apr 1909
Theatre Magazine 9:72-3+, Mar 1909

LONG, SUMNER ARTHUR

Angela
Productions:
Opened October 30, 1969 for 4 performances.
Reviews:
New York Theatre Critics' Reviews 1969:189
New York Times p. 33, Oct 31, 1969
     II, p. 1, Nov 9, 1969

Cradle and All (see Never Too Late)

Never Too Late
Productions:
Opened November 27, 1962 for 1,007 performances.

Reviews:
    America 108:53, Jan 12, 1962
    Nation 195:430, Dec 15, 1962
    New York Theatre Critics' Reviews 1962:187
    New York Times p. 42, Nov 28, 1962
                   p. 5, Dec 19, 1962
                   p. 48, Sep 25, 1963
    New Yorker 38:148, Dec 8, 1962
    Newsweek 60:58, Dec 10, 1962
    Theatre Arts 47:12-13, Jan 1963
    Time 80:72, Dec 7, 1962

LOOS, ANITA

Cheri (Based on Colette's Cheri and The Last of Cheri)
    Productions:
    Opened October 12, 1959 for 56 performances.
    Reviews:
    America 102:214+, Nov 14, 1959
    Nation 189:339, Nov 7, 1959
    New Republic 141:19-20, Oct 26, 1959
    New York Theatre Critics' Reviews 1959:267
    New York Times II, p. 1, Oct 11, 1959
                    p. 44, Oct 13, 1959
    New Yorker 35:91-2+, Oct 24, 1959
    Newsweek 54:116, Oct 26, 1959
    Saturday Review 42:26, Oct 31, 1959
    Theatre Arts 43:14-16, Nov 1959
                 43:84, Dec 1959
    Time 74:102+, Oct 26, 1959

The Fall of Eve (with John Emerson)
    Productions:
    Opened August 31, 1925 for 48 performances.
    Reviews:
    Life (NY) 86:18, Sep 17, 1925
    New Republic 44:95-6, Sep 16, 1925
    New York Times p. 18, Sep 1, 1925
                   VIII, p. 1, Sep 6, 1925
                   p. 13, Oct 17, 1926

Gentlemen Prefer Blondes (with John Emerson)
    Productions:
    Opened September 28, 1926 for 199 performances.
    Reviews:
    Bookman 64:479-80, Dec 1926
    Harper's Bazaar 60:117+, Oct 1926
    Life (NY) 88:23, Oct 21, 1926
    New Republic 48:245-6, Oct 20, 1926
    New York Times VIII, p. 1, Sep 3, 1926

                  p. 23, Sep 29, 1926
                VIII, p. 2, Oct 10, 1926
                  p. 32, Apr 3, 1928
Theatre Magazine 44:13+, Dec 1926
Vanity Fair 27:54+, Oct 1926

Gigi (Based on the novel by Colette)
  Productions:
    Opened November 24, 1951 for 219 performances.
  Reviews:
    Catholic World 174:309-10, Jan 1952
    Commonweal 55:254, Dec 14, 1951
    Nation 173:530, Dec 15, 1951
    New York Theatre Critics' Reviews 1951:159
    New York Times p. 20, Nov 26, 1951
               p. 27, May 24, 1956
    New Yorker 27:87, Dec 1, 1951
    Newsweek 38:60, Dec 3, 1951
    Saturday Review 34:32-3, Dec 15, 1951
    School and Society 75:107-8, Feb 16, 1952
    Theatre Arts 36:31, Feb 1952
             36:41-7+, Jul 1952
    Time 58:49, Dec 3, 1951

Happy Birthday
  Productions:
    Opened October 31, 1946 for 564 performances.
  Reviews:
    Catholic World 164:261, Dec 1946
    Commonweal 45:116, Nov 15, 1946
    Life 21:79-82, Nov 18, 1946
    Nation 163:565, Nov 16, 1946
    New Republic 115:662, Nov 18, 1946
    New York Theatre Critics' Reviews 1946:280
    New York Times VI, p. 27, Sep 22, 1946
               VI, p. 30, Oct 27, 1946
               p. 31, Nov 1, 1946
               II, p. 1, Nov 10, 1946
               II, p. 1, Jan 26, 1947
               II, p. 1, Apr 20, 1947
               II, p. 1, Oct 26, 1947
    New Yorker 22:55, Nov 9, 1946
    Newsweek 28:92, Nov 11, 1946
    Saturday Review 29:23, Dec 21, 1946
    School and Society 66:327-8, Oct 25, 1947
    Theatre Arts 31:18-19+, Jan 1947
    Time 48:56, Nov 11, 1946

*The King's Mare
  Reviews:
    New York Times p. 23, Jul 21, 1966

The Social Register (with John Emerson)
Productions:
    Opened November 9, 1931 for 97 performances.
Reviews:
    New York Times VIII, p. 2, Oct 4, 1931
                   p. 28, Nov 10, 1931

The Whole Town's Talking (with John Emerson)
Productions:
    Opened August 29, 1923 for 173 performances.
Reviews:
    Dramatist 14:1168-9, Jul 1923
    Metropolitan Magazine 58:38-9+, Dec 1923
    Nation 117:304, Sep 19, 1923
    New York Times p. 8, Aug 30, 1923
                   VII, p. 1, Sep 9, 1923
    Theatre Magazine 38:66, Oct 1923

LOWELL, ROBERT

Benito Cereno (see The Old Glory)

Endecott and the Red Cross
Productions:
    (Off Broadway) May 7, 1968 for 15 performances (American
        Place Theater).
Reviews:
    America 119:149, Aug 31, 1968
    Nation 206:710, May 27, 1968
    New York Times p. 50, May 7, 1968
    New Yorker 44:84-6+, May 11, 1968
    Newsweek 71:109-10, May 13, 1968
    Saturday Review 51:40, May 25, 1968
    Time 91:74, May 10, 1968
    See also reviews from the 1976 production of The Old Glory

My Kinsman, Major Molineux (see The Old Glory)

The Old Glory (Adapted from Nathaniel Hawthorne's My Kinsman,
        Major Molineux and Herman Melville's Benito Cereno. Some-
        times includes Endecott and the Red Cross.)
Productions:
    (Off Broadway) March 1, 1964 for one performance (American
        Place Theater).
    (Off Broadway) November 1, 1964 for 36 performances (Amer-
        ican Place Theater).
    (Off Broadway) April 9, 1976 for 41 performances (program
        included Endecott and the Red Cross).
Reviews:
    Catholic World 200:323-4, Feb 1965

Commentary 61:64-7, Jun 1976
Nation 199:390-1, November 23, 1964
    222:573, May 8, 1976
New Republic 151:28+, November 21, 1964
New York Magazine 9:79, May 3, 1976
New York Theatre Critics' Reviews 1976:268
New York Times p. 62, Nov 2, 1964
        II, p. 1, Nov 15, 1964
        II, p. 7, Dec 6, 1964
        p. 36, Apr 19, 1976
New Yorker 40:143-4, Nov 14, 1964
Newsweek 64:92, Nov 16, 1964
    87:83-4, May 3, 1976
Reporter 36:44-5, Jun 15, 1967
Vogue 145:68, Jan 1, 1965

*Phaedra (Adapted from Racine)
   Reviews:
      New York Times p. 50, May 22, 1967
           II, p. 3, Jun 11, 1967

*Prometheus Bound
   Reviews:
      Nation 204:829-30, Jun 26, 1967
        209:156, Aug 25, 1969
      New York Times p. 52, May 11, 1967
           II, p. 1, May 21, 1967
           II, p. 1, Jun 11, 1967
      Newsweek 69:109, May 22, 1967
      Reporter 36:44-6, Jun 15, 1967
      Saturday Review 50:49, May 27, 1967

LUCE, CLARE BOOTHE (see Boothe, Clare)

MacARTHUR, CHARLES

The Front Page (see entry under Hecht, Ben)

Johnny on a Spot (Based on a story by Parke Levy and Alan Lipscott)
   Productions:
      Opened January 8, 1942 for 4 performances.
      (Off Broadway) February 21, 1980 for 27 performances.
   Reviews:
      New York Magazine 13:66+, Mar 17, 1980
      New York Theatre Critics' Reviews 1942:391
      New York Times p. 24, Jan 9, 1942
           III, p. 3, Feb 29, 1980
      New Yorker 56:93-4, Mar 10, 1980

Ladies and Gentlemen (with Ben Hecht. Adapted from Twelve in a
    Box by L. Bush-Fekete)
    Productions:
    Opened October 17, 1939 for 105 performances.
    Reviews:
    Catholic World 150:337-8, Dec 1939
    Independent Woman 19:50, Feb 1940
    Life 7:30-32, Aug 21, 1939
    New York Theatre Critics' Reviews 1940:469
    New York Times IX, p. 2, Sep 24, 1939
                p. 30, Oct 18, 1939
                IX, p. 1, Oct 22, 1939
                IX, p. 1, Oct 29, 1939
    Newsweek 14:31-2, Jul 17, 1939
            14:38, Oct 30, 1939
    Theatre Arts 23:856, Dec 1939
    Time 34:50, Jul 24, 1939
        34:43, Oct 30, 1939

Lulu Belle (see entry under Sheldon, Edward)

Salvation (see entry under Howard, Sidney)

Swan Song (see entry under Hecht, Ben)

Twentieth Century (see entry under Hecht, Ben)

McCULLERS, CARSON

Ballad of the Sad Cafe (see entry under Albee, Edward)

The Member of the Wedding (Adapted from her novel)
    Productions:
    Opened January 5, 1950 for 501 performances.
    Opened January 2, 1975 for 12 performances.
    (Off Off Broadway) January 7, 1978 (Playwrights Horizons).
    Reviews:
    Catholic World 170:467, Mar 1950
    Commonweal 51:437-8, Jan 27, 1950
    Life 28:63-6, Jan 23, 1950
    Nation 170:44, Jan 14, 1950
    New Republic 122:28, Jan 30, 1950
    New York Theatre Critics' Reviews 1950:397
                                    1975:397
    New York Times II, p. 3, Jan 1, 1950
                p. 26, Jan 6, 1950
                II, p. 1, Jan 15, 1950
                II, p. 1, Sep 17, 1950
                p. 20, Feb 6, 1957
                p. 14, Jan 3, 1975
                XXIII, p. 4, Apr 27, 1980

New Yorker 25:46+, Jan 14, 1950
　　　　　　50:63-4, Jan 13, 1975
Newsweek 35:74, Jan 16, 1950
Playboy 21:24, Sep 1974
Saturday Review 33:27-9, Jan 28, 1950
School and Society 71:213-14, Apr 8, 1950
Theatre Arts 34:13, Mar 1950
Time 55:45, Jan 16, 1950

The Square Root of Wonderful
　Productions:
　　Opened October 30, 1957 for 45 performances.
　　(Off Broadway) April 19, 1963 for 9 performances (Equity Library Theater).
　Reviews:
　　America 98:299, Nov 30, 1957
　　Catholic World 186:306, Jan 1958
　　Christian Century 74:1425, Nov 27, 1957
　　Commonweal 67:288-9, Dec 13, 1957
　　Nation 185:394, Nov 23, 1957
　　New York Theatre Critics' Reviews 1957:199
　　New York Times p. 40, Oct 31, 1957
　　　　　　　　　p. 47, Mar 12, 1970
　　New Yorker 33:103-5, Nov 9, 1957
　　Theatre Arts 42:24, Jan 1958
　　Time 70:93-4, Nov 11, 1957

McENROE, ROBERT E.

Oliver Erwenter　(see The Silver Whistle)

The Silver Whistle
　Productions:
　　Opened November 24, 1948 for 219 performances.
　Reviews:
　　Catholic World 168:324, Jan 1949
　　Commonweal 49:258, Dec 17, 1948
　　Life 25:51-2, Dec 20, 1948
　　Nation 167:704, Dec 18, 1948
　　New Republic 119:31, Dec 13, 1948
　　New York Theatre Critics' Reviews 1948:139
　　New York Times p. 49, Nov 25, 1948
　　　　　　　　　II, p. 7, Dec 5, 1948
　　New Yorker 24:55, Dec 4, 1948
　　Newsweek 32:86-7, Dec 6, 1948
　　School and Society 69:232, Mar 26, 1949
　　Theatre Arts 33:16, Jan 1949
　　Time 52:90, Dec 6, 1948

McGUIRE, WILLIAM ANTHONY

*The Bad Penny
Reviews:
New York Times VIII, p. 1, Aug 23, 1931

A Good Bad Woman
Productions:
Opened April 8, 1919 for 31 performances.
Reviews:
Dramatist 16:1276, Jul 1925
Forum 61:628-9, May 1919
New York Times p. 9, Apr 9, 1919
Theatre Magazine 29:344-50, Jun 1919

The Heights
Productions:
Opened January 31, 1910 for 16 performances.
Reviews:
Dramatic Mirror 63:8, Feb 12, 1910
Green Book 3:770, Apr 1910
Life (NY) 55:284, Feb 17, 1910
Theatre Magazine 11:vii, Mar 1910

If I Was Rich
Productions:
Opened September 2, 1926 for 92 performances.
Reviews:
Life (NY) 88:19, Sep 30, 1926
New York Times p. 15, Sep 3, 1926
                VIII, p. 1, Sep 12, 1926
Overland 85:118, Apr 1927
Theatre Magazine 44:18, Nov 1926

It's a Boy!
Productions:
Opened September 19, 1922 for 63 performances.
Reviews:
Life (NY) 80:18, Oct 5, 1922
New York Clipper 70:39, Oct 4, 1922
New York Times p. 18, Sep 20, 1922

Six-Cylinder Love
Productions:
Opened August 25, 1921 for 344+ performances.
Reviews:
Dramatic Mirror 84:229, Aug 13, 1921
                84:341, Sep 3, 1921
Hearst 40:17-19+, Nov 1921
Independent 106:113, Sep 1921

Life (NY) 78:18, Sep 15, 1921
Nation 113:299, Sep 14, 1921
New York Clipper 69:17, Aug 31, 1921
New York Times p. 8, Aug 26, 1921
Theatre Magazine 34:291+, Nov 1921
Weekly Review 5:234-5, Sep 10, 1921

Twelve Miles Out
Productions:
Opened November 16, 1925 for 188 performances.
Reviews:
New York Times p. 29, Nov 17, 1925
VII, p. 6, Feb 21, 1926
VII, p. 1, Feb 20, 1927
Theatre Magazine 43:72, Apr 1926

MacKAYE, PERCY

Anti-Matrimony
Productions:
Opened September 22, 1910 for 20 performances.
Reviews:
Dramatic Mirror 64:6, Sep 28, 1910
Dramatist 4:374-5, Jul 1913
Everybody's 23:844+, Dec 1910
Hampton 25:680, Nov 1910
Leslies' Weekly 111:385, Oct 13, 1910
Life (NY) 56:364, Oct 6, 1910
Living Age 268:318, Feb 4, 1911
Nation 91:298, Sep 29, 1910

The Antick
Productions:
Opened October 4, 1915 in repertory (Washington Square Play-
ers).
Reviews:
Dramatic Mirror 74:9, Oct 16, 1915
74:2, Nov 6, 1915
New York Times p. 11, Oct 5, 1915

Caliban of the Yellow Sands
Productions:
Opened May 24, 1916 for 10 performances.
Reviews:
Book News 34:445-6, Jun 1916
Collier's 36:343-50, Jul 1, 1916
Current Opinion 60:408-10, Jun 1916
Dial 61:22, Jun 22, 1916
Dramatic Mirror 75:8, Jun 3, 1916
Independent 86:59-60, Apr 10, 1916
86:333, May 29, 1916

Literary Digest 52:1760-1, Jun 10, 1916
Nation 102:586, Jun 1, 1916
National Magazine 46:697-8, Aug 1917
Outlook 113:308+, Jun 7, 1916
Survey 36:343-50, Jul 1, 1916
Theatre Magazine 24:8-9, Jul 1916

George Washington
Productions:
Opened March 1, 1920 for 16 performances.
Reviews:
Dramatic Mirror 82:414, Mar 6, 1920
New York Clipper 68:14, Mar 10, 1920
New York Times p. 13, Feb 24, 1920
p. 9, Mar 2, 1920
Review 2:288-9, Mar 20, 1920
Theatre Magazine 31:247+, Apr 1920

Gettysburg
Productions:
(Off Off Broadway) December 1974 (American Theater Co.).
No Reviews.

*The Ghost of Elsinore
Reviews:
New York Times p. 10, Apr 16, 1949
II, p. 1, Apr 23, 1949

*Jeanne d'Arc
Reviews:
New York Times III, p. 13, Jun 7, 1914

*Sanctuary
Reviews:
New York Times p. 9, Feb 25, 1914

The Scarecrow
Productions:
Opened January 17, 1911 for 23 performances.
(Off Broadway) Season of 1953-54.
(Off Off Broadway) September 29, 1978 (Jean Cocteau).
Reviews:
Blue Book 12:1118-20, Apr 1911
Book News 27:358, Jan 1909
Bookman 23:28-9, Mar 1911
Collier's 46:33, Feb 25, 1911
Drama 4:216-22, Nov 1911
Dramatic Mirror 65:7-8, Jan 25, 1911
Everybody's 24:556-8, Jan 25, 1911
Hampton 26:360+, Mar 1911
26:640-3+, May 1911

Independent 70:406-7, Feb 23, 1911
Life (NY) 57:260-1, Feb 2, 1911
Munsey 44:871, Mar 1911
New Republic 128:23, Jun 29, 1953
New York Times p. 31, Jun 17, 1953
Pearson 25:387, Mar 1911
Red Book 16:1142-3+, Apr 1911
Theatre Magazine 9:xi-xii, Feb 1909
                11:56, Feb 1910
                13:71-2+, Mar 1911
World Today 20:281, Mar 1911

This Fine-Pretty World
    Productions:
        Opened December 26, 1923 for 33 performances.
    Reviews:
        Dial 76:288, Mar 1924
        Literary Digest 80:29-30, Jan 26, 1924
        Nation 118:68-9, Jan 16, 1924
        New York Times VII, pp. 2-3, Dec 23, 1923
                       p. 11, Dec 27, 1923

A Thousand Years Ago
    Productions:
        Opened January 6, 1914 for 87 performances.
    Reviews:
        American Magazine 77:43-4, Jun 1914
        Bookman 38:613-14, Feb 1914
        Colonnade 7:175-9, Feb 1914
        Current Opinion 56:188-92, Mar 1914
        Dramatic Mirror 71:22, Jan 14, 1914
        Dramatist 5:4845, Jul 1914
        Green Book 11:411, Mar 1914
                   11:526-7, Mar 1914
        Munsey 51:343-4, Mar 1914
        Nation 98:67, Jan 15, 1914
        New York Drama News 58:32, Jan 17, 1914
        New York Times p. 11, Jan 7, 1914
        Theatre Magazine 19:61+, Feb 1914

*Washington
    Reviews:
        New York Times p. 9, Feb 18, 1919

MacKAYE, STEELE
    No productions.

MacLEISH, ARCHIBALD

*Herakles

Reviews:
  Life 59:10, Dec 3, 1965
  New Republic 157:25-6+, Jul 22, 1967

J.B.
  Productions:
    Opened December 11, 1958 for 364 performances.
    (Off Broadway) March 17, 1962 for 9 performances (Equity Library Theater).
  Reviews:
    America 100:33, Oct 4, 1958
          100:502, Jan 24, 1959
    Catholic World 188:505, Mar 1959
          190:81-5, Nov 1959
    Christian Century 75:692-3, Jun 11, 1958
          75:926, Aug 13, 1958
          76:9-11, Jan 7, 1959
          76:21-2, Jan 7, 1959
          76:106-7, Jan 28, 1959
    Christianity Today 93:484-7, May 19, 1976
    Commentary 26:183-4, Aug 1958
          27:153-8, Feb 1959
    Commonweal 70:153-4+, May 8, 1959
    English Journal 61:653-7, May 1972
          61:658-62, May 1972
    Harper's Bazaar 218:77-8+, Apr 1959
    Library Journal 83:821, Mar 15, 1958
          84:36-7, Jan 1, 1959
    Life 45:171+, Dec 22, 1958
      46:124-5, May 18, 1959
    Nation 186:425-6, May 10, 1958
      188:19, Jan 3, 1959
    New York Theatre Critics' Reviews 1958:168
    New York Times p. 27, Jan 6, 1958
          p. 37, Apr 24, 1958
          II, p. 1, May 4, 1958
          p. 41, Nov 15, 1958
          II, p. 5, Dec 7, 1958
          p. 2, Dec 12, 1958
          II, p. 1, May 10, 1959
          p. 38, Nov 11, 1964
    New Yorker 34:70-2, Dec 20, 1958
    Newsweek 52:45, Dec 22, 1958
    Reporter 20:37, Jan 8, 1959
    Saturday Review 41:11-12+, Mar 8, 1958
          41:22, May 10, 1958
          42:22-3, Jan 3, 1959
          43:39+, Jan 30, 1960
    Theatre Arts 42:9-11, Aug 1958
          43:9, Feb 1959
          43:60-63, Apr 1959
          44:29-32, Feb 1960

Time 71:87-8, May 24, 1958
    72:53-4, Dec 22, 1958
    73:95, Apr 13, 1959

Panic
  Productions:
    Opened March 14, 1935 for 2 performances.
  Reviews:
    Nation 140:369-70, Mar 27, 1935
    New Republic 82:190-191, Mar 27, 1935
           82:217, Apr 3, 1935
    New York Times p. 18, Mar 16, 1935
           IX, p. 1, May 25, 1935
           p. 38, Nov 26, 1936
    Newsweek 5:29, Mar 23, 1935
    Saturday Review 11:545+, Mar 16, 1935
    Theatre Arts 19:325-7, May 1935
           21:103-5, Feb 1937
    Time 25:77, Mar 18, 1935
    Yale Review 24:839-41, Summer 1935

Scratch (Suggested by Steven Vincent Benet's "The Devil and Daniel
    Webster")
  Productions:
    Opened May 6, 1971 for 4 performances.
  Reviews:
    New York Theatre Critics' Reviews 1971:286
    New York Times p. 50, May 7, 1971
           p. 16, May 8, 1971
           II, p. 1, May 16, 1971
           II, p. 14, May 16, 1971
    New Yorker 47:102, May 15, 1971
    Newsweek 77:96, May 17, 1971
    Saturday Review 54:55, May 29, 1971

This Music Crept By Me on the Waters
  Productions:
    (Off Broadway) Season of 1959-60 (ANTA matinee).
  Reviews:
    New York Times p. 20, Oct 23, 1953
           p. 19, Nov 25, 1959

*The Trojan Horse
  Reviews:
    New York Times p. 20, Oct 23, 1953

McLELLAN, C. M. S.

The Fountain
  Productions:

Opened September 27, 1913 in repertory (The Princess Players).
Reviews:
New York Times III, p. 5, Feb 1, 1914

Judith Zaraine
Productions:
Opened January 16, 1911 for 16 performances.
Reviews:
Collier's 46:24, Feb 4, 1911
Dramatic Mirror 65:10, Jan 18, 1911
Green Book 5:481-519, Mar 1911

Leah Kleschna
Productions:
Opened April 21, 1924 for 32 performances.
Reviews:
American Mercury 2:242-3, Jun 1924
Bookman 59:580, Jul 1924
Dramatist 2:134-5, Jan 1911
New York Times p. 19, Apr 22, 1924
VIII, p. 1, Apr 27, 1924
Theatre Magazine 39:16, Jul 1924

McNALLY, TERRENCE

And Things That Go Bump in the Night
Productions:
Opened April 26, 1965 for 16 performances.
Reviews:
Commonweal 82:290, May 21, 1965
New York Theatre Critics' Reviews 1965:341
New York Times p. 27, Apr 27, 1965
II, p. 1, May 9, 1965
Saturday Review 48:24, May 15, 1965
Time 85:88-9, May 7, 1965

Bad Habits (Consists of Ravenswood and Dunelawn)
Productions:
(Off Off Broadway) Season of 1972-73 (New York Theater
Strategy).
(Off Broadway) February 4, 1974 for 96 performances and
transferred to Broadway.
Opened on Broadway May 5, 1974 for 273 performances.
Reviews:
New York Magazine 7:78, Feb 18, 1974
7:78, May 27, 1974
New York Theatre Critics' Reviews 1974:373
New York Times p. 29, Feb 5, 1974
II, p. 4, Feb 10, 1974
II, p. 1, Mar 10, 1974

p. 45, May 6, 1974
II, p. 3, May 12, 1974
New Yorker 49:74, Feb 18, 1974
Playboy 21:51, May 1974
Time 103:95, Feb 18, 1974

*Broadway, Broadway
Reviews:
New York Times III, p. 13, Jul 6, 1978
II, p. 1, Jul 24, 1978
XXI, p. 14, Jul 30, 1978

Cuba Sí
Productions:
(Off Broadway) December 9, 1968 for 2 performances (ANTA Matinee).
Reviews:
New York Times p. 53, Dec 10, 1968

Dunelawn (see Bad Habits)

The Lady of the Camellias (Based on a play by Giles Cooper)
Productions:
Opened March 20, 1963 for 13 performances.
Reviews:
Nation 196:333, Apr 20, 1963
New York Theatre Critics' Reviews 1963:305
New York Times p. 7, Mar 22, 1963
New Yorker 39:110, Mar 30, 1963
Newsweek 61:78, Apr 1, 1963
Theatre Arts 47:70-1, May 1963
Time 81:46, Mar 29, 1963

Next
Productions:
(Off Broadway) February 10, 1969 for 707 performances.
(Off Off Broadway) April 1976 (Drama Ensemble Co.).
Reviews:
Nation 208:282, Mar 3, 1969
New York Theatre Critics' Reviews 1969:269
New York Times p. 27, Feb 11, 1969
II, p. 5, Feb 23, 1969
p. 46, Mar 12, 1970
New Yorker 45:90+, Feb 22, 1969
Saturday Review 52:45, Mar 1, 1969
Time 93:42, Feb 21, 1969
Vogue 153:150, Apr 1, 1969

Noon
Productions:
Opened November 28, 1968 for 52 performances.

(Off Off Broadway) April 14, 1976 (Direct Theater).
Reviews:
    Commonweal 89:471-2, Jan 10, 1969
    Nation 207:665-6, Dec 16, 1968
    New York Theatre Critics' Reviews 1968:168
    New York Times p. 52, Nov 29, 1968
            II, p. 7, Dec 8, 1968
            p. 54, Dec 10, 1968
    New Yorker 44:139-40, Dec 7, 1968
    Time 92:71-2, Dec 6, 1968

Ravenswood (see Bad Habits)

The Ritz
    Productions:
    Opened January 20, 1975 for 400 performances.
    Reviews:
    New Republic 172:22, Mar 1, 1975
    New York Magazine 8:65, Feb 3, 1975
    New York Theatre Critics' Reviews 1975:376
    New York Times p. 40, Jan 21, 1975
            II, p. 5, Feb 2, 1975
    New Yorker 50:76-7, Feb 3, 1975
    Newsweek 85:75, Feb 10, 1975
    Playboy 22:42, May 1975
    Time 105:59, Feb 3, 1975

Sweet Eros
    Productions:
    (Off Broadway) November 21, 1968 for 78 performances.
    (Off Off Broadway) April 14, 1976 (Direct Theater).
    Reviews:
    Nation 207:665, Dec 16, 1968
    New York Times p. 38, Nov 22, 1968
            II, p. 34, Nov 24, 1968
    New Yorker 44:140+, Dec 7, 1968
    Newsweek 72:106, Dec 2, 1968
    Time 92:71, Nov 29, 1968

Tour
    Productions:
    (Off Broadway) May 8, 1968 for 80 performances.
    Reviews:
    Harper's Bazaar 237:113-15, Oct 1968
    Nation 206:772+, Jun 10, 1968
    New York Times p. 55, May 9, 1968
            II, p. 1, May 19, 1968
    New Yorker 44:74, May 18, 1968

Where Has Tommy Flowers Gone?
    Productions:

(Off Broadway) October 7, 1971 for 78 performances.
Reviews:
Nation 213:410-11, Oct 25, 1971
New York Theatre Critics' Reviews 1971:213
New York Times II, p. 3, Jan 24, 1971
            p. 32, Oct 8, 1971
            II, p. 3, Oct 17, 1971
            p. 59, Nov 30, 1971
New Yorker 47:101, Oct 16, 1971
Newsweek 78:108, Oct 18, 1971
Time 98:80, Oct 18, 1971

Whiskey
Productions:
(Off Off Broadway) April 29, 1973 for 7 performances (Theater at St. Clements).
Reviews:
New York Times p. 24, Apr 30, 1973
New Yorker 49:69, May 12, 1973

Witness
Productions:
(Off Broadway) November 21, 1968 for 78 performances.
(Off Off Broadway) September 15, 1978 (Gene Frankel).
Reviews:
Nation 207:665, Dec 16, 1968
New York Times p. 38, Nov 22, 1968
New Yorker 44:140+, Dec 7, 1968
Time 92:71+, Nov 29, 1968

MAILER, NORMAN

Barbary Shore (see entry under Gelber, Jack)

The Deer Park
Productions:
(Off Broadway) February 1, 1967 for 128 performances.
Reviews:
Commonweal 85:657-8, Mar 10, 1967
Life 62:8, Feb 24, 1967
Nation 204:252-3, Feb 20, 1967
New York Times II, p. 1, Jan 22, 1967
            p. 27, Feb 1, 1967
            II, p. 1, Feb 12, 1967
New Yorker 42:116, Feb 11, 1967
Newsweek 69:109+, Feb 13, 1967
Reporter 36:47-8, Apr 6, 1967
Saturday Review 50:45, Mar 4, 1967
Time 89:58, Feb 10, 1967
Vogue 149:94, Apr 1, 1967

MALTZ, ALBERT

Black Pit
    Productions:
        Opened March 20, 1935 for 85 performances.
    Reviews:
        Catholic World 141:213-4, May 1935
        Commonweal 21:654, Apr 5, 1935
        Nation 140:399-400, Apr 3, 1935
        New Republic 82:289, Apr 17, 1935
        New York Times p. 26, Mar 21, 1935
        Newsweek 5:29, Mar 30, 1935
        Theatre Arts 19:331-2, May 1935

Merry-Go-Round (with George Sklar)
    Productions:
        Opened April 22, 1932 for 48 performances.
    Reviews:
        Catholic World 135:339, Jun 1932
        Nation 134:552, May 11, 1932
        New Republic 71:70-72, Jun 1, 1932
        New York Times p. 11, Apr 23, 1932
                    p. 1, May 1, 1932
        North American Review 234:171-2, Aug 1932
        Stage 9:30-32, Jun 1932

Peace on Earth (see entry under Sklar, George)

Private Hicks
    Productions:
        (Off Broadway) Season of 1935-36.
    Reviews:
        New York Times p. 14, Jan 13, 1936

Rehearsal
    Productions:
        (Off Broadway) January 15, 1939 (New School for Social Re-
            search).
        (Off Broadway) April and May, 1939 (Flatbush Arts League).
        (Off Broadway) April, 1939 (New York Players).
        (Off Broadway) Spring, 1939 (International Workers Order).
    No Reviews.

MAMET, DAVID

American Buffalo
    Productions:
        (Off Off Broadway) January 23, 1976 (St. Clement American
            Repertory).
        Opened February 16, 1977 for 135 performances.

(Off Broadway) Opened June 3, 1981; suspended performances October 31, 1981. Reopened February 25, 1982 for 259+ performances (still running on June 1, 1982).

Reviews:

America 136:364, Apr 16, 1977
Los Angeles 23:218+, Mar 1978
Nation 224:313, Mar 12, 1977
  231:521-2, Nov 15, 1980
  233:353-4, Oct 10, 1981
New Leader 64:21-2, Jun 29, 1981
New West 3:SC-30, Mar 13, 1978
New York Magazine 10:71, Mar 7, 1977
  14:66, Jun 15, 1981
New York Theatre Critics' Reviews 1977:364
  1981:186
New York Times p. 30, Jan 28, 1976
  p. 50, Feb 17, 1977
  II, p. 3, Mar 6, 1977
  II, p. 4, Jul 23, 1978
  III, p. 8, Oct 21, 1980
  III, p. 3, Oct 26, 1980
  III, p. 19, Apr 29, 1981
  III, p. 1, May 22, 1981
  III, p. 3, Jun 5, 1981
  II, p. 3, Jun 14, 1981
  III, p. 1, Jul 2, 1981
New Yorker 51:81, Feb 9, 1977
  53:54+, Feb 28, 1977
  57:127, Jun 15, 1981
Saturday Review 4:37, Apr 2, 1977
Time 109:54+, Feb 28, 1977

The Best of a Marathon: A Sermon (see A Sermon)

Dark Pony (see Reunion)

Duck Variations

Productions:
(Off Off Broadway) May 27, 1975 (Theater at St. Clements).
(Off Broadway) June 16, 1976 for 273 performances.
(Off Broadway) April 16, 1978 for 3 performances.

Reviews:

Los Angeles 24:251, Jun 1979
New York Magazine 9:64, Jul 12, 1976
New York Times p. 15, Nov 1, 1975
  p. 10, May 20, 1978
  XXI, p. 14, Jul 13, 1980
New Yorker 51:135-6, Nov 10, 1975
Time 108:68, Jul 12, 1976

A Life in the Theater

Productions:

(Off Broadway) October 20, 1977 for 288 performances.
Reviews:
America 137:423, Dec 10, 1977
Los Angeles 25:219+, Mar 1980
Nation 225:504, Nov 12, 1977
New West 5:SC-17, Feb 25, 1980
New York Magazine 10:75+, Nov 7, 1977
New York Theatre Critics' Reviews 1977:121
New York Times p. 10, Feb 5, 1977
                   III, p. 3, Oct 21, 1977
                   II, p. 5, Oct 30, 1977
New Yorker 53:115-16, Oct 31, 1977
Time 110:94, Oct 31, 1977

Mr. Happiness

Productions:
Opened March 6, 1978 for 16 performances.
Reviews:
America 138:286, Apr 8, 1978
Commonweal 105:244+, Apr 14, 1978
Harper's 256:86-7, May 1978
New York Theatre Critics' Reviews 1978:333
New York Times p. 42, Mar 7, 1978
Saturday Review 5:41, Mar 4, 1978
Time 111:84, Mar 20, 1978

The Poet and the Rent

Productions:
(Off Off Broadway) January 13, 1979 (Henry St. Settlement).
Reviews:
New York Times III, p. 22, May 10, 1979

Reunion (Consists of The Sanctity of Marriage, Dark Pony, and Reunion)

Productions:
(Off Broadway) October 18, 1979 for 33 performances.
Reviews:
Nation 229:572, Dec 1, 1979
New York Magazine 12:87, Nov 5, 1979
New York Times III, p. 3, Oct 19, 1979
New Yorker 55:81, Oct 29, 1979

The Sanctity of Marriage (see Reunion)

A Sermon

Productions:
(Off Off Broadway) May-June 1981, as part of a bill called Marathon 1981 (Ensemble Studio Theater).
(Off Off Broadway) October 27, 1981 for 36 performances, called The Best of Marathon: A Sermon (Ensemble Studio Theater).

Reviews:
New York Magazine 14:71, Nov 9, 1981
New York Times III, p. 5, May 29, 1981

Sexual Perversity in Chicago
Productions:
(Off Off Broadway) September 29, 1975 (St. Clements American Repertory).
(Off Broadway) June 16, 1976 for 273 performances.
Reviews:
Los Angeles 24:251, Jun 1979
New York Magazine 8:83, Oct 20, 1975
9:64, Jul 12, 1976
New York Times p. 15, Nov 1, 1975
p. 29, Jun 17, 1976
II, p. 14, Aug 15, 1976
New Yorker 51:135-6, Nov 10, 1975
Time 108:68, Jul 12, 1976

Shoeshine
Productions:
(Off Off Broadway) November-December 1979 (Ensemble Studio Theater).
Reviews:
New York Times III, p. 5, Dec 21, 1979

The Water Engine
Productions:
(Off Broadway) December 20, 1977 for 63 performances.
Opened March 6, 1978 for 16 performances.
Reviews:
America 138:286, Apr 8, 1978
Commonweal 195:244+, Apr 14, 1978
Harper's 256:86-7, May 1978
Los Angeles 25:210+, Jan 1980
Nation 226:92, Jan 28, 1978
New York Magazine 11:60, Jan 30, 1978
New York Theatre Critics' Reviews 1978:333
New York Times p. 15, May 14, 1977
III, p. 3, Jan 6, 1978
II, p. 3, Jan 15, 1978
II, p. 3, Feb 19, 1978
p. 42, Mar 7, 1978
New Yorker 53:69, Jan 16, 1978
Newsweek 91:69, Jan 16, 1978
Saturday Review 5:41, Mar 4, 1978
Time 111:84, Mar 20, 1978

The Woods
Productions:
(Off Broadway) April 25, 1979 for 23 performances.

(Off Off Broadway) May 16, 1982 (Second Stage).
Reviews:
Nation 228:581-2, May 19, 1979
New York Magazine 12:75, May 14, 1979
15:93-4, May 31, 1982
New York Theatre Critics' Reviews 1979:250
New York Times III, p. 15, Apr 26, 1979
II, p. 5, May 13, 1979
III, p. 12, May 17, 1982
New Yorker 55:130, May 7, 1979

MARASCO, ROBERT

Child's Play
Productions:
Opened February 17, 1970 for 342 performances.
(Off Off Broadway) December 1976 (Stage Co.).
Reviews:
America 122:312-13, Mar 21, 1970
Commonweal 92:62-3, Mar 27, 1970
Life 68:18, Apr 10, 1970
Nation 210:285, Mar 9, 1970
New York Theatre Critics' Reviews 1970:367
New York Times p. 39, Feb 18, 1970
II, p. 1, Mar 1, 1970
New Yorker 46:77, Feb 28, 1970
Newsweek 75:77-8, Mar 2, 1970
Saturday Review 53:26, Mar 14, 1970
Time 95:69, Mar 2, 1970

MARKS, JOSEPHINE PRESTON PEABODY
No productions.

MARQUAND, JOHN P.

The Late George Apley (with George S. Kaufman. Based on Marquand's novel)
Productions:
Opened November 23, 1944 for 385 performances.
Reviews:
Catholic World 160:355, Jan 1945
Commonweal 41:230, Dec 15, 1944
Life 17:41-4, Dec 4, 1944
Nation 159:725, Dec 9, 1944
New Republic 111:798, Dec 11, 1944
New York Theatre Critics' Reviews 1944:77
New York Times p. 16, Oct 20, 1944
p. 25, Nov 7, 1944

VI, p. 28, Nov 19, 1944
p. 26, Nov 22, 1944
II, p. 1, Nov 26, 1944
II, p. 1, Dec 3, 1944
New York Times Magazine pp. 28-9, Nov 19, 1944
New Yorker 20:44, Dec 2, 1944
Newsweek 24:110, Dec 4, 1944
Saturday Review 27:24+, Dec 9, 1944
Scholastic 46:18, Mar 5, 1945
Theatre Arts 29:7, 11, Jan 1945
29:221-5, Apr 1945
Time 44:48, Dec 4, 1944

Point of No Return (see entry under Osborne, Paul)

MARQUIS, DON

The Dark Hours
    Productions:
        Opened November 14, 1932 for 8 performances.
    Reviews:
        Nation 135:542, Nov 30, 1932
        New York Times IX, p. 2, Nov 13, 1932
                        p. 24, Nov 15, 1932
        Vanity Fair 39:60, Feb 1933

Everything's Jake
    Productions:
        Opened January 16, 1930 for 76 performances.
    Reviews:
        Catholic World 130:79-80, Apr 1930
        New York Times p. 20, Jan 17, 1930
        Theatre Magazine 51:13+, Mar 1930
        Vogue 75:108, Mar 15, 1930

*Master of the Revels
    Reviews:
        New York Times p. 16, Aug 14, 1935

The Old Soak
    Productions:
        Opened August 22, 1922 for 423 performances.
    Reviews:
        Bookman 56:322-4, Nov 1922
        Collier's 70:26, Sep 30, 1922
        Dial 73:464, Oct 1922
        Dramatist 15:1199-1200, Jan 1924
        Life (NY) 80:20, Sep 14, 1922
        National Magazine 52:236, Oct 1923
        New York Clipper 70:20, Aug 30, 1922

New York Times p. 14, Aug 23, 1922
               VI, p. 1, Sep 3, 1922
Outlook 132:138-9, Sep 27, 1922
Theatre Magazine 36:296+, Nov 1922

Out of the Sea
    Productions:
    Opened December 5, 1927 for 16 performances.
    Reviews:
    New York Times p. 26, Dec 6, 1927
    Saturday Review 4:468-9, Dec 24, 1927
    Vogue 71:100, Feb 1, 1928

MAY, ELAINE

Adaptation
    Productions:
    (Off Broadway) February 10, 1969 for 707 performances.
    Reviews:
    Nation 208:281-2, Mar 3, 1969
    New York Theatre Critics' Reviews 1969:269
    New York Times p. 27, Feb 11, 1969
                   II, p. 1, Feb 23, 1969
                   p. 46, Mar 12, 1970
                   XXII, p. 20, May 7, 1978
    New Yorker 45:90+, Feb 22, 1969
    Saturday Review 52:45, Mar 1, 1969
    Time 93:42, Feb 21, 1969
    Vogue 153:50, Apr 1, 1969

*A Matter of Position
    Reviews:
    New York Times II, p. 1, Sep 23, 1962
                   p. 59, Oct 10, 1962

Not Enough Rope
    Productions:
    (Off Broadway) March 1, 1962 for 4 performances.
    (Off Off Broadway) June 18, 1974 (Circle Repertory).
    (Off Off Broadway) March 26, 1976 (IRT).
    (Off Off Broadway) April 26, 1976 (Theater at Noon).
    Reviews:
    New York Times p. 24, Mar 2, 1962
    New Yorker 38:83-4, Mar 10, 1962

MAYER, EDWIN JUSTUS

Children of Darkness
    Productions:

Opened January 7, 1930 for 79 performances.
(Off Broadway) Season of 1957-58.
(Off Off Broadway) November 21, 1975 (Counterpoint).
Reviews:
Catholic World 130:722, Mar 1930
              187:145, May 1958
Commonweal 68:105, Apr 25, 1958
Life (NY) 95:20, Jan 31, 1930
Nation 130:134, Jan 29, 1930
New Republic 62:20, Feb 19, 1930
New York Times VIII, p. 1, Jan 19, 1930
              VIII, p. 4, Feb 9, 1930
              p. 11, Mar 1, 1958
Theatre Arts 14:191+, Mar 1930
Theatre Magazine 51:72, Feb 1930
              51:32-5+, Apr 1930
Vogue 75:106, Mar 1, 1930

The Firebrand
Productions:
Opened October 15, 1924 for 261 performances.
(Off Broadway) December 10, 1965 for 9 performances (Equity
    Library Theater).
Reviews:
American Mercury 4:120-21, Jan 1925
Dramatist 16:1245-6, Jan 1925
Life (NY) 84:20, Nov 6, 1924
Nation 119:501-2, Nov 5, 1924
New York Times p. 33, Oct 16, 1924
              p. 16, Feb 10, 1926
Theatre Magazine 39:16, Dec 1924
              41:26+, May 1925

*Sunrise in My Pocket
Reviews:
New York Times IX, p. 1, Sep 28, 1941

MEDOFF, MARK

Children of a Lesser God
Productions:
Opened March 30, 1980 for 887 performances.
Reviews:
Commonweal 107:595-6, Oct 24, 1980
Los Angeles 24:386+, Dec 1979
Nation 230:508-9, Apr 26, 1980
New Republic 182:23-4, Jun 7, 1980
New West 4:SC-43, Dec 3, 1979
New York Magazine 13:85-6, Apr 14, 1980
New York Theatre Critics' Reviews 1980:301

New York Times III, p. 11, Mar 31, 1980
II, p. 1, Apr 13, 1980
II, p. 3, Jul 6, 1980
New Yorker 56:101, Apr 14, 1980
Newsweek 95:105, Apr 14, 1980
Texas Monthly 9:175+, Aug 1981
Time 115:112, Apr 14, 1980
116:62, Jul 7, 1980

*Firekeeper
Reviews:
Texas Monthly 6:136+, Jul 1978

The Halloween Bandit
Productions:
(Off Off Broadway) November 30, 1978 (Jewish Repertory Theatre).
Reviews:
New York Times III, p. 9, Dec 19, 1978

The Wager
Productions:
(Off Off Broadway) January 17, 1974 (Manhattan Theater Club).
(Off Broadway) October 21, 1974 for 104 performances.
(Off Off Broadway) March 31, 1978 (Drama Ensemble Co.).
Reviews:
Nation 219:476-7, Nov 9, 1974
New York Magazine 7:122, Nov 18, 1974
New York Theatre Critics' Reviews 1974:126
New York Times p. 48, Oct 22, 1974
II, p. 1, Nov 3, 1974
New Yorker 50:124, Nov 4, 1974
Newsweek 84:60+, Nov 4, 1974
Playboy 22:33, Feb 1975
Sports Illustrated 42:10, Jan 6, 1975
Time 104:120, Nov 4, 1974

When You Comin' Back, Red Ryder?
Productions:
(Off Off Broadway) November 5, 1973 (Circle Repertory Theater).
(Off Broadway) December 6, 1973 for 302 performances.
Reviews:
America 129:506, Dec 29, 1973
Nation 217:572, Nov 26, 1973
New York Magazine 6:72, Dec 24, 1973
New York Theatre Critics' Reviews 1973:141
New York Times p. 54, Nov 7, 1973
p. 31, Dec 7, 1973
II, p. 5, Dec 23, 1973
XI, p. 4, Feb 22, 1981
XXI, p. 17, Mar 7, 1982

New Yorker 49:99, Dec 17, 1973
Playboy 21:42, Apr 1974

MELFI, LEONARD

Ah! Wine!
Productions:
    (Off Off Broadway) January 14, 1974 (Drifting Traffic).
No Reviews.

Beautiful!
Productions:
    (Off Off Broadway) May 16, 1974 (Drifting Traffic).
No Reviews.

Birdbath
Productions:
    (Off Broadway) April 11, 1966 for 16 performances.
    (Off Off Broadway) Season of 1970-71 (ACSTA).
    (Off Off Broadway) Season of 1973-74 (Manhattan Theater Club).
    (Off Off Broadway) Season of 1975-76 (Courtyard Playhouse).
    (Off Off Broadway) January 6, 1978 (IRT).
    (Off Broadway) March 7, 1982 for 14 performances.
    (Off Off Broadway) Season of 1981-82 (La Mama ETC).
Reviews:
    Nation 202:404, Apr 4, 1966
    New York Times II, p. 15, Apr 10, 1966
                  p. 43, Apr 12, 1966
                   III, p. 20, Oct 14, 1981
    New Yorker 42:126, Apr 23, 1966

Butterfaces
Productions:
    (Off Off Broadway) February 5, 1981 for 20 performances
        (Theater for the New City).
Reviews:
    New York Times p. 54, Mar 1, 1981

The Dispossessed
Productions:
    (Off Off Broadway) May 6, 1982 (Theater for the New City).
Reviews:
    New York Times III, p. 15, May 11, 1982

Eddie and Susanna in Love
Productions:
    (Off Off Broadway) Season of 1972-73 (New York Theater Strat-
        egy).
No Reviews.

Fantasies at the Frick
    Productions:
        (Off Off Broadway) November 9, 1976 (Open Space in Soho).
    No Reviews.

Halloween
    Productions:
        (Off Off Broadway) Season of 1975-76 (Courtyard Playhouse).
        (Off Off Broadway) March 16, 1977 (Gene Frankel Theater Work-
            shop).
        (Off Off Broadway) November 2, 1977 (Cithaeron).
    No Reviews.

Lunchtime
    Productions:
        (Off Off Broadway) May 28, 1976 (IRT).
        (Off Off Broadway) March 6, 1978 (Quaigh Theater).
    No Reviews.

Night
    Productions:
        Opened November 28, 1968 for 52 performances.
    Reviews:
        Commonweal 89:471-2, Jan 10, 1969
        Nation 207:665-6, Dec 16, 1968
        New York Theatre Critics' Reviews 1968:168
        New York Times p. 52, Nov 29, 1968
                II, p. 7, Dec 8, 1968
                p. 54, Dec 10, 1968
        New Yorker 44:139-40, Dec 7, 1968
        Time 92:71-2, Dec 6, 1968

Porno Stars at Home
    Productions:
        (Off Off Broadway) January 28, 1976 (Courtyard Playhouse).
        (Off Broadway) November 28, 1978 for 66 performances.
    Reviews:
        New York Times p. 11, Feb 7, 1976
                III, p. 29, Nov 29, 1978

Rusty and Rico and Lena and Louie
    Productions:
        (Off Off Broadway) May 5, 1978 for 18 performances (IRT)
    No Reviews.

Stars and Stripes
    Productions:
        (Off Broadway) May 8, 1968 for 80 performances.
    Reviews:
        Harper's Bazaar 237:113-15, Oct 1968
        Nation 206:772+, Jun 10, 1968
        New York Times p. 55, May 9, 1968

II, p. 1, May 19, 1968
New Yorker 44:74, May 18, 1968

Taxi Tales
  Productions:
    Opened December 28, 1978 for 6 performances.
  Reviews:
    New York Theatre Critics' Reviews 1978:129
    New York Times p. 15, Dec 30, 1978

*Times Square
  Reviews:
    New York Times p. 16, Jan 27, 1968

MELONEY, ROSE (see Franken, Rose)

MICHAELS, SIDNEY

Dylan
  Productions:
    Opened January 18, 1964 for 273 performances.
    (Off Off Broadway) Season of 1970-71 (Assembly).
    (Off Broadway) February 7, 1972 for 48 performances.
  Reviews:
    America 110:238-9, Feb 15, 1964
    Catholic World 198:391-2, Mar 1964
    Commonweal 79:572-3, Feb 7, 1964
    Nation 198:176, Feb 17, 1964
    New York Theatre Critics' Reviews 1964:380
    New York Times II, p. 1, Jan 12, 1964
                    p. 18, Jan 20, 1964
                    p. 25, Feb 8, 1972
    New Yorker 39:72, Jan 25, 1964
               47:80, Feb 19, 1972
    Newsweek 63:58, Jan 27, 1964
    Saturday Review 47:22, Feb 8, 1964
    Time 83:54, Jan 31, 1964

The Elizabethans
  Productions:
    (Off Off Broadway) November 14, 1972 (New Dramatists Inc.).
  No Reviews.

Tchin-Tchin (Based on the play by François Billetdoux)
  Productions:
    Opened October 25, 1962 for 222 performances.
  Reviews:
    Nation 195:333-4, Nov 17, 1962
    New York Theatre Critics' Reviews 1962:227

New York Times p. 37, Oct 9, 1962
                p. 26, Oct 26, 1962
                II, p. 1, Nov 25, 1962
New Yorker 38:111, Nov 3, 1962
Newsweek 60:74, Nov 5, 1962
Saturday Review 45:28, Nov 10, 1962
Theatre Arts 46:11, Dec 1962
Time 80:82, Nov 2, 1962

Tricks of the Trade
    Productions:
    Opened November 6, 1980 for one performance.
    Reviews:
    Los Angeles 25:297, Nov 1980
    New York Theatre Critics' Reviews 1980:124
    New York Times III, p. 3, Nov 7, 1980
                    III, p. 3, Dec 12, 1980

MIDDLETON, GEORGE

Accused (Adapted from the play by Eugene Brieux)
    Productions:
    Opened September 29, 1925 for 95 performances.
    Reviews:
    Life (NY) 86:26, Oct 22, 1925
    Nation 121:446-7, Oct 14, 1925
    New York Times p. 20, Sep 30, 1925
    Theatre Magazine 42:16, Dec 1925

Adam and Eva (see entry under Bolton, Guy)

The Big Pond (with A. E. Thomas)
    Productions:
    Opened August 21, 1928 for 47 performances.
    Reviews:
    Life (NY) 92:13, Sep 14, 1928
    New York Times p. 25, Aug 22, 1928
    Outlook 150:743, Sep 5, 1928
    Review 48:41, Oct 1928
    Theatre Magazine 48:32-4+, Nov 1928
    Vogue 72:126, Oct 13, 1928

Blood Money (Based on a story by H. H. Van Loan)
    Productions:
    Opened August 22, 1927 for 64 performances.
    Reviews:
    Life (NY) 90:19, Sep 8, 1927
    New York Times p. 29, Aug 23, 1927
    Theatre Magazine 46:26-8+, Oct 1927
    Vogue 70:118, Oct 15, 1927

The Cave Girl (with Guy Bolton)
    Productions:
        Opened August 18, 1920 for 37 performances.
    Reviews:
        Dramatic Mirror   p. 9, Jul 3, 1920
                          p. 371, Aug 28, 1920
        Independent 103:261, Sep 4, 1920
        New York Clipper 68:19, Aug 25, 1920
        New York Times p. 12, Aug 19, 1920
        Theatre Magazine 32:242, Oct 1920

Hit-the-Trail-Holiday (see entry under Cohan, George M.)

The Light of the World (see entry under Bolton, Guy)

Madame Capet (Adapted from the French of Marcelle Maurette)
    Productions:
        Opened October 25, 1938 for 7 performances.
    Reviews:
        Commonweal 29:76, Nov 11, 1938

The Other Rose (Adapted from the French of Edouard Bourdet)
    Productions:
        Opened December 20, 1923 for 84 performances.
    Reviews:
        American Mercury 1:247, Feb 1924
        New York Times I, p. 2, Dec 16, 1923
                       p. 15, Dec 21, 1923
                       VII, p. 1, Dec 30, 1923
        Theatre Magazine 39:15, Feb 1924

Polly with a Past (see entry under Bolton, Guy)

The Road Together
    Productions:
        Opened January 17, 1924 for one performance.
    Reviews:
        New Republic 8:275-6, Oct 14, 1916
        New York Times p. 21, Jan 18, 1924

MILLAY, EDNA ST. VINCENT

Aria Da Capo
    Productions:
        (Off Broadway) Season of 1957-58 (ANTA).
        (Off Off Broadway) June 18, 1975 (New York Theater Ensemble).
        (Off Off Broadway) April 15, 1977 (4th Wall at Provincetown).
    Reviews:
        Drama 21:34, Mar 1931

New York Times p. 14, Dec 6, 1919
             p. 36, May 25, 1950
             p. 40, May 21, 1958
             p. 18, Jun 27, 1958

Conversation at Midnight
  Productions:
    Opened November 12, 1964 for 4 performances.
  Reviews:
    New York Theatre Critics' Reviews 1964:155
    New York Times p. 27, Nov 13, 1964

Launzi (Based on the play by Ferenc Molnar)
  Productions:
    Opened October 10, 1923 for 13 performances.
  Reviews:
    Life (NY) 82:20, Nov 1, 1923
    Nation 117:470, Oct 24, 1923
    New Republic 36:230-1, Oct 23, 1923
    New York Times p. 16, Oct 11, 1923
    Theatre Magazine 38:16, Dec 1923

Murder of Lidice
  Productions:
    (Off Off Broadway) June 18, 1975 (New York Theater Ensemble).
  No Reviews.

MILLER, ARTHUR

After the Fall
  Productions:
    Opened January 23, 1964 for 59 performances (Repertory Theatre of Lincoln Center).
  Reviews:
    America 110:322, Mar 7, 1964
    Commonweal 79:600-1, Feb 14, 1964
    Life 56:64A, Feb 7, 1964
    Nation 198:153-4, Feb 10, 1964
    National Review 16:289-90, Apr 7, 1964
    New Republic 150:26-8+, Feb 8, 1964
    New West 2:SC-20, Sep 12, 1977
    New York Theatre Critics' Reviews 1964:374
    New York Times p. 39, Oct 25, 1963
                  II, p. 1, Jan 19, 1964
                   p. 18, Jan 24, 1964
                   p. 14, Jan 31, 1964
                   II, p. 1, Feb 2, 1964
                   p. 37, Aug 11, 1964
                   p. 21, Jan 25, 1965
                   p. 26, Feb 1, 1966

New Yorker 39:59, Feb 1, 1964
Newsweek 63:49-52, Feb 3, 1964
Reporter 30:46+, Feb 27, 1964
Saturday Review 47:35, Feb 15, 1964
Theatre Arts 48:12-16+, Jan 1964
Time 83:54, Jan 31, 1964
Vogue 143:66, Mar 15, 1964

All My Sons
Productions:
Opened January 29, 1947 for 328 performances.
(Off Broadway) November 15, 1968 for 9 performances (Equity Library Theater).
(Off Broadway) September 27, 1974 for 60 performances.
Reviews:
Catholic World 164:552-3, Mar 1947
Commonweal 45:445-6, Feb 14, 1947
Forum 107:271-5, Mar 1947
Life 22:71-2+, Mar 10, 1947
Nation 164:191+, Feb 15, 1947
New Republic 116:42, Feb 10, 1947
New York Theatre Critics' Reviews 1947:475
New York Times p. 21, Jan 30, 1947
                II, p. 1, Feb 9, 1947
                II, p. 1, Apr 27, 1947
                II, p. 3, Jun 29, 1947
                II, p. 1, Sep 7, 1947
                II, p. 1, Sep 21, 1947
                II, p. 3, Oct 19, 1947
                p. 26, Oct 21, 1947
                II, p. 2, Jan 18, 1948
                p. 33, May 12, 1948
                p. 32, Oct 29, 1974
New Yorker 22:50, Feb 8, 1947
                50:106-7, Nov 11, 1974
Newsweek 29:85, Feb 10, 1947
Player's Magazine 25:47, Nov 1948
Saturday Review 30:22-24, Mar 1, 1947
School and Society 65:250, Apr 5, 1947
Theatre Arts 31:19, 50, Apr 1947
Time 49:68, Feb 10, 1947

The American Clock (Inspired by Studs Terkel's Hard Times)
Productions:
Opened November 20, 1980 for 12 performances.
Reviews:
Nation 231:652, Dec 13, 1980
New Leader 63:15-16, Dec 29, 1980
New York Magazine 13:92+, Dec 8, 1980
New York Theatre Critics' Reviews 1980:80
New York Times III, p. 7, May 27, 1980

III, p. 3, Nov 21, 1980
II, p. 5, Nov 30, 1980
III, p. 7, Dec 2, 1980
III, p. 17, Dec 4, 1980
III, p. 3, Dec 26, 1980
New Yorker 56:127, Dec 8, 1980
Newsweek 96:84, Dec 1, 1980
Saturday Review 8:79, Jan 1981
Time 115:65, Jun 9, 1980

The Creation of the World and Other Business
Productions:
Opened November 20, 1972 for 20 performances.
Reviews:
America 127:570, Dec 30, 1972
Commentary 55:83-5, Feb 1973
Commonweal 97:276, Dec 22, 1972
New Republic 167:26+, Dec 23, 1972
New York Theatre Critics' Reviews 1972:150
New York Times p. 28, Dec 1, 1972
II, p. 3, Dec 10, 1972
II, p. 5, Dec 17, 1972
II, p. 18, Jan 21, 1973
New Yorker 48:109, Dec 9, 1972
Newsweek 80:71, Dec 11, 1972
Saturday Review (Arts) 1:57, Jan 1973
Time 100:122, Dec 11, 1972

The Crucible
Productions:
Opened January 22, 1953 for 197 performances.
(Off Broadway) Season of 1957-58 for 571 performances.
Opened April 6, 1964 for 16 performances (National Repertory
    Theatre).
Opened April 27, 1972 for 44 performances.
(Off Off Broadway) May 16, 1974 (ACSTA).
(Off Off Broadway) November 26, 1975 (Gene Frankel Theater
    Workshop).
(Off Off Broadway) May 4, 1977 (Theater at St. Clements).
(Off Off Broadway) December 8, 1977 (Equity Library The-
    ater).
Reviews:
American Record Guide 29:508-9+, Mar 1963
Catholic World 176:465-6, Mar 1953
193:394-5, Sep 1961
Commentary 15:265-71, Mar 1953
16:83-4, Jul 1953
Commonweal 57:498, Feb 20, 1953
Life 34:87-8+, Feb 9, 1953
Nation 176:131, Feb 7, 1953
214:636-7, May 15, 1972

New Republic 128:22-3, Feb 16, 1953
166:22+, May 27, 1972
New York Magazine 9:61, Jul 5, 1976
New York Theatre Critics' Reviews 1953:383
1964:295
1972:296
New York Times II, p. 1, Jan 18, 1953
p. 15, Jan 23, 1953
II, p. 1, Feb 1, 1953
II, p. 3, Feb 8, 1953
VI, p. 20, Feb 15, 1953
p. 20, Jul 2, 1953
p. 8, Jul 29, 1955
p. 28, Apr 11, 1956
II, p. 3, Mar 9, 1958
p. 36, Mar 12, 1958
p. 21, Mar 17, 1958
II, p. 1, Jun 1, 1958
II, p. 1, May 17, 1959
p. 30, Apr 7, 1964
p. 35, Jan 20, 1965
p. 82, Jan 24, 1965
p. 36, Apr 28, 1972
III, p. 3, May 7, 1972
p. 31, Jun 17, 1976
II, p. 5, Jun 27, 1976
p. 16, Dec 10, 1977
New Yorker 28:47, Jan 31, 1953
48:54+, May 6, 1972
Newsweek 41:68, Feb 2, 1953
Saturday Review 36:24-6, Jan 31, 1953
36:41-2, Feb 14, 1953
55:62, May 20, 1972
School and Society 77:185-6, Mar 21, 1953
Theatre Arts 37:24-6, 65-9, Apr 1953
37:33-4, Oct 1953
40:80, Feb 1956
41:27, May 1957
Time 61:48, Feb 2, 1953
99:59, May 15, 1972

Death of a Salesman
Productions:
Opened February 10, 1949 for 742 performances.
Opened June 26, 1975 for 64 performances.
Reviews:
America 133:54, Aug 2, 1975
American Mercury 68:679-80, Jun 1949
Canadian Forum 29:86-7, Jul 1949
Catholic World 169:62-3, Apr 1949
171:110-16, May 1950

Commonweal 49:520-1, Mar 4, 1949
       81:670, Feb 19, 1965
Fortune 39:79-80, May 1949
Forum 111:219-21, Apr 1949
Harper's Bazaar 83:161, Mar 1949
House and Garden 95:218, May 1949
Life 26:115+, Feb 21, 1949
Nation 168:283-4, Mar 5, 1949
     221:59, Jul 19, 1975
New Republic 120:26-8, Feb 28, 1949
     173:20+, Jul 19, 1975
New York Magazine 8:74, Jul 7, 1975
New York Theatre Critics' Reviews 1949:358
     1975:221
New York Times II, p. 1, Feb 6, 1949
     p. 27, Feb 11, 1949
     II, p. 1, Feb 20, 1949
     VII, p. 12, May 29, 1949
     p. 12, Jul 29, 1949
     II, p. 1, Aug 7, 1949
     VI, p. 11+, Aug 28, 1949
     VI, p. 6, Sep 11, 1949
     II, p. 1, Feb 5, 1950
     p. 10, Mar 4, 1950
     II, p. 1, Mar 12, 1950
     p. 41, Mar 16, 1950
     p. 25, Apr 28, 1950
     p. 20, Sep 21, 1950
     p. 42, Dec 10, 1954
     p. 11, Jul 20, 1963
     p. 69, Apr 9, 1972
     p. 26, Jun 27, 1975
     II, p. 1, Jun 29, 1975
     p. 10, Mar 5, 1977
     XXII, p. 8, Mar 13, 1977
     XXI, p. 6, Jul 22, 1979
     XI, p. 21, Oct 5, 1980
     XXIII, p. 12, Jul 4, 1982
New Yorker 24:58+, Feb 19, 1949
     51:63, Jul 7, 1975
Newsweek 33:78, Feb 21, 1949
     86:61, Jul 7, 1975
Playboy 21:24, Sep 1974
Saturday Review 32:30-2, Feb 26, 1949
     46:34, Aug 24, 1963
School and Society 70:363-4, Dec 3, 1949
Theatre Arts 33:14-16, Apr 1949
     33:18-21, Oct 1949
     33:12-14, Nov 1949
Time 53:74-6, Feb 21, 1949
     54:59, Aug 8, 1949
     106:43, Jul 7, 1975

Vogue 113:157, Mar 1, 1949

An Enemy of the People (Adapted from Henrik Ibsen's play)
Productions:
Opened December 28, 1950 for 36 performances.
(Off Broadway) Season of 1958-59.
(Off Broadway) February 9, 1968 for 9 performances (Equity
Library Theater).
Opened March 11, 1971 for 54 performances (Repertory The-
ater, Lincoln Center).
Reviews:
Catholic World 172:387, Feb 1951
Christian Science Monitor Magazine p. 6, Jan 1951
Commonweal 53:374, Jan 19, 1951
Nation 172:18, Jan 6, 1951
212:411-13, Mar 29, 1971
New Republic 124:22, Jan 22, 1951
New York Theatre Critics' Reviews 1950:154
1971:334
New York Times II, p. 3, Dec 24, 1950
p. 14, Dec 29, 1950
II, p. 1, Jan 7, 1951
p. 24, Feb 5, 1959
p. 26, Mar 12, 1971
II, p. 3, Mar 21, 1971
New Yorker 26:44, Jan 13, 1951
34:68+, Feb 14, 1959
47:93, Mar 20, 1971
Newsweek 37:67, Jan 8, 1951
77:114, Mar 22, 1971
Saturday Review 42:34, Feb 21, 1959
School and Society 73:105, Feb 17, 1951
Theatre Arts 35:15, Mar 1951
Time 57:31, Jan 8, 1951
97:41, Mar 22, 1971

Fame
Productions:
(Off Off Broadway) Season of 1969-70 (New Theater Work-
shop).
No Reviews.

Incident at Vichy
Productions:
Opened December 3, 1964 for 99 performances (Repertory The-
ater of Lincoln Center).
(Off Off Broadway) May 16, 1981 (Jewish Repertory Theater).
Reviews:
America 112:147-9, Jan 23, 1965
Life 58:39-40+, Jan 22, 1965
Nation 199:504, Dec 21, 1964

New Republic 151:26-7, Dec 26, 1964
New York Theatre Critics' Reviews 1964:116
New York Times II, p. 1, Nov 29, 1964
    p. 44, Dec 4, 1964
    p. 45, Dec 7, 1964
    II, p. 3, Dec 20, 1964
    VI, p. 10, Jan 30, 1965
    p. 28, Jan 27, 1966
    III, p. 28, Jun 12, 1981
New Yorker 40:152, Dec 12, 1964
Newsweek 64:86, Dec 14, 1964
Saturday Review 47:24, Dec 19, 1964
Time 84:73, Dec 11, 1964
Vogue 145:27, Jan 15, 1965

The Man Who Had All the Luck
Productions:
 Opened November 23, 1944 for 4 performances.
Reviews:
 New York Theatre Critics' Reviews 1944:73
 New York Times p. 18, Nov 24, 1944

A Memory of Two Mondays
Productions:
 Opened September 29, 1955 for 149 performances.
 (Off Broadway) October 30, 1964 for 9 performances (Equity Library Theater).
 Opened January 26, 1976 for 33 performances.
Reviews:
 America 94:223, Nov 19, 1955
 Catholic World 182:144-5, Nov 1955
 Commonweal 63:117, Nov 4, 1955
 Life 39:166-7, Oct 17, 1955
 Nation 181:348-9, Oct 22, 1955
   222:189-90, Feb 14, 1976
 New York Theatre Critics' Reviews 1955:272
 New York Times p. 16, Aug 31, 1955
    VI, p. 78, Sep 18, 1955
    II, p. 1, Sep 25, 1955
    p. 21, Sep 30, 1955
    II, p. 1, Oct 9, 1955
    p. 35, Oct 12, 1955
    p. 34, Nov 9, 1956
    p. 9, Jan 29, 1971
    II, p. 17, Feb 7, 1971
    p. 26, Jan 27, 1976
    II, p. 5, Feb 8, 1976
 New Yorker 31:92+, Oct 8, 1955
   51:78, Feb 9, 1976
 Saturday Review 38:25-6, Oct 15, 1955
 Theatre Arts 39:18-19, Dec 1955
   40:31-2, Sep 1956

Time 66:53, Oct 10, 1955

The Price
Productions:
Opened February 7, 1968 for 429 performances.
(Off Broadway) April 19, 1979 for 34 performances and trans-
ferred to Broadway.
Opened on Broadway June 19, 1979 for 144 performances.
Reviews:
America 118:422-3, Mar 30, 1968
Atlantic 221:120-2, Jun 1968
Catholic World 207:74-5, May 1968
Christian Century 85:405-6, Mar 27, 1968
Commentary 45:74-6, Apr 1968
Commonweal 87:655, Mar 1, 1968
Life 64:18, Mar 8, 1968
Nation 206:281-3, Feb 26, 1968
National Review 20:511-12, May 21, 1968
New Republic 158:39-41, Feb 24, 1968
New York Magazine 12:94-5, Jul 9, 1979
New York Theatre Critics' Reviews 1968:334
    1968:352
    1979:202
New York Times II, p. 1, Jan 28, 1968
    p. 37, Feb 8, 1968
    II, p. 1, Feb 18, 1968
    p. 32, Mar 5, 1968
    II, p. 1, Apr 21, 1968
    p. 39, Oct 30, 1968
    p. 36, Mar 6, 1969
    III, p. 5, Apr 20, 1979
    III, p. 17, Jun 20, 1979
    II, p. 5, Jul 8, 1979
New Yorker 43:99, Feb 17, 1968
    55:96, Apr 30, 1979
Newsweek 71:104, Feb 19, 1968
Reporter 38:42+, Mar 21, 1968
Saturday Review 51:38, Feb 24, 1968
Time 91:76-7, Feb 16, 1968
    114:65, Jul 2, 1979

The Reason Why
Productions:
(Off Off Broadway) Season of 1969-70 (New Theater Workshop).
No Reviews.

A View from the Bridge
Productions:
Opened September 29, 1955 for 149 performances.
(Off Broadway) January 28, 1965 for 780 performances.
(Off Off Broadway) February 1975 (Classic Theater).

(Off Off Broadway) March 14, 1978 (South St. Theater Co.).
Reviews:
America 94:223, Nov 19, 1955
Catholic World 182:144-5, Nov 1955
Commonweal 63:117, Nov 4, 1955
      81:670, Feb 19, 1965
Life 39:166-7, Oct 17, 1955
Nation 181:348-9, Oct 22, 1955
New Republic 133:21-2, Dec 19, 1955
New York Theatre Critics' Reviews 1955:272
New York Times p. 16, Aug 31, 1955
      VI, p. 78, Sep 18, 1955
      II, p. 1, Sep 25, 1955
      p. 21, Sep 30, 1955
      II, p. 1, Oct 9, 1955
      p. 35, Oct 12, 1955
      p. 34, Nov 9, 1956
      p. 24, Jan 29, 1965
      II, p. 1, Aug 15, 1965
      p. 45, Dec 3, 1966
      XXII, p. 18, Jan 13, 1980
      III, p. 16, Dec 28, 1981
New Yorker 31:92+, Oct 8, 1955
      40:94, Feb 6, 1965
Newsweek 65:93, Mar 15, 1965
Saturday Review 38:25-6, Oct 15, 1955
Theatre Arts 39:18-19, Dec 1955
      40:31-2, Sep 1956
Time 66:53, Oct 10, 1955
Vogue 145:56, Apr 15, 1965

MILLER, JASON

Lou Gehrig Did Not Die of Cancer
Productions:
    (Off Off Broadway) March 2, 1970 for 3 performances (Equity Theater Informal).
No Reviews.

Nobody Hears a Broken Dream
Productions:
    (Off Broadway) March 19, 1970 for 6 performances.
Reviews:
New York Times p. 55, Mar 20, 1970
New Yorker 46:84+, Mar 28, 1970

That Championship Season
Productions:
    (Off Broadway) May 2, 1972 for 144 performances and transferred to Broadway.

Opened on Broadway September 14, 1972 for 700 performances (844 performances in all).
Reviews:
America 126:573-4, May 27, 1972
        127:264, Oct 7, 1972
Commonweal 97:60-1, Oct 20, 1972
Life 73:22, Jul 14, 1972
Nation 214:669, May 22, 1972
New Republic 166:33-4, Jun 3, 1972
New York Theatre Critics' Reviews 1972:250
                                   1972:259
New York Times p. 34, May 3, 1972
               II, p. 1, May 14, 1972
               p. 43, Sep 15, 1972
               II, p. 1, Sep 24, 1972
               II, p. 1, Oct 1, 1972
               II, p. 1, Jan 28, 1973
               p. 36, Mar 27, 1974
New Yorker 48:99-100, May 13, 1972
Newsweek 79:92, May 13, 1972
Saturday Review 55:66, Jun 3, 1972
Time 99:59, May 15, 1972

MITCHELL, LANGDON

Becky Sharp (Based on Thackeray's Vanity Fair)
    Productions:
        Opened March 20, 1911 for 16 performances.
        Opened June 3, 1929 for 8 performances.
    Reviews:
        Commonweal 10:189, Jun 19, 1929
        Dramatic Mirror 65:7, Mar 22, 1911
        Leslies' Weekly 112:423, Apr 13, 1911
        Life (NY) 93:22, Jun 28, 1929
        Literary Digest 101:23-4, Jun 29, 1929
        New York Times VIII, p. 2, Jun 2, 1929
                       p. 29, Jun 4, 1929
                       p. 24, Jun 10, 1929
        Outlook 152:313, Jun 19, 1929

The Kreutzer Sonata (Adapted from the play by Jacob Gordin)
    Productions:
        Opened May 14, 1924 for 38 performances.
    Reviews:
        American Mercury 2:373-4, Jul 1924
        New York Times p. 22, May 15, 1924
        Theatre Magazine 6:xv, Sep 1906
                         39:15, Jul 1924

Major Pendennis (Based on Thackeray's Vanity Fair)
    Productions:

Opened October 26, 1916 for 76 performances.
Reviews:
Current Opinion 62:24-8, Jan 1917
Dramatic Mirror 76:7, Nov 4, 1916
Green Book 17:7+, Jan 1917
Life (NY) 60:812, Nov 9, 1916
Literary Digest 53:1328-9, Nov 18, 1916
           53:1409, Nov 25, 1916
Nation 103:426-7, Nov 2, 1916
New Republic 9:21, Nov 4, 1916
New York Dramatic News 63:10-11, Nov 4, 1916
New York Times p. 7, Oct 27, 1916
          II, p. 6, Oct 29, 1916
          II, p. 7, Nov 5, 1916
          II, p. 6, Nov 26, 1916
Theatre Magazine 24:354+, Dec 1916

The New York Idea
Productions:
Opened September 28, 1915 in repertory (New York Playhouse Co.).
Opened March 22, 1933 for 3 performances.
(Off Broadway) March 18, 1977 for 28 performances.
Reviews:
Book News 34:123, Nov 1915
Bookman 42:263+, Nov 1915
Dramatic Mirror 74:8, Oct 6, 1915
Life (NY) 66:708, Oct 14, 1915
Nation 101:443, Oct 7, 1915
      224:476-7, Apr 16, 1977
New Republic 4:263, Oct 9, 1915
        119:31, Aug 30, 1948
New York Magazine 10:55, Apr 11, 1977
New York Theatre Critics' Reviews 1977:302
New York Times p. 13, Sep 29, 1915
          p. 29, Aug 18, 1948
          p. 12, Jul 13, 1963
          p. 40, Mar 28, 1977
          II, p. 5, Apr 3, 1977
          III, p. 17, Apr 6, 1977
New Yorker 53:81-2, Apr 4, 1977
Newsweek 89:110-11, Apr 11, 1977
Saturday Review 4:50-1, Jul 9, 1977
Smart Set 47:144-5, Dec 1915
Theatre Magazine 7:2-3, Jan 1907
         22:224, Nov 1915
Time 109:88, Apr 11, 1977

MITCHELL, THOMAS

Cloudy with Showers (see entry under Dell, Floyd)

Glory Hallelujah (with Bertram Bloch)
    Productions:
        Opened April 6, 1926 for 15 performances.
    Reviews:
        Bookman 63:468-9, Jun 1926
        Life (NY) 87:21, Apr 29, 1926
        New York Times p. 26, Apr 7, 1926
                        VIII, p. 1, Apr 11, 1926

Little Accident   (see entry under Dell, Floyd)

MONKS, JOHN, JR.

Brother Rat (with Fred F. Finklehoffe)
    Productions:
        Opened December 16, 1936 for 577 performances.
    Reviews:
        Catholic World 144:599, Feb 1937
        Commonweal 25:276, Jan 1, 1937
        Literary Digest 123:22-3, Jan 2, 1937
        New York Times XII, p. 6, Dec 6, 1936
                        p. 30, Dec 8, 1936
                        XI, p. 5, Dec 13, 1936
                        p. 34, Dec 17, 1936
                        X, p. 3, Oct 31, 1937
                        p. 26, Nov 6, 1941
        Newsweek 8:38, Dec 26, 1936
        Stage 14:64, Feb 1937
        Theatre Arts 21:97, Feb 1937
        Time 28:33, Dec 28, 1936

MOODY, WILLIAM VAUGHN

The Faith Healer
    Productions:
        Opened January 19, 1910 for 6 performances.
        (Off Off Broadway) Season of 1969-70 (American Theater Club).
    Reviews:
        Book News 27:61, Apr 1909
        Collier's 44:33, Feb 12, 1910
        Current Literature 48:311-7, Mar 1910
        Dramatic Mirror 69:7-8, Jan 29, 1909
        Dramatist 1:33-4, Jan 1910
        Hampton 24:561-5, Apr 1910
        Independent 68:989-90, May 5, 1910
        Life (NY) 55:205, Feb 3, 1910
        Nation 88:175-6, Feb 18, 1909
        Theatre Magazine 9:xii, Mar 1909

The Great Divide
    Productions:
        Opened February 7, 1917 for 53 performances.
        (Off Off Broadway) May 1, 1976 (Manhattan Lambda Prods.).
    Reviews:
        Book News 28:469, Feb 1910
        Dramatic Mirror 77:10, Feb 17, 1917
        Dramatist 4:354-6, Apr 1913
        Forum 43:90-92, Jan 1910
        Independent 67:932, Oct 21, 1909
        Nation 89:387, Oct 21, 1909
            104:197, Feb 15, 1917
        New Republic 10:137, Mar 3, 1917
        New York Times p. 11, Feb 8, 1917
            II, p. 2, Feb 11, 1917
            p. 105, Apr 18, 1971
        Theatre Magazine 6:282-3+, Nov 1906
            25:137+, Mar 1917

MOORE, EDWARD J.

The Sea Horse
    Productions:
        (Off Off Broadway) March 3, 1974 (Circle Repertory Theater
            Co.).
        (Off Broadway) April 15, 1974 for 128 performances.
    Reviews:
        Nation 218:381, Mar 23, 1974
        New York Magazine 7:81, Apr 29, 1974
        New York Theatre Critics' Reviews 1974:284
        New York Times p. 28, Mar 5, 1974
            p. 45, Apr 16, 1974
            p. 46, Apr 22, 1974
            XXI, p. 7, Feb 22, 1981
        New Yorker 50:63-4, Apr 29, 1974
        Playboy 21:22, Aug 1974
        Time 103:93, May 20, 1974

MOSEL, TAD

All the Way Home (Based on James Agee's novel A Death in the Fam-
    ily)
    Productions:
        Opened November 30, 1960 for 333 performances.
        (Off Broadway) December 1, 1976 for 37 performances.
        (Off Off Broadway) November 3, 1977 (Ensemble Studio The-
            ater).
        (Off Off Broadway) October 25, 1979 (Equity Library Theater).

Reviews:
America 104:480, Jan 14, 1961
Catholic World 193:206-8, Jun 1961
Commonweal 73:588, Mar 3, 1961
Life 50:93-4, Jan 27, 1961
Nation 191:491, Dec 17, 1960
New Republic 143:20-1, Dec 26, 1960
New York Theatre Critics' Reviews 1960:163
New York Times II, p. 1, Nov 27, 1960
                 p. 42, Dec 1, 1960
                 p. 46, Dec 9, 1960
                 II, p. 3, Dec 18, 1960
                 p. 26, Dec 27, 1960
                 III, p. 4, Jan 14, 1977
                 III, p. 23, Oct 19, 1977
                 II, p. 30, Oct 31, 1979
                 XI, p. 33, Nov 11, 1979
New Yorker 36:96+, Dec 10, 1960
Saturday Review 43:29, Dec 17, 1960
Theatre Arts 45:64-5+, Jun 1961
             45:10-11, Feb 1961
Time 76:76, Dec 12, 1960
Vogue 137:166-7, Feb 1, 1961

MOWATT, ANNA CORA

Fashion, or Life in New York
  Productions:
    Opened February 3, 1924 for 152 performances.
    (Off Broadway) Season of 1958-59.
    (Off Off Broadway) Season of 1972-73 (American Theater Co.).
    (Off Off Broadway) October 21, 1977 (Walden Theater).
  Reviews:
    America 100:613, Feb 21, 1959
    Bookman 59:202, Apr 1924
    Catholic World 189:60, Apr 1959
    Dial 76:383-4, Apr 1924
    Drama 15:124, Mar 1925
          15:154, Apr 1925
    Freeman 8:567-8, Feb 20, 1924
    Literary Digest 81:28-9, Apr 19, 1924
    Nation 118:213, Feb 20, 1924
    New Republic 37:313, Feb 13, 1924
    New York Times p. 21, Feb 5, 1924
                   VII, p. 1, Feb 10, 1924
                   VIII, p. 2, Mar 16, 1924
                   VII, p. 1, Jul 20, 1924
                   VII, p. 14, Aug 10, 1924
                   p. 19, Jul 15, 1939
                   p. 27, Jan 21, 1959
                   p. 61, Dec 6, 1973

New Yorker 34:64+, Jan 31, 1959
Theatre Magazine 25:143, Mar 1917
39:16+, Apr 1924
Time 73:66, Feb 16, 1959

MURRAY, JOHN

Room Service (with Alan Boretz)
Productions:
Opened May 19, 1937 for 500 performances.
Opened April 6, 1953 for 16 performances.
(Off Broadway) May 10, 1963 for 9 performances (Equity Library Theater).
(Off Broadway) May 12, 1970 for 71 performances.
(Off Off Broadway) July 25, 1974 (Queen's Playhouse).
Reviews:
America 89:116-17, Apr 25, 1953
122:638, Jun 13, 1970
Catholic World 145:472-3, Jul 1937
Commonweal 26:188, Jun 11, 1937
58:72, Apr 24, 1953
Life 2:56, Jun 28, 1937
Nation 144:628, May 29, 1937
210:701-2, Jun 8, 1970
New York Theatre Critics' Reviews 1953:322
New York Times p. 16, May 20, 1937
X, p. 1, May 30, 1937
X, p. 2, Jul 25, 1937
p. 35, Dec 16, 1937
X, p. 1, Jan 16, 1938
p. 34, Apr 7, 1953
p. 49, May 13, 1970
II, p. 3, May 24, 1970
II, p. 1, Jun 5, 1970
p. 36, Jul 13, 1970
p. 18, Jul 27, 1974
p. 7, Jan 1, 1980
XXI, p. 22, May 31, 1981
New Yorker 29:68+, Apr 18, 1953
46:73, May 23, 1970
Newsweek 9:23, May 29, 1937
12:21, Sep 26, 1938
Saturday Review 36:28, Apr 25, 1953
Theatre Arts 21:500, Jul 1937
37:89, Jun 1953
Time 29:34, May 31, 1937
32:36, Oct 3, 1938
61:72, Apr 20, 1953
95:62, May 25, 1970

NASH, N. RICHARD

Echoes
    Productions:
        (Off Broadway) March 26, 1973 for one performance.
    Reviews:
        Los Angeles 25:229, Jun 1980
        New York Theatre Critics' Reviews 1973:302
        New York Times p. 55, Mar 27, 1973
                        II, p. 1, Apr 1, 1973

Girls of Summer
    Productions:
        Opened November 19, 1956 for 56 performances.
    Reviews:
        Catholic World 184:305, Jan 1957
        Commonweal 65:382, Jan 11, 1957
        Nation 183:506, Dec 8, 1956
        New York Theatre Critics' Reviews 1956:197
        New York Times p. 45, Nov 20, 1956
        New Yorker 32:117-18, Dec 1956
        Newsweek 48:50, Dec 3, 1956
        Saturday Review 39:29, Dec 8, 1956
        Theatre Arts 41:30, Jan 1957
        Time 68:82, Dec 3, 1956

Handful of Fire
    Productions:
        Opened October 1, 1958 for 5 performances.
    Reviews:
        America 100:116+, Oct 25, 1958
        Commonweal 69:127-8, Oct 31, 1958
        New Republic 139:23, Oct 20, 1958
        New York Theatre Critics' Reviews 1958:285
        New York Times p. 45, Oct 2, 1958
        New Yorker 34:87-9, Oct 11, 1958
        Newsweek 52:112, Oct 13, 1958
        Theatre Arts 42:14+, Dec 1958

The Rainmaker
    Productions:
        Opened October 28, 1954 for 125 performances.
    Reviews:
        America 92:284, Dec 4, 1954
        Catholic World 180:227, Dec 1954
        Commonweal 61:251+, Dec 3, 1954
        Life 37:143-4+, Nov 15, 1954
        Nation 179:429, Nov 13, 1954
        New York Theatre Critics' Reviews 1954:264
        New York Times p. 28, Oct 29, 1954
                        II, p. 1, Nov 7, 1954

II, p. 1, Nov 21, 1954
p. 26, Jun 1, 1956
II, p. 9, Dec 9, 1956
XXI, p. 11, Jan 20, 1980
New Yorker 30:82+, Nov 6, 1954
Newsweek 44:60, Nov 8, 1954
Saturday Review 37:26, Nov 13, 1954
Theatre Arts 39:15, 20, Jan 1955
Time 64:59, Nov 8, 1954

Second Best Bed
Productions:
Opened June 3, 1946 for 8 performances.
Reviews:
New York Theatre Critics' Reviews 1946:371
New York Times p. 20, Jun 4, 1946
New Yorker 22:40+, Jun 15, 1946

See the Jaguar
Productions:
Opened December 3, 1952 for 5 performances.
Reviews:
Commonweal 57:333, Jan 2, 1953
New York Theatre Critics' Reviews 1952:164
New York Times p. 46, Dec 4, 1952
New Yorker 28:86+, Dec 13, 1952
Newsweek 40:63, Dec 15, 1952
Saturday Review 35:26, Dec 20, 1952
Theatre Arts 37:29, Feb 1953
Time 60:73, Dec 15, 1952

The Young and the Fair
Productions:
Opened November 22, 1948 for 48 performances.
Reviews:
Catholic World 168:323, Jan 1949
Commonweal 49:231, Dec 10, 1948
New Republic 119:38, Dec 6, 1948
New York Theatre Critics' Reviews 1948:143
New York Times p. 35, Nov 23, 1948
p. 14, Jul 1, 1949
New Yorker 24:55-7, Dec 4, 1948
Newsweek 32:86, Dec 6, 1948
School and Society 68:455, Dec 25, 1948
Theatre Arts 33:16, Jan 1949
Time 52:91, Dec 6, 1948

NICHOLS, ANNE

Abie's Irish Rose
Productions:

Opened May 23, 1922 for 2,327 performances.
Opened May 12, 1937 for 46 performances.
Opened November 18, 1954 for 20 performances.
Reviews:
Catholic World 180:309, Jan 1955
Classic 20:46, Oct 1924
Collier's 74:5+, Jul 26, 1924
Commonweal 26:160, Jun 4, 1937
Current Opinion 77:192, Aug 1924
Dial 78:432, May 1925
Dramatist 15:1214-15, Apr 1924
Ladies Home Journal 41:32+, Sep 1924
Life (NY) 85:20, May 21, 1925
        85:18, Jun 25, 1925
        85:19, Feb 3, 1927
Literary Digest 92:30, Feb 19, 1927
        93:27, May 14, 1927
Nation 125:467-8, Nov 2, 1927
National Magazine 55:12+, Sep 1926
New Republic 42:98-9, Mar 18, 1925
        51:18-19, May 25, 1927
New York Clipper 70:20, May 31, 1922
New York Theatre Critics' Reviews 1954:248
New York Times p. 22, May 24, 1922
        VIII, p. 1, May 13, 1923
        p. 6, Dec 18, 1925
        p. 14, May 22, 1926
        VII, p. 1, Aug 29, 1926
        p. 12, Nov 6, 1926
        p. 16, Jan 12, 1927
        p. 23, Mar 29, 1927
        p. 24, Apr 12, 1927
        VII, p. 1, May 8, 1927
        p. 23, May 24, 1927
        p. 10, Jul 16, 1927
        VII, p. 1, Jul 31, 1927
        p. 27, Aug 9, 1927
        II, p. 3, Sep 4, 1927
        p. 29, Sep 30, 1927
        VIII, p. 1, Oct 23, 1927
        VIII, p. 2, Oct 23, 1927
        p. 20, Oct 24, 1927
        VIII, p. 2, Jun 10, 1928
        X, p. 2, Aug 2, 1936
        XI, p. 2, May 2, 1937
        p. 30, May 13, 1937
        p. 19, Nov 19, 1954
        VI, p. 2, Dec 5, 1954
        II, p. 1, May 13, 1962
        p. 40, May 21, 1962
        p. 44, May 23, 1962

Newsweek 9:26+, May 22, 1937
Theatre Arts 31:66-7, Apr 1947
39:13+, Feb 1955
Theatre Magazine 36:95, Aug 1922
39:19+, Jul 1924
46:7-8, Jul 1927
Time 64:50, Nov 29, 1954
Vanity Fair 26:52+, May 1926

*Her Week-End
Reviews:
New York Times p. 28, Mar 20, 1936

Just Married (with Adelaide Matthews)
Productions:
Opened April 26, 1921.
Reviews:
Dramatic Mirror 83:733, Apr 30, 1921
Life (NY) 77:688, May 12, 1921
New York Clipper 69:23, May 4, 1921
Theatre Magazine 34:9+, Jul 1921

*Nearly Married (with Adelaide Matthews)
Reviews:
New York Times IX, p. 4, Sep 22, 1929

Pre-Honeymoon (with Alford VanRonkel)
Productions:
Opened April 30, 1936 for 255 performances.
Reviews:
New York Times p. 19, May 1, 1936
Time 27:28, May 11, 1936

NICHOLSON, KENYON

Apple of his Eye (with Charles Robinson)
Productions:
Opened February 5, 1946 for 118 performances.
Reviews:
Catholic World 162:553, Mar 1946
Life 20:107-10, Apr 8, 1946
New Republic 114:254, Feb 18, 1946
New York Theatre Critics' Reviews 1946:463
New York Times p. 18, Feb 6, 1946
New Yorker 22:50, Feb 16, 1946
Theatre Arts 30:135, Mar 1946
30:205, Apr 1946
Time 47:50, Feb 18, 1946

The Barker
Productions:

Opened January 18, 1927 for 172 performances.
Reviews:
Bookman 65:208, Apr 1927
Life (NY) 89:23, Feb 10, 1927
Nation 124:125, Feb 2, 1927
New York Times p. 20, Jan 19, 1927
VII, p. 1, Jan 23, 1927
Theatre Magazine 45:24+, Apr 1927
Vogue 69:138, Mar 15, 1927

Before You're 25
Productions:
Opened April 16, 1929 for 23 performances.
Reviews:
Life (NY) 93:24, May 10, 1929
New York Times p. 30, Apr 17, 1929
Outlook 152:32, May 1, 1929

Dance Night
Productions:
Opened October 14, 1938 for 3 performances.
Reviews:
New York Times p. 20, Oct 15, 1938

Eva the Fifth (with John Golden)
Productions:
Opened August 28, 1928 for 63 performances.
Reviews:
Life (NY) 92:13, Sep 14, 1928
New York Times VII, p. 1, Jul 22, 1928
p. 19, Aug 29, 1928
Outlook 150:785, Sep 12, 1928
Theatre Magazine 48:48, Nov 1928

The Flying Gerardos (with Charles Robinson)
Productions:
Opened December 29, 1940 for 24 performances.
Reviews:
New York Theatre Critics' Reviews 1940:165
1941:437
New York Times p. 21, Dec 30, 1940
Time 37:57, Jan 13, 1941

Love Is Like That (see entry under Behrman, S.N.)

Out West of Eighth
Productions:
Opened September 20, 1951 for 4 performances.
Reviews:
Commonweal 54:620, Oct 5, 1951
New York Theatre Critics' Reviews 1951:232

New York Times p. 20, Sep 21, 1951
New Yorker 27:66, Sep 29, 1951
Theatre Arts 35:8, Nov 12, 1951

Sailor, Beware! (with Charles Robinson)
Productions:
Opened September 28, 1933 for 500 performances.
Opened May 3, 1935 for 16 performances.
Reviews:
New Outlook 162:42, Nov 1933
New Republic 76:279, Oct 18, 1933
New York Times p. 24, Sep 29, 1933
              IX, p. 3, Jan 7, 1934
              IX, p. 2, Feb 4, 1934
              p. 22, Feb 7, 1935
              p. 28, May 7, 1935
Review of Reviews 89:47, Mar 1934
Stage 11:9-10+, Nov 1933
      11:10-11, Feb 1934
      11:29, Mar 1934
Theatre Arts 17:918-19, Dec 1933

Stepdaughters of War (Adapted from the novel by Helen Zenna Smith)
Productions:
Opened October 6, 1930 for 24 performances.
Reviews:
Bookman 72:297, Nov 1930
Commonweal 12:643-4, Oct 22, 1930
Life (NY) 96:18, Oct 24, 1930
Nation 131:451-2, Oct 22, 1930
New York Times p. 27, Oct 7, 1930
Outlook 156:314, Oct 22, 1930
Theatre Magazine 52:28+, Dec 1930

Swing Your Lady (with Charles Robinson)
Productions:
Opened October 18, 1936 for 105 performances.
Reviews:
New Republic 89:50, Nov 11, 1936
New York Times p. 22, Oct 19, 1936
Stage 14:49, Dec 1936
Theatre Arts 20:926+, Dec 1936
Time 28:47, Nov 2, 1936

Torch Song
Productions:
Opened August 27, 1930 for 87 performances.
Reviews:
Arts and Decoration 34:67, Nov 1930
Catholic World 132:206, Nov 1930
Life (NY) 96:16, Sep 19, 1930

Nation 131:303-4, Sep 17, 1930
National Magazine 59:136-7, Dec 1930
New Republic 64:152-3, Sep 24, 1930
New York Times VIII, p. 3, Aug 3, 1930
           p. 23, Aug 28, 1930
           IX, p. 1, Sep 7, 1930
           VIII, p. 4, Oct 4, 1930
Sketch Book 7:33, Oct 1930
Theatre Arts 14:909+, Nov 1930
Theatre Magazine 52:24, Nov 1930
           52:34-6+, Nov 1930
Vanity Fair 35:86+, Nov 1930
Vogue 76:83+, Oct 13, 1930

NORMAN, MARSHA W.

Getting Out
   Productions:
      (Off Broadway) October 19, 1978 for 22 performances.
      (Off Broadway) Reopened May 15, 1979 for 237 performances
         (259 performances in all).
   Reviews:
      Commonweal 106:559-60, Oct 12, 1979
      Los Angeles 23:246, Apr 1978
      Ms. 6:26-8, Jun 1978
      Nation 227:557, Nov 18, 1978
      New Republic 181:25, Jul 7, 1979
      New West 3:SC-79, Mar 13, 1978
      New York Magazine 11:152, Nov 13, 1978
                 12:98, May 28, 1979
      New York Theatre Critics' Reviews 1979:243
      New York Times III, p. 6, Jan 4, 1978
              III, p. 19, May 16, 1979
              II, p. 5, Jun 3, 1979
      New Yorker 54:152-3, Nov 6, 1978
      Newsweek 93:103, May 28, 1979
      Time 113:80, May 28, 1979

The Laundromat
   Productions:
      (Off Off Broadway) November-December 1979 as part of a bill
         called Invitational (Ensemble Studio Theater).
   Reviews:
      New York Times III, p. 5, Dec 21, 1979

'Night Mother
   Productions:
      (Off Off Broadway) November 9, 1981 (Circle Repertory Proj-
         ects).
   Reviews:
      Newsweek 101:41-2, Jan 3, 1983

NUGENT, ELLIOTT and J. C.

The Breaks
Productions:
Opened April 16, 1928 for 8 performances.
Reviews:
New York Times p. 26, Apr 17, 1928

By Request
Productions:
Opened September 27, 1928 for 28 performances.
Reviews:
Life (NY) 92:19, Oct 19, 1928
New York Times p. 30, Sep 28, 1928

Dream Child (J. C. Nugent alone)
Productions:
Opened September 27, 1934 for 24 performances.
Reviews:
New York Times p. 26, Sep 28, 1934

Dumb-Bell
Productions:
Opened November 26, 1923 for 2 performances.
Reviews:
New York Times p. 23, Nov 27, 1923
VIII, p. 1, Dec 2, 1923

Fast Service
Productions:
Opened November 17, 1931 for 7 performances.
Reviews:
New York Times p. 26, Nov 18, 1931

Human Nature
Productions:
Opened September 24, 1925 for 4 performances.
Reviews:
New York Times p. 24, Sep 25, 1925

Kempy
Productions:
Opened May 15, 1922 for 38+ performances.
Opened May 11, 1927 for 46 performances.
Reviews:
Current Opinion 73:213-20, Aug 1922
Everybody's 47:83-8, Nov 1922
Life (NY) 79:18, Jun 1, 1922
New York Clipper 70:20, May 24, 1922
New York Times p. 14, May 16, 1922
VI, p. 1, Jun 11, 1922

p. 25, May 12, 1927
VIII, p. 1, May 22, 1927
Theatre Magazine 36:30-31, Jul 1922
36:230+, Oct 1922

The Male Animal (see entry under Thurber, James)

*Mr. Shaddy (J. C. Nugent alone)
Reviews:
New York Times p. 14, Jul 15, 1936

Nightstick (with John Wray, and Elaine Sterne Carrington)
Productions:
Opened November 10, 1927 for 52 performances.
Reopened for 32 performances.
Reviews:
Life (NY) 90:21, Dec 8, 1927
New York Times p. 20, Nov 11, 1927
IX, p. 4, Nov 20, 1927
Vogue 71:100, Jan 1, 1928

A Place of Our Own (Elliott Nugent alone)
Productions:
Opened April 2, 1945 for 8 performances.
Reviews:
New York Theatre Critics' Reviews 1945:232
New York Times p. 23, Apr 3, 1945

The Poor Nut
Productions:
Opened April 27, 1925 for 32 performances.
Reviews:
Nation 120:556-7, May 13, 1925
New York Times p. 18, Apr 28, 1925
Theatre Magazine 42:15, Jul 1925
42:26+, Oct 1925

The Rising Son
Productions:
Opened October 27, 1924 for 16 performances.
Reviews:
Life (NY) 84:18, Nov 13, 1924
New York Times p. 27, Oct 28, 1924
Theatre Magazine 40:20, Jan 1925

That Old Devil (J. C. Nugent alone)
Productions:
Opened June 5, 1944 for 16 performances.
Reviews:
Commonweal 40:231, Jun 23, 1944
New York Theatre Critics' Reviews 1944:177

New York Times p. 14, Jun 6, 1944
New Yorker 20:44, Jun 17, 1944

The Trouper
Productions:
Opened March 18, 1926 for 24 performances.
Reviews:
New York Times p. 21, Mar 9, 1926
VIII, p. 1, Mar 14, 1926
Theatre Magazine 43:18, May 1926

*World's My Opinion
Reviews:
New York Times X, p. 1, Jun 16, 1935

ODETS, CLIFFORD

Awake and Sing!
Productions:
Opened February 19, 1935 for 209 performances.
Opened September 9, 1935 for 24 performances.
Opened March 7, 1939 for 45 performances.
(Off Broadway) May 27, 1970 for 41 performances.
(Off Off Broadway) January 23, 1975 (Joseph Jefferson).
(Off Off Broadway) March 18, 1977 (Counterpoint Theater Co.).
(Off Off Broadway) May 13, 1978 (Playwrights Horizons).
(Off Broadway) April 19, 1979 for 45 performances.
(Off Off Broadway) October 24, 1981 (Jewish Repertory Theater).
Reviews:
Catholic World 141:91, Apr 1935
149:217-18, May 1939
Commonweal 21:570, Mar 15, 1935
29:639, Mar 31, 1939
Literary Digest 119:18, Apr 6, 1935
Nation 140:314+, Mar 13, 1935
140:610, May 22, 1935
New Republic 82:134, Mar 13, 1935
New York Times p. 23, Feb 20, 1935
VIII, p. 1, Mar 10, 1935
p. 15, Feb 21, 1938
p. 16, Dec 23, 1938
p. 18, Mar 8, 1939
X, p. 1, Mar 26, 1939
VIII, p. 2, May 31, 1941
VIII, p. 2, May 31, 1942
p. 35, May 28, 1970
II, p. 1, Jun 5, 1970
II, p. 1, Jun 7, 1970
p. 83, Mar 9, 1972

p. 62, Sep 25, 1975
p. 27, Mar 16, 1976
III, p. 20, May 31, 1978
III, p. 20, May 16, 1979
p. 70, Nov 1, 1981
New Yorker 46:52, Jun 6, 1970
Newsweek 5:31, Mar 2, 1935
Stage 12:23, Apr 1935
Theatre Arts 19:254-6, Apr 1935
             23:323, May 1939
Time 25:39, Mar 4, 1935
       33:60, Mar 20, 1939
       95:76, Jun 8, 1970
Vanity Fair 44:24, Jun 1935

The Big Knife
    Productions:
        Opened February 24, 1949 for 108 performances.
        (Off Broadway) Season of 1959-60.
        (Off Off Broadway) Season of 1974-75 (ETC).
        (Off Off Broadway) January 9, 1976 (Amas Repertory Theater).
    Reviews:
        Catholic World 169:63, Apr 1949
        Commonweal 49:590-1, Mar 25, 1949
        Forum 111:286-7, May 1949
        Nation 168:340, Mar 19, 1949
        New Republic 120:28-9, Mar 14, 1949
        New York Theatre Critics' Reviews 1949:349
        New York Times p. 27, Feb 25, 1949
                  II, p. 1, Mar 6, 1949
                  p. 64, Jan 3, 1954
                  II, p. 4, Jan 17, 1954
                  p. 25, Nov 13, 1959
        New Yorker 25:56+, Mar 5, 1949
        Newsweek 33:84, Mar 7, 1949
        Saturday Review 32:34-5, Mar 19, 1949
        School and Society 69:340-1, May 7, 1949
        Theatre Arts 33:23-5, May 1949
        Time 53:58, Mar 7, 1949
        Vogue 113:206+, Apr 1, 1949

Clash by Night
    Productions:
        Opened December 27, 1941 for 49 performances.
        (Off Off Broadway) March 17, 1978 (IRT).
    Reviews:
        Catholic World 154:601, Feb 1942
        Commonweal 35:319-20, Jan 16, 1942
        Current History ns 1:566-8, Feb 1942
        Life 11:53-4, Nov 24, 1941
        Nation 154:45-6, Jan 10, 1942

New York Theatre Critics' Reviews 1941:161
New York Times IX, p. 1, Jan 11, 1942
　　　　　　　IX, p. 1, Jan 18, 1942
　　　　　　　IX, p. 3, Feb 1, 1942
New Yorker 17:28+, Jan 3, 1942
Newsweek 19:46, Jan 12, 1942
Player's Magazine 18:13, Feb 1942
Theatre Arts 26:150-2, Mar 1942

The Country Girl
Productions:
　Opened November 10, 1950 for 235 performances.
　(Off Broadway) March 12, 1968 for 15 performances. (Billed
　　as Winter Journey).
　Opened September 29, 1966 for 22 performances (City Center
　　Drama Company).
　Opened March 15, 1972 for 61 performances.
Reviews:
　American Mercury 72:350-1, Mar 1951
　Catholic World 172:310, Jan 1951
　Christian Science Monitor Magazine p. 4, Nov. 18, 1950
　Commonweal 53:196, Dec 1, 1950
　Life 29:77-80, Dec 4, 1950
　Nation 171:493, Nov 25, 1950
　　　　203:398, Oct 17, 1966
　National Review 19:99, Jan 24, 1967
　New Republic 123:29-30, Dec 11, 1950
　New York Theatre Critics' Reviews 1950:210
　　　　　　　　　　　　　　　　　1972:356
　New York Times II, p. 3, Nov 5, 1950
　　　　　　　　　p. 10, Nov 11, 1950
　　　　　　　　　II, p. 1, Nov 19, 1950
　　　　　　　　　II, p. 3, Nov 26, 1950
　　　　　　　　　p. 31, Apr 3, 1951
　　　　　　　　　p. 21, Apr 4, 1952
　　　　　　　　　II, p. 3, Apr 13, 1952
　　　　　　　　　p. 55, Sep 30, 1966
　　　　　　　　　p. 39, Mar 13, 1968
　　　　　　　　　p. 11, Dec 24, 1971
　　　　　　　　　p. 57, Mar 16, 1972
　　　　　　　　　II, p. 1, Mar 26, 1972
　　　　　　　　　p. 42, May 1, 1972
　New Yorker 26:77-9, Nov 18, 1950
　Newsweek 36:90, Nov 20, 1950
　Saturday Review 33:26-7, Dec 9, 1950
　School and Society 73:249-50, Apr 21, 1951
　Theatre Arts 35:14, Jan 1951
　Time 56:64, Nov 20, 1950

The Flowering Peach
Productions:
　Opened December 28, 1954 for 135 performances.

Reviews:
America 92:434, Jan 22, 1955
Catholic World 180:387, Feb 1955
Commentary 20:74-6, Jul 1955
Commonweal 61:502, Feb 11, 1955
Nation 180:57-9, Jan 15, 1955
New Republic 132:21, Jan 10, 1955
New York Theatre Critics' Reviews 1954:196
New York Times II, p. 1, Dec 26, 1954
                  p. 19, Dec 29, 1954
                  II, p. 1, Jan 9, 1955
                  II, p. 3, Mar 20, 1955
New Yorker 30:62+, Jan 8, 1955
Newsweek 45:62, Jan 10, 1955
Saturday Review 38:30, Jan 15, 1955
Theatre Arts 38:24-5, Oct 1954
              39:18, 23+, Mar 1955
Time 65:34, Jan 10, 1955

Golden Boy

Productions:
Opened November 4, 1937 for 250 performances.
Opened March 12, 1952 for 55 performances.
(Off Off Broadway) October 16, 1975 (Manhattan Theater Club).

Reviews:
Catholic World 146:342, Dec 1937
               175:148, May 1952
Commonweal 27:106, Nov 19, 1937
           55:614-15, Mar 28, 1952
Current History 48:54, Apr 1938
Life 4:24-7, Jan 17, 1938
Literary Digest 124:35, Nov 27, 1937
Nation 145:540, Nov 13, 1937
       174:285, Mar 22, 1952
New Republic 93:45, Nov 17, 1937
New York Theatre Critics' Reviews 1952:344
New York Times p. 18, Nov 5, 1937
               XI, p. 1, Nov 21, 1937
               p. 27, Jun 22, 1938
               IX, p. 1, Jul 10, 1938
               IX, p. 3, Oct 23, 1938
               X, p. 3, Mar 5, 1939
               II, p. 3, Mar 9, 1952
               p. 24, Mar 13, 1952
               II, p. 1, Mar 23, 1952
               p. 52, Nov 6, 1975
New Yorker 28:60, Mar 22, 1952
Newsweek 39:100, Mar 24, 1952
Saturday Review 35:26, Mar 29, 1952
School and Society 75:326-7, May 24, 1952
Scribner's Magazine 103:66, May 1938

Theatre Arts 22:11-13, Jan 1938
Time 30:25-6, Nov 15, 1937
        59:56, Mar 24, 1952

I Can't Sleep
    Productions:
        (Off Broadway) Season of 1967-68 in repertory (The Dove Company).
    No Reviews.

Night Music
    Productions:
        Opened February 22, 1940 for 20 performances.
        Opened April 8, 1951 for 8 performances.
    Reviews:
        Commonweal 31:435, Mar 8, 1940
                54:58, Apr 27, 1951
        Nation 150:316-7, Mar 2, 1940
        New Republic 102:377, Mar 18, 1940
                124:22, Apr 30, 1951
        New York Theatre Critics' Reviews 1940:385
                                          1951:300
        New York Times p. 18, Feb 23, 1940
                X, p. 1, Mar 3, 1940
                p. 29, Apr 9, 1951
        New Yorker 27:62+, Apr 21, 1951
        Newsweek 15:42, Mar 4, 1940
        Theatre Arts 24:230-1+, Apr 1940
        Time 35:34, Mar 4, 1940
        Yale Review 30:422, Winter 1941

Paradise Lost
    Productions:
        Opened December 9, 1935 for 73 performances.
    Reviews:
        Catholic World 142:600, Feb 1936
        Commonweal 23:244, Dec 27, 1935
        Forum 95:347, Jun 1936
        Literary Digest 120:20, Dec 21, 1936
        Nation 141:752, Dec 25, 1935
                142:27-8, Jan 1, 1936
                142:72-3, Jan 15, 1936
        New Republic 85:202, Dec 25, 1935
                86:283, Apr 15, 1936
        New York Times p. 31, Dec 10, 1935
                XI, p. 3, Dec 15, 1935
                IX, p. 1, Dec 29, 1935
                IX, p. 1, Jan 8, 1939
        Newsweek 6:39, Dec 21, 1935
        Stage 13:2+, Jan 1936

Theatre Arts 20:94-7, Feb 1936
20:465-6, Jun 1936
Time 26:31-2, Dec 23, 1935

Rocket to the Moon
Productions:
Opened November 24, 1938 for 131 performances.
(Off Off Broadway) Season of 1970-71 (American Theater Club).
(Off Off Broadway) March 5, 1976 (Counterpoint).
Reviews:
Catholic World 148:476, Jan 1939
Commonweal 29:190, Dec 9, 1938
Forum 101:72, Feb 1939
Nation 147:600-1, Dec 3, 1938
New Republic 97:173, Dec 14, 1938
New York Times p. 18, Nov 25, 1938
X, p. 5, Dec 4, 1938
p. 30, Mar 23, 1948
II, p. 3, Apr 11, 1948
XXI, p. 15, Sep 26, 1982
Newsweek 12:24, Dec 5, 1938
North American Review 247 no. 1:157-8, Mar 1939
One Act Play Magazine 2:599-602, Dec 1938
Theatre Arts 23:11-13, Jan 1939
Time 32:44, Dec 5, 1938

The Russian People (Adapted from the play by Konstantin Simonov)
Productions:
Opened December 29, 1942 for 39 performances.
Reviews:
Catholic World 156:599, Feb 1943
Commonweal 37:349, Jan 22, 1943
Current History ns 3:549, Feb 1943
Nation 156:103, Jan 16, 1943
New York Theatre Critics' Reviews 1942:127
New York Times p. 8, Jul 18, 1942
p. 17, Dec 30, 1942
Newsweek 21:66, Jan 11, 1943
Theatre Arts 27:70-1, Feb 1943
27:141-2+, Mar 1943

The Russians (see The Russian People)

The Silent Partner
Productions:
(Off Off Broadway) May 11, 1972 for 12 performances (Actors Studio).
Reviews:
New York Times II, p. 1, Apr 30, 1972

Till the Day I Die
Productions:

Opened March 26, 1935 for 136 performances.
Reviews:
Catholic World 141:328+, May 1935
Commonweal 21:682, Apr 12, 1935
Nation 140:428, Apr 10, 1935
New Republic 82:247, Apr 10, 1935
New York Times p. 24, Mar 27, 1935
X, p. 3, Sep 27, 1936
X, p. 10, Jan 10, 1937
Theatre Arts 19:328+, May 1935

Waiting for Lefty
Productions:
Opened March 26, 1935 for 168 performances.
Opened September 9, 1935 for 24 performances.
(Off Broadway) July 19, 1938 for one performance (Furrier's Worker's Union).
(Off Broadway) Season of 1967-68 in repertory (Roundabout Theatre).
(Off Off Broadway) April 1975 (ETC).
Reviews:
Catholic World 141:215, May 1935
Commonweal 21:682, Apr 12, 1935
Literary Digest 119:18, Apr 6, 1935
Nation 140:427-8, Apr 10, 1935
New Republic 82:247, Apr 10, 1935
New York Times p. 14, Feb 11, 1935
p. 24, Mar 27, 1935
p. 58, Dec 19, 1967
p. 42, Aug 16, 1973
Theatre Arts 19:327-8, May 1935
Time 25:38, Jun 1935

Winter Journey (see The Country Girl)

O'NEILL, EUGENE

Abortion (see The Lost Works of Eugene O'Neill)

Ah, Wilderness
Productions:
Opened October 2, 1933 for 289 performances.
Opened October 2, 1941 for 29 performances.
(Off Broadway) Season of 1952-53 (Equity Library Theater).
Opened September 18, 1975 for 77 performances.
Reviews:
America 133:283-4, Nov 1, 1975
Canadian Forum 14:188, Feb 1934
Catholic World 138:214-5, Nov 1933
154:212-213, Nov 1941

Commonweal 18:620, Oct 27, 1933
    34:613, Oct 17, 1941
Life 11:59-61, Nov 3, 1941
Literary Digest 116:24, Oct 28, 1933
     120:22, Dec 28, 1935
Nation 137:458-9, Oct 18, 1933
   153:381, Oct 18, 1941
   221:317-18, Oct 4, 1975
New Outlook 162:42, Nov 1933
New Republic 76:280, Oct 18, 1933
    85:198, Dec 25, 1935
    173:22-3, Oct 11, 1975
New York Magazine 8:68+, Oct 6, 1975
New York Theatre Critics' Reviews 1941:282
        1975:210
New York Times X, p. 1, Sep 10, 1933
     p. 26, Sep 26, 1933
     p. 28, Oct 3, 1933
     X, p. 1, Oct 8, 1933
     p. 26, Mar 20, 1934
     X, p. 2, Mar 25, 1934
     p. 26, Apr 10, 1934
     p. 26, May 1, 1934
     p. 23, Oct 30, 1934
     p. 18, Oct 31, 1934
     IX, p. 3, Jan 13, 1935
     VIII, p. 3, Jan 27, 1935
     p. 25, Aug 20, 1935
     p. 26, May 5, 1936
     IX, p. 2, Jun 7, 1936
     IX, p. 1, Jun 28, 1936
     p. 23, Aug 20, 1940
     p. 26, Oct 3, 1941
     p. 10, Feb 7, 1953
     II, p. 1, Feb 15, 1953
     p. 20, Aug 21, 1954
     II, p. 7, Mar 19, 1967
     p. 32, Dec 23, 1974
     p. 25, Sep 19, 1975
     II, p. 5, Sep 28, 1975
New Yorker 51:100, Sep 29, 1975
Newsweek 2:29, Oct 7, 1933
   3:23, May 12, 1934
   6:38, Dec 14, 1935
Review of Reviews 89:39, Feb 1934
Saturday Review 10:217, Oct 28, 1933
     52:62, Nov 22, 1969
Stage 11:7-9, Nov 1933
Theatre Arts 17:980-10, Dec 1933
   20:142-3, Feb 1936
   25:867-8, Dec 1941

Time 22:26-7, Oct 9, 1933
26:44, Dec 9, 1935
105:93, Jan 6, 1975
Vanity Fair 41:43+, Nov 1933

All God's Chillun Got Wings
Productions:
Opened May 15, 1924 (Provincetown Players).
Opened March 20, 1975 for 53 performances.
Reviews:
American Mercury 1:129-48, Feb 1924
2:113-4, May 1924
Bookman 59:582, Jul 1924
Life (NY) 83:18, Mar 27, 1924
Nation 118:664, Jun 4, 1924
220:442-3, Apr 12, 1975
New Republic 39:22, May 28, 1974
New York Magazine 8:78+, Apr 7, 1975
New York Theatre Critics' Reviews 1975:290
New York Times p. 22, Mar 3, 1924
p. 19, Mar 19, 1924
p. 21, Mar 20, 1924
IX, p. 5, May 11, 1924
p. 15, May 12, 1924
p. 22, May 16, 1924
VII, p. 1, May 18, 1924
p. 9, Aug 19, 1924
VII, p. 1, Aug 24, 1924
p. 19, Mar 14, 1933
p. 30, Mar 21, 1975
II, p. 1, Mar 30, 1975
New Yorker 51:47-8, Mar 31, 1975
Theatre Arts 8:497-8, Jul 1924
17:423-4, Jun 1933
Theatre Magazine 40:15, Jul 1924
Time 105:61, Mar 31, 1975

The Ancient Mariner
Productions:
Opened April 6, 1924 for 33 performances.
Reviews:
American Mercury 2:243-4, Jun 1924
Independent 112:259, May 10, 1924
New York Times p. 15, Apr 7, 1924
VIII, p. 1, Apr 13, 1924
Theatre Arts 8:357-8, Jun 1924
Theatre Magazine 39:19, Jun 1924

Anna Christie
Productions:
Opened November 2, 1921 for 177 performances.

Opened January 9, 1952 for 29 performances.
(Off Off Broadway) Season of 1970-71 (The Assembly).
(Off Off Broadway) January 30, 1976 (Soho Rep.).
Opened April 14, 1977 for 124 performances.
Reviews:
Catholic World 174:462-3, Mar 1952
Commonweal 55:399, Jan 25, 1952
Current Opinion 72:57-66, Jan 1922
Dial 71:724-5, Dec 1921
Dramatic Mirror 84:701, Nov 12, 1921
Hearst 41:45-7+, Mar 1922
Independent 107:326, Dec 3, 1921
Life (NY) 78:18, Nov 24, 1921
Life 32:82-4+, Feb 4, 1952
Literary Digest 77:28-9, May 26, 1923
Metropolitan Magazine 55:36-7, Jun 1922
Nation 113:626, Nov 30, 1921
　　　　120:242, Mar 4, 1925
　　　　174:92, Jan 26, 1952
　　　　224:538-9, Apr 30, 1977
New Republic 29:20, Nov 30, 1921
　　　　　　176:22-3, May 7, 1977
New York Magazine 10:68, May 2, 1977
New York Theatre Critics' Reviews 1952:395
New York Times p. 22, Nov 3, 1921
　　　　　　VI, p. 1, Nov 13, 1921
　　　　　　VI, p. 1, Dec 25, 1921
　　　　　　III, p. 3, Jan 15, 1922
　　　　　　p. 16, Apr 11, 1923
　　　　　　VII, p. 2, Apr 15, 1923
　　　　　　p. 18, Jun 24, 1924
　　　　　　p. 33, Jun 11, 1930
　　　　　　p. 30, Jun 12, 1930
　　　　　　IX, p. 1, Aug 10, 1941
　　　　　　p. 33, Jan 10, 1952
　　　　　　II, p. 1, Jan 20, 1952
　　　　　　p. 41, Nov 22, 1955
　　　　　　III, p. 3, Apr 15, 1977
　　　　　　II, p. 5, Apr 24, 1977
New Yorker 27:48, Feb 2, 1952
　　　　　53:92, Apr 25, 1977
Newsweek 89:89, Apr 25, 1977
Saturday Review 35:32-4, Feb 16, 1952
　　　　　　4:38-9, May 28, 1977
School and Society 75:107, Feb 16, 1952
Theatre Arts 36:70, Mar 1952
Theatre Magazine 35:29, Jan 1922
　　　　　　35:220+, Apr 1922
　　　　　　41:20, Apr 1925
Time 59:73, Jan 21, 1952
　　　109:84, Apr 25, 1977
See also reviews of Chris and Chris Christophersen

Before Breakfast
Productions:
Opened March 5, 1929 for 27 performances.
(Off Broadway) Season of 1957-58 (ANTA).
Reviews:
Arts and Decoration 81:104, May 1929
Drama Magazine 19:200, Apr 29, 1929
New York Times p. 33, Mar 6, 1929
p. 36, Mar 12, 1958
Theatre Arts 13:334, May 1924

Beyond the Horizon
Productions:
Opened February 2, 1920 for 111 performances.
Opened November 30, 1926 for 79 performances.
Reviews:
Current Opinion 68:339-45, Mar 1920
Drama 17:136, Feb 1927
Dramatic Mirror 82:258, Feb 14, 1920
Independent 101:382, Mar 13, 1920
Life (NY) 75:322, Feb 19, 1920
Literary Digest 64:33, Feb 28, 1920
Nation 110:241-2, Feb 21, 1920
123:646-7, Dec 15, 1926
New Republic 25:173-4, Jan 5, 1921
New York Clipper 68:21, Feb 11, 1920
New York Times p. 12, Feb 4, 1920
VIII, p. 2, Feb 8, 1920
p. 9, Mar 10, 1920
VI, p. 2, Apr 11, 1920
p. 28, May 23, 1926
p. 27, Nov 23, 1926
p. 24, Dec 1, 1926
XI, p. 3, Mar 20, 1938
p. 27, Oct 26, 1962
p. 18, Oct 12, 1974
Player's Magazine 26:46, Nov 1949
Review 2:185-6, Feb 21, 1920
Theatre Arts 4:286-9, Oct 1920
11:86, Feb 1927
Theatre Magazine 31:185, Mar 1920
43:185, Feb 1926

Bound East of Cardiff (see S. S. Glencairn for other productions)
Productions:
(Off Broadway) Summer of 1916 (Provincetown Players).
(Off Broadway) November 3, 1916 (Provincetown Players).
Reviews:
Commonweal 9:349, Jan 23, 1929
48:185, Jun 4, 1948
Current Opinion 61:323, Nov 1916

New Republic 118:27-9, Jun 7, 1948
New York Times p. 31, Nov 4, 1924
                VII, p. 1, Dec 28, 1924
                p. 24, Jan 10, 1929
                IX, p. 1, Jan 27, 1929
                p. 23, Oct 30, 1937
                p. 21, May 21, 1948
                II, p. 1, May 30, 1948
New Yorker 24:43, May 29, 1948
School and Society 67:478, Jun 26, 1948
Theatre Arts 13:172, Mar 1929
                27:400, Jul 1943
Theatre Guild Magazine 9:12, Nov 1931
Theatre Magazine 40:22, Jan 1925
Time 4:14, Nov 17, 1924
See also reviews of Three Plays of the Sea

*Chris (an early version of Anna Christie)
   Reviews:
      Dramatic Mirror 82:577, Mar 27, 1920

*Chris Christophersen (an early version of Anna Christie)
   Reviews:
      New York Times IV, p. 2, Jun 1, 1919

Days Without End
   Productions:
      Opened January 8, 1934 for 57 performances.
   Reviews:
      American Review 2:491-5, Feb 1934
      Catholic World 138:513-17+, Feb 1934
      Christian Century 51:191-2, Feb 7, 1934
                        51:258, Feb 21, 1934
                        73:950, Aug 15, 1956
      Commonweal 19:327-9, Jan 19, 1934
                  19:357, Jan 26, 1934
                  19:469, Feb 23, 1934
                  19:496-7, Mar 2, 1934
                  19:608, Mar 30, 1934
                  20:46, May 11, 1934
      Literary Digest 117:17, Feb 10, 1934
      Living Age 347:554-6, Feb 1935
      Nation 138:110-11, Jan 24, 1934
      New Outlook 163:48, Feb 1934
      New Republic 77:312, Jan 24, 1934
      New York Times p. 19, Jan 9, 1934
                     IX, p. 1, Jan 14, 1934
                     p. 26, Apr 24, 1934
                     p. 23, Feb 5, 1935
                     VIII, p. 1, Mar 3, 1935
      Newsweek 3:34, Jan 20, 1934

Saturday Review 10:419, Jan 20, 1934
Stage 11:16-18, Feb 1934
Theatre Arts 18:167-9+, Mar 1934
Vanity Fair 42:42, Mar 1934

Desire Under the Elms
  Productions:
    Opened November 11, 1924 for 208 performances.
    Opened January 16, 1952 for 46 performances.
    (Off Broadway) January 8, 1963 for 380 performances.
    (Off Off Broadway) Season of 1970-71 (ACSTA).
    (Off Off Broadway) Season of 1971-72 (ACSTA).
    (Off Off Broadway) Season of 1972-73 (ACSTA).
    (Off Off Broadway) March 9, 1974 (ACSTA).
    (Off Off Broadway) October 11, 1975 (Jean Cocteau Repertory).
    (Off Off Broadway) January 9, 1976 (ACSTA).
    (Off Off Broadway) April 30, 1982 (Urban Arts Theater).
  Reviews:
    America 108:275, Feb 23, 1963
    American Mercury 4:119, Jan 1925
    Bookman 60:621, Jan 1925
    Canadian Magazine 64:74, Apr 1925
    Catholic World 120:519-21, Jan 1925
                  174:464, Mar 1952
    Commonweal 55:423, Feb 1, 1952
               77:543, Feb 15, 1963
    Dial 78:82, Jan 1925
    Independent 114:51, Jan 10, 1925
    Life (NY) 84:18, Dec 11, 1924
    Life 32:82-4, Feb 4, 1952
    Literary Digest 86:23-4, Aug 8, 1925
    Nation 119:578-80, Nov 26, 1924
           120:346, Apr 1, 1925
           122:548-9, May 19, 1926
           196:106-7, Feb 2, 1963
    New Republic 41:44, Dec 3, 1924
                 148:26, Feb 2, 1963
    New York Theatre Critics' Reviews 1952:386
    New York Times p. 20, Nov 12, 1924
                   VIII, p. 5, Dec 7, 1924
                   p. 19, Feb 20, 1926
                   p. 15, Apr 10, 1926
                   p. 25, Apr 15, 1926
                   p. 8, Apr 16, 1926
                   p. 23, Aug 3, 1930
                   IX, p. 1, Nov 12, 1933
                   IX, p. 2, Feb 4, 1940
                   p. 45, Nov 22, 1951
                   p. 23, Jan 17, 1952
                   p. 17, May 23, 1952
                   II, p. 5, Mar 2, 1958

p. 5, Jan 11, 1963
p. 18, Apr 12, 1974
II, p. 5, Sep 5, 1976
New Yorker 27:53, Jan 26, 1952
38:62+, Jan 19, 1963
Newsweek 39:83, Jan 28, 1952
61:57, Jan 21, 1963
83:76-7, Jun 24, 1974
Saturday Review 35:32-4, Feb 16, 1952
46:32, Jan 26, 1963
School and Society 75:106-7, Feb 16, 1952
Survey 53:421-2, Jan 1, 1925
Theatre Arts 9:3-15, Jan 1925
36:70, Mar 1952
36:31-3, Apr 1952
47:10-11, Feb 1963
Theatre Guild Magazine 9:14, Nov 1931
9:12, Jan 1932
Theatre Magazine 41:22, Jan 1925
41:26+, Jun 1925
Time 59:44, Jan 28, 1952
81:42, Jan 18, 1963

Diff'rent

Productions:
  (Off Broadway) December 27, 1920 (Provincetown Players).
    Opened February 4, 1921 for 100 performances.
  (Off Broadway) Season of 1924-25.
  Opened January 25, 1938 for 4 performances (WPA Federal
    Theatre Project).
  (Off Broadway) October 17, 1961 for 88 performances.
Reviews:
  Bookman 52:565, Feb 1921
  Commonweal 1:466, Mar 4, 1925
  Independent 105:153, Feb 12, 1921
  Nation 193:459-60, Dec 2, 1961
  New Republic 42:45, Mar 4, 1925
  New York Clipper 68:19, Jan 5, 1921
  New York Times p. 8, Dec 29, 1920
      p. 19, Feb 11, 1925
      VII, p. 1, Mar 1, 1925
      p. 23, Oct 30, 1937
      II, p. 10, Nov 21, 1937
      p. 26, Jan 26, 1938
      p. 52, Oct 18, 1961
  New Yorker 37:137, Oct 28, 1961
  Review 4:207-9, Mar 2, 1921
  Theatre Arts 45:70-1, Dec 1961
  Theatre Magazine 33:261, Apr 1921
  Time 5:13, Feb 23, 1925
  Vanity Fair 16:33, Apr 1921
  Weekly Review 4:207-9, Mar 2, 1921

The Dreamy Kid
    Productions:
        (Off Broadway) October 31, 1919 (Provincetown Players).
        Opened February 11, 1925 for 28 performances.
        (Off Off Broadway) Season of 1975-76 (Di Pinto Di Blu).
    Reviews:
        New York Times VIII, p. 2, Nov 9, 1919

Dynamo
    Productions:
        Opened February 11, 1929 for 50 performances.
        (Off Off Broadway) October 29, 1976 (IRT).
    Reviews:
        American Mercury 16:119-20, Jan 1929
                         16:373-8, Mar 1929
        Arts and Decoration 30:72, Apr 1929
        Bookman 69:179-80, Apr 1929
        Catholic World 129:80-2, Apr 1929
        Commonweal 9:489-90, Feb 27, 1929
        Dial 86:349-50, Apr 1929
        Drama 19:201+, Apr 1929
        Life (NY) 93:24+, Mar 8, 1929
        Literary Digest 100:21-2, Mar 2, 1929
        Nation 128:264-6, Feb 27, 1929
        New Republic 58:43-4, Feb 27, 1929
        New York Times p. 22, Feb 12, 1929
                       VIII, p. 4, Mar 3, 1929
                       III, p. 22, Nov 12, 1976
        Outlook 151:331, Feb 27, 1929
        Review of Reviews 79:158-60, Apr 1929
        Theatre Arts 13:245-7, Apr 1929
        Theatre Magazine 49:45, May 1929
        Vanity Fair 31:62+, Feb 1929
        Vogue 73:61+, Mar 30, 1929

The Emperor Jones
    Productions:
        Opened November 1, 1920 for 204 performances.
        Opened February 11, 1925 for 28 performances.
        Opened February 16, 1926 for 35 performances.
        Opened November 10, 1926 for 61 performances.
        (Off Broadway) January 16, 1945 in repertory.
        (Off Off Broadway) Season of 1977-78 (Perry St. Theater).
    Reviews:
        Bookman 52:565, Feb 1921
        Current Opinion 70:55-64, Jan 1921
        Drama 14:132, Jan 1924
        Dramatist 14:1176-7, Jul 1928
        Everybody's 54:134-48, Apr 1926
        Independent 105:158-9, Feb 12, 1921
        Literary Digest 79:24-5, Dec 29, 1923

Nation 112:189, Feb 2, 1921
New York Clipper 68:19, Nov 24, 1920
New York Times VII, p. 1, Nov 7, 1920
      p. 24, Nov 1, 1923
      p. 18, Jan 10, 1924
      p. 18, May 7, 1924
      p. 16, Feb 12, 1925
      p. 20, Sep 11, 1925
      p. 11, Feb 17, 1926
      p. 28, May 18, 1926
      p. 23, Nov 11, 1926
      VII, p. 4, Feb 13, 1927
      p. 10, Apr 1, 1930
      p. 24, Aug 11, 1936
      p. 25, Jun 20, 1939
      p. 18, Jan 17, 1945
      II, p. 1, Jan 28, 1945
      p. 20, Aug 6, 1964
      II, p. 5, Aug 16, 1964
      III, p. 5, Sep 23, 1977
Outlook 126:710-11, Dec 22, 1920
Review of Reviews 3:567-8, Dec 8, 1920
Theatre Arts 5:5-7, Jan 1921
     17:172+, Mar 1933
Theatre Magazine 33:8, Jan 1921
Weekly Review 3:567-8, Dec 8, 1920

Exorcism
  Productions:
   (Off Broadway) March 26, 1920 (Provincetown Players).
  Reviews:
   New York Times VI, p. 6, Apr 4, 1920

The First Man
  Productions:
   Opened March 4, 1922 for 27 performances.
  Reviews:
   Bookman 52:284, May 1922
   Freeman 5:184-5, May 3, 1922
   New York Clipper 70:22, Mar 15, 1922
   New York Times p. 9, Mar 6, 1922
   Theatre Arts 6:182, Jul 1922
   Theatre Magazine 35:308, May 1922

The Fountain
  Productions:
   Opened December 10, 1925 for 28 performances.
  Reviews:
   American Mercury 7:247-9, Feb 1926
   Arts and Decoration 24:84-6, Feb 1926
   Bookman 62:704-5, Feb 1926

Commonweal 3:189, Dec 23, 1925
Dial 80:168-9, Feb 1926
Drama 16:175-6, Feb 1926
Life (NY) 86:18, Dec 31, 1925
New Republic 45:160-1, Dec 30, 1925
New York Times p. 26, Dec 11, 1925
New Yorker 1:17, Dec 19, 1925
Theatre Arts 10:77, Feb 1926
Theatre Magazine 43:15, Feb 1926
Vanity Fair 25:118, Feb 1926
Vogue 67:60-61, Feb 1, 1926

Gold
  Productions:
    Opened June 1, 1921 for 13 performances.
  Reviews:
    Bookman 53:528-30, Aug 1921
    Dramatic Mirror 83:1001, Jun 11, 1921
    Dramatist 13:1095-7, Jan 1922
    Independent 105:633, Jun 18, 1921
    Life (NY) 77:876, Jun 16, 1921
    Nation 112:902, Jun 22, 1921
    New York Clipper 69:19, Jun 8, 1921
    New York Times p. 14, Jun 2, 1921
    Review 4:584-5, Jun 18, 1921
    Theatre Magazine 34:97, Aug 1921

Great God Brown
  Productions:
    Opened January 23, 1926 for 271 performances.
    Opened October 6, 1959 for 32 performances.
    Opened December 10, 1972 for 19 performances.
  Reviews:
    America 102:139-40, Oct 31, 1959
            127:570-1, Dec 30, 1972
    American Mercury 7:503-4, Apr 1926
    Arts and Decoration 24:62, Mar 1926
    Catholic World 122:805-7, Mar 1926
    Commonweal 3:384, Feb 10, 1926
    Drama 16:206, Mar 1926
    Dramatist 17:1307-9, Jul 1926
    Independent 116:275, Mar 6, 1926
    Life (NY) 87:20, Feb 11, 1926
    Nation 122:164-5, Feb 10, 1926
           189:259-60, Oct 24, 1959
           216:28, Jan 1, 1973
    New Republic 45:329-30, Feb 10, 1926
                 141:29, Oct 19, 1959
    New York Magazine 6:54, Jan 1, 1973
    New York Theatre Critics' Reviews 1959:282
                                      1972:147

New York Times p. 26, Jan 25, 1926
    VII, p. 1, Jan 31, 1926
    VIII, p. 2, Feb 14, 1926
    p. 25, Apr 20, 1926
    VII, p. 1, Jul 24, 1927
    IX, p. 1, Jun 28, 1936
    II, p. 1, Oct 4, 1959
    p. 48, Oct 7, 1959
    II, p. 1, Oct 18, 1959
    p. 51, Dec 11, 1972
    II, p. 3, Dec 17, 1972
New Yorker 1:26, Feb 6, 1926
   35:131-3, Oct 17, 1959
   48:86, Dec 16, 1972
Newsweek 54:80, Oct 19, 1959
   80:54, Dec 25, 1972
Survey 56:43, Apr 1, 1926
Theatre Arts 10:145-6, Mar 1926
   43:88, Dec 1959
Theatre Magazine 43:18, Apr 1926
   44:26+, Nov 1926
Time 74:56, Oct 19, 1959
   100:35, Dec 25, 1972
Vanity Fair 26:78, Apr 1926
Vogue 67:106+, Mar 15, 1926

The Hairy Ape
 Productions:
  Opened March 9, 1922 for 108+ performances.
  (Off Off Broadway) January 10, 1976 (IRT).
 Reviews:
  Bookman 55:284, May 1922
  Catholic World 116:714, Feb 1923
  Century 104:748-9+, Sep 1922
  Current Opinion 72:768-76, Jun 1922
  Dial 72:548-9, May 1922
  Dramatist 13:1117-8, Jul 1922
  Freeman 5:449, Jul 19, 1922
  Independent 110:282-4, Apr 28, 1923
  Life (NY) 79:18, Mar 30, 1922
  Literary Digest 77:35, Apr 7, 1923
  Living Age 337:417-18, Dec 1, 1929
  Nation 114:349-50, Mar 22, 1922
  New Republic 30:112-13, Mar 22, 1922
  New York Clipper 70:22, Mar 22, 1922
  New York Magazine 9:75, Mar 15, 1976
  New York Times p. 18, Mar 10, 1922
      VI, p. 1, Apr 16, 1922
      VI, p. 1, Apr 23, 1922
      VIII, p. 4, Feb 19, 1928
      p. 27, Sep 23, 1929

p. 29, May 12, 1931
p. 17, Jan 14, 1976
Theatre Arts 6:182, Jul 1922
18:598, Aug 1934
Theatre Magazine 35:305, May 1922
35:370, Jun 1922
36:80+, Aug 1922

Hughie
Productions:
Opened December 22, 1964 for 51 performances.
(Off Off Broadway) August 9, 1973 (Lolly's Theater Club).
(Off Off Broadway) November 9, 1973 (American Theater Co.).
Opened February 11, 1975 for 31 performances.
(Off Off Broadway) January 14, 1980 for 8 performances (Hudson Guild Theater).
(Off Off Broadway) November 4, 1981 (South St. Theater Co.).
Reviews:
America 132:219, Mar 22, 1975
Commonweal 70:187-8, May 15, 1959
81:518, Jan 15, 1965
Nation 200:65, Jan 18, 1965
220:314-15, Mar 15, 1975
New York Magazine 8:64+, Mar 3, 1975
New York Theatre Critics' Reviews 1964:99
1975:354
New York Times p. 36, Sep 18, 1958
p. 24, Sep 19, 1958
VII, p. 5, Apr 19, 1959
p. 48, Oct 15, 1959
p. 29, Jun 11, 1963
p. 21, Dec 23, 1964
p. 35, Apr 9, 1974
p. 40, Aug 18, 1974
p. 48, Feb 12, 1975
II, p. 1, Feb 23, 1975
p. 28, Mar 5, 1975
New Yorker 40:58, Jan 2, 1965
51:95, Feb 24, 1975
Newsweek 65:52, Jan 4, 1965
Saturday Review 41:27, Oct 4, 1958
48:40, Jan 16, 1965
Theatre Arts 43:14-15, Aug 1959
Time 85:53, Jan 1, 1965
103:84, Apr 22, 1974

The Iceman Cometh
Productions:
Opened October 9, 1946 for 136 performances.
(Off Broadway) Season of 1955-56.
Opened December 13, 1973 for 85 performances.

Reviews:
    America 95:251, Jun 2, 1956
    Arizona Quarterly 3:293-300, Winter 1947
    Atlantic 178:64-6, Nov 1946
    Catholic World 164:168-9, Nov 1946
            183:310, Jul 1956
    Commonweal 45:44-6, Oct 25, 1946
            64:515, Aug 24, 1956
    Life 21:109-11, Oct 28, 1946
    Nation 163:481, Oct 26, 1946
            182:458, May 26, 1956
            218:29-30, Jan 5, 1974
    New Republic 115:517-8, Oct 21, 1946
    New York Magazine 7:84, Dec 31/Jan 7, 1973-74
    New York Theatre Critics' Reviews 1946:315
                                       1973:148
    New York Times VI, p. 27, Sep 22, 1946
            p. 31, Oct 10, 1946
            II, p. 1, Oct 13, 1946
            VI, p. 22, Oct 13, 1946
            II, p. 1, Oct 20, 1946
            II, p. 1, Oct 27, 1946
            II, p. 1, Nov 10, 1946
            p. 35, Jun 9, 1948
            p. 38, May 9, 1956
            II, p. 1, May 20, 1956
            VI, p. 31, Nov 11, 1956
            p. 18, Jan 30, 1958
            II, p. 1, Oct 8, 1959
            p. 58, Apr 1, 1968
            p. 65, Apr 30, 1972
            p. 41, May 1, 1972
            II, p. 5, Dec 9, 1973
            p. 54, Dec 14, 1973
            II, p. 3, Dec 23, 1973
            II, p. 3, Dec 30, 1973
            II, p. 5, Jul 18, 1976
    New York Times Magazine pp. 22-3, Oct 13, 1946
    New Yorker 22:53-7, Oct 19, 1946
            32:72+, May 26, 1956
            49:56+, Dec 24, 1973
    Newsweek 28:92, Oct 21, 1946
    Reporter 14:35-6, Jun 28, 1956
    Saturday Review 29:26-8+, Oct 19, 1946
            39:24, May 26, 1956
    Theatre Arts 30:635-6, Nov 1946
            30:684+, Dec 1946
            31:31, Jun 1947
            40:72-3, Oct 1956
    Time 48:71-2+, Oct 21, 1946
            102:57, Dec 24, 1973

'Ile
Productions:
Opened April 18, 1918 in repertory (Greenwich Village Players).
Reviews:
Dramatist 10:960, Jul 1919
New York Times p. 13, Apr 19, 1918
                IV, p. 2, May 11, 1919
Theatre Magazine 27:356, Jun 1918
                35:270, Apr 1922

In the Zone (see S.S. Glencairn for other productions)
Productions:
Opened October 31, 1917 in repertory (Washington Square Players).
Reviews:
Commonweal 9:349, Jan 23, 1929
            48:185, Jun 4, 1948
Current Opinion 65:159-62, Sep 1918
New Republic 118:27-9, Jun 7, 1948
New York Times p. 13, Nov 1, 1917
                p. 31, Nov 4, 1924
                VII, p. 1, Dec 28, 1924
                p. 24, Jan 10, 1929
                IX, p. 1, Jan 27, 1929
                p. 23, Oct 30, 1937
                p. 21, May 21, 1948
                II, p. 1, May 30, 1948
New Yorker 24:43, May 29, 1948
School and Society 67:478, Jun 26, 1948
Theatre Arts 13:172, Mar 1929
            27:400, Jul 1943
Theatre Guild Magazine 9:12, Nov 1931
Theatre Magazine 26:352, Dec 1917
                40:22, Jan 1925
Time 4:14, Nov 17, 1924
See also reviews of Three Plays of the Sea

*Lazarus Laughed
Productions:
Opened April 9, 1928 in Pasadena, California for 28 performances.
Reviews:
Arts and Decoration 27:68-9, Sep 1927
Catholic World 167:264, Jun 1948
Commonweal 48:674, Apr 30, 1948
Drama 18:244-6, May 1928
Nation 126:19, Jan 4, 1928
New York Times VIII, p. 1, Sep 11, 1927
                p. 33, Apr 10, 1928
                IX, p. 2, Apr 22, 1928
                p. 19, Nov 19, 1928
Review of Reviews 78:439-40, Oct 1928

Theatre Arts 12:447-8, Jun 1928
Theatre Magazine 48:42-4, Jul 1928

Long Day's Journey into Night
Productions:
    Opened November 7, 1956 for 390 performances.
    Opened May 15, 1962 for 2 performances (Royal Dramatic The-
      atre of Sweden).
    (Off Broadway) April 21, 1971 for 121 performances.
    (Off Off Broadway) December 10, 1973 (Actors Studio).
    (Off Off Broadway) December 1974 (Hudson Guild Theater).
    (Off Broadway) January 28, 1976 for 11 performances.
    (Off Off Broadway) April 7, 1978 (AST).
    (Off Broadway) March 18, 1981 for 87 performances.
Reviews:
    America 95:141, May 5, 1956
            126:377-8, Apr 8, 1972
    Catholic World 184:306, Jan 1957
    Christian Century 74:235, Feb 20, 1957
    Commonweal 63:614-5, Mar 16, 1956
            64:515, Aug 24, 1956
            65:467-8, Feb 1, 1957
    Harper's 212:96, Mar 1956
    Life 40:93-4+, Mar 12, 1956
        41:123-4+, Nov 19, 1956
    Los Angeles 22:192, Apr 1977
    Maclean's 93:69, Oct 20, 1980
    Mademoiselle 44:186, Feb 1957
    Nation 183:466, Nov 24, 1956
         212:605-6, May 10, 1971
    New Republic 134:20, Mar 5, 1956
            164:26+, Jun 12, 1971
    New West 2:SC-19+, Mar 14, 1977
    New York Theatre Critics' Reviews 1956:217
                               1962:285
                               1971:266
                               1976:343
                               1981:270
    New York Times p. 26, Jan 5, 1956
                p. 12, Feb 11, 1956
                II, p. 1, Feb 19, 1956
                VI, p. 56, Feb 19, 1956
                VI, p. 28, Sep 16, 1956
                p. 40, Oct 17, 1956
                II, p. 1, Nov 4, 1956
                p. 47, Nov 8, 1956
                II, p. 1, Nov 18, 1956
                II, p. 3, Nov 25, 1956
                II, p. 1, Mar 1957
                p. 14, Jul 3, 1957
                p. 9, Jul 6, 1957

II, p. 1, Aug 11, 1957
p. 40, Sep 9, 1958
p. 21, Sep 26, 1958
p. 42, Mar 10, 1959
p. 30, Apr 29, 1959
p. 35, May 16, 1962
p. 85, Sep 30, 1962
p. 25, Jun 27, 1963
p. 67, May 21, 1971
p. 36, Apr 22, 1971
II, p. 3, May 2, 1971
II, p. 26, Jun 13, 1971
p. 16, Dec 23, 1971
p. 53, Sep 7, 1972
II, p. 3, Dec 10, 1972
II, p. 5, Dec 31, 1972
II, p. 5, Jan 25, 1976
p. 26, Jan 29, 1976
XXI, p. 4, Mar 2, 1980
III, p. 10, Mar 3, 1981
III, p. 24, May 27, 1981
New York Times Magazine p. 56, Feb 19, 1956
p. 74, Oct 21, 1956
New Yorker 32:120+, Nov 24, 1956
47:94+, May 1, 1971
51:78+, Feb 9, 1976
Newsweek 47:92, Feb 20, 1956
48:117, Nov 19, 1956
77:122, May 10, 1971
87:52-3, Feb 9, 1976
97:104, Apr 20, 1981
Reporter 15:38-9, Dec 13, 1956
Saturday Review 39:15-16, Feb 25, 1956
39:58, Oct 20, 1956
39:30-1, Nov 24, 1956
Theatre Arts 40:25+, Apr 1956
40:65, May 1956
41:25-6, Jan 1957
Time 67:89, Feb 20, 1956
68:57, Nov 19, 1956
97:62, May 3, 1971
100:76-7, Sep 18, 1972
Vogue 128:105, Nov 15, 1956

Long Voyage Home (see S.S. Glencairn for other productions)
Productions:
(Off Broadway) November 2, 1917 (Provincetown Players).
(Off Broadway) December 4, 1961 for 32 performances.
Reviews:
Commonweal 9:349, Jan 23, 1929
48:185, Jun 4, 1948

New Republic 118:27-9, Jun 7, 1948
New York Times p. 31, Nov 4, 1924
        VII, p. 1, Dec 28, 1924
        p. 24, Jan 10, 1929
        IX, p. 1, Jan 27, 1929
        p. 23, Oct 30, 1937
        p. 21, May 21, 1948
        II, p. 1, May 30, 1948
        p. 49, Dec 5, 1961
        p. 17, Jan 14, 1976
New Yorker 24:43, May 29, 1948
School and Society 67:478, Jun 26, 1948
Theatre Arts 13:172, Mar 1929
        27:400, Jul 1943
Theatre Guild Magazine 9:12, Nov 1931
Theatre Magazine 40:22, Jan 1925
Time 4:14, Nov 17, 1924

The Lost Works of Eugene O'Neill ("Abortion," "Movie Man," "Sniper")
Productions:
    (Off Broadway) Season of 1959-60.
Reviews:
    New York Times p. 40, Oct 28, 1959

Marco Millions
Productions:
    Opened January 9, 1928 for 92 performances.
    Opened March 3, 1930 for 8 performances.
    (Off Broadway) Season of 1938-39 (Marionette Production).
    Opened February 20, 1964 for 38 performances (Repertory Theatre of Lincoln Center).
Reviews:
    America 110:656, May 9, 1964
    American Mercury 8:499-505, Aug 1926
    Arts and Decoration 28:62, Mar 1928
    Commonweal 80:89, Apr 10, 1964
    Drama 18:170, Mar 1928
    Dramatist 18:1341-2, Jul 1927
    Life (NY) 91:19, Jan 26, 1928
    Literary Digest 96:26-7, Feb 4, 1928
    Motion Picture Classic 27:31+, Apr 1928
    Nation 124:562-4, May 18, 1927
            126:104-5, Jan 25, 1928
            124:562-4, May 18, 1927
            126:104-5, Jan 25, 1928
            198:249-50, Mar 9, 1964
    New Republic 53:272-3, Jan 25, 1928
    New York Theatre Critics' Reviews 1964:338
    New York Times VIII, p. 2, Jan 8, 1928
                 p. 28, Jan 10, 1928

VIII, p. 1, Jan 22, 1928
VIII, p. 2, Jan 22, 1928
IX, p. 2, Apr 29, 1928
p. 24, Mar 4, 1930
p. 36, Nov 24, 1938
IX, p. 3, Jan 15, 1939
II, p. 1, Feb 16, 1964
p. 33, Feb 21, 1964
II, p. 1, Mar 1, 1964
New Yorker 40:106+, Feb 29, 1964
Newsweek 63:56, Mar 2, 1965
Saturday Review 4:590, Feb 11, 1928
47:23, Mar 7, 1964
Theatre Arts 12:163-6, Mar 1928
23:175, Mar 1939
Theatre Magazine 47:38, Mar 1928
47:45, Apr 1928
52:49, Aug 1930
53:42, Feb 1931
Time 83:61, Feb 28, 1964
Vanity Fair 30:52-3, Apr 1928
Vogue 71:82-3, Mar 1, 1928
143:40, Apr 1, 1964
Yale Review 17:173-4, Oct 1927

A Moon for the Misbegotten
Productions:
Opened May 2, 1957 for 68 performances.
(Off Broadway) June 12, 1968 for 199 performances.
Opened December 29, 1973; recessed July 13, 1974.
Reopened September 3, 1974 for a total of 314 performances.
Reviews:
America 97:270, May 25, 1957
130:33, Jan 19, 1974
Catholic World 185:308-9, Jul 1957
Christian Century 74:657, May 22, 1957
Commonweal 66:541, Aug 30, 1957
88:504-5, Jul 26, 1968
Life 42:109-10+, Jun 24, 1957
Nation 178:409, May 8, 1954
184:446, May 18, 1957
218:92-3, Jan 19, 1974
New Republic 170:22+, Jan 26, 1974
New York Magazine 7:53, Jan 21, 1974
New York Theatre Critics' Reviews 1957:277
1973:118
New York Times p. 16, Feb 21, 1947
p. 29, Mar 12, 1947
II, p. 1, Aug 24, 1952
II, p. 1, Apr 28, 1957
p. 21, May 3, 1957

II, p. 1, May 12, 1957
p. 10, Jun 7, 1958
p. 14, Jan 22, 1960
p. 55, Jun 13, 1968
p. 22, Dec 31, 1973
II, p. 1, Jan 13, 1974
II, p. 7, Oct 20, 1974
III, p. 19, Jul 21, 1977
XXI, p. 11, Mar 25, 1979
XI, p. 23, Nov 23, 1980
XXII, p. 16, Mar 1, 1981
New Yorker 33:84+, May 11, 1957
49:58, Jan 14, 1974
Newsweek 49:70, May 13, 1957
83:83, Jan 14, 1974
Playboy 21:42+, Apr 1974
Saturday Review 40:34, May 18, 1957
51:40, Jun 29, 1968
Theatre Arts 36:6-7+, Sep 1952
41:67-8+, May 1957
41:12-3, Jul 1957
Time 49:47, Mar 3, 1947
69:91, May 13, 1957
91:67, Jun 21, 1968
103:42, Jan 14, 1974
Vogue 152:70, Sep 15, 1968

Moon of the Caribees   (see S.S. Glencairn for other productions)
Productions:
(Off Broadway) December 20, 1918 (Provincetown Players).
(Off Off Broadway) Season of 1974-75 (WPA Theater).
Reviews:
Commonweal 9:349, Jan 23, 1929
48:185, Jun 4, 1948
New Republic 118:27-9, Jun 7, 1948
New York Times p. 13, Dec 21, 1918
p. 31, Nov 4, 1924
VII, p. 1, Dec 28, 1924
p. 24, Jan 10, 1929
IX, p. 1, Jan 27, 1929
p. 23, Oct 30, 1937
p. 21, May 21, 1948
II, p. 1, May 30, 1948
New Yorker 24:43, May 29, 1948
School and Society 67:478, Jun 26, 1948
Theatre Arts 13:172, Mar 1929
27:400, Jul 1943
Theatre Guild Magazine 9:12, Nov 1931
Theatre Magazine 34:60, Jul 1921
40:22, Jan 1925
Time 4:14, Nov 17, 1924
See also reviews of Three Plays of the Sea

More Stately Mansions
  Productions:
    Opened October 31, 1967 for 142 performances.
  Reviews:
    America 117:622, Nov 18, 1967
    Commonweal 87:335-6, Dec 8, 1967
    Life 63:63-4, Oct 13, 1967
    Nation 205:538-40, Nov 20, 1967
    National Review 20:43-4, Jan 15, 1968
    New York Theatre Critics' Reviews 1967:230
                                      1967:234
    New York Times p. 1, Mar 18, 1957
                   p. 35, Mar 21, 1957
                   p. 16, Nov 10, 1962
                   p. 82, Nov 11, 1962
                   p. 41, Feb 23, 1967
                   p. 32, Feb 28, 1967
                   II, p. 1, Oct 29, 1967
                   p. 40, Nov 1, 1967
                   II, p. 1, Nov 12, 1967
    New Yorker 43:127, Nov 11, 1967
    Newsweek 70:125, Nov 13, 1967
    Reporter 37:34-5, Nov 30, 1967
    Saturday Review 45:26, Dec 1, 1962
                    47:46, May 30, 1964
                    50:26+, Nov 18, 1967
    Time 90:76-7, Sep 22, 1967
    Vogue 151:62, Jan 1, 1968

Mourning Becomes Electra
  Productions:
    Opened October 26, 1931 for 150 performances.
    Opened May 9, 1932 for 16 performances.
    Opened November 15, 1972 for 55 performances.
  Reviews:
    Arts and Decoration 36:52+, Jan 1932
    Bookman 73:440-5, Dec 1931
            75:290-1, Jun 1932
    Catholic World 134:330-1, Dec 1931
    Commonweal 15:46-7, Nov 11, 1931
               15:386, Feb 3, 1932
    Dramatist 23:1439-46, Jan 1932
    Life (NY) 98:19, Nov 13, 1931
    Literary Digest 111:18-19, Nov 21, 1931
    Living Age 342:276, May 1932
    Nation 133:551-2, Nov 18, 1931
           134:210-11, Feb 17, 1932
           215:572-3, Dec 4, 1972
    New Republic 68:352-5, Nov 11, 1931
    New York Theatre Critics' Reviews 1972:182
    New York Times p. 25, Sep 9, 1931

p. 26, Oct 13, 1931
p. 22, Oct 27, 1931
p. 16, Oct 31, 1931
VIII, p. 1, Nov 1, 1931
p. 25, May 10, 1932
VIII, p. 1, May 22, 1932
p. 26, Jun 14, 1932
XI, p. 3, Dec 12, 1937
X, p. 1, Jan 30, 1938
II, p. 1, Sep 7, 1969
p. 60, Jul 1, 1971
II, p. 1, Jul 18, 1971
p. 57, Nov 16, 1972
II, p. 1, Nov 26, 1972
New Yorker 48:111, Nov 25, 1972
Newsweek 80:78, Nov 27, 1972
Outlook 159:343, Nov 11, 1931
Player's Magazine 8:11, Jan-Feb 1932
Saturday Review 8:257-8, Nov 7, 1931
          54:33, Aug 7, 1971
          55:72, Dec 16, 1972
Theatre Arts 16:13-16, Jan 1932
          22:101-7, Feb 1938
Theatre Guild Magazine 9:14-19, Dec 1931
          9:2, Jan 1932
          9:10, Mar 1932
Time 100:73, Nov 27, 1972
Town and Country 86:46, Dec 1, 1931
Vanity Fair 37:24+, Jan 1932
          37:46-7+, Jan 1932
Vogue 79:56-7+, Jan 1, 1932

Movie Man   (see The Lost Works of Eugene O'Neill)

The Rope
    Productions:
        (Off Broadway) April 26, 1918 (Provincetown Players).
    Reviews:
        Dramatic Mirror 78:730, May 25, 1918
        New York Times p. 11, May 14, 1918
        Theatre Magazine 27:358, Jun 1918

S.S. Glencairn ("Moon of the Caribees," "In the Zone," "Bound East
    for Cardiff," "Long Voyage Home")
    Productions:
        Opened November 3, 1924 for 105 performances.
        Opened January 9, 1929 for 90 performances.
        Opened October 29, 1937 for 68 performances (WPA Federal
            Theatre Project).
        Opened May 20, 1948 for 14 performances.

Reviews:
  Commonweal 9:349, Jan 23, 1929
            48:185, Jun 4, 1948
  New Republic 118:27-9, Jun 7, 1948
  New York Times p. 31, Nov 4, 1924
              VII, p. 1, Dec 28, 1924
              p. 24, Jan 10, 1929
              IX, p. 1, Jan 27, 1929
              p. 23, Oct 30, 1937
              p. 21, May 21, 1948
              II, p. 1, May 30, 1948
  New Yorker 24:43, May 29, 1948
  School and Society 67:478, Jun 26, 1948
  Theatre Arts 13:172, Mar 1929
             27:400, Jul 1943
  Theatre Guild Magazine 9:12, Nov 1931
  Theatre Magazine 40:22, Jan 1925
  Time 4:14, Nov 17, 1924

Sniper (see The Lost Works of Eugene O'Neill)

Strange Interlude
  Productions:
    Opened January 30, 1928 for 426 performances.
    Opened March 11, 1963 for 97 performances.
  Reviews:
    America 108:594, Apr 20, 1963
    American Mercury 11:499-506, Aug 1927
    Arts and Decoration 28:65, Apr 1928
    Catholic World 127:77-80, Apr 1928
    Commonweal 78:72-3, Apr 12, 1963
    Dial 84:348-51, Apr 1928
    Drama 18:170-71, Mar 1928
          19:174, Mar 1929
    Dramatist 19:1356-8, Jan 1928
    Life (NY) 91:21, Feb 16, 1928
    Literary Digest 96:26-7, Feb 25, 1928
              103:19-20, Oct 19, 1929
    Nation 126:192, Feb 15, 1928
        196:274-5, Mar 30, 1963
    New Republic 53:349-50, Feb 15, 1928
              148:28-9, Mar 30, 1963
    New York Theatre Critics' Reviews 1963:317
    New York Times p. 28, Jan 31, 1928
              VIII, p. 1, Feb 5, 1928
              p. 24, Apr 30, 1928
              IX, p. 1, May 13, 1928
              IV, p. 4, May 20, 1928
              p. 29, Jun 27, 1928
              IX, p. 1, Jan 27, 1929
              p. 18, Jan 30, 1929

p. 14, Apr 6, 1929
IX, p. 2, Oct 13, 1929
p. 1, Oct 18, 1929
III, p. 2, Nov 3, 1929
VIII, p. 1, Feb 22, 1931
VIII, p. 4, Mar 29, 1931
p. 19, Jan 5, 1937
p. 5, Mar 13, 1963
p. 34, Jun 18, 1963
New Yorker 39:73, Mar 23, 1963
Newsweek 61:97, Mar 25, 1963
Outlook 148:304-5, Feb 22, 1928
Overland ns 87:220, Jul 1929
Saturday Review 4:590, Feb 11, 1928
4:641, Mar 3, 1928
4:357-8, Sep 22, 1928
46:36, Mar 30, 1963
Theatre Arts 12:237-40, Apr 1928
15:286-9, Apr 1931
47:12-13, May 1963
Theatre Magazine 47:39, Apr 1928
53:25, Apr 1931
Time 81:74, Mar 22, 1963
Vanity Fair 30:52-3, Apr 1928
Virginia Quarterly Review 5:133-6, Jan 1929
Vogue 71:82-3+, Apr 1, 1928
72:62, Jul 1, 1928

The Straw
  Productions:
    Opened November 10, 1921 for 20 performances.
  Reviews:
    Bookman 54:463-4, Jan 1922
    Drama 12:152, Feb 1922
    Dramatic Mirror 84:737, Nov 19, 1921
    Independent 107:236, Dec 3, 1921
    Life (NY) 78:18, Dec 8, 1921
    Nation 113:626, Nov 30, 1921
    New York Clipper 69:20, Nov 16, 1921
    New York Times VI, p. 1, May 8, 1921
    p. 16, Nov 11, 1921
    Theatre Arts 6:6, Jan 1922
    Theatre Magazine 35:31, Jan 1922

Three Plays of the Sea (Consists of Moon of the Caribees, In the
    Zone, and Bound East for Cardiff)
  Productions:
    (Off Off Broadway) Season of 1970-71 (Masterworks Labora-
      tory Theater).
  Reviews:
    New York Times p. 39, Aug 20, 1970
    See also individual entries

A Touch of the Poet
    Productions:
        Opened October 2, 1958 for 284 performances.
        Opened May 2, 1967 for 5 performances (National Repertory
            Theatre).
        (Off Off Broadway) Season of 1971-72 (Workshop of the Play-
            er's Art).
        (Off Off Broadway) Season of 1974-75 (Manhattan Theater Club).
        (Off Off Broadway) February 17, 1976 (York Players).
        (Off Off Broadway) November 1976 (Irish Rebel Theater).
        Opened December 28, 1977 for 141 performances.
    Reviews:
        America 100:118, Oct 25, 1958
        Catholic World 188:243-4, Dec 1958
        Christian Century 75:252-4, Feb 26, 1958
                          75:1401-2, Dec 3, 1958
        Commonweal 69:151-3, Nov 7, 1958
        Life 42:116, Jun 24, 1957
        Nation 187:298-9, Oct 25, 1958
               226:60-1, Jan 21, 1978
        New Leader 61:25-6, Jan 30, 1978
        New Republic 136:21, Jun 3, 1957
                     139:23, Oct 20, 1958
                     178:24-5, Jan 28, 1978
        New York Magazine 11:57-8, Jan 16, 1978
        New York Theatre Critics' Reviews 1958:282
                                          1967:305
                                          1977:97
        New York Times p. 12, Mar 30, 1957
                       II, p. 3, Apr 7, 1957
                       II, p. 1, Sep 22, 1957
                       VII, p. 1, Sep 22, 1957
                       p. 23, Oct 3, 1958
                       II, p. 1, Oct 12, 1958
                       p. 85, Sep 30, 1962
                       p. 38, May 3, 1967
                       p. 36, Sep 24, 1971
                       p. 53, Mar 31, 1974
                       II, p. 2, Dec 25, 1977
                       III, p. 13, Dec 29, 1977
                       II, p. 5, Jan 8, 1978
        New York Times Magazine p. 49, Apr 28, 1957
        New Yorker 34:87, Oct 11, 1958
                   53:59, Jan 9, 1978
        Newsweek 49:66, Apr 8, 1957
                 52:112, Oct 13, 1958
                 91:71, Jan 9, 1978
        Reporter 19:37-8, Nov 13, 1958
        Saturday Review 40:24, Apr 13, 1957
                        40:21+, Sep 21, 1957
                        41:56, Oct 18, 1958
                        5:41, Mar 4, 1978

Theatre Arts 42:16-17+, Oct 1958
42:9-10, Dec 1958
Time 69:77, Apr 8, 1957
70:102+, Sep 30, 1957
72:89, Oct 13, 1958
111:68, Jan 9, 1978
Vogue 132:105, Nov 15, 1958

Welded
Productions:
Opened March 17, 1924 for 24 performances.
(Off Off Broadway) June 13, 1981 (Horace Mann Theater).
Reviews:
American Mercury 2:115-16, May 1924
Bookman 59:332, May 1924
Dramatist 15:1208-10, Apr 1924
Life (NY) 83:26, Apr 3, 1924
Nation 118:376-7, Apr 2, 1924
New York Magazine 14:39, Jun 29, 1981
New York Times VIII, p. 2, Mar 9, 1924
p. 24, Mar 18, 1924
VIII, p. 1, Mar 23, 1924
VIII, p. 2, Mar 23, 1924
p. 17, Mar 13, 1965
II, p. 5, Jun 7, 1981
III, p. 22, Jun 18, 1981
Outlook 137:238, Jun 11, 1924
Theatre Arts 8:497-8, Jul 1924
Theatre Magazine 39:16, May 1924

Where the Cross Is Made
Productions:
(Off Broadway) November 22, 1918 (Provincetown Players).
Reviews:
New York Times I, part 2, p. 5, Jun 3, 1923

OSBORN, PAUL

A Bell for Adano (Based on John Hersey's novel)
Productions:
Opened December 6, 1944 for 304 performances.
Reviews:
Catholic World 160:356, Jan 1945
Commonweal 41:254, Dec 22, 1944
Hollywood Quarterly 1:38-9, Oct 1945
Life 17:76-80+, Dec 18, 1944
Nation 159:781, Dec 23, 1944
161:67, Jul 21, 1945
New Republic 111:867, Dec 25, 1944
New York Theatre Critics' Reviews 1944:65

New York Times p. 24, Nov 10, 1944
　　　　　VI, p. 42, Nov 26, 1944
　　　　　II, p. 1, Dec 3, 1944
　　　　　p. 21, Dec 7, 1944
　　　　　p. 24, Dec 28, 1944
　　　　　p. 31, Sep 20, 1945
New Yorker 20:40+, Dec 16, 1944
Newsweek 24:78, Dec 18, 1944
　　　　　26:101, Jul 16, 1945
Photoplay 27:19, Aug 1945
Saturday Review 27:18-19, Dec 23, 1944
Theatre Arts 29:69-72+, Feb 1945
　　　　　29:583, Oct 1945
Time 44:75+, Dec 18, 1944
　　　　　46:86, Jul 2, 1945

Hotbed
　Productions:
　　Opened November 8, 1928 for 19 performances.
　Reviews:
　　New York Times p. 20, Nov 10, 1928
　　Theatre Magazine 49:46, Jan 1929

The Innocent Voyage (Adapted from a novel by Richard Hughes)
　Productions:
　　Opened November 15, 1943 for 40 performances.
　Reviews:
　　Catholic World 158:393-4, Jan 1944
　　Commonweal 39:172+, Dec 3, 1943
　　Nation 157:620, Nov 27, 1943
　　New Republic 109:746, Nov 29, 1943
　　New York Theatre Critics' Reviews 1943:224
　　New York Times p. 27, Nov 16, 1943
　　Player's Magazine 20:13, Jan 1944
　　　　　23:back cover, Nov-Dec 1946
　　　　　24:191, May 1948
　　Publishers' Weekly 144:2176, Dec 11, 1943
　　Theatre Arts 28:10+, Jan 1944
　　Time 42:42, Dec 6, 1943
　　Vogue 102:32-3, Dec 15, 1943

A Ledge (Suggested by Henry Holt's short story)
　Productions:
　　Opened November 18, 1929 for 16 performances.
　Reviews:
　　New York Times p. 26, Nov 19, 1929

*Maiden Voyage
　Reviews:
　　New York Times p. 15, Mar 9, 1957
　　　　　II, p. 1, Mar 10, 1957

Morning's at Seven
    Productions:
        Opened November 30, 1939 for 44 performances.
        (Off Broadway) Season of 1955-56.
        (Off Off Broadway) November 6, 1975 (Theater of the River-
            side Church).
        (Off Off Broadway) February 11, 1976 (Joseph Jefferson).
        Opened April 10, 1980 for 564 performances.
    Reviews:
        Catholic World 150:468-9, Jan 1940
                       181:64, Oct 1955
        Commonweal 31:186, Dec 15, 1939
                   62:469, Aug 12, 1955
                   107:335-6, Jun 6, 1980
        Nation 149:686+, Dec 16, 1939
               230:540, May 3, 1980
        New York Magazine 13:78, Apr 21, 1980
        New York Theatre Critics' Reviews 1940:445
                                          1980:286
        New York Times p. 30, Nov 7, 1939
                       IX, p. 1, Nov 12, 1939
                       p. 26, Dec 1, 1939
                       X, p. 5, Dec 10, 1939
                       IX, p. 3, Dec 17, 1939
                       p. 25, Jun 23, 1955
                       III, p. 3, Apr 11, 1980
                       II, p. 1, Jul 6, 1980
                       III, p. 5, Sep 12, 1980
        New Yorker 56:77, Apr 21, 1980
        Newsweek 95:112, Apr 21, 1980
        Theatre Arts 24:88+, Feb 1940
                     39:80, Oct 1955
        Time 34:48, Dec 11, 1939
             115:84, Apr 21, 1980

Oliver Oliver
    Productions:
        Opened January 5, 1934 for 11 performances.
    Reviews:
        New York Times p. 8, Jan 6, 1934
        Newsweek 3:35, Jan 13, 1934
        Stage 11:30, Feb 1934

On Borrowed Time (Based on the novel by Lawrence Edward Watkin)
    Productions:
        Opened February 3, 1938 for 321 performances.
        Opened February 10, 1953 for 78 performances.
    Reviews:
        Catholic World 146:727-8, Mar 1938
                       177:70, Apr 1953
        Commonweal 27:468, Feb 18, 1938
                   57:552, Mar 6, 1953

Life 4:39, Mar 28, 1938
Nation 146:225, Feb 19, 1938
    176:192, Feb 28, 1953
New Republic 94:74, Feb 28, 1953
New York Theatre Critics' Reviews 1953:365
New York Times p. 16, Feb 4, 1938
        X, p. 3, Feb 13, 1938
        p. 27, Oct 6, 1938
        IX, p. 1, Nov 6, 1938
        IX, p. 3, Nov 13, 1938
        p. 19, Jan 1, 1953
        p. 34, Feb 11, 1953
        p. 20, Feb 24, 1953
New Yorker 29:61, Feb 21, 1953
Newsweek 41:62, Feb 23, 1953
One Act Play Magazine 1:949, Feb 1938
Saturday Review 36:37, Feb 28, 1953
Stage 15:10, Jun 1938
Theatre Arts 22:180, Mar 1938
Time 31:36, Feb 14, 1938
    61:86, Feb 23, 1953
Vogue 91:108+, Mar 15, 1938

Point of No Return (Based on the novel by John P. Marquand)
    Productions:
        Opened December 13, 1951 for 364 performances.
        (Off Broadway) Season of 1956-57.
    Reviews:
        Catholic World 174:391, Feb 1952
        Commonweal 55:325, Jan 4, 1952
        Life 32:59-60+, Jan 7, 1952
        Nation 173:574, Dec 29, 1951
        New Republic 126:22-3, Jan 7, 1952
        New York Theatre Critics' Reviews 1951:140
        New York Times p. 32, Oct 31, 1951
                p. 84, Dec 2, 1951
                VI, p. 24, Dec 9, 1951
                p. 35, Dec 14, 1951
                II, p. 3, Dec 23, 1951
                p. 38, May 6, 1953
                p. 17, Mar 23, 1957
        New Yorker 27:47, Dec 22, 1951
        Newsweek 38:43, Dec 24, 1951
        Saturday Review 35:24-5, Jan 5, 1952
                     35:22, Jan 26, 1952
        Theatre Arts 36:73, Feb 1952
                37:31-3, Mar 1953
        Time 58:44, Dec 24, 1951

*Tomorrow's Monday
    Reviews:
        New York Times p. 15, Jul 16, 1936

The Vinegar Tree
  Productions:
    Opened November 19, 1930 for 229 performances.
  Reviews:
    Bookman 73:70, Mar 1931
    Catholic World 132:461, Jan 1931
    Drama Magazine 21:14, Feb 1931
    Life (NY) 96:18-19, Dec 12, 1930
    Nation 131:658, Dec 10, 1930
    National Magazine 59:172, Jan 1931
    New York Times p. 30, Nov 20, 1930
                   p. 9, May 30, 1931
                   VIII, p. 4, Nov 15, 1931
                   p. 16, Aug 14, 1935
    Theatre Arts 16:715, Sep 1932
    Theatre Magazine 53:25, Jan 1931
    Vogue 77:98, Jan 15, 1931

The World of Suzie Wong (Based on Richard Mason's novel)
  Productions:
    Opened October 14, 1958 for 508 performances.
  Reviews:
    Catholic World 188:246, Dec 1958
    Commonweal 69:272, Dec 12, 1958
    Life 45:95-6, Oct 6, 1958
    Nation 188:76, Jan 24, 1959
    New Republic 139:22, Oct 27, 1958
    New York Theatre Critics' Reviews 1958:266
    New York Times II, p. 3, Oct 12, 1958
                   p. 47, Oct 15, 1958
                   p. 74, Oct 16, 1958
                   II, p. 1, Oct 19, 1958
                   p. 49, Nov 18, 1959
    New Yorker 34:88+, Oct 25, 1958
    Newsweek 52:64, Oct 27, 1958
    Reporter 19:37-8, Nov 13, 1958
    Saturday Review 41:28, Nov 1, 1958
    Theatre Arts 42:10-11, Dec 1948
    Time 72:84, Oct 27, 1958
    Vogue 132:105, Nov 15, 1958

PARKER, DOROTHY

Close Harmony (with Elmer Rice)
  Productions:
    Opened December 1, 1924 for 24 performances.
  Reviews:
    Life (NY) 84:18, Dec 18, 1924
    Nation 119:686-7, Dec 17, 1924
    New York Times p. 23, Dec 2, 1924

Here We Are
  Productions:
    (Off Off Broadway) November 9, 1973 (American Theater Co.).
  No Reviews.

Into Love and Out Again
  Productions:
    (Off Off Broadway) October 10, 1975 (Drama Tree).
  No Reviews.

The Ladies of the Corridor (with Arnaud d'Usseau)
  Productions:
    Opened October 21, 1953 for 45 performances.
  Reviews:
    America 90:157, Nov 7, 1953
    Catholic World 178:230-1, Dec 1953
    Commonweal 59:197-8, Nov 27, 1953
    Nation 177:378, Nov 7, 1953
    New Republic 129:21, Nov 9, 1953
    New York Theatre Critics' Reviews 1953:244
    New York Times II, p. 1, Oct 18, 1953
                    VI, p. 65, Oct 18, 1953
                    p. 33, Oct 22, 1953
                    II, p. 1, Nov 1, 1953
    New Yorker 29:58-60, Oct 31, 1953
    Newsweek 42:65, Nov 2, 1953
    Saturday Review 36:32, Nov 7, 1953
                    36:47, Dec 12, 1953
    Theatre Arts 38:20, Jan 1954
    Time 62:82, Nov 2, 1953

PATRICK, JOHN

The Curious Savage
  Productions:
    Opened October 24, 1950 for 31 performances.
    (Off Off Broadway) October 17, 1976 (Malachy Co.).
  Reviews:
    Catholic World 172:227, Dec 1950
    Christian Science Monitor Magazine p. 8, Oct 28, 1950
    Commonweal 53:121, Nov 10, 1950
    Nation 171:418, Nov 4, 1950
    New Republic 123:21, Nov 13, 1950
    New York Theatre Critics' Reviews 1950:230
    New York Times p. 44, Oct 25, 1950
                   p. 17, May 29, 1953
                   p. 12, Mar 17, 1956
    New Yorker 26:76+, Nov 4, 1950
    Newsweek 36:88, Nov 6, 1950
    Theatre Arts 34:17, Dec 1950
    Time 56:57, Nov 6, 1950

Everybody Loves Opal
    Productions:
        Opened October 11, 1961 for 21 performances.
    Reviews:
        America 106:132, Oct 28, 1961
        New York Theatre Critics' Reviews 1961:234
        New York Times p. 40, Oct 12, 1961
        New Yorker 37:131, Oct 21, 1961
        Theatre Arts 45:70, Dec 1961
        Time 78:64, Oct 20, 1961

Good As Gold (Based on Alfred Toombs' novel)
    Productions:
        Opened March 7, 1957 for 4 performances.
    Reviews:
        Nation 184:262, Mar 23, 1957
        New York Theatre Critics' Reviews 1957:321
        New York Times p. 22, Mar 8, 1957
        New Yorker 33:79, Mar 16, 1957
        Saturday Review 40:24, Mar 23, 1957
                        40:7-8, Apr 6, 1957
        Theatre Arts 41:19, May 1957

The Hasty Heart
    Productions:
        Opened January 3, 1945 for 207 performances.
        (Off Broadway) Season of 1953-54.
        (Off Broadway) Season of 1959-60.
    Reviews:
        Catholic World 160:452-3, Feb 1945
        Commonweal 41:396, Feb 2, 1945
        Life 18:103-4, Feb 5, 1945
        Los Angeles 27:238, Jun 1982
        Nation 160:81, Jan 20, 1945
        New Republic 112:118, Jan 22, 1945
        New York Theatre Critics' Reviews 1945:298
        New York Times p. 14, Jan 4, 1945
                        II, p. 1, Jan 14, 1945
                        p. 10, Mar 13, 1954
                        p. 45, Sep 15, 1959
        New Yorker 20:38, Jan 13, 1945
        Newsweek 25:78, Jan 15, 1945
        Player's Magazine 22:10+, Nov-Dec 1945
                        23:23, Sep-Oct 1946
        Saturday Review 28:26-7, Mar 3, 1945
        Theatre Arts 29:138+, Mar 1945
        Time 45:55, Jan 15, 1945

Hell Freezes Over
    Productions:
        Opened December 28, 1935 for 25 performances.

Reviews:
Catholic World 142:602, Feb 1936
New York Times p. 14, Dec 30, 1935
Time 27:24, Jan 6, 1936

Lo and Behold
Productions:
Opened December 12, 1951 for 38 performances.
Reviews:
Catholic World 174:392-3, Feb 1952
Commonweal 55:300, Dec 28, 1951
Nation 173:574, Dec 29, 1951
New Republic 126:22, Jan 7, 1952
New York Theatre Critics' Reviews 1951:143
New York Times p. 45, Dec 13, 1951
New Yorker 27:48-9, Dec 22, 1951
Newsweek 38:43, Dec 24, 1951
Theatre Arts 36:73, Feb 1952
Time 58:44, Dec 24, 1951

Love Is a Time of Day
Productions:
Opened December 22, 1969 for 8 performances.
Reviews:
New York Theatre Critics' Reviews 1969:148
New York Times p. 21, Dec 23, 1969
II, p. 5, Jan 4, 1970

The Story of Mary Surratt
Productions:
Opened February 8, 1947 for 11 performances.
(Off Broadway) December 9, 1961 for 9 performances (Equity
Library Theater).
Reviews:
Catholic World 164:551, Mar 1947
Commonweal 45:491, Feb 28, 1947
Nation 164:226-7, Feb 22, 1947
New Republic 116:40, Feb 24, 1947
New York Theatre Critics' Reviews 1947:461
New York Times II, p. 1, Feb 2, 1947
p. 25, Feb 10, 1947
New Yorker 22:50-1, Feb 15, 1947
Newsweek 29:88, Feb 17, 1947
Theatre Arts 31:20, Apr 1947
Time 49:53, Feb 17, 1947

The Teahouse of the August Moon (Based on Vern Sneider's novel)
Productions:
Opened October 15, 1953 for 1,027 performances.
Opened November 8, 1956 for 14 performances.
Reviews:

America 90:186, Nov 14, 1953
Catholic World 178:228-9, Dec 1953
          184:306, Jan 1956
Commonweal 59:163, Nov 20, 1953
Life 35:129-30+, Nov 2, 1953
     36:101-2+, Jun 14, 1954
Nation 177:357-8, Oct 31, 1953
       178:429-30, May 15, 1954
New Republic 129:21, Oct 26, 1953
             130:28, May 17, 1954
New York Theatre Critics' Reviews 1953:254
                                  1956:214
New York Times II, p. 1, Oct 11, 1953
               p. 32, Oct 16, 1953
               II, p. 1, Oct 25, 1953
               VI, p. 17, Nov 15, 1953
               II, p. 3, Dec 20, 1953
               p. 30, Mar 10, 1954
               p. 23, Apr 23, 1954
               II, p. 3, May 2, 1954
               p. 37, May 20, 1954
               II, p. 1, Sep 12, 1954
               p. 13, Sep 18, 1954
               p. 13, Dec 18, 1954
               p. 22, Feb 17, 1955
               p. 35, Mar 22, 1955
               p. 24, May 10, 1955
               p. 60, Aug 7, 1955
               II, p. 1, Aug 14, 1955
               p. 32, May 29, 1956
               p. 25, Jun 4, 1956
               p. 33, Nov 9, 1956
New Yorker 29:66+, Oct 24, 1953
Newsweek 42:60, Dec 21, 1953
         42:92, Oct 26, 1953
Saturday Review 36:29, Oct 31, 1953
                36:45, Dec 12, 1953
Theatre Arts 37:22-4, Dec 1953
             39:32-3, Jun 1955
             41:31-2, Jan 1957
Time 62:72, Oct 26, 1953

The Willow and I
  Productions:
    Opened December 10, 1942 for 28 performances.
  Reviews:
    Commonweal 37:256, Dec 25, 1942
    Nation 156:32, Jan 2, 1943
    New York Theatre Critics' Reviews 1942:144
    New York Times p. 32, Dec 11, 1942
    New Yorker 18:37, Dec 19, 1942
    Theatre Arts 27:76-7, Feb 1943

PAYNE, JOHN HOWARD

Charles the Second; or, the Merry Monarch (with Washington Irving)
Productions:
(Off Off Broadway) March 26, 1977 (Stage Directors).
(Off Off Broadway) September 15, 1977 (Classic Theater).
No Reviews.

Love in Humble Life
Productions:
Opened March 9, 1937 in repertory (Federal Theatre Project).
Reviews:
New York Times p. 27, Mar 10, 1937

PETERSEN, LOUIS

Entertain a Ghost
Productions:
(Off Broadway) April 9, 1962 for 8 performances.
Reviews:
New York Times p. 48, Apr 10, 1962

Take a Giant Step
Productions:
Opened September 24, 1953 for 76 performances.
(Off Broadway) Season of 1956-1957.
(Off Off Broadway) November 30, 1978 (New Fed Th).
Reviews:
America 90:81, Oct 17, 1953
        96:56, Oct 13, 1956
Catholic World 178:148, Nov 1953
Commonweal 59:38, Oct 16, 1953
Nation 177:298, Oct 10, 1953
New York Theatre Critics' Reviews 1953:274
New York Times II, p. 1, Sep 20, 1953
              p. 16, Sep 25, 1953
              II, p. 1, Oct 4, 1953
              p. 30, Sep 26, 1956
              VI, p. 31, Nov 11, 1956
New Yorker 29:79, Oct 3, 1953
Newsweek 42:54, Oct 5, 1953
Saturday Review 36:33, Oct 10, 1953
              36:47, Dec 12, 1953
Theatre Arts 37:24, Nov 1953
Time 62:78, Oct 5, 1953

PIELMEIER, JOHN

Agnes of God
Productions:

Opened March 30, 1982 for 64+ performances (still running on
June 1, 1982).
Reviews:
America 146:382, May 15, 1982
New Leader 65:20, Apr 19, 1982
New York Magazine 15:71-2, Apr 12, 1982
New York Theatre Critics' Reviews 1982:321
New York Times III, p. 23, Mar 31, 1982
II, p. 3, Apr 11, 1982
New Yorker 58:125-6, Apr 12, 1982

Jass
Productions:
(Off Off Broadway) May 8-18, 1980 (Actors Studio).
(Off Off Broadway) June 24, 1981 (The New Dramatists).
No Reviews.

PINERO, MIGUEL

All Junkies
Productions:
(Off Broadway) August and September 1972 (Lincoln Center
Community Street Theater Festival).
Reviews:
New York Times p. 42, Aug 30, 1972

Eulogy for a Small-Time Thief
Productions:
(Off Off Broadway) November 7, 1977 for 16 performances
(Ensemble Studio Theater).
Reviews:
New York Times p. 41, Nov 28, 1977

The Guntower
Productions:
(Off Off Broadway) August 26, 1976 (Nuyorican Poets' Cafe).
No Reviews.

A Midnight Moon at the Greasy Spoon
Productions:
(Off Off Broadway) April 16, 1981 for 12 performances (The-
ater for the New City).
Reviews:
Los Angeles 22:191+, Apr 1977
New York Times III, p. 20, Apr 27, 1981

Short Eyes
Productions:
(Off Off Broadway) January 3, 1974 (Theater of the Riverside
Church).

(Off Broadway) February 1974 for 54 performances.
Opened May 23, 1974 for 156 performances.
Reviews:
America 130:457, Jun 8, 1974
Nation 218:445, Apr 6, 1974
National Review 26:764-5, Jul 5, 1974
New Republic 170:20, Apr 20, 1974
New York Magazine 7:74, Apr 1, 1974
                   7:76, Jun 10, 1974
New York Theatre Critics' Reviews 1974:258
New York Times p. 24, Jan 8, 1974
               p. 45, Mar 14, 1974
               II, p. 1, Mar 24, 1974
               II, p. 9, May 19, 1974
               p. 21, May 24, 1974
               p. 15, Aug 2, 1974
New Yorker 50:170, Mar 25, 1974
           50:68, Jun 3, 1974
Newsweek 83:81, Apr 8, 1974
Playboy 21:40, Jul 1974
Saturday Review 1:47, Jul 13, 1974

Straight from the Ghetto (with Neil Harris)
  Productions:
    (Off Off Broadway) January 10, 1977 (Theater for the New
      City).
    (Off Off Broadway) February 1977 (The Family).
  Reviews:
    New York Times III, p. 3, Jan 14, 1977

The Sun Always Shines for the Cool
  Productions:
    (Off Off Broadway) December 9, 1975 (New York Shakespeare
      Festival Public Theater).
    (Off Off Broadway) September 20, 1979 (78th St. Theater Lab).
  Reviews:
    Encore 8:36-7, Oct 1, 1979
    New York Times III, p. 5, Sep 28, 1979

POLLOCK, CHANNING

The Crowded Hour (see entry under Selwyn, Edgar)

The Enemy
  Productions:
    Opened October 20, 1925 for 203 performances.
  Reviews:
    Dramatist 17:1290-91, Jan 1926
    Nation 121:696, Dec 16, 1925
    New York Times p. 20, Oct 21, 1925

VII, p. 4, Oct 25, 1925
p. 27, Mar 3, 1926
VII, p. 1, Aug 19, 1928
Theatre Magazine 42:18-19, Dec 1925
43:26+, Mar 1926
Woman Citizen 10:20, Dec 1925

The Fool
Productions:
Opened October 23, 1922 for 272+ performances.
Reviews:
Bookman 58:60-61, Sep 1923
Dramatist 14:1155-6, Apr 1923
Everybody's 48:120-26, Mar 1923
Hearst 43:93-5+, Mar 1923
Life (NY) 80:18, Nov 9, 1922
New York Clipper 70:20, Nov 1, 1922
New York Times p. 18, Oct 24, 1922
VII, p. 1, Oct 29, 1922
VII, p. 1, Nov 19, 1922
Theatre Magazine 37:28+, Mar 1923

The House Beautiful
Productions:
Opened March 12, 1931 for 108 performances.
Reviews:
Arts and Decoration 35:88, May 1931
Catholic World 133:206, May 1931
Commonweal 13:610, Apr 1, 1931
Drama 21:10, May 1931
Life (NY) 97:23, Apr 3, 1931
Nation 132:360-1, Apr 1, 1931
New York Times p. 20, Mar 13, 1931
VIII, p. 1, Mar 22, 1931
VIII, p. 2, Mar 22, 1931
Theatre Arts 15:371-2, May 1931
Vogue 77:76-7+, May 15, 1931

Mr. Moneypenny
Productions:
Opened October 17, 1928 for 61 performances.
Reviews:
Catholic World 128:336-7, Dec 1928
New York Times p. 26, Oct 17, 1928
IX, p. 5, Oct 21, 1928
p. 1, Oct 28, 1928
Theatre Magazine 48:45-6, Dec 1928
Vogue 72:162, Dec 8, 1928

A Perfect Lady (with Rennold Wolf)
Productions:

Opened October 28, 1914 for 21 performances.
Reviews:
    Dramatic Mirror 72:9, Nov 4, 1914
    Dramatist 6:534-5, Jan 1915
    Green Book 13:121, Jan 1915
    Munsey 54:94, Feb 1915
    Nation 99:561, Nov 4, 1915
    New York Times p. 11, Oct 29, 1914
    Theatre Magazine 20:266-7, Dec 1914

Roads of Destiny (Suggested by O. Henry's story)
    Productions:
    Opened November 27, 1918 for 101 performances.
    Reviews:
    Dramatic Mirror 79:865, Dec 14, 1918
    Hearst 35:46-7+, Feb 1919
    New York Times p. 15, Nov 28, 1918
                    VII, p. 8, Dec 1, 1918
    Theatre Magazine 29:15+, Jan 1919

The Sign on the Door
    Productions:
    Opened December 19, 1919 for 187 performances.
    Reviews:
    Dramatic Mirror 81:2023, Jan 1, 1920
    Dramatist 11:1007-8, Jul 1920
    Forum 63:244-5, Feb 1920
    New York Times p. 14, Dec 20, 1919
                    IX, p. 2, Jan 4, 1920
    Theatre Magazine 31:99+, Feb 1920

Such a Little Queen
    Productions:
    Opened August 31, 1909 for 103 performances.
    Reviews:
    Collier's 44:23-4, Nov 6, 1909
    Current Literature 47:543-50, Nov 1909
    Dramatic Mirror 62:5, Sep 11, 1909
    Forum 42:361-2, Oct 1909
    Green Book 3:257-95, Feb 1910
    Hampton 23:693+, Nov 1909
    Harper's World 53:24, Oct 30, 1909
    Leslies' Weekly 109:274, Sep 16, 1909
    Life (NY) 54:379, Sep 16, 1909
    Metropolitan Magazine 31:262-3, Nov 1909
    Pearson 22:663-4, Nov 1909
    Theatre Magazine 10:103-4+, Oct 1909
    Vanity Fair 6:200, Nov 1909
    World Today 17:1269-79, Dec 1909

POMERANCE, BERNARD

The Elephant Man
    Productions:
        (Off Broadway) January 14, 1979 for 73 performances and trans-
            ferred to Broadway.
        Opened on Broadway April 19, 1977 for 916 performances.
    Reviews:
        America 140:135, Feb 24, 1979
        Christian Century 97:14-18, Jan 2, 1980
        Commentary 68:62-4, Jul 1979
        Commonweal 106:180-1, Mar 30, 1979
        Harper's 262:66-8, May 1981
        Horizon 22:16-24, Jun 1979
        Nation 228:156, Feb 10, 1979
        New Leader 62:23-4, May 7, 1979
        New Republic 180:24-6, Feb 17, 1979
                     180:24-5, May 12, 1979
        New West 5:SC-24, May 19, 1980
        New York Magazine 12:120-1, Jan 29, 1979
                          12:84-5, May 7, 1979
                          13:54-5, Oct 13, 1980
        New York Theatre Critics' Reviews 1979:274
        New York Times III, p. 13, Jan 15, 1979
                        II, p. 1, Jan 28, 1979
                        III, p. 5, Apr 20, 1979
                        p. 13, Apr 28, 1979
                        II, p. 1, May 6, 1979
                        III, p. 4, May 25, 1979
                        II, p. 1, Jul 1, 1979
                        II, p. 1, Dec 30, 1979
                        III, p. 15, Sep 29, 1980
        People 12:77+, Dec 10, 1979
        Rolling Stone pp. 8-11, Nov 13, 1980
        Saturday Review 6:60, Mar 17, 1979
        Texas Monthly 9:175+, Aug 1981
        Theatre Crafts 14:24-7+, Jan/Feb 1980
        Time 113:64, Jan 29, 1979

RABE, DAVID

The Basic Training of Pavlo Hummel
    Productions:
        (Off Broadway) May 20, 1971 for 363 performances.
        Opened April 24, 1977 for 107 performances.
    Reviews:
        Commonweal 96:14-15, Mar 10, 1972
        Nation 212:733, Jun 7, 1971
               224:602, May 14, 1977
        New York Magazine 10:63, May 9, 1977

New York Theatre Critics' Reviews 1971:258
                                 1977:254
New York Times p. 25, May 21, 1971
                II, p. 3, May 30, 1971
                II, p. 1, Jul 11, 1971
                p. 55, Dec 7, 1971
                p. 38, Apr 25, 1977
                II, p. 1, May 8, 1977
New Yorker 47:55, May 29, 1971
           53:91, May 2, 1977
Newsweek 77:70, Jun 14, 1971
         78:58+, Dec 20, 1971
Saturday Review 54:36, Jul 10, 1971
                55:43-4, Feb 26, 1972
Time 99:66, Apr 24, 1972
     109:50, May 9, 1977

Boom Boom Room   (see In the Boom Boom Room)

Burning
    Productions:
        (Off Broadway) April 13, 1974 (Joseph Papp's Public Theater
            Workshop).
    No Reviews.

Goose and Tomtom
    Productions:
        (Off Broadway) May 6, 1982 for 14 performances (New York
            Shakespeare Festival Public Theater).
    Reviews:
        New York Times p. 17, May 8, 1982

In the Boom Boom Room
    Productions:
        Opened November 8, 1973 for 37 performances.
        (Off Broadway) November 20, 1974 for 31 performances.
        (Off Off Broadway) December 18, 1975.
        (Off Off Broadway) November 1976.
    Reviews:
        America 129:485, Dec 22, 1973
        Commonweal 99:294-5, Dec 14, 1973
        Los Angeles 22:247, Aug 1977
        Nation 217:572, Nov 26, 1973
               217:603, Dec 3, 1973
               219:701, Dec 28, 1974
        National Review 26:90-1, Jan 18, 1974
        New West 4:SC-41, May 21, 1979
        New York Magazine 6:92, Nov 26, 1973
                          7:62, Dec 23, 1974
        New York Theatre Critics' Reviews 1973:196
        New York Times p. 31, Nov 9, 1973

II, p. 3, Nov 18, 1973
p. 55, Dec 5, 1974
p. 60, Dec 12, 1974
New Yorker 49:84, Nov 19, 1973
50:69, Dec 9, 1974
Newsweek 82:96, Nov 19, 1973
84:105, Dec 16, 1974
Time 102:96, Nov 19, 1973

The Orphan
Productions:
(Off Broadway) March 30, 1973 for 53 performances (New York Shakespeare Festival Public Theater).
Reviews:
America 128:444-5, May 12, 1973
New York Magazine 6:98, Apr 30, 1973
New York Theatre Critics' Reviews 1973:250
New York Times p. 51, Apr 19, 1973
II, p. 1, Apr 29, 1973
New Yorker 49:105, Apr 28, 1973
Newsweek 81:87, Apr 30, 1973
Time 101:90, Apr 30, 1973

Sticks and Bones
Productions:
(Off Broadway) November 7, 1971 for 121 performances and transferred to Broadway.
Opened on Broadway March 1, 1972 for 245 performances (366 performances in all).
Reviews:
America 126:295, Mar 18, 1972
Commonweal 96:14-15, Mar 10, 1972
Nation 213:539, Nov 22, 1971
New Republic 165:22+, Dec 4, 1971
New York Theatre Critics' Reviews 1971:162
1972:364
New York Times p. 53, Nov 8, 1971
p. 60, Nov 9, 1971
II, p. 1, Nov 14, 1971
II, p. 3, Dec 12, 1971
p. 33, Mar 2, 1972
II, p. 3, Mar 12, 1972
New Yorker 47:114+, Nov 20, 1971
48:82, Mar 11, 1972
Newsweek 78:110, Nov 29, 1971
78:58+, Dec 20, 1971
Saturday Review 54:70-1, Nov 27, 1971
Time 98:93, Nov 22, 1971

Streamers
Productions:

(Off Broadway) April 21, 1976 for 478 performances.
Reviews:
America 134:432, May 15, 1976
Atlantic 238:108-9, Dec 1976
Commentary 62:61-3, Jul 1976
Commonweal 103:334-5, May 21, 1976
Los Angeles 23:208, Feb 1978
Nation 222:574, May 8, 1976
New Republic 174:20, Jun 12, 1976
New York Magazine 9:78, May 10, 1976
New York Theatre Critics' Reviews 1976:264
New York Times p. 45, Feb 8, 1976
    II, p. 1, Feb 22, 1976
    p. 38, Apr 22, 1976
    II, p. 5, May 2, 1976
New Yorker 52:76-7, May 3, 1976
Newsweek 87:89+, Feb 23, 1976
Saturday Review 3:48, Apr 17, 1976
Time 107:75, May 3, 1976

RANDALL, BOB

6 Rms Riv Vu
Productions:
    Opened October 17, 1972 for 247 performances.
Reviews:
    Nation 215:444, Nov 6, 1972
    New York Theatre Critics' Reviews 1972:216
    New York Times p. 40, Oct 18, 1972
        II, p. 3, Oct 29, 1972
        p. 47, May 22, 1973
    New Yorker 48:119, Oct 28, 1972
    Playboy 20:34, Feb 1973
    Time 100:109, Oct 30, 1972

RAPHAELSON, SAMUEL

Accent on Youth
Productions:
    Opened December 25, 1934 for 229 performances.
    (Off Broadway) May 16, 1969 for 9 performances (Equity Library Theater).
Reviews:
    Catholic World 140:600, Feb 1935
    Commonweal 21:318, Jan 11, 1935
    Literary Digest 119:19, Jan 12, 1935
    Nation 140:83-4, Jan 16, 1935
    New Republic 81:336, Jan 30, 1935
    New York Times p. 19, Dec 26, 1934

IX, p. 3, Jan 6, 1935
p. 24, Jul 2, 1935
p. 21, Jul 9, 1935
p. 24, Jul 11, 1935
p. 20, Aug 13, 1935
p. 18, Jun 29, 1937
XXI, p. 11, Jul 4, 1982
Theatre Arts 19:99, Feb 1935
Time 25:40, Jan 7, 1935

Harlem (see White Man)

*The Heel
Reviews:
New York Times p. 33, May 27, 1954

Hilda Crane
Productions:
Opened November 1, 1950 for 70 performances.
Reviews:
American Mercury 72:351-3, Mar 1951
Catholic World 172:225-6, Dec 1950
Christian Science Monitor Magazine p. 8, Nov 11, 1950
Commonweal 53:171-2, Nov 24, 1950
Nation 171:444, Nov 11, 1950
New Republic 123:21-2, Nov 27, 1950
New York Theatre Critics' Reviews 1950:221
New York Times II, p. 1, Oct 29, 1950
p. 38, Nov 2, 1950
New Yorker 26:79, Nov 11, 1950
Newsweek 36:99, Nov 13, 1950
Theatre Arts 35:11, Jan 1951
Time 56:99, Nov 13, 1950

Jason
Productions:
Opened January 21, 1942 for 125 performances.
Reviews:
Catholic World 154:727-8, Mar 1942
Commonweal 35:393, Feb 6, 1942
Nation 154:173, Feb 7, 1942
New York Theatre Critics' Reviews 1942:377
New York Times p. 12, Jan 22, 1942
New Yorker 17:28+, Jan 31, 1942
Player's Magazine 18:12, Mar 1942
Theatre Arts 26:221-2, Apr 1942

The Jazz Singer
Productions:
Opened September 14, 1925 for 303 performances.
Opened April 18, 1927 for 16 performances.

Reviews:
>New York Times p. 29, Sep 15, 1925
>p. 25, Apr 19, 1927

The Perfect Marriage
Productions:
>Opened October 26, 1944 for 92 performances.

Reviews:
>Nation 159:624, Nov 18, 1944
>New York Theatre Critics' Reviews 1944:104
>New York Times p. 17, Oct 27, 1944
>II, p. 1, Nov 5, 1944
>Newsweek 24:104, Nov 6, 1944
>Theatre Arts 29:16, Jan 1945

Skylark
Productions:
>Opened October 11, 1939 for 256 performances.

Reviews:
>Catholic World 150:337, Dec 1939
>Commonweal 31:14, Oct 27, 1939
>Life 7:46-8, Nov 13, 1939
>Nation 149:448-9, Oct 21, 1939
>New Republic 100:368, Nov 1, 1939
>New York Theatre Critics' Reviews 1940:475
>New York Times XI, p. 2, Mar 19, 1939
>p. 32, Oct 12, 1939
>IX, p. 1, Oct 22, 1939
>X, p. 3, Dec 10, 1939
>p. 12, Jan 30, 1940
>VIII, p. 1, Apr 12, 1942
>North American Review 248 no. 2:404, Dec 1939
>Stage 16:18-19, Apr 1, 1939
>Theatre Arts 23:855, Dec 1939
>Time 34:36, Oct 23, 1939

White Man
Productions:
>Opened October 17, 1936 for 7 performances.

Reviews:
>New York Times X, p. 3, Oct 11, 1936
>p. 22, Oct 19, 1936
>Theatre Arts 20:932+, Dec 1936

The Wooden Slipper
Productions:
>Opened January 3, 1934 for 5 performances.

Reviews:
>New York Times p. 16, Jan 4, 1934

Young Love
Productions:

Opened October 30, 1928 for 87 performances.
Reviews:
Life (NY) 92:17, Nov 23, 1928
Nation 127:556-7, Nov 21, 1928
      128:397-8, Apr 3, 1928
New York Times VII, p. 1, Aug 12, 1928
             IX, p. 1, Oct 21, 1928
             p. 28, Oct 31, 1928
Vogue 72:82, Dec 22, 1928

RAYFIEL, DAVID

Nathan Weinstein, Mystic, Connecticut
Productions:
Opened February 25, 1966 for 3 performances.
Reviews:
New York Theatre Critics' Reviews 1966:355
New York Times p. 15, Feb 26, 1966

P.S. 193
Productions:
(Off Broadway) October 30, 1962 for 48 performances.
Reviews:
Commonweal 77:254-5, Nov 30, 1962
Nation 195:361-2, Nov 24, 1962
New York Times p. 33, Oct 31, 1962
New Yorker 38:146+, Nov 10, 1962
Saturday Review 45:48, Nov 17, 1962

REED, MARK

Mother's Day (see Yes, My Darling Daughter)

The Partisans (see She Would and She Did)

Petticoat Fever
Productions:
Opened March 4, 1935 for 137 performances.
Reviews:
Catholic World 141:90, Apr 1935
Commonweal 21:600, Mar 22, 1935
Literary Digest 119:16, Mar 16, 1935
New York Times IX, p. 3, Jan 13, 1935
            p. 22, Mar 5, 1935
            VIII, p. 2, Mar 10, 1935
            p. 14, Jun 25, 1935
            p. 24, Jul 12, 1935
            p. 21, Feb 21, 1936
            p. 14, Jul 8, 1936

II, p. 7, Mar 21, 1937
p. 23, Jul 6, 1937
p. 19, Jul 20, 1937
Newsweek 5:29, May 16, 1935
Stage 12:22-3, Apr 1935
Theatre Arts 19:325+, May 1935
Time 25:25, Mar 18, 1935

She Would and She Did
Productions:
Opened September 11, 1919 for 36 performances.
Reviews:
Dramatic Mirror 80:1504, Sep 25, 1919
New Republic 20:234, Sep 24, 1919
New York Times p. 18, Sep 12, 1919
IV, p. 2, Sep 21, 1919
Review 1:457-8, Oct 4, 1919

Skyrocket
Productions:
Opened January 11, 1929 for 11 performances.
Reviews:
New York Times p. 14, Jan 12, 1929

Yes, My Darling Daughter
Productions:
Opened February 9, 1937 for 405 performances.
(Off Broadway) May 10, 1968 for 9 performances (Equity Library Theater).
Reviews:
Catholic World 144:730-1, Mar 1937
Nation 144:249, Feb 27, 1937
New Republic 90:139, Mar 10, 1937
New York Times p. 19, Feb 10, 1937
XI, p. 1, Feb 28, 1937
XI, p. 1, Mar 14, 1937
p. 26, Jun 4, 1937
X, p. 2, Jun 12, 1938
p. 17, Jun 14, 1938
p. 17, Jul 13, 1938
Theatre Arts 21:262, Apr 1937
Time 29:46, Feb 22, 1937

REGAN, SYLVIA

The Fifth Season
Productions:
Opened January 23, 1953 for 654 performances.
Reviews:
Catholic World 176:468, Mar 1953

Look 17:4, Mar 10, 1953
Nation 176:132, Feb 7, 1953
New York Theatre Critics' Reviews 1953:380
New York Times p. 13, Jan 24, 1953
    II, p. 1, Jun 14, 1953
    p. 24, Feb 25, 1954
    II, p. 3, Sep 5, 1954
New Yorker 28:48, Jan 31, 1953
Saturday Review 36:25, Feb 7, 1953
Time 61:49, Feb 2, 1953

Morning Star
  Productions:
    Opened April 16, 1940 for 63 performances.
  Reviews:
    Catholic World 151:345-6, Jun 1940
    Commonweal 32:43, May 3, 1940
    New York Theatre Critics' Reviews 1940:328
    New York Times p. 26, Apr 17, 1940
        p. 22, Apr 18, 1940
    Newsweek 15:34, May 6, 1940
    Theatre Arts 24:402, Jun 1940
    Time 35:64, Apr 29, 1940

Zelda
  Productions:
    Opened March 5, 1969 for 5 performances.
  Reviews:
    New York Theatre Critics' Reviews 1969:336
    New York Times p. 38, Mar 6, 1969

REIZENSTEIN, ELMER (see Rice, Elmer)

RESNIK, MURIEL

Any Wednesday
  Productions:
    Opened February 18, 1964 for 982 performances.
  Reviews:
    America 110:466, Mar 28, 1964
        110:552, Apr 18, 1964
    Look 28:100-4, Jun 16, 1964
    New York Theatre Critics' Reviews 1964:342
    New York Times p. 34, Feb 19, 1964
        p. 24, Feb 20, 1964
        II, p. 1, Aug 1, 1965
        p. 45, Nov 11, 1965
        p. 48, Jun 28, 1966
    New Yorker 40:106, Feb 29, 1964

Newsweek 63:56, Mar 2, 1964
Saturday Evening Post 237:83-7, Apr 25, 1964
Saturday Review 47:23, Mar 7, 1964
Time 83:61, Feb 28, 1964

RICE, ELMER

The Adding Machine
    Productions:
    Opened March 19, 1923 for 72 performances.
    (Off Broadway) June 13, 1947 (Actor's Theatre).
    (Off Broadway) Season of 1948-49 (New York Repertory Group).
    (Off Broadway) Season of 1955-56.
    (Off Off Broadway) Season of 1970-71 (Workshop of the Play-
        ers Art).
    Reviews:
    Bookman 57:319-20, May 1923
            58:58, Sep 1923
    Dial 74:526-9, May 1923
    Drama 20:20, Oct 1929
    Freeman 7:184-5, May 2, 1923
            7:231-2, May 16, 1923
    Independent 110:270-2, Apr 14, 1923
    Life (NY) 81:20, Apr 12, 1923
    Nation 116:399, Apr 4, 1923
    New Republic 34:164-5, Apr 4, 1923
    New York Clipper 71:14, Mar 28, 1923
    New York Times p. 24, Mar 20, 1923
                VIII, p. 1, Mar 25, 1923
                VII, p. 1, Apr 1, 1923
                VII, p. 2, Apr 1, 1923
                X, p. 2, Dec 4, 1927
                VIII, p. 2, Jan 29, 1928
                p. 35, Nov 18, 1948
                p. 17, Feb 10, 1956
                VI, p. 28, Feb 12, 1956
                p. 40, Dec 5, 1970
    Theatre Magazine 37:19, May 1923
                37:30+, Jun 1923

American Landscape
    Productions:
    Opened December 3, 1938 for 43 performances.
    Reviews:
    Catholic World 148:472-3, Jan 1939
    Commonweal 29:273, Dec 30, 1938
    Nation 147:700, Dec 24, 1938
    New Republic 97:230, Dec 28, 1938
    New York Times p. 19, Dec 5, 1938
                X, p. 3, Dec 11, 1938
                IX, p. 3, Dec 25, 1938

North American Review 247 no. 1:155, Mar 1939
One Act Play Magazine 2:594-9, Dec 1938
Theatre Arts 23:86-9, Feb 1939
Time 32:31, Dec 12, 1938

Between Two Worlds
    Productions:
        Opened October 25, 1934 for 32 performances.
    Reviews:
        Catholic World 140:342-3, Dec 1934
        Nation 139:574, Nov 14, 1934
        New York Times p. 24, Oct 26, 1934
        Stage 12:28-9, Dec 1934
        Theatre Arts 18:900-2, Dec 1934
        Time 24:32, Nov 5, 1934
        Vogue 84:51, Dec 15, 1934

Black Sheep
    Productions:
        Opened October 13, 1932 for 4 performances.
    Reviews:
        New York Times p. 22, Oct 14, 1932
        Theatre Arts 16:961-2, Dec 1932

Close Harmony   (see entry under Parker, Dorothy)

Cock Robin   (see entry under Barry, Philip)

Counsellor-at-Law
    Productions:
        Opened November 6, 1931 for 292 performances.
        Opened September 12, 1932 for 104 performances.
        Opened May 15, 1933 for 16 performances.
        Opened November 24, 1942 for 258 performances.
        (Off Off Broadway) July 26, 1977 (Quaigh Theater).
        (Off Broadway) September 6, 1977 for 62 performances.
    Reviews:
        Arts and Decoration 36:68, Jan 1932
        Catholic World 134:470-1, Jan 1932
                      156:601, Feb 1943
        Commonweal 15:102, Nov 25, 1931
                   37:206, Dec 11, 1942
        Current History ns 3:457, Jan 1943
        Dramatist 23:1446-8, Jan 1932
        Independent Woman 22:155, May 1943
        Nation 133:621-2, Dec 2, 1931
        New Republic 69:69, Dec 2, 1931
        New York Magazine 10:61, Sep 26, 1977
        New York Theatre Critics' Reviews 1942:165
        New York Times p. 17, Nov 7, 1931
                      VIII, p. 3, Mar 27, 1932

p. 13, Sep 17, 1932
IX, p. 3, Nov 6, 1932
p. 24, Apr 11, 1933
IX, p. 2, May 6, 1933
p. 17, Nov 25, 1942
p. 14, Mar 26, 1943
III, p. 4, Jul 29, 1977
II, p. 15, Sep 8, 1977
North American Review 233:75, Jan 1932
Outlook 159:407, Nov 25, 1931
Theatre Arts 16:21-2, Jan 1932
27:16, Jan 1943
Theatre Guild Magazine 9:6-7+, Dec 1931
Time 40:55, Dec 7, 1942
Vanity Fair 37:24+, Jan 1932

Cue for Passion
    Productions:
        Opened November 25, 1958 for 39 performances.
    Reviews:
        Catholic World 188:418, Feb 1959
        New York Theatre Critics' Reviews 1958:192
        New York Times p. 25, Nov 26, 1958
                       II, p. 5, Dec 7, 1958
        New Yorker 34:116-17, Dec 6, 1958
        Newsweek 52:66, Dec 8, 1958
        Theatre Arts 43:21-2, Feb 1959
        Time 72:77, Dec 8, 1958

Dream Girl
    Productions:
        Opened December 14, 1945 for 348 performances.
        Opened May 9, 1951 for 15 performances.
    Reviews:
        Catholic World 162:454-5, Feb 1946
                       173:306, Jul 1951
        Commonweal 43:456-7, Feb 15, 1946
                   54:165, May 25, 1951
        Forum 105:564, Feb 1946
        Harper's Bazaar 79:128, Dec 1945
        Life 19:36-8, Dec 31, 1945
        Nation 162:54, Jan 12, 1946
        New Republic 113:903, Dec 31, 1945
                     124:23, May 28, 1951
        New York Theatre Critics' Reviews 1945:66
                                          1951:271
        New York Times p. 13, Dec 15, 1945
                       III, p. 3, Dec 23, 1945
                       II, p. 1, Mar 10, 1946
                       II, p. 1, Jun 9, 1946
                       p. 13, Sep 2, 1946

II, p. 1, Sep 8, 1946
p. 39, May 10, 1951
New Yorker 21:36, Dec 22, 1945
Newsweek 26:88, Dec 24, 1945
Theatre Arts 30:72, 78-9, Feb 1946
Time 46:77-8, Dec 24, 1945

Flight to the West
Productions:
Opened December 30, 1940 for 136 performances.
Reviews:
Catholic World 152:595, Feb 1941
Commonweal 33:328, Jan 17, 1941
Nation 152:53, Jan 11, 1941
New Republic 104:84, Jan 20, 1941
New York Theatre Critics' Reviews 1940:162
1941:434
New York Times p. 59, Dec 15, 1940
p. 19, Dec 31, 1940
IX, p. 1, Jan 19, 1941
New Yorker 16:33, Jan 11, 1941
Newsweek 17:52, Jan 13, 1941
Stage 1:10, Dec 1940
1:28-9, Feb 1941
Theatre Arts 25:112, Feb 1941
25:184-5, Mar 1941
Time 37:57, Jan 13, 1941

For the Defense
Productions:
Opened December 19, 1919 for 77 performances.
Reviews:
Dramatic Mirror 81:2023, Jan 1, 1920
Life (NY) 96:17, Aug 8, 1930
New York Times p. 14, Dec 20, 1919
Theatre Magazine 31:100+, Feb 1920

The Grand Tour
Productions:
Opened December 10, 1951 for 8 performances.
Reviews:
Commonweal 55:299, Dec 28, 1951
New York Theatre Critics' Reviews 1951:146
New York Times II, p. 5, Dec 9, 1951
p. 45, Dec 11, 1951
New Yorker 27:49, Dec 22, 1951
Newsweek 38:43, Dec 24, 1951
Theatre Arts 36:73, Feb 1952

The Home of the Free
Productions:

Opened October 31, 1917 in repertory (Washington Square Players).
Reviews:
Dramatic Mirror 78:620, May 4, 1918
New York Times p. 7, Apr 23, 1917
         p. 11, Apr 23, 1918
Theatre Magazine 27:355, Jun 1918

The Iron Cross
Productions:
Opened February 13, 1917 in repertory.
Reviews:
New York Times p. 9, Feb 12, 1917
Theatre Magazine 25:213-14, Apr 1917

It Is the Law (Adapted from the story by Hayden Talbot)
Productions:
Opened November 29, 1922 for 125 performances.
Reviews:
New York Clipper 70:20, Dec 6, 1922
New York Times p. 28, Nov 30, 1922
Theatre Magazine 37:19, Feb 1923

Judgment Day
Productions:
Opened September 12, 1934 for 93 performances.
Reviews:
Catholic World 140:89-90, Oct 1934
Commonweal 20:509, Sep 28, 1934
Golden Book Magazine 20:506, Nov 1934
Literary Digest 118:20, Sep 29, 1934
Nation 139:392, Oct 3, 1934
New York Times p. 26, Sep 13, 1934
         X, p. 1, Sep 23, 1934
         p. 16, May 20, 1937
         X, p. 1, Jun 20, 1937
         p. 21, Aug 20, 1937
         IX, p. 7, Dec 3, 1939
Newsweek 4:28, Sep 22, 1934
Theatre Arts 18:814-15, Nov 1934
Vogue 84:74, Oct 15, 1934

The Left Bank
Productions:
Opened October 5, 1931 for 242 performances.
Reviews:
Arts and Decoration 36:68, Dec 1931
Bookman 74:302, Nov 1931
Catholic World 134:210, Nov 1931
Nation 133:440-1, Oct 21, 1931
New Republic 68:264+, Oct 21, 1931

New York Times p. 35, Oct 6, 1931
                    VIII, p. 1, Oct 18, 1931
Outlook 159:248, Oct 21, 1931
Theatre Arts 15:983-4, Dec 1931
Theatre Guild Magazine 9:4, Jan 1932
Vogue 78:102, Dec 1, 1931

*Love Among the Ruins
    Reviews:
    New York Times p. 85, May 5, 1963

The Mongrel (Adapted from Herman Bahr's play)
    Productions:
    Opened December 15, 1924 for 32 performances.
    Reviews:
    Independent 114:51, Jan 10, 1925
    Living Age 324:70-76, Jan 3, 1925
    New York Times p. 28, Dec 16, 1924
    Theatre Magazine 40:62+, Feb 1925

A New Life
    Productions:
    Opened September 15, 1943 for 70 performances.
    Reviews:
    Catholic World 158:187, Nov 1943
    Commonweal 38:585, Oct 1, 1943
    Nation 157:388, Oct 2, 1943
    New Republic 109:426, Sep 27, 1943
    New York Theatre Critics' Reviews 1943:279
    New York Times VI, p. 14, Sep 12, 1943
                    p. 26, Sep 16, 1943
    Newsweek 22:90, Sep 27, 1943
    Theatre Arts 27:640-4, Nov 1943

Not for Children
    Productions:
    Opened February 13, 1951 for 7 performances.
    Reviews:
    Commonweal 53:541, Mar 9, 1951
    New York Theatre Critics' Reviews 1951:348
    New York Times p. 23, Nov 25, 1935
                    IX, p. 3, Dec 22, 1935
                    IX, p. 2, Dec 29, 1935
                    IX, p. 2, Mar 1, 1936
                    II, p. 1, Feb 4, 1951
                    p. 35, Feb 14, 1951
    New Yorker 27:66, Feb 24, 1951
    Newsweek 37:49, Feb 26, 1951
    Theatre Arts 35:19, Apr 1951
    Time 57:50, Feb 26, 1951

On Trial
    Productions:
        Opened August 19, 1914 for 365 performances.
        (Off Off Broadway) February 20, 1979 for 12 performances
          (Quaigh Theater).
    Reviews:
        American Heritage 16:46-9+, Apr 1965
        American Magazine 79:42+, Jan 1915
        American Playwright 3:300-303, Sep 1914
        Book News 33:91-2, Oct 1914
        Bookman 40:181-3, Oct 1914
        Colliers 54:10, Jan 2, 1915
        Current Opinion 57:249, Oct 1914
                   59:24-7, Jul 1915
        Dramatic Mirror 72:8, Aug 19, 1914
                72:8, Aug 26, 1914
        Dramatist 6:498-500, Oct 1914
        Everybody's 31:700-702, Nov 1914
        Green Book 12:772-84, Nov 1914
                12:886-8, Nov 1914
                12:901-3, Nov 1914
        Hearst 26:640-7, Nov 1914
        Life (NY) 64:395, Sep 3, 1914
        McClure's 44:18-21, Jan 1915
        Munsey 53:348-55, Nov 1914
        Nation 99:260-1, Aug 27, 1914
        New York Times p. 11, Aug 20, 1914
                    VIII, p. 6, Oct 18, 1914
                    p. 5, Apr 30, 1915
                    VII, p. 4, May 16, 1915
        Strand 48:685-8, Dec 1914
        Theatre Magazine 20:154+, Oct 1914
                      20:160+, Oct 1914

See Naples and Die
    Productions:
        Opened September 24, 1929 for 62 performances.
    Reviews:
        Life (NY) 94:26, Oct 18, 1929
        Nation 129:409, Oct 16, 1929
        New Republic 60:243-4, Oct 16, 1929
        New York Times p. 30, Sep 27, 1929
        Theatre Magazine 50:70, Nov 1929

Street Scene
    Productions:
        Opened January 10, 1929 for 601 performances.
        (Off Off Broadway) July 9, 1975 (Quaigh Theater).
        (Off Off Broadway) September 1975 (Drama Comm. Rep. The-
         ater).

Reviews:
    Catholic World 128:720-2, Mar 1929
    Commonweal 9:348-9, Jan 23, 1929
    Dial 86:245-6, Mar 1929
    Drama Magazine 19:170, Mar 1929
    Life (NY) 93:23, Feb 1, 1929
    Nation 128:142, Jan 30, 1929
          128:680-1, Jun 5, 1929
    New Republic 57:296-8, Jan 30, 1929
    New York Times p. 20, Jan 11, 1929
                 VIII, p. 1, Jan 20, 1929
                 IX, p. 4, Jan 27, 1929
                 IX, p. 4, Feb 24, 1929
                 IX, p. 1, May 19, 1929
                 p. 24, Jan 10, 1930
                 IX, p. 4, Mar 16, 1930
                 p. 14, Sep 10, 1930
                 VIII, p. 2, Sep 28, 1930
                 p. 45, Feb 29, 1976
    Outlook 151:140, Jan 23, 1929
    Saturday Review 30:24-6, Feb 1, 1947
    Theatre Arts 13:164-6, Mar 1929
          14:164-6, Feb 1930
          43:59-64+, Nov 1959
    Theatre Magazine 49:50, Mar 1929
            49:26-7+, Apr 1929
    Vogue 73:114, Mar 2, 1929

The Subway
    Productions:
    Opened January 25, 1929 for 35 performances.
    Reviews:
    New York Times p. 15, Jan 26, 1929
                p. 25, Jul 15, 1929
    Theatre Magazine 49:47, Apr 1929

Two on an Island
    Productions:
    Opened January 22, 1940 for 96 performances.
    Reviews:
    Catholic World 150:729-30, Mar 1940
    Commonweal 31:348, Feb 9, 1940
    Life 8:42-4, Feb 19, 1940
    Nation 150:136, Feb 3, 1940
    New York Theatre Critics' Reviews 1940:409
    New York Times p. 18, Jan 16, 1940
                p. 17, Jan 23, 1940
                IX, p. 1, Jan 28, 1940
                IX, p. 1, Feb 4, 1940
    Newsweek 15:34, Feb 5, 1940
    Player's Magazine 25:192, May 1949

Theatre Arts 24:167-8, Mar 1940
Time 35:41, Feb 5, 1940

Wake Up, Jonathan! (see entry under Hughes, Hatcher)

We, the People
    Productions:
        Opened January 21, 1933 for 49 performances.
    Reviews:
        Arts and Decoration 38:58, Mar 1933
        Christian Century 50:231, Feb 15, 1933
        Commonweal 17:411, Feb 8, 1933
        Literary Digest 115:15, Feb 11, 1933
                        115:19, Mar 4, 1933
        Nation 136:158-60, Feb 8, 1933
               136:172, Feb 15, 1933
        New Outlook 161:10, Mar 1933
        New Republic 74:18-19, Feb 15, 1933
        New York Times p. 9, Jan 23, 1933
                       IX, p. 1, Feb 5, 1933
        Stage 10:20-21, Mar 1933
        Theatre Arts 17:258-60, Apr 1933
        Time 21:22, Jan 30, 1933
        Vogue 81:73, Mar 15, 1933
        World Tomorrow 16:176, Feb 22, 1933

The Winner
    Productions:
        Opened February 17, 1954 for 30 performances.
    Reviews:
        America 90:664, Mar 20, 1954
        New York Theatre Critics' Reviews 1954:365
        New York Times II, p. 3, Feb 14, 1954
                       p. 34, Feb 18, 1954
        New Yorker 30:78-80, Feb 27, 1954
        Newsweek 43:71, Mar 1, 1954
        Saturday Review 37:25, Mar 6, 1954
        Theatre Arts 38:16, Apr 1954
        Time 63:76+, Mar 1, 1954

RICHARDSON, JACK

Christmas in Las Vegas (see Xmas in Las Vegas)

Gallows Humor
    Productions:
        (Off Broadway) April 18, 1961 for 40 performances.
        (Off Broadway) February 11, 1962 for 55 performances.
        (Off Off Broadway) April 7, 1978 (WPA Theater).

Reviews:
    Nation 192:399, May 6, 1961
    New York Times p. 35, Apr 19, 1961
    New Yorker 37:93, Apr 29, 1961
    Newsweek 57:62, May 1, 1961
    Saturday Review 44:39, May 6, 1961
    Theatre Arts 45:32, Jun 1961

Lorenzo
    Productions:
    Opened February 14, 1963 for 4 performances.
    Reviews:
    New Republic 148:29, Mar 9, 1963
    New York Theatre Critics' Reviews 1963:174
    New York Times p. 12, Jan 25, 1963
                   p. 5, Feb 16, 1963
    New Yorker 39:112+, Feb 23, 1963
    Newsweek 61:60, Feb 25, 1963
    Saturday Review 46:24, Mar 9, 1963
    Theatre Arts 47:13, Apr 1963
    Time 81:75, Feb 22, 1963

The Prodigal
    Productions:
    (Off Broadway) February 11, 1960 for 167 performances.
    Reviews:
    Esquire 55:47-8, Apr 1961
    Nation 190:214, Mar 5, 1960
    New York Times p. 23, Feb 12, 1960
                   II, p. 1, Feb 21, 1960
    New Yorker 36:104+, Feb 20, 1960
    Time 75:54, Apr 18, 1960

Xmas in Las Vegas
    Productions:
    Opened November 4, 1965 for 4 performances.
    Reviews:
    Commonweal 83:243, Nov 26, 1965
    New York Theatre Critics' Reviews 1965:284
    New York Times p. 31, Nov 5, 1965
    New Yorker 41:154, Nov 13, 1965

RICHMAN, ARTHUR

All Dressed Up
    Productions:
    Opened September 9, 1925 for 13 performances.
    Reviews:
    Life (NY) 86:18, Oct 1, 1925
    New York Times p. 28, Sep 10, 1925

Ambush
  Productions:
    Opened October 10, 1921 for 98 performances.
  Reviews:
    Bookman 54:374-5, Dec 1921
    Dramatic Mirror 84:557, Oct 15, 1921
    Everybody's 46:137-44, Apr 1922
    Independent 107:110, Oct 29, 1921
    Life (NY) 78:18, Nov 3, 1921
    Nation 113:484, Oct 26, 1921
           113:599, Nov 23, 1921
    New Republic 28:301, Nov 2, 1921
    New York Clipper Vol. 69, Oct 19, 1921
    New York Times p. 22, Oct 11, 1921
                   VI, p. 1, Oct 16, 1921
    Outlook 129:507, Nov 30, 1921
    Theatre Magazine 34:426+, Dec 1921
                     35:292+, May 1922

Antonia (Adapted from the play by Melchior Lengyel)
  Productions:
    Opened October 20, 1925 for 55 performances.
  Reviews:
    Dramatist 16:1280-81, Oct 1925
    New York Times p. 20, Oct 21, 1925

*Arelene Adair
  Reviews:
    New York Times p. 15, Jun 12, 1926

The Awful Truth
  Productions:
    Opened September 18, 1922 for 144 performances.
  Reviews:
    Life (NY) 80:18, Oct 5, 1922
    New York Clipper 70:20, May 1922
                     70:20, Nov 8, 1922
    New York Times p. 14, Sep 19, 1922
                   VI, p. 1, Sep 24, 1922
    Theatre Magazine 36:299, Nov 1922

The Far Cry
  Productions:
    Opened September 30, 1924 for 31 performances.
  Reviews:
    American Mercury 3:377, Nov 1924
    Life (NY) 84:18, Oct 23, 1924
    Nation 119:451, Oct 22, 1924
    New York Times p. 24, Oct 1, 1924
    Theatre Magazine 39:15-16, Dec 1924

Heavy Traffic
  Productions:
    Opened September 5, 1928 for 61 performances.
  Reviews:
    American Mercury 15:373-5, Nov 1928
    Life (NY) 92:17, Sep 28, 1928
    Nation 127:276-7, Sep 19, 1928
    New York Times p. 23, Sep 6, 1928
    Theatre Magazine 48:78, Nov 1928
    Vogue 72:108, Oct 27, 1928

Isabel (Adapted from a play by Curt Goetz)
  Productions:
    Opened January 13, 1925 for 31 performances.
  Reviews:
    Bookman 61:75, Mar 1925
    Life (NY) 85:18, Feb 12, 1925
    New York Times p. 19, Jan 14, 1925
    Theatre Magazine 40:64, Mar 1925

Not So Long Ago
  Productions:
    Opened May 4, 1920 for 31 performances.
  Reviews:
    Current Opinion 69:54-60, Jul 1920
    New York Times p. 14, May 5, 1920

A Proud Woman
  Productions:
    Opened November 15, 1926 for 7 performances.
  Reviews:
    New York Times p. 24, Nov 16, 1926

The Season Changes
  Productions:
    Opened December 23, 1935 for 8 performances.
  Reviews:
    New York Times p. 10, Dec 24, 1935

A Serpent's Tooth
  Productions:
    Opened August 24, 1922 for 36 performances.
  Reviews:
    Dial 73:463, Oct 1922
    Life (NY) 80:20, Sep 14, 1922
    New Republic 32:149-50, Oct 4, 1922
    New York Clipper 70:20, Aug 30, 1922
    New York Times p. 8, Aug 25, 1922
    Theatre Magazine 36:301, Nov 1922
                     36:310+, Nov 1922

RIGGS, LYNN

Big Lake
    Productions:
        Opened April 11, 1927 for 11 performances.
    Reviews:
        New York Times p. 17, Apr 9, 1927

Borned in Texas
    Productions:
        Opened August 21, 1950 for 8 performances.
    Reviews:
        Nation 171:213, Sep 2, 1950
        New Republic 123:23, Sep 4, 1950
        New York Times p. 23, Jun 4, 1945
                       p. 30, Aug 22, 1950

*Cherokee Night
    Reviews:
        New York Times p. 19, Jun 21, 1932
                       IX, p. 1, Jun 26, 1932

The Cream in the Well
    Productions:
        Opened January 20, 1941 for 24 performances.
    Reviews:
        Commonweal 33:375, Jan 31, 1941
        Nation 152:136, Feb 1, 1941
        New Republic 104:179, Feb 10, 1941
        New York Theatre Critics' Reviews 1941:404
        New York Times p. 19, Jan 21, 1941
        New Yorker 16:27, Feb 1, 1941
        Theatre Arts 25:190, Mar 1941

Green Grow the Lilacs
    Productions:
        Opened January 26, 1931 for 64 performances.
    Reviews:
        Arts and Decoration 34:84, Apr 1931
        Bookman 73:293-4, May 1931
        Catholic World 132:179, Mar 1931
        Commonweal 13:414, Feb 11, 1931
        Drama 21:11-12, Mar 1931
        Life (NY) 97:18, Feb 20, 1931
        Nation 132:164-5, Feb 11, 1931
        New Republic 66:19, Feb 18, 1931
        New York Times IX, p. 3, Dec 14, 1930
                       p. 21, Jan 27, 1931
                       VIII, p. 1, Feb 8, 1931
                       VIII, p. 3, Mar 1, 1931
                       p. 20, Jul 23, 1952

Outlook 157:234, Feb 11, 1931
Theatre Arts 15:272-3, Apr 1931
Theatre Magazine 53:26, Apr 1931
Vogue 77:108, Mar 15, 1931

*Lonesome West
Reviews:
New York Times p. 15, Jun 30, 1936

Roadside
Productions:
Opened September 26, 1930 for 11 performances.
(Off Broadway) June 3, 1947 in repertory (Actors Theatre).
Reviews:
Drama 21:17, Nov 1930
Life (NY) 96:19, Oct 17, 1930
New York Times p. 21, Sep 27, 1930

Russet Mantle
Productions:
Opened January 16, 1936 for 117 performances.
Reviews:
Catholic World 142:725-6, Mar 1936
Commonweal 23:386, Jan 31, 1936
Nation 142:168, Feb 5, 1936
New Republic 86:169, Mar 18, 1936
New York Times p. 15, Jan 17, 1936
               IX, p. 1, Jan 26, 1936
               p. 15, Aug 18, 1936
Newsweek 7:30, Jan 25, 1936
Stage 13:36-7, Mar 1936
Theatre Arts 20:176-8, Mar 1936
Time 27:43, Jan 27, 1936

*Year of Pilar
Reviews:
New York Times p. 14, Jan 7, 1952

RILEY, LAWRENCE

Personal Appearance
Productions:
Opened October 17, 1934 for 501 performances.
(Off Broadway) January 5, 1941 (Lighthouse Players).
Reviews:
Catholic World 140:341, Dec 1934
Commonweal 21:122, Nov 23, 1934
Literary Digest 118:20, Nov 10, 1934
Nation 139:517, Oct 31, 1934
New York Times p. 26, Oct 18, 1934

IX, p. 1, Oct 28, 1934
IX, p. 3, Nov 17, 1935
p. 23, Jun 16, 1936
p. 27, Jun 23, 1936
p. 17, Jul 9, 1936
Theatre Arts 18:896+, Dec 1934
Time 24:44-5, Oct 29, 1934

Return Engagement
Productions:
    Opened November 1, 1940 for 8 performances.
Reviews:
    New York Theatre Critics' Reviews 1940:230
    New York Times p. 19, Nov 2, 1940
    Time 36:44, Nov 11, 1940

RINEHART, MARY ROBERTS

The Bat (with Avery Hopwood)
Productions:
    Opened August 23, 1920 for 867 performances.
    Opened May 31, 1937 for 18 performances.
    Opened January 20, 1953 for 23 performances.
Reviews:
    Catholic World 176:467, Mar 1953
    Commonweal 57:473, Feb 13, 1953
    Dramatic Mirror p. 371, Aug 28, 1920
    Dramatist 12:1053, Apr 1921
    Independent 103:261, Sep 4, 1920
    Life (NY) 76:456, Sep 9, 1920
    Literary Digest 68:27-8, Feb 12, 1921
    New York Clipper 68:19, Sep 1, 1920
    New York Theatre Critics' Reviews 1953:390
    New York Times p. 6, Aug 24, 1920
            VI, p. 1, Nov 14, 1920
            p. 11, Jan 24, 1922
            VII, p. 1, Apr 30, 1922
            p. 5, Sep 3, 1922
            p. 27, Jun 1, 1937
            II, p. 3, Jan 18, 1953
            p. 28, Jan 21, 1953
    New Yorker 28:49, Jan 31, 1953
    Newsweek 41:68, Feb 2, 1953
    Saturday Review 36:25, Feb 7, 1953
    Theatre Magazine 32:240-2, Oct 1920
    Time 61:49, Feb 2, 1953

The Breaking Point
Productions:
    Opened August 16, 1923 for 68 performances.
Reviews:

New York Times p. 8, Aug 17, 1923
                    VI, p. 1, Aug 26, 1923
Theatre Magazine 38:16, Oct 1923

Cheer Up
    Productions:
        Opened December 30, 1912 for 24 performances.
    Reviews:
        Blue Book 16:1150-2, Apr 1913
        Dramatic Mirror 69:7, Jan 8, 1913
        New York Dramatic News 57:23, Jan 4, 1913

Seven Days (with Avery Hopwood)
    Productions:
        Opened November 10, 1909 for 397 performances.
    Reviews:
        American Mercury 71:271, Dec 1910
        Burr McIntosh Monthly 22:126, Feb 1910
        Cosmopolitan 48:484, Mar 1910
        Dramatist 1:15, Jan 1910
        Forum 43:183-4, Feb 1910
        Green Book 3:77-9, Jan 1910
        Hampton 24:135-6, Jan 1910
        Harper's Weekly 53:25, Nov 27, 1909
        Leslies' Weekly 109:535, Dec 2, 1909
                        110:107, Feb 3, 1910
        Life (NY) 54:473, Nov 25, 1909
        Lippincott 82:641-712, Dec 1908
        Metropolitan Magazine 31:822-3, Mar 1910
        Pearson 23:230, Feb 1910
        Theatre Magazine 10:xv+, Dec 1909

ROTTER, FRITZ

Letters to Lucerne (with Allen Vincent)
    Productions:
        Opened December 23, 1941 for 23 performances.
    Reviews:
        Commonweal 35:294, Jan 9, 1942
        New York Theatre Critics' Reviews 1941:168
        New York Times p. 47, Dec 9, 1941
                        p. 14, Dec 24, 1941
        New Yorker 17:28, Jan 3, 1942
        Newsweek 19:55, Jan 5, 1942
        Player's Magazine 18:14, Feb 1942
        Theatre Arts 26:155-6, Mar 1942

ROYLE, EDWIN MILTON

Her Way Out

Productions:
Opened June 23, 1924 for 24 performances.
Reviews:
New York Times p. 18, Jun 24, 1924
VII, p. 1, Jul 13, 1924

Launcelot and Elaine (Dramatized from Tennyson's "Idylls of the King")
Productions:
Opened September 12, 1921 for 32 performances.
Opened March 8, 1930 for 25 performances.
Reviews:
Dramatic Mirror 84:413, Sep 17, 1921
Independent 106:137, Sep 24, 1921
107:36, Oct 8, 1921
New York Times p. 12, Sep 13, 1921
p. 24, Mar 10, 1930
Theatre Magazine 34:340, Nov 1921

*Peace and Quiet
Reviews:
New York Times p. 9, Jun 20, 1916

The Silent Call
Productions:
Opened January 2, 1911 for 8 performances.
No Reviews.

The Squaw Man
Productions:
Opened January 9, 1911 for 8 performances.
Opened December 26, 1921 for 50 performances.
Reviews:
Dramatic Mirror 84:999, Dec 31, 1921
Dramatist 2:133, Jan 1911
New York Clipper 69:29, Jan 11, 1922
New York Times p. 10, Dec 27, 1921

The Unwritten Law
Productions:
Opened February 7, 1913 for 19 performances.
Reviews:
American Playwright 2:76-8, Mar 1913
Bookman 37:65, Mar 1913
Dramatic Mirror 69:6, Feb 12, 1913
Dramatist 3:265-6, Apr 1912
Life (NY) 61:374, Feb 20, 1913
New York Drama News 55:12, Apr 27, 1912
57:19, Feb 15, 1913
New York Times p. 13, Feb 8, 1913
Theatre Magazine 17:68+, Mar 1913

RYERSON, FLORENCE (Mrs. Colin Clements)

Glamour Preferred (with Colin Clements)
Productions:
Opened November 15, 1940 for 11 performances.
Reviews:
Commonweal 33:152, Nov 29, 1940
New York Theatre Critics' Reviews 1940:220
New York Times p. 13, Nov 16, 1940

Harriet (with Colin Clements)
Productions:
Opened March 3, 1943 for 377 performances.
Opened September 27, 1944 for 11 performances.
Reviews:
Catholic World 157:177-8, Apr 1943
Commonweal 37:568, Mar 26, 1943
Current Literature 4:156-8, Apr 1943
Independent Woman 22:65, Mar 1943
Life 14:37-8+, Apr 5, 1943
Nation 156:426, Mar 20, 1943
New Republic 108:381, Mar 22, 1943
New York Theatre Critics' Reviews 1943:364
New York Times p. 22, Jan 29, 1943
p. 24, Mar 4, 1943
II, p. 1, Mar 14, 1943
p. 15, Jun 29, 1943
II, p. 7, Dec 12, 1943
p. 26, Sep 28, 1944
VI, p. 16, Feb 14, 1943
New Yorker 19:43, Mar 13, 1943
Newsweek 21:82, Mar 15, 1943
Scholastic 44:13-16, Apr 24, 1944
Theatre Arts 27:265-7+, May 1943
Time 41:42, Mar 15, 1943

Morality Clause (see Glamour Preferred)

Strange Bedfellows (with Colin Clements)
Productions:
Opened January 14, 1948 for 229 performances.
Reviews:
Catholic World 166:552-3, Mar 1948
Commonweal 47:399, Jan 30, 1948
Life 24:71-2, Feb 16, 1948
New York Theatre Critics' Reviews 1948:386
New York Times p. 27, Jan 15, 1948
New Yorker 23:41, Jan 24, 1948
Newsweek 31:82, Jan 26, 1948
School and Society 67:243, Mar 27, 1948
Theatre Arts 32:22, Spring 1948
Time 51:64, Jan 26, 1948

SACKLER, HOWARD

Goodbye Fidel
  Productions:
    Opened April 23, 1980 for 6 performances.
  Reviews:
    New York Magazine 13:61, Aug 5, 1980
    New York Theatre Critics' Reviews 1980:280
    New York Times III, p. 19, Apr 24, 1980
                   III, p. 2, Apr 25, 1980
    New Yorker 56:109, May 5, 1980

The Great White Hope
  Productions:
    Opened October 3, 1968 for 556 performances.
  Reviews:
    America 119:528-30, Nov 23, 1968
    Commentary 47:22+, Feb 1969
    Commonweal 89:283-4, Nov 22, 1968
    Harper's 238:108-9, Jan 1969
    Nation 206:93-4, Jan 15, 1968
           207:446, Oct 28, 1968
    National Review 20:1282-3, Dec 17, 1968
    New Republic 159:36+, Oct 26, 1968
    New York Theatre Critics' Reviews 1968:222
    New York Times p. 58, Dec 14, 1967
                   II, p. 3, Dec 24, 1967
                   X, p. 3, Dec 24, 1967
                   p. 40, Oct 4, 1968
                   p. 39, Oct 5, 1968
                   II, p. 1, Oct 13, 1968
                   p. 54, Oct 29, 1968
                   p. 26, Sep 27, 1969
                   II, p. 3, Oct 26, 1969
    New Yorker 44:103, Oct 12, 1968
    Newsweek 70:73, Dec 25, 1967
             72:117, Oct 14, 1968
    Saturday Review 50:18, Dec 30, 1967
                    51:28, Oct 19, 1968
    Sports Illustrated 29:34-5, Oct 7, 1968
    Time 92:73, Oct 11, 1968
    Vogue 152:92, Nov 15, 1968

*Semmelweiss
  Reviews:
    New York Times III, p. 24, Nov 12, 1980
                   III, p. 26, May 13, 1981
                   III, p. 4, May 22, 1981
    Time 117:60, Jun 1, 1981

SAROYAN, WILLIAM

Across the Board on Tomorrow Morning (see Two by Saroyan)

The Beautiful People
    Productions:
        Opened April 21, 1941 for 120 performances.
        (Off Broadway) Season of 1955-56 (Theatre East).
    Reviews:
        Catholic World 153:342-3, Jun 1941
        Commonweal 34:38, May 2, 1941
        Life 10:128-31, May 19, 1941
        Nation 152:537, May 3, 1941
        New Republic 104:632, May 5, 1941
                     104:664, May 12, 1941
        New York Theatre Critics' Reviews 1941:328
        New York Times p. 27, Apr 22, 1941
                      p. 30, Apr 11, 1956
        New Yorker 17:30, May 3, 1941
        Newsweek 17:67, May 5, 1941
        Theatre Arts 25:411-13, Jun 1941
        Time 37:66+, May 5, 1941

The Cave Dwellers
    Productions:
        Opened October 19, 1957 for 97 performances.
        (Off Broadway) October 16, 1961 for six performances.
    Reviews:
        America 98:299, Nov 30, 1957
        Catholic World 186:305, Jan 1958
        Christian Century 74:1425, Nov 27, 1957
        Commonweal 67:287, Dec 13, 1957
        Nation 185:330-1, Nov 9, 1957
        New Republic 137:20, Nov 4, 1957
        New York Theatre Critics' Reviews 1957:211
        New York Times II, p. 1, Oct 13, 1957
                      p. 29, Oct 21, 1957
                      II, p. 1, Oct 27, 1957
                      p. 34, Oct 16, 1961
        New Yorker 33:85-7, Nov 2, 1957
                   37:138, Oct 28, 1961
        Saturday Review 40:22, Nov 2, 1957
        Texas Monthly 7:152+, Jul 1979
        Theatre Arts 41:20-1, Dec 1957
        Time 70:92, Oct 28, 1957

*Don't Go Away Mad
    Reviews:
        New York Times p. 28, May 10, 1949

Fat Man in a Famine (see Jim Dandy)

Floydada to Matador ("Hello Out There," "The Hungerers," "Opera
  Opera")
  Productions:
    (Off Broadway) Season of 1955-56.
  Reviews:
    New York Times II, p. 5, Dec 18, 1955
            p. 19, Dec 22, 1955

Get Away Old Man
  Productions:
    Opened November 24, 1943 for 13 performances.
  Reviews:
    Commonweal 39:205, Dec 10, 1943
    New Republic 109:851, Dec 13, 1943
    New York Theatre Critics' Reviews 1943:312
    New York Times p. 40, Nov 25, 1943
    Player's Magazine 20:13, Jan 1944
    Theatre Arts 28:77-8, Feb 1944
    Time 42:42, Dec 6, 1943

Hello, Out There
  Productions:
    Opened September 29, 1942 for 47 performances.
    (Off Broadway) Season of 1955-56 (see Floydada to Matador
      for reviews).
    (Off Off Broadway) Season of 1974-75 (Theater '77).
    (Off Off Broadway) February 17, 1980 (Encompass Theater).
  Reviews:
    Catholic World 156:214, Nov 1942
    Commonweal 36:615, Oct 16, 1942
    Nation 155:357, Oct 10, 1942
    New Republic 107:466, Oct 12, 1942
    New York Theatre Critics' Reviews 1942:223
    New York Times p. 20, Sep 11, 1941
            p. 28, Sep 30, 1942
    New Yorker 18:30, Oct 10, 1942
    Newsweek 20:82, Oct 12, 1942

*High Time Along the Wabash
  Reviews:
    New York Times p. 17, Dec 2, 1961
    Saturday Review 44:30, Dec 23, 1961

The Hungerers
  Productions:
    (Off Off Broadway) November 2, 1977 (Cithaeron).
  Reviews:
    See Floydada to Matador

*Jim Dandy
  Reviews:

Library Journal 67:229, Mar 1, 1941
New York Times p. 26, Oct 8, 1941
      p. 10, Nov 8, 1941
      IX, p. 5, Dec 14, 1941
Quarterly Journal of Speech 30:71-5, Feb 1944
Time 38:68, Nov 17, 1941
Vogue 110:129, Oct 15, 1947

*Life, Laughter and Tears (with Sean O'Casey)
 Reviews:
  New York Times p. 15, Feb 26, 1942

*London Comedy: or, Sam the Highest Jumper of Them All
 Reviews:
  New York Times p. 24, Apr 8, 1960
         p. 39, Apr 12, 1960
  Time 75:47, Mar 28, 1960

*A Lost Child's Fireflies
 Reviews:
  New York Times p. 11, Jul 16, 1954

Love's Old Sweet Song
 Productions:
  Opened May 2, 1940 for 44 performances.
  (Off Broadway) October 21, 1961 for 10 performances (Equity
   Library Theater).
 Reviews:
  Catholic World 151:344-5, Jun 1940
  Commonweal 32:82, May 17, 1940
  Nation 150:634-5, May 18, 1940
  New Republic 102:760, Jun 3, 1940
  New York Theatre Critics' Reviews 1940:319
  New York Times p. 44, Apr 7, 1940
        IX, p. 3, Apr 4, 1940
        p. 16, May 3, 1940
  New Yorker 16:28, May 11, 1940
  Newsweek 15:44-5, Apr 29, 1940
  Theatre Arts 24:832, Nov 1940
  Time 35:52, May 13, 1940

My Heart's in the Highlands
 Productions:
  Opened April 13, 1939 for 44 performances.
  (Off Broadway) Season of 1938-39 (Group Theatre).
  (Off Broadway) Season of 1949-50 (Equity Library Theater).
 Reviews:
  Catholic World 149:343-4, Jun 1939
  Commonweal 30:22, Apr 28, 1939
  Nation 148:538, May 6, 1939
  New Republic 98:379, May 3, 1939

New York Times p. 29, Apr 14, 1939
　　　　　　　X, p. 1, May 7, 1939
　　　　　　　p. 36, Nov 22, 1949
　　　　　　　p. 8, Feb 18, 1950
Newsweek 13:45, May 1, 1939
North American Review 247 no. 2:365, Jun 1939
Theatre Arts 23:396+, Jun 1939
　　　　　　　24:832, Nov 1940

Once Around the Block
　Productions:
　　(Off Broadway) Season of 1956-57.
　Reviews:
　　New York Times p. 36, May 25, 1950
　　　　　　　　p. 34, Oct 29, 1956
　　　　　　　　VI, p. 31, Nov 11, 1956

Opera Opera　(see Floydada to Matador)

The Rebirth Celebration of the Human Race at Artie Zabala's Off-
　Broadway Theater
　Productions:
　　(Off Off Broadway) July 10, 1975 (Shirtsleeve Theater).
　Reviews:
　　New York Times p. 16, Jul 12, 1975

*Sam Ego's House
　Reviews:
　　New York Times p. 43, Nov 11, 1954

*Sam Ego's House of Angels Aghast
　Reviews:
　　New York Times p. 11, Nov 1, 1947

Sam the Highest Jumper of Them All　(see London Comedy)

*Settled Out of Court (with H. Cecil)
　Reviews:
　　New York Times p. 44, Oct 20, 1960

*The Son
　Reviews:
　　Christian Science Monitor Magazine p. 7, Aug 19, 1950
　　New York Times p. 12, Apr 1, 1950
　　　　　　　　p. 24, Aug 16, 1950

*Sunset Sonata
　Reviews:
　　Newsweek 13:35, Jun 12, 1939

Talking to You　(see Two by Saroyan)

The Time of Your Life
   Productions:
      Opened October 25, 1939 for 185 performances.
      Opened September 23, 1940 for 32 performances.
      (Off Broadway) Season of 1946-47.
      Opened January 19, 1955 for 15 performances.
      Opened November 6, 1969 for 52 performances.
      Opened October 28, 1975 for 8 performances.
   Reviews:
      America 92:518, Feb 12, 1955
              121:622, Dec 20, 1969
      Catholic World 150:335, Dec 1939
                     180:467, Mar 1955
      Commonweal 31:78, Nov 10, 1939
                 32:512, Oct 11, 1940
                 49:20+, Mar 1970
      Life 7:46-9, Dec 4, 1939
      Nation 149:505-6, Nov 4, 1939
             180:124-5, Feb 5, 1955
             209:581, Nov 24, 1969
      New Republic 101:169, Nov 29, 1939
                   161:22+, Nov 22, 1969
      New York Theatre Critics' Reviews 1940:463
                                        1955:390
                                        1969:184
                                        1975:172
      New York Times p. 26, Oct 26, 1939
                     IX, p. 1, Nov 5, 1939
                     IX, p. 1, Nov 12, 1939
                     IX, p. 1, Nov 26, 1939
                     p. 27, Sep 24, 1940
                     II, p. 1, Jan 16, 1955
                     p. 35, Jan 20, 1955
                     II, p. 1, Jan 30, 1955
                     p. 37, Nov 7, 1969
                     II, p. 1, Nov 16, 1969
                     p. 26, Feb 25, 1972
                     p. 48, Oct 29, 1975
      New Yorker 30:44+, Jan 29, 1975
                 45:163, Nov 15, 1969
      Newsweek 14:30, Oct 23, 1939
               14:35, Nov 6, 1939
               45:80-1, Jan 31, 1955
               74:139, Nov 17, 1969
      North American Review 248 no. 2:403-4, Dec 1939
      One Act Play Magazine 3:175-9, Feb 1940
      Saturday Review 52:10, Nov 29, 1969
      Theatre Arts 23:842+, Dec 1939
                   24:11-13, Jan 1940
                   24:832, Nov 1940
                   30:351, Jun 1946

                39:22-4+, Jan 1955
                39:22, 25, Apr 1955
      Time 34:32, Nov 6, 1939
           65:71, Jan 31, 1955
           94:57, Nov 14, 1969
      Yale Review 30:422, Winter 1941

Two by Saroyan ("Talking to You" and "Across the Board on Tomor-
    row Morning")
    Productions:
      Opened August 17, 1942 for 8 performances.
      (Off Broadway) October 22, 1961 for 98 performances.
    Reviews:
      Nation 193:460, Dec 2, 1961
      New Republic 107:257, Aug 31, 1942
      New York Theatre Critics' Reviews 1942:252
      New York Times p. 13, Mar 21, 1942
                     p. 17, Aug 18, 1942
                     p. 22, Oct 23, 1961
      New Yorker 37:129-30, Nov 4, 1961
      Player's Magazine 17:8, Apr 1941
      Theatre Arts 25:526-9, Jul 1941
      Vogue 100:82-3, Sep 15, 1942

SCHARY, DORE

Brightower
    Productions:
      Opened January 28, 1970 for one performance.
    Reviews:
      New York Theatre Critics' Reviews 1970:388
      New York Times p. 32, Jan 29, 1970
      New Yorker 45:72-3, Feb 7, 1970

The Devil's Advocate (Based on Morris L. West's novel)
    Productions:
      Opened March 9, 1961 for 116 performances.
    Reviews:
      America 105:161-3, Apr 15, 1961
      Catholic World 193:8-12, Apr 1961
      Christian Century 78:458, Apr 12, 1961
      Commonweal 74:279, Jun 9, 1961
      Nation 192:312, Apr 8, 1961
      New York Theatre Critics' Reviews 1961:332
      New York Times II, p. 3, Mar 5, 1961
                     p. 20, Mar 10, 1961
                     II, p. 1, Mar 19, 1961
      New Yorker 37:126, Mar 18, 1961
      Newsweek 57:88, Mar 20, 1961
      Reporter 24:44, Apr 13, 1961
      Saturday Review 44:35, Mar 25, 1961

Theatre Arts 45:54-5, May 1961
Time 77:42, Mar 17, 1961

Herzl (with Amos Elon. Based on the biography by Amos Elon)
    Productions:
        Opened December 5, 1976 for 8 performances.
    Reviews:
        New York Magazine 9:85, Dec 20, 1976
        New York Theatre Critics' Reviews 1976:98
        New York Times III, p. 17, Dec 1, 1976

The Highest Tree
    Productions:
        Opened November 4, 1959 for 21 performances.
    Reviews:
        America 102:253, Nov 21, 1959
        New York Theatre Critics' Reviews 1959:235
        New York Times II, p. 1, Nov 1, 1959
                            p. 41, Nov 5, 1959
        New Yorker 35:117-18, Nov 14, 1959
        Reporter 21:39, Dec 10, 1959
        Saturday Review 42:34, Nov 21, 1959
        Time 74:57, Nov 16, 1959

One by One
    Productions:
        Opened December 1, 1964 for 7 performances.
    Reviews:
        New York Theatre Critics' Reviews 1964:123
        New York Times p. 60, Dec 2, 1964

Sunrise at Campobello
    Productions:
        Opened January 30, 1958 for 556 performances.
    Reviews:
        America 98:735, Mar 22, 1958
        Catholic World 187:67, Apr 1958
        Christian Century 75:622-3, May 21, 1958
        Commonweal 67:592, Mar 7, 1958
        Life 44:91-4, Feb 10, 1958
        Look 22:98-101+, Apr 1, 1958
        Nation 186:146, Feb 15, 1958
        New Republic 138:20, Feb 10, 1958
        New York Theatre Critics' Reviews 1958:378
        New York Times VI, p. 42, Jan 19, 1958
                        II, p. 1, Jan 26, 1958
                        p. 16, Jan 29, 1958
                        p. 25, Jan 31, 1958
                        II, p. 1, Feb 9, 1958
                        II, p. 3, Apr 20, 1958
                        II, p. 4, Jan 25, 1959

p. 17, Mar 26, 1959
p. 15, Jun 8, 1959
New York Times Magazine p. 42, Jan 19, 1958
New Yorker 33:93-6, Feb 8, 1958
Newsweek 51:69, Feb 10, 1958
Reporter 18:35, Mar 6, 1958
Saturday Review 41:28, Feb 15, 1958
Theatre Arts 42:15-16, Apr 1958
Time 71:57, Feb 10, 1958

Too Many Heroes
    Productions:
    Opened November 15, 1937 for 16 performances.
    Reviews:
    New York Times p. 26, Nov 16, 1937
    Theatre Arts 22:22, Jan 1938
    Time 30:36, Nov 29, 1937

SCHISGAL, MURRAY

All over Town
    Productions:
    Opened December 29, 1974 for 233 performances.
    Reviews:
    New York Theatre Critics' Reviews 1974:106
                                      1974:118
    New York Times p. 38, Dec 30, 1974
                   p. 46, Jan 2, 1975
                   II, p. 5, Jan 12, 1975
                   p. 50, Jun 5, 1975
    New Yorker 50:63, Jan 13, 1975
               50:76-7, Feb 3, 1975
    Playboy 22:46, Apr 1975
    Time 105:53, Jan 13, 1975

An American Millionaire
    Productions:
    Opened April 20, 1974 for 17 performances.
    Reviews:
    New York Magazine 7:80, May 6, 1974
    New York Theatre Critics' Reviews 1974:304
    New York Times p. 43, Apr 22, 1974
                   II, p. 1, May 5, 1974
    New Yorker 50:63, Apr 29, 1974

The Basement
    Productions:
    (Off Broadway) October 2, 1967 for 24 performances.
    Reviews:
    America 117:487-8, Oct 28, 1967

Christian Century 85:26+, Jan 3, 1968
New York Times p. 56, Oct 3, 1967
II, p. 3, Oct 15, 1967
New Yorker 43:151-2, Oct 14, 1967
Newsweek 70:106+, Oct 16, 1967

The Chinese and Dr. Fish (2 one-acts)
Productions:
Opened March 10, 1970 for 15 performances.
Reviews:
New York Theatre Critics' Reviews 1970:348
New York Times p. 42, Mar 11, 1970
II, p. 3, Mar 22, 1970
New Yorker 46:115, Mar 21, 1970

Dr. Fish (see The Chinese and Dr. Fish)

*Ducks and Lovers
Reviews:
New York Times p. 39, Oct 20, 1961

Fragments
Productions:
(Off Broadway) October 2, 1967 for 24 performances.
Reviews:
America 117:487-8, Oct 28, 1967
Christian Century 85:26+, Jan 3, 1968
New York Times p. 56, Oct 3, 1967
II, p. 3, Oct 15, 1967
New Yorker 43:151-2, Oct 14, 1967
Newsweek 70:106+, Oct 16, 1967

Invitational (see The Pushcart Peddlers)

Jimmy Shine
Productions:
Opened December 5, 1968 for 153 performances.
Reviews:
America 120:147-8, Feb 1, 1969
New Republic 160:32-4, Jan 25, 1969
New York Theatre Critics' Reviews 1968:152
1968:154
New York Times p. 52, Dec 6, 1968
II, p. 3, Dec 22, 1968
New Yorker 44:180-1, Dec 14, 1968
Newsweek 72:115, Dec 16, 1968
Saturday Review 51:13, Dec 21, 1968
Time 92:81, Dec 13, 1968

Luv
Productions:
Opened November 11, 1964 for 901 performances.

Reviews:
America 112:232-3, Feb 13, 1965
Catholic World 200:383, Mar 1965
Commonweal 81:389, Dec 11, 1964
Life 58:79-81+, Jan 8, 1965
Nation 199:415, Nov 30, 1964
New Republic 151:20, Dec 12, 1964
New York Theatre Critics' Reviews 1964:152
New York Times p. 43, Nov 12, 1964
           p. 26, Nov 13, 1964
           II, p. 1, Nov 22, 1964
           p. 56, Nov 16, 1965
           p. 20, Feb 3, 1966
           p. 36, Dec 22, 1966
New Yorker 40:143, Nov 21, 1964
Newsweek 64:102, Nov 23, 1964
Saturday Review 47:29, Nov 28, 1964
Time 84:81, Nov 20, 1964
Vogue 145:68, Jan 1, 1965

The Pushcart Peddlers
  Productions:
    (Off Off Broadway) November-December 1979, as part of a bill
    called Invitational (Ensemble Studio Theater).
  Reviews:
    New York Times III, p. 21, Nov 22, 1979

The Tiger
  Productions:
    (Off Broadway) February 4, 1963 for 200 performances.
  Reviews:
    Commonweal 77:665, Mar 22, 1963
    Nation 196:166-7, Feb 23, 1963
    New York Times p. 5, Feb 6, 1963
    New Yorker 38:116, Feb 16, 1963
    Newsweek 61:56, Feb 18, 1963
    Time 81:63, Feb 15, 1963

The Typists
  Productions:
    (Off Broadway) February 4, 1963 for 200 performances.
  Reviews:
    Commonweal 77:665, Mar 22, 1963
    Nation 196:166-7, Feb 23, 1963
    New York Times p. 5, Feb 6, 1963
    New Yorker 38:114+, Feb 16, 1963
    Newsweek 61:56, Feb 18, 1963
    Time 81:63, Feb 15, 1963

Walter & the Flatulist
  Productions:

(Off Off Broadway) March 1980 (Sanctuary Theater).
No Reviews.

SCHULBERG, BUDD

The Disenchanted (with Harvey Breit. Based on Schulberg's novel)
    Productions:
        Opened December 3, 1958 for 189 performances.
        (Off Broadway) January 6, 1962 for 9 performances (Equity
            Library Theater).
    Reviews:
        America 100:557, Feb 7, 1959
        Catholic World 188:419, Feb 1959
        Christian Century 75:1488, Dec 24, 1958
        Commonweal 69:386, Jan 9, 1959
        Nation 187:501, Dec 27, 1958
        New Republic 139:23, Dec 22, 1958
        New York Theatre Critics' Reviews 1958:180
        New York Times II, p. 4, Nov 4, 1958
                        p. 53, Dec 4, 1958
                        II, p. 1, Jan 11, 1959
        New Yorker 34:107-9, Dec 13, 1958
        Newsweek 52:63, Dec 15, 1958
        Reporter 20:36-7, Jan 8, 1959
        Saturday Review 41:31, Dec 20, 1958
        Theatre Arts 43:11+, Feb 1959
                        44:22-47, Aug 1960
        Time 72:44, Dec 15, 1958

SELWYN, EDGAR

Anything Might Happen
    Productions:
        Opened February 20, 1923 for 63 performances.
    Reviews:
        Life (NY) 81:18, May 5, 1923
        New York Clipper 71:14, Mar 7, 1923
        New York Times p. 22, Feb 21, 1923
                        VII, p. 1, Feb 25, 1923
        Theatre Magazine 37:16+, Apr 1923

The Arab
    Productions:
        Opened September 20, 1911 for 53 performances.
    Reviews:
        Dramatic Mirror 66:10, Sep 27, 1911
                        66:5, Oct 4, 1911
        Everybody's 25:818, Dec 1911
        Green Book 6:966, Nov 1911

Leslies' Weekly 113:493, Nov 2, 1911
Life (NY) 58:618, Oct 12, 1911
Munsey 46:282, Nov 1911
　　55:695, Sep 1915
New York Drama News 61:20, Jun 26, 1915
Red Book 18:379+, Dec 1911
Theatre Magazine 14:163, Nov 1911

The Country Boy
　Productions:
　　Opened August 30, 1910 for 143 performances.
　Reviews:
　　Canadian Magazine 36:287-8, Jan 1911
　　Dramatic Mirror 64:7, Sep 10, 1910
　　Dramatist 2:99-101, Oct 1910
　　Everybody's 23:702-3+, Nov 1910
　　Good Housekeeping 51:707, Dec 1910
　　Green Book 5:536-9, Mar 1911
　　　　　　5:1153-78, Jun 1911
　　Hampton 25:674-6, Nov 1910
　　Metropolitan Magazine 33:262-3, Nov 1910
　　Munsey 44:270-6, Nov 1910
　　Pearson 24:645, Nov 1910
　　Theatre Magazine 12:100-1+, Oct 1910
　　World Today 19:1224-35, Nov 1910

The Crowded Hour (with Channing Pollock)
　Productions:
　　Opened November 22, 1918 for 139 performances.
　Reviews:
　　Dramatic Mirror 79:831, Dec 7, 1918
　　Forum 61:114-15, Jan 1919
　　Hearst 35:42-3+, May 1919
　　New York Drama News 65:10, Nov 16-23, 1918
　　New York Times p. 13, Nov 26, 1918
　　　　　　　VII, p. 6, Dec 8, 1918
　　　　　　　VII, p. 8, Dec 8, 1918
　　Theatre Magazine 29:20+, Jan 1919

Dancing Mothers (with Edmund Goulding)
　Productions:
　　Opened August 11, 1924 for 312 performances.
　Reviews:
　　Bookman 60:211, Oct 1924
　　Canadian Magazine 64:104-5+, May 1925
　　Life (NY) 84:18, Aug 28, 1924
　　Theatre Magazine 39:15+, Oct 1924
　　　　　　　39:28-9+, Nov 1924

I'll Be Hanged If I Do (with William Collier)
　Productions:

Opened November 28, 1910 for 80 performances.
Reviews:
Blue Book 12:882-5, Mar 1911
Bookman 23:602, Feb 1911
Dramatic Mirror 64:7, Nov 30, 1910
64:9, Dec 14, 1910
Green Book 5:242-3+, Feb 1911
Munsey 44:710, Feb 1911
Pearson 25:260, Feb 1911
Red Book 16:764-8, Feb 1911

The Mirage
Productions:
Opened September 30, 1920 for 192 performances.
Reviews:
Dramatic Mirror p. 635, Oct 9, 1920
Independent 104:113, Oct 23, 1920
New York Clipper 68:29, Oct 6, 1920
New York Times p. 14, Oct 1, 1920
Theatre Magazine 32:349+, Dec 1920

Nearly Married
Productions:
Opened September 5, 1913 for 123 performances.
Reviews:
Blue Book 18:215-17, Dec 1913
Bookman 38:263, Nov 1913
Dramatic Mirror 70:6-7, Sep 10, 1913
Dramatist 5:440-1, Jan 1914
Green Book 10:870-1, Nov 1913
10:964-5, Dec 1913
Munsey 50:294-5, Nov 1913
New York Drama News 58:9, Sep 13, 1913
New York Times p. 7, Sep 6, 1913
Theatre Magazine 18:112-13+, Oct 1913

Possession
Productions:
Opened October 2, 1928 for 47 performances.
Reviews:
Life (NY) 92:19, Oct 19, 1928
New York Times VII, p. 1, Jul 22, 1928
IX, p. 2, Sep 23, 1928
p. 35, Oct 3, 1928

Rolling Stones
Productions:
Opened August 17, 1915 for 115 performances.
Reviews:
Bookman 42:159+, Oct 1915
Dramatic Mirror 74:8, Aug 25, 1915

Green Book 14:620-1, Oct 1915
Nation 101:269, Aug 26, 1915
New York Times p. 11, Aug 18, 1915
Theatre Magazine 22:169+, Oct 1915

Something to Brag About (with William LeBaron)
    Productions:
        Opened August 13, 1925 for 4 performances.
    Reviews:
        New York Times VII, p. 1, Jul 12, 1925
                        p. 14, Aug 14, 1925

SHAW, IRWIN

The Assassin
    Productions:
        Opened October 17, 1945 for 13 performances.
    Reviews:
        Commonweal 43:69, Nov 2, 1945
        New Republic 113:573, Oct 29, 1945
                      114:479-80, Apr 8, 1946
        New York Theatre Critics' Reviews 1945:138
        New York Times p. 13, Mar 23, 1945
                       II, p. 2, Apr 1, 1945
                       p. 20, Oct 18, 1945
        New Yorker 21:42, Oct 27, 1945
        Newsweek 26:90, Oct 29, 1945
        Theatre Arts 29:679+, Dec 1945
        Time 47:67, Mar 25, 1946

Bury the Dead
    Productions:
        Opened April 18, 1936 for 97 performances.
        (Off Off Broadway) Season of 1970-71 (Urban Arts Corps).
    Reviews:
        Catholic World 143:338-40, Jan 1936
        Commonweal 24:48, May 8, 1936
        Literary Digest 121:11, May 2, 1936
        Nation 142:592-3, May 6, 1936
        New Republic 87:21, May 13, 1936
        New York Times p. 21, Mar 16, 1936
                       p. 17, Apr 20, 1936
                       IX, p. 1, Apr 26, 1936
                       X, p. 1, May 3, 1936
                       XI, p. 3, Nov 15, 1936
                       II, p. 1, Aug 20, 1950
                       II, p. 3, Jun 27, 1971
        Newsweek 7:29, Apr 25, 1936
        Theatre Arts 20:417-19, Jun 1936
        Time 27:56, Apr 27, 1936

Children from Their Games
Productions:
Opened April 11, 1963 for 4 performances.
Reviews:
New York Theatre Critics' Reviews 1963:352
New York Times II, p. 7, Apr 7, 1963
p. 33, Apr 12, 1963
New Yorker 39:96, Apr 20, 1963
Newsweek 61:90, Apr 22, 1963
Saturday Review 46:27, Apr 27, 1963
Theatre Arts 47:65, Jun 1963

The Gentle People
Productions:
Opened January 5, 1939 for 141 performances.
(Off Broadway) July 5, 1947 (Actors' Theatre).
(Off Off Broadway) April 26, 1979 (Jewish Repertory Theater).
(Off Off Broadway) December 6, 1980 for 23 performances (Playwrights Horizons).
Reviews:
Catholic World 148:598, Feb 1939
Commonweal 29:358, Jan 20, 1939
Life 6:31, Feb 6, 1939
New Republic 97:343, Jan 25, 1939
New York Times p. 25, Jan 6, 1939
p. 12, Jul 7, 1939
IX, p. 1, Jul 30, 1939
p. 10, Apr 15, 1950
XXI, p. 13, Dec 21, 1980
III, p. 9, Dec 23, 1980
North American Review 247 no. 2:368-9, Jun 1939
Newsweek 13:26, Jan 16, 1939
One Act Play Magazine 2:675-7, Jan 1939
Stage 16:10-11, Feb 1939
Theatre Arts 23:170, Mar 1939
Time 33:41, Jan 16, 1939

Patate (Adapted from the play by Marcel Achard)
Productions:
Opened October 28, 1958 for 7 performances.
Reviews:
Nation 184:554, Jun 22, 1957
New York Theatre Critics' Reviews 1958:234
New York Times p. 31, Oct 29, 1958
New Yorker 34:91, Nov 8, 1958
Saturday Review 41:27, Nov 15, 1958
Theatre Arts 43:23-4, Jan 1959

Quiet City
Productions:
(Off Broadway) April 16 and 23, 1939 (Group Theatre).
No Reviews.

Retreat to Pleasure
    Productions:
        Opened December 17, 1940 for 23 performances.
    Reviews:
        New York Theatre Critics' Reviews 1940:188
        New York Times p. 32, Dec 18, 1940
                     p. 24, Dec 19, 1940
        New Yorker 16:29, Dec 28, 1940
        Newsweek 16:38, Dec 30, 1940
        Stage 1:54, Feb 1941
        Theatre Arts 25:96, Feb 1941

Siege
    Productions:
        Opened December 8, 1937 for 6 performances.
    Reviews:
        New York Times p. 31, Dec 9, 1937

Sons and Soldiers
    Productions:
        Opened May 4, 1943 for 22 performances.
    Reviews:
        Catholic World 157:300, Jun 1943
        Commonweal 38:123, May 21, 1943
        Nation 156:715, May 15, 1943
        New Republic 108:669, May 17, 1943
        New York Theatre Critics' Reviews 1943:325
        New York Times p. 22, May 5, 1943
        New Yorker 19:36, May 15, 1943
        Time 41:73, May 17, 1943

The Survivors (with Peter Viertel)
    Productions:
        Opened January 19, 1948 for 8 performances.
    Reviews:
        Catholic World 166:552, Mar 1948
        Commonweal 47:424, Feb 6, 1948
        Forum 109:156-8, Mar 1948
        New Republic 118:33, Feb 2, 1948
        New York Theatre Critics' Reviews 1948:374
        New York Times p. 27, Jan 20, 1948
                     II, p. 1, Jan 25, 1948
        New Yorker 23:38+, Jan 31, 1948
        Newsweek 31:73, Feb 2, 1948

SHELDON, EDWARD

Bewitched (with Sidney Howard)
    Productions:
        Opened October 1, 1924 for 29 performances.

Reviews:
New York Times p. 26, Oct 2, 1924
VIII, p. 1, Oct 5, 1924
Theatre Magazine 39:14+, Dec 1924

The Boss
Productions:
Opened January 30, 1911 for 88 performances.
(Off Broadway) Opened February 24, 1976 for 24 perform-
ances.
(Off Off Broadway) March 1976 (Playwrights Horizons).
Reviews:
Blue Book 13:22-4, May 1911
Bookman 23:32, Mar 1911
Collier's 46:16+, Feb 25, 1911
Dramatic Mirror 65:7, Feb 1, 1911
Dramatist 2:143-5, Apr 1911
Everybody's 24:670-3, May 1911
Leslies' Weekly 112:181, Feb 16, 1911
Life (NY) 57:308-9, Feb 9, 1911
Metropolitan Magazine 34:126, Apr 1911
Munsey 45:133-4, Apr 1911
Nation 222:382, Mar 27, 1976
New York Magazine 9:66, Mar 22, 1976
New York Times p. 17, Mar 5, 1976
II, p. 5, Mar 14, 1976
New Yorker 52:52, Mar 15, 1976
Pearson 25:502, Apr 1911
Theatre Magazine 13:72, Mar 1911
World Today 20:282, Mar 1911

The Czarina (Adapted from the Hungarian of Melchoir Lengyel and
Lajos Biro)
Productions:
Opened January 31, 1922 for 136 performances.
Reviews:
Hearst 41:45-7+, May 1922
New Republic 29:340-41, Feb 15, 1922
New York Clipper 70:20, Feb 8, 1922
New York Times p. 22, Feb 1, 1922
Theatre Magazine 35:211+, Apr 1922

Dishonored Lady (with Margaret Ayer Barnes)
Productions:
Opened February 4, 1930 for 127 performances.
Reviews:
Commonweal 11:453, Feb 19, 1930
Life (NY) 95:18, Feb 28, 1930
New Republic 62:20-1, Feb 19, 1930
New York Times VIII, p. 2, Jan 26, 1930
p. 27, Feb 6, 1930
IX, p. 2, May 25, 1930

Outlook 154:312, Feb 19, 1930
Theatre Arts 14:283-4, Apr 1930
Theatre Magazine 51:43, Apr 1930
Vogue 75:54+, Mar 29, 1930

The Garden of Paradise (Based on Hans Christian Andersen's "The
    Little Mermaid")
  Productions:
  Opened November 28, 1914 for 17 performances.
  Reviews:
    American Mercury 79:42-6, Apr 1915
    American Playwright 4:6-7, Jan 1915
    Book News 33:229, Jan 1915
    Bookman 40:548-9, Jan 1915
    Collier's 54:28, Jan 2, 1915
    Dial 60:75, Jan 20, 1916
    Dramatic Mirror 72:8, Dec 9, 1914
    Green Book 13:267-78, Feb 1915
    Life (NY) 64:1082, Dec 10, 1914
    Munsey 54:85-9+, Feb 1915
    Nation 9:669, Dec 3, 1914
    New Republic 1:23, Dec 5, 1914
    New York Times VII, p. 8, Jul 19, 1914
                    p. 9, Nov 30, 1914
                 IX, p. 2, Dec 6, 1914
    Smart Set 45:147-8, Feb 1915

The High Road
  Productions:
  Opened November 9, 1912 for 71 performances.
  Reviews:
    American Magazine 75:61, May 1913
    American Playwright 1:391-4, Dec 1912
    Book News 31:653-4, Apr 1913
    Bookman 36:536-8, Jan 1913
    Collier's 50:19, Dec 28, 1912
    Dramatic Mirror 68:6, Nov 27, 1912
    Dramatist 4:319-20, Jan 1913
    Everybody's 28:258, Feb 1913
    Green Book 9:200-201+, Feb 1913
              9:367-8, Feb 1913
    Literary Digest 46:183, Jan 25, 1913
    McClure's 40:66-9, Mar 1913
    Munsey 48:684-5, Jan 1913
    New York Drama News 67:11, Nov 30, 1912
    Red Book 20:689-96, Feb 1913
    Theatre Magazine 17:2+, Jan 1913

Jenny (with Margaret Ayer Barnes)
  Productions:
  Opened October 8, 1929 for 111 performances.

Reviews:
    Catholic World 130:332-3, Dec 1929
    Life (NY) 94:22, Nov 1, 1929
    Nation 129:504, Oct 30, 1929
    New York Times VIII, p. 1, Jun 2, 1929
                     p.34, Oct 9, 1929
    Outlook 153:314, Oct 23, 1929
    Theatre Magazine 50:15+, Dec 1929
    Vogue 74:164, Dec 7, 1929

Lulu Belle (with Charles MacArthur)
    Productions:
        Opened February 9, 1926 for 461 performances.
    Reviews:
        Bookman 63:215-16, Apr 1926
        Life (NY) 87:21, Mar 4, 1926
        New York Times p. 17, Jan 27, 1926
                      p. 20, Feb 10, 1926
                      VIII, p. 1, Feb 14, 1926
        Theatre Magazine 43:15, Apr 1926
        Vogue 67:116-17, Apr 1926

The Nigger
    Productions:
        Opened December 4, 1909 in repertory.
    Reviews:
        Burr McIntosh Monthly 22:220-1, Mar 1910
        Dramatic Mirror 62:5, Dec 11, 1909
        Dramatist 2:161-3, Apr 1911
        Forum 43:186-7, Feb 1910
        Green Book 3:392-4, Feb 1910
                 5:705-36, Apr 1911
        Hampton 24:272-3, Feb 1910
        Harper's Weekly 54:24, Jan 1, 1910
        Life (NY) 54:886, Dec 16, 1909
        Metropolitan Magazine 32:118-19, Apr 1910
        Theatre Magazine 10:3-5, Jan 1910

*Proud Princess (with Dorothy Donnelly)
    Reviews:
        New York Times VII, p. 2, Feb 17, 1924

Romance
    Productions:
        Opened February 10, 1913 for 160 performances.
        Opened February 28, 1921 for 106 performances.
    Reviews:
        Blue Book 17:242-4, Jun 1913
        Bookman 37:308, May 1913
        Current Opinion 54:379-83, May 1913
        Dramatic Mirror 69:6, Feb 19, 1913
                    83:408, Mar 5, 1921

Dramatist 5:468-9, Apr 1914
Editor 37:357-8, Jun 25, 1913
Everybody's 28:681-3, May 1913
Green Book 9:632-4, Apr 1913
          9:735-6, Apr 1913
         10:489-503, Sep 1913
Hearst 24:299-308, Aug 1913
Life (NY) 61:416, Feb 27, 1913
Munsey 49:148, Apr 1913
New York Clipper 69:23, May 9, 1921
New York Times VIII, p. 5, Feb 9, 1913
            p. 13, Feb 11, 1913
            p. 20, Jul 1, 1916
            p. 9, Oct 7, 1916
            p. 18, Mar 1, 1921
            VI, p. 1, Mar 6, 1921
            VIII, p. 2, Mar 11, 1928
            p. 23, Aug 27, 1935
            p. 23, Aug 17, 1937
Red Book pp. 113-16, May 1913
Theatre Magazine 17:65-6, Mar 1913

The Song of Songs (Based on Hermann Sudermann's novel)
   Productions:
      Opened December 22, 1914 for 191 performances.
   Reviews:
      Bookman 40:637-8, Feb 1915
      Current Opinion 58:97-8, Feb 1915
      Dramatic Mirror 72:8, Dec 30, 1914
      Green Book 13:478-9, Mar 1915
              13:570-1, Mar 1915
      Hearst 27:299-301+, Mar 1915
      Nation 100:87, Jan 21, 1915
      New Republic 1:25, Jan 2, 1915
      New York Times p. 13, Dec 23, 1914
                   VIII, p. 2, Dec 27, 1914
      Smart Set 45:453-4, Jan 1915
      Theatre Magazine 21:58+, Feb 1915

SHELLEY, ELSA

Foxhole in the Parlor
   Productions:
      Opened May 23, 1945 for 45 performances.
   Reviews:
      Commonweal 42:191, Jun 8, 1945
      New Republic 112:815, Jun 11, 1945
      New York Theatre Critics' Reviews 1945:210
      New York Times p. 15, May 24, 1945
      New Yorker 21:38, Jun 2, 1945
      Theatre Arts 29:389, Jul 1945

Pick-Up Girl
    Productions:
        Opened May 3, 1944 for 198 performances.
    Reviews:
        Catholic World 159:264-6, Jun 1944
        Commonweal 40:110-111, May 19, 1944
        Life 16:68-70, Jun 12, 1944
        New York Theatre Critics' Reviews 1944:196
        New York Times p. 25, May 4, 1944
        New Yorker 20:44, May 13, 1944
        Theatre Arts 28:572, Oct 1944

With a Silk Thread
    Productions:
        Opened April 12, 1950 for 13 performances.
    Reviews:
        New York Theatre Critics' Reviews 1950:314
        New Yorker 26:60+, Apr 22, 1950
        Newsweek 35:95, Apr 24, 1950
        Theatre Arts 34:17, Jun 1950

SHEPARD, SAM

Action
    Productions:
        (Off Broadway) April 4, 1975 for 34 performances.
        (Off Off Broadway) February 1979 (Soho Repertory).
        (Off Off Broadway) February 1980 (A New Space).
    Reviews:
        Nation 220:542, May 3, 1975
        New West 5:SC-24, May 19, 1980
        New York Times p. 54, Apr 16, 1975
                       III, p. 24, Mar 12, 1980
        New Yorker 51:81, May 5, 1975

Angel City
    Productions:
        (Off Off Broadway) October 21, 1977 for 15 performances (Play-
            wrights Horizons).
        (Off Off Broadway) May 18, 1978 (Theater Genesis).
    Reviews:
        Los Angeles 22:180+, Jun 1977
        New West 2:SC-48, May 23, 1977
        New York Times III, p. 23, Mar 9, 1977
                       III, p. 20, Nov 2, 1977

Back Bog Beast Bait
    Productions:
        (Off Broadway) April 29, 1971 (American Place Theater).
        (Off Off Broadway) March 1976 (Direct Theater).
    No Reviews.

Blue Bitch
    Productions:
        (Off Off Broadway) January 18, 1973 (Theater Genesis).
    No Reviews.

Buried Child
    Productions:
        (Off Off Broadway) October 12, 1978 for 20 performances (The-
            ater for the New City).
        (Off Broadway) Opened December 5, 1978 for 152 performances.
        (Off Broadway) Opened June 2, 1979 for 90 performances.
    Reviews:
        America 139:500, Dec 30, 1978
        Nation 227:621-2, Dec 2, 1978
        New York Magazine 11:117-18, Nov 27, 1978
        New York Theatre Critics' Reviews 1978:146
        New York Times p. 61, Nov 7, 1978
                      II, p. 3, Dec 10, 1978
                      III, p. 14, Jan 25, 1979
                      III, p. 18, Sep 13, 1979
        New Yorker 54:151-2, Nov 6, 1978
        Newsweek 92:106, Oct 30, 1978
        Texas Monthly 8:132, Feb 1980
        Time 112:76, Dec 18, 1978

Chicago
    Productions:
        (Off Broadway) April 12, 1966 for 16 performances.
    Reviews:
        Nation 202:403, Apr 4, 1966
        New York Times II, p. 15, Apr 10, 1966
                      p. 36, Apr 13, 1966

Cowboys 2
    Productions:
        (Off Off Broadway) March 15, 1976 (Theater Off Park).
        (Off Off Broadway) March 31, 1977 (Perry St. Theater).
    Reviews:
        New York Times p. 27, Aug 11, 1970

Curse of the Starving Class
    Productions:
        (Off Broadway) Opened February 14, 1978 for 62 performances.
    Reviews:
        America 138:286, Apr 8, 1978
        Nation 226:348-9, Mar 25, 1978
        New Republic 178:24-5, Apr 8, 1978
        New York Theatre Critics' Reviews 1978:340
        New York Times III, p. 3, Mar 3, 1978
                      II, p. 3, Mar 12, 1978
        New Yorker 54:57-8, Mar 13, 1978
        Time 111:84-5, Mar 20, 1978

Forensic and the Navigators
Productions:
(Off Broadway) Season of 1967-68 (Theater Genesis).
(Off Broadway) April 1, 1970 for 21 performances.
Reviews:
New York Times p. 43, Apr 2, 1970
New Yorker 46:83, Apr 11, 1970

Geography of a Horse Dreamer
Productions:
(Off Off Broadway) December 1975 (Manhattan Theater Club).
(Off Off Broadway) April 14, 1981 (Ensemble Studio Theater).
Reviews:
Nation 222:27, Jan 3, 1976
New York Times p. 21, Dec 13, 1975
New Yorker 51:60+, Dec 22, 1975

Hawk Moon #1
Productions:
(Off Off Broadway) July 1977 (Westbeth Theater Center).
No Reviews.

The Holy Ghostly
Productions:
(Off Off Broadway) November 29, 1972 (New Village Theater).
(Off Off Broadway) February 1977 (Direct Theater).
No Reviews.

Icarus's Mother
Productions:
(Off Off Broadway) November 29, 1972 (New Village Theater).
(Off Off Broadway) March 1976 (Direct Theater).
No Reviews.

Killer's Head
Productions:
(Off Broadway) Opened April 4, 1975 for 34 performances.
(Off Broadway) January/February 1982 for one performance.
Reviews:
Nation 220:542, May 3, 1975
New York Magazine 8:94, May 5, 1975
New York Times p. 54, Apr 16, 1975

Mad Dog Blues
Productions:
(Off Off Broadway) Season of 1970-71 (Theater Genesis).
Reviews:
America 124:408, Apr 17, 1971
New York Times p. 25, Mar 9, 1971

Melodrama Play
Productions:

(Off Broadway) Season of 1971-72 (La Mama ETC).
Reviews:
New York Times p. 37, Jun 28, 1971

Nightwalk (with The Open Theater, Jean-Claude van Itallie, and
    Megan Terry)
Productions:
    (Off Off Broadway) Season of 1972-73 (Open Theater).
    (Off Off Broadway) September 8, 1973 (Theater at St. Clem-
    ents).
Reviews:
    New York Magazine 6:92, Sep 24, 1973
    New York Times p. 55, Sep 11, 1973
                II, p. 3, Oct 7, 1973

Operation Sidewinder
Productions:
    Opened March 12, 1970 for 52 performances.
Reviews:
    America 122:398, Apr 11, 1970
    Commonweal 92:193-4, May 8, 1970
    Nation 210:380-1, Mar 30, 1970
    New York Theatre Critics' Reviews 1970:344
    New York Times p. 33, Mar 13, 1970
                II, p. 1, Mar 22, 1970
    New Yorker 46:115, Mar 21, 1970
    Newsweek 75:69, Mar 23, 1970
    Saturday Review 53:24, Mar 28, 1970
    Time 95:49, Mar 23, 1970

Red Cross
Productions:
    (Off Broadway) April 28, 1968 for 65 performances.
    (Off Off Broadway) Season of 1974-75 (Corner Loft Theater).
Reviews:
    Commonweal 88:384, Jun 14, 1968
    Nation 202:224, Feb 21, 1966
    New York Times p. 47, Apr 29, 1968
    New Yorker 44:91, May 11, 1968

Savage/Love (see Tongues and Savage/Love)

Seduced
Productions:
    (Off Broadway) Opened February 2, 1979 for 44 performances.
Reviews:
    Nation 228:221, Feb 24, 1979
    New York Theatre Critics' Reviews 1979:330
    New York Times III, p. 3, Apr 28, 1978
                III, p. 3, Feb 2, 1979
                II, p. 3, Feb 11, 1979

New Yorker 54:46, Feb 12, 1979
Newsweek 91:94, May 8, 1978

Suicide in B Flat
Productions:
(Off Off Broadway) March 31, 1977 (Circles Repertory).
(Off Off Broadway) February 16, 1979 (IRT).
Reviews:
New York Times p. 42, Oct 25, 1976
II, p. 3, Nov 7, 1976
III, p. 19, Mar 14, 1979
Newsweek 88:109, Nov 8, 1976

Tongues and Savage/Love (with Joseph Chaikin)
Productions:
(Off Off Broadway) November 7, 1979 for 18 performances (NY Shakespeare Festival Public Theater).
(Off Broadway) Opened November 15, 1979 for 44 performances.
Reviews:
New York Times III, p. 6, Nov 16, 1979
I, p. 3, Dec 9, 1979

The Tooth of Crime
Productions:
(Off Broadway) Opened March 7, 1973 for 123 performances.
(Off Off Broadway) March 8, 1973 (The Performance Group).
(Off Off Broadway) February 2, 1974 (The Performance Group).
(Off Off Broadway) November 1975 (The Performance Group).
Reviews:
America 128:290, Mar 31, 1973
Los Angeles 21:180, Sep 1976
Nation 216:411-12, Mar 26, 1973
New Republic 168:22+, Mar 24, 1973
New York Times p. 77, Nov 12, 1972
II, p. 8, Nov 19, 1972
p. 34, Mar 8, 1973
II, p. 3, Mar 18, 1973
New Yorker 49:92+, Mar 17, 1973
Newsweek 80:77, Nov 27, 1972
Time 100:73, Nov 27, 1972

True West
Productions:
(Off Broadway) Opened December 23, 1980 for 24 performances.
Reviews:
Nation 232:123-4, Jan 31, 1981
New Republic 184:21-3, Jan 31, 1981
New York Magazine 14:45-6, Jan 12, 1981
New York Theatre Critics' Reviews 1981:366
New York Times III, p. 9, Dec 24, 1980
II, p. 3, Jan 11, 1981

New Yorker 56:81-2, Jan 12, 1981
Newsweek 97:63, Jan 5, 1981
Time 117:92, Jan 5, 1981

La Turista
  Productions:
    (Off Broadway) March 4, 1967 for 29 performances (American
      Place Theatre).
  Reviews:
    Commonweal 90:204, May 2, 1969
    New York Times II, p. 5, Mar 5, 1967
                    II, p. 3, Apr 13, 1969

The Unseen Hand
  Productions:
    (Off Off Broadway) Season of 1969-70 (La Mama ETC).
    (Off Broadway) Opened April 1, 1970 for 21 performances.
    (Off Off Broadway) March 31, 1977 (Perry St. Theater).
    (Off Broadway) Opened January 27, 1982 for 127 performances.
    (Off Off Broadway) Season of 1981-82 (La Mama ETC).
  Reviews:
    New Republic 168:23, Apr 21, 1973
    New York Times p. 43, Apr 2, 1970
                 III, p. 20, Jan 6, 1982
    New Yorker 46:82-3, Apr 11, 1970

Up to Thursday
  Productions:
    (Off Broadway) February 10, 1965 for 23 performances (Theatre
      1965 New Playwrights Series).
  Reviews:
    New York Times II, p. 1, Feb 7, 1965
                    p. 45, Feb 11, 1965
    Newsweek 65:93, Feb 22, 1965

SHERMAN, MARTIN

Bent
  Productions:
    Opened December 2, 1979 for 240 performances.
  Reviews:
    America 142:64, Jan 26, 1980
    Commentary 69:74-5, Mar 1980
    Maclean's 94:63, Mar 30, 1981
    Nation 229:700+, Dec 29, 1979
    New Republic 182:24, Jan 5, 1980
    New York Magazine 12:110-11, Dec 17, 1979
    New York Theatre Critics' Reviews 1979:73
    New York Times II, p. 1, Dec 2, 1979
                 III, p. 15, Dec 3, 1979

> II, p. 3, Dec 16, 1979
> II, p. 1, Dec 30, 1979
> II, p. 1, Feb 3, 1980
> II, p. 2, Mar 14, 1980
> III, p. 16, Jun 19, 1980
> III, p. 23, Jun 25, 1980
> New Yorker 55:100, Dec 17, 1979
> Newsweek 94:115, Dec 17, 1979
> Saturday Review 6:56+, Dec 13, 1979
> 7:30+, Feb 2, 1980
> Time 114:84, Dec 17, 1979

Cracks
    Productions:
        (Off Broadway) February 10, 1976 for one performance.
        (Off Off Broadway) June 16, 1977 for 12 performances (Play-
            wrights Horizons).
    Reviews:
        New York Times p. 35, Feb 11, 1976
                        III, p. 22, Jun 23, 1977
                        III, p. 1, Jun 24, 1977
        New Yorker 52:82, Feb 23, 1976

Passing By
    Productions:
        (Off Off Broadway) March 5, 1974 (Playwrights Horizons).
    No Reviews.

Rio Grande
    Productions:
        (Off Off Broadway) November 11, 1976 (Playwrights Horizons).
    No Reviews.

SHERWOOD, ROBERT E.

*Acropolis
    Reviews:
        New York Times p. 25, Nov 24, 1933

Abe Lincoln in Illinois
    Productions:
        Opened October 15, 1938 for 472 performances.
        (Off Broadway) January 21, 1963 for 40 performances.
    Reviews:
        Canadian Forum 19:355-6, Feb 1940
        Catholic World 148:340-1, Dec 1938
        Commonweal 29:20, Oct 28, 1938
                    77:543, Feb 15, 1963
        Forum 101:72, Feb 1939
        Independent Woman 17:348, Nov 1938

Life 5:42+, Oct 31, 1938
Nation 147:487-8, Nov 5, 1938
    196:125-6, Feb 9, 1963
New Republic 97:18, Nov 9, 1938
    98:134, Mar 8, 1939
New York Times p. 20, Oct 4, 1938
    p. 12, Oct 17, 1938
    IX, p. 1, Oct 23, 1938
    X, p. 3, Apr 23, 1939
    IX, p. 1, Jul 30, 1939
    IX, p. 1, Oct 22, 1939
    p. 5, Jan 23, 1963
New Yorker 38:69-70, Feb 2, 1963
Newsweek 12:29, Oct 31, 1938
North American Review 246 no. 2:373-4, Dec 1938
Saturday Review 19:6, Feb 18, 1939
    46:20, Feb 9, 1963
Stage 16:7-9, Nov 1938
    16:48-9, Apr 1, 1939
Theatre Arts 22:853-5, Dec 1938
    47:58-9+, Mar 1963
Time 32:53, Oct 24, 1938
Vogue 92:45+, Nov 15, 1938

*Hannibal Ante Portas
  Reviews:
    New York Times VIII, p. 2, Jul 7, 1929

Idiot's Delight
  Productions:
    Opened March 24, 1936 for 300 performances.
    Opened August 31, 1936 for 179 performances.
    Opened May 23, 1951 for 15 performances.
    (Off Broadway) Season of 1956-57.
    (Off Off Broadway) Season of 1973-74 (Theater Arts Reper-
      tory Co.).
  Reviews:
    Catholic World 143:212, May 1936
        173:306-7, Jul 1951
    Commonweal 23:664, Apr 10, 1936
        24:104, May 22, 1936
        54:213, Jun 8, 1951
    Drama 16:117, May 1938
    Forum 95:348-9, Jun 1936
    Literary Digest 121:20, Mar 28, 1936
    Nation 142:490-2, Apr 15, 1936
    New Republic 86:253, Apr 8, 1936
    New York Theatre Critics' Reviews 1951:260
    New York Times p. 26, Mar 10, 1936
        p. 25, Mar 25, 1936
        IX, p. 1, Apr 12, 1936

                    IX, p. 3, Oct 4, 1936
                    p. 26, May 19, 1937
                    p. 22, Aug 10, 1937
                    p. 19, Mar 23, 1938
                    X, p. 2, Apr 10, 1938
                    IV, p. 8, Oct 23, 1938
                    p. 46, May 24, 1951
                    p. 14, Feb 23, 1957
                    p. 39, Mar 24, 1970
        Newsweek 7:32, Apr 4, 1936
                    9:24, May 29, 1937
        Pictorial Review 37:65, Jul 1936
        Player's Magazine 12:11+, May-Jun 1936
        Saturday Review 14:6-7, May 9, 1936
                        14:18, May 9, 1936
        Stage 13:26-8, Apr 1936
        Theatre Arts 20:340-1, May 1936
                     20:466-7, Jun 1936
                     22:410-11, Jun 1938
        Time 27:38, Apr 6, 1936

The Love Nest (Based on Ring Lardner's story)
    Productions:
        Opened December 22, 1927 for 23 performances.
    Reviews:
        New York Times p. 17, Dec 23, 1927
        Saturday Review 4:499-500, Jan 7, 1928

The Petrified Forest
    Productions:
        Opened January 7, 1935 for 197 performances.
        Opened November 1, 1943 for 8 performances.
        (Off Off Broadway) January 22, 1974 (Th. at St. Clements).
    Reviews:
        Canadian Forum 15:194, Feb 1935
        Catholic World 140:601-2, Feb 1935
        Commonweal 21:375, Jan 25, 1935
        Literary Digest 119:19+, Jan 19, 1935
        Nation 140:111, Jan 23, 1935
        New Republic 82:21, Feb 13, 1935
        New York Theatre Critics' Reviews 1943:242
        New York Times p. 31, Dec 21, 1934
                        IX, p. 1, Dec 30, 1934
                        p. 26, Jan 8, 1935
                        IX, p. 1, Jan 13, 1935
                        X, p. 1, Jan 20, 1935
                        X, p. 1, May 12, 1935
                        II, p. 9, Nov 24, 1935
                        II, p. 12, Mar 1, 1936
                        VIII, p. 1, Jan 10, 1943
                        p. 30, Nov 2, 1943

p. 6, Mar 19, 1955
p. 33, Jan 22, 1974
Saturday Review 11:572, Mar 23, 1935
Stage 12:4, Feb 1935
Theatre Arts 19:169-70, Mar 1935
Time 25:30, Jan 14, 1935
Vanity Fair 44:48, Mar 1935
Vogue 85:52-3, Feb 15, 1935

The Queen's Husband
Productions:
Opened January 25, 1928 for 125 performances.
Reviews:
Dial 84:351, Apr 1928
Life (NY) 91:19, Feb 9, 1928
New York Times p. 17, Jan 26, 1928
VIII, p. 4, Jan 29, 1928
VIII, p. 1, Feb 12, 1928
IX, p. 4, Apr 15, 1928
p. 23, Sep 6, 1928
VIII, p. 2, Nov 15, 1931
p. 23, Jun 2, 1936
Outlook 148:225, Feb 8, 1928
Theatre Magazine 47:28-30+, May 1928
Vogue 71:146+, Mar 15, 1928

Reunion in Vienna
Productions:
Opened November 16, 1931 for 264 performances.
Reviews:
Arts and Decoration 36:68, Jan 1932
Bookman 74:564, Jan 1932
Catholic World 134:467-8, Jan 1932
Commonweal 15:160, Dec 9, 1931
Dramatist 23:1448-9, Jan 1932
Nation 133:650, Dec 9, 1931
134:608, May 25, 1932
New Republic 69:70, Dec 2, 1931
New York Times p. 29, May 12, 1931
VIII, p. 4, Oct 18, 1931
p. 31, Nov 17, 1931
p. 17, Jan 4, 1934
IX, p. 3, Jan 28, 1934
North American Review 234:174, Aug 1932
Outlook 159:438, Dec 2, 1931
Sketch Book 8:19, Dec 1931
Theatre Arts 16:96-7, Feb 1932
Theatre Guild Magazine 9:3, Jan 1932
9:18-21, Mar 1932
Vanity Fair 37:74, Jan 1932
Vogue 79:68+, Jan 15, 1932

The Road to Rome
    Productions:
        Opened January 31, 1927 for 392 performances.
        Opened May 21, 1928 for 440 performances.
    Reviews:
        Bookman 65:205-6, Apr 1927
        Dramatist 18:1335-6, Apr 1927
        Life (NY) 89:19, Feb 17, 1927
        New Republic 50:70-1, Mar 9, 1927
        New York Times p. 24, Feb 1, 1927
                    VII, p. 1, Feb 6, 1927
                    VIII, p. 4, Feb 5, 1928
                    p. 19, May 22, 1928
                    p. 23, May 17, 1928
                    VIII, p. 3, Jun 3, 1928
                    VIII, p. 1, Jun 10, 1928
                    p. 22, Apr 15, 1929
                    X, p. 4, Nov 10, 1929
        Outlook 146:546-7, Aug 24, 1927
        Theatre Magazine 45:20, May 1927
                    45:28+, Jun 1927
        Vogue 69:84+, Apr 1, 1927

The Rugged Path
    Productions:
        Opened November 10, 1945 for 81 performances.
    Reviews:
        Catholic World 162:264, Dec 1945
        Commonweal 43:168, Nov 30, 1945
        Forum 105:468, Jan 1946
        Life 19:88-90, Dec 3, 1945
        Nation 161:562, Nov 24, 1945
        New Republic 113:711, Nov 26, 1945
        New York Theatre Critics' Reviews 1945:109
        New York Times p. 17, Oct 13, 1945
                    p. 17, Nov 12, 1945
                    II, p. 1, Nov 18, 1945
        New Yorker 21:47, Nov 17, 1945
        Newsweek 26:84, Nov 19, 1945
        Saturday Review 28:18-20, Nov 24, 1945
        Theatre Arts 30:6, 8-10, Jan 1946
        Time 46:63, Nov 19, 1945
        Vogue 106:61, Dec 15, 1945

Second Threshold (see entry under Barry, Philip)

Small War on Murray Hill
    Productions:
        Opened January 3, 1957 for 12 performances.
        (Off Off Broadway) May 1976 (Theater Off Park).

Reviews:
    Catholic World 184:470-1, Mar 1957
    Christian Century 74:201, Feb 13, 1957
    Commonweal 65:436+, Jan 25, 1957
    New York Theatre Critics' Reviews 1957:397
    New York Times II, p. 1, Dec 30, 1956
                   p. 19, Jan 4, 1957
                   II, p. 1, Jan 13, 1957
    New Yorker 32:58+, Jan 12, 1957
    Newsweek 49:58, Jan 14, 1957
    Saturday Review 40:48, Jan 19, 1957
    Theatre Arts 41:19, Mar 1957
    Time 69:68, Jan 14, 1957

There Shall Be No Night
    Productions:
    Opened April 29, 1940 for 115 performances.
    Reopened September 9, 1940 for 66 performances.
    Reviews:
    Catholic World 151:343-4, Jun 1940
    Commonweal 32:62, May 10, 1940
    Life 8:48+, May 13, 1940
    Nation 150:605-6, May 11, 1940
    New Republic 102:641, May 13, 1940
    New York Theatre Critics' Reviews 1940:322
    New York Times p. 11, Mar 30, 1940
                   p. 25, Apr 30, 1940
                   X, p. 1, May 5, 1940
                   IX, p. 1, May 12, 1940
                   IX, p. 1, Sep 22, 1940
                   IX, p. 1, Oct 13, 1940
                   IX, p. 3, Mar 30, 1941
                   p. 20, May 6, 1941
                   XI, p. 1, May 11, 1941
                   p. 34, Dec 16, 1943
                   II, p. 1, Jan 2, 1944
    New Yorker 16:28, May 11, 1940
    Newsweek 15:34, May 13, 1940
             22:80, Dec 27, 1943
    Survey Graphic 29:408, Jul 1940
    Theatre Arts 24:398-401+, Jul 1940
                 24:548, Aug 1940
                 25:788+, Nov 1941
                 28:209-10+, Apr 1944
    Time 35:52, May 13, 1940
    Yale Review 30:423, Winter 1941

This Is New York
    Productions:
    Opened November 28, 1930 for 59 performances.

Reviews:
    Bookman 72:516, Jan 1931
    Catholic World 132:464, Jan 1931
    Drama Magazine 21:13, Jan 1931
    Harper's Bazaar Vol. 162, Mar 1931
    Life (NY) 96:18, Dec 19, 1930
    New York Times p. 21, Nov 29, 1930
    Outlook 156:629, Dec 17, 1930
    Theatre Magazine 53:25, Feb 1931
    Vogue 77:118, Feb 15, 1931

Tovarich (Adapted from the play by Jacques Deval)
    Productions:
        Opened October 15, 1936 for 356 performances.
        Opened May 14, 1952 for 15 performances.
    Reviews:
        Catholic World 144:335-6, Dec 1936
                  175:309, Jul 1952
        Commonweal 25:20, Oct 30, 1936
              56:224, Jun 6, 1952
        Life 2:38-9, Jan 11, 1937
           3:22-3, Dec 20, 1937
        Literary Digest 122:22, Oct 31, 1936
        Nation 143:530, Oct 31, 1936
        New Republic 89:21, Nov 4, 1936
        New York Theatre Critics' Reviews 1952:281
        New York Times p. 19, Apr 25, 1935
                IX, p. 1, May 19, 1935
                p. 35, Sep 29, 1936
                IX, p. 2, Oct 4, 1936
                IX, p. 1, Oct 15, 1936
                p. 31, Oct 16, 1936
                X, p. 1, Oct 25, 1936
                X, p. 1, Jan 24, 1937
                X, p. 2, Apr 25, 1937
                p. 39, May 15, 1952
        Newsweek 8:40, Oct 24, 1936
            10:30, Dec 20, 1937
        Saturday Review 35:26, May 31, 1952
        Stage 14:48-9, Nov 1936
           15:95, Oct 1937
        Theatre Arts 19:481, Jul 1935
            20:919-23, Dec 1936
            21:833, Nov 1937
            36:82, Jul 1952
        Time 28:47, Oct 26, 1936
           31:29, Jan 3, 1938

Waterloo Bridge
    Productions:
        Opened January 6, 1930 for 64 performances.

Reviews:
  Life (NY) 95:20, Jan 24, 1930
  Nation 130:106, Jan 22, 1930
  New Republic 61:251, Jan 22, 1930
  New York Times X, p. 4, Dec 1, 1929
              p. 29, Jan 7, 1930
              VIII, p. 4, Nov 29, 1931
  Outlook 154:152, Jan 22, 1930
  Theatre Magazine 51:70+, Feb 1930
  Vogue 75:108, Mar 1, 1930

SHIPMAN, SAMUEL

Alley Cat (with Alan Dinehart. Based on an original script by Lawrence Pohle)
  Productions:
  Opened September 17, 1934 for 8 performances.
  Reviews:
  New York Times p. 18, Sep 18, 1934

Behind Red Lights (with Beth Brown. Adapted from Beth Brown's novel For Men Only)
  Productions:
  Opened January 13, 1937 for 177 performances.
  Reviews:
  New York Times p. 17, Jan 14, 1937
  Stage 14:64, Feb 1937

Cheaper to Marry
  Productions:
  Opened April 15, 1924 for 71+ performances.
  Reviews:
  Life (NY) 83:20, May 1, 1924
  New York Times p. 26, Apr 16, 1924
              VIII, p. 1, Apr 20, 1924
  Theatre Magazine 39:19, Jun 1924

Children of Today (with Clara Lipman)
  Productions:
  Opened December 1, 1913 for 24 performances.
  Reviews:
  Dramatic Mirror 70:6-7, Dec 3, 1913
  Theatre Magazine 19:46, Jan 1914

Creoles (with Kenneth Perkins)
  Productions:
  Opened September 22, 1927 for 28 performances.
  Reviews:
  New York Times p. 33, Sep 23, 1927

Crime (with John B. Hymer)
    Productions:
        Opened February 22, 1927 for 133 performances.
    Reviews:
        Bookman 65:331-2, May 1927
        Life (NY) 89:21, Mar 24, 1927
        New York Times p. 27, Feb 23, 1927
        Theatre Magazine 46:26+, Sep 1927
        Vogue 69:87+, Apr 15, 1927

Crime Wave (see Crime)

Crooked Gamblers (with Percival Wilde)
    Productions:
        Opened July 31, 1920 for 82 performances.
    Reviews:
        Dramatic Mirror p. 229, Aug 7, 1920
        New York Clipper 68:23, Aug 4, 1920
        New York Times p. 12, Aug 2, 1920
        Theatre Magazine 32:187-8, Oct 1920

The Crooked Square (with Alfred C. Kennedy)
    Productions:
        Opened September 10, 1923 for 88 performances.
    Reviews:
        New York Times p. 10, Sep 11, 1923
                      VII, p. 1, Sep 16, 1923
        Theatre Magazine 38:19, Nov 1923

East Is West (with John B. Hymer)
    Productions:
        Opened December 25, 1918 for 680 performances.
    Reviews:
        Dramatic Mirror 80:47, Jan 11, 1919
        Dramatist 11:1016, Jul 1920
        Forum 61:244-6, Feb 1919
        Hearst 35:46-7+, Jun 16, 1919
        Nation 108:104, Jan 18, 1919
        New York Times p. 9, Dec 26, 1918
        Theatre Magazine 29:78+, Feb 1919

Elevating a Husband (with Clara Lipman)
    Productions:
        Opened January 22, 1912 for 120 performances.
    Reviews:
        American Playwright 1:41-2, Feb 1912
        Blue Book 14:244-7, Dec 1911
        Dramatic Mirror 67:7, Jan 24, 1912
        Dramatist 3:237-8, Apr 1912
        Green Book 7:700-1+, Apr 1912
                    8:901-20, Nov 1912

Hampton 28:202+, Apr 1912
Munsey 46:902, Mar 1912
Theatre Magazine 15:75-6+, Mar 1912

Fast Life (with John B. Hymer)
Productions:
Opened September 26, 1928 for 21 performances.
Reviews:
Life (NY) 92:17, Oct 12, 1928
New York Times p. 35, Sep 27, 1928

First Is Last (with Percival Wilde)
Productions:
Opened September 17, 1919 for 62 performances.
Reviews:
Dramatic Mirror 80:1538, Oct 2, 1919
New York Times p. 14, Sep 18, 1919

Friendly Enemies (with Aaron Hoffman)
Productions:
Opened July 22, 1918 for 440 performances.
Reviews:
Dramatic Mirror 79:157, Aug 3, 1918
              79:225, Aug 17, 1918
Dramatist 9:899-900, Apr 1918
Forum 60:361-2, Sep 1918
Green Book 20:584-8, Oct 1918
Hearst 34:286-7+, Oct 1918
Leslies' Weekly 128:483, Apr 5, 1919
National Magazine 47:509-10, Oct-Nov 1918
New York Times p. 11, Jul 23, 1918
              III, p. 6, Aug 11, 1918
              III, p. 4, Aug 25, 1918
Theatre Magazine 28:87, Aug 1918
              28:143, Sep 1918

A Lady Detained (with John B. Hymer)
Productions:
Opened January 9, 1935 for 13 performances.
Reviews:
New York Times p. 23, Jan 10, 1935
Time 25:25, Jan 21, 1935

Lawful Larceny
Productions:
Opened January 2, 1922 for 190+ performances.
Reviews:
Current Opinion 73:354-62, Sep 1922
Dramatic Mirror 95:17, Jan 7, 1922
Life (NY) 79:18, Jan 26, 1922
New York Clipper 69:20, Jan 11, 1922

    New York Times p. 20, Jan 3, 1922
              VI, p. 1, Jan 8, 1922
    Theatre Magazine 35:167, Mar 1922

Nature's Nobleman (with Clara Lipman)
    Productions:
        Opened November 14, 1921 for 74 performances.
    Reviews:
        Dramatic Mirror 84:736, Nov 19, 1921
        New York Times p. 23, Nov 15, 1921

No More Women (with Neil Twomey)
    Productions:
        Opened August 3, 1926 for 6 performances.
    Reviews:
        New York Times p. 17, Aug 4, 1926
        Theatre Magazine 44:16, Oct 1926

Scarlet Pages (with John B. Hymer)
    Productions:
        Opened September 9, 1929 for 72 performances.
    Reviews:
        Life (NY) 94:22, Oct 4, 1929
        New York Times VIII, p. 1, Sep 1, 1929
                    p. 26, Sep 10, 1929
                    IX, p. 1, Sep 22, 1929
        Outlook 153:155, Sep 25, 1929
        Theatre Magazine 50:46, Nov 1929
        Vogue 74:128, Oct 26, 1929

She Means Business
    Productions:
        Opened January 26, 1931 for 8 performances.
    Reviews:
        New York Times p. 21, Jan 27, 1931

That French Lady (with Neil Twomey)
    Productions:
        Opened March 15, 1927 for 47 performances.
    Reviews:
        New York Times p. 29, Mar 16, 1927

Trapped (with Max Marcin)
    Productions:
        Opened September 11, 1928 for 15 performances.
    Reviews:
        New York Times p. 25, Sep 12, 1928

The Unwritten Chapter (with Victor Victor)
    Productions:
        Opened October 11, 1920 for 24 performances.

Reviews:
> Dramatic Mirror p. 683, Oct 16, 1920
> Life (NY) 76:768, Oct 28, 1920
> New York Clipper 68:373+, Dec 1920
> New York Times p. 18, Oct 12, 1920

The Woman in Room 13 (with Max Marcin)
Productions:
> Opened January 14, 1919 for 175 performances.
Reviews:
> Dramatic Mirror 80:125, Jan 25, 1919
> Forum 61:375, Mar 1919
> Independent 97:137, Feb 1, 1919
> Life (NY) 73:172, Jan 30, 1919
> New York Dramatic News 65:8, Jan 25, 1919
> New York Times p. 9, Jan 15, 1919
> Theatre Magazine 29:141+, Mar 1919

SHULMAN, MAX

The Tender Trap (with Robert Paul Smith)
Productions:
> Opened October 13, 1954 for 102 performances.
> (Off Broadway) Season of 1961-62.
Reviews:
> America 92:257, Nov 27, 1954
> Catholic World 180:227-8, Dec 1954
> Commonweal 61:166, Nov 12, 1954
> Nation 179:390, Oct 30, 1954
> New Republic 131:23, Nov 1, 1954
> New York Theatre Critics' Reviews 1954:282
> New York Times p. 37, Oct 14, 1954
>   p. 15, Aug 26, 1961
> New Yorker 30:83, Oct 23, 1954
> Newsweek 44:94, Oct 25, 1954
> Saturday Review 37:27, Oct 30, 1954
> Theatre Arts 38:25+, Dec 1954
> Time 64:41, Oct 25, 1954

SIMON, NEIL

Barefoot in the Park
Productions:
> Opened October 23, 1963 for 1,530 performances.
> (Off Off Broadway) March 12, 1970 for 12 performances (Equity
>   Library Theater).
Reviews:
> America 109:753, Dec 7, 1963
> Commonweal 79:226, Nov 15, 1963

New York Theatre Critics' Reviews 1963:221
New York Times p. 36, Oct 24, 1963
                p. 35, Oct 25, 1963
                II, p. 3, Nov 3, 1963
                p. 28, Mar 10, 1966
                p. 39, Jun 19, 1967
New Yorker 39:93, Nov 2, 1963
Newsweek 62:62, Nov 4, 1963
Saturday Review 46:32, Nov 9, 1963
Theatre Arts 48:68, Jan 1964
Time 82:74, Nov 1, 1963

California Suite (Visitor from New York, Visitor from Philadelphia,
    Visitors from London, Visitors from Chicago)
    Productions:
    Opened June 10, 1976 for 445 performances.
    Reviews:
    Los Angeles 21:167+, Jun 1976
    Nation 223:30, Jul 3, 1976
    New Republic 175:20, Jul 21, 1976
    New York Theatre Critics' Reviews 1976:224
    New York Times III, p. 3, Jun 11, 1976
                     II, p. 7, Jun 20, 1976
                     III, p. 1, Sep 10, 1976
                     III, p. 23, Jun 29, 1977
                     XXI, p. 7, Jul 29, 1979
    Newsweek 87:55, Jun 21, 1976
    Saturday Evening Post 250:52-3+, May 1978
    Time 107:43, Jun 21, 1976

Chapter Two
    Productions:
    Opened December 4, 1977 for 857 performances.
    Reviews:
    America 137:485, Dec 31, 1977
    Los Angeles 22:252+, Nov 1977
    Nation 225:699-700, Dec 24, 1977
    New Republic 178:25, Jan 7, 1978
    New West 2:SC-21, Nov 7, 1977
    New York Magazine 10:102, Dec 19, 1977
    New York Theatre Critics' Reviews 1977:108
    New York Times p. 52, Dec 5, 1977
                   II, p. 3, Dec 18, 1977
                   III, p. 23, Oct 24, 1979
                   XI, p. 13, Aug 10, 1980
                   XXII, p. 20, Sep 14, 1980
                   XXI, p. 18, Nov 30, 1980
                   XXI, p. 8, Sep 13, 1981
    New Yorker 53:91, Dec 12, 1977
    Newsweek 90:86, Dec 19, 1977
    Saturday Review 5:45, Feb 4, 1978
    Time 110:96, Dec 19, 1977

Come Blow Your Horn
    Productions:
        Opened February 22, 1961 for 677 performances.
        (Off Off Broadway) January 4, 1974 (Drama Tree Players).
    Reviews:
        America 105:355, May 20, 1961
        Nation 192:222, Mar 11, 1961
        New York Theatre Critics' Reviews 1961:356
        New York Times p. 31, Feb 23, 1961
                        II, p. 1, Mar 5, 1961
                        XXI, p. 13, Jan 11, 1981
        New Yorker 37:93, Mar 4, 1961
        Saturday Review 44:38, Mar 11, 1961
        Time 77:60, Mar 3, 1961

Fools
    Productions:
        Opened April 6, 1981 for 40 performances.
    Reviews:
        Los Angeles 26:409+, Dec 1981
        New Leader 64:20, May 4, 1981
        New York Magazine 14:54, Apr 20, 1981
        New York Theatre Critics' Reviews 1981:292
        New York Times II, p. 1, Apr 5, 1981
                        III, p. 11, Apr 7, 1981
                        II, p. 9, Apr 12, 1981
                        III, p. 17, Apr 16, 1981
                        III, p. 19, May 7, 1981
        New Yorker 57:133, Apr 20, 1981
        Time 117:63, Apr 20, 1981

The Gingerbread Lady
    Productions:
        Opened December 13, 1970 for 193 performances.
        (Off Off Broadway) November 13, 1976 (Assn. of Theater Art-
            ists).
        (Off Off Broadway) June 11, 1977 (Playwrights Horizons).
        (Off Off Broadway) March 8, 1978 (TRG Repertory Co.).
    Reviews:
        Nation 212:29, Jan 4, 1971
        New Republic 164:22+, Jan 16, 1971
        New York Theatre Critics' Reviews 1970:118
        New York Times p. 58, Dec 14, 1970
                        II, p. 3, Dec 20, 1970
                        XXI, p. 17, Dec 20, 1981
        New Yorker 46:96, Dec 19, 1970
        Newsweek 76:61, Dec 28, 1970
        Saturday Review 54:4, Jan 9, 1971
        Time 96:27, Dec 28, 1970

God's Favorite
    Productions:

Opened December 11, 1974 for 119 performances.
Reviews:
America 132:36, Jan 18, 1975
New Republic 172:33-4, Feb 22, 1975
New York Magazine 8:54+, Jan 13, 1975
New York Theatre Critics' Reviews 1974:145
                                    1974:154
New York Times p. 59, Dec 12, 1974
            II, p. 5, Dec 22, 1974
               p. 21, May 21, 1975
New Yorker 50:53-4, Dec 23, 1974
Newsweek 84:56, Dec 23, 1974
Playboy 22:45+, Apr 1975
Time 104:47, Dec 23, 1974

The Good Doctor (Adapted from stories by Anton Chekhov)
Productions:
Opened November 27, 1973 for 208 performances.
Reviews:
Nation 217:669, Dec 17, 1973
National Review 26:90, Jan 18, 1974
New York Magazine 6:88, Dec 17, 1973
New York Theatre Critics' Reviews 1973:156
New York Times p. 36, Nov 28, 1973
            II, p. 3, Dec 9, 1973
New Yorker 49:111-12, Dec 10, 1973
Newsweek 82:118, Dec 10, 1973
Playboy 21:40, Mar 1974
Time 102:88+, Dec 10, 1973

I Ought to Be in Pictures
Productions:
Opened April 3, 1980 for 324 performances.
Reviews:
Los Angeles 25:216+, Mar 1980
New West 5:127, Feb 11, 1980
New York Magazine 13:86, Apr 14, 1980
New York Theatre Critics' Reviews 1980:292
New York Times III, p. 3, Apr 4, 1980
             II, p. 3, May 18, 1980
            III, p. 19, Jan 6, 1981
Newsweek 95:106-7, Apr 14, 1980
Saturday Review 7:56+, May 1980
Time 115:112, Apr 14, 1980

Last of the Red Hot Lovers
Productions:
Opened December 28, 1969 for 706 performances.
(Off Off Broadway) June 1975 (Elysian Playhouse).
Reviews:
America 122:55, Jan 17, 1970

Commonweal 92:38-9, Mar 20, 1970
Nation 210:60-1, Jan 19, 1970
New Republic 162:25+, Feb 14, 1970
New York Theatre Critics' Reviews 1969:124
New York Times p. 37, Dec 29, 1969
                    II, p. 1, Jan 4, 1970
New Yorker 45:64, Jan 10, 1970
Newsweek 75:73, Jan 12, 1970
Saturday Review 53:28, Jan 17, 1970
Time 95:64, Jan 12, 1970

The Odd Couple
    Productions:
        Opened March 10, 1965 for 964 performances.
    Reviews:
        America 112:810-11, May 29, 1965
        Commonweal 82:51-2, Apr 2, 1965
        Life 58:35-6, Apr 9, 1965
        Los Angeles 21:116, Jan 1976
        Nation 200:373-4, Apr 5, 1965
        New York Theatre Critics' Reviews 1965:362
        New York Times VI, p. 42, Mar 7, 1965
                        p. 36, Mar 11, 1965
                        p. 25, Mar 12, 1965
                        II, p. 1, Mar 21, 1965
                        p. 28, Mar 10, 1966
                        p. 34, Jun 29, 1967
        New Yorker 41:83, Mar 20, 1965
        Newsweek 65:90-1, Mar 22, 1965
        Saturday Review 48:44, Mar 27, 1965
        Time 85:66, Mar 19, 1965
        Vogue 145:142, May 1965

Plaza Suite (Visitor from Mamaroneck, Visitor from Hollywood, Visitor from Forest Hills)
    Productions:
        Opened February 14, 1968 for 1,097 performances.
    Reviews:
        America 118:552, Apr 20, 1968
        Commonweal 88:597, Sep 6, 1968
        Nation 206:317, Mar 4, 1968
        New York Theatre Critics' Reviews 1968:346
        New York Times p. 49, Feb 15, 1968
                        p. 31, Feb 16, 1968
                        II, p. 1, Feb 25, 1968
                        p. 61, Dec 14, 1968
                        p. 90, Mar 22, 1970
        New Yorker 44:75-6, Feb 24, 1968
        Newsweek 71:56, Feb 26, 1968
        Saturday Review 51:39, Mar 2, 1968
        Time 91:54, Feb 23, 1968
        Vogue 151:132, Apr 1, 1968

Prisoner of Second Avenue
Productions:
Opened November 11, 1971 for 780 performances.
(Off Off Broadway) June 17, 1978 (Playwrights Horizons).
Reviews:
Commonweal 98:215-16, May 4, 1973
Nation 213:573, Nov 29, 1971
New York Theatre Critics' Reviews 1971:191
New York Times p. 55, Nov 12, 1971
     II, p. 1, Nov 21, 1971
     II, p. 5, Dec 19, 1971
     p. 58, Nov 9, 1972
New Yorker 47:111, Nov 20, 1971
Newsweek 78:86+, Nov 22, 1971
Saturday Review 54:20+, Dec 4, 1971
     55:66, Aug 26, 1972
Time 98:93, Nov 22, 1971

The Star-Spangled Girl
Productions:
Opened December 21, 1966 for 261 performances.
Reviews:
America 116:264, Feb 18, 1967
New York Theatre Critics' Reviews 1966:194
New York Times p. 38, Dec 22, 1966
     II, p. 8, Jan 8, 1967
New Yorker 42:59, Dec 31, 1966
Newsweek 69:66, Jan 2, 1967
Saturday Review 50:98, Jan 14, 1967
Time 88:45, Dec 30, 1966
Vogue 149:60, Feb 15, 1967

The Sunshine Boys
Productions:
Opened December 20, 1972 for 538 performances.
Reviews:
America 128:41, Jan 20, 1973
Commonweal 98:215-16, May 4, 1973
Nation 216:61, Jan 8, 1973
National Review 25:316-17, Mar 16, 1973
New Republic 168:26, Jan 27, 1973
New York Magazine 6:68, Jan 8, 1973
New York Theatre Critics' Reviews 1972:134
New York Times p. 31, Dec 21, 1972
     II, p. 1, Dec 31, 1972
New Yorker 48:47, Dec 30, 1972
Newsweek 81:52, Jan 1, 1973
Playboy 20:50, Apr 1973
Saturday Review (Arts) 1:59, Feb 1973
Time 101:64, Jan 1, 1973
Vogue 161:78, Feb 1973

Visitor from Forest Hills   (see Plaza Suite)

Visitor from Hollywood   (see Plaza Suite)

Visitor from Mamaroneck   (see Plaza Suite)

Visitor from New York   (see California Suite)

Visitor from Philadelphia   (see California Suite)

Visitors from Chicago   (see California Suite)

Visitors from London   (see California Suite)

SINCLAIR, UPTON

Cicero
    Productions:
        (Off Broadway) Season of 1960-61.
    Reviews:
        New York Times p. 37, Feb 9, 1961
        New Yorker 37:94-5, Feb 18, 1961

*Giant's Strength
    Reviews:
        New York Times p. 8, Jun 19, 1948

Singing Jailbirds
    Productions:
        Opened December 6, 1928 for 79 performances.
        (Off Broadway) November 24, 1934 in repertory.
    Reviews:
        New York Times VIII, p. 2, May 20, 1928
                        p. 34, Dec 5, 1928
                        VIII, p. 4, Dec 23, 1928
                        p. 20, Feb 10, 1929
        Theatre Magazine 49:50+, Feb 1929
        World Tomorrow 12:112, Mar 1929

SKINNER, CORNELIA OTIS

Edna His Wife (Adapted from the book by Margaret Ayer Barnes)
    Productions:
        Opened December 7, 1937 for 32 performances.
    Reviews:
        New York Times p. 30, Dec 8, 1937
        Time 30:33-4, Dec 20, 1937

The Loves of Charles II
    Productions:

Opened December 27, 1933 for 23 performances.
No Reviews.

Mansion on the Hudson
Productions:
Opened April 2, 1935 for 16 performances.
Reviews:
New York Times p. 20, Apr 3, 1935

The Pleasure of His Company (see entry under Taylor, Samuel)

Paris '90
Productions:
Opened March 4, 1952 for 87 performances.
Reviews:
New York Theatre Critics' Reviews 1952:348
New York Times p. 10, Feb 9, 1952
VI, pp. 10-11, Feb 24, 1952
VI, pp. 10-11, Mar 2, 1952
p. 33, Mar 5, 1952
II, p. 1, Mar 16, 1952

The Wives of Henry VIII
Productions:
Opened November 15, 1931 for 69 performances.
Reviews:
New York Times p. 22, Nov 16, 1931
p. 33, Jun 29, 1949
Theatre Guild Magazine 9:11, Dec 1931

SKLAR, GEORGE

*And People All Around (with B. T. Bradshaw, Jr.)
Reviews:
New York Times II, p. 1, Aug 7, 1966
p. 46, Feb 12, 1968

Laura (with Vera Caspary. Based on the novel by Vera Caspary)
Productions:
Opened June 26, 1947 for 44 performances.
Reviews:
Catholic World 165:458, Aug 1947
New York Theatre Critics' Reviews 1947:353
New York Times II, p. 1, Jun 22, 1947
p. 16, Jun 27, 1947
Newsweek 30:82, Jul 7, 1947
Time 50:56, Jul 7, 1947

Life and Death of an American
Productions:

Opened May 19, 1939 for 29 performances (WPA Federal Theatre
   Project).
Reviews:
   Catholic World 149:471-2, Jul 1939
   Commonweal 30:188, Jun 9, 1939
   New York Times p. 11, May 20, 1939

Merry-Go-Round (see entry under Maltz, Albert)

Peace on Earth (with Albert Maltz)
   Productions:
      Opened November 29, 1933 for 126 performances.
      Opened March 31, 1934 for 18 performances.
   Reviews:
      Catholic World 138:478, Jan 1934
      New Outlook 163:43, Jan 1934
      New Republic 77:169, Dec 20, 1933
      New York Times p. 39, Nov 30, 1933
                     p. 22, Mar 9, 1934
      Survey 23:240, May 1934
      Theatre Arts 18:88-91, Feb 1934
      Vanity Fair 41:41, Feb 1934
      World Tomorrow 17:19, Jan 4, 1934

Stevedore (with Paul Peters)
   Productions:
      Opened April 18, 1934 for 111 performances.
      Opened October 1, 1934 for 64 performances.
      (Off Broadway) Season of 1948-49.
   Reviews:
      Catholic World 139:342-3, June 1934
      Golden Book 20:246, Sep 1934
      Literary Digest 117:23+, May 5, 1934
      Nation 138:515-16, May 2, 1934
      New Outlook 163:44, Jun 1934
      New Republic 78:367, May 9, 1934
      New York Times p. 33, Apr 19, 1934
                     IX, p. 1, Apr 29, 1934
                     p. 18, Oct 2, 1934
                     IX, p. 3, Jan 13, 1935
                     p. 26, May 7, 1935
                     p. 20, Sep 23, 1935
                     p. 30, Feb 23, 1949
      Newsweek 3:38, Apr 28, 1934
      Review of Reviews 89:48, Jun 1934
      Saturday Review 10:797, Jul 7, 1934
      Stage 11:8, Jun 1934
      Theatre Arts 18:408-9+, Jun 1934
      Time 23:26, Apr 30, 1934

SMITH, HARRY JAMES

Blackbirds
Productions:
  Opened January 6, 1913 for 16 performances.
Reviews:
  American Playwright 2:40-2, Feb 1913
  Bookman 36:644-5, Feb 1913
  Dramatic Mirror 69:6, Jan 8, 1913
  Green Book 9:376+, Mar 1913
             9:498-9, Mar 1913
  Munsey 48:1005-6, Mar 1913
  New York Drama News 57:24, Jan 11, 1913
  New York Times p. 11, Jan 7, 1913

The Little Teacher
Productions:
  Opened February 4, 1918 for 128 performances.
Reviews:
  Dramatic Mirror 78:7, Feb 16, 1918
  Forum 59:362, Mar 1918
  Green Book 19:580+, Apr 1918
  Life (NY) 71:262, Feb 14, 1918
  New York Times p. 11, Feb 5, 1918

Mrs. Bumpstead-Leigh
Productions:
  Opened April 3, 1911 for 64 performances.
  Opened April 1, 1929 for 72 performances.
Reviews:
  Blue Book 13:462-3, Jul 1911
  Bookman 33:358-9, Jun 1911
  Commonweal 9:722-3, Apr 24, 1929
  Dial 86:531-2, Jun 1929
  Dramatic Mirror 65:7, Apr 5, 1911
  Dramatist 2:169-70, Jul 1911
  Leslies' Weekly 112:451, Apr 10, 1911
  Life (NY) 57:788, Apr 20, 1911
            93:20, Apr 26, 1929
  Metropolitan Magazine 34:353, Jun 1911
  Munsey 45:419-20, Jun 1911
  New Republic 58:252-3, Apr 17, 1929
  New York Times p. 28, Apr 2, 1929
                IX, p. 2, May 12, 1929
  Red Book 17:376-7+, Jun 1911
  Theatre Magazine 12:176, Dec 1910
                   13:142-3+, May 1911
  Vogue 73:104, Jun 8, 1929

A Tailor Made Man
Productions:

Opened August 27, 1917 for 398 performances.
Opened October 21, 1929 for 8 performances.
Reviews:
Current Opinion 63:311-14, Nov 1917
Dramatic Mirror 77:8, Sep 8, 1917
Dramatist 10:930, Jan 1919
Forum 59:360-1, Mar 1918
Green Book 18:778-82, Nov 1917
Hearst 32:378-80+, Nov 1917
Life (NY) 70:424, Sep 13, 1917
New York Drama News 64:3, Sep 1, 1917
New York Times p. 5, Aug 28, 1917
              IV, p. 5, Sep 2, 1917
              p. 26, Oct 22, 1929
Theatre Magazine 26:209+, Oct 1917

SMITH, WINCHELL

Bobby Burnit (Based on the novel by George R. Chester)
Productions:
Opened August 22, 1910 for 32 performances.
Reviews:
Dramatist 2:101-2, Oct 1910
Hampton 25:524, Oct 1910
Leslies' Weekly 111:271+, Sep 15, 1910
Metropolitan Magazine 33:120-1, Oct 1910
New York Dramatic News 64:5, Sep 3, 1910

The Boomerang (with Victor Mapes)
Productions:
Opened August 10, 1915 for 522 performances.
Reviews:
American Mercury 81:33+, Jan 1916
Book News 34:73-4, Oct 1915
Bookman 42:155+, Oct 1915
Current Opinion 59:240-3, Oct 1915
Dramatic Mirror 74:8, Aug 18, 1915
              75:2, Jan 1, 1916
              76:19, Oct 21, 1916
Dramatist 7:612-13, Oct 1915
Green Book 14:618-19, Oct 1915
          14:796, Nov 1915
Harper's Weekly 61:206-7, Aug 28, 1915
Hearst 28:266-9+, Oct 1915
Munsey 57:333, Mar 1916
       58:307, Jul 1916
Nation 101:240, Aug 19, 1915
New Republic 4:76, Aug 21, 1915
New York Dramatic News 61:16, Aug 21, 1915
New York Times p. 9, Aug 11, 1915

VI, p. 2, Aug 15, 1915
II, p. 5, May 28, 1916
Smart Set 47:146-8, Oct 1915
Theatre Magazine 22:107+, Sep 1915

The Fortune Hunter
    Productions:
        Opened September 4, 1909 for 345 performances.
    Reviews:
        Collier's 44:24, Oct 30, 1909
        Columbian 3:638-64+, Jan 1911
        Cosmopolitan 48:485, Mar 1910
        Current Literature 49:421-9, Oct 1910
        Dramatic Mirror 62:5, Sep 18, 1909
        Dramatist 1:20-21, Jan 1910
        Forum 42:437, Nov 1909
        Green Book 2:1015, Nov 1909
            3:421-5, Feb 1910
            4:257-85, Aug 1910
        Hampton 23:692-3+, Nov 1909
        Metropolitan Magazine 31:358-9, Nov 1909
        New York Dramatic News 55:10, May 18, 1912
        Pearson 22:664-6, Nov 1909
        Theatre Magazine 10:xiii, Oct 1909
        Woman's Home Companion 38:43, Feb 1911
        World Today 18:286-97, Mar 1910

A Holy Terror (with George Abbott)
    Productions:
        Opened September 28, 1925 for 32 performances.
    Reviews:
        New York Times p. 31, Sep 29, 1925

Lightnin' (with Frank Bacon)
    Productions:
        Opened August 26, 1918 for 1,291 performances.
        Opened September 15, 1938 for 54 performances.
    Reviews:
        Catholic World 148:212, Nov 1938
        Commonweal 28:589, Sep 30, 1938
        Current Opinion 65:227-30, Oct 1918
        Dramatic Mirror 78:33, Feb 2, 1918
            79:361, Sep 7, 1918
        Dramatist 12:1040-41, Jan 1921
        Everybody's 40:43, Jan 1919
        Green Book 20:786-7+, Nov 1918
        Hearst 34:454-5+, Dec 1918
        Illus World 38:502-4, Dec 1922
        Life (NY) 72:416, Sep 19, 1918
            78:18, Jul 21, 1921
        Literary Digest 84:31, Mar 14, 1925

Nation 113:253, Sep 7, 1921
New York Times p. 7, Aug 27, 1918
　　　　　　　IV, p. 2, Sep 8, 1918
　　　　　　　p. 10, Aug 24, 1921
　　　　　　　p. 13, Aug 19, 1938
　　　　　　　X, p. 2, Sep 11, 1938
　　　　　　　p. 17, Sep 16, 1938
Outlook 126:182, Sep 29, 1920
Theatre Arts 22:774+, Nov 1938
Theatre Magazine 28:203+, Oct 1918
　　　　　　　　　32:272+, Nov 1920
Time 32:39, Sep 26, 1938

Love Among the Lions (Based on a novel by F. Anstey)
　Productions:
　　Opened August 8, 1910 for 48 performances.
　Reviews:
　　Dramatic Mirror 64:6, Aug 20, 1910
　　Hampton 25:522+, Oct 1910
　　Leslies' Weekly 111:213, Sep 1, 1910
　　Life (NY) 56:399, Sep 8, 1910
　　Metropolitan Magazine 33:126-7, Oct 1910
　　Munsey 44:133-4, Oct 1910
　　Pearson 24:530, Oct 1910
　　Theatre Magazine 12:66-7+, Sep 1910

The New Henrietta (with Victor Mapes. Based on Bronson Howard's
　play)
　Productions:
　　Opened December 22, 1913 for 48 performances.
　Reviews:
　　Blue Book 18:1044-5, Apr 1914
　　Bookman 38:611-12, Feb 1914
　　Dramatic Mirror 70:10, Dec 24, 1913
　　　　　　　　　70:2, Dec 31, 1913
　　　　　　　　　71:2, Jan 21, 1914
　　Green Book 11:696-7, Apr 1914
　　Leslies' Weekly 118:59, Jan 15, 1913
　　Theatre Magazine 19:61-2+, Feb 1914
　　Woman's Home Companion 42:19, Nov 1915

The Only Son
　Productions:
　　Opened October 16, 1911 for 32 performances.
　Reviews:
　　American Playwright 1:21-3, Jan 1912
　　Blue Book 14:1140-3, Apr 1912
　　Bookman 34:367-8, Dec 1911
　　Dramatic Mirror 66:10, Oct 18, 1911
　　　　　　　　　66:2, Nov 1, 1911
　　Dramatist 3:218, Jan 1912

Everybody's 26:88-90, Jan 1912
Green Book 6:1200+, Dec 1911
Leslies' Weekly 113:493, Nov 2, 1911
     113:560, Nov 16, 1911
Life (NY) 58:762-3, Nov 2, 1911
Munsey 46:428-9, Dec 1911
Pearson 26:769-70, Dec 1911
Theatre Magazine 14:197+, Dec 1911

Thank You (with Tom Cushing)
 Productions:
  Opened October 3, 1921 for 257 performances.
 Reviews:
  Dramatic Mirror 84:556, Oct 15, 1921
  Independent 107:63, Oct 15, 1921
  New York Clipper 69:28, Oct 12, 1921
  New York Times p. 10, Oct 4, 1921
       VI, p. 1, Oct 16, 1921
  Theatre Magazine 34:438, Dec 1921
       35:103, Feb 1922

Turn to the Right (with John E. Hazard)
 Productions:
  Opened August 18, 1916 for 435 performances.
 Reviews:
  Collier's 58:8, Jan 27, 1917
  Current Opinion 61:240-4, Oct 1916
  Dramatic Mirror 76:8, Aug 26, 1916
       76:4, Oct 21, 1916
       76:9, Nov 11, 1916
       77:8, Jan 6, 1917
       77:4, Apr 7, 1917
  Dramatist 8:733-5, Oct 1916
  Everybody's 36:57-8, Jan 1917
  Green Book 16:790-3, Nov 1916
  Hearst 32:198-200+, Sep 1917
  Leslies' Weekly 123:629+, Dec 7, 1916
  McClure's 48:10, Jan 1917
  Munsey 59:286, Nov 1916
  Nation 103:183, Aug 24, 1916
  New York Times p. 7, Aug 18, 1916
  Theatre Magazine 24:140, Sep 1916
       24:205, Oct 1916
  Woman's Home Companion 44:24, Jan 1917

The Wheel
 Productions:
  Opened August 29, 1921 for 49 performances.
 Reviews:
  Dramatic Mirror 83:893, May 21, 1921
       84:341, Sep 3, 1921

Independent 106:113, Sep 17, 1921
New York Clipper 69:20, Sep 7, 1921
New York Times p. 10, Aug 30, 1921
Weekly Review 5:234, Sep 10, 1921

SPEWACK, SAMUEL

Boy Meets Girl (with Bella Spewack)
    Productions:
        Opened November 27, 1935 for 669 performances.
        Opened June 22, 1943 for 15 performances.
        Opened April 13, 1976 for 10 performances.
    Reviews:
        Catholic World 142:471, Jan 1936
        Commonweal 23:188, Dec 13, 1935
        Life 5:36-8, Aug 29, 1938
        Literary Digest 120:19, Dec 14, 1935
        New Republic 85:175, Dec 18, 1935
                    174:18, May 8, 1976
        New York Magazine 9:88, Apr 26, 1976
        New York Theatre Critics' Reviews 1943:316
                                          1976:302
        New York Times p. 27, Nov 19, 1935
                       p. 38, Nov 28, 1935
                       XI, p. 3, Dec 15, 1935
                       p. 18, May 28, 1936
                       IX, p. 1, Jun 28, 1936
                       X, p. 3, Nov 22, 1936
                       p. 23, Jul 6, 1937
                       p. 15, Jun 23, 1943
                       p. 31, Apr 14, 1976
                       II, p. 5, Apr 25, 1976
        New Yorker 52:111-12, Apr 26, 1976
        Newsweek 6:42, Dec 7, 1935
                 12:22-3, Sep 5, 1938
        Stage 13:2+, Jan 1936
        Theatre Arts 20:19, Jan 1936
        Time 26:53, Dec 9, 1935
             107:67, Apr 26, 1976
        Vogue 87:57, Jan 15, 1936

Clear All Wires (with Bella Spewack)
    Productions:
        Opened September 14, 1932 for 93 performances.
    Reviews:
        Arts and Decorations 38:44-5, Nov 1932
        Catholic World 136:209-10, Nov 1932
        Commonweal 16:512, Sep 28, 1932
        Literary Digest 114:21, Oct 15, 1932
        Nation 135:290-1, Sep 28, 1932

New Outlook 161:38, Oct 1932
New York Times p. 19, Sep 15, 1932
           IX, p. 1, Sep 25, 1932
           IX, p. 3, Oct 2, 1932
Stage 10:9-10, Oct 1932
Theatre Arts 16:865-6, Nov 1932
Town and Country 87:26, Oct 15, 1932
Vogue 80:32, Nov 1, 1932

Festival (with Bella Spewack)
  Productions:
    Opened January 18, 1955 for 23 performances.
  Reviews:
    America 92:545, Feb 19, 1955
    New Republic 132:22, Feb 7, 1955
    New York Theatre Critics' Reviews 1955:393
    New York Times p. 22, Jan 19, 1955
               p. 35, Jan 20, 1955
    New Yorker 30:46-7, Jan 29, 1955
    Saturday Review 38:24, Feb 12, 1955
    Time 65:71, Jan 31, 1955

The Golden State
  Productions:
    Opened November 25, 1950 for 25 performances.
  Reviews:
    Commonweal 53:253, Dec 15, 1950
    New York Theatre Critics' Reviews 1950:183
    New York Times p. 29, Nov 27, 1950
    New Yorker 26:82, Dec 2, 1950
    Newsweek 36:74, Dec 4, 1950
    Theatre Arts 35:14, Feb 1951
    Time 56:65, Dec 4, 1950

Miss Swan Expects (with Bella Spewack)
  Productions:
    Opened February 20, 1939 for 8 performances.
  Reviews:
    New York Times p. 15, Feb 21, 1939
    Newsweek 13:28, Mar 6, 1939

My 3 Angels (with Bella Spewack. Based on Albert Husson's La
    Cuisine des Agnes)
  Productions:
    Opened March 11, 1953 for 344 performances.
    (Off Broadway) Season of 1955-56.
    (Off Off Broadway) November 21, 1975 (T. Schreiber).
  Reviews:
    America 88:716-17, Nov 28, 1953
    Catholic World 177:149, May 1953
    Life 34:101-2+, May 11, 1953
    Nation 176:273, Mar 28, 1953

New York Theatre Critics' Reviews 1953:334
New York Times p. 23, Mar 12, 1953
        p. 24, Feb 4, 1956
        VI, p. 72, Feb 5, 1956
New Yorker 29:64+, Mar 21, 1953
Newsweek 41:98, Mar 23, 1953
Saturday Review 36:27, Mar 28, 1953
Theatre Arts 38:32-3, Jun 1954
Time 61:80, Mar 23, 1953

Once There Was a Russian
    Productions:
        Opened February 18, 1961 for one performance.
    Reviews:
        New York Theatre Critics' Reviews 1961:363
        New York Times II, p. 1, Feb 12, 1961
                p. 32, Feb 20, 1961

Poppa (with Bella Spewack)
    Productions:
        Opened December 24, 1928 for 96 performances.
    Reviews:
        New York Times p. 31, Dec 25, 1928
                VIII, p. 1, Dec 30, 1928
        Theatre Magazine 49:46, Apr 1929

Spring Song (with Bella Spewack)
    Productions:
        Opened October 1, 1934 for 40 performances.
    Reviews:
        Catholic World 140:214, Nov 1934
        New York Times p. 18, Oct 2, 1934
        Theatre Arts 18:817, Nov 1934

Two Blind Mice
    Productions:
        Opened March 2, 1949 for 157 performances.
    Reviews:
        Catholic World 169:64, Apr 1949
        Commonweal 49:592, Mar 25, 1949
        Life 26:141-2+, Apr 4, 1949
        New York Theatre Critics' Reviews 1949:342
        New York Times p. 32, Mar 3, 1949
        New Yorker 25:48+, Mar 12, 1949
        Newsweek 33:81, Mar 14, 1949
        School and Society 69:338, May 7, 1949
        Theatre Arts 33:23, 26, May 1949
        Time 53:38, Mar 14, 1949
        Vogue 113:138, Apr 1, 1949

Under the Sycamore Tree
    Productions:

(Off Broadway) March 7, 1960 for 41 performances.
Reviews:
Life 33:169, Oct 13, 1952
New York Times p. 38, Apr 24, 1952
                p. 37, Mar 8, 1960
New Yorker 36:121-2, Mar 19, 1960

The War Song (with Bella Spewack and George Jessel)
Productions:
Opened September 24, 1928 for 80 performances.
Reviews:
Nation 127:406, Oct 17, 1928
New York Times p. 39, Sep 25, 1928
Vogue 72:150, Nov 10, 1928

Woman Bites Dog (with Bella Spewack)
Productions:
Opened April 17, 1946 for 5 performances.
Reviews:
Commonweal 44:72, May 3, 1946
Forum 105:940-1, Jun 1946
New York Theatre Critics' Reviews 1946:407
New York Times II, p. 1, Apr 14, 1946
                 p. 21, Apr 18, 1946
New Yorker 22:44, Apr 27, 1946

SPIGELGASS, LEONARD

Dear Me, the Sky Is Falling (Based on a story by Gertrude Berg
    and James Yaffe)
Productions:
Opened March 2, 1963 for 145 performances.
Reviews:
Commonweal 78:47, Apr 5, 1963
Nation 196:254, Mar 23, 1963
New York Theatre Critics' Reviews 1963:366
New York Times p. 9, Mar 4, 1963
                p. 20, Jul 23, 1963
New Yorker 39:132, Mar 9, 1963
Newsweek 61:69, Mar 18, 1963
Saturday Review 46:28, Mar 23, 1963
Theatre Arts 47:10-12, Apr 1963
Time 81:70, Mar 15, 1963

A Majority of One
Productions:
Opened February 16, 1959 for 556 performances.
Reviews:
America 100:671, Mar 7, 1959
Catholic World 189:158, May 1959

Commonweal 69:625, Mar 13, 1959
Life 46:50+, Mar 9, 1959
Nation 188:215, Mar 7, 1959
New York Theatre Critics' Reviews 1959:370
New York Times II, p. 1, Feb 15, 1959
            p. 28, Feb 17, 1959
            II, p. 1, Feb 22, 1959
            p. 37, Mar 10, 1960
            p. 39, May 16, 1960
New Yorker 35:66+, Feb 28, 1959
Newsweek 53:82, Mar 2, 1959
Reporter 20:40, Mar 19, 1959
Saturday Review 42:29, Mar 7, 1959
Theatre Arts 43:11+, Apr 1959
Time 73:49, Mar 2, 1959

The Wrong Way Lightbulb
    Productions:
        Opened March 4, 1969 for 7 performances.
    Reviews:
        New York Theatre Critics' Reviews 1969:344
        New York Times p. 40, Mar 5, 1969

STALLINGS, LAURENCE

The Buccaneer   (see entry under Anderson, Maxwell)

*Eldorado (with George S. Kaufman)
    Reviews:
        New York Times VIII, p. 2, Oct 25, 1931

A Farewell to Arms (Adapted from Ernest Hemingway's novel)
    Productions:
        Opened September 22, 1930 for 24 performances.
    Reviews:
        Bookman 72:296, Nov 1930
        Life (NY) 96:18, Oct 10, 1930
        National Magazine 59:137, Dec 1930
        New Republic 64:208-9, Nov 8, 1930
        New York Times p. 30, Sep 17, 1930
                    p. 30, Sep 23, 1930
        Outlook 156:233, Oct 8, 1930
        Vanity Fair 35:46, Dec 1930
        Vogue 76:72+, Nov 10, 1930

First Flight   (see entry under Anderson, Maxwell)

The Streets Are Guarded
    Productions:
        Opened November 20, 1944 for 24 performances.

Reviews:
>   Commonweal 41:205, Dec 8, 1944
>   Nation 159:725, Dec 9, 1944
>   New Republic 111:746-7, Dec 4, 1944
>   New York Theatre Critics' Reviews 1944:79
>   New York Times p. 19, Nov 21, 1944
>   II, p. 1, Nov 26, 1944
>   New Yorker 20:44, Dec 2, 1944
>   Newsweek 24:111, Dec 4, 1944
>   Theatre Arts 29:11-13, Jan 1945
>   Time 44:48, Dec 4, 1944

What Price Glory? (see entry under Anderson, Maxwell)

STEIN, GERTRUDE

Brewsie and Willie (Adapted by Ellen Violett and Lisabeth Blake)
>   Productions:
>   (Off Off Broadway) Season of 1979-80 (Soho Rep.).
>   No Reviews.

Dr. Faustus Lights the Lights
>   Productions:
>   (Off Broadway) Season of 1951-52 (Living Theatre).
>   Reviews:
>   New York Times p. 19, May 26, 1952

If You Had Three Husbands
>   Productions:
>   (Off Off Broadway) February 1979 (Soho Rep.).
>   No Reviews.

In Circles
>   Productions:
>   (Off Broadway) November, 1967 for 222 performances.
>   (Off Broadway) June 25, 1968 for 56 performances (Judson
>   Poets Theater).
>   Reviews:
>   New York Times p. 12, Oct 14, 1967
>   II, p. 1, Nov 5, 1967
>   p. 49, Jun 21, 1968
>   p. 36, Jun 28, 1968

Listen to Me (music by Al Carmines)
>   Productions:
>   (Off Off Broadway) October 18, 1974.
>   Reviews:
>   New York Magazine 7:117, Nov 11, 1974
>   New York Times p. 31, Oct 29, 1974

Made by Two (music by William Turner)
Productions:
    (Off Off Broadway) March 12, 1980 (La Mama ETC).
Reviews:
    New York Times p. 12, Mar 15, 1980

The Mother of Us All (music by Virgil Thomson)
Productions:
    (Off Off Broadway) May 24, 1975 (Encompass Theater).
    (Off Off Broadway) March 20, 1976 (Encompass Theater).
No Reviews.

Photograph
Productions:
    (Off Off Broadway) September 15, 1977 for 18 performances
        (Open Space in Soho).
Reviews:
    New York Times III, p. 11, Dec 22, 1977

What Happened
Productions:
    (Off Broadway) September 26, 1963 for 12 performances (Jud-
        son Poets' Theater).
Reviews:
    Commonweal 79:227, Nov 15, 1963

Yes Is for a Very Young Man
Productions:
    (Off Broadway) June 1949.
    (Off Broadway) March 4, 1963 for one performance.
Reviews:
    New York Times p. 27, Jun 7, 1949
                p. 7, Mar 6, 1963
    Time 47:67, Mar 25, 1946

STEINBECK, JOHN

Burning Bright
Productions:
    Opened October 18, 1950 for 13 performances.
    (Off Broadway) Season of 1959-60.
Reviews:
    Catholic World 172:228, Dec 1950
    Commonweal 53:120, Nov 10, 1950
    Nation 171:396, Oct 28, 1950
    New York Theatre Critics' Reviews 1950:238
    New York Times II, p. 1, Oct 15, 1950
                p. 40, Oct 19, 1950
                II, p. 1, Oct 29, 1950
                p. 27, Oct 17, 1959

New Yorker 26:52+, Oct 28, 1950
Newsweek 36:78, Oct 30, 1950
Saturday Review 33:20-1, Nov 11, 1950
Theatre Arts 34:16, Dec 1950
Time 56:58, Oct 30, 1950

The Long Valley (Adapted by Robert Glenn)
Productions:
   (Off Off Broadway) January 6, 1974 (Matinee Theater Series).
No Reviews.

The Moon Is Down
Productions:
   Opened April 7, 1942 for 71 performances.
Reviews:
   Catholic World 155:213-14, May 1942
   Commonweal 36:14, Apr 24, 1942
   Current History ns 2:228-31, May 1942
   Harper's Bazaar 76:74, Apr 1942
   Life 12:32-4, Apr 6, 1942
   Nation 154:468, Apr 18, 1942
   New Republic 106:638-9, May 11, 1942
   New York Theatre Critics' Reviews 1942:318
   New York Times VII, pp. 6-7, Mar 29, 1942
                  p. 22, Apr 8, 1942
              VIII, p. 1, Apr 12, 1942
              VIII, p. 1, Apr 19, 1942
              VIII, p. 1, May 10, 1942
                II, p. 1, Jul 11, 1943
                   p. 5, Nov 15, 1963
   New Yorker 18:34+, Apr 18, 1942
   Newsweek 19:72, Apr 20, 1942
   Scholastic 40:19, Apr 27, 1942
   Theatre Arts 26:287-9, May 1942
   Time 39:36, Apr 20, 1942

Of Mice and Men
Productions:
   Opened November 23, 1937 for 207 performances.
   (Off Broadway) April 4, 1964 for 8 performances (Equity Li-
      brary Theater).
   (Off Off Broadway) September 21, 1972 (Theater at St. Cle-
      ments).
   (Off Off Broadway) October 11, 1973 (T. Schreiber)
   Opened December 18, 1974 for 61 performances.
Reviews:
   America 132:36, Jan 18, 1975
   Catholic World 146:468, Jan 1938
   Commonweal 27:191, Dec 10, 1937
                28:161, Jun 3, 1938
   Essence 5:7, Apr 1975
   Life 3:44-6, Dec 13, 1937

Literary Digest 124:34, Dec 18, 1937
Nation 145:663-4, Dec 11, 1937
    220:27, Jan 11, 1975
New Republic 93:170, Dec 15, 1937
    94:396, May 4, 1938
    172:18, Jan 25, 1975
New York Magazine 8:56, Jan 20, 1975
New York Theatre Critics' Reviews 1974:138
New York Times p. 20, Nov 24, 1937
    XII, p. 7, Dec 5, 1937
    XI, p. 3, Dec 12, 1937
    X, p. 1, Apr 24, 1938
    XI, p. 3, Apr 30, 1939
    p. 14, Jun 10, 1939
    p. 23, Jul 31, 1972
    p. 57, Dec 19, 1974
    II, p. 5, Dec 29, 1974
New Yorker 50:52, Dec 30, 1974
Newsweek 10:32, Dec 6, 1937
One Act Play Magazine 1:858-9, Jan 1938
Saturday Review 6:57, Jan 20, 1979
Scribner's Magazine 103:70, Feb 1938
Stage 15:50-51, Jan 1938
    15:54-5, Jan 1938
Theatre Arts 21:774-81, Oct 1937
    22:13-16, Jan 1938
Time 30:41, Dec 6, 1937
    104:53, Dec 30, 1974

Tortilla Flat (see entry under Kirkland, Jack)

STEWART, DONALD OGDEN

How I Wonder
    Productions:
        Opened September 30, 1947 for 63 performances.
    Reviews:
        Catholic World 166:170-1, Nov 1947
        Commonweal 47:16, Oct 17, 1947
        Forum 108:372, Dec 1947
        New Republic 117:37, Oct 13, 1947
        New York Theatre Critics' Reviews 1947:332
        New York Times p. 34, Oct 1, 1947
        New Yorker 23:53, Oct 11, 1947
        Newsweek 30:80, Oct 13, 1947
        Science Illustrated 2:22-5, Dec 1947
        School and Society 66:421, Nov 29, 1947
        Theatre Arts 31:20, Nov 1947
            31:14, Dec 1947
        Vogue 110:132, Oct 15, 1947
            110:190, Nov 15, 1947

*The Kidders
Reviews:
New York Times p. 40, Nov 13, 1957

Los Angeles (with Max Marcin)
Productions:
Opened December 19, 1927 for 16 performances.
Reviews:
New York Times p. 32, Dec 20, 1927

Rebound
Productions:
Opened February 3, 1930 for 114 performances.
Reviews:
Catholic World 131:80-1, Apr 1930
Commonweal 11:453, Feb 19, 1930
Life (NY) 95:16, Feb 21, 1930
Nation 130:254, Feb 26, 1930
New Republic 62:47-8, Feb 26, 1930
New York Times p. 29, Feb 4, 1930
p. 21, Feb 6, 1930
IX, p. 1, Feb 16, 1930
VIII, p. 4, Nov 1, 1931
Outlook 154:312, Feb 19, 1930
Theatre Magazine 51:42-3, Apr 1930
Vogue 75:90, Mar 29, 1930

STITT, MILAN

Back in the Race
Productions:
(Off Off Broadway) June 10, 1979 (Circle Repertory).
(Off Broadway) April 17, 1980 for 30 performances.
Reviews:
New York Times III, p. 3, Apr 18, 1980

Edie's Home
Productions:
(Off Off Broadway) Aug 20, 1975 (Triad Play. Co., in a bill called Triad Singles).
No Reviews.

The Runner Stumbles
Productions:
(Off Off Broadway) December 13, 1974 (Manhattan Theater Club).
Opened May 18, 1976 for 191 performances.
(Off Broadway) January 14, 1979 for 35 performances.
Reviews:
America 134:518, Jun 2, 1976

Commonweal 103:464-5, Jul 16, 1976
Horizon 22:30-5, Oct 1979
Nation 222:701, Jun 5, 1976
New York Magazine 9:77, Jun 7, 1976
New York Theatre Critics' Reviews 1976:237
New York Times p. 19, Jan 10, 1976
       p. 25, May 19, 1976
       II, p. 5, Jun 6, 1976
       p. 37, Oct 23, 1976
       XXI, p. 13, Oct 7, 1979
New Yorker 52:51, May 31, 1976

Triad Singles (see Edie's Home)

STONE, JOHN AUGUSTUS
No productions.

STRONG, AUSTIN

Bunny
 Productions:
  Opened January 4, 1916 for 16 performances.
 Reviews:
  Book News 34:322-3, Mar 1916
  Dramatic Mirror 75:7, Jan 15, 1916
  Green Book 15:440-2, Mar 1916
  Harper's Weekly 62:84, Jan 22, 1916
  Nation 102:56, Jan 13, 1916
  New York Dramatic News 62:17, Jan 8, 1916
  New York Times p. 13, Jan 5, 1916
  Theatre Magazine 23:64+, Feb 1916

The Dragon's Claw
 Productions:
  Opened September 14, 1914 for 8 performances.
 Reviews:
  Dramatic Mirror 72:8, Sep 23, 1914
  Munsey 53:357, Nov 1914

A Good Little Devil (Based on Un Bon Petit Diable by Rosemonde
  Gerard and Maurice Rostand)
 Productions:
  Opened January 8, 1913 for 133 performances.
 Reviews:
  American Playwright 2:75-6, Mar 1913
  Blue Book 17:30-2, May 1913
  Bookman 37:61-3, Mar 1913
  Collier's 50:20, Feb 8, 1913
  Dramatic Mirror 69:4, Jan 15, 1913

69:2, Jan 22, 1913
69:2, Apr 2, 1913
Everybody's 28:518-20, Apr 1913
Green Book 9:372-5+, Mar 1913
10:44-6+, Jul 1913
Harper's Weekly 57:19, Feb 8, 1913
Hearst 23:973-84, Jun 1913
Independent 74:303-4, Feb 6, 1913
Life (NY) 61:200-1, Jan 23, 1913
Munsey 48:1012-13, Mar 1913
New York Dramatic News 57:3, Jan 11, 1913
57:17, Jan 18, 1913
Red Book 20:1078-81, Apr 1913
Theatre Magazine 17:35+, Feb 1913

The Little Father of the Wilderness (with Lloyd Osborne)
Productions:
Opened June 2, 1930 for 8 performances.
Reviews:
New York Times p. 27, Jun 3, 1930

A Play Without a Name
Productions:
Opened November 26, 1928 for 48 performances.
Reviews:
Life (NY) 92:9, Dec 28, 1928
New York Times p. 30, Nov 26, 1928
IX, p. 4, Dec 16, 1928
Outlook 150:1355, Dec 19, 1928
Theatre Magazine 49:26+, Feb 1929
49:51, Feb 1929

Seventh Heaven
Productions:
Opened October 30, 1922 for 704 performances.
Reviews:
Current Opinion 74:441-7, Apr 1923
Dramatist 14:1160-61, Apr 1923
Hearst 43:93-5+, May 1923
Life (NY) 81:20, Feb 1, 1923
New Republic 33:97-8, Dec 20, 1922
New York Clipper 70:20, Nov 8, 1922
New York Times p. 11, Oct 31, 1922
VIII, p. 1, Nov 5, 1922
VIII, p. 1, Nov 12, 1922
Theatre Magazine 37:23, Jan 1923

Three Wise Fools
Productions:
Opened October 31, 1918 for 316 performances.
Opened March 1, 1936 for 9 performances.

Reviews:
Dramatic Mirror 79:723, Nov 16, 1918
79:827, Dec 7, 1918
Dramatist 11:1031, Oct 1920
Hearst 36:46-7+, Sep 1919
Life (NY) 72:712-13, Nov 14, 1918
New York Times p. 13, Nov 1, 1918
IV, p. 2, Nov 10, 1918
p. 25, Jan 14, 1936
p. 14, Feb 29, 1936
IX, p. 1, Mar 1, 1936
p. 12, Mar 2, 1936
Newsweek 7:30, Jan 25, 1936
Theatre Magazine 28:345, Dec 1918
29:8, Jan 1919

STURGES, PRESTON

Child of Manhattan
Productions:
Opened March 1, 1932 for 87 performances.
Reviews:
Arts and Decoration 37:56, May 1932
Nation 134:351-2, Mar 23, 1932
New Republic 70:127, Mar 16, 1932
New York Times p. 15, Mar 2, 1932
Theatre Arts 16:362, May 1932

The Guinea Pig
Productions:
Opened January 7, 1929 for 64 performances.
Reviews:
New York Times p. 35, Jan 8, 1929

Recapture
Productions:
Opened January 29, 1930 for 24 performances.
Reviews:
Life (NY) 95:16, Feb 21, 1930
New York Times VIII, p. 2, Jan 19, 1930
p. 16, Jan 30, 1930
Theatre Magazine 51:70, Mar 1930

Strictly Dishonorable
Productions:
Opened September 18, 1929 for 557 performances.
Reviews:
Commonweal 10:592, Oct 9, 1929
Drama 20:40, Nov 1929
Life (NY) 94:24, Oct 11, 1929
95:18, Jun 6, 1930

Nation 129:392-3, Oct 9, 1929
130:659-60, Jun 4, 1930
New Republic 60:270, Oct 23, 1929
New York Times p. 37, Sep 19, 1929
IX, p. 1, Sep 29, 1929
p. 23, Mar 11, 1931
VIII, p. 2, Mar 29, 1931
IX, p. 1, Apr 12, 1931
Outlook 153:232, Oct 9, 1929
Theatre Magazine 50:20+, Nov 1929
50:45, Nov 1929
Vogue 74:150, Nov 9, 1929

TARKINGTON, BOOTH

*Alice Adams
Reviews:
New York Times p. 9, Mar 9, 1946
p. 26, Aug 5, 1947

Beauty and Jacobin
Productions:
Opened November 29, 1912 for one matinee.
Reviews:
Dramatic Mirror 68:6-7, Dec 4, 1912
Harper's Weekly 125:390-9, 539-53, Aug 1912
125:539-53, Sep 1912

Cameo Kirby (with Harry Leon Wilson)
Productions:
Opened December 20, 1909 for 24 performances.
Reviews:
Dramatist 2:106-7, Oct 1910

Clarence
Productions:
Opened September 20, 1919 for 300 performances.
(Off Broadway) Opened December 23, 1975 for 64 perform-
ances.
Reviews:
Current Opinion 67:296-300, Dec 1919
Dramatic Mirror 80:1539, Oct 2, 1919
Forum 62:502-3, Oct-Nov 1919
Life (NY) 74:592, Oct 2, 1919
New York Theatre Critics' Reviews 1976:347
New York Times p. 8, Sep 22, 1919
IV, p. 3, Sep 28, 1919
p. 36, Jan 6, 1976
New Yorker 51:46, Jan 19, 1976

Colonel Satan
   Productions:
      Opened January 10, 1931 for 17 performances.
   Reviews:
      Nation 132:134, Feb 4, 1931
      New York Times p. 24, Jan 12, 1931
                  p. 25, Jan 19, 1931
      Vogue 77:88, Mar 1, 1931

The Country Cousin (with Julian Street)
   Productions:
      Opened September 3, 1917 for 128 performances.
   Reviews:
      Dramatic Mirror 77:5, Sep 15, 1917
      Green Book 18:780-3, Nov 1917
      Hearst 32:470-2+, Dec 1917
      Life (NY) 70:506-7, Sep 27, 1917
      New York Times p. 9, Sep 4, 1917
                   IV, p. 2, Sep 9, 1917
                   p. 12, Sep 11, 1917
      Theatre Magazine 26:203+, Oct 1917

Getting a Polish (with Harry Leon Wilson)
   Productions:
      Opened November 7, 1910 for 32 performances.
   Reviews:
      Blue Book 12:858-60, Feb 1911
              12:894-6, Mar 1911
      Dramatic Mirror 64:9, Dec 7, 1910
      Green Book 5:233+, Feb 1911
      Metropolitan Magazine 33:797, Mar 1911
      Munsey 44:560-1, Jan 1911
      Theatre Magazine 12:xvii+, Dec 1910

How's Your Health (with Harry Leon Wilson)
   Productions:
      Opened November 26, 1929 for 47 performances.
   Reviews:
      Catholic World 130:469-70, Jan 1930
      New York Times p. 30, Nov 27, 1929

The Intimate Strangers
   Productions:
      Opened November 7, 1921 for 91 performances.
   Reviews:
      Bookman 54:464-5, Jan 1922
      Dramatic Mirror 84:700, Nov 12, 1921
      Life (NY) 78:18, Dec 8, 1921
      New York Clipper 69:20, Nov 16, 1921
      New York Times p. 28, Nov 8, 1921
      Theatre Magazine 35:30, Jan 1922

*Karabash
    Reviews:
      New York Times IX, p. 3, Aug 27, 1939

Magnolia
    Productions:
      Opened August 27, 1923 for 40 performances.
    Reviews:
      Hearst 44:85-7+, Dec 1923
      Life (NY) 82:18, Sep 13, 1923
      Nation 117:273, Sep 12, 1923
      New York Times VII, p. 1, Jun 24, 1923
                    p. 12, Aug 28, 1923
                    VI, p. 1, Sep 2, 1923
                    p. 10, Jul 29, 1940

Mister Antonio
    Productions:
      Opened September 18, 1916 for 48 performances.
    Reviews:
      Dramatic Mirror 76:7, Sep 23, 1916
      Harper's Weekly 134:187-203, Jan 1917
                    134:374-87, Feb 1917
      Life (NY) 68:580, Oct 5, 1916
      Nation 103:330, Oct 5, 1916
      New York Times p. 9, Sep 19, 1916
                    II, p. 4, Sep 24, 1916
      Theatre Magazine 24:281+, Nov 1916

Monsieur Beaucaire (with E. G. Sutherland)
    Productions:
      Opened March 11, 1912 for 64 performances.
    Reviews:
      Blue Book 15:233-5, Jun 1912
      Dramatic Mirror 67:7, Mar 13, 1912
      Green Book 7:1098-9+, Jun 1912
      Life (NY) 59:631, Mar 28, 1912
      New York Drama News 55:24, Mar 16, 1912
      New York Times IV, p. 2, May 25, 1919

Poldekin
    Productions:
      Opened September 9, 1920 for 44 performances.
    Reviews:
      Current Opinion 69:481-8, Oct 1920
      Dramatic Mirror 82:415, Mar 6, 1920
                    82:503, Sep 18, 1920
      Dramatist 11:1025-6, Oct 1920
      Independent 104:1, Oct 2, 1920
      Life (NY) 76:582, Sep 30, 1920
      McClure's 52:8-11+, Mar 1920
                52:91, Apr 1920

New York Clipper 68:27, Sep 15, 1920
New York Times p. 12, Sep 10, 1920
        VI, p. 1, Sep 12, 1920
        VI, p. 1, Sep 19, 1920
Theatre Magazine 32:371+, Dec 1920
Weekly Review 3:275-6, Sep 29, 1920

Rose Briar
    Productions:
        Opened December 25, 1922 for 88 performances.
    Reviews:
        Nation 116:128, Jan 31, 1923
        New York Clipper 70:20, Jan 3, 1923
        New York Times p. 11, Dec 26, 1922
        Theatre Magazine 37:5+, Mar 1923

Springtime (with Harry Leon Wilson)
    Productions:
        Opened October 19, 1909 for 79 performances.
    Reviews:
        Collier's 44:23, Nov 6, 1909
        Dramatic Mirror 62:5, Oct 30, 1909
        Everybody's 22:273, Feb 1910
        Green Book 3:83-4, Jan 1910
                3:481-507, Mar 1910
        Hampton 24:133, Jan 1910
        Harper's Weekly 53:24, Nov 20, 1909
        Leslies' Weekly 109:439, Nov 4, 1909
        Metropolitan Magazine 31:532-3, Jan 1910
        Theatre Magazine 10:170+, Dec 1909

Tweedles (with Harry Leon Wilson)
    Productions:
        Opened August 13, 1923 for 96 performances.
    Reviews:
        Bookman 58:181, Oct 1923
        Current Opinion 75:445-50+, Oct 1923
        Life (NY) 82:18, Aug 30, 1923
        Nation 117:273, Sep 12, 1923
        New York Times p. 10, Aug 14, 1923
                VI, p. 1, Aug 19, 1923
                VI, p. 2, Aug 19, 1923
        Theatre Magazine 38:19, Oct 1923

Up from Nowhere (with Harry Leon Wilson)
    Productions:
        Opened September 8, 1919 for 40 performances.
    Reviews:
        Dramatic Mirror 80:1465, Sep 18, 1919
        Forum 62:501, Oct-Nov 1919
        New York Times p. 17, Sep 9, 1919

IV, p. 2, Sep 14, 1919
Theatre Magazine 30:280, Oct 1919

The Wren
    Productions:
        Opened October 10, 1921 for 24 performances.
    Reviews:
        Bookman 54:375-6, Dec 1921
        Life (NY) 78:18, Oct 27, 1921
        New York Clipper 69:20, Oct 19, 1921
        New York Times p. 22, Oct 11, 1921
            VI, p. 1, Oct 16, 1921

Your Humble Servant (with Harry Leon Wilson)
    Productions:
        Opened January 3, 1910 for 72 performances.
    Reviews:
        Dramatic Mirror 63:5, Jan 15, 1910
        Dramatist 1:17-20, Jan 1910
        Green Book 3:522, Mar 1910
        Hampton 24:409-10, Mar 1910
        Life (NY) 55:129, Jan 20, 1910
        Metropolitan Magazine 32:122-3, Apr 1910
        Munsey 42:891-2, Mar 1910
        Theatre Magazine 11:37, Feb 1910

TAYLOR, SAMUEL

Avanti!
    Productions:
        Opened January 31, 1968 for 21 performances.
    Reviews:
        New York Theatre Critics' Reviews 1968:365
        New York Times p. 29, Feb 1, 1968
        New Yorker 43:86+, Feb 10, 1968

Beekman Place
    Productions:
        Opened October 7, 1964 for 29 performances.
    Reviews:
        New York Theatre Critics' Reviews 1964:198
        New York Times p. 50, Oct 8, 1964
        New Yorker 40:108, Oct 17, 1964
        Saturday Review 47:30, Oct 24, 1964
        Time 84:77, Oct 16, 1964

First Love (Based on Romain Gary's Promise at Dawn)
    Productions:
        Opened December 25, 1961 for 24 performances.

Reviews:
  America 106:540, Jan 20, 1962
  New York Theatre Critics' Reviews 1961:143
  New York Times II, p. 5, Dec 17, 1961
           p. 20, Dec 26, 1961
  New Yorker 37:56-7, Jan 6, 1962
  Newsweek 59:45, Jan 8, 1962
  Reporter 26:45, Feb 1, 1962

The Happy Time (Based on the book by Robert Fontaine)
  Productions:
  Opened January 24, 1950 for 614 performances.
  Reviews:
  Catholic World 170:470, Mar 1950
  Commonweal 51:510, Feb 17, 1950
  Life 28:107-8+, Feb 6, 1950
  New Republic 122:20, Feb 27, 1950
  New York Theatre Critics' Reviews 1950:370
  New York Times p. 24, Jan 25, 1950
               II, p. 2, Feb 10, 1952
               p. 39, May 12, 1959
  New Yorker 25:50-1, Feb 4, 1950
  Newsweek 35:76, Feb 6, 1950
  Saturday Review 33:26-8, Feb 18, 1950
  Texas Monthly 7:136, Feb 1979
  Theatre Arts 34:12, Apr 1950
  Time 55:66, Feb 6, 1950

Legend
  Productions:
  Opened May 13, 1976 for 5 performances.
  Reviews:
  New York Theatre Critics' Reviews 1976:242
  New York Times III, p. 3, May 14, 1976
  New Yorker 52:103, May 24, 1976

Nina (Adapted from the play by André Roussin)
  Productions:
  Opened December 5, 1951 for 45 performances.
  Reviews:
  Commonweal 55:277, Dec 21, 1951
  New York Theatre Critics' Reviews 1951:152
  New York Times p. 44, Dec 5, 1951
             p. 36, Jun 24, 1952
  New Yorker 27:71, Dec 15, 1951
  Newsweek 38:69, Dec 17, 1951
  Theatre Arts 36:31+, Feb 1952
  Time 58:76, Dec 17, 1951

The Pleasure of His Company (with Cornelia Otis Skinner)
  Productions:
  Opened October 22, 1958 for 474 performances.

Reviews:
America 100:255, Nov 22, 1958
Catholic World 188:331, Jan 1959
New York Theatre Critics' Reviews 1958:245
New York Times p. 36, Oct 23, 1958
      II, p. 1, Nov 2, 1958
      p. 22, Apr 24, 1959
New Yorker 34:97-8, Nov 1, 1958
Newsweek 52:62-3, Nov 3, 1958
Reporter 19:36, Nov 27, 1958
Saturday Review 41:25, Nov 8, 1958
Theatre Arts 43:9, Jan 1959
Time 72:48+, Nov 3, 1958

Sabrina Fair
Productions:
Opened November 11, 1953 for 318 performances.
Reviews:
America 90:325+, Dec 19, 1953
Catholic World 178:306, Jan 1954
Commonweal 59:281, Dec 18, 1953
Nation 177:454, Nov 28, 1953
New Republic 129:20-1, Nov 23, 1953
New York Theatre Critics' Reviews 1953:217
New York Times p. 37, Nov 12, 1953
      II, p. 1, Nov 22, 1953
      p. 18, Aug 5, 1954
New Yorker 29:85, Nov 21, 1953
Newsweek 42:60, Dec 21, 1953
      42:64, Nov 23, 1953
Saturday Review 36:46, Dec 12, 1953
      36:29-30, Nov 28, 1953
Theatre Arts 38:24, Jan 1954
      38:26-9, Feb 1954
Time 62:78, Nov 23, 1953

Stop-Over (with Matt Taylor)
Productions:
Opened January 11, 1938 for 23 performances.
Reviews:
New York Times p. 16, Jan 12, 1938
Theatre Arts 22:177-8, Mar 1938
Time 31:46, Jan 24, 1938

THOMAS, A. E.

The Big Idea (with Clayton Hamilton)
Productions:
Opened November 16, 1914 for 24 performances.

Reviews:
American Playwright 3:398-9, Dec 1914
Book News 33:229-30, Jan 1915
Bookman 40:551-2, Jan 1915
Collier's 54:9-10, Jan 2, 1915
Current Opinion 58:29, Jan 1915
Dramatic Mirror 72:8, Nov 25, 1914
Green Book 13:379-80, Feb 1915
Munsey 53:812, Jan 1915
New Republic 1:24, Nov 21, 1914
New York Drama News 60:11, Nov 21, 1914
New York Times p. 13, Nov 17, 1914
VIII, p. 6, Nov 22, 1914
Theatre Magazine 21:7-8+, Jan 1915

The Big Pond (see entry under Middleton, George)

The Champion (with Thomas Louden)
Productions:
Opened January 3, 1921 for 175 performances.
Reviews:
Collier's 67:15, Feb 5, 1921
Dramatic Mirror 83:59, Jan 8, 1921
Life (NY) 77:136, Jan 27, 1921
New York Clipper 68:19, Jan 4, 1921
New York Times p. 11, Jan 4, 1921
VI, p. 1, Jan 9, 1921
VI, p. 1, Jan 16, 1921
Theatre Magazine 33:181+, Mar 1921

Come Out of the Kitchen (Based on Alice Duer Miller's story)
Productions:
Opened October 23, 1916 for 224 performances.
Reviews:
Collier's 58:37-8, Jan 27, 1917
Dramatic Mirror 76:7, Oct 28, 1916
Dramatist 8:761-2, Jan 1917
Green Book 17:8-9+, Jan 1917
Nation 103:427, Nov 2, 1916
New York Drama News 63:10, Oct 28, 1916
New York Times p. 14, Oct 24, 1916
Theatre Magazine 24:356+, Dec 1916

Embers (adapted from the French of Pierre Wolff and Henri Duver-
nois)
Productions:
Opened February 1, 1926 for 25 performances.
Reviews:
New York Times p. 20, Feb 2, 1926

Fool's Bells (Based on a story by Leona Dairymple)
Productions:

Opened December 22, 1925 for 5 performances.
Reviews:
New York Times p. 8, Dec 24, 1925

The French Doll (Adapted from the French of MM. Armont and Gerbidon)
Productions:
Opened February 20, 1922 for 120 performances.
Reviews:
New York Clipper 70:22, Mar 8, 1922
New York Times p. 20, Feb 21, 1922
Theatre Magazine 35:308, May 1922

Her Friend the King (with Harrison Rhodes)
Productions:
Opened October 7, 1929 for 24 performances.
Reviews:
New York Times p. 34, Oct 8, 1929
Theatre Magazine 50:68, Dec 1929

Her Husband's Wife
Productions:
Opened May 9, 1910 for 48 performances.
Opened January 8, 1917 for 32 performances.
(Off Broadway) February 1946 (Playhouse des Artistes).
Reviews:
Bookman 33:359, Jun 1911
Current Literature 49:192-7, Aug 1910
Dramatic Mirror 63:10, May 21, 1910
                77:7, Jan 20, 1917
Dramatist 6:516-17, Oct 1914
Everybody's 23:696+, Nov 1910
Green Book 4:99-100, Jul 1910
Life (NY) 55:922, May 19, 1910
            69:102, Jan 18, 1917
Metropolitan Magazine 32:542-3, Jul 1910
Nation 104:85, Jan 18, 1917
New York Drama News 63:2, Jan 13, 1917
New York Times p. 3, Jan 9, 1917
              II, p. 4, Jan 21, 1917
Pearson 24:92-4, Jul 1910
Theatre Magazine 11:175-7, Jun 1910
                25:88, Feb 1917

The Jolly Roger
Productions:
Opened August 30, 1923 for 52 performances.
Reviews:
Nation 117:304, Sep 19, 1923
New York Times p. 10, Aug 31, 1923
              VII, p. 1, Sep 9, 1923

Just Suppose
    Productions:
      Opened November 1, 1920 for 88+ performances.
    Reviews:
      Dramatic Mirror p. 880, Nov 6, 1920
      Life (NY) 76:960, Nov 25, 1920
      New York Clipper 68:32, Nov 17, 1920
      New York Times p. 15, Nov 2, 1920
                     VII, p. 1, Nov 7, 1920
                     p. 24, Jul 2, 1935
      Theatre Magazine 33:7+, Jan 1921
      Weekly Review 3:509-10, Nov 24, 1920

Lost (with George Agnew Chamberlain)
    Productions:
      Opened March 28, 1927 for 8 performances.
    Reviews:
      New York Times p. 22, Mar 29, 1927

Merely Murder (Based on Georgette Heyer's novel)
    Productions:
      Opened December 3, 1937 for 3 performances.
    Reviews:
      New York Times p. 26, Nov 16, 1937
                     p. 21, Dec 4, 1937

No More Ladies
    Productions:
      Opened January 23, 1934 for 162 performances.
      Opened September 3, 1934 for 16 performances.
    Reviews:
      Catholic World 138:732-3, Mar 1934
      Nation 138:167-8, Feb 7, 1934
      New Outlook 163:32, Mar 1934
      New York Times p. 20, Jan 24, 1934
                     p. 23, Sep 4, 1934
                     p. 14, Sep 19, 1934
                     p. 15, Aug 9, 1939
      Newsweek 3:36, Feb 3, 1934
      Review of Reviews 89:48, Apr 1934
      Stage 11:7-8, Mar 1934
      Theatre Arts 18:248, Apr 1934
      Time 23:35, Feb 5, 1934

Only 38
    Productions:
      Opened September 13, 1921 for 88 performances.
    Reviews:
      Dramatic Mirror 84:413, Sep 17, 1921
      Independent 107:36, Oct 8, 1921
      New York Times p. 22, Sep 14, 1921
      Theatre Magazine 34:422, Dec 1921

The Rainbow
    Productions:
        Opened March 11, 1912 for 104 performances.
    Reviews:
        American Playwright 1:110-12, Apr 1912
        Blue Book 15:246-8, Jun 1912
        Bookman 35:247-8, Jun 1912
        Collier's 49:24, Apr 13, 1912
        Current Literature 52:687-93, Jun 1912
        Dramatic Mirror 67:7, Mar 13, 1912
        Dramatist 3:245-7, Apr 1912
        Green Book 7:1072, May 1912
                  7:1088-90+, Jun 1912
        Hampton 28:294+, May 1912
        Hearst 21:2473-88, Jun 1912
        Munsey 47:281-2, May 1912
        National Magazine 37:780-5, Jan 1913
        New York Drama News 55:14, Mar 16, 1912
        Red Book 19:380-4, Jun 1912
        Theatre Magazine 15:108, Apr 1912

*Spin-Drift
    Reviews:
        New York Times p. 16, Feb 14, 1925

Vermont
    Productions:
        Opened January 7, 1929 for 15 performances.
    Reviews:
        New York Times p. 28, Jan 9, 1929
        Theatre Magazine 49:51, Mar 1929

What the Doctor Ordered
    Productions:
        Opened September 20, 1911 for 21 performances.
    Reviews:
        American Playwright 1:23-4, Jan 1912
        Bookman 33:359-60, Jun 1911
        Dramatic Mirror 66:10, Sep 27, 1911
        Life (NY) 58:567, Oct 5, 1911
                  90:19, Sep 8, 1927

THOMAS, AUGUSTUS

Arizona
    Productions:
        Opened April 28, 1913 for 40 performances.
    Reviews:
        Blue Book 17:659-61, Aug 1913
        Bookman 37:430-1, Jun 1913

Dramatic Mirror 69:6, Apr 30, 1913
Dramatist 3:252-3, Jul 1913
Green Book 10:19-21+, Jul 1913
Life (NY) 61:980, May 15, 1913
New York Times p. 11, Apr 30, 1913
Theatre Magazine 17:171, Jun 1913

As a Man Thinks
Productions:
    Opened March 13, 1911 for 128 performances.
Reviews:
    Blue Book 13:250-2, Jun 1911
    Book News 31:289, Dec 1912
    Bookman 33:354, Jun 7, 1911
    Current Literature 50:529-36, May 1911
    Dramatic Mirror 65:7, Mar 15, 1911
    Dramatist 2:142-3, Apr 1911
    Everybody's 25:688-89, Nov 1911
    Harper's Weekly 55:18, Apr 15, 1911
    Independent 70:664-5, Mar 30, 1911
    Leslies' Weekly 112:347, Mar 30, 1911
    Life (NY) 57:580, Mar 23, 1911
    Metropolitan Magazine 34:220, May 1911
    Munsey 45:282-3, May 1911
    Nation 93:197-8, Aug 31, 1911
    Outlook 97:714, Apr 1, 1911
    Pearson 25:663-72, May 1911
    Red Book 17:369-74, Jun 1911
    World Today 20:530, May 1911
            21:1247-54, Oct 1911

The Copperhead (Based on a story by Frederick Landis)
Productions:
    Opened February 18, 1918 for 120 performances.
Reviews:
    Art World 3:460, Mar 1918
    Bookman 47:291, May 1918
    Current Opinion 65:23-6, Jul 1918
    Dramatic Mirror 78:5, Mar 2, 1918
    Dramatist 9:896-7, Apr 1918
    Green Book 19:776-9, May 1918
    Hearst 34:42-4+, Jul 1918
    Life (NY) 71:382, Mar 7, 1918
    New Republic 14:267, Mar 30, 1918
    New York Times p. 11, Feb 19, 1918
            V, p. 4, Feb 24, 1918
            IV, p. 10, Mar 31, 1918
    Theatre Magazine 27:21+, Apr 1918

The Harvest Moon
Productions:
    Opened October 15, 1909 for 91 performances.

Reviews:
American Magazine 69:417, Jan 1910
Current Literature 47:661-8, Dec 1909
Dramatic Mirror 62:5, Oct 30, 1909
Dramatist 1:21-2, Jan 1910
Everybody's 22:130, Jan 1910
Forum 42:575-6, Dec 1909
Green Book 3:81-2, Jan 1910
3:705-49, Apr 1910
Hampton 24:128+, Jan 1910
Harper's Weekly 53:24, Nov 6, 1909
Independent 67:1123-4, Nov 18, 1909
Life (NY) 54:628, Nov 4, 1909
Metropolitan Magazine 31:536-7, Jan 1910
Nation 89:387, Oct 21, 1909
Outlook 93:571, Nov 13, 1909
Pearson 23:97-8, Jan 1910
Theatre Magazine 10:167-9+, Dec 1909
World Today 18:651-8, Jun 1910

Indian Summer
Productions:
Opened October 27, 1913 for 24 performances.
Reviews:
American Playwright 2:351-5, Nov 1913
Bookman 38:364-5, Dec 1913
Dramatic Mirror 70:6, Oct 29, 1913
Dramatist 5:420-1, Jan 1914
Harper's Weekly 58:24-5, Nov 22, 1913
Life (NY) 62:838-9, Nov 13, 1913
New York Times p. 11, Oct 28, 1913
Theatre Magazine 18:177-9, Dec 1913

Mere Man
Productions:
Opened November 25, 1912 for 8 performances.
Reviews:
American Playwright 1:399-400, Dec 1912
Dramatic Mirror 68:7, Nov 27, 1912
New York Drama News 56:26, Nov 30, 1912
Theatre Magazine 17:4, Jan 1913

The Model
Productions:
Opened August 31, 1912 for 17 performances.
Reviews:
American Playwright 1:288-90, Sep 1913
Blue Book 15:701-4, Aug 1912
Bookman 36:170-1, Oct 1912
Dramatic Mirror 68:6, Sep 4, 1912
Dramatist 3:252, Jul 1912

Everybody's 27:673, Nov 1912
Green Book 8:802-3, Nov 1912
8:898-9, Nov 1912
Life (NY) 60:1767, Sep 12, 1912
New York Drama News 55:18-19, Apr 13, 1912
56:12, Sep 14, 1912
Theatre Magazine 16:102+, Oct 1912

Nemesis
Productions:
Opened April 4, 1921 for 56 performances.
Reviews:
Dramatic Mirror 83:620, Apr 9, 1921
Dramatist 12:1051-2, Apr 1921
Everybody's 45:106-12, Jul 1921
Life (NY) 77:572, Apr 21, 1921
Nation 112:598, Apr 20, 1921
New York Clipper 69:19, Apr 6, 1921
New York Times p. 24, Apr 5, 1921
VI, p. 1, Apr 10, 1921
Theatre Magazine 33:395+, Jun 1921
Weekly Review 4:377-8, Apr 20, 1921

Palmy Days
Productions:
Opened October 27, 1919 for 50 performances.
Reviews:
Nation 109:640, Nov 15, 1919
New York Times p. 14, Oct 28, 1919
VIII, p. 2, Nov 2, 1919
Theatre Magazine 30:367+, Dec 1919

Rio Grande
Productions:
Opened April 4, 1916 for 55 performances.
Reviews:
Book News 34:401, May 1916
Bookman 43:343, May 1916
Dramatic Mirror 75:9, Mar 11, 1916
75:8, Apr 15, 1916
7:663-6, Apr 1916
Green Book 15:972-3+, Jun 1916
Hearst 30:97-9+, Aug 1916
Life (NY) 67:759, Apr 20, 1916
Nation 102:420, Apr 13, 1916
New Republic 6:353-4, Apr 29, 1916
New York Drama News 62:18, Apr 8, 1916
New York Times p. 11, Apr 5, 1916
Theatre Magazine 23:273-4+, May 1916

Still Waters
Productions:

Opened March 1, 1926 for 16 performances.
Reviews:
Catholic World 123:92-3, Apr 1926
New York Times p. 21, Sep 8, 1925
p. 29, Sep 10, 1925
p. 23, Sep 11, 1925
p. 24, Sep 15, 1925
p. 24, Feb 26, 1926
p. 23, Mar 2, 1926
VIII, p. 1, Mar 7, 1926
Theatre Magazine 43:16, May 1926

*When It Comes Home
Reviews:
New York Times VIII, p. 1, Jan 22, 1928

THOMPSON, ERNEST

On Golden Pond
Productions:
(Off Broadway) September 13, 1978 for 30 performances and transferred to Broadway.
Opened on Broadway February 28, 1979 for 126 performances (156 in all).
Opened September 12, 1979 for 252 performances.
Reviews:
Commonweal 106:403-4, Jul 6, 1979
Encore 7:28, Oct 16, 1978
Nation 227:357-8, Oct 7, 1978
New York Magazine 12:75, Mar 19, 1979
New York Theatre Critics' Reviews 1979:356
New York Times p. 73, Sep 19, 1978
III, p. 21, Dec 13, 1978
III, p. 13, Mar 1, 1979
II, p. 3, Mar 18, 1979
XI, p. 6, Oct 26, 1980
XXI, p. 7, Apr 11, 1982
New Yorker 54:67, Sep 25, 1978
55:107, Mar 12, 1979
Newsweek 93:103, Mar 12, 1979
Time 113:83, Mar 12, 1979

The West Side Waltz
Productions:
Opened November 19, 1981 for 126 performances.
Reviews:
Los Angeles 26:240+, Mar 1981
New Leader 65:20, Jan 11, 1982
New York Magazine 14:87, Nov 30, 1981
New York Theatre Critics' Reviews 1981:77

New York Times III, p. 5, Nov 20, 1981
                II, p. 3, Nov 29, 1981
New Yorker 57:95, Nov 30, 1981
Newsweek 98:110, Nov 30, 1981
Time 118:90, Nov 30, 1981

THURBER, JAMES

The Male Animal (with Elliott Nugent)
    Productions:
        Opened January 9, 1940 for 243 performances.
        Opened April 30, 1952 for 317 performances.
        (Off Off Broadway) April 20, 1974 (American Theater Co.).
        (Off Off Broadway) October 2, 1980 for 16 performances (Man-
            hattan Punch Line).
    Reviews:
        Catholic World 150:597, Feb 1940
                       175:228, Jun 1952
        Commonweal 31:307, Jan 26, 1940
                   56:173, May 23, 1952
        Life 8:27-8+, Jan 29, 1940
        Nation 150:81, Jan 20, 1940
               175:58, Jul 19, 1952
        New Republic 102:116, Jan 22, 1940
        New York Theatre Critics' Reviews 1940:424
                                          1952:297
        New York Times IX, p. 1, Jan 7, 1940
                           p. 17, Jan 10, 1940
                           IX, p. 1, Jan 21, 1940
                           p. 27, Jul 1, 1941
                           p. 24, Jul 9, 1941
                           II, p. 2, Apr 27, 1952
                           p. 35, May 1, 1952
                           II, p. 1, May 18, 1952
                           III, p. 11, Oct 13, 1980
        New Yorker 28:58, May 10, 1952
        Newsweek 14:34, Nov 6, 1939
                 15:32-3, Jan 22, 1940
                 39:84, May 26, 1952
        Saturday Review 35:28, May 17, 1952
        Theatre Arts 24:158-9+, Mar 1940
                     24:396+, Jun 1940
                     36:17, 32-5, Jul 1952
        Time 35:49, Jan 22, 1940
             59:58, May 12, 1952

A Thurber Carnival
    Productions:
        Opened February 26, 1960 for 127 performances.
        Opened September 5, 1960 for 96 performances.

(Off Broadway) October 1, 1965 for 9 performances (Equity Theater).
(Off Off Broadway) May 16, 1976 (Drama Comm. Rep Th).
Reviews:
America 103:322-3, May 28, 1960
Christian Century 77:489-90, Apr 20, 1960
Nation 190:236, Mar 12, 1960
New York Theatre Critics' Reviews 1960:342
New York Times II, p. 1, Feb 21, 1960
       p. 13, Feb 27, 1960
       II, p. 1, Mar 6, 1960
       VI, p. 18, Mar 6, 1960
       II, p. 3, Sep 4, 1960
       p. 41, Sep 13, 1960
       VI, p. 28, Oct 16, 1960
       p. 42, Apr 12, 1962
New Yorker 36:125-6, Mar 5, 1960
Newsweek 55:89, Mar 7, 1960
Saturday Review 43:26, Mar 19, 1960
Time 75:50, Mar 7, 1960

TOPOR, TOM

Answers
Productions:
(Off Off Broadway) April 1976 (Drama Ensemble Co.).
No Reviews.

But Not for Me
Productions:
(Off Off Broadway) May 10, 1976 (Theater at Noon).
(Off Off Broadway) December 1, 1978 for 12 performances
(Theater of the Riverside Church).
No Reviews.

Nuts
Productions:
(Off Off Broadway) June 1974 (Theater at St. Clements).
(Off Off Broadway) February 23, 1980 for 16 performances
(WPA Theater).
Opened April 28, 1980 for 96 performances.
Reviews:
California Magazine 6:138, Nov 1981
Los Angeles 26:304, Oct 1981
New York Theatre Critics' Reviews 1980:268
New York Times III, p. 7, Apr 29, 1980
       II, p. 3, Jun 8, 1980
New Yorker 56:69, May 12, 1980

Romance: Here to Stay
Productions:

(Off Off Broadway) December 1, 1978 for 12 performances (Theater of the Riverside Church).
No Reviews.

TOTHEROH, DAN

Distant Drums
　Productions:
　　Opened January 18, 1932 for 40 performances.
　Reviews:
　　Catholic World 134:712-13, Mar 1932
　　Commonweal 15:385, Feb 3, 1932
　　Literary Digest 112:17, Feb 6, 1932
　　Nation 134:177-8, Feb 10, 1932
　　New Republic 69:320-1, Feb 3, 1932
　　New York Times p. 24, Jan 19, 1932
　　　　　　　　　　　　VIII, p. 1, Jan 31, 1932
　　　　　　　　　　　　VIII, p. 1, Jan 24, 1932
　　Outlook 160:151, Feb 3, 1932
　　Player's Magazine 8:13, Mar-Apr 1932
　　Theatre Arts 16:190-1, Mar 1932
　　Theatre Guild Magazine 9:11, Mar 1932
　　Vogue 79:73+, Mar 15, 1932

Live Life Again
　Productions:
　　Opened September 29, 1945 for 2 performances.
　Reviews:
　　Catholic World 162:164, Nov 1945
　　New Republic 113:499, Oct 15, 1945
　　New York Theatre Critics' Reviews 1945:154
　　New York Times p. 14, Oct 1, 1945
　　New Yorker 21:50-1, Oct 6, 1945
　　Theatre Arts 29:621-2, 632-3, Nov 1945

Moor Born
　Productions:
　　Opened April 3, 1934 for 63 performances.
　Reviews:
　　Catholic World 134:213-4, May 1934
　　Commonweal 19:692, Apr 20, 1934
　　Literary Digest 117:24, Apr 21, 1934
　　Nation 138:453-4, Apr 18, 1934
　　New Outlook 163:43, May 1934
　　New Republic 78:275, Apr 18, 1934
　　New York Times p. 26, Apr 4, 1934
　　New Yorker 3:37-8, Apr 14, 1934
　　Review of Reviews 89:49, May 1934
　　Stage 11:6-7, May 1934
　　Theatre Arts 18:409, Jun 1934
　　Time 23:55-6, Apr 16, 1934

Mother Lode (with George O'Neil)
    Productions:
        Opened December 22, 1934 for 9 performances.
    Reviews:
        New York Times p. 16, Dec 24, 1934
        Theatre Arts 19:103, Feb 1935

*Rough an' Ready
    Reviews:
        New York Times II, p. 3, May 22, 1949

Searching for the Sun
    Productions:
        Opened February 19, 1936 for 5 performances.
    Reviews:
        New York Times IX, p. 2, Feb 16, 1936
                    p. 22, Feb 20, 1936

Wild Birds
    Productions:
        Opened April 9, 1925 for 44 performances.
    Reviews:
        American Mercury 5:247-8, Jun 1925
        Dramatist 16:1266-7, Apr 1925
        Independent 114:644, Jun 6, 1925
        New York Times p. 16, Apr 10, 1925
                    VIII, p. 1, Apr 26, 1925

*Wind in the Sails
    Reviews:
        New York Times p. 24, Aug 1, 1940

TREADWELL, SOPHIE

Gringo
    Productions:
        Opened December 12, 1922 for 35 performances.
    Reviews:
        Bookman 56:749-50, Feb 1923
        New York Times p. 26, Dec 15, 1922
                    VII, p. 1, Dec 24, 1922
        Theatre Magazine 37:19, Feb 1923

Hope for a Harvest
    Productions:
        Opened November 26, 1941 for 38 performances.
    Reviews:
        Catholic World 154:472-3, Jan 1942
        Nation 153:621, Dec 13, 1941
        New Republic 105:762, Dec 8, 1941

New York Theatre Critics' Reviews 1941:198
New York Times p. 18, Apr 5, 1941
                 p. 28, Nov 27, 1941
                 X, p. 5, Dec 7, 1941
Theatre Arts 26:12, Jan 1942
Time 38:39, Dec 8, 1941

Ladies Leave
    Productions:
        Opened October 1, 1929 for 15 performances.
    Reviews:
        New York Times p. 28, Oct 2, 1929
        Outlook 153:272, Oct 16, 1929
        Theatre Magazine 50:68, Dec 1929

Lone Valley
    Productions:
        Opened March 10, 1933 for 3 performances.
    Reviews:
        New York Times p. 18, Mar 11, 1933

*Lonely Lee
    Reviews:
        New York Times VIII, p. 2, Nov 11, 1923

Machinal
    Productions:
        Opened September 7, 1928 for 91 performances.
        (Off Broadway) Season of 1959-60.
        (Off Off Broadway) March 25, 1978 (Encompass Theater).
    Reviews:
        America 103:203, Apr 30, 1960
        American Mercury 15:376-7, Nov 28, 1928
        Commonweal 72:306, Jun 17, 1960
        Dial 85:445, Nov 1928
        Life (NY) 92:17, Sep 28, 1928
        Nation 127:302, Sep 26, 1928
        New Republic 56:299-300, Oct 31, 1928
                     142:21-2, Apr 25, 1960
        New York Times p. 10, Sep 8, 1928
                       III, p. 4, Sep 16, 1928
                       IX, p. 1, Sep 16, 1928
                       X, p. 1, Nov 25, 1928
                       p. 27, Apr 8, 1960
                       II, p. 1, Apr 17, 1960
        New Yorker 36:134-6, Apr 16, 1960
        Theatre Arts 12:774-80, Nov 1928
        Theatre Magazine 48:46, Nov 1928
                         49:20, Jan 1929
        Vogue 72:74+, Oct 27, 1928

O, Nightingale
  Productions:
    Opened April 15, 1925 for 29 performances.
  Reviews:
    New York Times p. 25, Apr 16, 1925

Plumes in the Dust
  Productions:
    Opened November 6, 1936 for 11 performances.
  Reviews:
    Catholic World 144:336-7, Dec 1936
    Commonweal 25:104, Nov 20, 1936
    New Republic 89:116, Nov 25, 1936
    New York Times p. 21, Oct 26, 1936
                   p. 14, Nov 7, 1936
                   XI, p. 1, Nov 15, 1936
    Newsweek 8:58+, Nov 14, 1936
    Time 28:89, Nov 16, 1936

TURNEY, ROBERT

Daughters of Atreus
  Productions:
    Opened October 14, 1936 for 13 performances.
  Reviews:
    Commonweal 25:20, Oct 30, 1936
    Nation 143:529-30, Oct 31, 1936
    New York Times p. 33, Oct 15, 1936
    Player's Magazine 13:8, Nov-Dec 1936
    Saturday Review 14:18, Oct 17, 1936
    Scribner's Magazine 100:78, Dec 1936
    Stage 14:68-9, Oct 1936
          14:72, Nov 1936
    Theatre Arts 20:924-5, Dec 1936
    Time 28:48, Oct 26, 1936
    Vogue 88:66, Nov 15, 1936

The Secret Room
  Productions:
    Opened November 7, 1945 for 21 performances.
  Reviews:
    Catholic World 162:263, Dec 1945
    Commonweal 43:140, Nov 23, 1945
    Life 19:51-2+, Nov 19, 1945
    New York Theatre Critics' Reviews 1945:124
    New York Times p. 16, Nov 8, 1945
    New Yorker 21:50+, Nov 17, 1945
    Newsweek 26:85, Nov 19, 1945
    Theatre Arts 30:13, Jan 1946
    Time 46:64, Nov 19, 1945

TYLER, ROYALL

The Contrast
    Productions:
        (Off Off Broadway) Season of 1971-72 (American Theater Co.).
        (Off Off Broadway) October 14, 1975 (York Players).
        (Off Off Broadway) March 8, 1977 (The Wooden O).
    Reviews:
        New York Times p. 27, Jul 20, 1948
                       p. 45, Jul 20, 1966
                       p. 51, Nov 28, 1972
                       II, p. 7, Dec 24, 1972
                       III, p. 4, Jul 16, 1976

VALE, MARTIN (MRS. BAYARD VEILLER)

The Two Mrs. Carrolls
    Productions:
        Opened August 3, 1943 for 585 performances.
    Reviews:
        Catholic World 157:635-7, Sep 1943
        Life 15:115-16+, Aug 23, 1943
        Nation 157:388, Oct 2, 1943
        New York Theatre Critics' Reviews 1943:304
        New York Times p. 14, Aug 14, 1943
        Newsweek 22:78, Aug 16, 1943
        Theatre Arts 27:575-6, Oct 1943
        Time 42:50, Aug 16, 1943

VAN DRUTEN, JOHN

After All
    Productions:
        Opened December 3, 1931 for 20 performances.
    Reviews:
        Arts and Decorations 36:56, Feb 1932
        Catholic World 134:468-9, Jan 1932
        Commonweal 15:187, Dec 16, 1931
        Nation 133:706, Dec 23, 1931
        New York Times IX, p. 1, May 26, 1929
                       p. 28, Dec 4, 1931
        Outlook 159:502, Dec 16, 1931
        Theatre Arts 16:101, Feb 1932
        Town and Country 86:22, Jan 1, 1932

*Behold We Live
    Reviews:
        New York Times p. 13, Aug 17, 1932
                       IX, p. 1, Sep 11, 1932

Bell, Book and Candle
    Productions:
        Opened November 14, 1950 for 233 performances.
        (Off Off Broadway) May 5, 1977 (American Ensemble Co.).
    Reviews:
        Catholic World 172:307, Jan 1951
        Christian Science Monitor Magazine p. 10, Nov 25, 1950
        Commonweal 53:197, Dec 1, 1950
        Hobbies 57:38, Oct 1952
        Life 29:111-12+, Dec 11, 1950
        Nation 171:493, Nov 25, 1950
        New Republic 123:22, Dec 25, 1950
        New York Theatre Critics' Reviews 1950:206
        New York Times II, p. 3, Nov 12, 1950
                        p. 37, Nov 15, 1950
                        II, p. 3, Dec 17, 1950
                        p. 86, Oct 11, 1953
                        p. 30, Oct 6, 1954
        New Yorker 26:62+, Nov 25, 1950
        Newsweek 36:76, Nov 27, 1950
        Saturday Review 33:24, Dec 16, 1950
        School and Society 73:104, Feb 17, 1951
        Theatre Arts 35:15, Jan 1951
                    36:50-75, Jun 1952
        Time 56:76+, Nov 27, 1950

The Damask Cheek (with Lloyd Morris)
    Productions:
        Opened October 22, 1942 for 93 performances.
    Reviews:
        Catholic World 156:335-6, Dec 1942
        Commonweal 37:71-2, Nov 6, 1942
        Independent Woman 21:368+, Dec 1942
        Life 13:68+, Nov 23, 1942
        Nation 155:599, Nov 28, 1942
        New Republic 107:609-10, Nov 9, 1942
        New York Theatre Critics' Reviews 1942:195
        New York Times p. 24, Oct 23, 1942
                    VIII, p. 1, Nov 8, 1942
                    VIII, p. 1, Dec 6, 1942
        New Yorker 18:30, Oct 31, 1942
        Newsweek 20:86, Nov 2, 1942
        Theatre Arts 26:740-1, Dec 1942
        Time 40:57, Nov 2, 1942

The Distaff Side
    Productions:
        Opened September 25, 1934 for 153 performances.
        Reopened for 24 performances.
    Reviews:
        Catholic World 140:212, Nov 1934

Commonweal 20:563, Oct 12, 1934
Golden Book Magazine 20:510, Nov 1934
Nation 139:418-9, Oct 10, 1934
New Republic 80:273, Oct 17, 1934
New York Times p. 24, Sep 6, 1933
          X, p. 1, Sep 24, 1933
          p. 17, Sep 26, 1934
          p. 22, Jul 7, 1936
Newsweek 4:22-3, Oct 6, 1934
Stage 12:15, Nov 1934
    12:12-13, Dec 1934
Theatre Arts 18:818, Nov 1934
Vanity Fair 43:45-6, Dec 1934

Diversion
Productions:
Opened January 11, 1928 for 62 performances.
Reviews:
Life (NY) 91:21, Feb 2, 1928
New York Times VII, p. 2, Aug 14, 1927
          p. 26, Jan 6, 1928
          p. 25, Jan 12, 1928
Vogue 71:114, Mar 1, 1928

The Druid Circle
Productions:
Opened October 22, 1947 for 70 performances.
Reviews:
Catholic World 166:265, Dec 1947
Commonweal 47:95, Nov 7, 1947
New Republic 117:36, Nov 3, 1947
New York Theatre Critics' Reviews 1947:288
New York Times II, p. 1, Oct 19, 1947
          p. 29, Oct 23, 1947
          II, p. 1, Nov 16, 1947
New Yorker 23:44+, Nov 1, 1947
Newsweek 30:76, Nov 3, 1947
Player's Magazine 25:191, May 1949
School and Society 66:507-8, Dec 27, 1947
Theatre Arts 31:14, Oct 1947
          32:11, Jan 1948
Time 50:68+, Nov 3, 1947
Vogue 110:133, Oct 15, 1947

Flowers of the Forest
Productions:
Opened April 8, 1935 for 40 performances.
Reviews:
Catholic World 141:216-18, May 1935
Commonweal 21:740, Apr 26, 1935
Nation 140:490-1, Apr 24, 1935

New Republic 82:316, Apr 24, 1935
New York Times p. 24, Oct 3, 1934
              p. 23, Nov 21, 1934
              X, p. 3, Dec 9, 1934
              p. 21, Apr 5, 1935
              p. 25, Apr 9, 1935
              IX, p. 1, Apr 14, 1935
Newsweek 5:17, Apr 20, 1935
Theatre Arts 19:3, Jan 1935
           19:400-1+, Jun 1935
Time 25:26, Apr 22, 1935

*Gertie Maude
  Reviews:
    New York Times p. 14, Aug 18, 1937
                X, p. 2, Sep 5, 1937
    Theatre Arts 21:847, Nov 1937

I Am a Camera (Based on the stories of Christopher Isherwood)
  Productions:
    Opened November 28, 1951 for 214 performances.
    (Off Broadway) Season of 1956-57.
    (Off Off Broadway) May 11, 1977 (Quaigh Theater).
    (Off Off Broadway) May 4, 1978 (Jewish Repertory Theater).
  Reviews:
    Catholic World 174:309, Jan 1952
    Commonweal 55:277, Dec 21, 1951
    Nation 173:554, Dec 22, 1951
    New Republic 125:22, Dec 24, 1951
    New York Theatre Critics' Reviews 1951:156
    New York Times p. 39, Nov 29, 1951
               II, p. 5, Dec 9, 1951
               p. 11, Mar 13, 1954
               II, p. 2, Apr 11, 1954
               p. 47, Oct 10, 1956
               p. 48, May 14, 1978
    New Yorker 27:62+, Dec 8, 1951
    Newsweek 38:50, Dec 10, 1951
    Saturday Review 34:26+, Dec 22, 1951
               35:27, Jul 5, 1952
    School and Society 75:41, Jan 19, 1952
    Theatre Arts 36:20-2, 30, Feb 1952
    Time 58:63, Dec 10, 1951

I Remember Mama (Adapted from Kathryn Forbes' Mama's Bank Ac-
    count)
  Productions:
    Opened October 19, 1944 for 714 performances.
    (Off Off Broadway) November 7, 1974.
  Reviews:
    Catholic World 160:259, Dec 1944

Commonweal 41:72, Nov 3, 1944
Life 17:104-6+, Nov 20, 1944
    18:79, Apr 9, 1945
Nation 159:568, Nov 4, 1944
New Republic 111:836, Dec 18, 1944
New York Theatre Critics' Reviews 1944:111
New York Times p. 16, Oct 20, 1944
                II, p. 1, Oct 29, 1944
                VI, p. 16, Dec 3, 1944
                VI, p. 24, Oct 14, 1945
                p. 79, Dec 15, 1946
                VI, p. 18, Mar 2, 1947
                p. 51, Jan 4, 1948
                II, p. 3, Apr 11, 1948
New Yorker 20:39, Oct 28, 1944
Newsweek 24:86, Oct 30, 1944
Player's Magazine 22:10, Nov-Dec 1945
Saturday Review 27:18+, Dec 16, 1944
Theatre Arts 28:692+, Dec 1944
            29:81-2, 87, Feb 1945
            29:215-17+, Apr 1945
Time 44:68, Oct 30, 1944

I've Got Sixpence

Productions:
Opened December 2, 1952 for 23 performances.
Reviews:
Commonweal 57:306, Dec 26, 1952
New York Theatre Critics' Reviews 1952:167
New York Times II, p. 1, Nov 30, 1952
                p. 44, Dec 3, 1952
                II, p. 5, Dec 7, 1952
New Yorker 28:86, Dec 13, 1952
Newsweek 40:62, Dec 15, 1952
Saturday Review 35:25, Dec 20, 1952
Theatre Arts 36:15, Dec 1952
            37:26, Feb 1953
Time 60:73, Dec 15, 1952

Leave Her to Heaven

Productions:
Opened February 27, 1940 for 15 performances.
Reviews:
Commonweal 31:455, Mar 15, 1940
New York Theatre Critics' Reviews 1940:379
New York Times p. 16, Feb 28, 1940
Newsweek 15:35, Mar 11, 1940
Theatre Arts 24:317, May 1940
Time 35:32, Mar 11, 1940

*London Wall

Reviews:

New York Times p. 23, May 2, 1931
            VIII, p. 1, May 24, 1931

Make Way for Lucia (Based on the novels of E. F. Benson)
    Productions:
        Opened December 22, 1948 for 29 performances.
    Reviews:
        Commonweal 49:352, Jan 14, 1949
        Nation 168:81, Jan 15, 1949
        New Republic 120:19, Jan 10, 1949
        New York Theatre Critics' Reviews 1948:115
        New York Times p. 23, Dec 23, 1948
        New Yorker 24:34, Jan 1, 1949
        Newsweek 33:54, Jan 3, 1949
        Time 53:49, Jan 3, 1949
        Vogue 113:115, Jan 1949

The Mermaids Singing
    Productions:
        Opened November 28, 1945 for 53 performances.
    Reviews:
        Catholic World 162:358, Jan 1946
        Commonweal 43:263, Dec 21, 1945
        Harper's Bazaar 79:128, Dec 1945
        New Republic 113:839, Dec 17, 1945
        New York Theatre Critics' Reviews 1945:86
        New York Times p. 26, Nov 29, 1945
                    II, p. 5, Dec 9, 1945
        New Yorker 21:56-8, Dec 8, 1945
        Newsweek 26:93, Dec 10, 1945
        Saturday Review 28:14-16, Dec 15, 1945
        Theatre Arts 30:7, Jan 1946
                    30:78, Feb 1946
        Time 46:76, Dec 10, 1945

Most of the Game
    Productions:
        Opened October 1, 1935 for 23 performances.
    Reviews:
        Nation 141:448, Oct 16, 1935
        New York Times p. 27, Oct 2, 1935
        Theatre Arts 19:823, Nov 1935
        Vanity Fair 45:40, Dec 1935

Old Acquaintance
    Productions:
        Opened December 23, 1940 for 170 performances.
    Reviews:
        Catholic World 152:597, Feb 1941
        Commonweal 33:303, Jan 10, 1941
        Nation 152:137, Feb 1, 1941

New York Theatre Critics' Reviews 1940:178
1941:448
New York Times p. 33, Dec 10, 1940
p. 18, Dec 24, 1940
IX, p. 2, Dec 28, 1941
Newsweek 17:52, Jan 6, 1941
Theatre Arts 25:93-4, Feb 1941
Time 37:41, Jan 6, 1941
Vogue 97:77, Mar 1, 1941

*Return of the Soldier
Reviews:
New York Times VIII, p. 1, Jul 8, 1928

Solitaire (Based on a novel by Edwin Corle)
Productions:
Opened January 27, 1942 for 23 performances.
Reviews:
Catholic World 154:730, Nov 1942
Commonweal 35:418, Feb 13, 1942
Nation 154:201-2, Feb 14, 1942
New Republic 106:204, Feb 9, 1942
New York Theatre Critics' Reviews 1942:362
New York Times p. 22, Jan 28, 1942
IX, p. 1, Feb 8, 1942
Newsweek 19:63+, Feb 9, 1942
Player's Magazine 18:12, Mar 1942
Theatre Arts 26:224-5, Apr 1942
Time 39:47, Feb 9, 1942

*Somebody Knows
Reviews:
New York Times VIII, p. 1, May 29, 1932

There's Always Juliet
Productions:
Opened February 15, 1932 for 108 performances.
Opened October 27, 1932 for 20 performances.
Reviews:
Bookman 74:667, Mar 1932
Catholic World 135:73, Apr 1932
Commonweal 15:495, Mar 2, 1932
Nation 134:266, Mar 2, 1932
New Republic 70:97, Mar 9, 1932
New York Times p. 26, Oct 13, 1931
VIII, p. 4, Nov 8, 1931
p. 24, Feb 16, 1932
VIII, p. 1, Feb 28, 1932
p. 23, Oct 28, 1932
North American Review 234:174-5, Aug 1932
Theatre Arts 16:270-1, Apr 1932

Theatre Guild Magazine 9:29-31, Apr 1932
Vogue 79:96B, Apr 15, 1932

The Voice of the Turtle
    Productions:
        Opened December 8, 1943 for 1,557 performances.
        (Off Broadway) Season of 1961-62.
        (Off Off Broadway) March 1976 (Manhattan Theater Club).
    Reviews:
        American Mercury 58:464-8, Apr 1944
        Catholic World 158:487-8, Feb 1944
        Collier's 113:16-17+, Apr 29, 1944
        Commonweal 39:253, Dec 24, 1943
        Life 15:45-6, Dec 27, 1943
        Nation 157:767, Dec 25, 1943
        New Republic 109:915, Dec 27, 1943
        New York Theatre Critics' Reviews 1943:199
        New York Times II, p. 5, Dec 5, 1943
                          p. 30, Dec 9, 1943
                          II, p. 3, Dec 19, 1943
                          II, p. 6, Dec 10, 1944
                          p. 27, Dec 19, 1944
                          p. 19, Feb 5, 1945
                          p. 16, Feb 6, 1945
                          II, p. 1, Jun 30, 1945
                          p. 16, Sep 3, 1946
                          II, p. 1, Sep 8, 1946
                          p. 35, Feb 26, 1947
                          II, p. 3, Jun 8, 1947
                          p. 12, Aug 22, 1947
                          II, p. 2, Aug 22, 1947
                          p. 41, Jun 28, 1961
                          III, p. 23, Nov 12, 1980
        New Yorker 19:44, Dec 18, 1943
        Newsweek 22:86, Dec 20, 1943
        Theatre Arts 28:73-5, Feb 1944
        Time 42:36, Dec 20, 1943

Young Woodley
    Productions:
        Opened November 2, 1925 for 260 performances.
    Reviews:
        Bookman 62:595, Jan 1926
        Dramatist 17:1292-3, Jan 1926
        Independent 115:713, Dec 19, 1925
        Nation 121:582+, Nov 18, 1925
                126:130, Feb 1, 1928
        New Republic 45:133-4, Dec 23, 1925
        New York Times p. 34, Nov 3, 1925
                        VIII, p. 1, Nov 8, 1925
                        VIII, p. 2, Nov 29, 1925

Outlook 141:508, Dec 2, 1925
Theatre Arts 10:10-11, Jan 1926
Theatre Magazine 43:15, Jan 1926
                43:19, Jan 1926
                43:26+, Feb 1926
Vogue 67:63, Jan 1, 1926

VAN ITALLIE, JEAN-CLAUDE

America Hurrah (Interview, T.V., and Motel)
    Productions:
        (Off Broadway) November 6, 1966 for 634 performances.
    Reviews:
        America 116:25, Jan 7, 1967
        Christian Century 84:596-7, May 3, 1967
        Commentary 43:87-8, Mar 1967
        Nation 203:587-8, Nov 28, 1966
        New Republic 155:31-3, Dec 3, 1966
        New York Times p. 66, Nov 7, 1966
                       II, p. 1, Nov 27, 1966
                       p. 59, Dec 20, 1966
                       p. 13, Aug 4, 1967
                       II, p. 3, Aug 13, 1967
                       p. 25, Sep 4, 1967
                       p. 55, Oct 10, 1967
        New Yorker 42:69-70, Jan 21, 1967
        Newsweek 68:114, Nov 21, 1966
        Reporter 36:49-50, Mar 9, 1967
        Time 88:79-80, Nov 18, 1966

Bag Lady
    Productions:
        (Off Off Broadway) November 21, 1979 (Theater for the New
            City).
    Reviews:
        New York Times III, p. 24, Nov 27, 1979

*Interview (See also America Hurrah)
    Reviews:
        New York Times p. 72, Dec 16, 1971

King of the United States (music by Richard Peaslee)
    Productions:
        (Off Off Broadway) Season of 1971-72 (Theater for the New
            City).
        (Off Off Broadway) November 19, 1974 (Theater at St.
            Clements).
    Reviews:
        New York Times p. 21, Nov 23, 1974

*Motel
  Productions:
    (Off Off Broadway) Season of 1981-82 (La Mama ETC).
    See also America Hurrah.
  No Reviews.

Mystery Play
  Productions:
    (Off Broadway) Opened January 3, 1973 for 14 performances.
  Reviews:
    America 128:41, Jan 20, 1973
    New York Magazine 6:58, Jan 22, 1973
    New York Times p. 34, Jan 4, 1973
    New Yorker 48:59-60, Jan 13, 1973

Nightwalk (with The Open Theater, Sam Shephard, and Megan
    Terry)
  Productions:
    (Off Off Broadway) Season of 1972-73 (Open Theater).
    (Off Off Broadway) September 8, 1973 (Theater at St. Cle-
      ments).
  Reviews:
    New York Times p. 55, Sep 11, 1973
                    II, p. 3, Oct 7, 1973

The Serpent: A Ceremony
  Productions:
    (Off Broadway) May 29, 1970 for 3 performances (Bill called
      The Open Theater).
  Reviews:
    America 121:160-1, Sep 13, 1969
    Nation 210:765-6, Jun 22, 1970
    New York Times p. 92, Mar 10, 1968
                    p. 56, May 6, 1968
                    II, p. 1, Feb 9, 1969
                    p. 35, Jun 2, 1970
    New Yorker 46:90, Jun 13, 1970

T.V. (see America Hurrah)

Thoughts on the Instant of Greeting a Friend on the Street
  Productions:
    (Off Broadway) May 8, 1968 for 80 performances.
  Reviews:
    Harper's Bazaar 237:113-15, Oct 1968
    Nation 206:772+, Jun 10, 1968
    New York Times p. 55, May 9, 1968
                    II, p. 1, May 19, 1968
    New Yorker 44:74, May 18, 1968

War
  Productions:

(Off Broadway) December 22, 1963 for 2 performances (Theatre
    1964 Playwrights Unit).
(Off Broadway) April 12, 1966 for 16 performances.
Reviews:
    Nation 202:404-5, Apr 4, 1966
    New York Times II, p. 15, Apr 10, 1966
                  p. 36, Apr 13, 1966

VARESI, GILDA

Enter Madame (with Dolly Byrne)
    Productions:
        Opened August 16, 1920 for 350 performances.
    Reviews:
        Bookman 53:412-13, Jul 1921
        Current Opinion 70:199-207, Feb 1921
        Drama 11:130, Jan 1921
        Dramatic Mirror p. 327, Jan 1921
        Dramatist 12:1037-8, Jan 1921
        Everybody's 44:38-9, Jan 1921
        Hearst 38:41-3+, Nov 1920
        New Republic 24:300, Nov 17, 1920
        New York Clipper 68:19, Aug 25, 1920
        New York Times p. 11, Aug 17, 1920
                      VI, p. 1, Aug 22, 1920
                      VI, p. 1, Oct 17, 1920
        Outlook 126:221, Oct 6, 1920
        Review 4:40, Jan 12, 1921
        Theatre Magazine 32:240, Oct 1920
        Weekly Review 5:40, Jan 12, 1921

VEILLER, BAYARD

Back Home (Based on Irvin S. Cobb's "Back Home" stories)
    Productions:
        Opened November 15, 1915 for 16 performances.
    Reviews:
        Dramatic Mirror 73:9, Jun 30, 1915
                       74:8-9, Nov 20, 1915
        Munsey 56:622, Jan 1916
        New York Drama News 61:17, Nov 20, 1915
        New York Times p. 13, Nov 16, 1915

Damn Your Honor (with Becky Gardiner)
    Productions:
        Opened December 30, 1929 for 8 performances.
    Reviews:
        New York Times p. 14, Dec 31, 1929
        Theatre Magazine 51:66-7, Feb 1930

The Fight
    Productions:
        Opened October 31, 1912 for 4 performances.
        Opened September 2, 1913 for 80 performances.
    Reviews:
        Bookman 38:133-4, Oct 1913
        Dramatic Mirror 70:6, Sep 10, 1913
        Everybody's 29:679-82, Nov 1913
        Green Book 10:764-6, Nov 1913
        Life (NY) 62:476, Sep 18, 1913
        Munsey 50:297, Nov 1913
        New York Drama News 58:18, Sep 13, 1913
        Theatre Magazine 18:116, Oct 1913

That's the Woman
    Productions:
        Opened September 3, 1930 for 29 performances.
    Reviews:
        Arts and Decoration 34:110, Nov 1930
        Life (NY) 96:18, Sep 26, 1930
        New York Times p. 27, Sep 4, 1930

The Thirteenth Chair
    Productions:
        Opened November 20, 1916 for 328 performances.
    Reviews:
        Book News 35:206, Jan 1917
                  36:64, Oct 1917
        Collier's 58:38, Jan 27, 1917
        Dramatic Mirror 76:4+, Dec 2, 1916
                        77:4, Apr 7, 1917
        Dramatist 8:791-2, Apr 1917
        Green Book 17:205+, Feb 1917
        Life (NY) 68:949, Nov 30, 1916
        McClure's 48:11, Mar 1917
        New York Dramatic News vol. 63, Nov 25, 1916
        New York Times p. 9, Nov 21, 1916
        Theatre Magazine 25:20+, Jan 1917

The Trial of Mary Dugan
    Productions:
        Opened September 19, 1927 for 437 performances.
    Reviews:
        Dial 83:530-31, Dec 1927
        Dramatist 18:1351-2, Oct 1927
        Independent 119:482, Nov 12, 1927
        Life (NY) 90:21, Oct 6, 1927
        Nation 125:406-7, Oct 12, 1927
        New York Times p. 33, Sep 20, 1927
                       VIII, p. 4, Oct 9, 1927
                       p. 28, Mar 7, 1928

IX, p. 1, Apr 1, 1928
p. 31, May 4, 1928
VIII, p. 1, Jun 24, 1928
p. 17, Jun 28, 1928
VII, p. 2, Sep 2, 1928
IX, p. 4, Sep 30, 1928
Theatre Magazine 46:22+, Nov 1927
46:28-30+, Dec 1927
Vogue 70:87, Nov 15, 1927

Within the Law

Productions:
Opened September 11, 1912 for 541 performances.
Opened Mar 5, 1928 for 16 performances.
Reviews:
American Playwright 1:315-16, Oct 1912
2:205-7, Jun 1913
Blue Book 15:682-5, Aug 1912
Book News 32:255-6, Jan 1914
Bookman 36:282, Nov 1912
Collier's 50:24+, Oct 5, 1912
Current Literature 53:682-9, Dec 1912
Dramatic Mirror 68:6, Sep 18, 1912
68:2, Oct 9, 1912
69:2, Jun 11, 1913
Dramatist 4:318-19, Jan 1913
Everybody's 27:675, Nov 1912
28:394, Mar 1913
Green Book 8:200-2, Aug 1912
8:984-7, Dec 1912
8:1005-6, Dec 1912
Harper's Weekly 56:20, Oct 12, 1912
Hearst 23:484-94, Mar 1913
Independent 76:250, Nov 6, 1913
Leslies' Weekly 115:411, Oct 24, 1912
115:613, Dec 12, 1912
Life (NY) 60:1858, Sep 26, 1912
Metropolitan Magazine 38:41-2, Jun 1913
Munsey 48:350-1, Nov 1912
49:819-20, Aug 1913
National Magazine 38:53, Apr 1913
New York Dramatic News 55:18, April 13, 1912
56:10-11, Sep 21, 1912
New York Times p. 20, Mar 6, 1928
Red Book 20:186-8+, Nov 1912
Stage 14:77, Aug 1937
Theatre Magazine 16:36, Aug 1912
16:97+, Aug 1912
Woman's Home Companion 40:24, Mar 1913

VEILLER, MRS. BAYARD (see Vale, Martin)

VIDAL, GORE

The Best Man
Productions:
Opened March 31, 1960 for 520 performances.
Reviews:
America 103:422, Jul 2, 1960
Commonweal 72:128-9, Apr 29, 1960
Life 48:55+, Apr 25, 1960
Nation 190:343, Apr 16, 1960
New Republic 142:21-2, Apr 18, 1960
New York Theatre Critics' Reviews 1960:308
New York Times p. 39, Apr 1, 1960
            II, p. 1, Apr 10, 1960
            VI, p. 27, May 22, 1960
            p. 44, Oct 5, 1960
            p. 1, Dec 7, 1960
New Yorker 36:88+, Apr 9, 1960
Newsweek 55:86, Apr 11, 1960
Reporter 22:38-9, Apr 28, 1960
Saturday Review 43:33, Apr 16, 1960
Time 75:85, Apr 11, 1960

An Evening with Richard Nixon And ...
Productions:
Opened April 30, 1972 for 16 performances.
Reviews:
Nation 214:669, May 22, 1972
National Review 24:652-3, Jun 9, 1972
New Republic 166:34, May 27, 1972
New York Theatre Critics' Reviews 1972:289
New York Times p. 41, May 1, 1972
            II, p. 1, May 7, 1972
            p. 25, May 12, 1972
New Yorker 48:54, May 6, 1972
Newsweek 79:92, May 15, 1972
Saturday Review 55:62-3, May 20, 1972
Time 99:59, May 15, 1972

*Fire to the Sea
Reviews:
New York Times p. 20, Nov 15, 1961

Romulus (Adapted from the play by Friedrich Duerrenmatt)
Productions:
Opened January 10, 1962 for 69 performances.
Reviews:
America 106:772-3, Mar 10, 1962
Christian Century 79:233, Feb 21, 1962
Nation 194:106-7, Feb 3, 1962
National Review 12:173-4, Mar 13, 1962
New Republic 146:20+, Jan 29, 1962

New York Theatre Critics' Reviews 1962:380
New York Times p. 27, Jan 11, 1962
                p. 25, Mar 2, 1962
New Yorker 37:63, Jan 20, 1962
Newsweek 59:50, Jan 22, 1962
Saturday Review 45:29, Jan 27, 1962
Theatre Arts 46:62-3, Mar 1962
Time 79:68+, Jan 19, 1962

Visit to a Small Planet
  Productions:
    Opened February 7, 1957 for 388 performances.
  Reviews:
    America 96:629, Mar 2, 1957
    Catholic World 185:68, Apr 1957
    Christian Century 74:918, Jul 31, 1957
    Commonweal 65:662-3, Mar 29, 1957
    Life 42:87-8, Mar 4, 1957
    Nation 184:174, Feb 23, 1957
    New York Theatre Critics' Reviews 1957:356
    New York Times p. 18, Feb 8, 1957
                   II, p. 1, Feb 24, 1957
    New Yorker 32:78+, Feb 16, 1957
    Newsweek 49:95, Feb 18, 1957
    Reporter 16:40, Mar 7, 1957
             17:35-6, Jul 11, 1957
    Saturday Review 40:29, Feb 23, 1957
    Theatre Arts 41:17, Apr 1957
    Time 69:60, Feb 18, 1957

Weekend
  Productions:
    Opened March 13, 1968 for 21 performances.
  Reviews:
    Commonweal 88:74-5, Apr 5, 1968
    Nation 206:454, Apr 1, 1968
    New York Theatre Critics' Reviews 1968:326
    New York Times p. 50, Mar 14, 1968
                   II, p. 1, Mar 31, 1968
    New Yorker 44:101, Mar 23, 1968
    Newsweek 71:100, Mar 25, 1968
    Saturday Review 51:20, Mar 30, 1968
    Time 91:64, Mar 22, 1968

VINCENT, ALLEN

Letters to Lucerne (see entry under Rotter, Fritz)

VOLLMER, LULA

The Dunce Boy
    Productions:
        Opened April 1, 1925 for 43 performances.
    Reviews:
        American Mercury 5:247, Jun 1925
        New York Times p. 20, Apr 4, 1925

The Hill Between
    Productions:
        Opened March 11, 1938 for 11 performances.
    Reviews:
        New York Times p. 12, Mar 12, 1938
        One Act Play Magazine 1:1120-21, Apr 1938
        Time 31:30, Mar 21, 1938

*Moonshine and Honeysuckle
    Reviews:
        New York Times p. 17, Jul 25, 1933

Sentinels
    Productions:
        Opened December 25, 1931 for 11 performances.
    Reviews:
        Commonweal 15:301, Jan 13, 1932
        New York Times p. 15, Dec 26, 1931
        Outlook 160:22, Jan 6, 1932

The Shame Woman
    Productions:
        Opened October 16, 1923 for 278 performances.
    Reviews:
        Nation 117:587-8, Nov 21, 1923
        New York Times p. 14, Oct 17, 1923
                        VIII, p. 1, Oct 21, 1923
        Theatre Magazine 38:68, Dec 1923

Sun Up
    Productions:
        Opened May 25, 1923 for 28+ performances.
        Opened October 22, 1928 for 101 performances.
    Reviews:
        Current Opinion 75:701-6+, Dec 1923
        Drama 17:116, Jan 1927
        New York Clipper 71:14, May 30, 1923
        New York Times p. 28, May 25, 1923
                        p. 18, Dec 21, 1923
                        VIII, p. 4, Dec 30, 1923
                        VII, p. 2, Jan 13, 1924
                        VII, p. 2, Feb 24, 1924

VIII, p. 2, Mar 30, 1924
p. 25, May 5, 1925
p. 13, Aug 14, 1925
p. 34, Sep 18, 1928
p. 33, Oct 23, 1928
IX, p. 4, Nov 4, 1928
p. 34, Jan 8, 1929
p. 22, Feb 19, 1929
p. 47, Mar 4, 1929
Theatre Magazine 38:16, Jul 1923
38:26+, Oct 1923

Trigger
    Productions:
        Opened December 6, 1927 for 47 performances.
    Reviews:
        Life (NY) 90:19, Dec 22, 1927
        New York Times p. 32, Dec 7, 1927
        Theatre Magazine 47:39-40, Feb 1928

Troyka (Adapted from the Hungarian of Imre Fazekas)
    Productions:
        Opened April 1, 1930 for 15 performances.
    Reviews:
        Life (NY) 95:18, Apr 18, 1930
        New York Times p. 32, Apr 2, 1930
        Outlook 154:631, Apr 16, 1930
        Theatre Magazine 51:70+, May 1930

WALKER, JOSEPH A.

Antigone Africanus
    Productions:
        (Off Off Broadway) March 1975 (Demi Gods).
    No Reviews.

The Harangues
    Productions:
        (Off Broadway) December 30, 1969 for 56 performances
            (Negro Ensemble Co.).
    Reviews:
        Nation 210:124-5, Feb 2, 1970
        New York Times p. 42, Jan 14, 1970
                        II, p. 1, Jan 25, 1970
        New Yorker 45:58, Jan 24, 1970
        Saturday Review 53:30, Feb 14, 1970

The Lion Is a Soul Brother
    Productions:
        (Off Off Broadway) April 24, 1976 (Gene Frankel).
    No Reviews.

The River Niger
Productions:
(Off Broadway) December 5, 1972 for 120 performances and transferred to Broadway.
Opened on Broadway March 27, 1973 for 280 performances (400 total performances).
Reviews:
Nation 215:668-9, Dec 25, 1972
216:541-2, Apr 23, 1973
New Republic 169:22+, Feb 1973
New York Magazine 6:94, Apr 9, 1973
New York Theatre Critics' Reviews 1973:298
New York Times p. 43, Dec 6, 1972
II, p. 5, Dec 17, 1972
p. 35, Mar 28, 1973
New Yorker 48:86+, Dec 16, 1972
49:57, Apr 7, 1973
Playboy 20:39, Jul 1973
Saturday Review (Arts) 1:59, Feb 1973
Time 101:64, Jan 1, 1973

Yin Yang
Productions:
(Off Broadway) May 1972 (Negro Ensemble Co.).
(Off Off Broadway) October 4, 1973 (Demi Gods).
(Off Off Broadway) October 1974 (Demi Gods).
Reviews:
New York Times p. 48, May 31, 1973

WALTER, EUGENE

The Challenge
Productions:
Opened August 5, 1919 for 72 performances.
Reviews:
Hearst 36:48+, Nov 1919
New York Times p. 7, Aug 6, 1919
IV, p. 2, Aug 10, 1919
Review 1:458, Oct 4, 1919
Theatre Magazine 30:223-5, Oct 1919

The Easiest Way
Productions:
Opened January 19, 1909 for 157 performances.
Opened September 6, 1921 for 63 performances.
Reviews:
Bookman 54:230-31, Nov 1921
Craftsman 15:739-41, Mar 1909
Current Literature 51:73-81, Jul 1911
Dramatic Mirror 61:3, Jan 30, 1909
84:377, Sep 10, 1921

Dramatist 4:379-80, Jul 1913
Forum 41:215-7, Mar 1909
Independent 66:191, Jan 28, 1909
Life (NY) 53:166, Feb 4, 1909
            57:682, Apr 6, 1911
Literary Digest 42:679-80, Apr 8, 1911
Munsey 41:578-9, Jul 1909
Nation 88:72, Jan 21, 1909
        113:381, Oct 5, 1921
New Republic 28:138-9, Sep 28, 1921
New York Clipper 69:23, Sep 14, 1921
New York Times p. 14, Sep 7, 1921
                    VI, p. 1, Sep 11, 1921
Stage 14:80, Aug 1937
Theatre Magazine 9:81-4, Mar 1909
Weekly Review 5:255, Sep 17, 1921

Fine Feathers
    Productions:
        Opened January 7, 1913 for 79 performances.
    Reviews:
        American Playwright 2:37-40, Feb 1913
        Blue Book 16:8-11, Nov 1912
        Bookman 36:643-4, Feb 1913
        Collier's 50:15+, Oct 26, 1912
        Current Literature 53:443-50, Oct 1912
        Dramatic Mirror 69:4, Jan 15, 1913
        Dramatist 4:321-2, Jan 1913
        Everybody's 28:520-1, Apr 1913
        Green Book 9:142-67, Jan 1913
                    9:432-4, Mar 1913
        Hearst 23:811-22, May 1913
        Life (NY) 61:200, Jan 23, 1913
        Munsey 48:1009-12, Mar 1913
        New York Drama News 57:19, Jan 18, 1913
        New York Times p. 11, Jan 8, 1913
        Smart Set 39:147-9, Mar 1913
        Theatre Magazine 16:194, Dec 1912
                        17:34+, Feb 1913
        Woman's Home Companion 40:24, Mar 1913

The Heritage
    Productions:
        Opened January 14, 1918 for 16 performances.
    Reviews:
        Dramatic Mirror 78:7, Jan 26, 1918
        Life (NY) 71:142, Jan 24, 1918
        New York Drama News 64:23, Jan 19, 1918
        New York Times p. 11, Jan 15, 1918
                        IV, p. 4, Jan 20, 1918

Jealousy (Based on the French of Louis Verneuil)
    Productions:
        Opened October 22, 1928 for 136 performances.
    Reviews:
        Life (NY) 92:17, Nov 9, 1928
        Nation 127:502, Nov 7, 1928
        New York Times p. 32, Oct 23, 1928
                        IX, p. 4, Nov 4, 1928
        Theatre Magazine 49:45-6, Jan 1929
                        49:30-31+, Feb 1929
        Vogue 72:146, Dec 8, 1928

Just a Wife
    Productions:
        Opened February 1, 1910 for 79 performances.
    Reviews:
        Bookman 31:142-4, Apr 1910
        Dramatic Mirror 63:6, Feb 12, 1910
        Dramatist 1:37-8, Apr 1910
        Green Book 3:765-6, Apr 1910
        Hampton 24:702-3, May 1910
        Life (NY) 55:284, Feb 17, 1910
        Theatre Magazine 11:vi, Mar 1910

Just a Woman
    Productions:
        Opened January 17, 1916 for 136 performances.
    Reviews:
        Bookman 43:164+, Apr 1916
        Dramatic Mirror 75:8, Jan 22, 1916
        Dramatist 7:678-9, Apr 1916
        Green Book 15:655+, Apr 1916
        Harper's Weekly 62:134, Feb 5, 1916
        Hearst 29:281-3+, Apr 1916
        Life (NY) 67:160-1, Jan 27, 1916
        Nation 102:115, Jan 27, 1916
        New Republic 5:336, Jan 29, 1916
        New York Drama News 62:17-18, Jan 22, 1916
        New York Times p. 12, Jan 8, 1916
        Theatre Magazine 23:124, Mar 1916

The Knife
    Productions:
        Opened April 12, 1917 for 84 performances.
    Reviews:
        Dramatic Mirror 77:4+, Apr 21, 1917
        Dramatist 8:821-2, Jul 1917
        Green Book 18:13-15, Jul 1917
        Life (NY) 69:728, Apr 26, 1917
        Nation 104:470, Apr 19, 1917
        New York Times p. 11, Apr 13, 1917
        Theatre Magazine 25:342+, Jun 1917

The Man's Name (with Marjorie Chase)
    Productions:
        Opened November 14, 1921 for 24 performances.
    Reviews:
        New York Times p. 22, Nov 16, 1921
                        p. 16, Nov 28, 1921

Nancy Lee (with H. Crowin Wilson)
    Productions:
        Opened April 9, 1918 for 63 performances.
    Reviews:
        Book News 36:377-8, Jun 1918
        Dramatic Mirror 78:548, Apr 20, 1918
        Green Book 19:977-8, Jun 1918
        Life (NY) 71:682, Apr 25, 1918
        Theatre Magazine 27:286, May 1918

Trail of the Lonesome Pine (Based on the novel by John Fox, Jr.)
    Productions:
        Opened January 29, 1912 for 32 performances.
    Reviews:
        American Playwright 1:35-8, Feb 1912
        Blue Book 14:478-80, Jan 1912
        Dramatic Mirror 67:6, Feb 7, 1912
        Dramatist 3:240-1, Apr 1912
        Everybody's 26:542, Apr 1912
        Green Book 7:26-7+, Jan 1912
                  7:798-9, Apr 1912
        Leslies' Weekly 114:205, Feb 22, 1912
        Munsey 47:130, Apr 1912
        Theatre Magazine 15:76, Mar 1912

WARREN, ROBERT PENN

All the King's Men
    Productions:
        (Off Broadway) Season of 1959-60.
        (Off Broadway) Season of 1966-67 for 9 performances (Equity
            Library Theater).
        (Off Off Broadway) May 14, 1974 (Urban Arts Corps).
    Reviews:
        New York Times p. 19, Jan 19, 1948
                        p. 25, Jul 19, 1950
                        p. 27, Oct 17, 1959
                        II, p. 1, Oct 25, 1959
                        p. 12, Jul 12, 1963

*Brothers to Dragons
    Reviews:
        New York Times p. 86, Dec 8, 1968

WATKINS, MAURINE

Chicago
    Productions:
        Opened December 30, 1926 for 172 performances.
    Reviews:
        American Mercury 10:375-6, Mar 1927
        Collier's 79:10, Jan 22, 1927
        Dramatist 18:1329-30, Jan 1927
        Life (NY) 89:19, Jan 20, 1927
        New York Times p. 7, Jun 7, 1926
                       p. 21, Dec 28, 1926
                       p. 10, Dec 29, 1926
                       p. 11, Dec 31, 1926
                       IX, p. 1, Dec 18, 1927
                       p. 19, Mar 14, 1935
        Overland 85:243, Aug 1927
        Vogue 69:80-81+, Mar 1, 1927

Revelry (Based on the novel by Samuel Hopkins Adams)
    Productions:
        Opened September 12, 1927 for 48 performances.
    Reviews:
        American Mercury 12:376-8, Nov 1927
        Life (NY) 90:19, Sep 29, 1927
        New Republic 52:148, Sep 28, 1927
        New York Times VII, p. 2, Sep 4, 1927
                       p. 37, Sep 13, 1927
                       VIII, p. 1, Sep 25, 1927

WATTERS, GEORGE MANKER

Burlesque (with Arthur Hopkins)
    Productions:
        Opened September 1, 1927 for 372 performances.
        Opened December 25, 1946 for 439 performances.
    Reviews:
        American Mercury 12:375-6, Nov 1927
        Catholic World 164:455, Feb 1947
        Independent 119:362, Oct 8, 1927
        Life (NY) 90:21, Sep 22, 1927
        Nation 125:295, Sep 21, 1927
        New Republic 52:123, Sep 21, 1927
        New York Theatre Critics' Reviews 1946:208
        New York Times p. 15, Sep 2, 1927
                       VIII, p. 1, Sep 11, 1927
                       IX, p. 4, Nov 20, 1927
                       p. 17, Jun 10, 1928
                       II, p. 3, Dec 22, 1946
                       p. 30, Dec 26, 1946
                       II, p. 1, Jan 5, 1947

New Yorker 22:44+, Jan 4, 1947
Newsweek 29:64, Jan 6, 1947
Saturday Review 30:22, Jan 4, 1947
Theatre Arts 31:17, Mar 1947
Theatre Magazine 46:22-4, Nov 1927
Time 49:56, Jan 6, 1947
Vogue 70:84-5+, Nov 1, 1927

WEITZENKORN, LOUIS

First Mortgage
  Productions:
    Opened October 10, 1929 for 4 performances.
  Reviews:
    New York Times p. 36, Oct 11, 1929

Five Star Final
  Productions:
    Opened December 30, 1930 for 175 performances.
  Reviews:
    Arts and Decoration 34:84, Mar 1931
    Catholic World 133:81-2, Apr 1931
    Commonweal 13:329, Jan 21, 1931
    Drama 21:9, Mar 1931
    Life (NY) 97:18, Jan 23, 1931
    Nation 132:53, Jan 14, 1931
    New York Times p. 11, Dec 31, 1930
                 VIII, p. 1, Jan 11, 1931
                 p. 32, Jun 9, 1931
    Outlook 157:112, Jan 21, 1931
    Theatre Arts 15:186, Mar 1931
    Vogue 77:88, Mar 1, 1931

*Name Your Poison
  Reviews:
    New York Times p. 27, Jan 21, 1936

WELLER, MICHAEL

Fishing
  Productions:
    (Off Broadway) February 1, 1975 for 46 performances.
    (Off Off Broadway) April 17, 1981 (Second Stage).
  Reviews:
    New York Magazine 8:78, Mar 10, 1975
    New York Times p. 41, Feb 13, 1975
                 II, p. 1, Feb 23, 1975
                 III, p. 20, Apr 27, 1981
    New Yorker 51:70, Mar 3, 1975

Loose Ends
    Productions:
        Opened June 6, 1979 for 284 performances.
    Reviews:
        Commentary 68:61, Aug 1979
        Nation 229:59-60, Jul 14, 1979
        New Leader 62:24, Jun 18, 1979
        New Republic 181:24-5, Jul 7, 1979
        New York Magazine 12:100+, Mar 5, 1979
        New York Theatre Critics' Reviews 1979:219
        New York Times III, p. 17, Feb 14, 1979
                       III, p. 17, Jun 7, 1979
                       II, p. 5, Jun 17, 1979
                       II, p. 1, Jul 1, 1979
                       II, p. 3, Aug 26, 1979
                       II, p. 1, Dec 30, 1979
        New Yorker 55:90+, Jun 18, 1979
        Newsweek 94:81, Jul 2, 1979
        Time 113:65, Feb 19, 1979

Moonchildren
    Productions:
        Opened February 21, 1972 for 16 performances.
        (Off Broadway) November 4, 1973 for 394 performances.
    Reviews:
        America 126:295-6, Mar 18, 1972
        Nation 214:349, Mar 13, 1972
               217:572, Nov 26, 1973
        New York Magazine 6:114, Nov 19, 1973
        New York Theatre Critics' Reviews 1972:372
        New York Times II, p. 9, Nov 21, 1971
                       p. 56, Nov 26, 1971
                       p. 45, Feb 22, 1972
                       p. 1, Feb 27, 1972
                       II, p. 6, Mar 19, 1972
                       p. 51, Nov 5, 1973
                       II, p. 3, Nov 11, 1973
        New Yorker 48:81, Mar 4, 1972
        Newsweek 78:114-15, Dec 13, 1971
        Playboy 21:46, Apr 1974
        Saturday Review 54:12+, Dec 11, 1971

More Than You Deserve
    Productions:
        (Off Off Broadway) April 13, 1973 (The Other Stage).
    No Reviews.

Now There's Just the Three of Us
    Productions:
        (Off Broadway) October 19, 1971 for 6 performances (bill
            called Four Americans).

Reviews:
    New York Times p. 29, Oct 22, 1971
                p. 50, Oct 28, 1971

Split
  Productions:
    (Off Off Broadway) April 1978 (Ensemble Studio Theater).
    (Off Off Broadway) April 4, 1980 (Sound Stage).
  Reviews:
    New York Times III, p. 12, Apr 7, 1980

Tira Tells Everything There Is to Know About Herself
  Productions:
    (Off Off Broadway) Season of 1975-76 (WPA Theater).
    (Off Off Broadway) October 23, 1978 (Quaigh Theater).
  No Reviews.

WEXLEY, JOHN

All the World Wondered (see The Last Mile)

The Last Mile
  Productions:
    Opened February 13, 1930 for 289 performances.
  Reviews:
    Catholic World 131:214, May 1930
    Collier's 85:25, May 3, 1930
    Commonweal 11:658-9, Apr 9, 1930
    Life (NY) 95:18, Mar 7, 1930
             95:18, Jun 6, 1930
    Literary Digest 105:18-19, Apr 5, 1930
    Nation 130:278, Mar 5, 1930
    New Republic 62:152-3, Mar 26, 1930
    New York Times p. 21, Feb 14, 1930
                 VIII, p. 1, Feb 23, 1930
                 VIII, p. 4, Mar 30, 1930
                 VIII, p. 3, Dec 21, 1930
                 VIII, p. 3, Feb 8, 1931
    Outlook 154:470, Mar 19, 1930
    Sketch Book 7:29, Jun 1930
    Theatre Arts 14:278-80, Apr 1930
    Theatre Magazine 51:43, Apr 1930
                    51:30, May 1930
                    51:14, Jun 1930
                    52:25, Aug 1930
    Vogue 75:92-3, Apr 12, 1930

Steel
  Productions:
    Opened November 17, 1931 for 14 performances.
    (Off Broadway) Fall, 1936 in repertory (Labor Stage, Inc.).

Reviews:
    Commonweal 15:160-1, Dec 9, 1931
    New York Times p. 26, Nov 19, 1931

They Shall Not Die
    Productions:
        Opened February 21, 1934 for 62 performances.
    Reviews:
        Catholic World 139:90-1, Apr 1934
        Commonweal 19:554, Mar 16, 1934
        Literary Digest 117:22, Mar 17, 1934
        Nation 138:284-5, Mar 7, 1934
        New Outlook 163:44, Apr 1934
        New Republic 78:134, Mar 14, 1934
        New York Times IX, p. 2, Feb 18, 1934
                      p. 24, Feb 22, 1934
                  IX, p. 2, Mar 4, 1934
                      p. 19, Mar 5, 1934
                   X, p. 1, Mar 11, 1934
        Newsweek 3:34, Mar 3, 1934
        Review of Reviews 89:48, Apr 1934
        Stage 11:15, Apr 1934
        Survey Graphic 23:240, May 1934
        Theatre Arts 18:323-5, May 1934
        Time 23:40, May 5, 1934

WILDER, THORNTON

Childhood (see Plays for Bleecker Street)

The Happy Journey to Trenton and Camden
    Productions:
        (Off Broadway) April 1939.
        (Off Broadway) February 9, 1948 (New Stages).
        Opened March 16, 1948 for 348 performances (presented with
            Sartre's The Respectful Prostitute).
        (Off Broadway) September 6, 1966 for 72 performances.
        (Off Off Broadway) November 25, 1977 (Counterpoint Theater
            Co.).
    Reviews:
        America 115:432, Oct 8, 1966
        Nation 203:334, Oct 3, 1966
        New York Times II, p. 1, Mar 21, 1948
                       p. 37, Apr 28, 1954
                       p. 53, Sep 7, 1966
        New Yorker 42:126, Sep 17, 1966
        Saturday Review 49:54, Sep 24, 1966

Infancy (see Plays for Bleecker Street)

*Life in the Sun
    Reviews:
        New York Times p. 34, Mar 18, 1955
                      p. 24, Aug 24, 1955
                      II, p. 1, Aug 28, 1955
        Saturday Review 38:42+, Sep 10, 1955

The Long Christmas Dinner
    Productions:
        (Off Broadway) September 6, 1966 for 72 performances.
        (Off Off Broadway) December 11, 1975 (IRT).
        (Off Off Broadway) November 25, 1977 (Counterpoint Theater
           Co.).
    Reviews:
        America 115:431, Oct 8, 1966
        Nation 203:334, Oct 3, 1966
        New York Times p. 53, Sep 7, 1966
        New Yorker 42:126, Sep 17, 1966
        Saturday Review 49:54, Sep 24, 1966

The Matchmaker
    Productions:
        Opened December 5, 1955 for 486 performances.
    Reviews:
        America 94:363, Dec 24, 1955
        Catholic World 182:386, Feb 1956
        Collier's 137:6, Mar 2, 1956
        Commonweal 63:379-80, Jan 13, 1956
        Holiday 19:85+, May 1956
        Life 40:131-2+, Jan 23, 1956
        Nation 181:562-3, Dec 24, 1955
        New Republic 134:21, Jan 2, 1956
        New York Theatre Critics' Reviews 1955:194
        New York Times p. 18, Aug 24, 1954
                      II, p. 3, Sep 5, 1954
                      p. 16, Nov 5, 1954
                      II, p. 3, Nov 14, 1954
                      II, p. 1, May 8, 1955
                      VI, p. 66, Nov 27, 1955
                      p. 45, Dec 6, 1955
                      II, p. 3, Dec 18, 1955
                      p. 14, Aug 20, 1959
                      II, p. 5, Sep 5, 1976
                      III, p. 18, Apr 5, 1979
        New Yorker 31:78-80, Dec 17, 1955
        Saturday Review 38:26, Dec 24, 1955
        Theatre Arts 40:14-15, Feb 1956
        Time 66:80+, Dec 19, 1955

The Merchant of Yonkers (Based on a play by Johann Nestroy)
    Productions:
        Opened December 28, 1938 for 39 performances.

Reviews:
    Catholic World 148:599-600, Feb 1939
    Commonweal 29:330, Jan 13, 1939
    Nation 148:74, Jan 14, 1939
    New York Times p. 30, Dec 13, 1938
              IX, p. 3, Dec 18, 1938
              p. 14, Dec 29, 1938
              IX, p. 1, Jan 8, 1939
    Newsweek 13:32, Jan 9, 1939
    Theatre Arts 23:173-4, Mar 1939
    Time 33:25, Jan 9, 1939

Our Town

Productions:
    Opened February 4, 1938 for 336 performances.
    Opened January 10, 1944 for 24 performances.
    (Off Broadway) Season of 1958-59.
    Opened November 27, 1969 for 36 performances.
Reviews:
    America 101:231, Apr 18, 1959
           121:622, Dec 20, 1969
    Atlantic 197:38-9, Apr 1956
    Canadian Forum 19:355-6, Feb 1940
    Catholic World 146:729, Mar 1938
           189:242-3, Jun 1959
    Christian Century 55:943-4, Aug 3, 1938
    Commentary 49:20+, Mar 1970
    Commonweal 27:496, Feb 25, 1938
           28:161, Jun 3, 1938
           39:373, Jan 28, 1944
           70:128-30, May 1, 1959
    Independent Woman 17:147, May 1938
    Nation 146:244-5, Feb 19, 1938
          188:324, Apr 11, 1959
          209:676, Dec 15, 1969
    National Review 25:1304, Nov 23, 1973
    New Republic 94:74, Feb 23, 1938
    New York Theatre Critics' Reviews 1969:163, 176
    New York Times II, p. 10, Jan 23, 1938
              p. 27, Jan 26, 1938
              X, p. 3, Jan 30, 1938
              p. 18, Feb 5, 1938
              X, p. 1, Feb 13, 1938
              p. 17, Sep 16, 1938
              p. 35, Jun 30, 1940
              p. 16, Jan 24, 1941
              p. 24, Jan 11, 1944
              II, p. 1, Jan 16, 1944
              p. 11, Feb 13, 1946
              p. 27, May 2, 1946
              p. 32, Mar 18, 1955

VI, p. 26, Nov 27, 1955
p. 46, Mar 24, 1959
p. 40, Mar 25, 1959
II, p. 1, Apr 5, 1959
II, p. 1, Aug 23, 1959
II, p. 3, Aug 21, 1960
p. 20, Aug 28, 1961
p. 14, Nov 4, 1961
p. 77, Sep 29, 1968
p. 62, Dec 14, 1968
p. 50, Nov 28, 1969
II, p. 7, Dec 7, 1969
p. 41, Oct 8, 1973
II, p. 1, Nov 18, 1973
p. 38, Jun 17, 1975
II, p. 5, Jul 20, 1975
New Yorker 35:80+, Apr 11, 1959
44:98, Oct 5, 1968
45:166, Dec 6, 1969
One Act Play Magazine 1:948, Feb 1938
Saturday Review 18:11, May 7, 1938
32:33-4, Aug 6, 1949
42:35, Apr 11, 1959
52:36, Dec 20, 1969
Scribner's Magazine 103:65, May 1938
Stage 15:34-6, Apr 1938
Theatre Arts 22:172-3, Mar 1938
24:815-24, Nov 1940
28:137, Mar 1944
29:234-9, Apr 1945
Time 31:36-7, Feb 14, 1938
94:84, Dec 12, 1969
105:68, Jun 30, 1975
Vogue 91:108-9, Mar 15, 1938
Yale Review 27:836-8, Summer 1938

Plays for Bleecker Street (Infancy, Childhood, and Someone from
Assisi)
Productions:
(Off Broadway) January 11, 1962 for 349 performances.
Reviews:
Commonweal 75:516-17, Feb 9, 1962
Nation 194:86-7, Jan 27, 1962
New Republic 146:30, Feb 5, 1962
New York Times p. 28, Jan 12, 1962
II, p. 1, Jan 21, 1962
New Yorker 37:64+, Jan 20, 1962
Newsweek 59:50, Jan 22, 1962
Reporter 26:48, Mar 1, 1962
Saturday Review 45:26, Feb 3, 1962
Theatre Arts 46:63, Mar 1962
Time 79:68, Jan 19, 1962

Pullman Car Hiawatha
    Productions:
        (Off Broadway) December 3, 1962 for 33 performances.
        (Off Off Broadway) July 1974 (Lion Theater Co.).
    Reviews:
        New York Times p. 46, Dec 4, 1962
        New Yorker 38:130+, Dec 15, 1962

Queens of France
    Productions:
        (Off Broadway) September 6, 1966 for 72 performances.
        (Off Off Broadway) November 1976 (National Arts Theater).
    Reviews:
        America 115:431, Oct 8, 1966
        Nation 203:334, Oct 3, 1966
        New York Times p. 53, Sep 7, 1966
        New Yorker 42:126, Sep 17, 1966
        Saturday Review 49:54, Sep 24, 1966

Skin of Our Teeth
    Productions:
        Opened November 18, 1942 for 359 performances.
        Opened August 17, 1955 for 22 performances.
        (Off Broadway) Season of 1960-61 (Equity Library Theater).
        Opened September 9, 1975 for 7 performances.
    Reviews:
        America 93:574, Sep 10, 1955
        Atlantic 171:121+, Mar 1943
        Catholic World 156:473-4, Jan 1943
                    166:73-4, Oct 1947
                    181:62-3, Oct 1955
        Commonweal 37:175-6, Dec 4, 1942
                    37:229, Dec 18, 1942
                    63:13, Oct 7, 1955
        Cosmopolitan 114:19, Apr 1943
        Current History ns 3:458-9, Jan 1943
        Independent Woman 21:368, Dec 1942
        Life 13:93-4+, Nov 30, 1942
                    39:71-2, Aug 29, 1955
        Nation 155:629, Dec 5, 1942
                    181:210, Sep 3, 1955
                    221:286, Sep 27, 1975
        New Republic 107:714, Nov 30, 1942
                    173:31-2, Aug 2, 1975
        New York Magazine 8:58, Jul 28, 1975
        New York Theatre Critics' Reviews 1942:173
                                      1955:293
                                      1975:216
        New York Times VII, p. 20, Nov 1, 1942
                    p. 29, Nov 19, 1942
                    VIII, p. 1, Nov 22, 1942

VIII, p. 1, Dec 13, 1942
VIII, p. 1, Jan 3, 1943
p. 22, Mar 20, 1945
II, p. 1, May 27, 1945
II, p. 2, Nov 18, 1945
p. 32, Nov 5, 1946
VI, p. 26, Aug 7, 1955
p. 16, Aug 18, 1955
II, p. 1, Aug 28, 1955
VI, p. 64, Nov 27, 1955
p. 24, Oct 14, 1960
II, p. 1, Mar 5, 1962
p. 30, Mar 6, 1961
p. 43, Mar 15, 1961
p. 32, Mar 20, 1961
p. 40, Mar 28, 1961
p. 24, Mar 30, 1961
p. 11, Apr 1, 1961
p. 29, Apr 21, 1961
p. 35, May 1, 1961
p. 22, May 19, 1961
p. 28, May 31, 1961
p. 27, Jun 16, 1961
p. 29, Aug 9, 1961
p. 20, Aug 21, 1961
p. 27, Aug 29, 1961
p. 37, Sep 18, 1961
p. 85, Oct 8, 1961
p. 13, Oct 14, 1961
p. 22, Oct 23, 1961
p. 51, Jun 2, 1966
p. 55, Sep 12, 1968
p. 17, Jul 12, 1975
II, p. 5, Jul 13, 1975
II, p. 5, Jul 27, 1975
p. 32, Sep 10, 1975
II, p. 5, Sep 14, 1975
New York Times Magazine pp. 20-1, Nov 1, 1942
                       pp. 26-7, Aug 7, 1955
New Yorker 18:35, Nov 28, 1942
          19:32, May 8, 1943
          19:34, Jun 12, 1943
          31:72+, Aug 27, 1955
Newsweek 20:86-7, Nov 30, 1942
         46:67, Aug 29, 1955
Player's Magazine 22:12-13, Sep-Oct 1945
Poet Lore 49:187, Summer 1943
Saturday Review 25:3-4, Dec 19, 1942
               38:22, Aug 27, 1955
Theatre Arts 27:9-11, Jan 1943
            27:334+, Jun 1943

30:704-5, Dec 1946
39:66-9, Sep 1955
Time 40:57, Nov 30, 1942
40:62, Dec 28, 1942
66:32, Aug 29, 1955

Someone from Assisi (see Plays for Bleecker Street)

The Trumpet Shall Sound
Productions:
Opened December 10, 1926 for 30 performances.
Reviews:
Life (NY) 89:21, Jan 13, 1927
New York Times p. 15, Dec 11, 1926

The Victors (Adapted from the play by Jean-Paul Sartre)
Productions:
(Off Broadway) Opened December 1948 (New Stages).
Reviews:
Commonweal 49:352, Jan 14, 1949
Forum 111:162-3, Mar 1949
New Republic 120:19, Jan 10, 1949
New York Times p. 17, Dec 27, 1948
II, p. 1, Jan 2, 1949
II, p. 2, Jan 9, 1949
School and Society 69:85, Jan 29, 1949
Theatre Arts 31:44, Feb 1947
33:17, Mar 1949
Time 53:49, Jan 3, 1949

WILLIAMS, JESSE LYNCH

And So They Were Married (see Why Marry?)

Lovely Lady
Productions:
Opened October 14, 1925 for 21 performances.
Reviews:
New York Times p. 27, Oct 15, 1925

Why Marry?
Productions:
Opened December 25, 1917 for 120 performances.
Reviews:
Book News 36:218, Feb 1918
Bookman 47:75, Mar 1918
Current Opinion 64:99-102, Feb 1918
Dramatic Mirror 77:31, Nov 17, 1917
78:7, Jan 5, 1918
Dramatist 9:917-18, Jul 1918

Green Book 19:389-94, Mar 1918
Hearst 33:362-4+, May 1918
Life (NY) 71:64, Jan 10, 1918
Nation 107:132, Aug 3, 1918
New York Times p. 7, Dec 26, 1917
              IV, p. 7, Jan 27, 1918
              V, p. 3, Feb 8, 1918
              V, p. 8, Feb 10, 1918
              V, p. 10, Mar 3, 1918
North American Review 207:278-81, Feb 1918
Theatre Magazine 27:85+, Feb 1918

Why Not?
Productions:
    Opened December 25, 1922 for 120 performances.
Reviews:
    Dramatist 14:1159-60, Apr 1923
    Nation 116:128, Jan 31, 1923
    New York Clipper 70:20, Dec 27, 1922
    New York Times p. 20, Dec 25, 1922
                   p. 13, Dec 30, 1922
                   VII, p. 1, Dec 31, 1922
                   VII, p. 1, Jan 7, 1923
                   p. 6, Jan 29, 1923
                   VIII, p. 1, Mar 11, 1923

WILLIAMS, SAMM-ART

The Frost of Renaissance
Productions:
    (Off Off Broadway) April 1979 for 12 performances (Theater of
        the Riverside Church).
No Reviews.

Home
Productions:
    (Off Broadway) December 14, 1979 for 82 performances and
        transferred to Broadway).
    Opened on Broadway May 7, 1980 for 197 performances (total
        of 279 performances).
    (Off Broadway) May 8, 1981 for 45 performances.
Reviews:
    Encore 9:36-7, Apr 1980
             9:43, Sep 1980
    Essence 10:22, Apr 1980
              11:17+, Aug 1980
    New York Magazine 13:60-1, May 19, 1980
    New York Theatre Critics' Reviews 1980:243
    New York Times III, p. 20, Oct 26, 1979
                   III, p. 12, Dec 20, 1979

II, p. 1, Jan 6, 1980
II, p. 5, Mar 16, 1980
III, p. 20, May 8, 1980
III, p. 1, May 22, 1981
XI, p. 10, May 2, 1982
Saturday Review 7:67-8, Jul 1980
Time 115:52, May 19, 1980

A Love Play
    Productions:
        (Off Broadway) April 13, 1976 for 8 performances.
    Reviews:
        New York Times p. 24, Apr 15, 1976

The Sixteenth Round
    Productions:
        (Off Broadway) October 7, 1980 for 40 performances.
    Reviews:
        New York Times III, p. 14, Oct 20, 1980
        New Yorker 56:166, Nov 3, 1980

Welcome to Black River
    Productions:
        (Off Broadway) May 20, 1975 for 8 performances.
    Reviews:
        New York Times p. 35, May 22, 1975

WILLIAMS, TENNESSEE

*a/k/a Tennessee (fragments from twelve plays)
    Reviews:
        New York Times III, p. 17, Sep 28, 1982

At Liberty
    Productions:
        (Off Off Broadway) Season of 1977-78, as part of a bill called
            3 Small Plays by Big Playwrights (Quaigh Theater).
    No Reviews.

Battle of Angels
    Productions:
        (Off Off Broadway) October 27, 1974 (Circle Repertory The-
            ater Co.).
    Reviews:
        New York Times p. 18, Dec 31, 1940
                       IX, p. 1, Jan 5, 1941
                       p. 51, Nov 4, 1974
                       II, p. 5, Nov 17, 1974

Camino Real
    Productions:

Opened March 19, 1953 for 60 performances.
(Off Broadway) Season of 1959-60.
Opened January 8, 1970 for 52 performances.
(Off Off Broadway) August 1975 (Drama Comm. Repertory
    Theater).
Reviews:
    America 89:25, Apr 4, 1953
            89:59, Apr 11, 1953
            103:422-4, Jul 2, 1960
            122:140+, Feb 7, 1970
    Catholic World 177:148, May 1953
    Commentary 49:20+, Mar 1970
    Commonweal 58:51-2, Apr 17, 1953
    Look 17:17, May 5, 1953
    Nation 176:293-4, Apr 4, 1953
           210:93-4, Jan 26, 1970
    New Republic 128:30-1, Mar 30, 1953
    New York Theatre Critics' Reviews 1953:330
                                       1970:395
    New York Times II, p. 1, Mar 15, 1953
                    p. 26, Mar 20, 1953
                    II, p. 1, Mar 29, 1953
                    p. 21, Mar 21, 1955
                    p. 41, Apr 9, 1957
                    II, p. 1, May 15, 1960
                    p. 42, May 17, 1960
                    II, p. 1, May 29, 1960
                    p. 42, Jan 9, 1970
                    p. 8, Jul 7, 1979
    New Yorker 29:69, Mar 28, 1953
               36:92+, May 28, 1960
               45:50+, Jan 17, 1970
    Newsweek 41:63, Mar 30, 1953
             75:82, Jan 19, 1970
    Saturday Review 36:28-30, Apr 18, 1953
                    53:24, Jan 24, 1970
    Theatre Arts 37:88, Jun 1953
    Time 61:46, Mar 30, 1953
         95:61, Jan 19, 1970

The Case of the Crushed Petunias (see a/k/a/ Tennessee)

Cat on a Hot Tin Roof
    Productions:
        Opened March 24, 1955 for 694 performances.
        Opened September 24, 1974 for 160 performances.
    Reviews:
        America 131:194, Oct 12, 1974
        Catholic World 181:147-8, May 1955
        Collier's 137:6, Mar 2, 1956
        Commonweal 62:230-1, Jun 3, 1955

Life 38:137-8+, Apr 18, 1955
Los Angeles 26:341+, Nov 1981
Nation 180:314, Apr 9, 1955
      219:349-50, Oct 12, 1974
New Republic 132:28, Apr 11, 1955
            132:22, Apr 18, 1955
            132:23, Apr 25, 1955
            171:16+, Oct 19, 1974
New York Magazine 7:48+, Aug 12, 1974
New York Theatre Critics' Reviews 1955:342
                                 1974:242
New York Times p. 18, Mar 25, 1955
              II, p. 1, Apr 3, 1955
              II, p. 3, Apr 17, 1955
              p. 37, Dec 20, 1956
              p. 24, Jan 31, 1958
              p. 23, Oct 23, 1959
              p. 50, Nov 12, 1973
              p. 40, Jul 22, 1974
              II, p. 3, Jul 28, 1974
              p. 26, Sep 25, 1974
              II, p. 1, Oct 6, 1974
              p. 27, Jan 23, 1975
              XI, p. 9, Nov 9, 1980
New Yorker 31:68+, Apr 2, 1955
          50:73, Oct 7, 1974
Newsweek 45:54, Apr 4, 1955
Playboy 22:41, Mar 1975
Saturday Review 38:32-3, Apr 9, 1955
               38:26, Apr 30, 1955
Theatre Arts 39:18-19, 22-3+, Jun 1955
           39:74-7, Jul 1955
Time 65:98, Apr 4, 1955
     104:107, Oct 7, 1974

Clothes for a Summer Hotel
   Productions:
   Opened March 26, 1980 for 15 performances.
   Reviews:
   Horizon 23:66-71, Apr 1980
   Nation 230:477, Apr 19, 1980
   New York Magazine 13:82+, Apr 7, 1980
   New York Theatre Critics' Reviews 1980:310
   New York Times III, p. 9, Jan 8, 1980
                 II, p. 1, Mar 23, 1980
                 III, p. 15, Mar 27, 1980
                 II, p. 1, Jun 22, 1980
   New Yorker 56:116+, Apr 7, 1980
   Newsweek 95:95, Apr 7, 1980

Creve Coeur   (see A Lovely Sunday for Creve Coeur)

The Eccentricities of a Nightingale (revised version of Summer and
    Smoke)
    Productions:
        Opened November 23, 1976 for 24 performances.
        (Off Off Broadway) November 25, 1978 (Playwrights Horizons).
        See productions of Summer and Smoke.
    Reviews:
        New West 4:SC-39, Mar 12, 1979
        New York Magazine 9:116, Dec 13, 1976
        New York Theatre Critics' Reviews 1976:107
        New York Times p. 23, Nov 24, 1976
                II, p. 3, Dec 5, 1976
        New Yorker 52:134-5, Dec 6, 1976
        Time 108:98, Dec 6, 1976
        See also reviews of Summer and Smoke

*Evening of Tennessee Williams (Consists of Portrait of a Madonna,
    27 Wagons Full of Cotton, and I Rise in Flame, Cried the Phoe-
    nix)
    Reviews:
        New York Times p. 31, Apr 9, 1976

Garden District (see Something Unspoken and Suddenly Last Sum-
    mer)

The Glass Menagerie
    Productions:
        Opened March 31, 1945 for 561 performances.
        Opened November 21, 1956 for 15 performances.
        Opened May 4, 1965 for 175 performances.
        (Off Off Broadway) February 23, 1974 (Amas Repertory The-
            ater).
        Opened December 18, 1975 for 78 performances.
        (Off Off Broadway) November 4, 1980 (Twin Oak).
    Reviews:
        America 112:888, Jun 19, 1965
                134:75, Jan 31, 1976
        Catholic World 161:166-7, May 1945
                   161:263-4, Jun 1945
                   184:307, Jan 1957
        Christian Science Monitor Magazine p. 8, Apr 15, 1950
        Commonweal 42:16-17, Apr 20, 1945
               82:356-7, Jun 4, 1965
        Life 18:81-3, Apr 30, 1945
           18:12-14, Jun 11, 1945
           58:16, May 28, 1965
        Nation 160:424, Apr 14, 1945
              199:60, Aug 10, 1964
              222:28, Jan 3, 1976
        New Republic 112:505, Apr 16, 1945
                  174:28, Jan 17, 1976

New York Magazine 9:71, Jan 12, 1976
New York Theatre Critics' Reviews 1945:234
1956:190
1965:332
1975:125
New York Times II, p. 2, Jan 14, 1945
p. 15, Apr 2, 1945
II, p. 1, Apr 8, 1945
II, p. 1, Apr 15, 1945
II, p. 1, Sep 9, 1945
II, p. 1, Jan 27, 1946
II, p. 1, Mar 31, 1946
II, p. 2, Jun 2, 1946
VI, p. 18, Mar 2, 1947
p. 17, Jul 29, 1948
p. 50, Nov 22, 1956
II, p. 1, Dec 2, 1956
p. 30, Mar 6, 1960
II, p. 1, Mar 5, 1961
p. 30, Mar 6, 1961
p. 32, Mar 20, 1961
p. 32, Mar 28, 1961
p. 11, Apr 1, 1961
p. 43, Apr 11, 1961
p. 29, Apr 21, 1961
p. 35, May 1, 1961
p. 22, May 19, 1961
p. 28, May 31, 1961
p. 27, Jun 16, 1961
p. 20, Aug 21, 1961
II, p. 1, Mar 28, 1965
p. 53, May 5, 1965
II, p. 1, May 16, 1965
p. 52, Dec 19, 1975
II, p. 5, Dec 28, 1975
II, p. 6, Feb 14, 1980
p. 14, Sep 26, 1980
III, p. 19, Oct 30, 1980
III, p. 16, Nov 6, 1980
New York Times Magazine pp. 28-9, Mar 4, 1945
New Yorker 21:40, Apr 7, 1945
41:158, May 15, 1965
Newsweek 25:86, Apr 9, 1945
65:92, May 17, 1965
82:61, Dec 17, 1973
Player's Magazine 22:5+, Sep-Oct 1945
Saturday Review 28:34-6, Apr 14, 1945
39:29, Dec 8, 1956
50:71, Nov 25, 1967
Theatre Arts 29:263, May 1945
29:325-7+, Jun 1945

29:554, Oct 1945
31:38-9, Aug 1947
41:24, Feb 1957
Time 45:86, Apr 9, 1945
85:64, May 14, 1965
107:61, Jan 12, 1976

Gnädiges Fräulein (see The Latter Days of a Celebrated Soubrette
and Slapstick Tragedy)

Hello from Bertha
    Productions:
        (Off Off Broadway) March 26, 1976 (IRT).
        See also Promises, Lies and Delusions.
    Reviews:
        See Promises, Lies and Delusions

I Can't Imagine Tomorrow
    Productions:
        (Off Off Broadway) Season of 1974-75 (WPA Theater).
        (Off Off Broadway) August 1977 (Academy Arts Theater Co.).
        (Off Off Broadway) April 14, 1978 (Academy Arts Theater
            Co.).
    No Reviews.

I Rise in Flame, Cried the Phoenix
    Productions:
        (Off Broadway) Season of 1958-59.
    Reviews:
        New York Times p. 30, Apr 15, 1959
        Saturday Review 42:23, Apr 25, 1959
        See also reviews of Evening of Tennessee Williams

In the Bar of a Tokyo Hotel
    Productions:
        (Off Broadway) May 11, 1969 for 25 performances.
        (Off Off Broadway) Season of 1974-75 (Jean Cocteau Repertory).
        (Off Off Broadway) March 9, 1979 (Jean Cocteau Repertory).
    Reviews:
        Life 66:10, Jun 13, 1969
        Nation 208:709-10, Jun 2, 1969
        New York Theatre Critics' Reviews 1969:262
        New York Times p. 54, May 12, 1969
                    II, p. 5, May 25, 1969
        Newsweek 73:133, May 26, 1969
        Saturday Review 52:18, May 31, 1968
        Time 93:75, May 23, 1969

The Lady of Larkspur Lotion
    Productions:

(Off Off Broadway) September 1975 (Direct Theater).
See also Promises, Lies and Delusions and Three by Tennes-
see
Reviews:
See Promises, Lies and Delusions and Three by Tennessee

The Latter Days of a Celebrated Soubrette (new version of The
Gnädiges Fräulein)
Productions:
(Off Off Broadway) May 16, 1974 (Central Arts Cabaret The-
ater).
Reviews:
New York Times p. 48, May 29, 1974

Life Boat Drill
Productions:
(Off Off Broadway) November 14-December 30, 1979 (Ensemble
Studio Theater).
Reviews:
New York Times III, p. 5, Dec 21, 1979

A Lovely Sunday for Creve Coeur
Productions:
(Off Broadway) January 17, 1979 for 30 performances.
Reviews:
America 140:135, Feb 24, 1979
Commonweal 106:146-7, Mar 16, 1979
Nation 228:156-7, Feb 10, 1979
New York Magazine 11:60-1, Jun 26, 1978
New York Theatre Critics' Reviews 1979:337
New York Times III, p. 19, Jun 7, 1978
            III, p. 15, Jan 22, 1979
            II, p. 26, Feb 4, 1979
            II, p. 1, Jul 1, 1979
New Yorker 54:99-100, Feb 5, 1979
Newsweek 93:68, Feb 5, 1979
Time 111:84, Jun 12, 1978

The Milk Train Doesn't Stop Here Anymore
Productions:
Opened January 16, 1963 for 69 performances.
Opened January 1, 1964 for 5 performances.
Reviews:
America 108:449, Mar 30, 1963
Commonweal 77:515-17, Feb 8, 1963
Nation 196:106, Feb 2, 1963
National Review 14:291+, Apr 9, 1963
New Republic 148:27, Feb 2, 1963
New York Theatre Critics' Reviews 1963:391
                                   1964:397
New York Times p. 19, Jul 12, 1962

p. 7, Jan 18, 1963
p. 32, Sep 18, 1963
p. 33, Jan 2, 1964
p. 25, Jul 27, 1965
New Yorker 38:72, Jan 26, 1963
Newsweek 61:79, Jan 28, 1963
        63:70, Jan 13, 1964
Reporter 28:48, Apr 25, 1963
Saturday Review 46:20-1, Feb 2, 1963
            47:22, Jan 18, 1964
Theatre Arts 47:66, Feb 1963
Time 80:40, Jul 20, 1962
    81:53, Jan 25, 1963
    83:52, Jan 10, 1964

Moony's Kid Don't Cry
Productions:
   (Off Off Broadway) September 1, 1980 (Urban Arts Theater).
No Reviews.

The Mutilated
Productions:
   (Off Off Broadway) September 17, 1975 (New York Theater
      Ensemble).
Reviews:
   See Slapstick Tragedy.

The Night of the Iguana
Productions:
   Opened December 28, 1961 for 316 performances.
   (Off Broadway) Season of 1966-67 for 9 performances (Equity
      Library Theatre).
   (Off Off Broadway) July 1976 (Drama Comm. Repertory The-
      ater).
   Opened December 16, 1976 for 77 performances.
Reviews:
   America 106:604, Feb 3, 1962
        136:20, Jan 8, 1977
   Catholic World 194:380-1, Mar 1962
   Christian Century 79:169, Feb 7, 1962
   Commonweal 75:460, Jan 26, 1962
   Life 52:67+, Apr 13, 1962
   Nation 194:86, Jan 27, 1962
        224:28, Jan 1, 1977
   New Republic 146:20+, Jan 22, 1962
   New York Magazine 10:63, Jan 10, 1977
   New York Theatre Critics' Reviews 1961:131
                          1976:62
   New York Times VI, pp. 34-5, Oct 29, 1961
              II, p. 5, Dec 24, 1961
              p. 10, Dec 29, 1961

II, p. 1, Jan 7, 1962
III, p. 2, Dec 17, 1976
II, p. 3, Dec 19, 1976
XI, p. 12, Nov 8, 1981
XXI, p. 17, Nov 22, 1981
New Yorker 37:61, Jan 13, 1962
52:52, Dec 27, 1976
Newsweek 59:44, Jan 8, 1962
Reporter 26:45, Feb 1, 1962
Saturday Review 42:23, Apr 25, 1959
45:36, Jan 20, 1962
Texas Monthly 6:124, Apr 1978
Theatre Arts 46:57, Mar 1962
Time 79:53, Jan 5, 1962
108:39, Dec 27, 1976

*The Notebook of Trigorin
Reviews:
Los Angeles 27:266+, Sep 1982

Orpheus Descending
Productions:
Opened March 21, 1957 for 68 performances.
(Off Broadway) Season of 1958-59.
(Off Broadway) Season of 1959-60.
(Off Off Broadway) October 1976 (Drama Comm. Repertory Theater).
Reviews:
America 97:148-50, Apr 27, 1957
Catholic World 185:226-7, Jun 1957
189:192-3, Jun 1959
Christian Century 74:455, Apr 10, 1957
Commonweal 66:94-7, Apr 26, 1957
Harper's 214:76-7, May 1957
Nation 184:301-2, Apr 6, 1957
New Republic 136:21, Apr 8, 1957
New York Theatre Critics' Reviews 1957:310
New York Times II, p. 1, Mar 17, 1957
p. 28, Mar 22, 1957
II, p. 1, Mar 31, 1957
p. 44, Mar 18, 1959
p. 23, May 15, 1959
p. 45, Oct 6, 1959
p. 21, Aug 28, 1961
New Yorker 33:84+, Mar 30, 1957
Newsweek 49:81, Apr 1, 1957
Reporter 16:43, Apr 18, 1957
Saturday Review 40:26, Mar 30, 1957
Theatre Arts 41:20, May 1957
42:25-6, Sep 1958
Time 69:61, Apr 1, 1957

Out Cry (revised version of Two Character Play)
Productions:
    Opened March 1, 1973 for 12 performances.
    (Off Off Broadway) June 1974 (13th St. Repertory Co.).
    (Off Off Broadway) August 1975 (Quaigh Theater).
    (Off Off Broadway) August 7, 1979 (Shelter West).
Reviews:
    America 128:242, Mar 17, 1973
    Nation 216:380, Mar 19, 1973
    New Republic 168:22, Mar 24, 1973
    New York Magazine 6:66, Mar 19, 1973
    New York Theatre Critics' Reviews 1973:343
    New York Times p. 18, Mar 2, 1973
                  II, p. 1, Mar 11, 1973
                  II, p. 6, Apr 8, 1973
    Time 101:89, Mar 12, 1973
    See also reviews of Two Character Play

A Perfect Analysis Given by a Parrot
Productions:
    (Off Off Broadway) Season of 1975-76 (Di Pinto Di Blu).
    (Off Off Broadway) June 7, 1976 (Quaigh Theater).
    (Off Off Broadway) October 13, 1977 (Academy Arts Theater
        Co.).
Reviews:
    Esquire 80:288-90+, Oct 1973

Period of Adjustment
Productions:
    Opened November 10, 1960 for 132 performances.
Reviews:
    America 104:410-11, Dec 17, 1960
    Catholic World 192:255-6, Jan 1961
    Christian Century 77:1536, Dec 28, 1960
    Commonweal 74:255, Jun 2, 1961
    Horizon 3:102-3, Mar 1961
    Nation 191:443-4, Dec 3, 1960
           195:59, Aug 11, 1962
    New Republic 143:38-9, Nov 28, 1960
    New York Theatre Critics' Reviews 1960:176
    New York Times p. 34, Nov 11, 1960
                  II, p. 1, Nov 20, 1960
                  p. 25, Jan 3, 1962
                  p. 24, Jun 14, 1962
    New Yorker 36:93, Nov 19, 1960
    Newsweek 56:79, Nov 21, 1960
    Reporter 23:35, Dec 22, 1960
    Saturday Review 43:28, Nov 26, 1960
    Theatre Arts 45:57-8, Jan 1961
    Time 73:54+, Jan 12, 1959
         76:75, Nov 21, 1960

Portrait of a Madonna
    Productions:
        Opened April 15, 1959 for 37 performances.
        (Off Off Broadway) Season of 1974-75 (Manhattan Theater
           Club).
    Reviews:
        New York Theatre Critics' Reviews 1959:320
        New York Times p. 21, Apr 1, 1957
                    p. 28, Apr 16, 1959
                    II, p. 1, Apr 26, 1959
        Theatre Arts 43:9, Jun 1959
        See also Evening of Tennessee Williams

*Promises, Lies and Delusions (Consists of This Property Is Con-
    demned, Hello from Bertha, The Unsatisfactory Supper, and
    The Lady of Larkspur Lotion)
    Reviews:
        Los Angeles 26:249, Jul 1981
        Los Angeles Times VI, p. 3, Jun 11, 1981

The Purification
    Productions:
        (Off Broadway) Season of 1959-60.
        (Off Off Broadway) November 26, 1975 (Mama Gail's).
        (Off Off Broadway) February 10, 1977 (Perry St. Theater).
    Reviews:
        New York Times p. 12, May 29, 1954
                    II, p. 1, Jun 6, 1954
                    p. 57, Dec 9, 1959
                    p. 56, Dec 10, 1975

*The Red Devil Battery Sign
    Reviews:
        Maclean's 93:70+, Nov 3, 1980
        New York Times p. 39, Jul 15, 1975
        Playboy 21:40, Mar 1974

The Rose Tattoo
    Productions:
        Opened February 3, 1951 for 306 performances.
        Opened October 20, 1966 for 76 performances (City Center
           Drama Co.).
    Reviews:
        America 115:786, Dec 10, 1966
        Catholic World 172:467-8, Mar 1951
        Commonweal 53:492-4, Feb 23, 1951
        Encore 8:40-1, Sep 4, 1979
        Life 30:80+, Feb 26, 1951
        Nation 172:161, Feb 17, 1951
                 203:493, Nov 7, 1966
        National Review 19:99, Jan 24, 1967

New Republic 124:22, Feb 19, 1951
New York Theatre Critics' Reviews 1951:363
New York Times II, p. 1, Jan 28, 1951
      p. 19, Feb 5, 1951
      II, p. 1, Feb 11, 1951
      II, p. 3, Mar 25, 1951
      II, p. 1, Jun 3, 1951
      p. 23, Feb 21, 1952
      p. 36, Oct 21, 1966
      II, p. 1, Nov 20, 1966
      p. 27, May 9, 1977
      III, p. 3, Aug 10, 1979
New Yorker 26:58+, Feb 10, 1951
Newsweek 37:72, Feb 12, 1951
Saturday Review 34:22-4, Mar 10, 1951
      49:60, Nov 26, 1966
School and Society 73:181-3, Mar 24, 1951
Theatre Arts 35:16, Apr 1951
Time 57:53-4, Feb 12, 1951
      88:80, Nov 18, 1966

The Seven Descents of Myrtle
 Productions:
  Opened March 27, 1968 for 29 performances.
 Reviews:
  Commonweal 88:208-9, May 3, 1968
  Nation 206:516-17, Apr 15, 1968
  New York Theatre Critics' Reviews 1968:313
  New York Times p. 54, Mar 28, 1968
        II, p. 1, Apr 7, 1968
  New Yorker 44:109, Apr 6, 1968
  Newsweek 71:131, Apr 8, 1968
  Saturday Review 51:30, Apr 13, 1968
  Time 91:72, Apr 5, 1968

Slapstick Tragedy (The Mutilated and The Gnädiges Fräulein)
 Productions:
  Opened February 22, 1966 for 7 performances.
 Reviews:
  Commonweal 84:82, Apr 8, 1966
  Nation 202:309, Mar 14, 1966
  New Republic 154:34, Mar 26, 1966
  New York Theatre Critics' Reviews 1966:359
  New York Times p. 42, Feb 23, 1966
        p. 15, Feb 26, 1966
        II, p. 1, Mar 6, 1966
  New Yorker 42:83, Mar 5, 1966
  Newsweek 67:90, Mar 7, 1966
  Reporter 34:49-50, Mar 24, 1966
  Saturday Review 49:28, Mar 12, 1966
  Time 87:88, Mar 4, 1966
  Vogue 147:109, Apr 1, 1966

Small Craft Warnings
    Productions:
        (Off Broadway) April 2, 1972 for 200 performances.
        (Off Off Broadway) November 6, 1975 (Association of Theater
            Artists).
        (Off Off Broadway) January 8, 1976 (Washington Market Play-
            house).
    Reviews:
        America 126:462, Apr 29, 1972
        Commonweal 96:214-16, May 5, 1972
        Nation 214:540-1, Apr 24, 1972
        New Republic 166:24, Apr 29, 1972
                    168:22, Mar 17, 1973
        New York Theatre Critics' Reviews 1972:271
        New York Times p. 50, Apr 3, 1972
                    II, p. 8, Apr 16, 1972
        New Yorker 48:110, Apr 15, 1972
        Saturday Review 55:22-4, Apr 22, 1972
        Time 99:72, Apr 17, 1972

Something Cloudy, Something Clear
    Productions:
        (Off Off Broadway) August 25, 1981 (Jean Cocteau Repertory).
    Reviews:
        America 114:262-3, Nov 1981
        New York Times III, p. 17, Aug 13, 1981
                    III, p. 3, Sep 11, 1981
                    II, p. 3, Sep 27, 1981
        Time 118:65, Sep 21, 1981

Something Unspoken
    Productions:
        (Off Broadway) Season of 1957-58, billed as Garden District.
        (Off Off Broadway) December 6, 1973, billed as Three by
            Tennessee (Lolly's Theater Club).
        (Off Off Broadway) May 20, 1977 (National Arts Theater).
    Reviews:
        Catholic World 186:469-70, Mar 1958
        Christian Century 75:136, Jan 29, 1958
        Commonweal 68:232-3, May 30, 1958
        Nation 186:86-7, Jan 25, 1958
        New Republic 138:20, Jan 27, 1958
        New York Times p. 23, Jan 8, 1958
                    II, p. 1, Jan 19, 1958
                    p. 44, Sep 17, 1958
        New Yorker 33:66+, Jan 18, 1958
        Newsweek 51:84, Jan 20, 1958
        Reporter 18:42-3, Feb 6, 1958
        Saturday Review 41:26, Jan 25, 1958
        Theatre Arts 42:13, Mar 1958
        Time 71:42, Jan 20, 1958

*Stairs to the Roof
  Reviews:
    New York Times p. 35, Feb 26, 1947
    Theatre Arts 31:12, Jul 1947

A Streetcar Named Desire
  Productions:
    Opened December 3, 1947 for 855 performances.
    Opened May 23, 1950 for 16 performances.
    (Off Broadway) Season of 1954-55.
    Opened February 15, 1956 for 15 performances.
    Opened April 26, 1973 for 110 performances.
    Opened October 4, 1973 for 53 performances.
    (Off Off Broadway) September 1975 (National Arts Theater).
    (Off Off Broadway) April 9, 1976 (ACSTA).
    (Off Off Broadway) February 19, 1977 (Association of The-
      ater Artists).
    (Off Off Broadway) March 4, 1977 (AST).
  Reviews:
    America 128:495, May 26, 1973
    Atlantic 186:94-5, Jul 1950
    Catholic World 166:358, Jan 1948
              183:67, Apr 1956
    Commonweal 47:254, Dec 19, 1947
    Forum 109:86-8, Feb 1948
    Life 23:101-2+, Dec 15, 1947
        27:66, Dec 19, 1949
    Nation 165:686, Dec 20, 1947
          216:635-6, May 14, 1973
    New Republic 117:34-5, Dec 22, 1947
    New York Magazine 6:97, May 14, 1973
    New York Theatre Critics' Reviews 1947:249
                                 1956:362
                                 1973:224, 281
    New York Times VI, p. 14, Nov 23, 1947
                  p. 42, Dec 4, 1947
                  II, p. 3, Dec 14, 1947
                  II, p. 1, Jun 6, 1948
                  II, p. 1, Jun 12, 1949
                  p. 38, Sep 29, 1949
                  p. 33, Oct 13, 1949
                  p. 36, May 24, 1950
                  p. 18, Mar 4, 1955
                  p. 24, Feb 16, 1956
                  p. 27, Feb 19, 1965
                  II, p. 1, Dec 3, 1972
                  II, p. 1, Apr 1, 1973
                  p. 31, Apr 27, 1973
                  II, p. 1, May 6, 1973
                  p. 19, Oct 5, 1973
                  p. 59, Oct 23, 1973

p. 16, Aug 17, 1974
p. 34, Oct 11, 1976
XI, p. 6, Aug 12, 1979
New Yorker 23:50+, Dec 13, 1947
          32:90+, Feb 25, 1956
          49:81, May 5, 1973
Newsweek 30:82-3, Dec 15, 1947
         81:109-10, May 7, 1973
Saturday Review 30:22-4, Dec 27, 1947
                39:22, Mar 3, 1956
School and Society 67:241-3, Mar 27, 1948
Theatre Arts 31:18, Dec 1947
             32:10-11, 13, Jan 1948
             32:35, Feb 1948
             32:30, Apr 1948
             32:21, Oct 1948
             33:44, Jun 1949
             33:14, Nov 1949
             40:24, Apr 1956
Time 50:85, Dec 15, 1947
     54:54, Oct 31, 1949
     67:61, Feb 27, 1956
     101:88+, May 7, 1973

Suddenly Last Summer
Productions:
  (Off Broadway) Season of 1957-58, billed as Garden District.
  (Off Broadway) October 30, 1964 for 9 performances (Equity
    Library Theater).
  (Off Off Broadway) Season of 1973-74 (Manhattan Theater
    Club).
  (Off Off Broadway) Season of 1974-75 (Jean Cocteau Reper-
    tory).
  (Off Off Broadway) September 1974 (T. Schreiber Studio).
Reviews:
  Catholic World 186:469-70, Mar 1958
  Christian Century 75:136, Jan 29, 1958
  Commonweal 68:232-3, May 30, 1958
  Nation 186:86-7, Jan 25, 1958
  New York Times p. 23, Jan 8, 1958
               II, p. 1, Jan 19, 1958
               p. 44, Sep 17, 1958
  New Yorker 33:66+, Jan 18, 1958
  Newsweek 51:84, Jan 20, 1958
  Reporter 18:42-3, Feb 6, 1958
  Saturday Review 41:26, Jan 25, 1958
  Theatre Arts 42:13, Mar 1958
  Time 71:42, Jan 20, 1958

Summer and Smoke
Productions:

Opened October 6, 1948 for 100 performances.
(Off Broadway) Season of 1951-52.
(Off Broadway) September 16, 1975 for 64 performances (Round-
about Theater Co.).
(Off Off Broadway) February 1976 (Drama Comm. Repertory
Theater).
Reviews:
America 133:340, Nov 15, 1975
Catholic World 168:161, Nov 1948
176:148-9, Nov 1952
Commonweal 49:68-9, Oct 29, 1948
Forum 110:352-3, Dec 1948
Life 25:102-3, Oct 25, 1948
Nation 167:473-4, Oct 23, 1948
New Republic 119:25-6, Oct 25, 1948
119:27-8, Nov 15, 1948
New York Magazine 8:83, Oct 20, 1975
New York Theatre Critics' Reviews 1948:205
New York Times p. 18, Jul 9, 1947
p. 21, Aug 1, 1947
II, p. 1, Aug 10, 1947
II, p. 1, Oct 3, 1948
p. 33, Oct 7, 1948
II, p. 1, Oct 17, 1948
II, p. 7, Dec 5, 1948
p. 21, Aug 9, 1949
II, p. 3, Oct 29, 1950
p. 32, Nov 23, 1951
p. 13, Jan 25, 1952
p. 19, Apr 25, 1952
II, p. 1, May 4, 1952
p. 44, Oct 7, 1975
II, p. 1, Oct 19, 1975
New York Times Magazine pp. 66-7, Sep 26, 1948
New Yorker 24:51, Oct 16, 1948
Newsweek 32:88, Oct 18, 1948
Saturday Review 31:31-3, Oct 30, 1948
35:28, May 10, 1952
School and Society 68:303-4, Oct 30, 1948
Theatre Arts 31:11, Sep 1947
33:10-11+, Jan 1949
Time 52:82-3, Oct 18, 1948
See also reviews of The Eccentricities of a Nightingale

Sweet Bird of Youth
Productions:
Opened March 10, 1959 for 375 performances.
(Off Broadway) December 3, 1975 for 15 performances (Brook-
lyn Academy of Music).
Opened December 29, 1975 for 48 performances.
(Off Off Broadway) January 28, 1978 (Association of Theater
Artists).

Reviews:
  America 101:55-6, Apr 4, 1959
  Catholic World 189:158-9, May 1959
            189:191-4, Jun 1959
  Christian Century 76:726, Jun 17, 1959
            76:854, Jul 22, 1959
  Life 46:71-3, Apr 20, 1959
  Los Angeles 25:238+, Feb 1980
  Nation 188:281-3, Mar 28, 1959
            221:700, Dec 27, 1975
  New Republic 140:21-2, Apr 20, 1959
            174:28-9, Jan 17, 1976
  New York Magazine 9:67, Jan 19, 1976
  New York Theatre Critics' Reviews 1959:347
            1975:110
  New York Times p. 27, Apr 17, 1956
            p. 39, Mar 11, 1959
            p. 26, Mar 12, 1959
            II, p. 1, Mar 22, 1959
            p. 27, Oct 27, 1961
            p. 53, Dec 4, 1975
            II, p. 5, Dec 21, 1975
  New Yorker 35:98-100, Mar 21, 1959
  Newsweek 53:75, Mar 23, 1959
  Reporter 20:34, Apr 16, 1959
  Saturday Review 42:26, Mar 28, 1959
  Theatre Arts 40:66-7, Aug 1956
            43:21-2, May 1959
  Time 73:58, Mar 23, 1959
            106:71, Dec 15, 1975

Talk to Me Like the Rain
  Productions:
    (Off Off Broadway) February 13, 1976 (Malachy Co.).
    (Off Off Broadway) March 26, 1976 (IRT).
    (Off Off Broadway) September 1, 1980 (Urban Arts Theater).
    See also Three by Tennessee.
  No Reviews.

This Property Is Condemned
  Productions:
    (Off Broadway) Season of 1956-57.
    (Off Off Broadway) Season of 1974-75 (Manhattan Theater Club).
    (Off Off Broadway) February 27, 1976 (ACSTA).
    (Off Off Broadway) May 20, 1977 (National Arts Theater).
  Reviews:
    New York Times p. 34, Oct 29, 1956
            IV, p. 31, Nov 11, 1956

Three by Tennessee (Consists of The Lady of Larkspur Lotion, Talk to Me Like the Rain, and Something Unspoken)

Productions:
(Off Off Broadway) December 6, 1973 (Lolly's Theater Club).
No Reviews.

Twenty-Seven Wagons Full of Cotton
Productions:
Opened April 19, 1955 for 47 performances.
Opened January 26, 1976 for 33 performances.
Reviews:
America 93:193, May 14, 1955
Catholic World 181:227, Jun 1955
Commonweal 62:255, Jun 10, 1955
Nation 222:188-90, Feb 14, 1976
New Republic 132:22, May 2, 1955
New York Theatre Critics' Reviews 1955:325
                                   1976:382
New York Times p. 23, Jan 19, 1955
              p. 40, Apr 20, 1955
              II, p. 1, Apr 24, 1955
              p. 26, Jan 27, 1976
              II, p. 5, Feb 8, 1976
New Yorker 31:69-71, Apr 30, 1955
          51:78, Feb 9, 1976
Saturday Review 38:26, May 14, 1955
Theatre Arts 39:17, 23+, Jul 1955
Time 65:78, May 2, 1955
See also reviews of Evening of Tennessee Williams

*Two Character Play (original version of Out Cry)
Reviews:
Los Angeles 22:193, Apr 1977
New York Times p. 54, Dec 13, 1967
Time 90:63, Dec 22, 1967
See also reviews of Out Cry

The Unsatisfactory Supper (see Promises, Lies and Delusions)

Vieux Carré
Productions:
Opened May 11, 1977 for 7 performances.
Reviews:
America 136:506, Jun 4, 1977
Nation 224:669, May 28, 1977
New York Magazine 10:92, May 30, 1977
New York Theatre Critics' Reviews 1977:244
New York Times III, p. 22, May 12, 1977
              II, p. 5, May 22, 1977
New Yorker 53:83, May 23, 1977
Time 109:108, May 23, 1977

*Will Mr. Merriwether Return from Memphis?
Reviews:

New York Times p. 12, Jan 26, 1980
Time 115:61, Feb 4, 1980

You Touched Me (with Donald Windham. Suggested by a short story
    by D. H. Lawrence)
Productions:
Opened September 25, 1945 for 109 performances.
Reviews:
Catholic World 162:166, Nov 1945
Commonweal 42:623, Oct 12, 1945
Nation 161:349, Oct 6, 1945
New Republic 113:469, Oct 8, 1945
New York Theatre Critics' Reviews 1945:164
New York Times II, p. 2, Oct 17, 1943
              VI, p. 28, Sep 23, 1945
              p. 27, Sep 26, 1945
              II, p. 1, Sep 30, 1945
New York Times Magazine pp. 28-9, Sep 23, 1945
New Yorker 21:48, Oct 6, 1945
Theatre Arts 29:618-21, Nov 1945
             29:680, Dec 1945
Time 46:77, Oct 8, 1945

WILLIAMS, WILLIAM CARLOS

Many Loves
Productions:
(Off Broadway) Season of 1958-59 (Living Theatre).
(Off Broadway) October 13, 1961 for 19 performances.
(Off Off Broadway) April 29, 1976 (Drama Ensemble Co.).
Reviews:
Nation 188:125, Feb 7, 1959
New York Times p. 28, Jan 14, 1959
              p. 29, Jun 16, 1961

WILSON, LANFORD

Be Who You Are
Productions:
(Off Off Broadway) March 17, 1978 (Academy Arts Theater
    Co.).
No Reviews.

Brontosaurus
Productions:
(Off Broadway) March 9, 1978 for 21 performances as part
    of a program called Two from the Late Show.
Reviews:
Nation 225:571, Nov 26, 1977

Confluence (see Thymus Vulgaris)

The Family Continues
    Productions:
        (Off Off Broadway) May 21, 1972 (Circle Theater Co.).
        (Off Off Broadway) September 30, 1976 (New York Theater
            Ensemble).
        See also Three New Plays by Lanford Wilson.
    Reviews:
        New York Times p. 43, May 22, 1972.

Fifth of July
    Productions:
        (Off Broadway) April 27, 1978 for 159 performances.
        Opened November 5, 1980 for 511 performances.
    Reviews:
        Los Angeles 24:308+, Oct 1979
        Nation 226:579-80, May 13, 1978
                231:588-9, Nov 29, 1980
        New Republic 184:26, May 23, 1981
        New West 4:SC-32+, Sep 24, 1979
        New York Magazine 11:77, May 15, 1978
                            13:65, Nov 17, 1980
        New York Theatre Critics' Reviews 1980:126
        New York Times II, p. 5, Apr 23, 1978
                        III, p. 3, Apr 28, 1978
                        II, p. 5, May 7, 1978
                        III, p. 19, Nov 6, 1980
                        p. 3, Nov 16, 1980
                        III, p. 3, Dec 26, 1980
                        III, p. 20, Apr 9, 1981
                        III, p. 13, Jan 22, 1982
        New Yorker 54:90, May 8, 1978
                    56:172-3, Nov 17, 1980
        Newsweek 96:129, Nov 24, 1980
        Time 116:109, Nov 17, 1980

The Gingham Dog
    Productions:
        Opened April 23, 1969 for 5 performances.
        (Off Off Broadway) December 1977 (Urban Arts Corps).
    Reviews:
        New York Theatre Critics' Reviews 1969:304
                                          1969:306
        New York Times II, p. 18, Oct 13, 1968
                        p. 41, Apr 24, 1969
                        II, p. 22, May 4, 1969
        New Yorker 45:107, May 3, 1969
        Saturday Review 51:32+, Oct 26, 1968

The Great Nebula in Orion
    Productions:

(Off Off Broadway) May 21, 1972 (Circle Theater Co.).
(Off Off Broadway) February 22, 1977 (West Park Theater).
See also Three New Plays by Lanford Wilson.
Reviews:
New York Times p. 43, May 22, 1972

Home Free
Productions:
(Off Broadway) February 10, 1965 for 23 performances (The-
atre 1965 New Playwrights Series).
(Off Off Broadway) December 3, 1976 (Drama Ensemble Co.).
(Off Off Broadway) Season of 1976-77 (Circle Repertory).
(Off Off Broadway) June 31, 1977 (Quaigh Theater).
Reviews:
New York Times II, p. 1, Feb 7, 1965
p. 45, Feb 11, 1965
Newsweek 65:93, Feb 22, 1965

The Hot l Baltimore
Productions:
(Off Off Broadway) January 27, 1973 (Circle Theater Co.).
(Off Broadway) March 22, 1973 for 1,166 performances.
Reviews:
Mademoiselle 77:88, Aug 1973
Nation 216:313-14, Mar 5, 1973
New Republic 168:33, Apr 14, 1973
New York Magazine 6:94, Apr 9, 1973
New York Theatre Critics' Reviews 1973:306
New York Times p. 37, Feb 8, 1973
II, p. 3, Mar 4, 1973
p. 21, Mar 23, 1973
XXI, p. 9, May 27, 1979
New Yorker 49:77, Mar 31, 1973
Newsweek 81:91, Feb 26, 1973
Playboy 20:39, Jul 1973
Time 101:96, Apr 23, 1973

Ikke, Ikke, Nye, Nye, Nye
Productions:
(Off Off Broadway) May 21, 1972 (Circle Theater Co.).
(Off Off Broadway) December 3, 1976 (Drama Ensemble Co.).
(Off Off Broadway) Season of 1976-77 (Circle Repertory).
See also Three New Plays by Lanford Wilson.
Reviews:
New York Times p. 43, May 22, 1972

Lemon Sky
Productions:
(Off Broadway) May 17, 1970 for 17 performances.
(Off Off Broadway) January 12, 1973 (Central Arts Cabaret).
(Off Off Broadway) February 4, 1976 (T. Schreiber).
(Off Off Broadway) March 2-14, 1976 (T. Schreiber Studio).

Reviews:
>   Nation 210:668, Jun 1, 1970
>   New Republic 162:18+, Jun 13, 1970
>   New York Theatre Critics' Reviews 1970:207
>   New York Times p. 40, May 18, 1970
>   p. 28, Mar 3, 1976
>   New Yorker 46:72, May 30, 1970
>   Time 95:63, Jun 1, 1970

Ludlow Fair

Productions:
>   (Off Broadway) March 22, 1966 for 15 performances.
>   (Off Off Broadway) November 11, 1974 (Theater at Noon).
>   (Off Off Broadway) September 30, 1976 (New York Theater
>   Ensemble).
>   (Off Off Broadway) November 1976 (IRT).
>   (Off Off Broadway) November 1976 (13th St. Repertory The-
>   ater).
>   (Off Off Broadway) March 17, 1978 (Academy Arts Theater
>   Co.).

Reviews:
>   Commonweal 84:178, Apr 29, 1966
>   New York Times p. 42, Mar 23, 1966
>   New Yorker 42:124, Apr 2, 1966

The Madness of Lady Bright

Productions:
>   (Off Broadway) March 22, 1966 for 15 performances.
>   (Off Off Broadway) September 30, 1976 (New York Theater
>   Ensemble).
>   (Off Off Broadway) November 1976 (13th St. Repertory Co.).

Reviews:
>   Commonweal 84:178, Apr 29, 1966
>   New York Times p. 42, Mar 23, 1966
>   New Yorker 42:124, Apr 2, 1966

The Mound Builders

Productions:
>   (Off Off Broadway) February 1, 1975 (Circle Repertory The-
>   ater Co.).

Reviews:
>   Nation 220:315-16, Mar 15, 1975
>   New Republic 172:22, Mar 1, 1975
>   New West 2:SC-20, Jun 20, 1977
>   New York Times p. 35, Feb 3, 1975
>   New Yorker 50:84-5, Feb 17, 1975

Nebula in Orion

Productions:
>   (Off Off Broadway) May 1978 (Academy Arts Theater Co.).

Reviews:
>   See Great Nebula in Orion

The Rimers of Eldritch
  Productions:
    (Off Broadway) February 20, 1967 for 32 performances.
    (Off Off Broadway) April 1, 1976 (Equity Library Theater).
    (Off Off Broadway) Season of 1981-82 (La Mama ETC).
  Reviews:
    America 116:354-5, Mar 11, 1967
    New York Times p. 53, Feb 21, 1967
                   p. 30, Apr 6, 1976
    New Yorker 43:132+, Mar 4, 1967
    Saturday Review 50:30, Mar 11, 1967
    Time 89:52, Mar 3, 1967

Serenading Louie
  Productions:
    (Off Broadway) May 2, 1976 for 33 performances.
  Reviews:
    New York Magazine 9:78, May 24, 1976
    New York Times p. 45, May 6, 1976
    New Yorker 52:125, May 17, 1976

Sextet (Yes)
  Productions:
    (Off Off Broadway) Season of 1970-71 (Circle Theater Co.).
  No Reviews.

A Tale Told
  Productions:
    (Off Broadway) June 11, 1981 for 30 performances (Circle
      Repertory Co.).
  Reviews:
    America 145:35, Jul 18-25, 1981
    Commonweal 108:500-1, Sep 11, 1981
    New York Magazine 14:46-7, Jun 22, 1981
    New York Theatre Critics' Reviews 1981:182
    New York Times III, p. 3, Jun 12, 1981
                    III, p. 17, Jun 18, 1981
                    II, p. 3, Jun 21, 1981
    New Yorker 57:86-7, Jun 22, 1981
    Newsweek 97:64, Jun 22, 1981
    Saturday Review 8:46-7, Sep 1981
    Time 117:48, Jun 22, 1981

The Talley Family (see Fifth of July, Talley's Folly, and A Tale
      Told)

Talley's Folly
  Productions:
    (Off Broadway) May 1, 1979 for 44 performances and transferred
      to Broadway.
    Opened on Broadway February 20, 1980 for a total of 277 per-
      formances.

Reviews:
Commonweal 108:182, Mar 28, 1980
Los Angeles 24:308+, Oct 1979
Nation 228:609, May 26, 1979
230:316, Mar 15, 1980
New Republic 180:24, Jun 9, 1979
182:28, Apr 5, 1980
New West 4:SC-32+, Sep 24, 1979
New York Magazine 12:76, May 21, 1979
13:87, Mar 10, 1980
New York Theatre Critics' Reviews 1979:247
1980:360
New York Times III, p. 3, May 4, 1979
II, p. 5, May 13, 1979
III, p. 3, Jun 1, 1979
II, p. 1, Jul 1, 1979
II, p. 1, Dec 30, 1979
III, p. 15, Feb 21, 1980
II, p. 3, Jul 6, 1980
XI, p. 29, Mar 14, 1982
New Yorker 55:84+, May 14, 1979
56:62, Mar 3, 1980
Newsweek 95:53, Mar 3, 1980
Time 113:113, May 14, 1979

This Is the Rill Speaking
Productions:
(Off Broadway) April 11, 1966 for 16 performances.
(Off Off Broadway) September 1975 (Back East).
Reviews:
Nation 202:403-4, Apr 4, 1966
New York Times II, p. 15, Apr 10, 1966
p. 43, Apr 12, 1966

Three New Plays by Lanford Wilson (Consists of Great Nebula in
Orion, Ikke, Ikke, Nye, Nye, Nye, and The Family Continues)
Productions:
(Off Off Broadway) October 12, 1972 (Circle Theater Co.).
Reviews:
See individual entries

Thymus Vulgaris
Productions:
(Off Broadway) January 10, 1982 for 36 performances, as part
of a bill called Confluence (Circle Repertory Theater).
Reviews:
New York Magazine 15:56, Jan 25, 1982
New York Theatre Critics' Reviews 1982:360
New York Times III, p. 14, Jan 11, 1982
II, p. 3, Jan 24, 1982

Two for the Late Show (see Brontosaurus)

Untitled Play
    Productions:
        (Off Broadway) Season of 1967-68, in repertory (Judson Poet's
            Theatre).
    No Reviews.

Wandering
    Productions:
        (Off Broadway) May 8, 1968 for 80 performances.
    Reviews:
        Harper's Bazaar 237:113-15, Oct 1968
        Nation 206:772+, Jun 10, 1968
        New York Times p. 55, May 9, 1968
                       II, p. 1, May 19, 1968
        New Yorker 44:74, May 18, 1968

WINCELBERG, SHIMON

Kataki
    Productions:
        Opened April 9, 1959 for 20 performances.
        (Off Broadway) Season of 1959-1960.
    Reviews:
        New York Theatre Critics' Reviews 1959:326
        New York Times p. 24, Apr 10, 1959
                       p. 55, Dec 16, 1959
        New Yorker 35:79, Apr 18, 1959
        Newsweek 53:75, Apr 20, 1959
        Saturday Review 42:23, Apr 25, 1959
        Theatre Arts 43:10-11, Jun 1959
        Time 73:71, Apr 20, 1959

WISHENGRAD, MORTON

The Rope Dancers
    Productions:
        Opened November 20, 1957 for 189 performances.
        (Off Broadway) Season of 1958-59.
    Reviews:
        America 98:437, Jan 11, 1958
        Catholic World 186:384, Feb 1958
        Christian Century 74:1514, Dec 18, 1957
        Commonweal 67:616, Mar 14, 1958
                   67:640, Mar 21, 1958
        Nation 185:442, Dec 7, 1957
        New York Theatre Critics' Reviews 1957:174
        New York Times II, p. 1, Nov 17, 1957
                       p. 39, Nov 21, 1957
                       II, p. 1, Dec 1, 1957

p. 26, Mar 14, 1959
p. 26, Jul 15, 1959
New Yorker 33:94+, Nov 30, 1957
Newsweek 50:70-1, Dec 2, 1957
Reporter 17:34, Dec 26, 1957
Saturday Review 40:51, Dec 7, 1957
Theatre Arts 42:21-2, Feb 1958
Time 70:77, Dec 2, 1957

WOLFSON, VICTOR

American Gothic (Based on Wolfson's The Lonely Steeple)
    Productions:
        (Off Broadway) Season of 1953-54.
    Reviews:
        America 90:251, Nov 28, 1953
        Catholic World 178:309, Jan 1954
        New Republic 129:21, Nov 30, 1953
        New York Times p. 35, Nov 11, 1953
        New Yorker 29:85-6+, Nov 21, 1953
        Saturday Review 36:30, Nov 28, 1953

Bitter Stream (Based on Ignazio Silone's Fontamara)
    Productions:
        Opened March 30, 1936 for 61 performances.
    Reviews:
        Commonweal 23:696, Apr 17, 1936
        Literary Digest 121:18, Apr 11, 1936
        New York Times p. 16, Mar 31, 1936
        Newsweek 7:43, Apr 11, 1936
        Theatre Arts 20:339, Apr 11, 1936

Excursion
    Productions:
        Opened April 9, 1937 for 116 performances.
    Reviews:
        Catholic World 145:214-15, May 1937
        Commonweal 26:20, Apr 20, 1937
        Literary Digest 123:22, Apr 24, 1937
        New Republic 91:74-5, May 26, 1937
        New York Times p. 11, Apr 10, 1937
                     XI, p. 1, Apr 18, 1937
                     p. 24, Jul 27, 1937
        Newsweek 9:32, Apr 17, 1937
        Stage 14:49, May 1937
        Theatre Arts 21:422-4, Jun 1937
        Time 29:62, Apr 19, 1937

The Family (Based on Nina Fedorova's novel)
    Productions:

Opened March 30, 1943 for 7 performances.
Reviews:
New York Theatre Critics' Reviews 1943:344
New York Times p. 22, Mar 31, 1943
Theatre Arts 27:333-4, Jan 1943

Pastoral
Productions:
Opened November 1, 1939 for 14 performances.
Reviews:
New York Times p. 26, Nov 2, 1939
Newsweek 14:32, Nov 13, 1939

Prides' Crossing
Productions:
Opened November 20, 1950 for 8 performances.
Reviews:
Christian Science Monitor Magazine p. 10, Nov 25, 1950
Commonweal 53:231, Dec 8, 1950
New York Theatre Critics' Reviews 1950:198
New York Times p. 37, Nov 21, 1950
New Yorker 26:83, Dec 2, 1950
Theatre Arts 35:17, Jan 1951
Time 56:65, Dec 4, 1950

WOUK, HERMAN

The Caine Mutiny Court-Martial (Adapted from Wouk's novel)
Productions:
Opened January 20, 1954 for 415 performances.
(Off Off Broadway) December 8, 1969 for 3 performances
    (Equity Theater Informals).
Reviews:
America 90:516+, Feb 13, 1954
Catholic World 178:466, Mar 1954
Collier's 132:50-3, Nov 13, 1953
Commonweal 59:523, Feb 26, 1954
Life 35:75-6+, Dec 14, 1953
Nation 178:138, Feb 13, 1954
        178:260-1, Mar 27, 1954
New Republic 130:21, Feb 15, 1954
New York Theatre Critics' Reviews 1954:382
New York Times p. 35, Oct 14, 1953
            p. 52, Dec 15, 1953
            II, p. 1, Jan 17, 1954
            p. 27, Jan 21, 1954
            II, p. 1, Jan 31, 1954
            VI, p. 12, Mar 21, 1954
            pp. 12-13+, Mar 21, 1954
            p. 6, Apr 4, 1954

p. 13, Dec 8, 1954
p. 40, Jun 14, 1956
p. 49, Apr 5, 1981
New Yorker 29:66+, Jan 30, 1954
Newsweek 43:73, Feb 1, 1954
Saturday Review 37:24+, Feb 6, 1954
Theatre Arts 38:18-19, Apr 1954
39:58-61, Jan 1955
Time 63:36, Feb 1, 1954

Nature's Way
    Productions:
        Opened October 16, 1957 for 61 performances.
    Reviews:
        Christian Century 74:1384, Nov 20, 1957
        Nation 185:310, Nov 2, 1957
        New York Theatre Critics' Reviews 1957:219
        New York Times VI, p. 29, Aug 25, 1957
                        p. 42, Oct 17, 1957
        New Yorker 33:96-8, Oct 26, 1957
        Theatre Arts 41:25-6, Dec 1957
        Time 70:92, Oct 28, 1957

The Traitor
    Productions:
        Opened April 4, 1949 for 67 performances.
    Reviews:
        Catholic World 169:145, May 1949
        Commonweal 50:45-6, Apr 22, 1949
        New Republic 120:30, Apr 18, 1949
        New York Theatre Critics' Reviews 1949:322
        New York Times p. 30, Apr 1, 1949
                      II, p. 1, Apr 10, 1949
        New Yorker 25:55, Apr 9, 1949
        Newsweek 33:79+, Apr 11, 1949
        Saturday Review 32:34-6, May 21, 1949
        School and Society 69:339, May 7, 1949
        Theatre Arts 33:13, Jun 1949
        Time 53:87, Apr 11, 1949

WRIGHT, RICHARD

Daddy Goodness
    Productions:
        (Off Broadway) June 4, 1968 for 64 performances (Negro En-
            semble).
    Reviews:
        New York Times p. 37, Jun 5, 1968

The Long Dream (see entry under Frings, Ketti)

Native Son   (see entry under Green, Paul)

WYCHERLY, MARGARET   (see Vale, Martin)

YORDAN, PHILIP

Anna Lucasta
    Productions:
        (Off Broadway) June 16, 1944 in repertory (American Negro
            Theatre).
        Opened August 30, 1944 for 957 performances.
        Opened September 22, 1947 for 32 performances.
        (Off Broadway) Season of 1955-56.
        (Off Off Broadway) November 10, 1978.
    Reviews:
        Catholic World 160:71-2, Oct 1944
        Commonweal 40:517, Sep 15, 1944
        Life 17:69-72, Oct 4, 1944
             18:79, Apr 9, 1945
        New Republic 111:334-40, Sep 18, 1944
        New York Theatre Critics' Reviews 1944:143
        New York Times p. 10, Jun 17, 1944
                       p. 15, Aug 31, 1944
                       II, p. 1, Sep 10, 1944
                       II, p. 1, Sep 24, 1944
                       II, p. 1, Mar 3, 1946
                       II, p. 1, Aug 25, 1946
                       II, p. 3, Sep 21, 1947
                       p. 31, Oct 7, 1947
                       p. 31, Oct 30, 1947
                       p. 21, Apr 13, 1956
                       III, p. 30, Nov 15, 1978
        New Yorker 20:40, Sep 4, 1944
        Newsweek 24:107-9, Sep 11, 1944
                 30:74, Nov 10, 1947
        Theatre Arts 28:632-4, Nov 1944
        Time 43:56, Jun 26, 1944

Any Day Now
    Productions:
        (Off Broadway) June 3, 1941.
    Reviews:
        New York Times p. 28, Jun 10, 1941

ZINDEL, PAUL

And Miss Reardon Drinks a Little
    Productions:
        Opened February 25, 1971 for 108 performances.

Reviews:
Nation 212:347-8, Mar 15, 1971
New York Theatre Critics' Reviews 1971:341
New York Times p. 29, Feb 26, 1971
p. 28, Mar 2, 1971
II, p. 1, Mar 7, 1971
New Yorker 47:67, Mar 6, 1971
Saturday Review 54:10, Mar 20, 1971
Time 97:47, Mar 8, 1971

A Dream of Swallows
Productions:
(Off Broadway) April 14, 1964 for one performance.
Reviews:
New York Times p. 46, Apr 15, 1964
p. 42, Apr 16, 1964

The Effect of Gamma Rays on Man-in-the-Moon Marigolds
Productions:
(Off Broadway) April 7, 1970 for 819 performances.
(Off Off Broadway) February 18, 1973 (Actors Studio).
Opened March 14, 1978 for 16 performances.
Reviews:
Commonweal 93:49, Oct 9, 1970
Life 69:8-9, Jul 4, 1970
Nation 210:476, Apr 20, 1970
New York Theatre Critics' Reviews 1970:242
1978:330
New York Times p. 32, Apr 8, 1970
II, p. 1, Apr 19, 1970
p. 24, Apr 9, 1971
p. 25, May 12, 1972
p. 56, May 24, 1973
III, p. 25, Mar 15, 1978
New Yorker 46:82+, Apr 18, 1970
54:95, Mar 27, 1978
Newsweek 75:64, Apr 27, 1970
Saturday Review 53:12, May 2, 1970
Time 95:51, Apr 20, 1970
97:66, May 17, 1971

Ladies at the Alamo
Productions:
(Off Off Broadway) May 29, 1975 (Actors Studio).
Opened April 7, 1977 for 20 performances.
Reviews:
New York Magazine 10:71, Apr 25, 1977
New York Theatre Critics' Reviews 1977:284
New York Times III, p. 3, Apr 8, 1977
II, p. 3, Apr 17, 1977
New Yorker 53:102, Apr 18, 1977

Texas Monthly 6:136, Jun 1978
Time 109:31, Apr 18, 1977

The Ladies Should Be in Bed
Productions:
(Off Off Broadway) April 29, 1982 (Nat Horne Musical Theater).
No Reviews.

Let Me Hear You Whisper
Productions:
(Off Off Broadway) April 29, 1982 (Nat Horne Musical The-
ater).
No Reviews.

The Secret Affairs of Mildred Wild
Productions:
Opened November 14, 1972 for 23 performances.
Reviews:
Nation 215:573, Dec 4, 1972
New York Theatre Critics' Reviews 1972:186
New York Times p. 38, Nov 15, 1972
II, p. 32, Dec 3, 1972
New Yorker 48:111-12, Nov 25, 1972
Newsweek 80:77, Nov 27, 1972
Time 100:73, Nov 27, 1972

Zindel x 2 (see Let Me Hear You Whisper and The Ladies Should Be in Bed)

ABOUT THE DRAMATISTS

Name	Birthplace	Dates
Abbott, George	Hamburg, N.Y.	born 1887
Ade, George	Kentland, Ind.	1866-1944
Akins, Zoë	Humansville, Mo.	1886-1958
Albee, Edward	Washington, D.C.	born 1928
Alfred, William	New York	born 1922
Allen, Woody	New York	born 1935
Anderson, Maxwell	Atlantic, Pa.	1888-1959
Anderson, Robert	New York	born 1917
Anspacher, Louis K.	Cincinnati	1878-1947
Archibald, William	Trinidad, West Indies	1919-1970
Ardrey, Robert	Chicago	1908-1980
Atlas, Leopold	New York	born 1907
Aurthur, Robert Alan	Freeport, N.Y.	1922-1978
Axelrod, George	New York	born 1922
Babe, Thomas	Buffalo, N.Y.	born 1941
Balderston, John	Philadelphia	1889-1954
Baldwin, James	New York	born 1924
Baraka, Imamu Amiri	Newark, N.J.	born 1934
Barry, Philip	Rochester, N.Y.	1896-1949
Beach, Lewis	Saginaw, Mich.	born 1891
Behrman, S. N.	Worcester, Mass.	1893-1973
Belasco, David	San Francisco	1859-1931
Bellow, Saul	Lachine, Quebec	born 1915
Benet, Steven Vincent	Bethlehem, Pa.	1898-1943
Berg, Gertrude	New York	born 1899
Berrigan, Daniel	Two Harbors, Minn.	born 1921
Bolton, Guy	England	1881-1979
Boothe, Clare	New York	born 1903
Boucicault, Dion	Dublin, Ireland	1820-1890
Bowles, Jane	New York	1917-1973
Breit, Harvey	New York	1910-1968
Browne, Porter Emerson	Beverly, Mass.	1879-1934
Buck, Pearl S.	Hillsboro, West Va.	1892-1973
Bullins, Ed	Philadelphia	born 1935
Burrows, Abe	New York	born 1910
Caldwell, Erskine	White Oak, Ga.	born 1903

Name	Birthplace	Dates
Capote, Truman	New Orleans	born 1924
Carter, Steve	New York	born 1929
Chase, Mary Coyle	Denver	1907-1981
Chayefsky, Paddy	New York	1923-1981
Chodorov, Edward	New York	born 1904
Chodorov, Jerome	New York	born 1911
Coburn, D. L.	Baltimore	born 1938
Cohan, George M.	Providence, R.I.	1878-1942
Conkle, E. P.	Peru, Neb.	born 1899
Connelly, Marc	McKeesport, Pa.	1890-1980
Coxe, Louis O.	Manchester, N.H.	born 1918
Craven, Frank	Boston	1880-1945
Cristofer, Michael	Trenton, N.J.	born 1946
Crothers, Rachel	Bloomington, Ill.	1878-1958
Crouse, Russel	Findlay, Ohio	1893-1966
Crowley, Mart	Vicksburg, Miss.	born 1935
Cummings, E. E.	Cambridge, Mass.	1894-1962
Daly, Augustin	Plymouth, N.C.	1838-1899
Davis, Bill C.	Ellenville, N.Y.	born 1951
Davis, Ossie	Cogdell, Ga.	born 1921
Davis, Owen	Portland, Maine	1874-1956
Dell, Floyd	Barry, Ill.	1887-1969
Dodd, Lee Wilson	Franklin, Pa.	1879-1933
Dos Passos, John	Chicago	born 1896
Dreiser, Theodore	Indiana	1871-1945
Duberman, Martin	New York	born 1930
Dunlap, William	Perth Amboy, N.J.	1766-1839
Dunning, Philip	Meriden, Conn.	1890-1968
Durang, Christopher	Montclair, N.J.	born 1949
d'Usseau, Arnaud	Los Angeles	born 1916
Eliot, T. S.	St. Louis	1888-1965
Emery, Gilbert	Naples, N.Y.	1875-1945
Faulkner, William	New Albany, Miss.	1897-1962
Feiffer, Jules	New York	born 1929
Ferber, Edna	Kalamazoo, Mich.	1885-1968
Ferris, Walter	Green Bay, Wis.	born 1882
Fields, Joseph	New York	1895-1966
Fierstein, Harvey	Brooklyn	born 1954
Fitch, Clyde	Elmira, N.Y.	1865-1909
Fitzgerald, F. Scott	St. Paul, Minn.	1896-1940
Flavin, Martin	San Francisco	1883-1967
Forbes, James	Salem, Ontario, Canada	1871-1938
Foster, Paul	Salem, N.J.	born 1931
Franken, Rose	Dallas	born 1895
Freeman, David	Cleveland	born 1941

Name	Birthplace	Dates
Friedman, Bruce Jay	New York	born 1930
Frings, Ketti	Columbus, Ohio	1916-1981
Frost, Robert	San Francisco	1874-1963
Fuller, Charles	Philadelphia	born 1939
Gale, Zona	Portage, Wis.	1874-1938
Gardner, Herb	Brooklyn	born 1934
Gelbart, Larry	Chicago	born 1928
Gelber, Jack	Chicago	born 1932
Gershe, Leonard		
Gibbs, Wolcott	New York	1902-1958
Gibson, William	New York	born 1914
Gillette, William	Hartford, Conn.	1855-1937
Gilroy, Frank D.	New York	born 1925
Glaspell, Susan	Davenport, Iowa	1882-1948
Gleason, James	Alameda, Calif.	1886-1959
Goetz, Augustus	Buffalo, New York	1901-1957
Goetz, Ruth	Philadelphia	born 1912
Goldberg, Dick	Winston-Salem, N.C.	born 1947
Goldman, James	Chicago	born 1927
Goldsmith, Clifford	East Aurora, N.Y.	born 1900
Goodrich, Frances	Belleville, N.Y.	born 1933
Gordon, Ruth	Wollaston, Mass.	born 1896
Gordone, Charles	Elkhart, Ind.	born 1925
Gow, James	Iowa	1907-1952
Green, Paul	Lillington, N.C.	1894-1981
Guare, John	New York	born 1938
Gurney, A. R., Jr.	Buffalo, N.Y.	born 1930
Hackett, Albert	New York	born 1900
Haines, William Wister	Des Moines, Iowa	born 1908
Hanley, William	Lorain, Ohio	born 1931
Hansberry, Lorraine	Chicago	1930-1965
Hart, Moss	New York	1904-1961
Hayden, John	Hartford, Conn.	born 1889
Hayes, Alfred	London	born 1911
Hayes, Joseph	Indianapolis	born 1918
Hecht, Ben	New York	1893-1964
Heggen, Thomas	Fort Dodge, Iowa	1918-1949
Heller, Joseph	Brooklyn	born 1923
Hellman, Lillian	New York	born 1905
Hemingway, Ernest	Oak Park, Ill.	1899-1961
Henley, Beth	Jackson, Miss.	born 1952
Herbert, F. Hugh	Vienna	1897-1958
Herne, James A.	Cohoes, N.Y.	1839-1901
Heyward, Dorothy	Wooster, Ohio	1890-1961
Heyward, Dubose	Charleston, S.C.	1885-1940
Hopkins, Arthur	Cleveland	1878-1950
Howard, Bronson	Detroit	1842-1908

Name	Birthplace	Dates
Howard, Sidney	San Francisco	1891-1939
Howells, William Dean	Martin's Ferry, Ohio	1837-1920
Hoyt, Charles Hale	Concord, N.H.	1860-1900
Hughes, Hatcher	North Carolina	1886-1945
Hughes, Langston	Joplin, Mo.	1902-1967
Hurlbut, William	Belvedere, Ill.	born 1883
Huston, John	Nevada, Mo.	born 1906
Hwang, David Henry	Los Angeles	born 1957
Inge, William	Independence, Kan.	1913-1973
Innaurato, Albert	Philadelphia	born 1948
James, Daniel Lewis	Kansas City, Mo.	born 1911
James, Henry	New York	1843-1916
Jeffers, Robinson	Pittsburgh	1887-1962
Jones, Preston	Albuquerque, N.M.	1936-1979
Kanin, Fay	New York	born 1917
Kanin, Garson	Rochester, N.Y.	born 1912
Kaufman, George S.	Pittsburgh	1889-1961
Kelly, George	Philadelphia	1887-1974
Kennedy, Charles Rann	England	1871-1950
Kerr, Jean	Scranton, Pa.	born 1923
Kesselring, Joseph O.	New York	1902-1967
Kingsley, Sidney	New York	born 1906
Kirkland, Jack	St. Louis	1902-1969
Kober, Arthur	Brody, Austria-Hungary	1900-1975
Koch, Howard	New York	born 1902
Kopit, Arthur L.	New York	born 1937
Kramm, Joseph	Philadelphia	born 1928
Krasna, Norman	Long Island	born 1909
Kummer, Clare	Brooklyn	1873-1958
Lapine, James	Mansfield, Ohio	born 1949
Lardner, Ring	Niles, Mich.	1885-1933
Laurents, Arthur	New York	born 1918
Lavery, Emmet	Poughkeepsie, N.Y.	born 1902
Lawrence, Jerome	Cleveland	born 1915
Lawson, John Howard	New York	1895-1977
Lee, Robert E.	Elyria, Ohio	born 1918
Levin, Ira M.	New York	born 1919
Levitt, Saul	Hartford, Conn.	1911-1977
Lewis, Sinclair	Sauk Center, Minn.	1885-1951
Lindsay, Howard	Waterford, N.Y.	1892-1968
Logan, Joshua	Texarkana, Texas	born 1908
Long, John Luther	Pennsylvania	1861-1927
Loos, Anita	Sisson, Calif	1893-1981
Lowell, Robert	Boston, Mass.	1917-1977

Name	Birthplace	Dates
MacArthur, Charles	Scranton, Pa.	1895-1956
McCullers, Carson	Columbus, Ga	1917-1967
McEnroe, Robert E.	New Britain, Conn.	born 1916
McGuire, William Anthony	Chicago	1887-1940
MacKaye, Percy	New York	1875-1956
MacLeish, Archibald	Glencoe, Ill.	1892-1982
McLellan, C. M. S.	Maine	1865-1916
McNally, Terrence	Corpus Christi, Texas	born 1939
Mailer, Norman	Long Branch, N.J.	born 1923
Maltz, Albert	Brooklyn	born 1908
Mamet, David	Flossmore, Ill.	born 1947
Marasco, Robert	Bronx	born 1937
Marquand, John P.	Wilmington, Del.	born 1893
Marquis, Don	Walnut, Ill.	1878-1937
May, Elaine	Philadelphia	born 1932
Mayer, Edwin Justus	New York	1897-1960
Medoff, Mark	Mount Carmel, Ill.	born 1940
Michaels, Sidney	New York	born 1927
Middleton, George	Paterson, N.J.	1880-1967
Millay, Edna St. Vincent	Maine	1892-1950
Miller, Arthur	New York	born 1915
Miller, Jason	Scranton, Pa.	born 1940
Mitchell, Langdon	Philadelphia	1862-1935
Mitchell, Thomas	Elizabeth, N.J.	born 1895
Moody, William Vaughn	Spencer, Ind.	1869-1910
Moore, Edward J.	Chicago	born 1935
Mosel, Tad	Steubenville, Ohio	
Mowatt, Anna Cora	Bordeaux, France	1819-1870
Nichols, Anne	Dales Mills, Ga.	1899-1966
Nicholson, Kenyon	Crawfordsville, Ind.	born 1894
Norman, Marsha W.	Louisville, Ky.	born 1947
Nugent, Elliott	Dover, Ohio	1900-1980
Odets, Clifford	Philadelphia	1906-1963
O'Neill, Eugene	New York	1888-1953
Osborn, Paul	Evansville, Ind.	born 1901
Parker, Dorothy	West End, N.J.	1893-1967
Patrick, John	Louisville, Ky.	born 1910
Peterson, Louis	Hartford, Conn.	born 1922
Pielmeier, John	Altoona, Pa.	born 1949
Pinero, Miguel	Puerto Rico	born 1946
Pollock, Channing	Washington, D.C.	1880-1946
Pomerance, Bernard	New York	born 1940
Rabe, David	Dubuque, Iowa	born 1940
Randall, Bob	New York	born 1937

Name	Birthplace	Dates
Raphaelson, Samuel	New York	born 1896
Rayfiel, David	Brooklyn	born 1923
Reed, Mark	Chelmsford, Mass.	born 1893
Rice, Elmer	New York	1892-1967
Richardson, Jack	New York	born 1935
Richman, Arthur	New York	1886-1944
Riggs, Lynn	Claremore, Ok.	1899-1954
Riley, Lawrence	Bradford, Pa.	1897-1975
Rinehart, Mary Roberts	Pittsburgh	1876-1958
Royle, Edwin Milton	Lexington, Mo.	1862-1942
Ryerson, Florence	Glendale, Calif	1895-1965
Sackler, Howard	New York	born 1930
Saroyan, William	Fresno, Calif	1908-1981
Schary, Dore	Newark, N.J.	1905-1980
Schisgal, Murray	New York	born 1926
Schulberg, Budd	New York	born 1914
Selwyn, Edgar	Canada	1875-1944˙
Shaw, Irwin	New York	born 1912
Sheldon, Edward	Chicago	1886-1946
Sherman, Martin	Philadelphia	
Sherwood, Robert E.	New Rochelle, N.Y.	1896-1955
Shipman, Samuel	New York	1888-1937
Shulman, Max	St. Paul, Minn.	born 1919
Simon, Neil	New York	born 1927
Sinclair, Upton	Baltimore	1878-1968
Skinner, Cornelia Otis	Chicago	born 1901
Sklar, George	Meriden, Conn.	born 1910
Smith, Harry James	New Britain, Conn.	1880-1918
Smith, Winchell	Hartford, Conn.	1871-1933
Spewack, Bella	Hungary	born 1899
Spewack, Samuel	Russia	1899-1971
Stallings, Laurence	Macon, Ga.	1894-1968
Stein, Gertrude	San Francisco	1874-1946
Steinbeck, John	Salinas Valley, Calif.	1902-1968
Stewart, Donald Ogden	Columbus, Ohio	1894-1980
Stitt, Milan	Detroit	born 1941
Strong, Austin	San Francisco	1881-1952
Sturges, Preston	Chicago	1898-1959
Tarkington, Booth	Indianapolis, Ind.	1869-1946
Taylor, Samuel	Chicago	born 1912
Thomas, A. E.	Chester, Mass.	1872-1947
Thomas, Augustus	St. Louis, Mo.	1857-1934
Thompson, Ernest	Bellows Falls, Vt.	born 1949
Thurber, James	Columbus, Ohio	1894-1961
Topor, Tom	Vienna	born 1938
Totheroh, Dan	California	1894-1976
Treadwell, Sophie	California	1890-1970
Turney, Robert	Nashville, Tenn.	born 1900

Name	Birthplace	Dates
Van Druten, John	London, England	1902-1957
van Itallie, Jean-Claude	Brussels	born 1936
Varesi, Gilda	Milan, Italy	born 1887
Veiller, Bayard	Brooklyn	1869-1943
Vidal, Gore	West Point, N.Y.	born 1925
Vollmer, Lula	North Carolina	1898-1955
Walker, Joseph A.	Washington, D.C.	born 1935
Walter, Eugene	Cleveland	1874-1941
Warren, Robert Penn	Guthrie, Ky.	born 1905
Watkins, Maurine	Kentucky	1901-1969
Watters, George Manker	Rochester, N.Y.	1891-1943
Weitzenkorn, Louis	Wilkes-Barre, Pa.	1893-1943
Weller, Michael	New York	born 1942
Wexley, John	New York	born 1902
Wilder, Thornton	Madison, Wis.	1897-1975
Williams, Jesse Lynch	Sterling, Ill.	1871-1929
Williams, Samm-Art	Burgaw, N.C.	born 1946
Williams, Tennessee	Columbus, Miss.	born 1914
Williams, William Carlos	New Jersey	born 1883
Wilson, Lanford	Lebanon, Mo.	born 1938
Wincelberg, Shimon	Germany	born 1915
Wishengrad, Morton	New York	1913-1963
Wolfson, Victor	New York	born 1910
Wouk, Herman	New York	born 1915
Wright, Richard	Natchez, Miss.	born 1909
Yordan, Philip	Chicago	born 1914
Zindel, Paul	Staten Island	born 1936

LONG-RUNNING AMERICAN PLAYS

Performances	Play and Year of Production	Author
3,224	Life with Father (1939)	Lindsay
3,182	Tobacco Road (1933)	Kirkland
2,327	Abie's Irish Rose (1922)	Nichols
*1,809	Deathtrap (1978)	Levin
1,788	Gemini (1977)	Innaurato
1,775	Harvey (1944)	Chase
1,642	Born Yesterday (1946)	Kanin
1,572	Mary, Mary (1961)	Kerr
1,557	Voice of the Turtle (1943)	Van Druten
1,530	Barefoot in the Park (1963)	Simon
1,444	Arsenic and Old Lace (1941)	Kesselring
1,291	Lightnin' (1918)	W. Smith
1,234	Cactus Flower (1965)	Burrows
1,166	Hot l Baltimore (1973)	Wilson
1,157	Mister Roberts (1948)	Logan
1,141	Seven Year Itch (1952)	Axelrod
1,128	Butterflies Are Free (1969)	Gershe
1,097	Plaza Suite (1968)	Simon
1,027	Teahouse of the August Moon (1953)	Patrick
1,007	Never Too Late (1962)	Long
1,000	Boys in the Band (1968)	Crowley
982	Any Wednesday (1964)	Resnik
964	Odd Couple (1965)	Simon
957	Anna Lucasta (1944)	Yordan
956	Kiss and Tell (1943)	Herbert
925	Dracula (1977)	Balderston
924	Moon Is Blue (1951)	Herbert
916	Elephant Man (1979)	Pomerance
901	Luv (1964)	Schisgal
887	Children of a Lesser God (1980)	Medoff

*Still playing on June 1, 1982

Performances	Play and Year of Production	Author
867	Bat (1920)	Rinehart
865	My Sister Eileen (1940)	Fields
857	Chapter Two (1977)	Simon
855	Streetcar Named Desire (1947)	T. Williams
844	That Championship Season (1972)	J. Miller
837	You Can't Take It with You (1936)	Hart
835	Three Men on a Horse (1935)	Abbott
832	Subject Was Roses (1964)	Gilroy
819	Effect of Gamma Rays on Man-in-the-Moon Marigolds (1970)	Zindel
806	Inherit the Wind (1955)	Lawrence
796	No Time for Sergeants (1955)	Levin
789	Ladder (1926)	J. E. Davis
780	Forty Carats (1968)	J. Allen
780	View from the Bridge (1965)	Miller
780	Prisoner of Second Avenue (1971)	Simon
765	State of the Union (1945)	Lindsay
760	First Year (1920)	Craven
755	You Know I Can't Hear You When the Water's Running (1967)	R. Anderson
750	Two for the Seesaw (1958)	Gibson
742	Death of a Salesman (1949)	Miller
739	Man Who Came to Dinner (1939)	Hart
722	Connection (1959)	Gelber
722	Claudia (1941)	Franken
717	Diary of Anne Frank (1955)	Goodrich
714	I Remember Mama (1944)	Van Druten
712	Tea and Sympathy (1953)	R. Anderson
710	Junior Miss (1941)	J. Chodorov
707	Next (1969)	McNally
707	Adaptation (1969)	May
706	Last of the Red Hot Lovers (1969)	Simon
704	Seventh Heaven (1922)	Strong
700	Miracle Worker (1959)	Gibson
694	Cat on a Hot Tin Roof (1955)	T. Williams
692	Scuba Duba (1967)	Friedman
691	Children's Hour (1934)	Hellman
687	Dead End (1935)	Kingsley
683	Dear Ruth (1944)	Krasna
680	East Is West (1918)	Shipman

Performances	Play and Year of Production	Author
677	Come Blow Your Horn (1961)	Simon
671	Doughgirls (1942)	Fields
670	Impossible Years (1965)	Fisher
669	Boy Meets Girl (1935)	Spewack
664	Who's Afraid of Virginia Woolf? (1962)	Albee
657	Women (1936)	Boothe
654	Fifth Season (1953)	Regan
642	Janie (1942)	Bentham
640	Green Pastures (1930)	Connelly
639	Auntie Mame (1956)	Lawrence
634	America Hurrah (1966)	Van Itallie
623	Tenth Man (1959)	Chayefsky
618	Is Zat So? (1925)	Gleason
615	Anniversary Waltz (1954)	J. Chodorov
614	Happy Time (1950)	Taylor
613	Separate Rooms (1940)	Carole
607	Hogan's Goat (1965)	Alfred
603	Broadway (1926)	Dunning
601	Street Scene (1929)	Rice
600	Kiki (1921)	Belasco
598	Don't Drink the Water (1966)	W. Allen
585	Two Mrs. Carrolls (1943)	Vale
582	Zoo Story (1960)	Albee
581	Detective Story (1949)	Kingsley
577	Brother Rat (1936)	Monks
571	Crucible (1957)	Miller
571	Show Off (1924)	Kelly
564	Happy Birthday (1946)	Loos
564	Look Homeward, Angel (1957)	Frings
564	Morning's at Seven (1980)	Osborn
561	Glass Menagerie (1945)	T. Williams
557	Strictly Dishonorable (1929)	Sturges
556	Majority of One (1959)	Spigelgass
556	Sunrise at Campobello (1958)	Schary
556	Great White Hope (1968)	Sackler
556	Toys in the Attic (1960)	Hellman
541	Within the Law (1912)	Veiller
538	What a Life (1938)	Goldsmith
538	Sunshine Boys (1972)	Simon
530	Raisin in the Sun (1959)	Hansberry
526	Solid Gold Cadillac (1953)	Kaufman
522	Boomerang (1915)	W. Smith
520	Best Man (1960)	Vidal
517	Gin Game (1977)	Coburn
511	Fifth of July (1980)	Wilson
508	World of Suzie Wong (1958)	Osborn
501	Member of the Wedding (1950)	McCullers
501	Personal Appearance (1934)	Riley

Performances	Play and Year of Production	Author
500	Room Service (1937)	Murray
500	Sailor, Beware! (1933)	Nicholson
500	Tomorrow the World (1943)	Gow
495	Sly Fox (1976)	Gelbart
493	In White America (1963)	Duberman
486	Matchmaker (1955)	Wilder
478	Bus Stop (1955)	Inge
478	Streamers (1976)	Rabe
477	Deep Are the Roots (1945)	d'Usseau
477	Middle of the Night (1956)	Chayefsky
477	Picnic (1953)	Inge
474	Pleasure of His Company (1958)	Taylor
472	Abe Lincoln in Illinois (1938)	Sherwood
471	Sherlock Holmes (1974)	Gillette
468	Dark at the Top of the Stairs (1957)	Inge
461	Lulu Belle (1926)	Sheldon
453	Play It Again, Sam (1969)	W. Allen
446	Goodbye, My Fancy (1948)	Kanin
445	California Suite (1976)	Simon
444	Will Success Spoil Rock Hunter? (1955)	Axelrod
440	Friendly Enemies (1918)	Shipman
440	Road to Rome (1928)	Sherwood
439	Burlesque (1946)	Watters
438	Family Business (1978)	Goldberg
437	Trial of Mary Dugan (1927)	Veiller
435	Turn to the Right (1916)	W. Smith
429	Price (1968)	Miller
428	Thousand Clowns (1962)	Gardner
426	Strange Interlude (1928)	O'Neill
424	Get-Rich-Quick Wallingford (1910)	Cohan
423	John Loves Mary (1947)	Krasna
423	Old Soak (1922)	Marquis
417	Jacobowsky and the Colonel (1944)	Behrman
417	Philadelphia Story (1939)	Barry
417	Tunnel of Love (1957)	J. Fields
415	Caine Mutiny Court-Martial (1954)	Wouk
411	Twin Beds (1914)	Field
410	Heiress (1947)	Goetz
410	Little Foxes (1939)	Hellman
409	Cocktail Party (1950)	Eliot
408	Command Decision (1947)	Haines
406	Once in a Lifetime (1930)	Kaufman
405	Yes, My Darling Daughter (1937)	Reed

Performance	Play and Year of Production	Author
400	Little Murders (1969)	Feiffer
400	River Niger (1973)	Walker
400	Ritz (1975)	McNally
398	Hatful of Rain (1955)	Gazzo
398	Tailor Made Man (1917)	H. J. Smith
397	Seven Days (1909)	Rinehart
394	Moonchildren (1973)	Weller
392	Road to Rome (1927)	Sherwood
390	Long Day's Journey into Night (1956)	O'Neill
388	Visit to a Small Planet (1957)	Vidal
385	Late George Apley (1944)	Marquand
382	Oh, Men! Oh, Women! (1953)	E. Chodorov
380	Desire Under the Elms (1963)	O'Neill
380	To Be Young, Gifted and Black (1969)	Hansberry
378	Prime of Miss Jean Brodie (1968)	J. Allen
378	Watch on the Rhine (1941)	Hellman
377	Harriet (1943)	Ryerson
375	Sweet Bird of Youth (1959)	T. Williams
373	Mulatto (1935)	L. Hughes
372	Burlesque (1927)	Watters
372	Having Wonderful Time (1937)	Kober
370	American Dream (1961)	Albee
367	Porgy (1927)	Heyward
367	Season in the Sun (1950)	Gibbs
366	Coquette (1927)	Abbott
366	Sticks and Bones (1971)	Rabe
365	On Trial (1914)	Rice
364	J. B. (1958)	MacLeish
364	Point of No Return (1951)	Osborn
363	Basic Training of Pavlo Hummel (1971)	Rabe
360	Craig's Wife (1925)	Kelly
360	She Loves Me Not (1933)	Lindsay
359	Skin of Our Teeth (1942)	Wilder
356	Tovarich (1936)	Sherwood
351	Men in White (1933)	Kingsley
350	Enter Madame (1920)	Varesi
350	Mrs. McThing (1952)	Chase
349	Plays for Bleecker Street (1962)	Wilder
348	Dream Girl (1945)	Rice
348	Happy Journey to Trenton and Camden (1948)	Wilder
345	Fortune Hunter (1909)	W. Smith
345	Royal Family (1927)	Kaufman
344	Six-Cylinder Love (1921)	McGuire

Performance	Play and Year of Production	Author
344	Another Language (1932)	Franken
344	My 3 Angels (1953)	Spewack
342	Bad Man (1920)	Browne
342	Child's Play (1970)	Marasco
337	House of Blue Leaves (1971)	Guare
336	Hit-the-Trail-Holiday (1915)	Cohan
336	Lunatics and Lovers (1954)	Kingsley
336	Our Town (1938)	Wilder
333	All the Way Home (1960)	Mosel
332	Bad Seed (1954)	M. Anderson
328	All My Sons (1947)	Miller
328	Death of Bessie Smith (1961)	Albee
328	Thirteenth Chair (1916)	Veiller
324	I Ought to Be in Pictures (1980)	Simon
322	One Sunday Afternoon (1933)	Hagan
321	On Borrowed Time (1938)	Osborn
320	Seven Keys to Baldpate (1913)	Cohan
318	Sabrina Fair (1953)	Taylor
318	Searching Wind (1944)	Hellman
317	Male Animal (1952)	Thurber
316	Night of the Iguana (1961)	T. Williams
315	Polly with a Past (1917)	Bolton
315	Shadow Box (1977)	Cristofer
314	Moon for the Misbegotten (1973)	O'Neill
312	Thieves (1974)	H. Gardner
312	No Place to Be Somebody (1970)	Gordone
312	Adam and Eva (1919)	Bolton
312	Dancing Mothers (1924)	Selwyn
312	Forever After (1918)	Owen Davis
310	Saturday's Children (1927)	M. Anderson
307	Eve of St. Mark (1942)	M. Anderson
306	Rose Tattoo (1951)	T. Williams
305	Old Maid (1935)	Akins
304	Bell for Adano (1944)	Osborn
303	Jazz Singer (1925)	Raphaelson
303	Little Accident (1928)	Dell
302	When You Comin' Back, Red Ryder? (1973)	Medoff
300	Clarence (1919)	Tarkington
300	Idiot's Delight (1936)	Sherwood
299	Generation (1965)	Goodhart
299	What Price Glory? (1924)	M. Anderson
295	Tom Paine (1968)	Foster
292	Counsellor-at-Law (1931)	Rice
289	Ah, Wilderness (1933)	O'Neill

Performance	Play and Year of Production	Author
289	Last Mile (1930)	Wexley
288	Shannons of Broadway (1927)	Gleason
288	Susan and God (1937)	Crothers
288	Life in the Theater (1977)	Mamet
286	Anne of the Thousand Days (1948)	M. Anderson
286	Kiss the Boys Good-Bye (1938)	Boothe
284	Touch of the Poet (1958)	O'Neill
284	Loose Ends (1979)	Weller
283	Biography (1934)	Behrman
279	Home (1980)	Samm-Art Williams
279	King of Hearts (1954)	Kerr
279	Nervous Wreck (1923)	Owen Davis
278	Shame Woman (1923)	Vollmer
277	Talley's Folly (1980)	Wilson
273	Bad Habits (1974)	McNally
273	Duck Variations (1976)	Mamet
273	Sexual Perversity in Chicago (1976)	Mamet
273	Dylan (1964)	Michaels
273	June Moon (1929)	Lardner
272	Fool (1922)	Pollock
272	Anastasia (1954)	Bolton
271	Far Country (1961)	Denker
271	Great God Brown (1926)	O'Neill
267	Biography (1932)	Behrman
265	For Love or Money (1947)	Herbert
265	Life with Mother (1948)	Lindsay
264	Margin for Error (1939)	Boothe
264	Reunion in Vienna (1931)	Sherwood
264	Table Settings (1980)	Lapine
263	Time of the Cuckoo (1952)	Laurents
262	Lunch Hour (1980)	Kerr
261	Dracula (1927)	Balderston
261	Firebrand (1924)	Mayer
261	Purlie Victorious (1961)	Ossie Davis
261	Star-Spangled Girl (1966)	Simon
260	Young Woodley (1925)	Van Druten
*259	American Buffalo (1981)	Mamet
259	Getting Out (1979)	Norman
258	Counsellor-at-Law (1942)	Rice
257	Déclassée (1919)	Akins
257	Thank You (1921)	W. Smith
256	Skylark (1939)	Raphaelson
256	U.S.A. (1959)	Dos Passos
255	Pre-Honeymoon (1936)	Nichols
255	You Can't Take It with You (1965)	Hart

Performance	Play and Year of Production	Author
253	Greeks Had a World for It (1930)	Akins
253	Soldier's Wife (1944)	Franken
252	Little Journey (1918)	Crothers
252	On Golden Pond (1979)	Thompson
250	Golden Boy (1937)	Odets
250	No Place to Be Somebody (1969)	Gordone
248	Mary of Scotland (1933)	M. Anderson
248	Merton of the Movies (1922)	Kaufman
248	Tarnish (1923)	Emery
247	Sister Mary Ignatius Explains It All for You (1981)	Durang
247	Actor's Nightmare (1981)	Durang
247	6 Rms Riv Vu (1972)	Randall
246	Dulcy (1921)	Kaufman
246	First Lady (1935)	Dayton
246	I Know My Love (1949)	Behrman
243	Butter and Egg Man (1925)	Kaufman
243	Male Animal (1940)	Thurber
242	Case of Libel (1963)	Denker
242	Left Bank (1931)	Rice
240	Bent (1979)	Sherman
239	Crimes of the Heart (1981)	Henley
236	Gideon (1961)	Chayefsky
235	Country Girl (1950)	Odets
234	Paris Bound (1927)	Barker
233	Bell, Book and Candle (1950)	Van Druten
233	All over Town (1974)	Schisgal
232	Royal Family (1975)	Kaufman
232	Dinner at Eight (1932)	Kaufman
232	Tommy (1927)	Lindsay
231	Return of Peter Grimm (1911)	Belasco
229	Accent on Youth (1934)	Raphaelson
229	Berkeley Square (1929)	Balderston
229	Holiday (1928)	Barker
229	Lark (1955)	Hellman
229	Strange Bedfellows (1948)	Ryerson
229	Vinegar Tree (1930)	Osborn
228	Rollo's Wild Oat (1920)	Kummer
224	Come Out of the Kitchen (1916)	A. E. Thomas
224	Her Master's Voice (1933)	Kummer
224	Late Christopher Bean (1932)	S. Howard
223	Son-Daughter (1919)	Belasco
223	Star Wagon (1937)	M. Anderson
223	Too Many Cooks (1914)	Craven
222	In Circles (1967)	Stein
222	Tchin-Tchin (1962)	Michaels
221	Calculated Risk (1962)	J. Hayes

Performance	Play and Year of Production	Author
221	Over 21 (1944)	Gordon
*221	Soldier's Play (1981)	Fuller
220	Sinners (1915)	Owen Davis
219	Gigi (1951)	Loos
219	Silver Whistle (1948)	McEnroe
216	Light Up the Sky (1948)	Hart
214	I Am a Camera (1951)	Van Druten
214	Medea (1947)	Jeffers
212	Desperate Hours (1955)	J. Hayes
212	Winged Victory (1943)	Hart
210	Immoralist (1963)	Goetz
209	Awake and Sing (1935)	Odets
208	Desire Under the Elms (1924)	O'Neill
208	Who Was That Lady I Saw You With? (1958)	Krasna
208	Good Doctor (1973)	Simon
207	Hasty Heart (1945)	Patrick
207	Of Mice and Men (1937)	Steinbeck
206	Tomorrow and Tomorrow (1931)	Barker
206	Years Ago (1946)	Gordon
204	Emperor Jones (1920)	O'Neill
204	Indian Wants the Bronx (1968)	Horovitz
204	It's Called the Sugar Plum (1968)	Horovitz
203	Enemy (1925)	Pollock
200	In Abraham's Bosom (1926)	Green
200	Tiger (1963)	Schisgal
200	Typists (1963)	Schisgal
200	Small Craft Warnings (1972)	T. Williams

ANTOINETTE PERRY (TONY) AWARDS
FOR BEST PLAY

1946-47   All My Sons, by Arthur Miller

1947-48   A Streetcar Named Desire, by Tennessee Williams (Best
             New American Play)

             Mister Roberts, by Joshua Logan and Thomas Heggen
             (the Outstanding Play)

1948-49   Death of A Salesman, by Arthur Miller

1949-50   The Cocktail Party, by T. S. Eliot

1950-51   Darkness at Noon, by Sidney Kingsley

1951-52   No American winners.

1952-53   The Crucible, by Arthur Miller

1953-54   Teahouse of the August Moon, by John Patrick

1954-55   The Desperate Hours, by Joseph Hayes

1955-56   The Diary of Anne Frank, by Frances Goodrich and
             Albert Hackett

1956-57   Long Day's Journey into Night, by Eugene O'Neill

1957-58   Sunrise at Campobello, by Dore Schary

1958-59   J.B., by Archibald MacLeish

1959-60   The Miracle Worker, by William Gibson

1960-61   No American winners.

1961-62   No American winners.

1962-63   Who's Afraid of Virginia Woolf?, by Edward Albee

1963-64   No American winners.

1964-65	The Subject Was Roses, by Frank D. Gilroy
1965-66	No American winners.
1966-67	A Delicate Balance, by Edward Albee
1967-68	No American winners.
1968-69	The Great White Hope, by Howard Sackler
1969-70	No American winners.
1970-71	No American winners.
1971-72	Sticks and Bones, by David Rabe
1972-73	That Championship Season, by Jason Miller
1973-74	The River Niger, by Joseph A. Walker
1974-75	No American winners.
1975-76	No American winners.
1976-77	Shadow Box, by Michael Cristofer
1977-78	No American winners.
1978-79	The Elephant Man, by Bernard Pomerance
1979-80	Children of a Lesser God, by Mark Medoff
1980-81	No American winners.
1981-82	No American winners.

NEW YORK DRAMA CRITICS' CIRCLE AWARDS

(Best American Play)

1935-36   Winterset, by Maxwell Anderson

1936-37   High Tor, by Maxwell Anderson

1937-38   Of Mice and Men, by John Steinbeck

1938-39   No Award.

1939-40   The Time of Your Life, by William Saroyan

1940-41   Watch on the Rhine, by Lillian Hellman

1941-42   No Award.

1942-43   The Patriots, by Sidney Kingsley

1943-44   Jacobowsky and the Colonel, adapted by S. N. Behr-
           man (considered as Best Foreign Play)

1944-45   The Glass Menagerie, by Tennessee Williams

1945-46   No Award.

1946-47   All My Sons, by Arthur Miller

1947-48   A Streetcar Named Desire, by Tennessee Williams

1948-49   Death of a Salesman, by Arthur Miller

1949-50   The Member of the Wedding, by Carson McCullers
           The Cocktail Party, by T. S. Eliot (considered as
              Best Foreign Play)

1950-51   Darkness at Noon, by Sidney Kingsley

1951-52   I Am a Camera, by John Van Druten

1952-53   Picnic, by William Inge

1953-54   Teahouse of the August Moon, by John Patrick

1954-55   Cat on a Hot Tin Roof, by Tennessee Williams

1955-56   The Diary of Anne Frank, by Frances Goodrich and
              Albert Hackett

1956-57   Long Day's Journey into Night, by Eugene O'Neill

1957-58   Look Homeward, Angel, by Ketti Frings

1958-59   A Raisin in the Sun, by Lorraine Hansberry

1959-60   Toys in the Attic, by Lillian Hellman

1960-61   All the Way Home, by Tad Mosel

1961-62   *The Night of the Iguana, by Tennessee Williams

1962-63   Who's Afraid of Virginia Woolf?, by Edward Albee

1963-64   No Award.

1964-65   The Subject Was Roses, by Frank D. Gilroy

1965-66   No Award.

1966-67   No Award.

1967-68   No Award.

1968-69   *The Great White Hope, by Howard Sackler

1969-70   The Effect of Gamma Rays on Man-in-the-Moon Mari-
              golds, by Paul Zindel

1970-71   The House of Blue Leaves, by John Guare

1971-72   *That Championship Season, by Jason Miller

1972-73   The Hot l Baltimore, by Lanford Wilson

1973-74   Short Eyes, by Miguel Pinero

1974-75   The Taking of Miss Janie, by Ed Bullins

1975-76   Streamers, by David Rabe

1976-77   American Buffalo, by David Mamet

1977-78   No Award.

---

*Best Play, regardless of category.

1978-79   *The Elephant Man, by Bernard Pomerance

1979-80   *Talley's Folly, by Lanford Wilson

1980-81   Crimes of the Heart, by Beth Henley

1981-82   A Soldier's Play, by Charles Fuller

PULITZER PRIZE WINNERS

(American Drama)

1917-18	Why Marry?, by Jesse Lynch Williams
1918-19	No Award.
1919-20	Beyond the Horizon, by Eugene O'Neill
1920-21	Miss Lulu Bett, by Zona Gale
1921-22	Anna Christie, Eugene O'Neill
1922-23	Icebound, by Owen Davis
1923-24	Hell-bent fer Heaven, by Hatcher Hughes
1924-25	They Knew What They Wanted, by Sidney Howard
1925-26	Craig's Wife, by George Kelly
1926-27	In Abraham's Bosom, by Paul Green
1927-28	Strange Interlude, by Eugene O'Neill
1928-29	Street Scene, by Elmer Rice
1929-30	The Green Pastures, by Marc Connelly
1930-31	Alison's House, by Susan Glaspell
1931-32	musical
1932-33	Both Your Houses, by Maxwell Anderson
1933-34	Men in White, by Sidney Kingsley
1934-35	The Old Maid, by Zoë Akins
1935-36	Idiot's Delight, by Robert E. Sherwood
1936-37	You Can't Take It with You, by Moss Hart and George S. Kaufman

1937-38	Our Town, by Thornton Wilder
1938-39	Abe Lincoln in Illinois, by Robert E. Sherwood
1939-40	The Time of Your Life, by William Saroyan
1940-41	There Shall Be No Night, by Robert E. Sherwood
1941-42	No Award.
1942-43	The Skin of Our Teeth, by Thornton Wilder
1943-44	No Award.
1944-45	Harvey, by Mary Chase
1945-46	State of the Union, by Howard Lindsay and Russel Crouse
1946-47	No Award.
1947-48	A Streetcar Named Desire, by Tennessee Williams
1948-49	Death of a Salesman, by Arthur Miller
1949-50	musical
1950-51	No Award.
1951-52	The Shrike, by Joseph Kramm
1952-53	Picnic, by William Inge
1953-54	The Teahouse of the August Moon, by John Patrick
1954-55	Cat on a Hot Tin Roof, by Tennessee Williams
1955-56	The Diary of Anne Frank, by Frances Goodrich and Albert Hackett
1956-57	Long Day's Journey into Night, by Eugene O'Neill
1957-58	Look Homeward, Angel, by Ketti Frings
1958-59	J.B., by Archibald MacLeish
1959-60	musical
1960-61	All the Way Home, by Tad Mosel
1961-62	musical

1962-63	No Award.
1963-64	No Award.
1964-65	The Subject Was Roses, by Frank D. Gilroy
1965-66	No Award.
1966-67	A Delicate Balance, by Edward Albee
1967-68	No Award.
1968-69	The Great White Hope, by Howard Sackler
1969-70	No Place to Be Somebody, by Charles Gordone
1970-71	The Effect of Gamma Rays on Man-in-the-Moon Marigolds, by Paul Zindel
1971-72	No Award.
1972-73	That Championship Season, by Jason Miller
1973-74	No Award.
1974-75	Seascape, by Edward Albee
1975-76	musical
1976-77	The Shadow Box, by Michael Cristofer
1977-78	The Gin Game, by D. L. Coburn
1978-79	Buried Child, by Sam Shepard
1979-80	Talley's Folly, by Lanford Wilson
1980-81	Crimes of the Heart, by Beth Henley
1981-82	A Soldier's Play, by Charles Fuller

INDEX OF CO-AUTHORS, ADAPTERS, AND
ORIGINAL AUTHORS

INDEX OF TITLES